The Crisis of Russian Der

MW00777111

The view that Russia has taken a decisive shift towards authoritarianism may be premature, but there is no doubt that its democracy is in crisis. In this original and dynamic analysis of the fundamental processes shaping contemporary Russian politics, Richard Sakwa applies a new model based on the concept of Russia as a dual state. Russia's constitutional state is challenged by an administrative regime that subverts the rule of law and genuine electoral competitiveness. This has created a situation of permanent stalemate: the country is unable to move towards genuine pluralist democracy but, equally, its shift towards full-scale authoritarianism is inhibited. Sakwa argues that the dual state could be transcended either by strengthening the democratic state or by the consolidation of the arbitrary power of the administrative system. The future of the country remains open.

RICHARD SAKWA is Professor of Russian and European Politics at the University of Kent.

The Crisis of Russian Democracy

The Dual State, Factionalism and the Medvedev Succession

Richard Sakwa

CAMBRIDGE
UNIVERSITY PRESS

CAMBRIDGE UNIVERSITY PRESS
Cambridge, New York, Melbourne, Madrid, Cape Town, Singapore,
São Paulo, Delhi, Dubai, Tokyo, Mexico City

Cambridge University Press
The Edinburgh Building, Cambridge CB2 8RU, UK

Published in the United States of America by
Cambridge University Press, New York

www.cambridge.org
Information on this title: www.cambridge.org/9780521145220

First published 2011

Printed in the United Kingdom at the University Press, Cambridge

A catalogue record for this publication is available from the British Library

Library of Congress Cataloging-in-Publication Data

Sakwa, Richard.
The crisis of Russian democracy : the dual state, factionalism, and the Medvedev
succession / Richard Sakwa.
    p.   cm.
  Includes bibliographical references and index.
  ISBN 978-0-521-76842-9 (Hardback) – ISBN 978-0-521-14522-0 (Pbk.)
1. Presidents–Succession–Russia (Federation)   2. Democracy–Russia
(Federation)   3. Russia (Federation)–Politics and government–1991–
I. Title.
  JN6540.S25 2010
  320.947–dc22
2010029495

ISBN 978-0-521-76842-9 Hardback
ISBN 978-0-521-14522-0 Paperback

Contents

Tables

Preface

Russia has been in 'crisis' for as long as anyone can remember. Several generations became accustomed to viewing the tsarist system as fundamentally dysfunctional, and for many no less illegitimate. The imbalance between the claims of the autocracy to undivided power and the demands of an increasingly dynamic society for a share in that power was partially resolved after the 1905 revolution with the creation of the constitutional monarchy. The principle of popular sovereignty and representative government came into contradiction with the continuing claims by the autocracy in the person of Nicholas II that sovereignty resided in the crown. The crisis of power ultimately provoked the overthrow of the monarchy in February 1917. The Provisional Government was in permanent crisis, and overshadowed by the demands of war. The seizure of power by the Bolsheviks in October 1917 began the experiment of Communist governance that lasted seventy-four years, and was marked by no less intense structural contradictions. The new social order claimed to give power to the people, but instead a political elite claimed tutelary rights over the nation in the name of the higher ideals of building socialism, and became an ever more corrupt and self-aggrandising group. Despite Mikhail Gorbachev's efforts to reform the communist order during *perestroika* from 1985, the system collapsed in 1991. Since then, Russia has been engaged in the no less grandiose experiment of attempting to build a capitalist democracy from scratch.

Russia, it seems, is trapped in a permanent crisis. For well over a century, the country has been looking for a viable social order combining economic dynamism with political legitimacy. After 1991, the newly independent state set out on the path of constitutional democracy and market capitalism and gave up attempts to create an alternative system to that found in the west. Instead, it sought to adapt its institutions to those found in most of the developed world and to integrate into the dominant institutions of the modern era. In the 1990s, under the leadership of President Boris Yeltsin, this proved highly traumatic, but the basic institutions of a capitalist democracy were established. On coming to power in

2000, President Vladimir Putin continued along the broad policy direction established by Yeltsin, but now with more emphasis on reasserting the assumed prerogatives of the central state and its status in the world. The 'crisis', clearly, was not over, and by the end of the second four-year term of Putin's presidency, the country's domestic order and international politics was subjected to similar levels of criticism to that of its late tsarist and Communist predecessors. The accession of Dmitry Medvedev to the presidency in May 2008, although accompanied by a more liberal domestic rhetoric, solved none of the systemic problems. Various modernisation strategies have been pursued by different political regimes, yet Russia remains a resolute laggard in competitive terms compared to the advanced western industrial societies.

This book will seek to analyse the features of the crisis in Russian democracy as revealed in the transition from Putin to Medvedev. It will not be an exhaustive political history of post-communist Russia, let alone of the various systems that preceded it. Instead, the work focuses on the specific crisis features of the Russian political system at the moment of succession in 2007–8. The fundamental premise of the work is that succession acts as a prism to reveal the underlying structures of power. The book is an interpretative analysis of contemporary Russian politics, with the focus on the transition from Putin to Medvedev and the systemic problems faced by the latter. It is a study of the specific problems of *Russian* democracy, and not a general study of the problems facing democracy in Russia, although clearly the two are linked. In other words, the focus is not on democratisation as such, let alone on what could be considered a general crisis of democratic governance in the advanced capitalist systems, but on the operation of Russian politics during a specific period.

The broad model that will be applied is that of the dual state. I argue that a dual state has emerged in which the legal-normative system based on constitutional order is challenged by shadowy arbitrary arrangements, dubbed in this book the 'administrative regime', populated by various conflicting factions. The tension between the two is the defining feature of contemporary Russian politics. No society is without such features, but in Russia dualism assumed systemic forms. As the succession struggle from around 2005 to 2008 demonstrated, neither of the two orders predominated over the other. The interaction between the constitutional state and the administrative regime is the critical arena in which politics is conducted; and as long as each retains a distinctive identity, then Russian political evolution remains open-ended. The tension between the two pillars is the matrix through which the Russian political landscape can be understood.

The 1993 constitution limited Putin to a maximum of two consecutive terms as president, and therefore a new person would assume office in 2008 accompanied by elite fears that a change of leader would entail a change of regime. Given the extraordinary concentration of powers vested in the presidency, at the heart not only of political power but also of patronage and policy-making in foreign and domestic affairs, the stakes as 2008 approached could not have been higher. Succession conflicts are certainly nothing new in Russian imperial and Soviet history.[1] The hereditary mechanism on more than one occasion (notably with the accession of Catherine II in 1762 and Alexander I in 1801) was trumped by a brutal struggle that changed or accelerated the order of succession. Following Lenin's death in January 1924, the Soviet Union entered a prolonged succession struggle which effectively lasted to 1929, and in a sense the purges of the 1930s were a reflection of that crisis as Joseph Stalin systematically liquidated his potential rivals. Stalin's death in March 1953 led to an interregnum before Nikita Khrushchev was able to consolidate his power, accompanied by the judicial murder of Lavrenty Beria, the leader of the secret police, to remove him as a potential leader before the struggle between various groups continued in a more peaceful way. With the crushing of the so-called 'anti-party group' in 1957, Khrushchev emerged as the clear victor, before he in turn was overthrown by a high-level conspiracy by a party plenum in October 1964.[2] Leonid Brezhnev emerged as part of a leadership *troika*, but by around 1968 he greatly overshadowed the president, Nikolai Podgorny, and the prime minister, Alexei Kosygin.[3] Brezhnev's death in November 1982 following a long decline was accompanied by an extended leadership contest, which finally saw Gorbachev emerge triumphant as General Secretary of the Communist Party of the Soviet Union (CPSU) in March 1985.

He in turn was soon challenged by Yeltsin, a contest which began as a struggle over the pace of the reform of the communist system but ended as a struggle between the declining Soviet state and a number of rising nations, pre-eminent among which was the idea of an independent Russia.[4] This new version of 'dual power' was based on two states and

---

[1] For a vivid and informative overview, see Petr Romanov, *Preemniki ot Ivana III do Dmitriya Medvedeva* (St Petersburg: Amfora, 2008).

[2] Uri Ra'anan (ed.), *Flawed Succession: Russia's Power Transfer Crises* (Lanham, MD: Lexington Books, 2006), describes these events and other succession crises.

[3] Seweryn Bialer, *Stalin's Successors, Leadership, Stability, and Change in the Soviet Union* (Cambridge: Cambridge University Press, 1980).

[4] John B. Dunlop, *The Rise of Russia and the Fall of the Soviet Empire* (Princeton, NJ: Princeton University Press, 1993).

differing visions of the future. With the disintegration of the USSR in December 1991, Russia finally emerged as an independent state, but it was immediately plunged into an extended succession crisis in which personal conflicts were overshadowed by a struggle between institutions, primarily the presidency versus parliament. In this period of 'phoney democracy', the constitution-drafting process became the main issue of contention, which certainly marked an advance over the bullet used earlier, but in the end also took a violent turn in the form of bloody battles in October 1993.[5] The victor once again was Yeltsin, but the price paid was a heavy one, above all the relative isolation of the regime from accountability to parliament and to organised social forces, notably political parties. Yeltsin's leadership lacked an organised mass political base, and thus it was precisely in this period that the foundations were laid of the post-communist administrative regime. A new constitution was finally adopted in December 1993, but it bears the scars of the presidential victory, and thus the struggle for genuine constitutionalism continues. The legal-normative order represented by the constitution has not been able to constrain the administrative regime.

Only the Russian parliamentary election of March 1990 and the presidential election of June 1991, in which Yeltsin was elected Russia's first president, were genuinely open competitions. The December 1993 parliamentary election and referendum on the new constitution established a pattern in which the electoral process was suborned by a force standing outside the competition. In 1996 the regime managed to organise Yeltsin's re-election, and in late 1999 the succession passed to a nominee of the regime, Putin. The electoral process underwent a dual adaptation: while formally conducted within the framework of law and electoral pluralism, the regime used elections (that were typically hard-fought) to legitimate its own power rather than subjecting that power to the openness of outcomes that is the characteristic feature of free and fair political competition.

The dualism of the electoral process is accompanied by factionalism in politics. Political succession in post-communist Russia has been attended by factional conflicts, usually conducted in the shadowy corridors of power but with a public form played out using the formal political institutions and processes. The outcome of these struggles shaped the nature of the system. In the 1990s, succession took the form of the vivid interplay of secret and public politics, but in the 2000s, although this duality remained, the process was increasingly internalised

---

[5] Richard Sakwa, *Russian Politics and Society*, 4th edn (London: Routledge, 2008), Part I.

as the regime imposed restrictive regulations on public politics. Fearing the untrammelled exercise of electoral democracy, regime perpetuation trumped the formal constitutional procedures for the transfer of power in a process independent of the regime itself. In other words, instead of the competitive selection of alternative governments within the framework of a given constitutional order, the power system (the administrative regime) found ways of constraining the electoral process to ensure its own survival. The moment of change – Yeltsin's re-election in 1996, the succession to Putin in 1999–2000, once again re-election in 2003–4 when Putin easily won a second term, and intensely in 2007–8 when a successor had to be found – became a test for the regime and the stability of the political system, but had little to do with competitive elections even in a minimalist Schumpeterian sense in which the incumbents have a real chance of losing.

The constitutional order, nevertheless, exercises a constraining and normative function. Limited to two terms, Putin repeatedly declared that he would leave the presidency in conformity with the constitution. As the succession approached, tensions within the system became increasingly apparent, taking the form of factional conflict and ideological struggles. The battle between powerful interests was not limited to the formal institutional rules of political conduct but spilled over into the parallel sphere of para-constitutional competition. Fearing that the emergence of a new leader would be accompanied by power and property redistribution, incumbent elites sought to avoid this at all cost. The succession, in other words, brought to the surface hidden patterns of political behaviour and economic concerns.

The battle for the succession was at the same time a struggle between the two pillars: the formal constitutional order, and the second world of factional conflict and para-constitutional political practices. We use the term 'para-constitutional' deliberately, because the political regime and its factions did not repudiate the formal constitutional framework but operated within its formal constraints while subverting much of its spirit. The struggle between the two systems gave birth to the dual state, with much of politics taking place in the charged zone between them. This is a dynamic model of Russian politics that moves away from the typological transitology typical of the 'democracy with adjectives' school of analysis.[6] It seeks to endow a sense of agency to the hybrid order that has emerged in post-communist Russia, accompanied by a clear conceptual hierarchy. Rather than qualifying Russian democracy with a modifying adjective,

---

[6] Cf. David Collier and Steven Levitsky, 'Democracy with Adjectives: Conceptual Innovation in Comparative Research', *World Politics* 49, 1997, pp. 430–51.

denoting some sort of unified order, we adopt a spatial approach in which the political terrain is contested by two sub-systems, neither of which in present conditions can gain uncontested dominance over the other.

We define democracy as a set of institutions and a set of norms and practices, with the two in constant interaction. The institutional level has a validity of its own, and without falling into the trap of the legal-constitutional positivism characteristic of continental institutionalism, even formal compliance with the normative order associated with democratic institutions is no mean achievement. Russia's Constitutional Court has not been as courageous as some would like, yet it has delivered qualified judgments against the regime.[7] As Bernard Crick reminds us, 'An ounce of law is worth a ton of rhetoric if a court will recognize certain liberties and order their preservation against the State itself.'[8] The formal provisions of Russia's constitution are wholly in line with the requirements of a liberal democratic order, although there are disputes (as we shall see) over specific provisions, notably the excessive powers of the presidency. The legal-constitutional pillar has real substance, and it is to the normative order associated with it that within-system reformers appeal. Practices of the administrative regime, however, foster the egregious abuse of law and weaken democratic competitiveness. The administrative regime is able to suborn the courts in cases of vital importance to it, as the Yukos trials attest, and to manipulate the electoral process. The administrative regime, as we shall detail later in this book, is far from a unitary actor, and indeed fragmentation is its defining feature, riven by factionalism as political and economic interests combine and collide.

The dual state in Russia today has some of the characteristics of the period of constitutional monarchy between 1906 and the overthrow of tsarism in February 1917, although of course the historical circumstances are very different. Nicholas II only grudgingly accepted the adoption of a constitution (Basic Law) following the 1905 revolution, and the results of the first two elections to the Imperial Duma in 1906 and 1907 were rejected until a more amenable parliament was elected. The tsar still insisted on his supra-constitutional status. In other words, sovereignty for him was not derived from a popular mandate but from the will of God. Elements of this tutelary approach are evident in the behaviour of the administrative regime today, claiming an

---

[7] Marie-Elisabeth Baudoin, 'Is the Constitutional Court the Last Bastion in Russia Against the Threat of Authoritarianism?', *Europe-Asia Studies* 58, 5, July 2006, pp. 679–99; Alexei Trochev, *Judging Russia: The Role of the Constitutional Court in Russian Politics 1990–2006* (Cambridge: Cambridge University Press, 2008).

[8] Bernard Crick, *In Defence of Politics* (Harmondsworth: Penguin Books, 1964), p. 65, from whom my definition of democracy is drawn.

extra-constitutional mandate to govern in what it perceives to be the best interests of the country. This principle was at the heart of Communist rule, and thus quasi-tsarist attitudes are reinforced by neo-Soviet practices. These 'best interests' are defined by the regime itself and thus the mass of the population, who are not trusted to achieve the right results at the ballot box (the so-called 'democracy paradox'), is infantilised and the legal-constitutional order suborned. The power of the administrative regime is based on a combination of this appeal to extra-democratic sovereignty and its own socio-political interests, which generates not just what we call *venal corruption* (the use of bribes and the like), but also systemic abuse that I call *meta-corruption*, where the logic of one order (for example the market system or administrative rationality) invades another (notably, the judicial system).

The two pillars of rule in contemporary Russia are in rough balance. If the administrative regime abandoned even its formal appeal to democratic legitimacy, then Russia would set out on the path of an overtly authoritarian system. If, however, the constitutional state could extend its authority and repulse the encroachments of the administrative system, as the democratic reformers of the Medvedev era tried to do, then Russia would become more of a consolidated democracy. The essence of the Putin system, however, was to keep the two pillars in parity, while balancing the factions within the administrative system (the two types of balance were mutually reinforcing). The forces favouring normative-constitutional renewal undoubtedly existed, both within government and beyond (notably in the world of non-governmental organisations and parts of the rising middle class), but they were stymied by the entrenched power of the bureaucracy and the pragmatic-technocratic rationality of the administrative system. This has given rise to a political and developmental stalemate, whose features will be explored later.

The power of the administrative regime in part resides in its ability to depoliticise the sources of its own power and to appeal to a 'centrist' pragmatic type of governmentality. Its opponents were weakened by a fundamental division, reminiscent of the late Soviet period, between those who argue for an evolutionary strategy of within-system reform, warning that a revolutionary attack on the administrative regime threatened to bring down the whole constitutional order, and the radicalised outsiders, who argue for the destruction of the whole rotten edifice. If the latter prevailed, Russia would once again, for the third time in a century, have to start again from scratch. As we know, revolutions only tend to perpetuate in new forms the old authoritarianism, whereas an evolutionary transcendence of the gulf between democratic institutions and the corrupt practices of the administrative regime, the strategy advocated by Medvedev although only tenuously implemented, promised more enduring perspectives for long-term democratic transformation.

From the perspective of the dual state model, it would be incorrect to label Putin's Russia an authoritarian regime *tout court*, since not only did it remain formally committed to constitutional democracy and liberal capitalism, and these remained the source of its popular legitimacy, but these commitments moderated its behaviour and allowed the formal constitutional framework to structure and influence the conduct of politics. Although many of the regime's actions were authoritarian in spirit, the formal niceties of a constitutional democracy remained pre-eminent and the legitimating framework for the system as a whole. There was no systematic national political repression, and a degree of political competition and media pluralism remained. It would be a grave mistake to lump Russia in with, say, semi-authoritarian regimes of the likes of Egypt, where Hosni Mubarak in 2005 won yet another term after twenty years in power.[9] Thus we have a peculiar hybrid, in which formal constitutional norms come into conflict and interact with para-constitutional practices. In the dual state, the two levels exist as discrete systems but at the same time operate in constant interaction with each other; and it is this which endows Russian governance with its peculiar kaleidoscopic character, constantly changing yet fundamentally remaining the same.

It also provoked the crisis of Russian democracy. We use the word 'crisis' in three senses. The first draws on the Greek word *krisis* to suggest a period of reflection in the life of the community, suggesting a turning point and moment of decision.[10] The succession struggle forced the Russian political establishment, as well as voters, to take a look at what had been created. The outcome of the two ballots, for parliament on 2 December 2007 and for the new president on 2 March 2008, suggests that not all that they saw was considered bad. The Putinist political order not only survived but was able to perpetuate itself in new forms. Putin's approach to politics and his plans for the future won the approval of the overwhelming majority of the population. However, critical observers were less impressed, and for many the 2007–8 electoral cycle represented conclusive proof of the political bankruptcy of the

---

[9] See Marina Ottaway, *Democracy Challenged: The Rise of Semi-Authoritarianism* (Washington, DC: Carnegie Endowment, 2003).

[10] Note also the complementary Greek term *krinein*, meaning (1) to separate, to divide, to classify, to distinguish, to select, to approve, to define, to determine; (2) to judge, to discern, to explicate, to believe, to interpret; (3) to pass judgment, to decide, to sentence; and (4) to investigate, to explore. Despite the capaciousness of the term, the underlying sense, as with *krisis*, suggests a moment of decision based on judgment.

regime and the failure of democracy to take root in Russia's harsh climate.

Used in a second and conventional modern sense, evidence of a 'crisis' in Russia's democracy was apparent at this time. The inability of the opposition to put forward its views in the mass media, the suffocating predominance of the administrative regime in the political campaign, the ability of the authorities to interfere in the management of electoral procedures and of the election itself, and in general the high level of 'manual' manipulation of the whole formal process was apparent throughout. The succession acted as a catalyst that brought out the deeper inner workings of the regime and showed just how far para-constitutional practices could influence constitutional norms. Above all, the factionalised nature of the regime became increasingly obvious. While parties could fight for seats in parliament and the whole panoply of the Central Election Commission (CEC) and ever more elaborate rules governed the formal electoral process, a second para-constitutional struggle was being waged between factions.

As we shall see, the factional model as applied in this book is not just descriptive but is a dynamic model that allows us to understand the interactions of groups and institutions. The succession revealed the system at its most vulnerable and brought to the surface subterranean processes. It also brought to the fore the ideological assertion of a distinct Russian model of society. The notion of 'sovereign democracy' provided the intellectual legitimation of the para-constitutional order. Not surprisingly, defenders of unadulterated constitutionalism, including Medvedev, baulked at the term. The debate revealed the tension between two schools of thought: partisans of Russia as a normal liberal capitalist democracy, governed by the rule of law and effective constitutional constraints on the exercise of power accompanied by formal procedures of popular account-ability; and adherents of the view that Russia as a great power should be more assertive in world politics and practise elements of exceptionalism at home as a preparatory phase for a more self-sustaining liberal democracy at some unspecified point in the future.

This brings us to the third sense in which the term is used. This draws on the Chinese approach that depicts a crisis as both a danger and an opportunity. The risks attending the succession crisis of 2007–8 were at the forefront of the regime's approach to the elections, seeing the threat of an 'orange' revolution everywhere (referring to the event in autumn 2004 in which popular mobilisation forced a third round in the Ukrain-ian presidential election), and doing all in its power to stamp out inde-pendent popular mobilisation, as well as warning of the danger of foreign interference. The risk was that the regime would not be able to

perpetuate itself, and even that the country would fall prey to disintegra-
tive tendencies. At the same time, the opportunity was provided by the
forced transparency that the election provided. It brought out the fever,
to shift to a medical metaphor, and as in the turning point of an illness,
could prove cathartic: either the patient would be healed, or they would
die. Thus crisis in this sense means not sclerosis but the struggle for life.

After taking a long look at itself during the succession, Russian democracy did not simply revert to the status quo ante. The rampant factionalism
clearly represented a danger to the coherence of the state, and the insidious
nature of para-constitutional practices eroded not only the effectiveness
but also the legitimacy of the formal constitutional order. The new leadership recognised that the gap between the two would have to be narrowed, if
not closed, and the regime would have to subordinate itself to the formal
rules to which it professed loyalty. This was the fundamental challenge
facing the new president from 2008, and one which Medvedev acknowledged in his condemnation of 'legal nihilism' and attempts to curb pervasive corruption. Although it would be too simple to assign Putin the role as
unmitigated defender of the administrative regime, his glowering presence
as prime minister from May 2008 inhibited the struggle to overcome the
'legal nihilism' and meta-corruption.

Russia may have endured a permanent crisis lasting well over a century, but there is also a crisis in the way that we analyse the country.
A crisis in crisis studies can be identified, with a ready recourse to
stereotypes and the abstract identification of faults and flaws in the
country; while Russian politicians and scholars have no less of a procliv-
ity to apply ontological characteristics to matters more readily explained
by temporal factors. In this study we will avoid both praise and condemnation, and instead try to free analysis of the whiff of Cold War thinking
that pervades so much analysis today. In methodological terms, this
work is based on a close reading of the Russian and western scholarly
literature and academic analysis, the study of the secondary literature,
current affairs periodicals and newspapers (the 'first draft of history'),
and above all on interviews and discussions with Russian politicians and
scholars. It makes use of polling and survey data, which provide a
singular, although invaluable, approach to the study of the highly complex reality that is contemporary Russia. The crisis of Russian democracy is unlikely to be resolved soon, but as long as it remains a crisis and
not a breakdown, there remains the possibility of renewal and revival.

Canterbury,
December 2009

Acknowledgements

Many scholars have shared their time and expertise with me. I am especially grateful to Oksana Antonenko, Yitzhak Brudny, Philip Boobbyer, Sam Charap, Timothy Colton, Piotr Dutkiewicz, Oksana Gaman-Golutvina, Kathryn Hendley, Svyatoslav Kaspe, Andrew Kuchins, Bobo Lo, Boris Makarenko, Vitaly Merkushev, Vyacheslav Nikonov, Sergei Peregudov, Nikolai Petrov, Thomas Remington, Neil Robinson, Peter Rutland, Dmitry Trenin and Alexei Zudin. Collaboration with the Institute of Law and Public Policy in Moscow, under the directorship of Olga Sidorovich, as always has been most helpful, and I thank all those who have helped in the development of this work. I am particularly grateful to Karen Dawisha at Miami University, Ohio, Clifford Gaddy at the Brookings Institution, Philip Hanson of the Royal Institute of International Affairs, Boris Kapustin at Yale/Moscow, Marlene Laruelle in Paris, and my colleague at the University of Kent, Adrian Pabst. The faults and views, of course, remain my own. I am most grateful for the help provided by Anna Miller in the Templeman Library and for the secretarial and other assistance of Gemma Chapman, Ann Hadaway, Jean Hudson, Nicola Huxtable and Suzie Robinson in the Department of Politics and International Relations at the University of Kent. The work of David Johnson deserves special mention, since his *Johnson's Russia List* provides scholars with a daily comprehensive and balanced coverage of developments in Russia and its region. It is my great pleasure to acknowledge the support of British Academy Small Research Grant SG-47170 in the development of the work. I am also pleased to acknowledge the support of the Kennan Institute of the Woodrow Wilson International Center for Scholars, Washington, DC, which provided a stimulating environment to work while undertaking a Short-Term Fellowship there in autumn 2007, and where this book was born.

Note on transliteration

In this book I follow the Library of Congress system of transliteration in its adapted British form. In transliterating Cyrillic, I use conventional English-language spelling of commonly used Russian proper names. The 'iu' letter becomes 'yu', 'ia' becomes 'ya', and at the beginning of names 'e' become 'ye' (Yevgeny rather than Evgeny). Thus, El'tsin becomes Yeltsin, Ekaterinburg is Yekaterinburg, and Riiazan is Ryazan. I have tried to be consistent without being pedantic. Anglicised name forms tend to be used (so 'Alexei', 'Dmitry, 'Alexander' and 'Yuri', rather than 'Aleksei', Dmitrii', 'Aleksandr' and Yurii), but for bibliographical references in the notes and Bibliography I have used transliterations of the Russian names.

1 The dual state in Russia

The debate over Russian politics remains as contested as ever, but with an emerging consensus that by the end of Vladimir Putin's second presidential term in 2008, Russian democracy was in crisis. The system in formal institutional terms was undoubtedly a liberal democracy, but practice fell short of declared principles. Views differed over the reasons for, and nature of, the crisis. This chapter will focus on two key issues. First, it will provide a theoretical framework in which the features of the crisis can be examined; and second, the fundamental processes characterising the crisis will be analysed. The combination of methodological and substantive analysis will allow us not only to examine developments, but also to frame how best to think about contemporary Russian politics. Our dual state model, which contrasts the constitutional state with the administrative regime, suggests that it is premature to write off the democratising impulse in Russia altogether. Instead, we shall argue that in an intensely contradictory but nonetheless substantive manner, the potential for democratic renewal within the existing constitutional order has not been exhausted; but at the same time authoritarian consolidation remains possible.

Politics in the 'gray zone'

The crisis of Russian democracy does not take place in a vacuum, and reflects the broader challenges facing the post-communist world. The instrumental use of the democratisation agenda in the post-Cold War world has provoked something of a backlash against the whole notion of a staged transition to democracy. The democratisation 'industry' has also been called into question.[1] The reality on the ground has prompted

---

[1] Sarah L. Henderson, *Building Democracy in Contemporary Russia: Western Support for Grassroots Organizations* (Ithaca and London: Cornell University Press, 2003); Marina Ottaway and Thomas Carothers (eds.), *Funding Virtue: Civil Society Aid and Democracy Promotion* (Washington, DC: Carnegie Endowment for International Peace, 2000); Peter J. Schraeder, *Exporting Democracy: Rhetoric vs. Reality* (Boulder, CO: Lynne Rienner, 2002); Janine R. Wedel, *Collision and Collusion: The Strange Case of Western Aid to Eastern Europe 1989–1998* (Basingstoke and London: Macmillan, 1998).

some rethinking, since much of the post-Soviet region appears trapped between an authoritarian past and an unclear future. Against this background, Thomas Carothers announced 'The end of the transition paradigm'.[2] In his view, early work on 'transitology' in the 1980s was later adopted as a 'universal paradigm' based on a number of assumptions: 'that any country moving *away* from dictatorial rule can be considered a country in transition *toward* democracy';[3] 'that democratisation tends to unfold in a set sequence of stages', with an *opening* followed by a *breakthrough*, with *consolidation* coming along at the end of the process; a belief in 'the determinative importance of elections';[4] that structural factors, such as level of economic development, institutional legacies, cultural traditions and the like will not be decisive; and finally, that the transitions were taking place in viable states.[5] Carothers notes that 'Of the nearly 100 countries considered as "transitional" in recent years, only a relatively small number – probably fewer than 20 – are clearly en route to becoming successful, well-functioning democracies ...'[6] Russia is not one of these.

Elections and managed democracy

The other countries find themselves in what Carothers calls the 'gray zone'. These are characterised by a number of syndromes, including 'feckless pluralism', notably in Latin America but not only there, where 'the whole class of political elites, though plural and competitive, are profoundly cut off from the citizenry, rendering political life an ultimately hollow, unproductive exercise'.[7] Another syndrome is 'dominant-power politics', where there is some formal contestation, but a group, 'whether it is a movement, a party, an extended family, or a single leader – dominates the system in such a way that there appears to be little prospect of alternation of power in the foreseeable future'.[8] He notes that in dominant-power systems, there is 'the blurring of the line between the state and the ruling party (or ruling political forces)',[9] a feature that is characteristic of Russian politics. As a description of contemporary Russian politics, Carother's analysis can hardly be bettered, yet it lacks a conceptual appreciation of the dynamics of the system.

As Yeltsin's rule came to a close in 1999, it looked as if with his political demise the whole system established during the decade would

[2] Thomas Carothers, 'The End of the Transition Paradigm', *Journal of Democracy* 13, 1, January 2002, pp. 5–21.
[3] *Ibid.*, p. 6.   [4] *Ibid.*, p. 7.   [5] *Ibid.*, p. 8.   [6] *Ibid.*, p. 9.   [7] *Ibid.*, p. 11.
[8] *Ibid.*, pp. 11–12.   [9] *Ibid.*, p. 11.

also pass with him. As the succession approached, factional conflict intensified, to the point that the entire regime appeared under threat from insurgent elites in the capital and the regions, which forged an alliance to storm the Kremlin. In the event, the regime and its associated elites managed to survive, but it was a close-run thing. In the 2000 presidential election, Putin came to power and thereafter consolidated what came to be known as 'managed democracy', accompanied in his second term, from 2004, by the notion of 'sovereign democracy'. The rampant elite struggles of the 1990s gave way to a system in which elite conflict was internalised within the regime and an 'imposed consensus' prevailed in society.[10] In the 'gray zone', elections help sustain authoritarian regimes and, at the same time, constrain the opportunities for outsider groups to come to power. The 2007–8 electoral cycle and its associated succession was by now a smoothly managed process, although there were a few alarms on the way.

There is a process of 'dual adaptation' in Russian politics, reflecting the bifurcated nature of the system in its entirety. The electoral system operates at two levels, corresponding to the formal constitutional and nominal para-constitutional (administrative) levels. On the one hand, elections are held according to the appropriate legal-normative framework, the sphere of public politics and political contestation. On the other hand, a parallel para-constitutional system operates, in which the regime imposes its preferences and where factions seek to influence outcomes through a closed and shadow political system. The most successful actors are those who can operate successfully at both levels. The electoral process and parties are forced to adapt to both the formal and the informal levels, hence the emergence of a dual adaptive system.

Features of this emerged from the very first days of post-communist competitive politics (for an overview of the electoral performance of the main parties since 1993, see Table 1.1). No election in post-communist Russia can be considered to have been free and fair.[11] The December 1993 election and referendum on the constitution was condemned as fraudulent, with widespread ballot stuffing, accompanied by inflated

---

[10] The term 'imposed consensus' is from Vladimir Gel′man, 'Vtoroi elektoral′nyi tsikl i transformatsiya politicheskogo rezhima v Rossii', in V. Ya. Gel′man, G. V. Golosov and E. Yu. Meleshkina (eds.), *Vtoroi elektoral′nyi tsikl v Rossii: 1999–2000gg.* (Moscow: Ves′ mir, 2002).

[11] For the various methods employed to adapt elections to desired outcomes, see Mikhail Myagkov, Peter C. Ordeshook and Dimitry Shakin, 'Fraud or Fairytales: Russia and Ukraine's Electoral Experience', *Post-Soviet Affairs* 21, 2, 2005, pp. 91–131. Their arguments are developed at greater length in Mikhail Myagkov, Peter C. Ordeshook and Dimitry Shakin, *The Forensics of Election Fraud: Russia and Ukraine* (Cambridge: Cambridge University Press, 2009).

Table 1.1 *Vote distribution between major parties (PR vote), 1993–2007*

	1993	1995	1999	2003	2007
Turnout (%)	54.8	64.4	61.7	55.7	64.1
The 'against all' vote	4.22	2.77	3.30	4.70	n.a
Five elections					
Communist Party (CPRF)	11.6	22.3	24.3	12.6	11.6
Liberal Democratic Party (LDPR)	21.4	11.2	6.0	11.5	8.1
Yabloko	7.3	6.9	5.9	4.3	1.59
Four elections					
Agrarian Party	7.4	3.8	n.a	3.6	2.3
Three elections					
Women of Russia	7.6	4.6	2.0	n.a	n.a
Union of Right Forces (SPS)	n.a	n.a	8.5	4.0	0.96
Two elections					
Russia's Choice	14.5	3.9	n.a	n.a	n.a
Russian Unity and Concord (PRES)	6.3	0.4	n.a	n.a	n.a
Cedar	0.7	1.4	n.a	n.a	n.a
Our Home is Russia (NDR)	n.a.	10.1	1.2	n.a	n.a
Communist Workers for Russia	n.a	4.5	2.2	n.a	n.a
Congress of Russian Communities (KRO)	n.a	4.3	0.6	(see Rodina)	n.a
United Russia (Unity + OVR)	n.a	n.a	(see Edinstvo)	37.6	64.3
One election					
Democratic Party of Russia (DPR)	5.1	n.a	n.a	n.a	n.a
Edinstvo (Unity)	n.a	n.a	23.3	n.a	(see UR)
Fatherland – All Russia (OVR)	n.a	n.a	13.3	(see UR)	(see UR)

Rodina (Motherland)	n.a	n.a	n.a	9.0	(see JR)
Social Justice Party	n.a	n.a	n.a	3.1	n.a
Party of Russia's Rebirth	n.a	n.a	n.a	1.9	(see Patriots of Russia)
People's Party	n.a	n.a	n.a	1.2	n.a
Just Russia (JR)	n.a	n.a	n.a	n.a	7.74
Civic Force	n.a	n.a	n.a	n.a	1.05
Patriots of Russia	n.a	n.a	n.a	n.a	0.89
Party of Social Justice	n.a	n.a	n.a	n.a	0.22
Democratic Party	n.a	n.a	n.a	n.a	0.13
Other parties/against all/invalid	18.1	26.6	12.7	11.2	n.a
TOTAL (%)	100	100	100	100	100

Sources: Adapted from Richard Rose, Neil Munro and Stephen White, 'Voting in a Floating Party System: The 1999 Duma Election', *Europe-Asia Studies* 53, 3, May 2001, pp. 419–43, at p. 424; with 2003 data from *Vybory deputatov gosudarstvennoi dumy federal'nogo sobraniya Rossiiskoi Federatsii 2003: elektoral'naya statistika*, Central Electoral Commission (Moscow: Ves' Mir, 2004), pp. 29, 141, 192; and 2007 data from www. cikrf.ru.

turnout figures to ensure that the 50 per cent minimum was achieved to allow the constitution to be adopted.[12] The authors of a study of the December 1995 Duma elections note that 'The new Duma's own composition changed after the election in ways that bore little relation to the "will of the people" it was meant to have embodied.'[13] As always, the electoral system was condemned, with particular criticism of the excessively large numbers of parties and alliances that participated. By 2007 the opposite criticism was levelled: too few groupings were allowed to take part. There is also a broader institutional problem in that parties fight for representation in the Duma and not for power, since Russia's version of the separation of powers creates a disjuncture between parliamentary representation and government formation. Of course, strong representation may translate into veto power and allow access to governmental posts, but this is a matter of presidential choice and not a systemic characteristic.

At first, however, the 1999–2000 electoral cycle looked as if it would have the uncertainty of outcome that characterises genuinely free and fair elections. A multitude of forces rushed to fill what was perceived to be a developing vacuum as Yeltsin prepared to leave the scene. First, there were a number of ambitious regional leaders. These included Moscow mayor Yury Luzhkov, who allied with President Mintimir Shaimiev of Tatarstan and some others to create the Fatherland – All Russia (Otechestvo – Vsya Rossiya, OVR) electoral bloc, which by mid-1999 looked as if it would sweep all before it. The OVR threat was immeasurably strengthened when former prime minister Yevgeny Primakov in August 1999 agreed to act as the opposition's figurehead in the parliamentary elections and the putative candidate in the presidential ballot. Primakov had served as foreign minister from January 1996 and as prime minister from September 1998 to May 1999, and signalled the return of Soviet-era officials to prominence, ousting the new generation of 'democrats'. This shift in appointment patterns reinforced the consolidation of the administrative regime.

Second, the 1990s had spawned what were colloquially known as 'oligarchs', a new class of super-rich individuals who held a large part of the Russian economy in their hands. Boris Berezovsky, the most egregiously political of them all, crowed that seven bankers had been responsible for Yeltsin's re-election in 1996 and controlled 50 per cent of

---

[12] Richard Sakwa, 'The Russian Elections of December 1993', *Europe-Asia Studies* 47, 2, March 1995, pp. 195–227.

[13] Stephen White, Matthew Wyman and Sarah Oates, 'Parties and Voters in the 1995 Russian Duma Election', *Europe-Asia Studies* 49, 5, 1997, pp. 793–4.

the Russian economy.[14] Some of these had become very close to Yeltsin (although people like Berezovsky greatly exaggerated their proximity to the throne) and had virtually merged with the political system to create the 'family', the nexus of business and economic links. Even those not part of the 'family' network had a large stake in the Yeltsin succession. The alliance of regional leaders and big business sponsored what Henry Hale calls 'party substitutes', para-political groupings representing not social interests but acting as vehicles to seize the Kremlin.[15] We shall return to this issue below.

Third, the forthcoming electoral cycle was considered a contest between 'chekists of the Andropov school' and the democrats, with the Berezovsky-sponsored mass media warning that a 'communist restoration' would be catastrophic for the country. The liberal media was shocked by Primakov's suggestion that gubernatorial elections should be abolished, but the idea brought into focus fears that the security services were beginning to set the national agenda.[16] Such concerns had already been prompted by the role played by the 'party of war' in launching the first assault against Chechnya in December 1994, and again in the prominent role played by Yeltsin's 'bodyguard', Alexander Korzhakov, in 1996, when he advocated cancelling the presidential elections and fought against the liberal reformers in government. Putin's role at the head of the Federal Security Service (FSB, the successor to the KGB) in assisting Yeltsin dismiss Yury Skuratov as prosecutor general in spring 1999 signalled the growing role of the security services and brought Putin into the frame as a potential presidential nominee. Alexander Voloshin, who replaced Valentin Yumashev as head of the presidential administration on 19 March 1999, was the first to suggest that Putin could become president.[17] Primakov's dismissal on 12 May, on the eve of the Duma vote on Yeltsin's impeachment, signalled the beginning of Russia's first succession operation. The appointment of Sergei Stepashin as the new prime minister was considered no more than an interim measure, and he was replaced by Putin on 9 August. Rem Vyakhirev, at the head of the giant gas production and distribution monopoly, Gazprom, was immediately hauled over the coals for having

---

[14] The seven bankers were Boris Berezovsky, Vladimir Potanin, Mikhail Khodorkovsky, Vladimir Gusinsky, Alexander Smolensky, Mikhail Fridman and Pyotr Aven. Chrystia Freeland, John Thornhill and Andrew Gowers, 'Moscow's Group of Seven', *The Financial Times*, 1 November 1997.

[15] Henry E. Hale, *Why Not Parties in Russia? Democracy, Federalism and the State* (Cambridge: Cambridge University Press, 2006).

[16] Mikhail Zygar' and Valeri Panyushkin, *Gazprom: Novoe russkoe oruzhie* (Moscow: Zakharov, 2008), p. 70.

[17] *Ibid.*, p. 72.

financed Luzhkov and Primakov.[18] Even before Putin's accession, public
politics had been marginalised and the Kremlin had become the main
focus of decision-making at the political as well as the administrative
level: 'Chinovniki with endless papers glided along the red carpets,
glancing in the mirrors. This was already Byzantium.'[19] The semi-
autonomous administrative regime had taken shape during the period
of 'phoney democracy' between late 1991 and 1993, and it now came
into its own.

The fourth, and by far the weakest, collective actor in the succession
were the actual political parties. The Communist Party of the Russian
Federation (CPRF) had declined significantly since its powerful challenge in 1996, when the presidency seemed within its grasp, and the
party remained locked in a time warp of Soviet concerns and an increasingly outmoded leadership, personified by its head, Gennady
Zyuganov.[20] The liberal groupings, above all Yabloko and the Union of
Right Forces (SPS), were weakened by their endemic failure to unite.
Yabloko, headed from its foundation in 1993 to 2008 by Grigory
Yavlinsky, is typically characterised as the party of the intelligentsia
losers,[21] while the SPS is taken to represent the vulgar 'bourgeois'
winners. In the event, in autumn 1999 the regime created its own
para-political electoral machine, Unity, that managed to wrest the initiative from the other 'party substitutes' and forged a link between presidential leadership and party politics that had been missing throughout
the 1990s. Unity became the core of the pro-presidential United Russia
(UR) party, formed on 1 December 2001 when it incorporated the
remnants of OVR, and went on to dominate the parliamentary elections
in December 2003 and 2007.

The tension between popular choice and managed democracy has
been the subject of considerable analysis. The regime's creation and
sponsorship of Unity provided the instrument to shape the succession
operation and allow the designated successor, Putin, to come to power.
Colton and McFaul aptly call this 'the transition within the transition'.[22]
Although around 70 million people voted in each stage of the 1999–
2000 electoral cycle, a 'pre-selection' had taken place that eliminated

---

[18] *Ibid.*, p. 77. For various reasons Berezovsky was the loudest in calling for Vyakhirev's
resignation; *ibid.*, p. 78.
[19] *Ibid.*, p. 79.
[20] Luke March, 'The Contemporary Russian Left after Communism: Into the Dustbin of
History?', *The Journal of Communist Studies and Transition Politics* 22, 4, December 2006,
pp. 431–56.
[21] David White, *The Russian Democratic Party Yabloko* (Aldershot: Ashgate, 2006).
[22] Timothy J. Colton and Michael McFaul, *Popular Choice and Managed Democracy: The
Russian Elections of 1999 and 2000* (Washington, DC: Brookings Institution Press, 2003).

such powerful candidates as Luzhkov and Primakov by the time votes were cast in March 2000. Six months before the election, OVR looked set to equal the Communist vote, but after having been trashed by Sergei Dorenko and others on the main television channel (ORT), the party managed only third place with 13.3 per cent of the vote, compared to the CPRF's 24.3 per cent, while Unity gained 23.3 per cent, a major success given that it had been established only a few months earlier (Table 1.1). The Yabloko vote declined in December 1999 to 5.9 per cent compared to 6.9 per cent in 1995, and in the 2000 presidential election Yavlinsky scored two points lower than his party in the Duma election, confirming a secular decline that saw the party fail to enter parliament in 2003. Independent parties were crushed by the titanic struggle between Moscow and regional bureaucratic alliances.

Once in office, Putin developed the system of managed democracy as part of his project of technocratic modernisation. He had clearly taken to heart the classic argument of Samuel Huntington in his *Political Order in Changing Societies* about the dangers of excessive mobilisation in a period of change, a key text of the era before the modernisation paradigm gave way to the discourse of democratisation and globalisation.[23] As Colton and McFaul argue, 'Putin's minitransition inside the transition is a regression away from some of the democratic gains of the 1980s and 1990s – a backtracking and not merely stalling of forward motion.'[24] According to Gel'man, the 2003–4 electoral cycle demonstrated that an equilibrium had been reached in Russian politics, in a 'non-democratic consolidation' of a dominant party and suppression of the intense elite struggles that characterised Yeltsin's presidency.[25] For Richard Rose and his colleagues, this equilibrium represented the 'resigned acceptance of an incomplete democracy', with the regime enjoying majority approval and with no majority for any alternative.[26] The persistence of a regime, they stress, does not necessarily betoken viability. The East European communist regimes travelled the road from stability to collapse in a matter of months.[27] From our dual state perspective,

[23] Samuel Huntington, *Political Order in Changing Societies* (New Haven, CT: Yale University Press, 1968).
[24] Colton and McFaul, *Popular Choice and Managed Democracy*, p. 16.
[25] V. Ya. Gel'man, 'Evolyutsiya elektoral'noi politiki v Rossii: Na puti k nedemokraticheskoi konsolidatsii', in V. Ya. Gel'man (ed.), *Tretii elektoral'nyi tsikl v Rossii, 2003–2004 gody: Kollektivnaya monografiya* (St Petersburg: European University, 2007), pp. 17–38.
[26] Richard Rose, Neil Munro and William Mishler, 'Resigned Acceptance of an Incomplete Democracy: Russia's Political Equilibrium', *Post-Soviet Affairs* 20, 3, 2004, pp. 195–218.
[27] *Ibid.*, p. 212.

we argue that by 2003–4 the two pillars had become locked in a stalemate that endures to the present.

Colton and McFaul nevertheless suggest that it is wrong to dismiss
Russian elections as meaningless and as entirely staged. The 1999–2000
electoral cycle (just like the 2007–8 cycle, but in a far more overt
manner) was accompanied by real struggles over 'power, position and
policy'.[28] The argument can be applied to the 2003–4 cycle, although
the presidential election was more of a plebiscite than a contest with real
alternatives.[29] Once in power, Putin's government dominated the political system, the political agenda and increasingly the whole political
process. This in part embodied aspirations to manage the political
situation, but it also reflected the inability of the political opposition to
respond to the changing dynamics of Russian politics in order to forge an
effective and credible political alternative. Even Mikhail Khodorkovsky,
the head of Russia's largest private oil company, Yukos, about whose
destruction by the administrative regime we shall have much to say later,
came to this view in the wake of the 2003–4 elections.[30] The split in the
liberal wing between SPS and Yabloko meant that neither entered the
Fourth Duma. The electoral failure of independent political forces is
pre-eminently because of the manipulative techniques employed by the
administrative regime, but the 'democrats' themselves also contributed
to what Vladimir Ryzhkov, a Duma deputy between 1993 and 2007,
called the 'liberal débâcle' of 2003–4, above all by their failure to unite
and inability to distance themselves from the chaos of the 1990s.[31]

For Colton and McFaul, the concept of 'managed democracy' accurately reflects the nature of the emerging system. There remains a degree
of popular choice and accountability, but this is combined with constraints on the free play of political forces and the contestation of policy
options. As they note, 'If it is too early to sign the death certificate for
democracy, it is too late to ignore tokens of a backing away from the
liberal and democratic ideals in whose name the Soviet regime was
overthrown.'[32] Their data demonstrate the gulf between the normative
orientation towards democracy of the Russian population and their

---

[28] Colton and McFaul, *Popular Choice and Managed Democracy*, p. 11.
[29] Richard Sakwa, 'The 2003–2004 Russian Elections and Prospects for Democracy',
Europe-Asia Studies 57, 3, May 2005, pp. 369–98.
[30] Mikhail Khodorkovskii, 'Krizis liberalizma v Rossii', *Vedomosti*, 29 March 2004; an
English version was published as Mikhail Khodorkovsky, 'Liberalism in Crisis: What
Is to Be Done?', *Moscow Times*, 31 March, 1 April 2004.
[31] Vladimir Ryzhkov, 'The Liberal Debacle', *Journal of Democracy* 15, 3, July 2004,
pp. 52–8.
[32] Colton and McFaul, *Popular Choice and Managed Democracy*, p. 207.

perception of what was really happening.[33] While people support democracy, they do not think Russia is one.

The party line

There are two main approaches to explaining Russia's stunted party development. The first focuses on social and cultural factors 'from below': the weakness of an independent civil society, blurred class identities, a cultural resistance to party affiliation, and weak civic subjectivity. The second prioritises institutional design 'from above', notably the 'superpresidential' system, which towers above the government, parliament and the judicial system and reproduces a 'monocentric' system to which all socio-political life is subordinated.[34] These are exogenous factors, and there is also the endogenous approach, focusing on the behaviour of parties themselves. One of the best examples of this is the work by Riggs and Schraeder, who argue that the precipitate fall of the Soviet system disrupted the evolutionary emergence of a stable party system by cutting its links to society, and thus the party system was reconstituted from above by elites, a pattern that was reinforced by subsequent elections. Thus the party system was largely the outcome of elite interactions and would remain stunted until parties were able to re-establish genuine reciprocal links with society.[35] In a later study of the 2003–4 electoral cycle, they concluded that the elite-driven party system had only intensified and accelerated the 'Mexicanisation' of Russian politics, the establishment of a one-party dominant political system.[36] Clearly, any convincing study of the Russian party system must combine endogenous with exogenous factors, and as Putin took an active managerial approach to party development, exogenous factors became decisive.

Parties in Russia fulfil few of the classical functions of such organisations. Parties have limited political reach and fail to provide the framework for the institutionalisation of political competition or the integration of regional and national politics.[37] They are not the source

---

[33] *Ibid.*, pp. 220 and *passim.*

[34] See Boris Makarenko, '"Nanopartiinaya" sistema', *Pro et Contra* 11, 4–5, July–October 2007, pp. 43–57, for a discussion of these two approaches.

[35] Jonathan W. Riggs and Peter J. Schraeder, 'Russia's Political Party System as an Impediment to Democratization', *Demokratizatsiya* 12, 2, Spring 2004, pp. 265–93.

[36] Jonathan W. Riggs and Peter J. Schraeder, 'Russia's Political Party System as a (Continued) Impediment to Democratization: The 2003 Duma and 2004 Presidential Elections in Perspective', *Demokratizatsiya* 13, 1, Winter 2005, pp. 141–51.

[37] Kathryn Stoner-Weiss, 'Weak National Parties, Weak Central State', in *Resisting the State: Reform and Retrenchment in Post-Soviet Russia* (Cambridge: Cambridge University Press, 2006), pp. 111–46.

of governmental formation, personnel appointments or policy generation, and neither are they, more broadly, 'system-forming', in the sense
of providing the framework for political order. Although parties are the
main actors in parliamentary elections, they are at best accessories to
processes taking place within the regime. This applies to UR as much as
to other parties, hence its role as a 'dominant party' is limited. The
regime's monopoly over political resources and its control over the
distribution of rents was systematically reinforced by Putin, resulting in
the marginalisation of other parties and institutions, to the degree that
the very term 'opposition' can be used only conditionally.[38] Medvedev
took the opposite tack, stressing endogenous weakness when he argued
that the problem lay with the opposition itself, notably its leading representatives, the CPRF and the Liberal Democratic Party of Russia
(LDPR), headed by the flamboyant Vladimir Zhirinovsky, and insisted
that 'our citizens have outgrown our opposition', and the failure to
advance coherent and popular alternative programmes led to the 'marginalisation of the opposition', which had nothing to do with state
actions under Putin.[39] He noted that 'The degradation of the opposition, above all on the right [i.e., the liberals], began much earlier,
basically in the late 1990s.' He was particularly concerned about the
absence of a serious rightist opposition but stressed that UR's legislation
was 'in essence right-conservative in content'.[40]

We have mentioned Hale's idea of party substitutes. He examines the
question in terms of a political market where voters and political elites
are seen as consumers courted by suppliers of various types. Hale argues
that Russian political parties were unable to close out the electoral
market, and that various non-party alternatives such as factions, cliques
and other informal aggregations as well as corporate groups were able to
take on quasi-party functions to offer alternative paths to power. Parties
in his view organise on the basis of two types of capital: ideational,
drawing on issues of identity and values that attract people to the party;
and administrative, which includes offices and power that can attract
ambitious politicians. Russian parties have not been able to establish a
monopoly on these sources of political capital and are thus challenged by
non-party alternatives. Although parties do perform important functions, including structuring electoral competition, they have not been
able to establish dominance over the political system. There are

---

[38] For informative discussions on the fate of the opposition in Russia, held under the aegis
of the 'Panorama' centre, see E. Mikhailovskii (ed.), *Rossiya Putina: Ruiny i rostki
oppozitsii*, 'Managed Democracy' series (Moscow: Panorama, 2005).
[39] Nikolai Svanidze and Marina Svanidze, *Medvedev* (St Petersburg: Amfora, 2008), p. 85.
[40] *Ibid.*, p. 86.

institutional reasons for this, above all the strong presidency which undermines incentives for party affiliation, and instead personal patronage and informal networks bypass the party system. Hale accepts that parties have the potential to dominate the electoral market, and in his view UR began to develop as a programmatic party and thus moved away from its project party roots.[41]

Our dual state model suggests that, with all its failings, UR was never simply a clientelist organisation, and indeed, in terms of distributing patronage remains subordinate to the administrative regime, but in the sphere of the constitutional state it acts as the main player in the electoral market place, in which it competes with a putative second party of power, Just Russia (Spravedlivaya Rossiya, JR), as well as the Communist and liberal oppositional parties. The electoral sphere was severely constrained by the interventions of the administrative regime and by the dominance of UR, yet it retained a fundamental level of competitiveness, if only because of the shifting and uncertain tactics of the administrative regime, as well as its fear that the excessive applications of administrative resources would undermine its own legitimacy (something that was strongly in evidence in the 11 October 2009 regional elections, see Chapter 9). Ironically, if the normative sphere were to achieve full autonomy and the administrative regime to shrivel away, then the dominance of UR would probably become absolute, given its accumulated reserves of political and administrative capital. A speedy return to genuine constitutionalism and the abolition of the tutelary aspects of the administrative regime entailed certain political risks, as the exponents of managed democracy and even the Medvedevite reformers were well aware.

One of Putin's priorities on coming to power was to restructure the party system. The aim was to reduce the number of parties and to ensure that those remaining actively participated in national and regional elections. The party law of July 2001 and subsequent amendments (notably in October 2004) meant that from 1 January 2006 parties required a minimum of 50,000 members and were to have regional branches with no fewer than 500 members each in more than half of Russia's regions where the population exceeds 500,000, and branches with no fewer than 250 people in the others. This was reinforced by a federal law of May 2002 stipulating that regional parliaments were to be formed on the party principle, with no fewer than half (and in many cases it was more than half) to be elected by proportional representation and the other part from single-mandate

---

[41] Hale, *Why Not Parties in Russia?*

constituencies.[42] Putin spectacularly achieved his aim of defragmenting the party system. In September 2007 the Federal Registration Service published a list with only fifteen parties eligible to fight the election, down from thirty-five in 2003 (see Table 7.1). Notable victims of the cull included Ryzhkov's Republican Party of Russia and a number of leftist parties. The disparate 'Other Russia' grouping was unable to meet the relevant conditions, and former prime minister, Mikhail Kasyanov, left in disappointment.

There were now fewer parties, and those that remained were stronger in physical terms, but their independence had waned. Stronger parties did not mean a stronger democracy. Instead of autonomously aggregating and articulating popular concerns and giving free vent to criticism, the regime parties turned into the opposite: the top-down mobilisation of the vote. Their prestige, never very high, also remained poor in terms of popular confidence ratings. In 2006 only 24 per cent considered that political parties played an important role in Russia, while 64.5 per cent thought that they played an insignificant or non-existent role. Only 17 per cent thought that a genuine multi-party system had been created, while 41.6 per cent saw only one real party, United Russia.[43] In late October 2007, Putin's presidency enjoyed an 80–83 per cent approval rating, followed rather surprisingly by the media and then the armed forces, while political parties, the State Duma and the courts came in bottom and rated around 17 per cent. A third of respondents at that time considered Russian elections unfair.[44] A later longitudinal study tracing trust in the main Russian social and political institutions found parties stuck firmly at the bottom (Table 1.2). Participatory institutions, intended to represent public interests, were trusted less than governmental and security agencies. The multi-party system was clearly in deep crisis, with Putin's reforms having reduced competitiveness accompanied by the monopolisation of party political representation by United Russia.

Nearly two decades after the fall of communism, it is still not entirely clear how the standard western political spectrum can be mapped on to the Russian political scene. The left–right division does apply and indicates the broad perspectives of a party, although drastically modified by Russian specificities. The CPRF espouses right-wing nationalist values

---

[42] For a good overview and evaluation, see Kenneth Wilson, 'Party-System Development Under Putin', *Post-Soviet Affairs* 22, 4, October–December 2006, pp. 314–48.

[43] All data from the All-Russia Centre for the Study of Public Opinion (VTsIOM), Leontii Byzov, 'Drugaya "Edinaya Rossiya"?', *Profil'*, 4 September 2006, pp. 36–7, at p. 36.

[44] Nadezhda Kevorkova, interview with the head of VTsIOM, Valeri Fedorov, 'Rossiya segodnya: Strana nizkikh energii i slabykh emotsii', *Gazeta*, 2 November 2007, p. 10.

Table 1.2 *Trust in state and social institutions, 1998–2009*

Institution	1998	2001	2004	2008	2009
President	14	67	70	73	63
Government	11	30	32	60	54
Church	43	38	44	52	51
Army	33	53	42	63	50
Television	32	–	31	34	35
Press (newspapers, journals)	31	–	28	26	26
State Duma	11	13	19	29	23
Federation Council	14	21	21	31	23
Police	11	18	12	24	22
Judicial system	13	-	15	21	20
Trade unions	21	23	22	23	18
Political parties	7	6	9	13	11

Source: M. K. Gorshkov, R. Krumm and V. V. Petukhov (eds.), *Rossiya na novom perelome: Strakhi i trevogi*, Friedrich Ebert Foundation and RAN Institute of Sociology (Moscow: Al'fa-M, 2009), p. 59.

while propounding a left-wing agenda of social justice and limited markets, and the LDPR advances a radical patriotic agenda. The LDPR was Russia's oldest political party, established in 1989, whereas the CPRF was re-established in 1993, the same year in which Yabloko was established. Under Putin significant evolution took place, and the rudiments of a western-style political landscape emerged, but in some ways the pre-revolutionary political map of the constitutional monarchy period fits better, although admittedly comparisons are tenuous. The liberal, but oppositional, Yabloko party replayed the role of the Constitutional Democrats (Kadets), firmly opposed to the authorities and refusing to engage in dialogue with them, while SPS took the part of the Octobrists, more willing to work with the regime. Putin brought the liberal conservatives over to his side, espousing a statist agenda of strong government and foreign-policy independence, and thus separating them from the more classically liberal parties.

The ideological grid, however, has to be supplemented by an administrative one, indicating a party's relationship with the regime. Four broad types can be identified. The first is *programme* parties, those with a clear platform adopted by some sort of inner-party democracy and pursued independently by the leadership and consistently presented to the public. The CPRF and Yabloko are the best examples, but their increasing marginalisation illustrated the decline of this type of autonomous party. The second is *project* parties, created typically not long before elections as part of an ulterior strategy of competing elite groups. A classic project party was the patriotic-leftist Rodina in the 2003 election, designed to draw votes away from the Communists. The LDPR began as a project party, and although it still works with the regime it has developed its own programmatic autonomy; and thus we recognise that parties may display hybrid qualities. The third category is various government-sponsored groupings to represent the system itself. This type can be described as *regime* parties, when they are sponsored by the ruling group, established to manipulate and shape political space and in some cases to act as what is called 'the party of power'. In 1995 Our Home is Russia (Nash Dom Rossiya, NDR) was an early and undeveloped prototype, but Unity in the 1999 election was rather more successful, as was its successor United Russia in 2003 and 2007, and in 2006 was joined by another regime-based project party, Just Russia. The fourth type is *spoiler* parties, which have little chance of success in their own right but which are designed to cause confusion in a political niche and to draw votes away from opposition groupings. The dominance of project and regime parties inhibited the development of a competitive and structured multi-party system and undermined genuine programme parties. This weakness was reinforced by the structure of electoral politics, with parties counting for little in presidential elections. In the 2000 election, the leaders of all main political parties threw in their hats, but in 2004 they did not even bother to do this, while in 2008 various inducements came into operation to ensure the semblance of competition.

The grouping led by Luzhkov and his allies in 1999, OVR, can be considered a distinctive subtype, the *oppositional project* party. It was certainly dealt some harsh blows by Yeltsin's government during the campaign, but as Colton and McFaul note, it also suffered endogenous weakness and failed to develop as a popular movement, relying too much on the mobilisational resources of regional governors and not developing a coherent political programme. The 'OVR vowed essentially to substitute one set of veteran officeholders for another and dangled no vision of rebirth.'[45] Much the same can be said of the CPRF, which squandered the opportunity presented by the economic crash of August 1998 and failed to build an opposition coalition. Instead of turning towards social democracy, the party sought allies on the nationalist flank while remaining far to the left of the median voter, and thus became increasingly marginalised. Putin was implacable in his refusal to engage with the Communists' ideology and ensured that they played no part in setting the political agenda. On the other flank, by 2003 the chronic

---

[45]   Colton and McFaul, *Popular Choice and Managed Democracy*, p. 107.

sectarianism of Yabloko and SPS prevented them from crossing the 5 per cent representation threshold, and they failed to enter the Duma as organised parties.[46] Putin's domination of an expanding centrist position was thus given free rein.

The 2003 Duma election witnessed the halving of support for the CPRF, while neither of the two main liberal parties entered parliament. The liberal vote had been steadily falling since 1993 (see Table 1.3), a decline that was vividly apparent in the Moscow City Duma elections on 11 December 2005. In the country's richest city with a strong middle class, the liberal parties could barely muster a fifth of the vote. They did, however, cross the 10 per cent barrier because Yabloko and SPS campaigned together;[47] a lesson on the importance of unity that was lost in the national parliamentary elections two years later. Most estimates suggested that the core liberal vote was no more than 7–10 per cent; this was the same proportion who accepted market values, that 'the state's main task is to defend the freedom of citizens, and that the state itself was the greatest threat to their freedom'.[48] The liberal opposition largely failed to renew its leadership, notably Boris Nemtsov and Grigory Yavlinsky who were tainted with past failures and not associated with forward-looking strategies. Only the SPS brought in a fresh personality in Nikita Belykh, their young but inexperienced new leader from Perm. In May 2005 he took over from former deputy prime minister Nemtsov at the head of SPS and adopted a much stronger anti-Putin stance that included joining the non-systemic opposition headed by the former world chess champion, Garry Kasparov. The strategy of intra-systemic opposition, however, also gave poor results, and the 2007 election once again saw organised liberalism excluded from parliament.

The history of the Rodina party illustrates faction-fighting in action. Established in September 2003, the bloc from the first was torn between internal leadership struggles, notably between its social democratically inclined Sergei Glaz'ev and the more nationalist Dmitry Rogozin. The party's fate in the end was determined less by internal rather than by exogenous factors, notably a 'struggle between the towers [of the Kremlin]', with at least two of the Kremlin's factions coming into conflict. Rodina gained the support of Igor Sechin, a deputy head of the presidential administration and Putin's loyal associate, on behalf of the

---

[46] *Ibid.*, p. 140.
[47] For a study of the Moscow Duma election as a rehearsal for the national elections, see Andrei Ryabov, 'Vybory v Moskve i politicheskaya perspektiva', *Svobodnaya mysl'*, No. 1, January 2006, pp. 44–52; on the success of liberal unity, pp. 47–8.
[48] Andrei Gromov and Tat'yana Gurova, 'Kapital'nyi remont konservatizma', *Ekspert*, No. 17, 9 May 2005, in *Ekspert: Luchshie materialy*, No. 2, 2007, pp. 106–13, at p. 111.

Table 1.3 Secular trends in party list voting

	1993	1995		1999		2003		2007	
	% total	% total	Change on previous election	% total	Change on previous election	% total	Change on previous election	% total	Change on previous election
Communists (parties)	20.3 (2)	30.6 (3)	+10.3 (+1)	28.1 (5)	−2.5 (+2)	19.3 (3)	−8.8 (−2)	11.57 (1)	−7.73 (−2)
Centrists (parties)	23.1 (5)	24.8 (13)	−1.7 (+8)	41.9 (9)	+17.1 (−4)	41.1 (5)	−0.8 (−4)	74.47 (4)	+33.37 (+4)
Liberals (parties)	27.3 (3)	16.1 (11)	−11.2 (+8)	15.0 (3)	−1.1 (−8)	8.5 (3)	−6.5 (no change)	3.6 (3)	−4.9 (no change)
National Patriots (parties)	22.8 (1)	21.8 (9)	−1.0 (+8)	7.4 (5)	−14.4 (−4)	23.0 (8)	+15.8 (+3)	9.25 (3)	−13.75 (−5)
Against all	4.2	2.8	−1.4	3.3	+0.5	4.7	+1.4	n.a	n.a
Turnout	54.8	64.4	+9.6	61.9	−2.5	55.7	−6.2	64.1	+8.4

Sources: Yitzhak Brudny, 'Continuity or Change in Russian Electoral Patterns? The December 1999–March 2000 Election Cycle', in Archie Brown (ed.), *Contemporary Russian Politics: A Reader* (Oxford: Oxford University Press, 2001), p. 164; Viktor Sheinis, 'Vybory i politicheskoe razvitie', in M. McFaul, N. Petrov and A. Ryabov (eds.), *Rossiya v izbiratel'nom tsikle 1999–2000 godov* (Moscow: Gendal'f and Moscow Carnegie Center, 2000), pp. 385–6; Yusup Abdurakhmanov, 'Ideological Orientations of the Russian Electorate in Duma Elections', *Perspectives on European Politics and Society* 6, 2, 2004, pp. 209–37, at p. 220; materials from Central Election Commission 2003 and 2007.

Note: The ideological groups are collated as follows (main parties only):

Communists: Communist Party of the Russian Federation (CPRF); Agrarian Party of Russia (APR) until 2003; Communists – Toiling Russia – For the Soviet Unionl; Russian Party of Pensioners and Party of Social Justice.

Centrists: Women of Russia; Party of Russian Unity and Concord (PRES); Democratic Party of Russia (DPR); Party of Workers' Self-Management; Our Home is Russia (NDR); Unity/Medved; Fatherland – All Russia (OVR); United Russia; Just Russia; Agrarian Party (in 2007); Democratic Party.

Democrats Reformers: Russia's Choice; Democratic Choice of Russia (DVR); Russian Movement for Democratic Reforms; Russian Constitutional Democratic Party; Union of Right Forces (SPS); Yabloko; Civic Force.

National Patriots: Liberal Democratic Party of Russia (LDPR); Congress of Russian Communities (KRO); Rodina (Popular Patriotic Union); Patriots of Russia; Party of Social Justice.

siloviki (from *silovye struktury*, the security apparatus writ large, people with a security service background and affiliated individuals). Democratic statists such as Vladislav Surkov, the deputy head of the presidential administration responsible for managing domestic political affairs, had never been keen on Rodina, and for him it would have been enough for the party to draw some 5 per cent of the vote from the Communists in December 2003, whereas its 9 per cent gave it a confidence that threatened to turn into uncontrollability. Sechin and the *siloviki* were quite happy to have a nationalistic presence in the Duma, but Surkov considered Rogozin's independence a threat.[49] Rodina's crude espousal of nationalist motifs in the 2005 Moscow City Duma elections demonstrated the rise in 'nationalist great Russian sentiments'.[50] One of its campaign slogans called for the city to be cleansed of 'trash', with the graphics indicating that the target was Caucasians (in the Russian sense). The administrative regime has been deeply concerned about the emergence of an independent nationalist movement, which would threaten its autonomy and possibly its very existence. Rodina's unpredictability and nationalism led to various splits being engineered, and in due course its remnants merged with the new Kremlin project party, JR.

Some in the Kremlin began to fear an excessively strong UR, and this was one reason for the creation of an alternative regime party, this time intended to represent the centre-left of the political spectrum. If Surkov was behind the development of UR, JR was sponsored by the *siloviki*, and for that reason its establishment was opposed by Surkov. Rodina formally merged with the Party of Life and the Party of Pensioners on 28 October 2006 to create JR, with the People's Party joining in February 2007. The new party was headed by the speaker of the Federation Council and the former head of the Party of Life, Sergei Mironov (another of Putin's colleagues from St Petersburg), while Alexander Babakov, the former chairman of Rodina, became secretary of the new party's central council presidium. Like Rodina in 2003, the aim was to wean part of the membership and electorate from the Communists and Zhirinovsky's Liberal Democrats, and thus the new organisation was pre-eminently a project party. There was also a spoiler aspect, designed to fill a niche and thus crowd out a genuine independent left-of-centre party.[51] Voters loyal to the Kremlin now had greater choice, but a side effect was the blurring of UR's monopoly. The creation of JR reflected

---

[49] Alexei Titkov, *'Party Number Four' – Rodina: Whence and Why?* (Moscow: Panorama, 2006), pp. 34–5.
[50] Ryabov, 'Vybory v Moskve i politicheskaya perspektiva', p. 48.
[51] Stephen Sestanovich, 'Putin's Invented Opposition', *Journal of Democracy* 18, 2, April 2007, p. 123.

tensions between various groups in the Kremlin and attempts to encompass a broader range of the electorate without conceding control. It cannot, however, be regarded simply as an attempt to formalise factional conflict, although that was a possible outcome. It was, as Luke March notes, an example of a 'parastatal' party effectively controlled by the state that sought to channel opposition into non-threatening forms.[52] The aim was to damp down elite competition, not to manage or even stimulate it.

In the wake of the liberal failure in the 2003 elections, Yabloko and SPS were left a tiny rump of single-mandate MPs in parliament. Ryzhkov and Nemtsov took the lead in trying to create a united liberal party, above all by facilitating the union of SPS with Yabloko, possibly on the basis of Ryzhkov's Republican Party.[53] One thing was clear, confirmed by numerous polls: a party created from scratch would stand no chance of entering the Duma in 2007, especially since by then the representation threshold had been raised to 7 per cent. If they wished to become a serious political force, the various liberal groups (including Irina Khakamada's Our Choice, as well as the Ryzhkov–Kasparov protogrouping) had to unite into a single organisation, but even then success would be far from guaranteed. However, the liberal 'veterans' insisted that Yabloko would have to take the lead in whatever group emerged, and that Anatoly Chubais, the architect of the 1990s privatisation programme, would have to be expunged from SPS. On these two conditions the unity negotiations foundered.[54]

Following the 2003–4 electoral cycle, the more doughty non-systemic opposition gathered in Other Russia, which evolved from 'Committee 2008' formed in March 2004 to ensure fair elections. Russian ruling elites at this time had a heightened fear that external forces could mobilise popular opposition to managed elections. The tension between the democratic forms and covert practices had become evident during elections in a number of countries, which provoked splits in the ruling group accompanied by mass mobilisation, typically sponsored from abroad, known as 'colour revolutions'. In Serbia in November 2000, Slobodan Milošević was overthrown after his attempt to fix the presidential election; in the so-called Rose revolution in Georgia in

---

[52] Luke March, 'Managing Opposition in a Hybrid Regime: Just Russia and Parastatal Opposition', *Slavic Review* 68, 3, Fall 2009, p. 508.
[53] Nicklaus Laverty, 'Limited Choices: Russian Opposition Parties and the 2007 Duma Election', *Demokratizatsiya* 16, 4, Fall 2008, pp. 366–9, discusses the reasons for the failure to unite.
[54] Editorial, 'Russia: A Union of "Lords" and "Comrades"', *Moscow News*, 9 February 2007, p. 1.

November 2003, Eduard Shevardnadze was overthrown after a clumsy election and replaced by his former protégé, Mikheil Saakashvili; in Ukraine in late 2004, Leonid Kuchma was forced by a massive popular mobilisation to cede power to the representative of the Orange revolution, Victor Yushchenko, rather than to his favoured candidate, Victor Yanukovich;[55] while the Tulip revolution in Kyrgyzstan in February 2005 saw insurgent regional elites take over from President Askar Akaev. In these countries regime change was achieved by a combination of elite pressure and popular mobilisation, and there was considerable speculation whether such a fate awaited Russia as well. Although exaggerated, fear of a Russian colour revolution overshadowed the Medvedev succession and prompted heavy-handed police actions to control the streets and social movements.[56]

The inaugural conference of the Other Russia movement, which neither Yabloko nor SPS attended, was held on the eve of the St Petersburg G8 summit in St Petersburg in July 2006. The slogan of one of its first 'march of the irreconcilables' (*marsh nesoglasnikhov*) on 14 April 2007 was 'No anti-constitutional restrictions on the 2007 Duma elections!' Not a snappy slogan, but one that reflected the appeal to the constitutional state against the para-political machinations of the administrative regime. It also reflected the spirit of the late Soviet dissidents, who appealed to the regime to observe the principles that it had signed up to in the Helsinki Final Act of August 1975. One of the main leaders of Other Russia was Kasparov, the head of the virulently anti-regime United Civic Front (OGF), who argued that Russia's government was fundamentally illegitimate, thus suggesting that any form of struggle was appropriate to bring it down.[57] He argued that 'Today the Kremlin is a mafia-style operation',[58] and warned that when Putin's term came to an end in 2008, 'his efficient political machine is threatening to explode'.[59]

Kasparov, the former world chess champion, hoped to break the stalemate in Russian politics with a characteristically decisive move. He was on the editorial board of the *Wall Street Journal*, a council member of the Centre for Security Policy, and he had close links with American

[55] David Lane, 'The Orange Revolution: "People's Revolution" or Revolutionary Coup', *The British Journal of Politics and International Relations* 10, 4, November 2008, pp. 525–49.

[56] Graeme B. Robertson, 'Managing Society: Protest, Civil Society, and Regime in Putin's Russia', *Slavic Review* 68, 3, Fall 2009, pp. 528–47.

[57] This was the theme of various OGF position documents, and repeated by Kasparov at a breakfast meeting with the author and others, Holiday Inn Vinogradova, 13 September 2008.

[58] Garry Kasparov, 'Battling KGB, Inc.', *Journal of Democracy* 18, 2, April 2007, p. 115.

[59] *Ibid.*, p. 117.

neo-conservatives.[60] Other Russia included Eduard Limonov's National Bolshevik Party, hardened in street demonstrations and various spectacular political interventions. Limonov served two years in jail from April 2001 for illegal arms purchases, having advocated 'Serbian tactics' to reunite Russian-populated parts of the former Soviet Union with Russia.[61] As well as intransigent anti-communists, Other Russia included cultural figures such as Victor Shenderovich, the creator of the *Kukly* (*Puppets*) satire show that so enraged Putin, as well as 'pragmatic' political scientists like Georgy Satarov, the head of the Indem research foundation. They pointed to the broad co-operation of diverse political forces that had led to success in the Orange revolution in Ukraine in late 2004. However, the attempt to unite the liberals and national communists on an anti-Kremlin platform smacked of a lack of principle. Kasyanov was associated with Other Russia until he, too, left in 2007 after it had failed to rally behind his presidential ambitions. Yabloko and SPS kept their distance, until in the last stages of the 2007 campaign SPS came out as a street-fighting party in a final desperate appeal to dissident sentiments.

United Russia and the dominant-party system

Anna Gryzmala-Busse argues that in contrast to the declining parties of western Europe, in the post-communist world parties perform vital state-building functions.[62] They are less about the struggle for office than creating the conditions for the functioning of democratic institutions, including the writing of electoral rules and establishing the foundations of market democracy; and thus they perform a *preparatory* rather than a representative role. However, unlike some of the countries Gryzmala-Busse studies, parties in Russia have not been able to exploit the state and instead have been dependent on state support or else cast into the wilderness. Parties in Russia are very much a subaltern subsystem, and although increasingly UR became the route to office, the party is certainly not yet the main avenue for enrichment and power.

The motives stimulating Putin's efforts to reshape Russia's party system have been much debated, including the argument that the

---

[60] Nicolai N. Petro, 'Why Russian Liberals Lose', www.nationalinterest.org, 3 December 2007.

[61] For Limonov's views and an account of his struggles against various regimes, including a virulent critique of Putin's policies and personality, see Eduard Limonov, *Takoi president nam ne nuzhen!* (Moscow: no publisher indicated, 2005), and his *Limonov protiv Putina* (Moscow: Novyi Bastion, 2006).

[62] Anna Gryzmala-Busse, *Rebuilding Leviathan: Party Competition and State Exploitation in Post-Communist Democracies* (Cambridge: Cambridge University Press, 2008).

elimination of inconvenient parties played a role, as well as the more positive view that reform of Russia's party system was overdue. What is not in question is that a streamlined party system helped ensure systemic continuity across the great divide of 2008. The main instrument to achieve this was the 'party of power', United Russia. As a recent history of the party notes, in 2000 Russia gained a 'tsar', and in 2001 the 'tsar's party'.[63] The 'portfolio putsch' of spring 2002 saw UR take the majority of committee chairmanships in the Duma, and the pre-eminent position of the party was thereafter confirmed as the regime and Putin personally identified with the party. This marked a considerable evolution of what had previously been a presidential personality-based system. Yeltsin refused to join a particular party, claiming to be president of the whole nation and feared that too close identification with a party would constrain his freedom of manoeuvre. Although suggestions that the dominant party could in due course form a government of the parliamentary majority had been mooted in 2003, the idea had thereafter been dropped.[64]

Unlike Yeltsin, Putin associated himself with the dominant party. In August 2003 UR completed the process of establishing branches throughout Russia. Regional legislatures were increasingly dominated by UR as a result of the rule from 2003 that at least half of deputies had to be elected from party lists.[65] This was reinforced by the abolition of gubernatorial elections in December 2004 and the shift to presidential nomination, ratified by regional assemblies. The dominant party was allowed to nominate governors from December 2005, and the great majority joined the UR bandwagon. By the time of the December 2007 election, UR claimed to have a membership of 1.66 million, an increasing proportion of whom were young people. The social basis of the party, however, overwhelmingly remained the bureaucracy, with nearly two-thirds of its membership service employees. Its core values reflected those of this class, combining anti-communism with liberal conservatism and embedded capitalism. Its unswerving loyalty to Putin was expressed by the party's leader, Boris Gryzlov, who, in a wide-ranging article called 'Contemporary Russia is Putin', argued that 'A "Russia without Putin" is a Russia without leadership, a Russia

[63] Vitalii Ivanov, *Partiya Putina: Istoriya 'Edinoi Rossii'* (Moscow: Olma Media Grupp, 2008), p. 8.
[64] Richard Sakwa, *Putin: Russia's Choice*, 2nd edn (London and New York: Routledge, 2008), p. 127.
[65] Aleksandr Kynev, *Vybory parlamentov rossiiskikh regionov 2003–2009: Pervyi tsikl vnedreniya proportsional'noi izbiratel'noi sistemy* (Moscow: Panorama, 2009).

without will, a Russia that can be divided up and to whom you can do anything you like.'[66]

Up to 2004 it was forbidden for ministers or regional leaders to be party members, which forced the UR statutes to permit non-party individuals to assume leadership positions and become members of its High Council. The exemption allowed the minister of internal affairs, Gryzlov, to head the party as the non-party chair of the Council. A UR-sponsored amendment to the law on government that came into force in October 2004 finally allowed ministers and top-ranking officials to join parties.[67] There was no rush to join, however, since the 'non-party' character of Russian governance had become deeply ingrained. In April 2008, out of twenty-two ministers only three were UR members: Vice Premier Alexander Zhukov, the natural resources minister, Yury Trutnev, and the agriculture minister, Alexei Gordeev. One of the co-chairs of the party's Council Sergei Shoigu, who was also the long-standing head of the emergency situations ministry, was not a party member; and neither was another of the co-chairs, Shaimiev; while it was unclear whether the third co-chair, Luzhkov, had ever joined. They enjoyed enough political capital not to need party membership. Some ministers were resolutely opposed to becoming party members, reflecting the characteristic post-communist hostility to party life. As the industry minister, Victor Khristenko, put it: 'I have never in my life been a party member, and after 50 years I do not plan to change my style of thinking and therefore do not plan to join any party; I am and always will be non-party.'[68]

Gryzlov developed the theme already announced by Surkov at a meeting on 7 February 2006 with UR activists. Surkov argued that the fall of communism had given birth to a 'deformed democracy', dominated by corrupt oligarchs and susceptible to western subversion. Putin's election in 2000 represented the first step on Russia's road to recovery, but western forces had regrouped in the guise of 'colour revolutions', notably in Ukraine, and sought to achieve the 'soft conquest of Russia'. To prevent democracy becoming the instrument of Russia's weakening, he advanced the idea of 'sovereign democracy'. 'Sovereignty', Surkov insisted, 'is a synonym for competitiveness'.[69] As the 2007 Duma

---

[66] Boris Gryzlov, 'Vladimir Putin ostanetsya national'nym liderom – nezavisimo ot posta, kotory on budet zanimat'', *Rossiiskaya gazeta*, 17 October 2007.

[67] The Law on Parties bans membership only for judges, the procuracy, investigators and members of the interior ministry (MVD).

[68] Nadezhda Ivanitskaya and Kira Latukhina, 'Pravitel'stvo partii', *Vedomosti*, 16 April 2008, p. 3.

[69] Vladislav Surkov, 'Suverenitet: Politicheskii sinonim konkurentosposobnosti', in Vladislav Surkov, *Teksty 97–07* (Moscow: Evropa, 2008), pp. 143–7; for an interesting

election approached, a vigorous debate focused on whether a single party could represent all social groups. Addressing business leaders at the Stolypin Club on 30 October 2007, Surkov insisted that Russia did not need 'a party of business', or even competing parties representing separate interest groups. As far as he was concerned, as a catch-all party UR could represent all of society.[70] The so-called oligarchs had now been effectively incorporated into governmental structures, and by the same token government became imbricated into business life.

As in Russian politics as a whole, where the dominance of the regime over political forces and institutions prompted the development of factions, so, too, factionalism emerged within UR in the form of platforms, reflecting its ideological heterogeneity. The 'social club' was headed by the chair of the State Duma committee for labour and social policy, Andrei Isaev; the liberal-conservative club, called '4 November', was led by the head of the Duma's constitutional legislation and state construction committee, Vladimir Pligin, the editor of *Ekspert*, Valery Fadaev, and the former justice minister, Pavel Krasheninnikov; while the conservative-patriotic club was headed by Yury Shuvalov and favoured a social-conservative policy.[71] The leadership stressed that ultimately the party was united in its hostility to left- and right-wing populism, but the idea of dividing UR into separate factions, each with some hundred deputies representing different flanks of the political spectrum, was taken seriously. This was facilitated by an amendment sponsored by UR in October 2007 that allowed party groups with over a hundred deputies to be divided into sub-factions. As the election approached, however, attempts to formalise inner-party factionalism were frozen and the party fought its putative ally, JR, to remain the exclusive presidential party. Gryzlov and Mironov struggled to be closest to Putin. United Russia was allowed to bring out a collection of Putin's speeches under the rubric 'Putin's plan' (see later), signalling their favoured status.[72]

Although Putin sponsored the creation and development of UR, at the same time he shared the concerns of all presidents that the party could become too independent and powerful, and thus curb presidential autonomy. This helps explain some of the hesitancies in his behaviour, and even when he agreed to head UR's national party list in the 2007

discussion, see Vladimir Rudakov, 'Ideologiya vos'mogo goda', *Profil'*, No. 12, 3 April 2006, pp. 24–33.

[70] Elena Ivanova, 'Sami vy reidery!', *Vedomosti*, 31 October 2007; Konstantin Sonin, 'The Party of Business', *Moscow Times*, 6 November 2007, p. 10.

[71] Marlène Laruelle, *Inside and Around the Kremlin's Black Box: The New Nationalist Think Tanks in Russia*, Institute for Security and Development Policy, Stockholm Paper, October 2009, pp. 25–31; www.isdp.eu.

[72] Elena Rudneva and Anna Nikolaeva, 'Vse kak u Putina', *Vedomosti*, 16 May 2007, p. A2.

parliamentary election, he stressed that he was not a party member. While UR sought to transform itself from a 'party of power' into a genuine ruling party, this was resisted by those in the Kremlin who well understood this would also transform the party from an obedient Kremlin tool into an independent political force and source of patronage. The party's authority came from its close identification with Putin, but it also began to develop claims to autonomous sources of power. At UR's ninth (emergency) conference on 14–15 April 2008, Putin finally bit the bullet and took on the post of party leader, but he still refused to become a party member. Fundamental programmatic and personnel issues were not decided by the party, and thus it remained a subaltern organisation. Its function was to gather the vote and pass laws, and anything more was resisted. From an instrument of representation, United Russia increasingly became a mechanism for mobilisation.

It remains unclear which is the most appropriate model to characterise UR's role. The idea of a 'cartel party', advanced by Katz and Mair in the mid-1990s, describes the interpenetration of state and party and the accompanying collusion between parties that reduces competition and lessens the danger of outside challenges.[73] Their approach, however, is more appropriate for a mature party system, where the model suggests progression from mass catch-all to cartel parties, whereas Russia's constantly changing scene has not only not yet reached that stage but may never do so, since it is developing in a very different context. Sartori developed the model of a 'predominant party system', an idea developed in the Russian context by Gel'man.[74] Atsushi Ogushi advances the notion of a 'government-party regime', in which the ruling party merges with the executive authorities and takes advantage of state resources to consolidate its predominance while reducing the scope for outsider parties to challenge the regime.[75] He compares Russian developments with the situation in a number of Asian countries: the predominance of the Liberal Democratic Party (LDP) in Japan, Golkar in Indonesia, the United Malays National Organisation (UNMO) in Malaysia, the People's Action Party (PAP) in Singapore and the Kuomingtang in Taiwan. In all these systems, the party acted as an adjunct to the state, and in turn the privileges and administrative resources of the state

---

[73] Richard S. Katz and Peter Mair, 'Changing Models of Party Organization and Party Democracy: The Emergence of the Cartel Party', *Party Politics* 1, 1, 1995, pp. 5–28.

[74] Vladimir Gel'man, 'From "Feckless Pluralism" to "Dominant Power Politics"? The Transformation of Russia's Party System', *Democratization* 13, 4, August 2006, pp. 545–61.

[75] Atsushi Ogushi, 'Toward a Government-Party Regime? United Russia in Perspective', paper delivered to the Annual Convention of the AAASS, New Orleans, 15 November 2007.

allowed the party repeatedly to win elections. For seven decades, from 1929 to 2000, a similar situation prevailed in Mexico, in which the Institutional Revolutionary Party (PRI) won every presidential election, dominated parliament and won most governorships in the thirty-one states, and ruled almost every municipality. Intra-party factionalism substituted for competitive party pluralism, and this could be a path followed by Russia.

Comparisons with Turkey raise some interesting parallels. Russia's 'independence' in 1991 was accompanied by an avalanche of material on Turkey's development in the twentieth century, including a number of mostly laudatory accounts (although some were quite critical) of Kemal Atatürk. A recent book on Atatürk argues that under his leadership, Turkey began to achieve 'political stability and economic prosperity'.[76] The book, however, also made no bones about calling him a 'dictator', which may well in part have been a coded call for more authoritative leadership in Russia after the chaos of the 1990s. Atatürk himself took great umbrage at being called a dictator. He insisted that there was a 'line between single-party rule, which he had come to see as inevitable, and a full-blown totalitarian dictatorship'.[77] This came after his attempt to create a type of managed opposition party. Atatürk was at the head of the ruling Republican People's Party but insisted that this did not impair his impartiality as president. He even sponsored the creation of an opposition party in 1930, the Free Republican Party, whose name he chose and whose programme he vetted.[78]

The experiment did not last long and the Free Republican Party was dissolved after little more than three months. As with the creation of Just Russia to provide some managed competition with United Russia, the Free Republicans were caught in an impossible trap: if they campaigned too vigorously as a genuine opposition, they risked splitting the elite and provoking anti-regime mobilisation; but if they remained too passive and obsequious, there was hardly any point in the exercise. As Mango observes in a comment that is as valid for Turkey in the 1930s and 1940s as it is for Russia today: 'Progress came in two stages: first rights with fraud, then rights without fraud.'[79] Atatürk also blocked attempts by the Republican People's Party to place itself above the state, in a process that elsewhere saw exclusive one-party rule established in the Soviet Union, Germany and Italy: 'In Turkey, it was the state and not the party which was the master.'[80] As Mango notes, 'Turkey in the 1930s, in

---

[76] Aleksandr Ushakov, *Fenomenon Atatyurka: Turetskii pravitel', tvorets i diktator* (Moscow: Tsentropoligraf, 2002).
[77] Andrew Mango, *Atatürk* (London: John Murray, 1999), p. 479.
[78] *Ibid.*, p. 472.   [79] *Ibid.*, p. 473.   [80] *Ibid.*, p. 501.

the last phase of his rule, was a disciplined country under an unopposed pragmatic government which respected the forms of constitutional democracy.'[81] Ultimately, this is the great difference with Russia in the twentieth century. Following its creation as an independent republic in the early 1920s, Turkey was spared the great cataclysms that beset Russia and even managed to keep out of the Second World War, whereas Russia is only now beginning to recover from its political and social disasters. Russia, however, has been transformed into a mature industrial society whose major challenge is 'redevelopment', whereas Turkey remains in the modernisation stage.

In this context, at the meeting with business leaders at the Stolypin Club, Surkov argued that:

We are too quick to jump to conclusions. How long has United Russia been in existence? Six years. Why are we rushing to declare that Russia is becoming a few-party system, a one-and-a-half party system, or even a one-party system? We have a normal system, which will eventually and inevitably develop into a system with two dominant parties and several smaller parties – just like the systems in most European countries. In Germany, one party was in power for 18 years after the war. In America, the Democrats held a majority in the House of Representatives for 40 years. Why don't people apply these one-party descriptions to the American or German systems?

That is the difference between democratic procedures and revolutionary or totalitarian practices: democratic procedures avoid force and coercion as far as possible. Only very patient people are capable of governing and maintaining public order by means of persuasion and explanation.[82]

Surkov could hardly be more explicit about the long-term role he envisaged for the party, but he failed to identify the differences. United Russia was not a party *in* power, but a party *of* power, something very different. Although UR began to enjoy extensive electoral success, unlike the PRI it was not the primary mechanism for leadership succession, or even the main instrument for managing factional conflict (the role of the LDP in Japan), and remains a subaltern body to an administrative regime whose power derives from the mix of normative authority derived from an authoritative presidency and its ability independently to access the power of the state. Although subordinate to the administrative regime, UR became hegemonic in the other pillar of Russian political society regulated by the constitutional state.

The Kremlin factions appealed to parties for the first time in 2007–8, but only hesitantly. Indeed, to a degree, 'parties reflect the interests of

[81] *Ibid.*, p. 480.
[82] Aleksandr Protopopov, 'V lyubom sluchae vse budet khorosho', *Ekspert*, No. 41, 5 November 2007, p. 67.

various Kremlin factions, rather than different groups of voters'.[83] This was evident in Surkov's distrust of JR, fearing that its creation (sponsored by a Kremlin faction suspicious of him) would jeopardise his project, United Russia. Just Russia declared its support for Putin, but advanced a more left-wing programme in contrast to UR's centre-right programme, and thus tried to identify itself more as a 'party of the people' than a party of power. Just Russia was initially sponsored by the *siloviki*, to balance the influence of the democratic statists predominant in United Russia. However, under Mironov's leadership JR moved beyond social democratic positions to embrace a range of socialist and nationalist policies, at which point Putin withdrew his public support and identified himself more closely with UR. An equally pertinent consideration was the fear that the presence of two regime parties would split officialdom along partisan lines. The creation of JR as a reserve 'party of power' introduced a degree of bureaucratic pluralism that had the potential to become genuinely competitive.

The crisis of Russian democracy

We can now step back and examine the dilemmas facing Russian politics, and in particular the features of the dual state, split as we have seen between a constitutional order and the administrative regime. A regime denotes both a type of governmental system and the identification of a ruling group. In the latter sense, a regime combines formal constitutional institutions with the personal preferences of individual leaders and the way that these interact with formal provisions. A regime is thus a combination of formal and informal rules, stressing the embedded nature of leadership in a set of institutions. It is on the basis of this tension between regime and system that the Russian dual order has emerged. The regime is far from an autonomous actor, and thus has the potential to evolve into a constitutional democratic government; however, it can also become a closed self-perpetuating system of rule, at which point the duality would be transcended and the time of equivocation over whether Russia is a democracy would be over.

Russia's passive revolution

Democracy in Russia is faced with the task of creating the conditions for its own existence; to which postulate Putin implicitly added that this

[83] Dmitrii Kamyshev, 'Natsionalisticheskii national'nyi proekt', *Kommersant-Vlast'*, No. 50, 18 December 2006.

could not be done by following the logic of democracy itself. An administrative regime emerged between the institutions of the constitutional state and the accountability structures of civil society, above all parties and parliament. The regime claimed a tutelary role over the process of democratic development – not repudiating the goal of democracy but standing outside the democratic process. This imbued the whole system with a profound duality – between the stated goals of the regime and its practices, which permanently subverted the principles which it proclaimed. Putin's team modified the network of business and regional relationships that had developed under Yeltsin, although in policy terms there was significant continuity between the two periods. Where power relations are concerned, however, the two leaderships are distinct (the factional power balance within the regime will be the subject of Chapters 3 and 4).

Putin recruited former associates from St Petersburg (liberal lawyers and security officials) and built a team, focused on the presidential administration in the Kremlin, that drove through the new agenda. The power of the most egregiously political oligarchs was reduced, and from their exile in London and Tel Aviv they plotted their revenge, further stoking the paranoia of the *siloviki*. With the fear of oligarchic Jacobites abroad, the insurgency in Chechnya spreading across the north Caucasus and the spectre of colour revolutions, the regime exhibited symptoms of a siege mentality, and its Metternich-style legitimism assumed an increasingly conservative hue. Paradoxically, as Putin centralised power, he imported into the Kremlin the conflicts that in a more pluralistic system are played out in society. Conflicts 'between parliament and the executive; between the left and the right; between the state and the oligarchs; and between the center and the provinces' allowed the executive to tower over all other political institutions;[84] but the evisceration of procedurally regulated pluralistic competition in the public sphere fostered informal antagonistic conflict in the shadow realm. It was not the executive alone that dominated, although clearly it was a central component of the administrative regime. Structural dualism was complemented by a fundamental dualism within the administrative regime itself, as the presidency mediated between the meta-factions of the liberals versus the *siloviki*. This double dualism after 2003 engendered systemic stalemate, a theme to which we shall return.

The common refrain of studies of the 1990s in Russia was the weakness of the state, but its ability to recuperate was much under-rated.

---

[84] Leon Aron, 'After the Leviathan', *Journal of Democracy*, 18, 2, April 2007, p. 120.

Already by the end of the period, there were clear attempts to reconstitute state powers, and under Putin this was achieved, although in a highly ambiguous manner. As Stoner-Weiss asserts, this was 'an attempt to build authoritarianism without an authoritative state – authoritarianism without authority'.[85] Putin not only denied that he was building an authoritarian system but even repudiated the charge of excessive centralisation, defending his approach as one of 'rationalisation'.[86] Russia is far from the only country where there is a gulf between the formal democratic institutional framework and the realities of political practice.[87] The problem of systemic hybridity, as we shall see, is prevalent in 'transitional' states. In Russia, laws are passed according to the appropriate procedures, yet the political process is characterised by tension between vitality and stasis. The presidency remains the source of vitality, but its very pre-eminence paralyses all other institutions and creates a system where initiative from below is inhibited.

Anyone who has had contact with the Russian bureaucracy knows that even minor decisions are constantly referred upwards, and the whole system is geared towards the mind-numbing implementation of exhaustively detailed regulations, thus lacking creativity and the ethos of personal responsibility. The autonomy of the administrative apparatus prompted Alexander Pogorelsky, the director of the Institute for East European Studies, to argue that a 'sovereign bureaucracy' had become established in Russia. As he argued, 'The bureaucracy has ceased to be servile; it has become sovereign. It has spiraled out of control politically and is now imposing its will on the country's leaders. The real master of the country today is this quasi-class, together with business interests that are closely associated with the authorities.'[88] Mao Zedong's Cultural Revolution from 1966 had destroyed the political power of the bureaucracy, and this is often considered the essential condition for China's reforms to develop successfully. In Russia, not only has the bureaucracy survived the transition from communism to capitalism, but it has been

---

[85] Stoner-Weiss, *Resisting the State*, p. 147.

[86] Meeting with foreign scholars and journalists in Valdai Discussion Club, Catherine Hall, the Kremlin, 5 September 2005, personal notes.

[87] For a good comparative analysis of the conundrum, see Tim Haughton (ed.), *Constraints and Opportunities of Leadership in Post-Communist Europe* (Aldershot: Ashgate, 2005). For a radical critique of American practices, see Sheldon S. Wolin, *Democracy Incorporated: Managed Democracy and the Specter of Inverted Totalitarianism* (Princeton, NJ: Princeton University Press, 2008).

[88] Alexander Pogorelsky, 'Russian Bureaucracy Needs to Be Brought Back to Reality', interviewed by Liubov Ulianova, *Russian Journal*, No. 23 (37), 30 September 2009, p. 6.

penetrated by business interests that thrived on monopolistic and rent-seeking practices.[89]

I have argued elsewhere that the word 'regime' (rather than government or administration) is the preferred term to describe the power system that came into existence around the middle period of Yeltsin's governance and which was consolidated under Putin. The notion of regime in this sense has a long pedigree in political science and is used to contrast an under-institutionalised power system in contrast with a government, which sits firmly in some sort of legal-constitutional regulation of power relations. A regime is inadequately constrained by the constitutional state from above and lacks effective accountability to the institutions of mass representation from below (parliament, political parties and civil society generally).[90] A regime represents a defined structural and operational pattern that in its own way creates a parallel constitution, although one without formal codification but reflecting the internal balance of forces within the power system.[91] In the Russian case, it is certainly an oversimplification to suggest that the *siloviki* constitute a 'state within the state', yet they are an important constituent element of the shifting constellation that we call 'the regime'. However, the nature of 'the regime', its constituent elements and dynamics, remain under-theorised. It is more than personalised leadership, but less than an institutionalised law-governed system.

More specifically, Putin remained the linchpin of the system, and in his absence many feared that vitality would give way to generalised stasis. Even during his presidency there was no lack of manifestations of the latter. As Vyacheslav Nikonov noted, over 1,800 of Putin's presidential decrees (not instructions or appointments, but policy-forming decisions) had not been implemented by the time he left office.[92] At the same time, Putin's personalised leadership helped maintain the delicate factional balance. The succession in 2007–8 was as much about how to ensure

---

[89] In purely numerical terms, the number of government officials (national and regional) in relation to the size and population of the country is not that enormous, having doubled in size by October 2008 to reach 1.2 million (down from 1.3 million in 2004). For a discussion, see Robert J. Brym and V. Gimpelson, 'The Size, Composition and Dynamics of the Russian State Bureaucracy in the 1990s', *Slavic Review* 63, 1, Spring 2004, pp. 90–113.

[90] Sakwa, *Russian Politics and Society*, pp. 466–70; Sakwa, *Putin*, Chapter 5; see also Richard Sakwa 'The Regime System in Russia', *Contemporary Politics* 3, 1, 1997, pp. 7–25.

[91] This definition of an alternative 'constitution' is applied fruitfully by Philip G. Roeder, *Red Sunset: The Failure of Soviet Politics* (Princeton, NJ: Princeton University Press, 1993).

[92] Vyacheslav Nikonov, president of the Russkii Mir Foundation, keynote speech to BASEES conference, Cambridge, 30 March 2008, and personal discussions.

stability within the regime as it was about leadership renewal, accompanied by fears that changes in factional power would entail property redistribution. Putin emerged as faction manager in a system where the reconstitution of governance remained tenuous and property rights unconsolidated. These features were exacerbated by the predations of the administrative regime. The system had been brought into existence in response to genuine governance problems, notably during the phoney democracy period, but the consolidation of the administrative pillar provoked a range of pathologies that could only be overcome by the strengthening of the constitutional state.

Russia's dominant-power system has some distinctive characteristics. From the time Putin came to power in 2000, the regime took on an ever stronger tutelary aspect, claiming the right to manage not only the sphere of policy, the usual job of governments, but also the exclusive right to manage political processes as a whole. This is what distinguishes a 'regime' from a normal 'government'. Fearing for the stability, and indeed for the very existence, of the state, Putin's regime represented a powerful shift from mobilisational to pacificatory politics; from encouraging independent civic activism to controlling and regulating it; and in the process suffocating not only political pluralism but also eroding the sources of regime renewal. This was the system known as 'managed democracy'. Popular inclusion in the Putin period did take place, but in an archaic manner reminiscent of Soviet practices. This was not modern civic participation of an active citizenry accompanied by the pluralistic representation of divergent interests. Putin's mutuality was top-down, mobilisational and paternalistic, and vitiated by the internally hierarchical power system. Inclusion at the economic level was even more partial, with small businesses remaining at the mercy of the bureaucracy, while big business was incorporated as a subaltern partner of the regime. The modernisation agenda from above was not accompanied by the necessary modernisation from the middle, represented by a competitive party system, an entrepreneurial and independent business culture, and a vibrant public sphere.

In his first annual address to the Federal Assembly (the two houses of parliament) on 8 July 2000, Putin used the term 'vertical' three times, although he never mentioned the word again in his seven subsequent addresses. A 'power vertical' was established to which the electoral and party systems adapted.[93] Putin's consolidation of the guardianship role

---

[93] For details of the 'democratic degradation', see Aleksandr Verkhovskii (ed.), *Demokratiya vertikali* (Moscow: Inform.-analiticheskii tsentr 'Sova' and Inform. issled. tsentr 'Demos', 2006).

of the state undermined the quality of democracy. As far as Putinites were concerned, the precondition for any democracy was the restoration of state autonomy and capacity, a view recently echoed by Marc Plattner.[94] The problem, however, is that it was not so much the autonomous operation of the state that was reconstituted, but the independent powers of the regime, concentrated in the hands of a relatively small ruling group. The regime developed an ever larger sphere of autonomy, encroaching in the one direction against independent agencies of the constitutional state, above all the courts and regulatory bodies; while in the other direction the accountability institutions of mass representative democracy were undermined. The development of regime autonomy in conditions of democratic deficit fostered its own pathologies, above all bureaucratic arbitrariness and corruption. Stability was bought at the price of the erosion of civic engagement, pluralism and active citizenship.[95] Russian democracy looked ever more lifeless and empty. The conflicts that modern institutions of representative democracy are designed to regulate and constrain through formalised rituals became internalised, taking the form of intra-regime factional conflict.

The Yukos 'affair' from 2003 marked a watershed in Putin's presidency. Dominating the middle part of his rule, the struggle against Khodorkovsky and his associates threw the spotlight on Putin's political style, the groups able to seize the policy agenda, and the tensions in the whole Putinist 'project'. Coming at a time when energy prices were rising to their historically second highest point (in relative terms), the Kremlin was showered with the accompanying bonanza, provoking intense competition over the appropriation and application of these resources. The *silovik* faction took full advantage of this to press forward their attack on one of the most egregiously independent business leaders. These two factors – the struggle against the 'over-mighty' oligarch and competition over control of rents – exacerbated fissures that are inherent in Russia's political system and intensified the struggles at the heart of Russian politics. As we shall argue later, it would be misleading to describe these as battles between 'clans', since that would suggest a permanence and depth to the various groups that is probably

---

[94] Marc F. Plattner, 'A Skeptical Perspective', in Larry Diamond and Leonardo Morlino (eds.), *Assessing the Quality of Democracy* (Baltimore, MD: The Johns Hopkins University Press, 2005), pp. 77–81.

[95] For an exploration of associated themes, see Richard Rose and Neil Munro, *Elections Without Order: Russia's Challenge to Vladimir Putin* (Cambridge: Cambridge University Press, 2002); Richard Rose, William Mishler and Neil Munro, *Russia Transformed: Developing Popular Support for a New Regime* (Cambridge: Cambridge University Press, 2006).

exaggerated. Instead, we argue that a model focused on 'factionalism' is more appropriate. The corollary of this is that the Yukos affair in the end did not mark a transformation of the regime – that is, the triumph of one faction over all others – but the temporary dominance of one faction to pursue a particular case; and factional balance was soon restored in the government reshuffle of November 2005 (see Chapter 5) and the broadly liberal macroeconomic policy continued to be applied. The Yukos affair, however, did signal the subordination of the business class to the regime and thus joined regional elites as subaltern elements of the administrative regime. It also greatly accelerated the degradation of the rule of law and demonstrated to any petty local bureaucrat that legal arbitrariness could be exercised with impunity.

The emergence of a relatively autonomous power system appealing to a centrist ideology to transcend the politics of left and right has parallels elsewhere. Developed in late nineteenth-century Italy, the concept of *trasformismo* describes the opportunistic acceptance of political support from any quarter and is also a synonym for corruption and stagnation. In Italy, as in contemporary Russia, left and right united in support of putatively non-ideological government from the centre that proclaimed the reconciliation of extremes for the good of the nation. In Italy a distinctive type of governance regime emerged in a society in which organised interests were simultaneously weak and divisive, where a hegemonic middle class was lacking and in which depoliticisation became endemic. Pragmatic leadership degenerated into unprincipled expediency. Equally, Putin's administration claimed to stand above the historic divisions of the modern era, and indeed, purposely sought to reconcile the forces that had torn Russia apart in the twentieth century. The democratic process was managed by a force standing outside democracy, co-opting elements of political society willing to compromise and marginalising the rest. This was a type of passive revolution, which for Antonio Gramsci entailed 'an abortive or incomplete transformation of society'. This can take a number of forms, including one where an external force provokes change, but this lacks a sufficiently strong domestic constituency and runs into the resistance of entrenched interests. When the forces are equally balanced, a stalemate emerges, giving rise to a situation of 'revolution/restoration'.[96] We have a Bonapartist situation where class forces are equally balanced, allowing the regime to

---

[96] Antonio Gramsci, 'Notes on Italian History', in *Selections From the Prison Notebooks of Antonio Gramsci*, ed. and trans. Quintin Hoare and Geoffrey Nowell Smith (London: Lawrence & Wishart, 1971), pp. 104–20; see also Robert W. Cox, 'Civil Society at the Turn of the Millennium: Prospects for an Alternative World Order', *Review of International Studies* 25, 1999, p. 16.

act with autonomy. The Russian government continued the revolution in property and power begun in the late Gorbachev years but, at the same time, restored elements of the previous regime. Promoted as the ideology of reconciliation, the inconclusive nature of the system took the form of a dual state, with all of its inherent contradictions and accompanying stalemate.

Although methodologically flawed,[97] the annual Freedom House 'Nations in Transit' rankings do at least provide a comparative dimension. Russia's democracy score had been declining since 1999: from 4.58 in that year (on a scale of 1–7, with 1 the best) down to 5.86 in 2007 and 5.98 in 2008, following the elections. The electoral process had declined even more sharply and showed the worst indicators, from 4 in 1999 to 6.75 in 2008 – threatening to fall off the scale if matters deteriorated much further.[98] Robert Orttung, the author of the report, asserted that 'Intimidation is now a central feature of the political system', and he warned that amendments to the Law on Extremism adopted in July 2007 rendered the 'public slander of state officials', 'humiliating national pride', 'hampering the lawful activity of state organisations' and 'hooliganism committed for political or ideological motives' extremist acts.[99] Although the situation was painted in lurid and exaggerated tones, the underlying analysis was correct. An accompanying report noted that 'The post-Soviet authoritarian bloc represents part of a larger, global phenomenon of oil-fueled authoritarian influence. Propelled by a surge of hydrocarbon wealth, Russia in particular has become the leading antidemocratic force in the region.'[100] There was very little 'bloc' politics in the region, but Russia's growing economic strength certainly fuelled greater resistance to western hegemony as the country navigated the tortuous dialectic of international adaptation and exceptionalism, the foreign-policy equivalent of the domestic 'gray zone'.

Putin remained committed to a moderate state-led modernisation process, accompanied by a constrained liberal democratisation project, but lacked the resources or the will to achieve either full-scale Thermidorean reaction or breakthrough into pluralistic liberal democracy. The system was a classic instance of the passive revolution. Putin's departure

---

[97] For a review, see Gerardo L. Munck and Jay Verkuilen, 'Conceptualizing and Measuring Democracy: Evaluating Alternative Indices', *Comparative Political Studies* 35, 1, February 2002, pp. 5–34.

[98] Robert W. Orttung, 'Russia', in *Nations in Transit 2008* (Washington, DC: Freedom House, 2008), p. 495.

[99] *Ibid.*, pp. 500, 507.

[100] Christopher Walker and Jeannette Goehring, 'Nations in Transit 2008: Petro-Authoritarianism and Eurasia's New Divides', in *Nations in Transit 2008* (Washington, DC: Freedom House, 2008), p. 26.

in 2008 according to the letter of the constitution was a great advance for democracy, but his shaping of the succession and the new administration at best made this a partial triumph for the spirit of constitutionalism. Fear that his designated successor would not be so adroit in balancing the various factions prompted Putin to take on the post of prime minister. How he would manage the succession was the pre-eminent question as the country entered the 2007–8 elections, and this is the focus of later chapters in this book.

A new dual state

States in the 'gray zone' legalise opposition parties and allow competitive elections, but the process is manipulated to the advantage of incumbent elites. Hybrid regimes subordinate democratic procedures to authoritarian practices.[101] By definition they are characterised by the operation of two systemic logics, and thus are dual orders. Russia is one of these hybrid systems, combining democratic and authoritarian features.[102] Lacking the tradition of 'constitutional liberalism', defined by Zakaria as the combination of the rule of law and individual liberty, Russia in his view has become a classic case of 'illiberal democracy'. The mix of democracy and authoritarianism allows relatively free elections, but the absence of independent parties, in his view, means that 'politics becomes a game for individuals, interest groups, and strongmen'.[103] Furman takes the argument further when he describes many of the states in post-Soviet Eurasia as 'imitation democracies', a 'combination of democratic constitutional forms with a reality of authoritarian rule'. Such systems emerge 'when conditions in a given society are not ripe for democracy, and yet there is no ideological alternative to it'. This is the classic stalemate situation, as noted, of a passive revolution. The duality, moreover, is reflected in popular attitudes, with 51 per cent in 2005 supporting the view that Russia needed a president who could exert the 'firm hand' to govern the country, while 44 per cent favoured a leader who 'strictly observed the constitution'.[104] Furman argues, moreover, that imitation democracies 'are not simply transitional forms, but rather distinct systems, functioning and developing according to their own

---

[101] Terry Lynn Karl, 'The Hybrid Regimes of Central America', *Journal of Democracy* 6, 3, 1995, pp. 72–87. For a discussion, see Larry Diamond, 'Thinking About Hybrid Regimes', *Journal of Democracy* 13, 2, 2002, pp. 21–35.

[102] Lilia Shevtsova, 'Russia's Hybrid Regime', *Journal of Democracy* 12, 4, October 2001, pp. 65–70.

[103] Fareed Zakaria, *The Future of Freedom* (New York: W. W. Norton, 2003), p. 94.

[104] Poll taken on 14–17 October 2005 with 1600 representative respondents in forty-six regions, www.levada.ru/press/2005110901.html.

logic'.[105] Although the model provides much acute insight into the comparative development of post-Soviet states, it fails to provide a lexicon to distinguish between developments in Commonwealth of Independent States (CIS) countries, other than suggesting that some countries are more imitative than others.[106]

In itself, however, this tells us little about how such a system is organised and operated, and the normative weight to be granted to each of the elements, or the dynamics of politics. No modern democracy is without its coercive features, and hybridity is the essence of contemporary states, but Russia is undeniably at the authoritarian end of the spectrum. Equality before the law, impartial operation of administration and electoral competitiveness are weak. As long as a system is hybrid, however, democratic mechanisms have an independent normative value, however much eroded in practice. As Furman concedes, imitation democracies 'are significantly closer to real democracy than tsarist autocracy or the Soviet system'.[107] The 'real democracy' element in Russia has certain structural and procedural features but is constrained by the arbitrariness of the administrative regime. It is the dynamics of this tension that the dual state model developed in this book seeks to capture.

The interaction of real constitutionalism and nominal para-constitutionalism in Russia can be contrasted with the development of the dual state in Germany in the 1930s. Ernst Fraenkel described how in Nazi Germany the prerogative state acted as a separate law system of its own, although the formal constitutional state was not dismantled. Two parallel systems of law operated, where the 'normative state' operated according to sanctioned principles of rationality and impartial legal norms; while the 'prerogative state' exercised power arbitrarily and without constraints, unrestrained by law.[108] In Fraenkel's words, 'By the Prerogative State we mean that governmental system which exercises unlimited arbitrariness and violence unchecked by any legal guarantees, and by the Normative State an administrative body endowed with elaborate powers for safeguarding the legal order as expressed in statutes, decisions of the courts, and activities of the administrative agencies.'[109]

[105] Dmitrii Furman, 'Imitation Democracies: The Post-Soviet Penumbra', *New Left Review*, No. 54, November–December 2008, p. 39.
[106] Dmitrii Furman, *Politicheskaya sistema Rossii v ryadu drugikh postsovetskikh system*, Report No. 233 (Moscow: Institute of Europe, 2009).
[107] Dmitrii Furman, 'Dilemmy i stradaniya liberalov', *Nezavisimaya gazeta*, 28 March 2008, p. 11.
[108] Ernst Fraenkel, *The Dual State: A Contribution to the Theory of Dictatorship*, trans. from the German by E. A. Shils, in collaboration with Edith Lowenstein and Klaus Knorr (New York: Oxford University Press, 1941; repr. The Lawbook Exchange Ltd, 2006).
[109] *Ibid.*, p. xiii.

The Nazi regime breached the formal rules with impunity, but where the authorities chose not to assert their prerogatives, 'private and public life are regulated either by the traditionally prevailing or newly enacted law'.[110] The normative state was largely concerned with regulating the capitalist economy, while the prerogative state dealt with the regime's enemies and controlled political activity. Court records studied by Fraenkel demonstrated that as time passed, the prerogative state encroached ever more on the impartial rules of the normative state.[111]

Gordon Smith notes that in the Soviet period the duality was strongly developed as well, and in particular 'The legal system in the USSR under Stalin clearly resembled Fraenkel's "dual state".'[112] This has been described in detail by Robert Sharlet, noting that 'Soviet legal culture under Stalinism can be most clearly understood within what can be described as a dual system of law and terror...'[113] This took the form of a permanent tension between the principles of *partiinost'* (party-mindedness) and *zakonnost'* (legality), with the prerogative state 'governed directly by the rule of force', while the normative state was 'regulated through a system of sanctioned legal norms prescribing the permissible boundaries of interpersonal relations and citizen-state relations'. There was a fundamental distinction between ordinary and 'political' cases, with *partiinost'* unequivocally taking precedence in the latter,[114] a differentiated application of law that also applies to post-communist Russia. In the post-Stalin years the boundary of *zakonnost'* expanded, but in keeping with Carl Schmitt's postulate that the sovereign is the one who can decide on the exception,[115] the persecution of dissent in the Brezhnev era was firmly located in the realm of *partiinost'*.

Crucially, however, Sharlet stresses the differences between the Soviet and German models of the dual state. First, in Germany the prerogative state was introduced by decree, whereas Sharlet argues that in Russia it was 'basically received from pre-revolutionary Russia'. Second, the development of the dual state in Germany marked a shift 'from political rationality to political radicalism', whereas 'the Soviet dual state

[110] *Ibid.*, p. 57.
[111] *Ibid.*, pp. 241–4.
[112] Gordon B. Smith, *Reforming the Russian Legal System* (Cambridge: Cambridge University Press, 1996), p. 34.
[113] Robert Sharlet, 'Stalinism and Soviet Legal Culture', in Robert C. Tucker (ed.), *Stalinism: Essays in Historical Interpretation* (New York: W. W. Norton, 1977), p. 155.
[114] Sharlet, 'Stalinism and Soviet Legal Culture', p. 156.
[115] Defined by Carl Schmitt, the 'exception' is the ability of the sovereign to make decisions outside the framework of normative law. As he put it in the opening of his work on the subject, 'Sovereign is he who decides on the exception': *Political Theology: Four Chapters on the Concept of Sovereignty* (Chicago and London: University of Chicago Press, 1985), p. 5.

reflected the constant, dynamic interaction of these tendencies'. Third, the Nazi party was the constitutive element of the prerogative state, while the Soviet Communist Party, both in theory and mostly in practice, 'has been outside of, and in control of, the dual state'. This is a feature of the dual state in Russia today, with the presidency representing a force that is implicated in both pillars of the dual state but controlled by neither. Fourth, in Germany the prerogative state was typically restricted to the political sphere, while the normative state operated mainly in the non-political private part of society; in Soviet Russia, however, the distinction between public and private spheres barely held (except possibly for the brief period of the New Economic Policy in the 1920s) and instead, Sharlet notes, 'the dual state has exercised jurisdiction over different sectors of a fundamentally politicized society'. Finally, the German normative state was grounded in private law and modern German history, whereas in the Soviet Union the public/private law distinction was irrelevant, and therefore what there was of the Soviet normative state already lacked deep roots in the pre-revolutionary system and was based on public law.[116]

In the post-Stalin era, there was an increasing emphasis on 'socialist legality', and although egregiously politicised trials of dissidents demonstrated the enduring power of prerogative authority, there was a growing recognition of the importance of independent courts, reflected in notions of 'developed socialism' and the 'people's state'.[117] The normative importance of the rule of law became one of the overriding concerns of *perestroika*. Gorbachev's reforms were one of the most profound attempts to overcome state duality by bringing the political regime within the ambit of constitutional authority.

The dual state model can be fruitfully applied to developments in post-communist Russia. Robert Amsterdam, international defence council for Khodorkovsky, has drawn attention to the parallels, and his analysis contains many insights on the way that the rule of law was subverted in the Yukos case to drive through the requisite convictions. Amsterdam notes that 'The prerogative state accepted that the courts were necessary to assure entrepreneurial liberty, the sanctity of contracts, private property rights and competition, but this did not mean that the courts or the law were inviolable.'[118] For Fraenkel, the

[116] Sharlet, 'Stalinism and Soviet Legal Culture', pp. 155–6, fn 2.
[117] For a classic discussion, see Fyodor Burlatsky, *The Modern State and Politics* (Moscow: Progress Publishers, 1978), esp. Chapter 3, 'The Political System of Developed Socialism, pp. 99–158, with comments on law at p. 125.
[118] Robert R. Amsterdam, *The Dual State Takes Hold in Russia*, mimeo, Royal Institute for International Affairs, 7 February 2008, p. 2.

destruction of legal independence was the central feature of the prerogative state.[119] As Knoops and Amsterdam put it, 'the concept of the Dual State implies that, despite the normative value and safeguards of certain legal mechanisms in terms of checks and balances, the entire legal system can become or de facto function as an instrument at the disposal of the political authorities'.[120] This is indeed the case, but the process also works in the reverse direction, with the normative state in Russia tempering the arbitrariness of the administrative regime, our synecdoche for the prerogative state.

There are obvious limits, recognised by Amsterdam, to the applicability of the model to Russia, above all because of the 'uniquely horrific' way in which it was applied by the Nazis, and the application of the dual state model does not imply any moral or political equivalence. Even within the realm of political practices, there are stark differences. In Germany the regime openly proclaimed the priority of non-constitutional imperatives as the guiding principles of the state, above all the word and will of the Führer, whereas in Russia the fundamental legitimacy of the regime is derived from it being embedded in a constitutional order that it is sworn to defend. On the other side, Germany had a long history of robust constitutionalism, whereas Russia lacks a strong constitutional culture, and thus the rule of law and the independence of the judiciary are at best tenuous. The two wings of dualism are less pronounced than in Germany, where dualism took the form of the open assault of the prerogative state on the entrenched constitutional order. Nevertheless, the tension between the two systems defines the political order in Russia.

Social relations in the prerogative state tended to be personalised, while impartial rules are the operative code of the normative order. In Nazi Germany the constitutional and prerogative states coexisted but with the prerogative state firmly in the ascendant, whereas in Russia the two are roughly matched and their *interaction* is the defining feature of the regime. These are discrete subsystems, but the two are not insulated, and hence Russian politics today is a dyadic order in which the two are in a constant interaction, the essence of its hybridity. Although the rule of law in Russia remains fragile and, as the Yukos affair amply demonstrated, is susceptible to manipulation by the political authorities, no fully fledged prerogative state emerged with anything like the same powers as in Germany. Instead we have a diffuse yet powerful

---

[119] Fraenkel, *The Dual State*, p. 24.
[120] Geert-Jan Alexander Knoops and Robert R. Amsterdam, 'The Duality of State Cooperation Within International and National Criminal Cases', *Fordham International Law Journal* 30, 2007, p. 263.

administrative regime, recognising its subordination to the normative state on the one side and its formal accountability to the institutions of mass representative democracy on the other.

For this reason we avoid the term 'prerogative state' and instead use the concept of 'administrative regime' as the protagonist of the normative state. We have no prerogative state as such in Russia, constituted through formal but extra-constitutional decrees or laws, but instead we have informal behaviour by an administrative regime that fulfils some of the functions of the prerogative state but has no independent legal or institutional status of its own. The administrative regime is both a network of social relations, in which political and economic power are entwined in a shifting landscape of factional politics, and also an actor in the political process. It thus has a passive element, acting as an arena of intra-bureaucratic contestation (since the social basis of the administrative regime overwhelmingly lies in Russia's burgeoning bureaucracy), but it also has agency features, allowing active purposive behaviour. As we shall describe in later chapters, the presidency is only one element, although obviously a crucial one, of the administrative regime.

Equally, the struggle for genuine constitutionalism is the cornerstone of the 'normative' pillar of our political diarchy, and hence we argue that the 'constitutional state' is the protagonist of the administrative regime. The constitutional state is based pre-eminently on the formal order of institutions, and thus its practices are unlike the factionalised politics of the administrative regime. Its adherents are found in legal-constitutional structures, among the liberal intelligentsia and those who have advanced into the elite up the electoral ladder. The latter route for independent politicians was increasingly blocked, as we shall see, by the suffocating regulations imposed on the electoral process by the administrative regime. By definition the defenders of constitutionalism and the rule of law appeal to openness and due process, although that does not preclude some faction-fighting of their own. The goal of universalistic law has been proclaimed by all leaders since Gorbachev, and both Putin and Medvedev, with their legal background, have proclaimed the supremacy of law (*gospodstvo zakona*), although the achievement falls far short of the ambition. Post-communist Russia has been in a permanent state of exception, exercised not through constitutional provisions of some sort defining a state of emergency but through an informal and undeclared derogation from constitutional principles. This is exercised by the administrative regime, which in the long term undermines the viability of constitutionalism as a whole. Elsewhere, notably in Malaysia and Singapore, regimes of exception have been unable 'to return to a state of normalcy'.[121] In Russia, however, the state of exception has not become the norm and coexists with the normal exercise of law, and thus the situation remains liminal and open-ended.

It is for this reason that Kathryn Hendley makes the convincing case that 'Over the last two decades, with surprisingly little fanfare, the legislative base and institutional infrastructure of the Russian legal system have undergone a remarkable transformation.'[122] This is demonstrated by a dramatic increase in Russians' use of the courts, with a doubling in the number of civil (non-criminal cases) in the last decade. However, when powerful business or political interests are involved, courts are avoided; and the persistence of 'telephone law' means that 'the Kremlin has been able to dictate the outcome of cases in which it takes a strong interest', with the Yukos affair only the best-known example.[123] This has given rise to a 'dual legal system': there is some measure of predictability in normal circumstances, and the courts 'can be relied on to handle mundane cases' but are suborned by the powerful in 'exceptional' instances, rendering the system a 'far cry from the rule-of-law-based state that was the initial goal'.[124] Thus 'rule by law' coexists with 'rule of law', a feature that in Hendley's view 'has been a reality in Russian life for decades, if not centuries'.[125] Studies of the late tsarist and Khrushchev eras reveal the same process at work. There is now equilibrium between the two systems, which in her view could last a long time, since 'In its current form, the Russian legal system meets the short-term needs of both state and society.'[126] This is a crucial feature of the stalemate that we discussed above. However, there are external factors at work which reinforce the legal-constitutional pillar in Russia, notably membership of the Council of Europe. As Trochev shows, 'the Russian courts draw on the ECtHR [European Court of Human Rights] to support both their independence from law enforcement authorities and their judicial power in the sense of requiring government agencies to carry out judicial decisions'.[127]

---

[121] Kanishka Jayasuriya, 'The Exception Becomes the Norm: Law and Regimes of Exception in East Asia', *Asian-Pacific Law & Policy Journal* 2, 1, Winter 2001, p. 110.

[122] Kathryn Hendley, 'Rule of Law, Russian-Style', *Current History*, October 2009, p. 339.

[123] Kathryn Hendley, '"Telephone Law" and the "Rule of Law": The Russian Case', *Hague Journal on the Rule of Law*, No. 1, 2009, p. 257.

[124] Hendley, 'Rule of Law, Russian-Style', p. 340.

[125] Hendley, '"Telephone Law" and the "Rule of Law"', p. 258.

[126] *Ibid.*, p. 262.

[127] Alexei Trochev, 'All Appeals Lead to Strasbourg?: Unpacking the Impact of the European Court of Human Rights on Russia', *Demokratizatsiya* 17, 2, Spring 2009, p. 166.

The Yukos affair revealed the ability of the regime to apply
'telephone law'; that is, to influence judicial outcomes.[128] The Yukos
affair was a classic case of a 'prosecution to order' (*zakazannoe delo*)
accompanied by the malpractices that became known as 'Basmanny
justice'.[129] These were indeed defined as malpractices by the Russian
public sphere and ultimately remained susceptible to remedy. However
imperfect the 1993 constitution may be, it provides the framework for
the development of a pluralistic political society and open public
sphere, and as long as the system remains dual, there remains a
dynamic of renewal. Under Putin, especially in the early years, considerable effort was devoted to strengthening the judiciary as an institution and the legal system as a whole. Measures included the
adoption of a new Criminal Procedural Code, shifting the power of
detention from prosecutors to the courts, significant wage rises for
judges to insulate them from the pressure of bribes, an increase in
the number of judges by a quarter, and an extensive programme of
court building and refurbishment. The legal-constitutional pillar was
reinforced in institutional terms, but the independence of the judiciary
was undermined by the continued application of Basmanny justice
(meta-corruption) and numerous varieties of venal corruption, including the use of 'intermediaries' to help fix outcomes. Meta-corruption
in Russia, moreover, was fostered by 'the inseparability of power and
ownership as well as the dominance of the bureaucracy in the system
of public decision-making'.[130]

In Russia both systems emerged at the same time and are therefore
more in balance than the earlier German, or even Soviet, model.
Whether the two are commensurate is a fundamental question, and
one which remains hotly contested. My argument is that the two pillars
of rule are more than a façade, with each carrying defined political
weight. Both subsystems are hegemonic, in the sense that they are each
associated with what Gramsci would call a 'historical bloc', a vision of
the appropriate social order carried by specific social groups and elites.
The tragedy of Russian post-communism is that these two blocs have
become locked into stalemate, preventing a radical move towards a more
genuinely open and competitive political system and a debureaucratised
economy. The triumph of Russian post-communism, however, is that

[128] Alena Ledeneva, 'Telephone Justice in Russia', *Post-Soviet Affairs* 24, 4, October–
December 2008, pp. 324–50.
[129] *Basmannoe pravosudie: Uroki samooborony: Posobie dlya advokatov* (Moscow:
Publichnaya reputatsiya, 2003); www.ip-centre.ru/books/Basmannoe.pdf.
[130] V. L. Rimsky, 'Bureaucracy, Clientelism and Corruption in Russia', *Russian Polity: The
Russian Political Science Yearbook (2007–2008)* (Moscow: Politeia, 2009), p. 105.

the stalemate has also prevented regression towards full-blown authoritarian restoration. The factional structure of the administrative regime does not predominate over formal political institutions. Instead, the system remains liminal, with its further evolution to be determined by the changing balance of power between the constitutional state and the administrative regime. The dynamics of the two systems will be explored later in this book.

Para-constitutionalism and para-politics

Rather than structures and rules providing the framework for order, political actors bend structures and rules for their own purposes and, at the same time, create new ones that sustain the administrative regime while bypassing the formal constitutional order. The experience of the period of 'phoney democracy' in the early 1990s up to the adoption of the constitution in December 1993, when the Russian parliament acted as a permanent constituent assembly, shifted Russia's executive towards a position of para-constitutional innovation. From the very first days of post-Soviet governance, the problem of duplication of administrative structures was apparent, initially focused on the dual executive (cabinet and presidency) replicating their functions.[131] The rush to the market in the 1990s, designed to dismantle the institutions of the planned economy in the shortest historical time, entailed a high degree of 'institutional nihilism': 'At that time, people tended to think that the market needed little in the way of management.'[132]

The development of administrative strategies was in part provoked by flaws in Russia's institutional design. Colton and Skatch note that 'Russian semi-presidentialism was of the most conflict-ridden sub-type – divided minority government.'[133] Krasnov argues that the constitution itself acts as the source of pathological behaviour, above all in promoting the excessive presidentialisation of politics.[134] As he notes in a later co-authored work, there is even a question about whether the presidency is a branch of power or stands entirely outside of the separation of powers. A strict reading of the constitution suggests that the presidency does not even head the executive but stands above and beyond the governmental

[131] Eugene Huskey, 'The State-Legal Administration and the Politics of Redundancy', *Post-Soviet Affairs* 11, 2, 1995, pp. 115–43.
[132] Igor Y. Yurgens, *Russia's Future Under Medvedev*, English edn, ed. Professor Lord Skidelsky (Warwick: Centre for Global Studies, 2008), p. 36.
[133] Timothy J. Colton and Cindy Skatch, 'The Russian Predicament', *Journal of Democracy* 16, 3, July 2005, p. 117.
[134] Mikhail Krasnov, 'Konstitutsiya v nashei zhizni', *Pro et Contra* 11, 4–5, July–October 2007, pp. 30–42, in particular p. 32.

system.[135] The weak or indeed absent separation of powers was accompanied by the strong concentration of power in the administrative system. This means that parliament does not act as the focus of consensual politics and instead veered from sullen resistance in the 1990s to passive obeisance in the 2000s. A great mass of reformist legislation was passed even in the 1990s, but in institutional terms the Duma is at the margins both of decision-making and of national political identity.[136]

When in the 2000s the regime began to reassert the assumed prerogatives of the state, it did so in a distinctive way. On the one hand, it appealed to the spirit of the constitution and the rule of law, a theme taken up by Putin in his early speeches in 2000 that stressed the 'dictatorship of law', and by Medvedev in his condemnation of 'legal nihilism' in his campaign speeches in 2008. These and numerous other measures entailed the *reconstitution* of the state, based on a return to constitutional norms and provisions. At the same time, by establishing a strong 'vertical' concentration of power and numerous control mechanisms over business and society, the process took the form of *reconcentration*. The logic of reconcentration was intended to overcome the institutional nihilism of the earlier period, but in practice it reproduced nihilism in new forms. The characteristic feature of institutional nihilism was the creation of a number of para-constitutional institutions that undermined the spirit of the 1993 constitution, but provided important integrative functions. Formal hierarchical structures were unable to generate adequate ordering mechanisms, while the lack of development of intermediate political structures opened up a gulf between state and society that threatened both to isolate the state and to marginalise social forces. The creation of para-constitutional agencies attempted to fill the gap by manual means, reflecting neither spontaneous social development nor the formal provisions of constitutional law while not repudiating those provisions. The political analyst and former political adviser Sergei Kurginyan precisely analyses this politics behind the scenes, which he calls *parapolitika* or 'under the carpet' politics.[137]

Putin's key goal was to enhance state capacity, defined as the ability of state agents to achieve a desired effect on 'existing non-state resources, activities, and interpersonal connections'.[138] Tilly highlights the possible

[135] M. A. Krasnov and I. G. Shablinskii, *Rossiiskaya sistema vlasti: Treugol'nik s odnom uglom* (Moscow: Institut prava i publichnoi politiki, 2008), p. 30.

[136] Paul Chaisty and Petra Schleiter, 'Productive but Not Valued: The Russian State Duma, 1994–2001', *Europe-Asia Studies* 54, 5, 2002, pp. 701–24. See also Paul Chaisty, *Legislative Politics and Economic Power in Russia* (Basingstoke: Palgrave, 2006).

[137] Sergei Kurginyan, *Kacheli: Konflikt elit ili razval Rossii?* (Moscow: Eksperimental'nyi tvorcheskii tsentr, 2008); and personal discussion, Yaroslavl, 14 September 2009.

[138] Charles Tilly, *Democracy* (Cambridge: Cambridge University Press, 2007), p. 34.

paradoxical effect of Putin's consolidation of state authority. By reducing the power of autonomous power clusters, notably 'capitalists who had acquired extraordinary independence from state control',[139] democratisation could be enhanced by achieving a more direct relationship between the state and its citizens. The elimination of alternative sources of coercive power had already been achieved with the weakening of the power of 'violent entrepreneurs',[140] and the field was clear for citizens to gain greater collective capacity. Thus Tilly notes that 'If, in the future, the Russian state again becomes subject to protected, mutually binding consultation in dialogue with a broad, relatively equal citizenry, we may look back to Putin as the autocrat who took the first undemocratic steps toward that outcome.'[141] This indeed remains possible, but the first step would be the subordination of the administrative regime to the institutions of the constitutional state. Alternative power sources in society had been weakened, but pluralism was internalised into the administrative regime in the form of factionalism, and thus public pluralism gave way to intra-regime contestation leaving popular social movements out in the cold.

In the administrative regime, para-constitutional behavioural norms predominate that, while not formally violating the letter of the constitution, undermine the spirit of constitutionalism. This is a feature that was already identified in American presidentialism in the 1980s,[142] and it has if anything intensified since then. As in America, para-constitutional behaviour gets things done, but it is ultimately counter-productive because reliance on bureaucratic managerialism undermines popular trust and promotes self-interested behaviour on the part of elites. This is more than the politics of duplication that was prevalent under Yeltsin, notably in the case of the development of the presidential administration as a type of surrogate government.[143] During Putin's presidency the practices of para-constitutionalism were sharply accentuated. His regime, in the main, was careful not to overstep the bounds of the letter of the constitution, but the ability of the system of managed democracy to conduct itself with relative impunity and lack of effective accountability means that it was firmly located in the grey area of para-constitutionalism. The Russian form of managed democracy is far from being a soft variant

---

[139] *Ibid.*, p. 137.
[140] Vadim Volkov, *Violent Entrepreneurs: The Use of Force in the Making of Russian Capitalism* (Ithaca, NY: Cornell University Press, 2002).
[141] Tilly, *Democracy*, p. 137.
[142] Cf. F. Riggs, 'The Survival of Presidentialism in America: Para-Constitutional Practices', *International Political Science Review* 9, 4, 1988, pp. 247–78.
[143] Eugene Huskey, *Presidential Power in Russia* (Armonk, NY: M. E. Sharpe, 1999).

of the Soviet system, *pace* Furman, but an entirely new order with its own regularities and practices.[144]

A number of key institutions were involved in the practice of para-constitutionalism. The first is the establishment of the seven federal districts in 2000, which were subordinated to the presidency and thus technically did not require constitutional validation. However, the insertion of an administrative tier between the central authorities and the subjects of the federation could not but change the nature of Russian federalism. The second was the establishment of the State Council in September 2000, a body comprised of the heads of Russia's regions but running in parallel with the upper chamber of Russia's parliament, the Federation Council. The third para-constitutional body is the 'Presidential Council for the Implementation of the National Projects', established in autumn 2005 to advance the four national projects in housing, education, health and agriculture announced in September of that year. The Council was chaired by the president and consisted of forty-one members, and was responsible for an initial budget of $4.6 billion. Medvedev was appointed to head the national projects and was thus provided with a platform to launch his bid for the presidency. The Council worked in parallel to the government and clearly undermined the authority of the prime minister. By bringing together the various executive and legislative agencies in this way, the Council also undermined the separation of powers.[145]

The fourth main para-constitutional body is the Public Chamber (Obshchestvennaya Palata). In his speech of 13 September 2004, which announced a whole raft of measures in the wake of the Beslan hostage crisis, Putin argued that a Public Chamber would act as a platform for broad dialogue, to allow civic initiatives to be discussed, state decisions to be analysed and draft laws to be scrutinised. It would act as a bridge between civil society and the state.[146] The Chamber monitors draft legislation and the work of parliament, reviews the work of federal and regional administrations, and offers non-binding recommendations to parliament and the government on domestic issues, investigates possible breaches of the law and requests information from state agencies.[147] The

---

[144] Dmitry Furman, 'A Silent Cold War', *Russia in Global Affairs* 4, 2, April–June 2006; http://eng.globalaffairs.ru/numbers/15/1020.html.

[145] Hans Oversloot, 'Reordering the State (Without Changing the Constitution): Russia Under Putin's Rule, 2000–2008', *Review of Central and East European Law* 32, 2007, pp. 61–3.

[146] 'Ob Obshchestvennoi Palate Rossiiskoi Federatii', http://document.kremlin.ru/index.asp.

[147] For details, see James Richter, 'Putin and the Public Chamber', *Post-Soviet Affairs* 25, 1, January–March 2009, pp. 39–65.

Public Chamber introduced a new channel of public accountability against overbearing officialdom and thus usurped what should have been one of parliament's key roles. Work that should properly have been the preserve of the State Duma was transferred to this new body, a type of non-political parliament. It acted as a type of 'collective ombudsman' to act as a feedback mechanism since formal channels were blocked. It also allowed steam to be let off before conflicts took on a regime-threatening character. It acted as a 'lightning rod' that was designed not just to legitimise the existing order and to mobilise support, but also 'to elicit but also to contain popular initiatives that contribute to the effective governance of Russian society'.[148] Some of the Chamber's members proved quite bold in their criticism of the authorities, and their access to key officials and public opinion allowed them to exert significant leverage in some high-profile cases.[149]

The Public Chamber diminished the role of parliament, which democratic theory suggests should act as the primary tribune for the expression of popular concerns. Similar bodies were established in Russia's more authoritarian neighbours. In Kazakhstan a Public Chamber was established to include representatives of the parties that failed to enter the republic's parliament in the December 2006 elections; and since only the presidential party Nur Otan had crossed the threshold (winning no less than 94 per cent of the vote), this para-constitutional body became more representative than the official parliament. In Belarus a people's congress (*Vsenarodnoe sobranie*) was established, consisting of President Alexander Lukashenko's personal nominations. The dominance of personal power in the republic at first did not allow Russian-style factionalism to emerge, but in later years it became more apparent. The creation of these social corporatist bodies of managed representation harked back to the era of fascism in the 1930s, as well as to Soviet-style controlled participatory mechanisms.

Para-constitutional accretions to the constitution were designed to enhance efficacy but in practice undermined the development of a self-sustaining constitutional order, the emergence of a vibrant civic culture and civil society, and above all denied the supremacy of the normative state. The spirit of constitutionalism was undermined by the failure of sections of the Russian political class to subordinate themselves to the constitution. This has been a problem in other countries. In Brazil, for example, Tosto notes that 'constitutions have represented the fleeting

---

[148] Richter, 'Putin and the Public Chamber', p. 61.
[149] Alfred B. Evans Jr, 'The First Steps of Russia's Public Chamber: Representation or Coordination?', *Demokratizatsiya* 16, 4, Fall 2008, pp. 345–62.

interests of those in power; they have not underpinned and defended the liberties of ordinary citizens'.[150] Instead of an impartial normative framework, patronage politics dominated. Expectations that Brazil's insertion into the global economy would allow depersonalised neo-liberal values to overcome entrenched oligarchies, above all in the regions, were disappointed. In Russia patronage politics differed from those predominant in developing countries because of the lack of a traditional autonomous social class whose power derived from historic-ally accumulated wealth rather than access to the state. The political order in these countries is used primarily to defend accrued privileges rather than to serve as an instrument of wealth-creation. In Russia, the political order defended the privileges of the political regime, which in a patrimonial way itself became the organiser, if not the outright owner, of economic property and thus the regulator of enrichment.

Para-constitutional innovations were accompanied by the luxuriant development of what may be termed para-political practices. These are forms of political activism not envisaged by the constitution, notably formal party politics and pluralistic elections, and instead it is a form of politics that is hidden and factional. By contrast with public politics, para-politics focuses on intra-elite intrigues and the mobilisation not of popular constituencies and open interests but of organisational and situational capital. The creation of 'parastatal' political parties, notably Just Russia, is a classic example of the way that para-politics works.[151] The regime devised para-political operative rules on political life that deprived it of the grounded antagonistic competition that is an inherent feature of a genuinely open political process. This rendered the 2007–8 electoral cycle a sterile arena for the enactment of decisions that were made elsewhere. The performance, however, was not deprived of a certain legitimating logic and competition over popular preferences, and thus a degree of genuine engagement remained that was reflected in a relatively high turnout. The regime on the whole did not need to have recourse to overt coercion, and its undoubted reliance on adminis-trative resources to ensure popular participation was more in the nature of an insurance policy. Even without this intervention, the regime would have achieved its goals – a strong parliamentary majority and the election of the appropriate successor.

The institutions of democracy remain central to political practice, and democracy remains the legitimating ideology of the regime, but politics

---

[150] Milton Tosto, 'The Future of Democracy in Brazil', *CSD Bulletin*, University of Westminster, 9, 1, Winter 2001–2, p. 9.
[151] March, 'Managing Opposition in a Hybrid Regime'.

operate at two levels, the formal constitutional (the normative state) and the nominal para-constitutional and para-political (the administrative regime). The persistence of a strong constitutional level is reflected in the agonism that is much in evidence in the discourse of the public sphere, where intellectuals, scholars, journalists and politicians conduct a vigorous debate, tolerated by the regime as long as this does take structured independent form. It is precisely the interaction of the two levels that gives ample scope for the 'two camps' in the study of Russian politics, the 'democratic evolutionists', who stress the evolutionary potential of the system to move towards greater constitutionalism and political pluralism,[152] and the 'failed transitionists', who argue that democracy has been 'derailed' in Russia,[153] to put forward their arguments with some credibility.[154] The two levels have their own institutional logic and legitimating discourses. It is this dualism that gives Russian politics its permanent sense of a double bottom.

[152] See, for example, Elena Chebankova, 'The Evolution of Russia's Civil Society Under Vladimir Putin: A Cause for Concern or Grounds for Optimism?', *Perspectives on European Politics and Society* 10, 3, September 2009, pp. 394–416.

[153] M. Steven Fish, *Democracy Derailed in Russia: The Failure of Open Politics* (New York: Cambridge University Press, 2005), p. 1.

[154] Richard Sakwa, 'Two Camps? The Struggle to Understand Contemporary Russia', *Comparative Politics* 40, 4, July 2008, pp. 481–99.

Adam Przeworski defines democracy as 'a system in which parties lose elections' in which 'outcomes depend on what participants do but no single force controls what occurs'. For him 'The decisive step toward democracy is the devolution of power from a group of people to a set of rules.'[1] In keeping with the hybrid nature of the Russian system, the rules governing Russian elections are exhaustive, but their operation in the end does depend on a 'single force', namely the administrative regime. This was vividly in evidence in the struggle for the presidency, the highest goal in the Russian political system. In 2008 Vladimir Putin came to the end of his period in office as president and insisted that he would step down within the terms stipulated in the constitution. The fundamental question was whether the succession would be limited to just the change of leader, or would it represent a change of regime. Could the system built by Putin survive beyond his presidency?

Operation successor

It is a Russian tradition for a new leader to repudiate the legacy of the previous incumbent and to build up their own power by denigrating the achievements of their predecessor. This is what Putin had done on coming to power in 2000, although in a relatively mild manner without attacking Yeltsin personally; while Yeltsin's whole political programme focused on a critique of the inadequacies of Gorbachev's restructuring (*perestroika*) of the Soviet system between 1985 and 1991. On coming to power in October 1964, Brezhnev subjected his predecessor to withering critique, while Khrushchev had promoted elements of de-Stalinisation.[2] The post-Putin succession had a much less open character than Yeltsin's surge to power in 1989–91, reflecting the shift

---

[1] Adam Przeworski, *Democracy and the Market* (Cambridge: Cambridge University Press, 1991), pp. 10, 11, notes 1, 12, 14.
[2] See Ra'anan (ed.), *Flawed Succession*.

from *glasnost'* (openness) in Russian politics to *skrytnost'* (lack of transparency). The struggle over the succession took the form of factional conflicts, reminiscent of Winston Churchill's alleged characterisation of Soviet politics: 'It's like watching two bloodhounds fighting under a carpet. You can detect a furious battle but you have no idea who's winning.'[3] The succession in 2007–8 was as much over what aspects of the Putin period would be maintained as over the character of the individual who would occupy Russia's highest office.

Succession operations

Russian history is littered with examples of savage court intrigues and murders as one monarch gave way to another. The Soviet period was no different, with the post-Lenin succession lasting some five years from January 1924 until Stalin emerged triumphant. This succession had fundamental policy implications, and its outcome determined the shape of the Soviet Union. As D'Agostino observed, even though the Soviet Union lacked a legal mechanism for leadership succession, this 'does not mean, aside from personalities, the process is devoid of rhyme or reason'. He notes 'a succession of policies alongside the success of leaders'.[4] In his view, party programmes alternated between a 'Moscow line', somewhat nativist and neo-populist, accompanied by stability in the state system (adumbrated by Nikolai Bukharin, Georgy Malenkov and Alexei Kosygin); and a 'Leningrad line', advocating a harsh revolutionary internationalism (whose advocates included Grigory Zinoviev, Andrei Zhdanov, Frol Kozlov and Grigory Romanov).[5] Thus in D'Agostino's view, the struggle between Stalin and Trotsky occluded a more profound struggle over policy and modes of governance. Although it would be going too far to call these 'lines' factions, the division indicates the possibility of a type of pluralism in the Soviet institutional system. Stalin's death on 5 March 1953 was followed by four months of bloody intrigues until Khrushchev emerged triumphant. As always in the

---

[3] The quotation does not appear in Richard Langworth's book *Churchill by Himself: The Life, Times and Opinions of Winston Churchill* (London: Ebery Press; New York: Public Affairs, 2008), which contains 4,120 entries, all of which are authenticated, and it did not come up when he scanned his digital archive of Churchill's 15 million published words (books, articles, speeches, letters and papers) plus 35 million more words about him, written or said by colleagues, biographers and friends. My thanks to Hugh Lunghi and Richard Langworth for their efforts on my behalf in trying to trace the source of what appears to be an apocryphal saying.

[4] Anthony D'Agostino, *Soviet Succession Struggles: Kremlinology and the Russian Question from Lenin to Gorbachev* (Boston: Unwin Hyman, 1988), p. xi.

[5] *Ibid.*, pp. xiii, 4–5 and *passim*.

Soviet system, conflicts over practical matters were invariably couched in theoretical and Marxist forms of discourse. In this case, the struggle over the appropriate degree of de-Stalinisation remained the central policy issue in Soviet politics until its final days.

Post-communist succession struggles have been conducted without bloodshed but with no fewer intrigues. In his foreword to *Flawed Succession*, Robert Conquest notes that 'the crux is the takeover of power by an individual, or a small group, in circumstances in which civic society is either non-existent or very weak, and that the contestants are the few already in a position to secure and use the mechanisms of the state for their own purpose'.[6] Stephen Blank, who in that collection examined Putin's rise to power in 1999–2000, certainly concurs, arguing that Putin's accession in effect amounted to a *coup d'état*, which he compares to Napoleon III's rise following the 1848 revolution in France.[7] In another study of the same events, he argues that Russia's 'authoritarian constitution' (by which he denotes informal arrangements) means that 'succession will inevitably engender permanent crises'.[8] Intra-elite struggles accompanied by the deinstitutionalisation of the state, in his view, means that 'Succession struggles remain the Achilles heel of the system because, for all of Putin's undoubted successes, they force an ever-clearer exposure of its fault lines and inherent fragilities.'[9]

According to Ra'anan and his colleagues, the absence of a mechanism for legitimate succession provokes intense struggles as the time for leadership change approaches. Bunce notes that the succession problem encouraged intra-elite conflict in communist systems[10] and 'open[ed] up regimes to new directions'.[11] It would be a mistake, however, to transfer Soviet practices directly to the post-communist period. The 1993 constitution is a far more authoritative document than anything that preceded it in the Soviet years, and thus the weight of the constitutional state, and with it the rules and procedures for leadership change, have immeasurably increased. The formal electoral procedure is far from a sham and does, however imperfectly, reflect popular preferences; but as noted, a second succession process was conducted

[6] Robert Conquest, 'Foreword', in Ra'anan (ed.), *Flawed Succession*, p. xii.

[7] Stephen Blank, 'The 18th Brumaire of Vladimir Putin', in Ra'anan (ed.), *Flawed Succession*, pp. 133–61.

[8] Stephen Blank, 'The Putin Succession and Its Implications for Russian Politics', *Post-Soviet Affairs* 24, 3, July–September 2008, pp. 231–2.

[9] *Ibid.*, p. 233, repeated on p. 259.

[10] Valerie Bunce, *Subversive Institutions: The Design and the Destruction of Socialism and the State* (Cambridge: Cambridge University Press, 1999), p. 26.

[11] *Ibid.*, p. 57.

in the shadows, and it is the interaction of the two contests that renders the 2007–8 electoral cycle so fascinating.

The search for a successor (*preëmnik*) had begun almost as soon as Putin was elected for a second term in March 2004. The ban on more than two consecutive terms by the same person (Art. 81.3) had also exercised Yeltsin soon after his re-election for a second term in mid-1996, and he had gone through a whole list of possible successors until he settled on Putin.[12] Yeltsin did not hide his 'main political goal: to quietly lead the country to 2000 and the presidential elections. Then, as I saw it, we would find a strong, young politician and pass the political baton to him … Together, we would help him win the elections.'[13] Putin's nomination as prime minister on 9 August 1999 was accompanied by an open television declaration by Yeltsin that 'a worthy candidate for the presidential elections in 2000' had been found.[14] From Yeltsin's perspective, Putin had several advantages, notably his loyalty and air of independent authority, but also because he was affiliated with none of the factions existing at that time, a pattern that was to be repeated in 2007–8. Although Putin came from a security service background, he had spent the first half of the 1990s as deputy to the liberal mayor of St Petersburg, Anatoly Sobchak.[15] Yeltsin's surprise resignation on 31 December 1999 opened the way to pre-term elections in March 2000, in which the acting president, Putin, enjoyed all the advantages of incumbency.[16] Although 'operation successor 2' in 2007–8 would take a very different form, the stakes were no less high. As one of the potential candidates, Medvedev, noted in April 2005, 'Unless we consolidate the elites, Russia could disappear as a single state.'[17] He went on to note that 'the history of Russia demonstrates that the legal transition of power was never straightforward'.[18] The succession process that brought him to power proved the verity of this observation.

Economic context

Russia had changed dramatically during Putin's two presidential terms (see Table 2.1). Between 2000 and 2007, Russia enjoyed economic

---

[12] Blank, 'The 18th Brumaire of Vladimir Putin', pp. 133–9.
[13] Boris Yeltsin, *Midnight Diaries* (London: Weidenfeld & Nicolson, 2000), p. 205.
[14] *Ibid.*, p. 334.   [15] Sakwa, *Putin*, Chapter 1.
[16] A nuanced insider's analysis of late Soviet succession operations and Putin's rise to power is provided by the former KGB official, Evgenii Strigin, *Vladimir Putin: Vnedrenie v kreml* (Moscow: Algoritm, 2006).
[17] Interviewed by Valerii Fadeev, 'Sokhranit effektivnoe gosudarstvo v sushchestvuyushchikh granitsakh', *Ekspert*, No. 13, 4 April 2005, in *Ekspert: Luchshie materialy*, No. 2, 2007, pp. 100–5, at p. 101.
[18] *Ibid.*, p. 102.

Table 2.1 *How Russia changed under Putin*

	1999	2007
Population	146 m	141 m
GDP	$183 bn	$1,024 bn
Foreign reserves	$6 bn (end year)	$400 bn
External (sovereign) foreign debt	$130 bn	$70 bn
Average monthly wage	R1,500	R13,810
Stabilisation Fund	N/A	$130 bn
Military budget	$6 bn	$32 bn
Oil price	$9 (Urals blend)	$88
Oil production (barrels per day)	6 million	10 million
Number of billionaires	0	53

Source: Luke Harding and Tom Parfitt, 'Putin wants to Go On and On, and the Voters Agree', *The Guardian*, 6 October 2007, p. 28, modified and updated.

growth averaging an annual 7 per cent that saw its gross domestic product (GDP) grow by 72 per cent, while real incomes grew by 141 per cent. In 2000–5 growth had mainly come from the export sector (pre-eminently energy, and within that overwhelmingly oil),[19] but from late 2006 growth was more investment-led. In 2007 Russia at last regained its GDP of 1990 and became the world's eighth largest economy. However, it ranked 51st in terms of competitiveness (the United States was in first place),[20] and the country faced some fundamental challenges, listed by Aron: a commodity-dependent economy, neglected human capital, declining life expectancy, a looming pensions crisis, corruption, rising crime, dysfunctional armed forces and an increasingly ungovernable North Caucasus.[21] The lessons of the economic crisis of 1998, however, had been taken to heart, and despite windfall energy rents the Putin administration pursued sound fiscal policies. Russia's recovery owed as much to prudent policy as to the commodity price boom of the period, including diverting resources into counter-cyclical reserves and from 2003 into the Stabilisation Fund rather than into immediate expenditure or consumption.[22]

[19] Rudiger Ahrend, 'Russia's Post-Crisis Growth: Its Sources and Prospects for Continuation', *Europe-Asia Studies* 58, 1, January 2006, p. 5.

[20] World Economic Forum, 'Global Competitiveness Index Rankings and 2007–2008 Comparisons', www.weforum.org/pdf/gcr/2008/rankings.pdf.

[21] Leon Aron, *The Vagaries of the Presidential Succession*, Russian Outlook (Washington, DC: American Enterprise Institute, Spring 2007), pp. 3–5.

[22] Hilary Appel, 'Is It Putin or Is It Oil? Explaining Russia's Fiscal Recovery', *Post-Soviet Affairs* 24, 4, October–December 2008, pp. 301–23.

Andrei Shleifer and Daniel Treisman argue that Russia's economic and political development has been typical of a normal middle-income country, not that of a gangster or criminal state, and thus akin to Brazil or Mexico, and not Colombia. In economic terms Russia was just another middle-income country with high dependence on natural resources, like Argentina and Mexico, while in normative terms Russia's faults were typical of a country at its level of development. This implied that much criticism of the country was ill-conceived. Russia's flawed democracy, they insisted, was perfectly normal for a country at its level of development, and sustained economic growth would elevate Russia to the lower ranks of developed countries to rank with the likes of Poland and Hungary.[23] While acting as a useful corrective to some of the more extravagant criticisms of the Putinite system, this application of traditional modernisation theory neglects the unique challenge facing Russia as it engages with the challenge of remodernisation, the third attempt (building on late tsarist and Soviet modernisation projects) to combine political and economic modernity to create a viable social order. Rather than facing the challenges of development, Russia is a *redevelopmental* state, struggling to overcome the legacy of Soviet mis-modernisation, with all of the distinctive pathologies that entails. In particular, the development of an independent public sphere (*obshchestvennost'*) and middle class was squeezed between an overweening state and its bureaucracy, on the one hand, and a subservient bourgeoisie, on the other. Civil society assumed peculiarly Russian characteristics, with a strong residual Soviet element. It remains state-centred with a constrained civic character.[24] Russia, according to the World Bank, is an 'upper-middle-income country', but its business environment is much harsher than most of its economic peers, including the permanent threat of unpredictable, if not outright corrupt, behaviour by state agencies, including the manipulation of environmental, tax and other regulations.[25]

---

[23] Andrei Shleifer and Daniel Treisman, 'A Normal Country', *Foreign Affairs* 83, 2, March–April 2004, pp. 20–39; Andrei Shleifer, *A Normal Country: Russia After Communism* (Cambridge, MA: Harvard University Press, 2005).

[24] For a general discussion of the dilemmas facing post-communist civil society, see Marc Morje Howard, *The Weakness of Civil Society in Post-Communist Europe* (Cambridge: Cambridge University Press, 2002). On Russian developments, see Alfred B. Evans Jr, Laura A. Henry and Lisa McIntosh Sundstrom (eds.), *Russian Civil Society: A Critical Assessment* (Armonk, NY: M. E. Sharpe, 2005) and Anders Uhlin, *Post-Soviet Civil Society: Democratization in Russia and the Baltic States* (London: Routledge, 2006).

[25] Philip Hanson, *Russia to 2020*, Finmeccanica Occasional Paper, RIIA, November 2009, pp. 14–15.

Table 2.2 *Level of inequality in the world, 2005*

	Russia	USA	Germany	Poland	Brazil
GDP per capita, $ thousand	12.1	43.4	31.1	14.9	9.1
Bottom 20%	5.5	5.4	8.5	7.5	2.6
Second 20%	10.2	10.7	11.4	13.7	11.9
Top 20%	46.4	45.8	36.9	42.2	62.1
Gini coefficient*	0.405	0.408	0.283	0.345	0.58

Source: Igor Y. Yurgens, *Russia's Future Under Medvedev*, English edn, ed. Professor Lord Skidelsky (Warwick: Centre for Global Studies, 2008), p. 28; calculated from World Bank and IMF data by the Institute of Economy and Finance.
*Gini coefficient – 0 if all have the same income, 1 if one person owns everything.

From the relative egalitarianism of the Soviet Union, in less than two decades Russia was transformed 'to a society with an Anglo-Saxon structure of income and a Latin-American structure of property'. In terms of the latter, Russia even outdid Latin America, and income inequality moved in the same direction.[26] Rosstat data reveal that the Gini index increased from .289 in 1992 to .395 in 2000 and .422 in 2007; although as Table 2.2 shows, this is still below the American, let alone the Brazilian, level, but is higher than in the European welfare states. Up to the crisis of late 2008, the proportion of the population in poverty fell consistently, from over a third when Putin came to power to 13.4 per cent in 2007 (18.9 million). A surprisingly large proportion of Russian private property was held by nominal offshore proprietors, a practice that predates the Yukos affair but intensified because of increased fears about the security of private property. Thus Putin's economic achievement is mixed, but the mass of the population improved their economic wellbeing, and this is the basis for his enduring popularity.

Putin's state of the nation speeches varied in tone and emphasis, yet he remained remarkably consistent in outlining a coherent set of policy goals, which in 2007 became the basis for the 'Putin plan'.[27] In the economic sphere, the plan included diversifying the economy away from its traditional focus on primary material exports towards manufacturing and knowledge-based industries; and supporting the strategic

[26] Yurgens, *Russia's Future Under Medvedev*, p. 28.
[27] All state of the nation speeches up to 2005 are in *Ezhegodnye poslaniya prezidenta RF federal'nomu sobraniyu 1994–2005* (Novosibirsk: Sibirskoe universitetskoe izdatel'stvo, 2006).

development of new industries, particularly in the area of technology and information services. In the social sphere, the programme included reducing the enormous income differential; reducing the number of people living below the poverty line; ensuring that wages and benefits were paid regularly and on time; addressing Russia's demographic problems, above all the high death-rate, the low birth-rate, the growing proportion of pensioners, and the declining workforce; and improving the social infrastructure, with greater investments in healthcare, education and housing. The latter was part of the €4 billion 'national projects' programme using Stabilisation Fund resources. We shall return to these issues where appropriate in due course.

The legal framework

On 2 December 2007, Russian citizens went to the polls to elect the Fifth State Duma, sitting for a four-year term. The 2007 campaign was formally launched with the publication of a presidential decree on 5 September, followed in short order by the preparation of the party lists that were to be submitted by 5 October. With the formal registration of the parties taking place by the end of the month, full-scale campaigning began on 3 November. Eleven parties won the right to contest the election, the smallest number ever: in December 1993 fourteen parties were on the ballot paper, in 1995 it was forty-three, in 1999 twenty-six and in 2003 twenty-three.

Numerous innovations were made to the legal framework governing elections, codified by the election law of May 2005, subsequently modified no fewer than eight times to become a lengthy document covering every angle in exhaustive detail.[28] The main changes included raising the representation threshold from 5 to 7 per cent; the abolition of mixed-member representation by moving to a wholly proportional closed list system, thus ending representation from 225 single-mandate constituencies – all 450 deputies were now elected by proportional representation (PR); changes to the funding regime, enhancing support for parties winning over 3 per cent of the vote; the banning of electoral blocs; the deletion of the 'against all' box on the ballot paper; and the

---

[28] The electoral law adopted by the State Duma on 26 October 1994 was thirty-one pages long: *Federal'nyi zakon 'Ob osnovnykh garantiyakh izbiratel'nykh prav grazhdan Rossiiskoi Federatsii'* (Moscow: Yuridicheskaya literatura, 1995). By late 2005 the law ran to 192 pages: *Federal'nyi zakon: O Vyborakh deputatov gosudarstvennoi dumy federal'nogo sobraniya rossiiskoi federatsii* (Moscow: Os'-89, 2005); updated versions available on the CEC website www.cikrf.ru.

abolition of a minimum turnout requirement.[29] The earlier rule that the 7 per cent threshold would apply only if a minimum of four parties qualified and if together they represented over 50 per cent of turnout now stipulated that the 7 per cent barrier applied as long as two parties qualified and represented over 60 per cent of those who voted. If a number of parties crossed the 7 per cent threshold but won less than 60 per cent in total, the next party entered parliament even if it had not obtained 7 per cent, and the process continued until the 60 per cent threshold was reached. In addition, it was made much harder to register for parliamentary elections. Registration could be refused if 5 per cent of signatures (250,000 were now required) on nomination lists were found to be invalid (it had been 25 per cent earlier). The registration deposit for those parties requiring it was raised from 37.5 million roubles (about €1 million) to R60 million.[30] Parties already represented in the Duma remained exempt from the need to gather signatures or lodge a deposit, representing a Premier League who increased their comparative advantage over the rest. Independent social organisations were no longer able to observe polling stations but had to go through political parties. There were now some forty reasons to refuse registration or ban candidates from party lists.[31]

Reinforcing all the other changes, in December 2004 gubernatorial elections were abolished in favour of a system of presidential nomination and approval by regional legislatures. The shift to a wholly proportional system was part of the larger plan to achieve a cohesive pro-presidential majority in the Duma, and thus to ensure continuity in the succession. It also reflected the tendency towards stronger presidentialism in Russia.[32] The closed nature of party lists, moreover, means that the order of names is decided not by voters but by party officials. This leaves little room for independent politicians, let alone those with radical ideas. One controversial rule allowed 'locomotives' to remain on party lists. Typically, these were leading national and regional leaders who headed party lists but had no intention of taking up their seats. This amounted to public deception but compensated for the lack of attractive public

---

[29] For details, see Ian McAllister and Stephen White, '"It's the Economy, Comrade!" Parties and Voters in the 2007 Russian Duma Election', *Europe-Asia Studies* 60, 6, August 2008, pp. 933–6.

[30] 'Federal'nyi zakon Rossiiskoi Federatsii ot 18 maya 2005g.', *Rossiiskaya gazeta*, 24 May 2005; http://document.kremlin.ru/doc.asp?ID=027816.

[31] Vladimir Ryzhkov, 'Lenivye i truslivye', *Pro et Contra* 11, 4–5, July–October 2007, p. 61.

[32] N. V. Anokhina and E. Yu. Meleshkina, 'Proportsional'naya izbiratel'naya sistema i opasnosti prezidentsializma: Rossiiskii sluchai', *Polis*, No. 5, 2007, pp. 8–24.

politicians in the regime parties. Harsh rules were introduced against negative campaigning, perhaps the most restrictive in the democratic world. In 2004 the presidential candidate and speaker of the First Duma, Ivan Rybkin, had made serious allegations against Putin, and the new legislation was in part designed to prevent personal attacks against Putin and his associates.

While there was little resistance to most of the election rule changes, the abolition of the 'against all' box was not popular and its abolition saw a rise in those stating that they would abstain.[33] In response, the regime's attempts to achieve a high turnout became a central feature of elections. The proportion of people voting 'against all' in the party list elections averaged 3.74 per cent, peaking at 4.7 per cent in 2003 (Table 1.1), while in some of the single-mandate seats this reached 40 per cent. The 2005 Moscow Duma election saw a turnout of only 35 per cent, and in response in 2007 the regime used its whole arsenal of 'administrative resources' (the use by officials of administrative and financial mechanisms to advance their cause and to undermine their opponents) to ensure a high turnout. Another response was to spoil ballot papers, but in the event the abolition of the 'against all' category did not lead to a significant increase. In the fourteen regional elections in March 2007, spoiled ballots made up 3–4 per cent of those cast, in line with previous elections. Even where favoured parties were excluded from the ballot, as with Rodina's exclusion from the 2005 Moscow Duma election, there were only 5.2 per cent in this category, while Yabloko's controversial exclusion from the March 2007 ballot in St Petersburg saw no spike in spoiled papers at 3 per cent. The abolition of 'against all', however, increased the proportion of 'used votes', those cast for parties crossing the representation threshold, which reached 88 per cent in the March 2007 vote.[34] The 'against all' option tended to be used as a protest vote, and thus the LDPR stood to gain – especially since a vote for Zhirinovsky was considered in any case a vote 'against all'.

The double vortex: parliamentary and presidential elections

Although overshadowed by a powerful presidency, Russia's parliament in the 1990s contained a strong opposition presence and was far from a

[33] A VTsIOM poll saw only 27% in support and 61% against. In 2006 between 9–12% firmly stated that they would not take part in the Duma elections, but after the deletion of the 'against all' option at the end of that year, the percentage of declared abstainers rose to 15–18%, Georgii Il'ichev, '"Protiv vsekh" – eto za kogo?, *Izvestiya*, 10 September 2007, pp. 1–2.

[34] Makarenko, '"Nanopartiinaya" sistema', p. 55.

supine instrument of the executive, with the threat of impeachment permanently hanging over Yeltsin's leadership. The First Duma, elected in 1993, had eight factions and five deputy groups, and the assembly remained fractious and pluralistic throughout the 1990s. The presidential dream of a centrist parliament was achieved only under Putin. The Third Duma, elected in December 1999, was dominated by Unity (Edinstvo), the grouping that was to become United Russia. The dominance of UR was complete in the Fourth Duma, elected in December 2003, enjoying a 'constitutional majority' (two-thirds of the 450 deputies). Not only did UR choose the speaker (Gryzlov, who also remained head of the UR faction), but it also took six out of nine seats on the Duma Council. Under Putin the inner life of the Duma changed dramatically from the turbulent years under Yeltsin. Enjoying a pro-presidential parliamentary majority, Putin used parliament to push through an extensive legislative programme. Pluralism within parliament, however, was drastically reduced, even though the efficiency with which laws were adopted much improved – although the quality of much of the legislation left something to be desired.

In 2003, as noted, Russia came close to adopting laws that would have stipulated that the government is created by the parliamentary majority, but at the last moment Putin baulked at the change. The necessary amendments were adopted in neighbouring Ukraine following the Orange revolution in December 2004, and the government is now formed by the parliamentary majority, an experience that has led to governmental instability and repeated pre-term elections. Although separated from governmental formation, except in the approval of the president's nominee as prime minister, the Duma is the heart of the law-making process.[35] It is for this reason that the Kremlin devoted so much effort to ensuring a strong majority in 2007, but by the same token parliament is no longer the regulator of the political temperature of the country.

Although United Russia comfortably won the 2005 Moscow Duma elections, taking all fifteen single-mandate seats and 47.25 per cent of the PR vote, the whole contest revealed the dual process at work in Russian elections. As Ryabov notes, in a genuinely competitive environment the UR win would not have been so convincing, and hence 'there was a danger of creating a new political space, parallel to the real one'.[36]

---

[35] Thomas F. Remington, *The Russian Parliament: Institutional Evolution in a Transitional Regime* (New Haven, CT: Yale University Press, 2001). See also his 'The Russian Federal Assembly, 1994–2004', *The Journal of Legislative Studies* 13, 1, March 2007, pp. 121–41.

[36] Ryabov, 'Vybory v Moskve i politicheskaya perspektiva', p. 51.

Table 2.3 *Presidential election of 14 March 2004*

Candidate	Vote	Percentage
Putin, Vladimir	49,565,238	71.31
Kharitonov, Nikolai (CPRF)	9,513,313	13.69
Glaz'ev, Sergei	2,850,063	4.10
Khakamada, Irina	2,671,313	3.84
Malyshkin, Oleg (LDPR)	1,405,315	2.02
Mironov, Sergei	524,324	0.75
Against all	2,396,219	3.45

Sources: Central Electoral Commission, *Vybory prezidenta Rossiiskoi Federatsii 2004: elektoral'naya statistika* (Moscow: Ves' mir, 2004), p. 106; Central Electoral Commission: www.pr2004.cikrf.ru/index.html.

The closed system sought to ensure the preservation and reproduction of the regime, using the usual carrots and sticks.[37] The Moscow and other regional elections acted as trial runs for the national contest, providing lessons that were applied later. Regional legislative elections were certainly monitored closely by the Kremlin, and the lessons were incorporated into subsequent national policies.

Parliamentary elections are inevitably overshadowed by the even greater prize of the presidency. The presidential succession struggle and the parliamentary election campaign are organically interlinked. Traditionally Duma elections have acted as a type of primary for the later presidential poll, acting as a filter for potential presidential candidates. The relatively poor performance of his OVR electoral bloc in December 1999 destroyed Primakov's candidacy in the succeeding presidential campaign. By the time of the 2003–4 electoral cycle, Putin's overwhelming predominance meant that no serious alternatives emerged, and in March 2004 he ran as the only serious candidate (see Table 2.3).[38] In 2007 the primary element was negligible since the competitive character of the electoral process had been so reduced. Putin's towering presence precluded an outsider candidate making a credible run, while the application of administrative resources was no longer the exception but had become 'normalised' as part of the *modus operandi* of the administrative state.

In 2007 Putin insisted on his supra-political right to ensure that a candidate was chosen who would continue his work. Russia's next

---

[37] *Ibid.*, p. 52.
[38] William A. Clark, 'Russia at the Polls: Potemkin Democracy', *Problems of Post-Communism* 51, 2, March–April 2004, pp. 22–9.

president effectively boiled down to Putin's choice, although at one point there was speculation that he would allow a number of favoured candidates to compete against each other. The abrupt dismissal of Mikhail Fradkov's government on 12 September 2007 signalled that Putin would closely manage the succession process. The appointment of his old colleague Mikhail Zubkov to head the new government meant that the scenario that had brought him to the presidency would not be repeated. Putin had used his appointment as prime minister in August 1999 as the launch pad for his presidential bid in March 2000. As we shall see (Chapter 5), Zubkov let drop enigmatic hints, endorsed by Putin, that if he succeeded in his post as premier then he might try a run for the presidency, but in the end this was no more than a diversion intended to dampen the ambitions of other potential successors and to ensure that Putin remained in control of the process.

Succession dynamics

In its review of international affairs in 2007, the Russian foreign ministry explicitly, and rather surprisingly, gave voice to regime fears: 'In view of the parliamentary and presidential elections in Russia the inadmissibility of interference from outside in our internal affairs, including the electoral process, became the unconditional priority of our foreign policy work.'[39] Concern over the application of 'colour technologies', however, was overshadowed by signs of internal elite fragmentation. As the succession approached there were increasing manifestations of factional struggle, accompanied by the intensification of Putin's attempts to manage the process. Despite his personal popularity, Putin feared that his ability to shape the succession would be undermined by elite fragmentation and popular alienation. A poll conducted by the Levada Center in March 2005 found that only 30 per cent said they would vote for the person nominated by Putin, while 20 per cent said they would not vote for the favoured candidate as a matter of principle. Forty per cent insisted that they would make up their minds irrespective of whether the candidate had the backing of the Kremlin.[40] In the event, the 'Putin effect' became stronger as his departure approached.

Russian politics is characterised by the paradoxical effect that as the efficiency of the political machine increases, its legitimacy declines. One

---

[39] 'Vneshnepoliticheskaya i diplomaticheskaya deyatel'nost' Rossiiskoi Federatsii v 2007 godu: Obzor MID Rossii', Moscow, March 2008, www.mid.ru/brp_4.nsf/0/9B6D03B7DC298E37C325741000339BEC.

[40] Results reported by Kseniya Solyanskaya in Gazeta.ru, 22 April 2005, in *Johnson's Russia List* (henceforth *JRL*), No. 9128, 2005, Item 10.

indicator of this law of diminishing returns was the number of abstentions in presidential elections, which increased in every election since 1991. In June of that year 16 per cent abstained, by 1996 (second round) this had risen to 29 per cent, in 2000 to 31 per cent and in 2004 to 35 per cent. Abstention was highest among young people, which in 2004 reached 52 per cent among those aged 18–19, and 55 per cent for those aged 20–24, while the most active voters were the over-60s, with an abstention rate of only 22 per cent.[41] One of the Kremlin's greatest fears in 2007–8 was that in the absence of convincing opposition parties and candidates, voters would express their opinions by staying at home, thus jeopardising the legitimacy of the outcome.

The March 2004 presidential election demonstrates the decline of competition, illustrating what Colton calls the 'attenuation of Russian democracy'.[42] Facing an exceptionally weak range of opponents (all other heavyweight political leaders withdrew), Putin gathered almost three-quarters of all votes cast (see Table 2.3). Colton argues that the incumbent stifled not only rival bids, but also the space from which such a bid could be launched. He is certainly right to stress that the sphere of public discourse had been substantially impoverished, and that few parties were able to sustain themselves as autonomous and effective shapers of public politics. Part of the responsibility lies with the failure of parties, such as the Communists and the liberals writ large, to redefine themselves in the new circumstances, to shape effective leadership structures, or to devise appropriate programmes (the endogenous approach discussed earlier); but the Kremlin's creation of a harsh environment for genuinely competitive politics must bear a large part of the blame. Very few politicians emerged who adapted their strategies to the real needs of the day. Ryzhkov's brave, and ultimately unsuccessful, attempt to create a broad liberal and democratic coalition on the basis of the old Republican Party was one of the few exceptions to this rule.

Fears that Just Russia would split the elite were reinforced by its strong performance in municipal and regional elections. At its first outing in October 2006, JR won the mayoral elections in Samara, but the 11 March 2007 regional elections saw the steady march of UR across the country, coming top in thirteen out of the fourteen regional legislature elections, winning on average 46 per cent of the vote. Nevertheless, on

[41] Youri Levada, 'Les élections présidentielles', in 'La Russie de Poutine', *Pouvoirs: Revue française d'études constitutionnelles et politiques*, No. 112, 2005, p. 146.

[42] Timothy J. Colton, 'Putin and the Attenuation of Russian Democracy', in Alex Pravda (ed.), *Leading Russia: Putin in Perspective* (Oxford: Oxford University Press, 2005), pp. 103–18.

occasion the Kremlin's creation of an alternative to UR worked rather too well. Just Russia's success in taking control of the legislature in Stavropol region acted as a warning of what could happen. United Russia received only 23 per cent of the vote, its lowest poll results to date. The March 2007 regional elections acted as a dry-run for the parliamentary election later that year and demonstrated that the creation of JR had split the vast army of officialdom, with politicians in the regions adopting a hedging strategy between the two putative parties of power and playing one off against the other. The emergence of JR changed the terms of political trade. Just Russia would now fight with UR to become the president's party, and possibly even the party of power. By late 2007 the regime had clearly changed its strategy, fearing splits within the elite, and no longer backed two horses but threw its weight entirely behind UR, although JR managed to scrape into the Duma.

The March 2007 elections were marked by a number of scandals, with seventeen party lists either disqualified or blocked from registering, demonstrating the tight control exercised by the Kremlin. The CPRF had initially been refused registration in Dagestan and Tyumen, although later with assistance 'from above' they were reinstated, demonstrating that the Kremlin needed to keep the ineffectual Communists as a toothless opposition party. The CPRF demonstrated that it was not entirely a spent force, coming second in half of the contests. The SPS had similar problems in Vologda, Pskov, Tyumen and Dagestan, but was able to overturn a decision to bar it in Samara region. Yabloko was barred from running in its heartland region of St Petersburg because of alleged irregularities, with more than 10 per cent invalid signatures on its nomination lists. The abolition of gubernatorial elections had removed one channel whereby strong independent politicians could emerge, and now the authorities sought to ensure that powerful independent parties did not act as an alternative channel for upward political mobility.

The role of ideology became more attenuated with each election. The SPS, for example, in these regional elections moved dramatically to the left, and this paid off, winning between 7–9 per cent of the vote where it stood. For much of 2007 it looked as if the SPS had become the natural party to represent the liberal part of the electorate, while at the same time broadening its appeal by overcoming the stigma of the 1990s. In the final fortnight before the Duma vote on 2 December, the SPS went even further and became a street-fighting radical opposition party, disappointed that the Kremlin had reneged on its apparent promise to allow it to enter parliament.

The 2007 parliamentary election was accompanied by an almost paranoid fear of external destabilisation, and Putin's speeches frequently referred to the perceived danger. In terms of public opinion, his fears were not entirely groundless. A poll earlier that year found that 42 per cent did not exclude the possibility of a colour revolution. A third considered that Russia lacked an independent and authoritative opposition, while 43 per cent stated that they would vote for the current authorities. Most worrying, only a third was satisfied with the existing political and economic policies. Nevertheless, while dissatisfied with the existing order, only 5 per cent stated that they would take part in protest actions. Why, then, all the talk of colour revolutions? The Kremlin took the view that colour revolutions were an instrument of destabilisation from outside. The fall of governments in Serbia, Georgia, Ukraine, Kyrgyzstan, together with the Andijan events of May 2005 in Uzbekistan (in which the authorities crushed an alleged popular uprising with heavy loss of life), sent the signal that the incumbent regimes across post-Soviet Eurasia were far from safe. Despite the Russian government's attempts to portray these revolutions as the work of foreign agents, few in Russia believed that this was indeed the case and instead were well aware that colour events had been provoked, at least in part, by attempts to steal elections. This did not translate into support for Russian oppositionists: only 7 per cent took the opposition seriously, and only 23 per cent sympathised with it. There was a yawning absence of new people, new ideas and new perspectives. Both the CPRF and SPS were tainted by failure, while Yabloko hardly registered as a serious national electoral challenge.[43]

From the failed democratisation perspective, a revolution is required to bridge the gulf between popular aspirations and the nascent authoritarian regimes; however, for democratic evolutionists, the only effective and durable way to bring the *pays légal* and the *pays réel* into alignment is through the gradual and patient establishment of the social and political structures that can sustain a democratic polity. This certainly was Putin's view, and it is the one that he pursued in the 2007–8 electoral cycle to avert a Russian colour revolution and to ensure policy continuity beyond the succession. The heavy-handed way in which this was done, however, undermined social sources of political renewal and to a degree discredited the political process in its entirety.

---

[43] Polling data from VTsIOM, Valerii Vyzhutovich, 'Oranzhevyi mirazh', *Novye izvestiya*, 10 May 2007, p. 2.

No third term

'Constitutionalism', Angelika Nussberger reminds us, 'is the art of creating legal rules to tame power', and one of the most important of these is establishing term limits on the person heading the executive. They were established throughout the post-communist world, but in most of Eurasia they proved ineffective.[44] In Russia the ban on more than two consecutive terms provoked many calls for the constitution to be amended to allow Putin a third term. This would require a change to Article 81.3, which given Putin's popularity and the extent of his support among the elite, entrenched in a near-constitutional majority in parliament, could easily have been done. The changes concern Chapter 4 of the constitution and, contrary to popular wisdom, do not require a referendum. According to Article 134, amendments to the constitution may be initiated by the president, the speaker of the Duma, the head of the Federation Council, groups of deputies numbering no fewer than one-fifth of either chamber, or finally by the legislative assembly of any one of Russia's regions. Amendments are adopted in the same way as federal constitutional laws, namely, they must be approved by two-thirds of the Duma, three-quarters of the Federation Council, and then ratified by two-thirds of Russia's regional assemblies (Art. 128.2). Unlike federal constitutional laws, however, the president's signature is not required. A simpler option would have been to change the law on elections, which prohibits a president who resigns before the end of their term from participating in pre-term elections. While legal, these various stratagems would have undermined the spirit of the constitution.

Elections in post-communist Eurasia have become the site of geopolitical contestation. The ideology of democratisation became bound up with security interests, while the notion of colour revolutions – the combination of popular resentment against hijacked elections accompanied by elite splits and international intervention – provided a vocabulary for forced change. Transnational actors helped shape the transition in numerous countries, and fears that they would do so in Russia evoked a sharp response from the regime.[45] The view that elections are the continuation of Cold War struggles by other means certainly influenced

---

[44] Angelika Nussberger, 'Ogranicheniya prezidentskoi vlasti v postkommunisticheskikh stranakh', *Sravnitel'noe konstitutsionnoe obozrenie*, No. 5 (66), 2008, pp. 53–68, quotation at p. 53.

[45] For arguments about the crucial role of transnational actors, called the 'dark matter', that shaped the transitions, see Mitchell A. Orenstein, Stephen Bloom and Nicole Lindstrom (eds.), *Transnational Actors in Central and East European Transitions* (Pittsburgh: University of Pittsburgh Press, 2008).

Putin's view of the 2007–8 elections. Vladislav Surkov, the deputy head of the presidential administration responsible for relations with social movements and the management of domestic political processes, and typically described as the 'Kremlin's grey cardinal',[46] warned of two possible dangers: the threat of 'oligarch revenge' by the 'offshore aristocracy', and nationalist mobilisation by 'national-isolationists';[47] to which Putin added a third threat: a colour revolution funded by the west. The three, in his view, threatened his ability to negotiate the electoral rapids that would allow a smooth transition not only to a new leader but also from stabilisation to a new era of modernisation. Once again Samuel Huntington's 'two turnover test', whereby 'a democracy may be viewed as consolidated if the party or group that takes power in the initial election at the time of transition loses a subsequent election and turns over power to those election winners, and if those election winners then peacefully turn over power to the winners of a later election', would not be achieved.[48] Yeltsin's refusal in 1996, as he faced re-election, to contemplate leaving office set Russia on a different path from that of Ukraine, where Leonid Kravchuk in 1994 accepted his second-round defeat and meekly went into retirement.[49] Yeltsin, however, did not cancel the elections, as recommended by his *silovik* associate Korzhakov, and instead fought a vigorous campaign that formally observed the constitutional proprieties while in practice suborning the electoral process.

Putin resolutely opposed all plans to change the normative framework for his own convenience. A number of post-Soviet Eurasian countries, including Belarus, Kazakhstan, Kyrgyzstan, Turkmenistan, Tajikistan and Uzbekistan, had used 'continuation' referendums to prolong the term in office of incumbent presidents, especially when there were constitutional prohibitions on being re-elected twice. Constitutions had been changed in Belarus and in Uzbekistan to allow Alexander Lukashenko and Islam Karimov, respectively, to consolidate their authoritarian rule.[50] On 17 October 2004, the referendum in Belarus on removing presidential term limits was accompanied by massive

[46] Aleksandr Rar [Rahr], *Rossiya zhmet na gaz: Vozvrashchenie mirovoi derzhavy* (Moscow: Olma-Press, 2008), p. 107.
[47] Surkov, 'Suverenitet: Politicheskii sinonim konkurentosposobnosti', in Vladislav Surkov, *Teksty 97–07* (Moscow: Evropa, 2008), pp. 143–7.
[48] Samuel Huntington, *The Third Wave: Democratization in the Late Twentieth Century* (Norman: University of Oklahoma Press, 1991), pp. 266–7.
[49] David C. Brooker, 'Kravchuk and Yeltsin at Re-Election', *Demokratizatsiya* 16, 3, 2008, pp. 294–304.
[50] For details of extension referendums, see Sakwa, *Russian Politics and Society*, Chapter 8.

violations. In South Korea, General Park Chung Hee, who in 1961 came to power in a coup, in 1969 changed the constitution to allow himself a third term, and it was downhill all the way thereafter: in 1972 he declared martial law, dissolved parliament and parties, and imposed strict censorship. He replaced elections with a handpicked electoral college that allowed him to rule to 1979, when he was accidentally shot by his own police chief who was busy suppressing worker protests. Historical experience illustrates that a leader who over-stays their welcome ends up badly, as President Ferdinand Marcos in the Philippines found to his cost in 1986 and General Suharto in Indonesia in 1998. Putin's peers in the CIS, nevertheless, encouraged him to stay on for fear that he would set an unwelcome precedent in the region by stepping down on time and in the manner duly prescribed by the relevant statutes – fearing demands for them to leave as well. Putin, however, refused to place himself in their company. Although relations with the west had soured by the end of his presidency, Putin still valued his international reputation. Putin's self-image is that of a European leader, and thus he resisted all blandishments to take an 'Asian' short cut to remaining in power.[51] Some loyal followers, including his biographer Roy Medvedev, continued to agitate for a third term despite Putin's protestations.[52]

While there were high reputational and substantial risks associated with any attempt to shape the constitutional rules to allow Putin to stay in power, the risks associated with the change were no less grave. It is for this reason that Putin sought to manage the process in a classic para-political manner. On 13 May 2006, Putin asserted that as a citizen of Russia he would announce his preferred candidate but would not actively campaign for that candidate or impose him on the country.[53] In the event, as we shall see, Putin took a vigorous part in the campaign. After 2008 Russia would find itself with a new president, but one that Putin hoped would be able to maintain continuity. As Sergei Markov notes, 'In Russia we lack traditions, political traditions of peaceful transfer of power from one leader to another.' On the same occasion he stressed the risks associated with 'the 2008 problem'. At the top of the list of dangers facing the country, he placed 'the risk of chronic destabilisation as a result of a clash of clans'. His second danger lay in the

---

[51] Compare, for example, the arguments applied to maintain Karimov in power in Uzbekistan, Andrew F. March, 'From Leninism to Karimovism: Hegemony, Ideology, and Authoritarian Legitimation', *Post-Soviet Affairs*, 19, 4, 2003, pp. 307–36.

[52] Roi Medvedev, *Vladimir Putin: Tret'ego sroka ne budet?* (Moscow: Vremya, 2007), pp. 334–42.

[53] Eberhard Schneider, 'Putin's Successor', *The EU-Russia Review*, No. 3, 'After Putin … What Next?' (Brussels: The EU-Russia Centre, March 2007), p. 14.

selection of a weak leader, which would tempt the authorities to use 'administrative resources' to manage the elections, provoking a Russian 'orange revolution'.[54] Later, Markov identified a third threat, 'an attempt at oligarchic revenge':

Vladimir Putin's team, which has been well consolidated over these years, may split up because of the fight between clans for the next leader. If this happens, they will start appealing to outside groups, seeking their support, basically appealing to oligarchic groups. Therefore I think in this case a return of oligarchy would be quite feasible, it may creep into the Kremlin amidst the fight between clans for the heir ... An alliance of clans with old oligarchs may provide one of the ways for bringing oligarchs back to power ... It would be a serious political mistake if oligarch groups are allowed to take part in deciding who should be Russia's president after 2008.[55]

One of the determinants governing the succession process, according to critics, was the fear that dark matters would be discovered if the incumbent regime lost power. As with Yeltsin earlier, the paramount consideration was to ensure that Putin's successor did not launch any hostile actions against him, his associates and the groups that had prospered during his leadership. While this was certainly a far from negligible consideration, Putin's overt concern was to ensure policy continuity while excluding the danger that the presidency would fall into the hands of what he considered extremists of one stripe or another. To that extent, his concern to oversee the process can be seen as basically altruistic, and the argument that the whole exercise was designed from the beginning to keep him in power for an unconstitutional third term is flawed. 'Operation successor 2008' was indeed designed to ensure continuity by locking in 'Putinism without Putin', but as the moment of changeover approached, the regime's options appeared to narrow. At least one of the factions began to fear that without Putin the Putin system would be doomed, and the calls for him to stay in authority, if not in power, became increasingly insistent.

Leadership and political values

The political institutions of post-communist democracy, regulated by the 1993 constitution, have been unable to generate an independent legitimacy. We have seen how low the trust ratings in the major

---

[54] Press conference with Sergei Markov at *Argumenty i fakty* press centre, 16 November 2005, in *JRL*, No. 9299, 2005, Item 15.
[55] Roundtable held on 6 June 2006, 'Sud'ba Khodorkovskogo koe-kogo nichemu ne nauchila', *Izvestiya.ru*, 6 June 2006; www.izvestia.ru/press/article3093549/index.html.

institutions of the Russian state have been, and only the presidency stood out as a body in which people could place their faith. However, it was not so much the institution that was trusted but the person occupying the post, and when he moved to the premiership in May 2008, trust in the government commensurately increased. Unlike Japan, which also has a type of managed democracy, fundamental political decisions emerge not out of hierarchical representative institutions of modernity, but out of a rather archaic system of court politics. Shevtsova argues that Putin's system of governance was based on factions fighting for his favour, but at the same time he allowed them to treat the state as their private patrimony, and thus their private ambitions and greed inhibited modernisation of the economy and polity.[56]

Leaderism and the Putin phenomenon

As with many two-term presidencies, Putin's second term differed from the first. The reform drive began to falter, accompanied by the Yukos affair. The market economy was given a more detailed legal framework through the adoption of a significant body of legislation in a now docile legislature. Putin was accused of building a personal authoritarian system in which he took all the major decisions himself, often with the minimum of consultation with his colleagues. The centralisation of power in the hands of the presidency was undoubted. There is also no question that Putin became rather more isolated, with no readily identifiable group of people on whom he would rely. As far as Bjorkman was concerned, Putin's policies were leading Russia into a dead-end and the country had become at best an electoral democracy.[57] It would be going too far to suggest, as Anders Åslund does, that a 'personal authoritarian system' had been created.[58] He is right, however, to suggest that Putin's presidency undermined the autonomy of other political institutions, and even to a degree their legitimacy. The whole system became pivoted on Putin personally, and hence the moment of succession posed a fundamental problem for the system to perpetuate itself.

Although Putin played an enormous role, it would be a mistake to characterise the system as personalistic. Russia was not Belarus; in the latter the public sphere was destroyed, the political elite fragmented,

---

[56] Lilia Shevtsova, *Russia – Lost in Transition: The Yeltsin and Putin Legacies* (Washington, DC: Carnegie Endowment for International Peace, 2007).

[57] Tom Bjorkman, *Russia's Road to Deeper Democracy* (Washington, DC: Brookings Institution Press, 2003).

[58] Anders Åslund, 'Unmasking President Putin's Grandiose Myth', *Moscow Times*, 28 November 2007, p. 9.

leadership posts wholly subordinated to Lukashenko's will, institutions suborned and policies generated by the one man. In both cases, however, totalising power was not based solely on charismatic or personal characteristics but was sustained by a system in which the leader was not so much the architect as its product.[59] A fully personalistic system does indeed face the fundamental problem of perpetuation at a time of leadership change. In Russia, however, we have a dual system where formal constitutional institutions interact with para-constitutional behaviour. Personalistic aspects of the system operate within the framework of formal institutions, both reinforcing and undermining each other. Individuals trump institutions only in certain circumstances; while institutions partially constrain individual preferences.

Drawing on opinion poll material, Surkov asserted that 'the level of trust in political institutions directly depends on their degree of personification and proximity to the supreme centre'.[60] This is probably the case, but this does not make Russia a personalistic system, where leadership preferences permanently trump institutional constraints. Russian governance under Putin was nevertheless highly personalised, provoking in turn *ad hominem* attacks. To quote Åslund again, 'Putin has established a purely personal dictatorship. He rules through the presidential administration and competing secret police forces without ideology ... Personal authoritarianism rarely survives its founder ... Putin's regime may be described as a group of clans, consisting of state-dominated corporations, such as Gazprom, Rosneft, Vneshtorgbank, Rosoboroneksport, and the Russian Railways, together with the security agencies.'[61] Under his leadership the state eroded economic freedoms and engaged in 'velvet reprivatisation', a period that saw the share of GDP coming from the private sector declining from 70 per cent to 65 per cent. Åslund, like Shevtsova, is right to note the importance of group politics in the Putin system but provides no analysis of the dynamics of 'clan' conflict or the role of the presidency, something we shall examine in Chapters 3 and 4 based on our model of the dual state discussed in Chapter 1.

---

[59] Cf. Wolin, *Democracy Incorporated*, in particular pp. 238–48 and 287, who makes the argument on the basis of the development of a new totalising power in advanced democracies.

[60] Vladislav Surkov, *'Russkaya politicheskaya kul'tura: Vzglyad iz utopii'*, in Konstantin Remchukov (ed.), *Lektsiya Vladislav Surkova 'Russkaya politicheskaya kul'tura: Vzglyad iz utopii': Materialy obsuzhdeniya v 'Nezavismoi gazete'* (Moscow: Nezavisimaya gazeta, 2007), p. 10.

[61] Anders Åslund, 'Putinomics', http://commentisfree.guardian.co.uk, 3 December 2007.

A notable example of a personal attack on Putin is the article by Sergei Kovalëv, the courageous human rights campaigner in the Soviet years and Yeltsin's first human rights ombudsman, who bravely condemned the assault on Grozny in the early days of the first Chechen war in December 1994. Kovalëv's intense personal distaste of Putin meant that his piece was more a diatribe than a useful analysis; and although many of the points are well made, the article reflects an extreme version of the failed democratisation approach to Russian politics. 'I should begin by saying that I find the current president of Russia and his policies extremely offensive. I believe that Vladimir Putin is the most sinister figure in contemporary Russian history. From the very beginning of his rule he has directed – and almost completed – a broad antidemocratic counterrevolution in Russia.'[62] Kovalëv adduces four reasons for the resilience of the 'Putin phenomenon'. The first is founded on achievements, above all 'relative stability and relative security', compared to the chaotic 1990s, such as the payment of wages on time and the end of economic decline, but he believed that Putinite stability was fragile. Much of the opposition in the last succession period in 1999–2000 had promised the same things, so 'Why did the voters prefer a homely colonel with fishlike eyes?' His second reason was that Putin's popularity was founded on a vote against the chaos of the 1990s, when democracy became a dirty word. Kovalëv will have none of this, arguing that it was not democracy that brought the country to its knees in that dark decade, but its absence: 'I believe, on the contrary, that the catastrophes of the 1990s were the result of the absence of genuine freedom in the country. The trouble with Yeltsin's first team of politicians and administrators was not that they were ineffective as democrats, but that in truth they weren't democrats at all.'

In that context Putin was not elected as a remedy for the evils of the 1990s but 'as a member of Yeltsin's team, as his "heir"', and his view of democracy, qualified by the adjectives 'managed' or 'sovereign', continues to 'undermine the very idea of democracy'.[63] The third explanation is nostalgia for Soviet times, with Putin having 'in effect created a myth of the imperial state – a myth derived from elements of pre-revolutionary Russian history and the Soviet past – that serves as a substitute for historical memory'. The fourth explanation is Putin's alleged 'charisma', but he questions this: 'Is the 71 per cent of the vote he received in 2004 convincing evidence of his popularity? I have never

---

[62] Sergei Kovalëv, 'Why Putin Wins', trans. Jamey Gambrel, *New York Review of Books*, 22 November 2007, p. 64.
[63] *Ibid.*, p. 65.

met anyone who likes Putin as a person.' So, the riddle of Putin's electoral success 'is quite simple and quite sad':

For virtually the first time in history, Russian citizens were given the primary instrument of political democracy: direct and competitive elections. But they do not know why they need this instrument or how to make use of it. Eleven hundred years of history have taught us only two possible relationships to authority, submission and revolt.

This is a classic statement of the 'democracy paradox': given the vote, people chose a non-democratic option. With the people fed up with revolution, Kovalëv argued, 'Energy for revolt' had not built up and thus submission triumphed. 'The ideological ingredients of Putinism existed in the consciousness of the population long before Putin's rule: his "team" transformed them into usable modern propaganda and aggressively rebroadcast them to the whole country.' Thus a political culture of passivity is abetted by the skilful exploitation of popular expectations and fears. 'For this reason it really doesn't matter what will be the outcome of the current intrigue over the different "scenarios" for the presidential election of 2008', since Putin's replacement would be no more than a figurehead as Putin holds on to the reins of power as prime minister. Kovalëv was not clear what was to be done, and each person would have to decide for themselves:

I imagine – with both sorrow and certainty – that the Byzantine system of power has triumphed in Russia. It's too late to remove it from power by a normal democratic process, for democratic mechanisms have been liquidated, transformed into pure imitation. I am afraid that few of us will live to see the reinstatement of freedom and democracy in Russia.[64]

The argument was in keeping with the 'Leninist liberalism' that typified Russia's 'democratic' opposition in the later Putin years, accepting the logic of 'the worse the better' to get rid of a regime they loathed. The extremism of Kovalëv's position reflects the broader problem of the 'political culture of Russian "democrats"', the title of a study by Alexander Lukin. In his view, the liberal and democratic movements learnt how to use western concepts and practices, but in effect assimilated them to the deeper authoritarian structures of Russian political culture.[65] Just as the Russian party and electoral systems adapted to the exigencies of regime politics, so the main actors of Russia's democratic

---

[64] *Ibid.*, p. 66.
[65] Alexander Lukin, *The Political Culture of the Russian 'Democrats'* (Oxford: Oxford University Press, 2000).

revolution adapted to the country's primordial authoritarianism. As we shall see, this is not a satisfactory argument.

Political values

Stephen Whitefield has examined the conundrum of Putin's popularity. If indeed Putin is responsible for the dismantlement of Russian democracy, then how can we explain his sustained popularity?[66] Whitefield examines a number of hypotheses to explain this phenomenon: Putin's popularity reflects the illiberal and undemocratic sentiments of Russians; Putin's leadership has changed the views of his supporters *because* of the illiberal outcomes, while his opponents take a more negative view; this leads to a bifurcated system of supports, for and against Putin. Whitefield suggests that a 'system performance' analysis is more convincing, in which Putin's popularity is based on perceived improved political and economic performance. His survey data discounts the growing illiberalism hypothesis, and the argument that Putin is supported by those with anti-democratic values is not sustained either. The data suggest that Russians on the whole do not hold the view that there has been significant democratic backsliding, while popular support for democratic norms and values has remained more or less constant. Opponents of democracy do not in the main support Putin, while those who seek the consolidation of government do not necessarily hold undemocratic views. In conclusion, Whitefield notes that 'Putin's popularity does not appear to rest on an "authoritarian" mass political culture.'[67] In a later study, Whitefield stresses that 'Russians do not see democratic performance on a single dimension',[68] and although Russians are consistently critical of the quality of their democracy, there has been little change over time to reflect prevalent western views about a decline in the performance of Russian democracy.[69]

These findings were confirmed by a Levada Center poll conducted in November 2007. Although the headline findings suggest a preference for order over democracy, the understanding that order and freedom were linked and not opposed reveals a deeper popular comprehension of the

---

[66] Stephen Whitefield, 'Putin's Popularity and Its Implications for Democracy in Russia', in Alex Pravda (ed.), *Leading Russia: Putin in Perspective* (Oxford: Oxford University Press, 2005), pp. 139–60.

[67] *Ibid.*, p. 157.

[68] Stephen Whitefield, 'Russian Citizens and Russian Democracy: Perceptions of State Governance and Democratic Practice, 1993–2007', *Post-Soviet Affairs* 25, 2, April–June 2009, p. 100.

[69] Whitefield, 'Russian Citizens and Russian Democracy', pp. 107–12.

substantive meaning of democracy than superficial analysis would suggest. While the majority of Russians were ready to sacrifice elements of democracy to safeguard law and order, this was balanced by a similar majority arguing that the authorities had to be controlled by society. The poll found that 68 per cent believe that order was the priority for Russia, even if this entailed some infringements of democratic standards. For 18 per cent of respondents, democracy was more important, even at the price of giving freedom to destructive and criminal elements. A solid 66 per cent believed that the authorities must be controlled by civil society, although 27 per cent considered that if the authorities acted in the interests of the people, they did not need to be controlled. The residues of Soviet-style thinking were strong when it came to the most appropriate type of economic system, with 54 per cent in favour of state planning and government-controlled distribution, up by 11 per cent since 1997. A total of 29 per cent supported private property and market relations, a fall from 40 per cent in 1997.

As for the fundamental question whether 'order' and 'democracy' are compatible in Russia, 40 per cent of respondents stated that one was impossible without the other; 17 per cent said that one contradicted the other; 12 per cent considered that order was possible without democracy but democracy was impossible without order; 9 per cent said that order was possible without democracy and democracy was possible without order; 8 per cent considered that democracy was possible without order but order was impossible without democracy; and 15 per cent were undecided. For 44 per cent of respondents, the word 'democracy' meant freedom of expression, the press and religious beliefs; 30 per cent associated it with order and stability; and 26 per cent with economic prosperity. Law and order were the priority for 21 per cent, balanced by the 17 per cent who said that all top state officials should be elected by the people. A sceptical stance was adopted by 11 per cent, who considered 'democracy' to be no more than 'empty talk'; 10 per cent thought it was the framework for everyone to do what they wanted; and 6 per cent considered it was about guaranteeing the rights of the minority. Four per cent thought that democracy meant anarchy and absence of authority, and 3 per cent said that it meant the minority had to be subordinated to the majority.[70] Bjorkman found that while the first priority for Russians was to 'restore order', this was not synonymous with authoritarianism and there was deep-rooted support for democratic values.[71] On the basis

[70] 'The State, Order and/or Freedom', poll of 1,600 people conducted 20–23 November 2007, published 5 December 2007, www.levada.ru/press/2007120502.html.
[71] Bjorkman, *Russia's Road to Deeper Democracy*, pp. 25–7 and *passim*.

of a major study, Mikhail Afanasiev asks 'Is the Russian craving for real order in the country an obstacle to modernization? Not at all; on the contrary it facilitates it.'[72] He finds a demand for modernisation in the country in which the state would play a leading role, but not a state built on the 'power vertical', and hence there is a demand for 'quality of government'.[73]

Political disengagement continues to be an issue in Russia, accompanied by alienation from the discourse of human rights.[74] A large-scale comparative study in 2007 found that 47 per cent of Russians valued stability above freedom of speech,[75] suggesting that there was some basis to the much-vaunted 'values gap' between Russia and the west, but its size was exaggerated. Although studies demonstrate that Russian values remain tolerant, and that pluriculturalism, based on the existence of over 150 autochthonous peoples, is part of Russian reality, there is a profound counter-movement based on exclusionary principles that privilege the notion of 'Russia for Russians'.[76] The notion of 'Russian', they insist, is capable of different interpretations. A survey by Gallup's Russian partner, Romir, in June 2007 found that 64 per cent of Russians affirmed that democracy was the best political system, with the figure rising to 71 per cent for those aged under thirty, but fell to below 50 per cent among those above 65 years of age. However, only 57 per cent said that they were satisfied with democracy in Russia, compared to a worldwide average of 69 per cent who were happy with democracy in their countries. Some 80 per cent of respondents doubted whether Russia was

---

[72] Mikhail Afanasiev, 'Is There a Demand for Modernization in Russia?', *Russia in Global Affairs* 7, 3, July–September 2009, p. 24.

[73] *Ibid.*, pp. 28–33.

[74] Maria Ordzhonikidze, 'Russians' Perceptions of Western Values', *Russian Social Sciences Review* 49, 6, November–December 2008, pp. 4–29.

[75] The survey was conducted by GlobeScan Incorporated for the BBC. Over 11,000 citizens were questioned on media freedom in the USA, UK, Germany, Russia, India, Kenya, Brazil, Venezuela, Egypt, Mexico, Nigeria, Singapore, United Arab Emirates and South Africa. Russian views tended to be closer to those in Asia than in western Europe. Forty-six per cent of Russians considered the Russian press free (world average 56%), and only 18% thought that press freedom in Russia was inadequate. Russians were particularly concerned about ownership structure, with only 27% considering that ownership did not affect the objectivity of information. Only 29% considered that the free expression of their views on current affairs was important, the lowest of all fourteen countries surveyed (average 56%). www.newsru.com/russia/10dec2007/freed.html. The Russian part of the survey was conducted by the Levada Center. The full report is available at www.newizv.ru/news/2007–10–16/78078/.

[76] See, for example, G. V. Kozhevnikova, O. A. Sibireva, A. M. Verkhovskii, *Xenophobia, Freedom of Conscience and Anti-Extremism in Russia in 2007: A Collection of Annual Reports by the SOVA Center for Information and Analysis* (Moscow: Informatsionno-analiticheskii tsentr 'Sova', 2008).

governed by the will of the people, a higher proportion than the 63 per cent worldwide.[77] Although order was consistently rated above democracy, the two were not seen as mutually exclusive, and a strong majority favoured the retention of democratic freedoms.[78]

Another study examined generational differences, finding that those who came of age in the post-Soviet period were generally more supportive of democratic values and institutions and a market economy than those who had matured in the Soviet years, a predictable finding. However, the younger generation placed more emphasis on capitalism rather than democracy and took a wholly instrumental view of freedom as a way of advancing their own interests, while support for the principles underlying the public good was secondary.[79] The generation that came of age after the fall of communism takes a more positive view of developments than older cohorts, with far greater endorsement of economic over political changes.[80] The study took issue with scholars who took a pessimistic view of the prospects for the development of democracy in Russia, with the younger generation demonstrating relatively higher levels of trust in public institutions and a greater belief in their own political efficacy.[81] Although educated and skilled young people are likely to share western values, this is accompanied by a robust patriotism.[82] This is precisely the Medvedev mix.

Polling data are only one way of understanding the mood of contemporary Russia. Perhaps a more interesting way is to examine the vigorous debates in the Russian public sphere. These reveal a powerful current of thought critical of western modernity. Even intellectuals within one family were torn. For example, Alexei Kara-Murza, at the Institute of Philosophy, propounded strongly liberal views based on his magisterial studies of the history of liberalism in the country. At the same time, his brother Sergei Kara-Murza was a favourite of the Russian patriotic movement and had a whole section of his works on the shelves of the 'Molodaya Gvardiya' national-minded bookshops. Similarly, Anatoly

---

[77] Jonas Bernstein, 'Almost Two-thirds of Russians Believe Democracy Is the Best Political System', *Eurasia Daily Monitor* (henceforth *EDM*), 5, 8, 16 January 2008.

[78] Timothy J. Colton and Michael McFaul, *Are Russians Undemocratic?* Carnegie Endowment for International Peace, Russian Domestics Politics Project, Russian and Eurasian Program, Working Paper No. 20, June 2001; republished in *Post-Soviet Affairs* 18, 2, 2002, pp. 91–121.

[79] Jeffrey W. Hahn and Igor Logvinenko, 'Generational Differences in Russian Attitudes Towards Democracy and the Economy', *Europe-Asia Studies* 60, 8, October 2008, pp. 1345–69.

[80] *Ibid.*, p. 1365.   [81] *Ibid.*, p. 1367.

[82] V. E. Semonov, 'The Value Orientations of Today's Young People', *Russian Social Sciences Review* 49, 6, September–October 2008, pp. 38–52.

Chubais had been at the head of the liberal attack on the Soviet economic system, masterminding the privatisation process and then helping establish the SPS liberal party, yet his brother Igor Chubais took a far more nativist approach to the question of Russia's developmental path.[83]

At the time of the election, a second volume of the *Proekt Rossiya* (*Project Russia*) book was published, which like the first was anonymous.[84] The first volume had come out in 2006 and represented the most coherent and influential defence of the argument that democracy, in the form it was practised in the west, was inappropriate for Russia. The book condemned the universal dominance of market relations, with the mass media undermining spiritual values and expounding utilitarian and consumerist thinking.[85] The second book was written in a similarly accessible but relatively sophisticated style. It called for the establishment of an Orthodox monarchical system, in which the powers of the sovereign would be limited by spiritual principles: altar and throne would work together to save Russia. As for who would take up the throne, this would be a matter for the people and God, but the shift should be achieved gradually and all forms of revolutionary excess avoided. The key idea was an honest and just Orthodox autocracy.[86] Although polls suggested that the majority of the Russian population opposed the restoration of the monarchy, the proportion in favour was on the rise. The monarchy here was purely symbolic and represented a shift to conservative nativism.

There remains a fundamental question concerning any necessary correlation between the extent of popular support for democracy and regime outcomes. Lucan Way notes that surveys conducted in the 1990s found greater public support in Belarus, which in the event took an authoritarian turn, and least in Moldova, which has enjoyed several cycles of incumbent turnover.[87] Russia was clearly divided on its fate

---

[83] Igor' Chubais, *Rossiya v poiskakh sebya: Kak my preodoleem ideinyi krizis* (Moscow: Izd-vo NOK 'Muzei bumagi', 1998).

[84] It is still not known who was behind the project, but rumours pointed to Vladimir Yakunin, head of Russian Railways. Formally, it was published by the Centre for Dynamic Conservatism, financed by a foundation called The Russian Entrepreneur. Another programme in 2007 with a similar name, the 'Russian Project' within United Russia headed by Ivan Demidov, focused on problems facing ethnic Russians, but following official disapproval in 2008 it was merged with the less ethnocratic social conservative State-Patriotic Club, one of the three recognised platforms in UR. Laruelle, *Inside and Around the Kremlin's Black Box,* p. 30.

[85] *Proekt Rossiya* (Moscow: Olma-Press, 2006).

[86] *Proekt Rossiya: Vybor puti,* vtoraya kniga (Moscow: Eksmo, 2007).

[87] Lucan A. Way, 'Authoritarian State Building and the Sources of Regime Competitiveness in the Fourth Wave: The Cases of Belarus, Moldova, Russia, and Ukraine', *World Politics* 57, January 2005, p. 246.

and place in the world. This was more than a simple dualism, for or against the market, democracy and international integration; it represented a complex multi-planed response to complex challenges. While not rejecting the importance of political values, Ellen Carnaghan critiques the simplistic application of political culture approaches and thus turns the question on its head – asking not whether 'Russians are democratic enough for their new institutions' but 'whether Russian institutions encourage people to be democrats'.[88] This indeed is the fundamental question, underpinned (Carnaghan notes) by aspirations for the restoration of a stable order, but not at the expense of democracy (although the appreciation of democratic procedures tends to be rather blunt). This serves as a short definition of Putinism.

The big turn or change delayed

On 7 October 2007, Putin celebrated his fifty-fifth birthday in the best of health and with the prospect of many years of active political life ahead of him. Some governors urged Putin to remain in power, and a number of popular demonstrations on 24 October 2007 were held across Russia, notably in Chechnya with some 30,000 participants, encouraging Putin to stay, despite his oft-declared intention not to do so.[89] It appears that Sechin tried to convince Putin to take on a third term, but when Putin dismissed such arguments, Sechin devised a plan whereby Putin would be replaced by a 'technical' president who would either resign pre-term or act as Putin's puppet until he could legally take on the post for two more terms.[90] The rather colourless premier, Fradkov, was considered ideal for this role. He was a classical 'technical' prime minister, reflecting the depoliticisation of the administration. Once again the idea of Putin taking over as the head of a new political unit, for example the joint Russo-Belarusan state, was advanced. In the event, the various conflicts with Lukashenko over energy prices and other issues meant that in 2007 the possibility of a unified Russian-Belarusan state to act as the springboard for Putin to stay in power (or even for Lukashenko to extend his authority) was discounted.

---

[88] Ellen Carnaghan, *Out of Order: Russian Political Values in an Imperfect World* (University Park: Pennsylvania State University Press, 2007), p. 24.

[89] For details, Anna Smolchenko, 'Putin Won't be Pulling the Strings Next Year', *Moscow Times*, 26 October 2007; and for a sceptical view that 'administrative resources' forced people to attend these rallies, 'Officials Linked to Putin Rallies', *Moscow Times*, 30 October 2007, p. 2.

[90] Rar, *Rossiya zhmet na gaz*, p. 218.

Once it was accepted that Putin would not change the constitution to stay in power, all sorts of ideas were floated about how he could retain influence while not infringing the law.[91] Ingenious schemes were devised by Vitaly Tret'yakov, the editor of the journal *Politicheskii klass*.[92] He was one who considered the retention of Putin in one capacity or another essential, including possibly as prime minister or leader of the dominant party (in the event Putin did both). As the succession approached, a number of scenarios were advanced. All were predicated on some sort of managed process, and they reveal the thinking at the time.[93] The ability of the dominant party, United Russia, to shape the succession was also minimal, despite enjoying a large majority in parliament. Russia did not take the path of institutionalising constraints on executive leadership of the sort practised in Japan or Mexico in the days of PRI. Instead, typically for Putin, he chose an individual whose policy preferences and political instincts were very close to his own and in the end remained part of a reconfigured governing team.

The presidential election in 2008 was only the final point of a succession operation conducted the previous year, and in practice the culmination of the emergence of Putin as the core of a new system of power. As Gleb Pavlovsky noted, 'He [Putin] is the single source of political communication in the country. Hence the mystique of the name – Putin is not simply a man or an office, but a political production complex.'[94] This was both a measure of his achievement, but also an indication of his failure to create a self-reproducing political system. Power had a tendency to transform itself into a neo-monarchical system, accompanied by the associated court politics and intrigues. To perpetuate itself, the regime engaged in manual intervention in the political process. The 'sheer enormity of the stakes involved', as Aron notes, 'subverted the mediating institutions that endow both the process and the result of transition with legitimacy'.[95] Not only power but also enormous financial flows were at stake in the battle of the factions.

---

[91] For an early discussion of the possibilities, see Boris Mazo, *Preemnik Putina, ili kogo my budem vybirat' v 2008 godu* (Moscow: Algoritm, 2005).

[92] Vitalii Tret'yakov, 'Nuzhen li nam Putin posle 2008 goda?', *Nezavisimaya gazeta*, 23 June 2005, p. 7. For a collection of his articles on the subject, see Vitalii Tret'yakov, *Nuzhen li nam Putin posle 2008 goda? Sbornik statei* (Moscow: Rossiiskaya gazeta, 2005).

[93] Aleksei Makarkin, 'Vybory-2008: Trebuetsya silovik s piterskim proshlym', *Ogonek*, 8 March 2004, p. 17, runs through a number of alternatives.

[94] Interview with Gleb Pavlovsky by Iskander Khisamov, 'Predstavitel' nepredstavlennykh', *Ekspert*, No. 16, 22 April 2002, in *Ekspert: Luchshie materialy*, No. 2, 2007, pp. 50–5, at p. 51.

[95] Aron, *The Vagaries of the Presidential Succession*, p. 1.

The fundamental question was whether the 2007–8 electoral cycle would represent a fundamental change, effectively from a regime of managed democracy to something else, ideally from the western perspective a more open and pluralistic type of democracy, although fear that a more xenophobic, populist and demagogic leadership could emerge was one reason for Putin's obsession to manage the process. Vladimir Pastukhov argues that such a fundamental cultural shift would only take place around 2012, when new elites emerge: 'A generation will enter active social life who were born after communism, a generation for whom the Soviet past will be little more than a legend.' This new generation, in his view, would have an entirely different, although unpredictable, world-view and will 'be able to create a new reality'. Hence he is unequivocal: 'No, not 2008, but 2012 will be decisive for Russia.'[96] The answer to the question of what will happen to Russia in 2008 was 'Nothing! Everything will remain as it is. It's a matter of historical, not political, choice. No choice is available to us because there is no realistic alternative to the current policy course in Russia.'[97] The social changes would ripen and by 2012 prepare the way for a change of regime. The key factors determining the change would be economic decline, the activisation of the masses and a crisis of governance.

Pastukhov also tackled another crucial issue – just how much depended on Putin personally. Pastukhov argued that the necessary restoration of statehood in Russia was achieved 'by the corporation that he [Putin] represented. This was fully a "corporate matter".'[98] The corporation he had in mind were the 'Chekists' (special services), whose 'deficiencies were a continuation of their qualities'.[99] They remained the spine of Russian statehood, but the bone was made out of Soviet material. They were able to restore some sort of order, but they did this in a Soviet manner, as evidenced by the Yukos affair.

This was borne out by events, and the succession of 2007–8 in the main represented 'change without change'. This is precisely the outcome that Pavlovsky had long predicted. The new leadership in 2000 had 'to secure the existence of Russia as such', but the 2008 succession was intended to do no more than 'realise a prosaic agenda', to maintain stability and continuity.[100] The era of extraordinary politics would give way to routine. However, the passage to the new presidency was

---

[96] V. B. Pastukhov, 'Temnyi vek: Postkommunizm kak "chernaya dyra" russkoi istorii', *Polis*, No. 3, 2007, p. 38.

[97] Vladimir Pastukhov, 'Pokolenie 2012', *Argumenty nedeli*, 17 May 2007.

[98] Pastukhov, 'Temnyi vek', p. 34, fn 2.

[99] *Ibid.*, p. 34.

[100] Interview with Gleb Pavlovsky by Andrei Gromov, *Ekspert*, No. 36, 2 October 2006.

characterised by the interpenetration of the extraordinary and the mundane, reflecting the two arms of the dual state. The crypto-elections were accompanied by covert para-political competition between factions. The old elite remained in power, the party system remained moribund, parliament was overshadowed by the power system that operated beyond its walls and, above all, Putin retained a decisive voice in Russian politics, although a position now shared with Medvedev. The succession operation allowed evolution to take place within the system and endowed Russia with a strong administration that would allow the period of unprecedented stability to continue. However, this stability was built on a fragmented political class and unstable foundations, to which we shall now turn.

3   Political power and factionalism

In the exit from communism many had called for a 'firm hand', even of the Pinochet type where political liberty is traded in exchange for economic growth. Others stressed the Bonapartist features of Putin's rule, a system defined in Marxist terms as 'an authoritarian government that temporarily gains relative independence and reigns above the classes of society, mediating between them'.[1] Medushevsky, for example, has developed this model, arguing that the presidential representatives at the head of the seven federal districts (*polpredy*) acted as the functional equivalents of Napoleonic prefects.[2] Zyuganov also argued that 'In recent years Russia has seen the emergence and strengthening of the Russian variety of Bonapartism. The regime emerged as a result of a fierce power struggle between clans of oligarchs. It is trying to balance between comprador capital and the mass of the population robbed by capital and the bureaucrats that are in its service.'[3] He insisted that like all Bonapartist regimes, it was unstable and could not resolve the fundamental problems facing the country. Our model suggests that rather than a clear-cut Bonapartist regime, balanced between the established bureaucratic classes and the nascent middle class and bourgeoisie, the presidency seeks to retain its independence by manoeuvring between factions and quasi-class structures. The presidency has a dual valence: applying elements of the liberal democratic lexicon while itself remaining outside the norms of accountability represented by that tradition; an ambivalent position that fostered the shadow practices of the administrative regime. Unable to take political form in society, conflicts were imported into the managerial system, undermining the coherence of the regime. Two parallel systems emerged: a sphere of public politics,

---

[1] The definition is from Alexander Lukin, 'Putin's Regime: Restoration or Revolution?', *Problems of Post-Communism* 48, 4, July–August 2001, p. 47.
[2] Andrei Medushevskii, 'Bonapartistskaya model' vlasti dlya Rossii?', *Konstitutsionnoe pravo: Vostochnoevropeiskoe obozrenie*, No. 4 (33)/No. 1 (34), 2001, p. 28.
[3] G. Zyuganov, 'Political Report of the CPRF Central Committee to the 13th Party Congress', 29 November 2008, http://kprf.ru/party_live/61739.html.

regulated by formal constitutional norms and populated by characteristic elements of a representative system, above all parties and parliament; and a second sphere of clandestine intra-elite contestation for power and property. The presidency participates in both, undermining the autonomy of public politics while seeking to retain its independence in the sphere of factional politics by appealing, typically instrumentally, to the impartiality inherent in the constitutional order.

History of factionalism

The great paradox of communist systems was that highly authoritarian social orders were accompanied by relatively weak systems of public administration. Party and ministerial bureaucracies undermined the autonomy and efficacy of Weberian administration. In Russia it proved hard to change from a system where command and coercion predominated to one governed by law, compromise and the constraints of institutional governance. The creation of a new set of political institutions could not immediately change deeper patterns of political behaviour and the entrenched power of Soviet-style bureaucracies; and thus certain cultural traits reasserted themselves against the institutional engineering of the early post-communist years. Public contestation and participation, the two fundamental features of democracy identified by Dahl,[4] were emptied of substance, and in their place para-political practices predominated. The dualism of the dual state is reflected in the neo-institutional approach, in which the formal institutional level is modified by informal behavioural practices.

Factionalism in the Yeltsin era

Victor Sheinis, one of the creators of the 1993 political system, stresses the influence of what he calls 'shadow structures': 'The defining feature of the organisation of power under both Russian presidents is the interaction of official and shadow structures. People from the president's "inner circle", because of their personal ties, gain influence that far exceeds the authority granted by law to their post.'[5] This was a type of court politics where Byzantine manoeuvrings within the administration and in the interface between regime and society substituted for a more

[4] Robert Dahl, *Polyarchy: Participation and Opposition* (New Haven, CT: Yale University Press, 1971), p. 5.
[5] V. L. Sheinis, 'Dvizhenie po spirali: Prevrashcheniya rossiiskogo parlamenta', *Obshchestvennye nauki i sovremennost'*, No. 5, 2004, p. 47.

open form of public politics, overshadowing parliament and other political institutions. Parties competed with other forms of political aggregation, including patronage and friendship networks as well as factions and the 'party substitutes' identified by Hale. The dominant party in the form of United Russia does not yet act as a mechanism to externalise and manage conflicts within the regime. The various 'columns' within UR gave political form to debates over public policy, and to that extent represented a potential bridge between the worlds of open and closed politics. In the meantime, the struggle for control over policy and the ideological orientations of the system took the form of factional struggle. We use the term 'faction' rather than 'clan' advisedly, since factions are far less substantive and enduring than clans. We shall return to definitions after a brief historical and analytical detour.

From Muscovy to the imperial autocracy, Russian politics were characterised by the struggle of cliques and what in modern parlance are called networks.[6] Even in Russia's most centralised and authoritarian periods, factional conflicts were present.[7] As Stalin consolidated his power in the 1920s, contending groups in the Soviet leadership appealed to provincial party committees to bolster support.[8] Patron–client relations fostered the networks on which Stalin based his power.[9] Khlevniuk argues that the Soviet system alternated between periods of oligarchic and dictatorial rule. For most of its existence the Soviet system was oligarchic, but in the period between 1935 and 1953 Stalin exercised dictatorial power. He finds no evidence of factional conflict within the top leadership in this period, or even that a division between radicals and moderates is warranted, but with the exception of the most intense phase of Stalin's dictatorship, elements of oligarch rule were prevalent.[10] Even under Stalin, however, leaders had their own 'tails' which they brought with them on assuming high office.[11] Stalin also had a perennial fear of alternative groupings, such as in Leningrad after the war, or

---

[6] See, for example, Marc Raeff, *Understanding Imperial Russia* (New York: Columbia University Press, 1984).

[7] Gerald M. Easter, *Reconstructing the State: Personal Networks and Elite Identity in Soviet Russia* (Cambridge: Cambridge University Press, 2000).

[8] Aleksandr Livshin and Igor′ Orlov, *Vlast′ i obshchestvo: Dialog v pis′makh* (Moscow: Rosspen, 2002), pp. 66, 82.

[9] T. H. Rigby, 'The Origins of the Nomenklatura System', in T. H. Rigby, *Political Elites in the USSR* (Aldershot: Edward Elgar, 1990).

[10] Oleg V. Khlevniuk, *Master of the House: Stalin and His Inner Circle* (New Haven, CT: Yale University Press, 2009).

[11] For example, on taking over the NKVD in 1936, Nikolai Yezhov brought his own people with him to the ministry: see J. Arch Getty and Oleg V. Naumov, *Yezhov: The Rise of Stalin's 'Iron Fist'* (New Haven, CT: Yale University Press, 2008).

'departmental' factions, such as the secret-police-based alliance involving the minister, V. S. Abakumov.[12]

The functional role of factions as a substitute for the integrative and expressive role of political parties has deep roots in the Soviet system.[13] A brilliant study revealed the structure of local fiefdoms and patron–client relationships in Stalin-era Abkhazia.[14] The memoirs of Dmitry Shepilov describe the importance of networks, or 'tails', and illustrate how loyalty to an individual took precedence over loyalty to institutions.[15] The predominance of the Dnepropetrovsk 'mafia', those associated in one way or another with Brezhnev in the region during his long leadership (and in Ukrainian politics afterwards), is well known as an example of patronage politics. As a recent commentary puts it, 'Power, that is groups of people taking crucial state decisions, has been formed in Russia-USSR with few exceptions on the clan principle. In the twentieth century this has declared and imitated "democratic" procedures.'[16] The lack of regulated open competition within the elite to win the right to run the country encouraged factional conflict. The very notion of elite, from the Latin 'eligo', assumes competitiveness, but when combined with the notion of clan, modern and pre-modern notions of governance come into conflict. A clan is typically defined as a group of blood relations connected to some real or mythical forebear, usually encompassing a number of families and led by some sort of traditional leader. Elements of this emerged in some Central Asian states (see below), but in Russia this is not an appropriate term, even in a metaphorical sense.

The power of the Soviet state derived as much from informal networks as it did from formal institutions, and this in the end helped precipitate

---

[12] Y. Gorlizki and O. Khlevniuk, *Cold Peace: Stalin and the Soviet Ruling Circles 1945–53* (Oxford: Oxford University Press, 2004), p. 89; see also pp. 148–51 for the post-Lenin succession.

[13] For a review of the subject, see John P. Willerton, *Patronage and Politics in the USSR* (Cambridge: Cambridge University Press, 1992). For earlier studies, see T. H. Rigby and Bohdan Harasymiw (eds.), *Leadership Selection and Patron–Client Relations in the USSR and Yugoslavia* (London: Allen & Unwin, 1983); Bohdan Harasymiw, *Political Elite Recruitment in the Soviet Union* (London: Macmillan, 1984); and for classic studies of how Soviet institutions worked in practice, see Merle Fainsod, *How Russia Is Ruled* (Oxford: Oxford University Press, 1963), and J. F. Hough, *The Soviet Prefects: The Local Party Organs in Industrial Decision-Making* (Cambridge, MA: Harvard University Press, 1969).

[14] Timothy Blauvelt, 'Abkhazia: Patronage and Power in the Stalin Era', *Nationalities Papers* 35, 2, May 2007, pp. 203–32.

[15] Dmitri Shepilov, *The Kremlin's Scholar: A Memoir of Soviet Politics Under Stalin and Khrushchev*, ed. Stephen V. Bittner (New Haven, CT: Yale University Press, 2007).

[16] Evgenii Andryushchenko, 'Za klanom klan?', *Literaturnaya gazeta*, No. 2 (6154), 23–29 January 2008, p. 3.

its collapse in 1991. What remained of organisational structures were removed, exposing fluid relationships that quickly adapted to new circumstances, and indeed in the absence of effective new institutions swiftly became the dominant operative system. Easter sums this up nicely when he states that 'If one argued ... that the [state] building process was driven by the intersection of informal and formal structures, then both the building phase and the subsequent collapse could be explained.'[17] Even within the Soviet carapace, the tension between formal political organisations and informal social structures generated elements of duality, which in the post-communist era became more delineated in the form of our dual state. As Easter stresses, it is the *intersection* of the two subsystems that compensated for the weakness of the post-revolutionary Soviet state from Stalin to Brezhnev; and equally, in the post-communist era the *interaction* of the normative state and administrative regime provided the new state with infrastructural capacity while at the same time inhibiting the complete predominance of one or the other.

Even in the Soviet system there were informal rules against the development of 'family clans' (*semeistvennost'*) (observed largely in the breach in Central Asia and the Caucasus), whereby close relatives were forbidden to be directly subordinate to each other. This did not mean that family members were not appointed to high positions, particularly in the long years of Brezhnevite stability that gave way to *zastoi* (stagnation), but direct subordination of family members was avoided by ensuring at least one other managerial level in between. Article 21 of the federal law on state service now makes this a formal requirement: 'A citizen may not be appointed to state service or remain in state service in cases of ... a close family relationship with another state servant, if their state service involves direct subordination of one to the other.' Despite this, a recent study revealed thirty-five examples of family connections in national and regional administration, a total that included a high proportion in state-controlled businesses. For example, the son (Alexei) of Sergei Bogdanchikov, the president of Rosneft (75 per cent state-owned), was in charge of investments in the oil company.[18]

The unity of the Russian political elite swiftly fragmented after August 1991, and although elected president in June 1991 with a strong mandate, Yeltsin was unable to impose his vision of the constitution or other projects on a fractious ruling group. The violence of October 1993

---

[17] Gerald M. Easter, 'Personal Networks and Postrevolutionary State Building: Soviet Russia Reexamined', *World Politics* 48, July 1996, p. 576, and see p. 557.

[18] *Kommersant-vlast'*, No. 37, 24 September 2007.

cleared the way for the development of a hegemonic presidency, but competing cliques did not disappear. Even within the presidential administration, Yeltsin pursued a policy of divide and rule, with the liberal faction in the early years headed by Chief of Staff Sergei Filatov, balanced against the statists represented by Victor Ilyushin and the *siloviki* headed by the head of the presidential security apparatus, Korzhakov. In the end Korzhakov overshadowed the other factions and was able to impose his ally, Nikolai Yegorov, as chief of staff, and together the 'party of war' encouraged Yeltsin to launch a full-scale assault on Chechnya in December 1994. Korzhakov was defeated by a liberal counter-coup headed by Anatoly Chubais during the presidential election of 1996, until the latter in turn fell victim to further factional conflict, this time led by oligarchic combinations. This was accompanied by the dominance of opposition parties, above all the CPRF, in the first two Dumas up to December 1999. With the exception of Chechnya, after 1993 Yeltsin repudiated coercive strategies and instead developed a range of what Gel'man calls 'cartel-like deals', notably with regional elites but also with business groupings.[19] Political resources were not monopolised by the administration, and on the eve of the 1999 election, a coalition of regional and business leaders once again prepared to do battle for the presidency. With Putin's help Yeltsin outwitted the political insurgents, and henceforth elite fragmentation no longer manifested itself in open contestation for power but in intra-regime factional conflict.

Thomas Graham in the mid-1990s suggested that clan-type structures had emerged as the shaping force in Russian politics. Various economic structures struggled for access to the president and thus to state resources in order 'to engineer a political stability that would ensure their hold on power and the country's financial resources'.[20] Graham noted that the major associative unit in post-communist Russian politics was not the political party, the interest group or formal political institutions, but personality-based interest constellations vying to influence the president.[21] Lukin considered clans the foundation of the system emerging from what he called the 'reforms' of the Gorbachev and Yeltsin

---

[19] Vladimir Gel'man, 'Out of the Frying Pan, into the Fire? Post-Soviet Regime Changes in Comparative Perspective', *International Political Science Review* 29, 2, 2008, p. 174.

[20] Thomas Graham, 'Novyi russkii rezhim', *Nezavisimaya gazeta*, 23 November 1995, p. 5.

[21] The point is reinforced by Janine Wedel in discussing American aid programmes to Russia, 'Cliques and Clans and Aid to Russia', *Transitions*, July 1997, pp. 66–71. For a full-length treatment of Russian 'clans' and western aid agencies, see Wedel, *Collision and Collusion*.

years. He identified 'criminal-clanism' as 'a system built around tightly knit groups struggling for power, all connected to the criminal world', while 'electoral-clanism' 'underscores that these groups use the electoral system as a key tool in their struggle for power'.[22] The notion of clan politics was probably an exaggeration even at the time when Graham was writing, although undoubtedly various interests sought to impose their views on policy by mobilising networks. These included the traditional industrialists represented by Prime Minister Victor Chernomyrdin, regional leaders and in particular the 'Moscow group' headed by the city's mayor, Luzhkov, the 'party of war', including Korzhakov, and the various 'westernisers' who shaped Russia's liberal economic programme. The dominance of the 'family', a grouping of oligarchs, relatives and administration officials in Yeltsin's last years, was always unstable and represented little more than a fluid grouping based on immediate interests, although sharing in broad terms a commitment to a set of policy preferences (above all, keeping the Communists and their allies out of power).

The emergence of the so-called family at the intersection of private and political networks pointed to the persistence across the post-communist divide of non-political networks of family and friends that compensated for the lack of efficacy in the public arena. The network of favours (*blat*) in the era of central planning acted as the functional substitute for a developed consumer economy.[23] Personal contacts provided access to scarce goods and services, as well as acting as a type of 'social capital' that could be exploited for career advancement. Ledeneva calls this an 'economy of favours' in which friends were used instrumentally. This introduced an exploitative factor into the heart of an arena that by convention is based on altruism and disinterested reciprocity. This is what may be called 'soft informality', where the focus is on patterns of personal interaction; whereas our factional model is based rather more on 'hard informality', porous but relatively durable informal political networks. 'Bonding' social capital (the strengthening of intra-group solidarity, as opposed to 'bridging' between groups) developed extensively within civil society,[24] dividing the social arena into 'ours' (*nashi* or *svoi*) and 'theirs' (*chuzhie*), a principle that extended into the heart of the operating practices of the Putin regime. This in part helps

[22] Lukin, 'Putin's Regime', p. 40.
[23] Alena V. Ledeneva, *Russia's Economy of Favours: Blat, Networking and Informal Exchange* (Cambridge: Cambridge University Press, 1998).
[24] Robert D. Putnam and Kristin A. Goss, 'Introduction', in Robert D. Putnam (ed.), *Democracies in Flux: The Evolution of Social Capital in Contemporary Society* (Oxford: Oxford University Press, 2002), p. 11.

explain the distinctive way that civil society developed in Russia, with the state itself becoming the arena for competing societally based networks based on factional loyalty. In this context, trust was something reserved for known individuals, while public institutions not colonised by *svoi* were distrusted and alien.[25] The terrain between the state and civil society was bridged politically by the development of regime relations, and socially by interest-based factions where personal loyalty took precedence over disinterested affiliation.

Applying a network analysis of elites during Yeltsin's presidency, Andrew Buck argues that rather than forming a unified block they 'clustered into distinct subgroups or factions'. Factions were a subset of networks with qualitatively different patterns of affiliation. Factions were distinguished by 'distinct structural properties' as well as 'world-views that reinforced network differences', and this lay at the base of the fragmentation and elite conflict that characterised Yeltsin's leadership.[26] On this basis Buck identified three main factions: the reformers, the national-communists and the centrists, based on 'substantive knowledge of politics in the locality and the kinds of civic organisations associated with each'.[27] Buck's work is an important attempt to link ideological factors to patterns of civic engagement at the regional level. The interaction of world-views and factional affiliation is also crucial at the national level, but by the time we come to the mature Putin system, centrism had ballooned to occupy a large part of the political bandwidth, and thus both the ideational and organisational features of factional politics had changed. Politically relevant factionalism was now largely an intra-bureaucratic phenomenon, focusing on administrative resources and nuances within the dominant coalition and with little overt ideological contestation.

This does not mean that ideas no longer mattered, and contrary to Lewis Namier's view of politics in the age of George III, which argued that personalities and not policies were the key in the relentless struggle for power, disputes remained over matters of principle in the leadership's court. Indeed, with the suffocation of public politics, it was precisely behind the Kremlin's walls that fundamental issues of political principle were decided by factions with differing interpretations of the public good but without recourse to grand theorising. Neo-Kremlinology, like Namier, reduces politics to a single

[25] Alena V. Ledeneva, *How Russia Really Works: The Informal Practices that Shaped Post-Soviet Politics and Business* (Ithaca, NY, and London: Cornell University Press, 2006).
[26] Andrew D. Buck, 'Elite Networks and Worldviews During the Yel'tsin Years', *Europe-Asia Studies* 59, 4, June 2007, p. 659.
[27] *Ibid.*, p. 651.

axis of struggle, whereas the reality, in post-communist Russia as in eighteenth-century England, is far more complex.[28] The factional interpretation of Russian politics has its basis in the struggle of object-ive groups with different views. While there is a danger of slipping into the subjectivism typical of Kremlinology (that is, imputing views and personal struggles on the basis of minor signals), shifts in the adminis-trative regime and its relationship with the constitutional state reflect real changes in factional balance.

In the state socialist system, social networks were an essential mech-anism to obviate shortages and bureaucratic rigidities, but the degree to which these have been perpetuated into the post-communist market-based era remains a matter of considerable controversy.[29] With the demise of the communist order, Russia entered a period of institutional indeterminacy, allowing informal groups operating across the blurred boundaries between the economy and the state to lever enormous com-petitive advantages by exploiting network capital. An economy of rents emerged in which access to government resources (financial, informa-tional and situational, as in the right to privatise state assets) rather than profits in market competition became the key to primary economic accumulation. Network capital coalesced in the form of informal groups that in some cases became factions. These factions were not simply semi-criminal agents exploiting the weakness of the state (although there was no shortage of these), but they colonised the space in which inter-actions between the state and the economy took place. In this model, a faction could comprise a number of 'clans'. Wedel, for example, notes how the liberal economists from St Petersburg became known as the 'Chubais clan', united by a commonality of views and loyalty to the informal leader whose influence was dispersed across numerous insti-tutions.[30] Indeed, loyalty according to Wedel is accorded more to the clan than to the institution with which the individual is formally associ-ated. This gave rise in her view to 'flex organisations' that are 'empowered by informal groups to cross-cut and mediate institutional spheres and domains'.[31] These networks gave rise to what Ledeneva calls the *sistema*, patterned informal behaviour that may also carry a

---

[28] For a recent critique of Namier's view, see Edward Pearce, *The Great Man: Sir Robert Walpole – Scoundrel, Genius and Britain's First Prime Minister* (London: Jonathan Cape, 2007).

[29] For a rich empirical and theoretical analysis, see Anna-Maria Salmi, *Social Networks and Everyday Practices in Russia* (Helsinki: Kimora Publications, 2006).

[30] Janine R. Wedel, 'Flex Organizing and the Clan-State', in William Alex Pridemore (ed.), *Ruling Russia: Law, Crime, and Justice in a Changing Society* (Lanham, MD: Rowman & Littlefield, 2005), p. 104.

[31] Wedel, 'Flex Organizing and the Clan-State', p. 106.

positive modernising dynamic.[32] The line between state and private interests is barely recognised, provoking not just what we have called venal corruption but above all the meta-corruption that undermines the coherence of the social order based on the normative state. The duality between the constitutional state and administrative regime permeates institutions as well as the social roles of individuals.

Thus any model based on the notion of 'state capture', whereby laws and other regulations and benefits are shaped to the advantage of private interests or the personal benefit of state officials, is too mechanistic. In the Russian context there is a permanent two-way interaction between the public and private spheres. Neo-patrimonial processes work not just from the state down to society, but also upwards into the very heart of governance. In post-communist Russia the lines between state service and economic entrepreneurship were blurred from the very start. In the parallel world of factional politics, it made little difference if someone was directly employed by the state, like Petr Aven, or worked at its side, like Roman Abramovich. Some moved between the two, like Vladimir Potanin and Berezovsky, and Aven later made a successful career in the banking sector. By the late 1990s, this carousel had created a distinctive state–private constellation known by the moniker of 'the family', the group around Yeltsin that included his blood relatives, notably his daughter Tatyana Dyachenko. Court politics in the Yeltsin years were pronounced, and the whole history of the period can be written in neo-monarchical terms.[33] While the political space associated with the normative state is populated by traditional aggregative institutions such as parties, the terrain of the administrative regime is populated by competing factions. Thus any notion of a 'clan state' or the like is misleading since it assumes a single integrated state–society arena. The reality is that of a bifurcated system in which the most profound contest is between the two social orders rather than between the actors limited to a single arena.

A perceptive analysis by Martin Walker in the late 1990s argued that the development of such a fungible political and economic system could

---

[32] Alena Ledeneva, 'From Russia with *Blat*: Can Informal Networks Help Modernize Russia?', *Social Research* 76, 1, Spring 2009, pp. 268–70.

[33] For a revealing account of the intrigues of the period, see the memoirs by Aleksandr Korzhakov, *Boris Yeltsin: Ot rassveta do zakata* (Moscow: Interbuk, 1997); an extended version of which appeared as Aleksandr Korzhakov, *Boris El'tsin: Ot rassveta do zakata – Posleslovie* (Moscow: DetektivPress, 2004). For a more analytical account, see Liliya Shevtsova, *Rezhim Borisa El'tsina* (Moscow: Rosspen, 1999), and her *Yeltsin's Russia: Myths and Reality* (Washington, DC: Carnegie Endowment for International Peace, 1999). See also Igor' Klyamkin and Liliya Shevtsova, *Vnesistemnyi rezhim Borisa II: Nekotorye osobennosti politicheskogo razvitiya postsovetskoi Rossii* (Moscow: Carnegie Centre, 1999).

develop in two possible directions. The optimistic scenario would be reminiscent of the oligarchic Whig system, referred to above, dominant in late seventeenth- and eighteenth-century England and with a lasting influence well into the twentieth century. Powerful grandees dominated the political system and established personal networks that acted as party substitutes.[34] The pessimistic scenario looks to a mafia model, where crime groups mimic the economic relations of the official sector but act beyond the law, a theme that has been treated by other authors.[35] The two share a common model of a 'power structure dominated by a handful of financial clans, with overlapping interests in virtually every sector of the Russian political and economic system'.[36] Walker identified the Gazprom clan, from whence came the long-serving prime minister, Chernomyrdin; the Gusinsky clan, based on his 'Media-Most' media and banking empire, including the NTV television station; the Berezovsky clan, also with media (notably a share in Russia's main channel, known at the time as ORT) and banking interests but also involved in the energy and automobile industries; and the Potanin clan, based on the Oneksimbank group and telecommunications. We should also add Khodorkovsky's Menatep-Rosprom-Yukos holding. These groups united to ensure Yeltsin's re-election in 1996, using overwhelming media and financial advantage to fight off what was a serious challenge from Zyuganov's Communists, and then entered government.[37] Business groups were joined in Walker's view by the military-industrial complex; and various regional clans, above all the Moscow clan focused on Luzhkov, who in 1996 launched his own television channel and the *Rossiya* newspaper.

The various factions aggregated interests, but not in a political way (the ideal in western liberal democracy), nor in a bureaucratic manner (Putin's ideal, subordinate to the regime), but in an informal 'subversive' way, since the basis of their *modus operandi* was to lever advantage by establishing non-transparent personalised relations that transcended the

---

[34] See Dorothy Marshall, *Eighteenth Century England* (London: Longman, 1962), pp. 60–3.

[35] Federico Varese, *The Russian Mafia: Private Protection in a New Market Economy* (Oxford: Oxford University Press, 2001); see also Volkov, *Violent Entrepreneurs*.

[36] Martin Walker, 'After Yeltsin: Russia Faces Free-Fall', *Transitions*, June 1998, p. 22.

[37] In August 1996 a meeting of business and political leaders in Davos, Switzerland, delegated Potanin to join the government as a deputy prime minister, but instead of acting as their representative he lobbied the interests of his own Oneksimbank, winning a number of lucrative government contracts and the Svyazinvest telecommunications company in July 1997. Under pressure from other banking interests, he was sacked from the government, but his economic interests continued, now transformed into the Interros holding company that owns Norilsk Nickel, the world's largest nickel producer, the Sidanko oil company, Svyazinvest and many other companies.

norms established by the constitutional system. As Ludmila Telen noted, 'Berezovskii openly counts on his business investments to pay political dividends, and vice-versa.' For example, it is alleged that he exploited his post as deputy secretary of the Security Council in 1997 to profit from the oil and construction industries in Chechnya.[38] It was Berezovsky who brought the various factions together in Davos in early 1996 to back Yeltsin's re-election, and then apparently claimed the requisite pay-back.[39] Yeltsin, however, disliked Berezovsky, and the latter was not even as close to his daughter, Dyachenko, as Berezovsky liked to make out.[40] The undoubted pluralism of the 1990s largely amounted to the struggle between oligarchic, mafia and regional groups, fought in their media outlets by mobilising various lobbying agencies and *piarshchiki* (from the word PR, public relations, but denoting the highly developed world of political technologies).[41] A world of 'fake-structures' emerged which encompassed not just politics but also non-commercial organisations, especially when funded from abroad, endowing civil society with elements of the 'virtuality' that characterised party competition.[42] A perceptive commentator already noted in 1998: 'Amid this Machiavellian carnival, ordinary Russians are left with the unpleasant sensation that they have little to do with the decisions determining their futures.'[43] All of this intensified as Yeltin approached the end of his allotted two terms.[44] The established parties operated in a parallel universe, bounded by the formal institutions of a constitutional democracy, but had remarkably little traction in shaping policy at the level of the regime. This was in part a flaw of institutional design, but it also reflected the predominance of informal political practices. At times of succession, these two universes came into conflict, with unpredictable consequences.

[38] Ludmila Telen, 'The Kingmakers: Oligarchs Jockey for Position Behind Their Candidates of Choice', *Transitions*, June 1998, p. 33.
[39] See Paul Klebnikov, *Godfather of the Kremlin: Boris Berezovsky and the Looting of Russia* (New York: Harcourt, 2000); a Russian version of which came out as Pavel Khlebnikov, *Krestnyi otets Kremlya Boris Berezovskii, ili Istoriya razgrableniya Rossii* (Moscow: DetektivPress, 2001).
[40] Timothy J. Colton, *Yeltsin: A Life* (New York: Basic Books, 2008), pp. 404–5.
[41] Their work is the focus of Andrew Wilson, *Virtual Politics: Faking Democracy in the Post-Soviet World* (New Haven, CT: Yale University Press, 2005).
[42] Maksim Grigor'ev, *Fake-struktury: Prizraki rossiiskoi politiki* (Moscow: Evropa, 2007). This is a polemical work, but its attack on 'fake-opposition' in the form of 'Other Russia' and allegedly fake human rights organisations at least has the merit of extending the notion of 'virtual politics' to the whole spectrum of political life and stresses the 'irresponsible' nature of much of the opposition in Russia.
[43] Askold Krushnelnycky, Moscow correspondent for *The European*, 'In the Wake of the Storm', *Transitions*, June 1998, p. 6.
[44] James Meek, 'Secrets of Yeltsin Clan Fuel War for Succession', *The Guardian*, 27 November 1998, p. 19.

Factionalism enters the Putin period

We discussed the factional struggles on the eve of the 1999–2000 succession in Chapter 1. Here let us note the forms of political struggle, and in particular the active involvement of Gazprom in supporting the attempted insurgency by outsider groups. Already in 1996 Gazprom had actively supported Chernomyrdin's Our Home is Russia, and in the 1999 election Gazprom supported around 130 candidates.[45] On Primakov's dismissal as prime minister in May 1999, his relations with the administration deteriorated further, and he joined the veteran Luzhkov and Gusinsky in opposition to the Kremlin. They were funded by Rem Vyakhirev, the head of Gazprom, who, according to the chief of staff at the time, Voloshin, felt much greater sympathy for the opposition than for Yeltsin.[46] One issue over which the conflict became apparent was at the Gazprom shareholders' meeting on 30 June 1999, when the new prime minister, Stepashin, and Voloshin tried to increase the number of state representatives to the board from four to five, whereas Vyakhirev insisted that since the state owned only 37.4 per cent of Gazprom shares, it was only entitled to four out of the eleven seats. Stepashin and Voloshin also tried to get the former head of Gazprom, Chernomyrdin, elected chair of the board. Chernomyrdin's antipathy to Primakov and Luzhkov was well known, and his feelings were intensified by their attempts to keep Vyakhirev away from the president.

In the event, only four state representatives were elected to the board, and although Chernomyrdin took over as chair, the act of defiance was not forgiven by Voloshin, although Stepashin was willing to forget.[47] This was one reason for Stepashin's dismissal as prime minister in August of that year, as well as for allowing the formal alliance of Primakov with Luzhkov and some regional leaders in that month (the alliance of Otechestvo with Vsya Rossiya to create OVR), generously funded by Gazprom. Stepashin had been proposed by Voloshin to All Russia to become their leader, but Stepashin refused and insisted that he would remain above electoral blocs. This flight from the field of battle was not forgotten, and he was dismissed on 9 August.[48] At the earliest opportunity, on 30 May 2001, Putin replaced Vyakhirev by one of his loyal St Petersburgers, Alexei Miller (who unlike Vyakhirev had no background in the gas industry), and in due course Chernomyrdin was replaced by another Petersburger, Dmitry Medvedev.[49] Miller had

---

[45] Jonathan P. Stern, *The Future of Russian Gas and Gazprom* (Oxford: Oxford University Press for the Oxford Institute for Energy Studies, 2005), p. 172.
[46] Zygar′ and Panyushkin, *Gazprom*, p. 74.
[47] *Ibid.*, pp. 74–6.   [48] *Ibid.*, p. 77   [49] *Ibid.*, pp. 106–15.

worked with Putin in the mayor's office in St Petersburg and later became a deputy minister in the energy ministry. Miller then set about breaking up the professional Gazprom elite loyal to Vyakhirev.[50] The management change at Gazprom, according to Konstantin Simonov, represented one of the few major victories for the Petersburg *siloviki* (until the Yukos affair), and the company went on to become one of their main financial backers.[51]

The stark role of Gazprom in Russia's system of political power was revealed by a secret memorandum written by Russian foreign-policy and energy experts in 2003. At the time there was discussion about breaking up the company, an initiative prompted by some of Yeltsin's former liberal advisers in the Ministry of Economic Development and Trade (MERT), concerned that under its new management led by Miller the Putinites were using Gazprom too much as an instrument of foreign policy as well as the source of funding for Putin's political projects at home. The consequences of the management shake-out at Gazprom included the weakening of the liberals in the ministry (although Elvira Nabiullina and other liberals remained influential) and the consolidation of the *siloviki* in Gazprom itself. They ensured that the sole export channel to Europe was Gazprom, thus excluding competition from independent gas producers, and allowed Gazprom to be used as an instrument to punish and reward countries as required. Various Gazprom-sponsored companies, such as Itera, Sibur, Stroitransgaz and Regiongazholdings, were brought back under direct Gazprom control, thus greatly expanding its financial base and levers of control. The memo also noted the strategy of support for Rosneft, which under *silovik* sponsorship (especially after Igor Sechin took over as chair of the board of directors in July 2004) grew from a relatively minor producer into Russia's largest oil company as it absorbed most of Yukos.[52] The struggle over Gazprom continued into the Medvedev era, with the company maintaining its domestic monopoly (thus excluding access to the gas market by Russia's few remaining independent oil companies, who produce gas as a by-product), while Putin was adamant that only Gazprom would be allowed to export gas. Despite having chaired the board at Gazprom, Medvedev's influence was limited and the company remained a bastion of Putinite power, both at home and abroad.

---

[50] Aleksei Makarkin, *Politiko-ekonomicheskie klany sovremennoi Rossii* (Moscow: Tsentr politicheskikh tekhnologii, 2003), p. 86.

[51] Konstantin Simonov, *Russkaya neft': Poslednii peredel* (Moscow: Eksmo Algoritm, 2005), p. 140.

[52] Roman Kupchinsky, 'Russian Energy Strategy: The Domestic Political Factor', *EDM* 6, 185, 8 October 2009.

The experience of Gazprom's independent political stance was undoubtedly one reason why Putin sent so many state and administration officials to the boards of the major companies. Just as he later ensured that there would be no popular orange revolution, so too he did all in his power to avert another elite *fronde*. The strategy, however, had the unintended consequence of reinforcing the link between power and property; and, indeed, where power became the key to winning and controlling property; and where property at a certain point could threaten power, as in the case of Khodorkovsky. The whole Yukos affair was designed to ensure that the business elite were subordinate to the political authorities. While the defeat of the supposed 'criminal oligarchs', like Berezovsky, of the Yeltsin era could be justified in terms of overcoming what was perceived to be 'state capture' and the end of what the left-nationalist opposition in Russia likes to call 'comprador capitalism', Khodorkovsky represented a different type of capitalism and threatened the autonomy of the regime as a whole. Even though Khodorkovsky had benefited no less than the criminal oligarchy from the anarcho-capitalism of the 1990s, he now came to represent the nascent industrial bourgeoisie. The flexing of his political muscles in 2003 can be seen as the attempt by this new bourgeoisie to emerge from the shadows of the state and to exist as an autonomous force in Russian politics.[53] Hence the clipping of the wings of the oligarchs in 2000–1 was very different from the process three years later.[54] The second event ultimately changed the nature of the post-communist state. Putin's *dirigisme* was now intensified to become a more tutelary form of neo-patrimonialism. Elements of state corporatism were introduced, which saw the state's share of market capitalisation rising from 20 to over 35 per cent (in part reflecting the rise in energy prices at the time), and its holdings of voting shares in Russia's twenty largest enterprises rose from 11 to over 40 per cent between the start of the attack on Yukos in 2003 and 2009.[55]

The inherent tendency for para-political depoliticisation to provoke fragmentation was compensated for by the generation of informal mechanisms to maintain regime coherence.[56] The Putinite dual state,

---

[53] Vladimir Shlapentokh, 'Big Money as an Obstacle to Democracy in Russia', *Journal of Communist Studies and Transition Politics* 24, 4, December 2008, p. 519.

[54] Richard Sakwa, *The Quality of Freedom: Khodorkovsky, Putin and the Yukos Affair* (Oxford: Oxford University Press, 2009).

[55] Samuel Charap, 'No Obituaries Yet for Capitalism in Russia', *History Today*, October 2009, p. 334.

[56] Cf. Andrey S. Makarychev, 'Politics, the State, and De-Politicization: Putin's Project Reassessed', *Problems of Post-Communism* 55, 5, September–October 2008, p. 66.

as we have seen, placed a high premium on the concept of 'loyalty'.[57] Perceived 'disloyalty' or opposition to the strategic goals of the political elite was met with direct intervention, commercial disruption, factional struggle and the perverted use of the legal system to weaken the opponent politically and socially, and to expropriate their assets. Baev argues that personal loyalty was the key criterion in selecting Putin's staff,[58] and on that basis he outlines the factions, emphasising the role of the *chekisty-siloviki* and their ability to draw St Petersburg economists and various statists into their orbit. The admittedly amorphous concept of loyalty plays an important role in the shaping of factions and the development of Russian policy in its entirety. For example, Dmitry Skarga was appointed director-general of Sovkomflot, Russia's largest open water shipping company, at Sechin's behest at the very young age of twenty-nine on 6 May 2000. His appointment was determined by the patronage of the oil trader Gennady Timchenko (about whom more later) and Sechin, the latter assuming that Skarga would be 'his' man in the company. However, when Skarga pursued independent policies and made choices that he considered to be in the best interests of the company, he was dismissed on 7 October 2004 and later prosecuted. His refusal to participate in the attack on Yukos, resistance to the merger with Novoship and some other incidents can be considered in this light. His main crime, ultimately, was 'disloyalty'; and this in part explains the unremitting nature of the attack against him.

In a different way, Yury Nikitin, an early partner in Timchenko's trading companies but who developed a shipping business of his own, was also considered disloyal to the broader interests of the Russian shipping industry, being based abroad and not flying the Russian flag. Equally, Tagir Izmailov's appointment to head Novoship, the second largest Russian shipping company, based in Novorossiisk, was sponsored by Sechin, and the latter did not hesitate to stress that this entailed obligations to him, including support for the merger with Sovkomflot, the funding of loyal deputies in the December 2003 parliamentary elections, and the partial privatisation of the Novorossiisk and Tuapse ship repair plants that would have seen shares transferred to FSB-controlled private companies. It was precisely these acts of 'velvet reprivatisation' that Oleg Shvartsman brought into the open on the eve of the 2007 Duma election (see Chapter 6). Direct contacts with senior officials and even with the president were frowned upon. Izmailov fought

---

[57] A key theme of Makarkin, *Politiko-ekonomicheskie klany sovremennoi Rossii.*

[58] Pavel K. Baev, 'The Evolution of Putin's Regime: Inner Circles and Outer Walls', *Problems of Post-Communism* 51, 6, November–December 2004, p. 5.

for the independence of Novoship, which seen from the perspective of those who considered a merger with Sovkomflot desirable, came to be seen as an act of disloyalty.[59]

While a claim of loyalty to the generic Russian state is understandable, in the administrative regime this takes the form of demands for loyalty to a particular team or group of individuals, and it is this which undermined public politics and encouraged the development of the covert half-world of factional politics. The inculcation of a technocratic theory of state development, which from 2005 reduced regional governors to little more than branch managers of the central state, also rendered the central state a type of expanded enterprise, Russia Ltd, based on loyalty and hierarchical subordination. The political logic of accountability and impersonal subordination to impartial rules typical of a genuine constitutional state was subverted by the para-political practices of the depoliticised administrative regime. The rise of factionalism compensated for the decay of 'the political'. Factional and elite conflicts provoked the archaisation of Russian politics, returning to a shadowy world of Byzantine networks operating in parallel to the formal world of constitutional politics.

Putin was brought into the Kremlin as a representative of the 'family', but he quickly 'emancipated' himself from their control. Putin was not a member of the 'family', and neither was he part of the Moscow elite that it represented.[60] Arkhangel'skaya and her colleagues estimate that out of the 150 individuals making up the top elite in July 2000, Putin controlled only about 15 per cent; he was able to impose Kudrin as finance minister to counter Kasyanov as prime minister, but he could not get his candidate Dmitry Kozak appointed prosecutor general, and he initially failed to have his colleague Medvedev appointed chair of the Gazprom board against the family's candidature of Chernomyrdin to that post. In launching an anti-business campaign at this time, the family hoped to gain some prime companies (Abramovich's interest in Norilsk Nickel was mentioned), and at the same time they would isolate Putin from the business community: 'The president, in allowing such illegitimate actions that do not spare the country's best companies, is an enemy of business.' There was even talk at that time of finding a new president. Their conclusion was simple: 'Russia today lacks a single source of power.' Putin's opponents were using his own words about 'Taking

---

[59] Material on the Sovkomflot and Novoship cases draws on confidential material provided to the author by the participants.

[60] Andrei Bunich, *Osen' oligarkhov: Istoriya prikhvatizatsii i budushchee Rossii* (Moscow: Yauza-Eksmo, 2006), p. 392.

responsibility for all that happens in the country' to discredit him.[61] The early Putin presidency was thus locked in conflict with factions before he was able to establish some sort of balance that allowed the presidency to emerge as arbiter. By 2003 the 'family' faction was breaking up, and it was 'removed from the commanding heights in politics and business'. For Ryabov this was a positive phenomenon, since the group had been associated with 'nepotism, favouritism, handing out state property for a fraction of its value, restricting competition in politics and the economy, brazen manipulation of public opinion', and the family's continued dominance would have 'doomed the nation to endless stagnation'.[62]

The general position is summed up well by an OECD report, noting that 'The Soviet administrative hierarchy, despite its complex and seemingly well-defined formal institutions, relied heavily on an informal structure of personal networks within the party-state apparatus to function.' The authority of offices was transferred to individual office-holders, encouraging patron–client ties and fostering rent-seeking and corruption.[63] Thus the Russian bureaucracy emerges as a highly person-alised system, and even as the state strengthened, the phenomenon of a 'weak state but strong officials' was not overcome. As an earlier OECD report put it, 'It [Russia] will need a strong state, capable of protecting individual rights, of interpreting the law impartially and of enforcing it effectively. But a state strong enough to perform these functions might succumb to the temptation to act arbitrarily itself. So the establishment of the rule of law will require not only a strong state but also strong institutions capable of constraining it. Russia lacks such institutions.'[64] Indeed, as the state under Putin gathered the powers lost in the 1990s, the phenomenon of a 'strong state and strong officials' only intensified the ability of individuals to mobilise institutional resources to advance factional interests. 'Institutions', as the 2006 OECD report noted, 'end up serving the interests of those who staff and run them'.[65] The para-political practices of the administrative regime colonised the state apparatus and fostered venal as well as meta-corruption.

---

[61] Natal'ya Arkhangel'skaya *et al.*, 'Provokatsiya', *Ekspert*, No. 27, 17 July 2000, in *Ekspert: Luchshie materialy*, No. 2, 2007, pp. 14–16, at p. 16.

[62] Andrei Ryabov, 'The Decline of the Family', *Vremya MN*, 8 August 2003; in *JRL*, No. 7281, 2003, Item 8.

[63] OECD, 'Improving the Quality of Public Administration', Chapter 3 of *Russian Federation*, OECD Economic Surveys (Paris: OECD Publishing, 2006), pp. 115–46, at p. 118.

[64] OECD, *Russia: Building Rules for the Market*, OECD Reviews of Regulatory Reform (Paris: OECD Publishing, 2005), pp. 51–2.

[65] OECD, 'Improving the Quality of Public Administration', p. 118.

Definitions

Factions are personal networks that exploit organisational structures and institutional procedures but do not entirely substitute for the formal system. As in the Soviet period, factions provide extra-systemic functional resources for the operation of the formal order, but their existence stymies autonomous institutional development.[66] Given their opaque nature, they eschew public politics and operate in the shadowy world of intra-bureaucratic struggle. Their aim is to extend their influence within politico-administrative structures, and by the same token they undermine formal public political processes. They may have enhanced institution building in the Soviet era, as argued by Easter, but in a democratising society they not only weaken institutional development, but they also inhibit open politics and a public sphere of impartial debate about crucial issues of policy.

Factions, informality and autonomy

The prominence of politico-bureaucratic groups in Russian politics is now clearly established and we are at the point where we can attempt some fundamental definitions. Factions are characterised by six key elements:

1. Their informal character, and thus while they exploit institutional opportunities they do not themselves take on formal institutional forms or develop long-term affective ties.
2. Their roots lie in bureaucratic politics where administrative and political resources are fused. Factions are politically rather than socially generated. Conflicts are restricted to the bureaucratic elite and business allies and do not appeal to the broader public or seek the support of any of the parties of power or their auxiliaries. A faction is therefore very different from a clan, which for Collins 'have their roots in a culture of kin-based norms and trust', 'in which actual or notional kinship based on blood or marriage forms the central bond among members'.[67] By contrast, a faction assumes a rather more functional role, helping political actors and bureaucratic elites to reduce transaction costs and to respond to changing circumstances to overcome uncertainty.[68]

[66] Graeme Gill makes a similar argument about the ultimately destructive character of informal relations in the Soviet system in Graeme Gill, *The Origins of the Stalinist Political System* (Cambridge: Cambridge University Press, 1990).
[67] Katherine Collins, 'Clans, Pacts, and Politics in Central Asia', *Journal of Democracy* 13, 3, July 2002, p. 142.
[68] Vladimir Gel'man, 'The Unrule of Law in the Making: The Politics of Informal Institution Building in Russia', *Europe-Asia Studies* 56, 7, 2004, pp. 1021–40.

3. Broad unity in strategic goals, which distinguish them from other factions.
4. In general terms they share ideological orientations, usually along the axis of support for greater or lesser state interventionism and international integration.
5. Their temporary and situational character. If they take on greater institutional or regional permanence, then a faction takes on 'clantype' characteristics or becomes a clientelistic network and is thus no longer a faction.
6. Last but far from least, the predominance of horizontal loyalty to the team or network, which can be drawn from many separate administrative structures. Vertical loyalty within an organisation, to a specific patron or indeed a region, the classic hallmark of a clientelistic system, is of lesser significance although undoubtedly important. Equally, there is almost no vertical relationship between elite and non-elite members, which further distinguishes factions from clans. Factions are relatively small elite alliances, whereas clans can be large-scale social organisations.

Factions are coalescences (coalitions would be too strong a term) united by common loyalties and instrumental goals. These coalescences are unstable and formed in an ad hoc manner in response to specific circumstances, but the long period of Putinite stabilisation from 2000 endowed them with an enduring quality that was not an inherent characteristic. Factions are not the same as clientelistic groups, which tend to be vertically integrated leadership-based associations based on the exchange of services between patron and client, typically support and loyalty to the patron in exchange for office and promotion.[69] Regional ethnic-based patronage networks in Central Asia and elsewhere ultimately hollowed out Soviet power, allowing the effective fusion of economic and political power in conditions of scarcity, and contributed to the fall of the communist order.[70] By contrast, factions act as an informal mechanism to prevent elite defection, binding individuals to a power system by ties of informal loyalty and reward while eschewing more demanding indicators of group membership. The costs of defection can be high, as Kasyanov, the former prime minister, discovered; but on the whole, as long as no political challenge was involved, a soft landing was found for former members of the Putin elite.

---

[69] For a historical and political study of clientelism and Russian state development, see M. N. Afanas'ev, *Klientizm i rossiiskaya gosudarstvennost'*, 2nd edn (Moscow: MONF, 2000).
[70] Gregory Gleason, 'Fealty and Loyalty: Informal Authority Structures in Soviet Asia', *Soviet Studies* 43, 4, 1991, pp. 613–28.

This is not caciquismo, the 'boss [*cacique*] politics' that has been so prominent in Mexico, where clientelism and charismatic authority combined to subvert the formal political sphere of parties and elections.[71] While the notion of 'competitive clientalism' (*sic*) has been identified as one of the pathologies besetting contemporary democracies,[72] Russian politics is characterised more by 'competitive factionalism', although competition is constrained by the constitutional pillar of the dual state and the moderating role of the presidency. Formal institutions and strong political leaders have to date inhibited the rampant overspill of factionalism into state institutions. This is also why it is a mistake in Russia to identify factions with networks of fiefdoms and rackets. A faction has network elements but is more than just an opportunistic network focused on self-enrichment.

Factional activity is focused on state structures, exploiting weakly developed institutional frameworks to advance their interests, but their very fluidity means that, unlike Central Asian clans, they can only partially colonise the constitutional state, and the state bureaucracy retains a degree of autonomy. Equally, although weakly institutionalised, the constitutional state retains sufficient independence to inhibit the development of a fully fledged 'faction state'. The courts do come under the influence of factions, but in systemic terms only when this reflects the preferences of powerful political leaders. Factions are generated by the political system and shape the nature of the regime but cannot entirely subvert the normative state. In the context of the managerial division of labour rather than a constitutional separation of powers, factions are mutually interested in maintaining balance; the instinct of self-preservation where politics within the administrative region is not a zero-sum game ensures that no single group entirely captures the state. Thus the oligarchs earlier or the *siloviki* under Putin were unable completely to dominate, let alone eradicate, other factions to establish their undisputed predominance or to achieve state capture. Factional balance, however, was precarious, and hence all were united in ensuring a strong presidency that could act as arbiter; but by the same token, the factions inhibited the president from aligning unequivocally with any single faction. Thus the tendency towards bureaucratic stagnation of the Russian polity was reinforced by the permanent compromise in the sphere of the administrative regime and an impaired constitutional state.

[71] See Alan Knight and Wil Panster (eds.), *Caciquismo in Twentieth-Century Mexico* (London: Institute for the Study of the Americas, 2006).

[72] Ellen Lust-Okar, 'Competitive Clientalism', in Anthony J. Langlois and Karol Edward Soltan (eds.), *Global Democracy and Its Difficulties* (London and New York: Routledge, 2008), pp. 130–45.

Factions are not coterminous with networks, which have a more accidental character of personal acquaintance based on shared educational, workplace and career patterns, or on residential association. Putin certainly was at the centre of a network of relationships based on his personal life and career path, and at all crucial junctions he drew on this network to staff agencies, and ultimately the state, for which he was responsible. The career pattern of Sechin in this respect is exemplary. But Putin did not allow a faction to become a clan, and their influence depended on access to the presidency. Putin's network was divided by various factional affiliations and was far from a homogeneous body, although focused on personal loyalty to him. It would also not be accurate to describe his associates as a clientelistic network, since for the most part they could have developed their careers quite successfully without him acting as patron; although of course his patronage was crucial in making them part of his vertiginous rise to the top.

The distinction between formal institutions and informal practices is clearly an arbitrary one, since all institutions operate with a degree of informality, while social practices such as clientelism, corruption and *blat* (networks of influence and social reciprocity) can assume relatively stable forms that mimic the operation of more formal institutions.[73] Equally, the assumption of a stark opposition between a formal constitutional sphere and a 'parallel reality' occludes the mutually constitutive relationship between the two. When we argue that a dual state has emerged in Russia, the key point is that the interaction between the two arms of the duality is crucial. Thus we can agree with North in adopting a broad definition of what constitutes an 'institution', essentially the 'rules of the game'; but the definition of what constitutes a 'rule' is perhaps excessively constrictive, basically those assuming a formal character; while at the minimum a two-level 'game' is in play.[74] Institutions are indeed 'patterned human behaviour',[75] in which constitutional institutions interact with political practices within the framework of specific historical traditions and social configurations. At the same time, there remains significant controversy over what precisely makes a social practice 'informal'. Helmke and Levitsky argue that informal institutions are 'socially shared rules, usually unwritten, that

---

[73] For a useful exploration, see Yaroslav Startsev, '"Informal" Institutions and Practices: Objects to Explore and Methods to Use for Comparative Research', *Perspectives on European Politics and Society* 6, 2, 2005, pp. 331–51.

[74] Douglass North, *Institutions, Institutional Change and Economic Performance* (Cambridge: Cambridge University Press, 1990).

[75] The term is Jeanne Kirkpatrick's.

are created, communicated, and enforced outside of officially sanctioned channels', whereas formal institutions are, by contrast, 'created, communicated, and enforced through channels widely accepted as official'.[76] At the centre of their analysis is the problem of conceptualising precisely the link between formal and informal institutions. The priority traditionally devoted to formal institutions is derived from the positivistic legal-constitutional tradition, although the behavioural revolution from the 1950s went too far in prioritising the social over the political. Social sciences did indeed have to 'bring the state back in',[77] but how and in what way remains a matter of controversy.

The typology of a dual state suggests a normative preference for the constitutional state over the informal sphere that drives the actions of the administrative regime. The informal sphere is thus something that compensates for the inadequacies of formal institutions. It is therefore in one way or another '*complementary, substitutive, accommodating* or even *competing*', in relation to formal institutions.[78] An ideal is established against which complex reality is measured, opening the door to subjectivism and, when dealing with non-western societies, an implicit tutelary judgmentalism that is pronounced in Russian studies. Gel'man notes that 'informal institutionalism' in contemporary Russian politics is probably more than a temporary 'defect' (deviating from the 'correct' path of development), but more likely a long-term feature of Russian modernisation.[79] Startsev has tried to overcome this methodological trap by proposing that when discussing institutions the pair 'formal – informal' is replaced by the binary 'inclusiveness – exclusiveness'. Institutions are inclusive if they '(a) are discursive (verbalised), and by this can be easily communicated to the interested public; (b) have no access barriers to be integrated in; (c) have no exit costs for individuals or collective actors who wish to leave the institution'. Exclusive institutions exhibit a set of opposed characteristics: 'they (a) are non-discursive, (b) have barriers for access, are difficult to overcome, and (c) have high exit costs'.[80] Membership in a political party is primarily an inclusive institutionalised practice, but membership in an organised criminal group is exclusive. There are all sorts of non-discursive rules (those that

[76] G. Helmke and S. Levitsky, 'Informal Institutions and Comparative Politics: A Research Agenda', *Perspectives on Politics* 2, 4, 2004, pp. 725–40.

[77] P. Evans, D. Rueschemeyer and T. Skocpol, *Bringing the State Back In* (Cambridge: Cambridge University Press, 1985).

[78] Startsev, '"Informal" Institutions and Practices', p. 334, drawing on Helmke and Levitsky.

[79] V. Ya. Gel'man, 'Institutsional'noe stroitel'stvo i neformal'nye instituty v sovremennoi rossiiskoi politike', *Polis*, No. 4, 2003, pp. 6–25.

[80] Startsev, '"Informal" Institutions and Practices', p. 335.

tend to be tacit and not verbalised) in contemporary Russia that shape factional behaviour.[81]

As for exit costs, including deviations from the operative norms of a particular group, the formal constitutional sphere has ultimately coercive properties, but this is not entirely lacking in the informal sphere. Although operating more through socialisation, there is a punitive regime that, even though lacking a formally codified character, can exact stiff penalties, as Khodorkovsky, Skarga and Nikitin discovered to their cost. In the dual state, the predominant factions can employ the coercive power of the law and state agencies, as the victims of the Yukos affair well know, and thus as it were 'borrow' the coercive power of the state; but it is always ultimately a loan and does not have an autonomous character. The parasitic nature of the 'loan' degrades the institution from which the loan is made, notably the courts. The disciplinary character of operative codes of the administrative regime under Putin was highly developed. In the economic sphere this took the form of 'deprivatisation'; allowing an economic agent freedom to conduct business and own property, but a degree of fealty to the regime and the appropriate faction was required. In the political sphere this took the form of 'de-autonomisation'; a political rent, in a form even as exiguous as loyalty, was demanded by the regime, which was applied even to avowedly opposition parties such as the CPRF as to more pliable groupings such as the LDPR. All of this sucked life out of the formal institutions located in the sphere of the constitutional state.

There is one more crucial issue to be addressed, namely the *site* of factionalism. Charap has usefully developed the notion of 'executive strength', applying the literature on state capacity but focusing specifically on the moving force of the Russian state, its executive.[82] The central executive in Russia has three facets, the presidency, the government (*pravitel'stvo*) and the ministries, each at the head of administrative empires. For Charap executive strength has two key variables: 'the relative power of the executive vis-à-vis other political institutions', including parliament, the judiciary, interest groups and regional governments; and 'the level of fragmentation within the executive'.[83] Fragmentation can take many forms, including traditional bureaucratic rivalry between departments, rival party or other affiliations and personal conflicts, as well as the projection onto the executive of competing social and

---

[81] A. B. Daugavet, 'Neformal'nye praktiki rossiiskoi elity (Aprobatsiya kognitivnogo podkhoda)', *Polis*, No. 4, 2003, pp. 26–38.

[82] Samuel Charap, 'Inside Out: Domestic Political Change and Foreign Policy in Vladimir Putin's First Term', *Demokratizatsiya* 15, 3, 2007, pp. 335–52.

[83] *Ibid.*, p. 336.

economic interests, which in extreme cases can take the form of 'state capture', or at least the hijacking of parts of the executive to serve the interests of particularistic groups. This is what Putin suggested had happened in the 1990s, but in tackling these identifiable aspects of fragmentation, he presided over the development of factional groupings within the executive that once again interacted with social interests but at a different level of aggregation. The political economy of factionalism under Putin differed in form from that under Yeltsin, but politico-economic groupings continued to exercise a crucial role. State institutions were no longer taken hostage by economic interest groups, but the reverse proposition would also be misleading: instead, in keeping with our dual state model, it is the terrain in between where factionalism flourishes, based on the coalescence of business and state interests.

We can distinguish between 'external equidistance', distancing the economic magnates from the heart of the Kremlin's policy-making process (the programme advanced by Putin between 2000 and 2003 before the Yukos affair upset the balance); and 'internal equidistance', the attempt by the presidency to keep the factions balanced so that none can dominate the policy agenda. The corollary of this is the distinction between internal and external autonomy. Internal autonomy refers to the transformation of a Kremlin faction into a clan, with a self-sustaining dynamic that significantly limits the freedom of manoeuvre of the executive. External autonomy refers to the freedom of action and ability to influence the policy process by civic associations, including business groupings and political parties; it also encompasses the aspiration of the presidency to maintain its superiority over the factions. At a time when the ability of political actors to act as independent agents was reduced through a not-so-subtle and at times brutal system of rewards and punishments, and the economic bases of independent political activity were systematically dismantled, so too the presidency struggled to retain its internal autonomy. The 'imposed consensus' of Russia's elite, as Gel'man notes, was achieved through the Kremlin's use of 'selective punishment of some elite sections and selective cooptation of others';[84] but even the 'Kremlin' itself was a far from unitary actor.

Comparative perspectives

The clan phenomenon is far less pronounced in Russia than in Ukraine and some other countries. Clans are groups connected by ties of blood

---

[84] Vladimir Gel'man, 'Political Opposition in Russia: A Dying Species?', *Post-Soviet Affairs* 21, 3, July–September 2005, p. 242.

and 'tribal' loyalties, and this sort of network is prevalent in most of Russia's republics, notably in Tatarstan and Mordovia, but only rarely encountered in 'Russian' regions.[85] Clans and kinship groups are highly ramified in the North Caucasus, but their role is not our concern here.[86] Unlike in Ukraine, where clan-type structures represent a combination of social, regional, economic and even ideological differences,[87] in Russia the political regime is more dominant, and interests less defined. In Ukraine regional clans wielded considerable power even in the Soviet period, notably in Donetsk and Dnepropetrovsk, and they have been able to reproduce themselves over generations and advance their own policy agenda. Following independence in 1991, they became a constituent element of the party system. Indeed, according to Balmaceda, Kuchma's policy-making was based on a strategy of 'president-as-balancer' between powerful business-administrative groups.[88] The classic case in Ukraine, as noted, was the long-established 'Dnepropetrovsk mafia'. The existence of several such deeply entrenched communities helps explain Ukraine's relative democratisation, but whether they can be characterised as 'clans' remains controversial. The semi-presidential system in Ukraine, as in the CIS as a whole, 'fitted the clientelist characteristics of these countries' politics'.[89]

Although Russia and Ukraine until 2004 shared broadly similar political systems, differences in the aggregation and representation of interests shaped the divergent democratisation trajectories in the two countries. Entrenched regional and business interests in Ukraine provided the bedrock for deep societal pluralism, whereas in Russia, despite its vast size, the socio-political landscape is far less contoured. Equally, in neighbouring Belarus, as Kimitaka Matsuzato notes, the absence of anything approximating clan-type formations is one reason why the Lukashenko regime was able to maintain its independence and to pursue populist practices in which the leadership appealed directly to the people without substantive intermediary aggregations.[90] This was reinforced by

---

[85] Oksana Gaman-Golutvina, 'Regional'nye elity Rossii: Personal'nyi sostav i tendentsii evolyutsii (I)', *Polis*, No. 2, 2004, pp. 14–15.

[86] Darrell Slider, 'Putin's "Southern Strategy": Dmitriy Kozak and the Dilemmas of Recentralization', *Post-Soviet Affairs* 24, 2, April–June 2008, pp. 182–3.

[87] See Kimitaka Matsuzato, 'Semipresidentialism in Ukraine: Institutionalist Centrism in Rampant Clan Politics', *Demokratizatsiya* 13, 1, Winter 2005, pp. 45–58.

[88] Margarita M. Balmaceda, *Energy Dependency, Politics and Corruption in the Former Soviet Union: Russia's Power, Oligarchs' Profits and Ukraine's Missing Energy Policy, 1995–2006* (London and New York: Routledge, 2008), p. 39.

[89] *Ibid.*, p. 48.

[90] Kimitaka Matsuzato, 'A Populist Island in an Ocean of Clan Politics: The Lukashenko Regime as an Exception Among CIS Countries', *Europe-Asia Studies* 56, 2, March 2004, pp. 235–61.

the development of a 'national ideology' that repudiated titular elite consolidation in favour of a state-centred developmental model based on egalitarian nationalism.[91]

In some Central Asian countries, clan structures (based on kinship ties and regional identities) and political administrations to all intents and purposes merged, and this in turn gave rise to yet another type of political regime.[92] Schatz criticises attempts to impose simplistic transition or democratisation models on Central Asia, while stressing that clan politics are not necessarily antithetical to the development of a modern state. For example, while the Kazakhstan regime condemned clans, it took an active part in shaping clan identities.[93] In other words, clan identities can be part of the modernisation process and not just an obstacle. While regional and ethnic factors were undoubtedly important in the civil war in Tajikistan from 1992 to 1997, a recent study has convincingly demonstrated that the mobilisation of networks was the crucial factor.[94] The debate about the role of clans in Central Asian politics continues, with arguments suggesting that they can provide a positive integrative function balanced by critiques of the destructive effect they have on formal institutions.[95] Collins places the debate over the role of clans firmly in the comparative social science literature while providing detailed empirical analysis of the practical way in which they operate in Central Asia. She argues that they are not a perverse inversion of standard accounts of institutional development but a rational way for social groups to interact in a specific collectivist institutional and cultural setting characterised by late state formation, weak national identities and under-developed capitalist market relations. Collins is at pains to stress that clans should not be reduced to state organisations or ethnic ties.[96]

---

[91] Natalia Leshchenko, 'The National Ideology and the Basis of the Lukashenka Regime in Belarus', *Europe-Asia Studies* 60, 8, October 2008, pp. 1419–33.

[92] See, for example, Edward Schatz, *Modern Clan Politics: The Power of "Blood" in Kazakhstan and Beyond*, Jackson School Publications in International Studies (Seattle: University of Washington Press, 2004); Edward Schatz, 'Reconceptualizing Clans: Kinship Networks and Statehood in Kazakhstan', *Nationalities Papers* 33, 2, 2005, pp. 231–54.

[93] Schatz, *Modern Clan Politics*, p. 161.

[94] Idil Tunçer Kilavuz, 'The Role of Networks in Tajikistan's Civil War: Network Activation and Violence Specialists', *Nationalities Papers* 37, 5, September 2009, pp. 693–717.

[95] See Collins, 'Clans, Pacts, and Politics in Central Asia'; Katherine Collins, 'The Logic of Clan Politics: Evidence from the Central Asian Trajectories', *World Politics* 56, 2, January 2004, pp. 224–61; V. Khanin, 'Political Clans and Political Conflicts in Contemporary Kyrgyzstan', in Yaacov Ro'i (ed.), *Democracy and Pluralism in Muslim Eurasia* (London: Frank Cass, 2004), pp. 215–32.

[96] Katherine Collins, *Clan Politics and Regime Transition in Central Asia* (New York: Cambridge University Press, 2006), p. 56.

She stresses that 'Far from being irrational relics of a bygone age, the informal ties and networks of clan life reduce the high transaction costs of making deals in an environment where impersonal institutions are weak or absent and stable expectations are hard to form.'[97] A similar argument may be made about the functional role of factions in Russia.

In Ukraine there is a clear regional and sectoral basis to relatively stable groupings with a defined stance on public policy issues, but the degree to which a stable 'clan' system has emerged can be questioned. Similarly, the attempt to apply a clan model to Kazakhstan politics has been questioned on the basis of the lack of empirically testable evidence.[98] The applicability of the clan model to Russia is even more problematical, since here things are far more situational, permeable and malleable. Executive authorities in the centre and the regions build up their own factions through personalised patterns of appointment, as seen most vividly in Putin's 'tail' from St Petersburg, but it would be far-fetched to call them a 'clan'. Elsewhere in the country the recruitment mechanism of the great majority of regional officials does not conform to any Weberian stereotype and is far from competitive, being dominated by 'informal relations and personalised practices'.[99] The reason for this in part lies in the absence of what one author calls 'instruments of mass vertical mobility', primarily effective political parties, and thus 'politics', that is, 'activity to achieve influence and power, is hostage to the amorphous structure of Russian society [*sotsium*]'.[100] To a large degree, as Gaman-Golutvina notes, in the 1990s 'property became the key for recruitment into power (*vlast'*). The state and elite status were privatized.'[101] The development of UR as a dominant party may well render it an instrument of 'vertical mobility' in due course.

The internalisation of factional conflict within a dominant party is a well-known phenomenon in international politics. The Liberal Democratic Party (LDP), Japan's ruling party since 1955 with a brief break in 1992 until its defeat on 30 August 2009, had some six clearly identifiable

[97] Collins, 'Clans, Pacts, and Politics in Central Asia', p. 142.
[98] Jonathan Murphy, 'Illusory Transition? Elite Reconstitution in Kazakhstan, 1989–2002', *Europe-Asia Studies* 58, 4, June 2006, pp. 523–54. For a recent fruitful analysis of Kazakhstani politics using the factional approach, see Rico Isaacs, 'Between Informal and Formal Politics: Neopatrimonialism and Party Development in Kazakhstan', Ph.D., Department of IR, Politics and Sociology, Oxford Brookes University, 2009.
[99] A. E. Chirikova, 'Ispolnitel'naya vlast' v regionakh: Pravila igry formal'nye i neformal'nye', *Obshchestvennye nauki i sovremennost'*, No. 3, 2004, p. 73.
[100] A. G. Vishnevskii, 'Modernizatsiya i kontrmodernizatsiya: Ch'ya voz'met?', *Obshchestvennye nauki i sovremennost'*, No. 1, 2004, pp. 17–25, at p. 23.
[101] Oksana Gaman-Golutvina, 'Posle Imperii', *Nezavisimaya gazeta: NG-Stsenarii*, 27 March 2007, p. 13.

factions, which took turns to nominate the prime minister. Although their influence has declined in recent years, a faction (*ha*, or *habatsu*) focused on a particular leader where policy differences were less salient than power-brokering activities accompanied by fund-raising and resource distribution in a system based on an 'iron triangle' of politicians, bureaucracy and big business. Above all, cabinet reshuffles were preceded by bargaining with the prime minister over the distribution of ministerial and party posts.[102] Single-party dominance was accompanied by the weakness of opposition, but even the main alternative, the Democratic Party of Japan (DPJ), was also factionalised, although not quite in such an institutionalised form as the LDP.[103] The development of United Russia as a Japanese-style dominant party could take this form. Already in the Fourth Duma there was much speculation about splits in UR, but instead, as we have seen, it grew various 'wings' that gradually hardened into three policy platforms: liberal, social and conservative. The idea of UR marching into the 2007 parliamentary election in three columns was even mooted, but in the event it fought as a single united body. Nevertheless, there may come a time when the dominant party subsumes and incorporates factional conflict as a way of managing party and societal pluralism. Just Russia may in part be seen as a type of 'external faction', a wing of the broader ruling group, but within UR no Japanese-style formalisation of factionalism has yet occurred. Instead, factional conflicts occupy a parallel sphere, subverting the official world of public politics but at the same time constrained by the formal rules of the game.

Elites, factions and the succession

The shift from Yeltsinite conflict to Putinite stability can be likened to Stalinist consolidation after the political struggles of the 1920s.[104] By the early 1930s, Stalin had defeated the various groups led by Trotsky, Kamenev, Zinoviev and Bukharin and also treated those with foreign links, including agents of the Comintern, with suspicion. The analogy, however, in at least two ways is inadequate. Although inter-departmental struggles continued under Stalin, they did not take the form of factional conflict, whereas Putin's regime represented a shift from the open competing lobbying networks of the Yeltsin years to intra-regime factional

[102] J. A. A. Stockwin, *Governing Japan: Divided Politics in a Resurgent Economy*, 4th edn (Oxford: Blackwell Publishing, 2008), pp. 139–40.
[103] Sarah Hyde, *The Transformation of the Japanese Left: From Old Socialists to New Democrats* (London: Nissan Institute/Routledge Japanese Studies, 2009), pp. 62–9.
[104] Cf. Easter, *Reconstructing the State*.

conflict. Second, appointments in Stalin's system were constrained by the *nomenklatura* system, whereas Putin was forced to rely on a highly developed network of personal contacts to ensure at least a minimum cadre of people loyal to him.

Like the Party-state in the Soviet era, the administrative regime has its own 'constitution' to prevent intra-elite struggles growing into internecine warfare or even blood-letting of the type that afflicted the country under Stalin and in 1993. The Putin 'constitution' regulated the behaviour of the administrative regime and sought to manage intra-elite conflict. In a system where the winner did not take it all, every faction had enough of a stake to ensure their loyalty, and none was allowed to gain such a predominance as would threaten the existence of the others. This was a type of intra-elite pluralism that compensated for the weakness of formal institutions. Democracy may well have emerged to regulate intra-elite conflict, but it is not always the most efficient way of doing this, especially in times of crisis.[105]

A study by Henry Hale focuses on the concept of 'patronal presidentialism', where an elected president disposes not only enormous formal power resources but also 'immense informal authority based on pervasive patron-client relationships and machine politics'.[106] Putin stood at the centre of a massive patron–client network, with various 'teams' advanced on the basis of personal acquaintance. By late 2007, sixty-five of the top posts in the thirty main federal ministries and agencies had at some point worked with him in St Petersburg.[107] These relationships are structured around groups: 'Patronal presidents like Russia's Boris Yeltsin and Ukraine's Leonid Kuchma, for example, were famous for balancing key groups of supporters against each other, and current Russian president Vladimir Putin has long done the same with informal Kremlin "groups", such as those sometimes referred to as the *Siloviki* and the "St. Petersburg lawyers".'[108] Hale's central argument is that the moment of succession is the most dangerous one for patronal presidencies, potentially exposing the regime to a range of threats. He notes that some leaders, such as Heidar Aliev in Azerbaijan, avoided the 'succession trap', which he defines as 'the need to choose the successor from among the several competing elite groups that were all part of the

[105] Cf. Dankwart A. Rustow, 'Transitions to Democracy: Toward a Dynamic Model', *Comparative Politics* 2, 3, 1970, pp. 337–63.
[106] Henry E. Hale, 'Democracy or Autocracy on the March? The Colored Revolutions as Normal Dynamics of Patronal Presidentialism', *Communist and Post-Communist Studies* 39, 2006, p. 307.
[107] Andryushchenko, 'Za klanom klan?', p. 3.
[108] Hale, 'Democracy or Autocracy on the March?', p. 308.

presidential team', by appointing his own son, Ilham, as successor.[109] In Russia, Yeltsin pre-empted a crisis by ensuring that his nominated successor, Putin, was able to cruise into power.

Where elites are split and the succession election is mismanaged, however, 'colour' revolutions have broken out to reclaim disputed elections. Putin devoted much of his second term to foreclosing such an eventuality, including imposing restrictions on foreign-financed NGOs and creating youth movements (notably Nashi on 1 March 2005) to occupy the space from whence anti-regime movements could emerge. In the immediate pre-succession period, according to Hale, 'The [orange] revolutions are actually triggered primarily by splits in the elite brought about by a lame duck syndrome and unpopular leadership under patronal presidential institutions', and not by the various civic activists and western intervention, as feared by many of the post-Soviet leaders.[110] Putin ensured that he did not become a lame duck president by keeping his succession strategy close to his chest, and by adapting that strategy as events unfolded, while remaining enormously popular and refusing to share that popularity with his successor until the last moment. The greatest danger in the Putin succession was not so much a 'colour revolution' as the defection of elite factions and social groups. As we shall see, much of the succession was focused on forestalling this eventuality. Factions were balanced and neutralised, while regional bosses and business leaders suborned.

Putin took care not to create a group of alienated ex-officials who could act as the focus of elite opposition and popular movements. Sacked officials were usually found an alternative post, and only in very rare cases were they removed from the elite appointment system in its entirety. Yeltsin had been less careful in this respect, although he too tended to find a sinecure for dismissed officials. One of the few people under Putin not appointed to a reasonably commensurate post was the former prime minister, Kasyanov, who went on to try to play the role that a former prime minister of Ukraine had done – to take over the presidency. However, while Victor Yushchenko stormed into the presidency through a forced third round of the presidential election with the help of mass mobilisation, Putin spent much of his second term precisely doing everything in his power to forestall a colour revolution, and that included keeping the great bulk of the elite on board. Even Voloshin, who resigned as chief of staff on 30 October 2003 following Khodorkovsky's arrest, went on to head the board at the state-owned electricity monopoly (Russian Share Company Edinye Energosistemy,

---

[109] *Ibid.*, p. 310.   [110] *Ibid.*, pp. 320–1.

RAO UES), headed by Chubais until its privatisation in July 2008. While the recycling of appointments under Putin may not always have ensured that the best qualified people were in the appropriate posts, it did at least ensure stability. This was monitored by Victor Ivanov, the head of the Kremlin's personnel appointment system, who in 2004–6 in effect conducted a purge of officials appointed as a result of factional lobbying, and they were replaced by specialists, notably in the financial and social spheres. As a cadre reserve, he brought in new people from the regions. At the top level, these regional appointments included Sergei Sobyanin, who became head of the presidential administration following Medvedev's move into the government (see Chapter 5), and Yury Trutnev, the natural resources minister.[111]

The executive under Putin was careful to maintain its pre-eminence by standing above factions, and indeed part of its power derived from its ability to arbitrate between different elements of the regime. The presidency feared becoming the puppet of any particular faction but was more than a neutral referee in factional conflict; it was an active player whose autonomy was constrained by factional conflict, although its power was not simply a function of those struggles. As Andrei Ryabov puts it, 'In post-communist Russia the presidency, in which all fundamental authoritative functions are concentrated, is traditionally balanced, and often even opposed, to the interests of various elite groups. Conflicting groups have to appeal to the supreme arbiter for support. The president also wishes to maintain such a state of affairs, which works to strengthen his power and extends the field for political manoeuvre.'[112] This is a Bonapartist model of politics, although tempered by the constraints imposed by the legal-constitutional order and focused on preventing factions gaining excessive internal autonomy. According to Glebova, 'The ruling layer of the new Russia is divided into groups engaged in a permanent "war" for access to resources and superprofitable output. All these groups participated (and participate) in the creation of supermonopolies – raw materials, telecommunications and so on, which are easily controlled. The state is one of the players in this field and always wins any fights.'[113] However, the state itself was fragmented and outcomes uncertain since it was never clear whether the formal procedures of the constitutional state or the arbitrariness of the administrative regime would predominate in any particular case.

[111] Vitalii Tseplyaev, *Argumenty i fakty*, No. 45, November 2007.
[112] Andrei Ryabov, 'Poslanie prezidenta kuda podal'she', *Novaya gazeta*, No. 33, 4–10 May 2006, p. 2.
[113] I. I. Glebova, 'Politicheskaya kultura sovremennoi Rossii: Obliki novoi russkoi vlasti i sotsial'nye raskoly', *Polis*, No. 1, 2006, p. 40.

The factions

The Yukos case became an instrument in the factional struggles in the Kremlin, with a particular section intent on using the affair to assert its authority and to build a property empire of its own.[114] The attack on Yukos, like the 2007–8 succession later, exposed the outlines of factional configuration, but there is no consensus on the precise breakdown of factional conflict in the Kremlin. Bremmer and Charap argue that at least ten Kremlin factions can be identified, although they suggest that three primary groups predominate, liberals, technocrats and *siloviki*.[115] The overall picture is of two meta-groups, the liberal-technocrats and the *siloviki*, which Putin maintained in rough balance throughout his presidency. There was a broad division of labour between the two, with the liberal-technocrats predominant in economic and financial management, while the *siloviki* took responsibility for 'strategic' industries, the energy sector and defence policy. Within that overarching framework, some six factions may be identified, a categorisation combining, in a non-exclusive manner, place of origin, professional background, policy orientation and, ultimately, actor motivation. Clearly Putin's colleagues from St Petersburg (the *Pitertsy*) are one of the most recognisable groups in his administration, while those with a background in the security services are also an identifiable group. Regional background, career path, professional occupation and beliefs came together in unexpected ways to shape factional allegiance and the contour of politics.[116]

The *siloviki*

The first of our factions, and the focus of most analysis, are the *siloviki*, representatives of the security apparatus and to a lesser extent the military. The *siloviki* is a category broader than the *chekisty* (the Cheka is the abbreviated name for the Extraordinary Commission, the first secret police organisation established by Lenin in December 1917), those who had served specifically in the KGB or its successors, and denotes quite a broad spectrum of statist-patriotic sentiment. From the very first years of post-communist Russia, the continued power of the

---

[114] For a discussion of the struggles of members of the presidential administration, see Pavel K. Baev, 'Putin's Team in Disarray over Oil Money', *EDM* 2, 55, 21 March 2005.

[115] Ian Bremmer and Samuel Charap, 'The *Siloviki* in Putin's Russia: Who They Are and What They Want', *The Washington Quarterly* 30, 1, Winter 2006–7, p. 85.

[116] For a broad review, see Klaus Segbers (ed.), *Explaining Post-Soviet Patchworks*, 3 vols. (Aldershot: Ashgate, 2001).

security services was condemned. Yevgenia Albats writes that 'The years since the August 1991 coup have proved that our victory at the walls of the Russian parliament lasted only a few days or, at best, months. The Party was defeated in that battle, but the other two structures of the oligarchy, the KGB and the MIC [military-industrial complex], regained their footing. And, to our misfortune, they are growing stronger every day.'[117] This view was repeated in a typically misleading and lurid account in *The Economist*, which talked of a shift 'from oligarchy to spookocracy'.[118]

Contrary to much ill-informed commentary, Putin's KGB past did not automatically make him leader of a newly militant security apparatus thirsting for revenge. Putin worked in the KGB from 1975 to 1990 and briefly returned as head of the FSB in 1998–9. Nevertheless, Putin's *silovik* background, even though tempered by his work under the liberal mayor of St Petersburg, Sobchak, in the early 1990s and then in the presidential administration under Yeltsin, no doubt predisposed him to statist rather than pluralist approaches to public policy issues. The *siloviki* viewpoint is an important one in reinforcing dirigiste trends in Russian political economy and a 'securitarian' approach in public affairs. The *siloviki* stress the need to restore the coherence of the state and have strong views about how the economy should be run. The concept of a cohesive 'militocracy' is exaggerated, but the general *silovik* view that the state should take the priority over the anarchy of the market in strategic economic issues and over the unpredictability of the democratic representation of civil society in politics is something that is close to Putin's heart. Putin brought the *siloviki* back into the heart of the power system, something that was already beginning in the late Yeltsin years, but by the same token imported traditions of secrecy and bureaucratic arbitrariness back into government. The *siloviki* were particularly concerned to ensure the consolidation of their power and the perpetuation of their rule even after Putin had left the presidency.

Numerous studies have noted the increased role of the *siloviki* under Putin. The standard figure is that about 6,000 former security service operatives, including Putin himself, entered government service in his first term. As a recent work has demonstrated, the federal and regional

[117] Yevgenia Albats, *KGB: State Within a State* (London: I. B. Tauris, 1995), p. 329. For a development of the argument, see Amy Knight, *Spies Without Cloaks: The KGB's Successors* (Princeton, NJ: Princeton University Press, 1996).
[118] The title was 'Putin's People: The Spies Who Run Russia', *The Economist*, 25–31 August 2007, with the cover story on p. 11, with the main feature 'The Making of a Neo-KGB State', pp. 25–8, with the notion of a 'spookocracy' on p. 27.

elite structures now have a significant security component.[119] The *siloviki* made up to 70 per cent of staff in the seven federal districts.[120] According to Kryshtanovskaya and White, the proportion of those with a security, military or other law-enforcement agencies background in leadership positions rose from 4 per cent under Gorbachev to 11 per cent under Yeltsin, and then increased to 25 per cent by the end of Putin's first term as president, with the proportion even higher in the national government.[121] Rivera and Rivera demonstrated that while the number of *siloviki* in responsible government positions had indeed increased, this rise was not as big as Kryshtanovskaya and White had suggested – a threefold increase since 1998 rather than the reported sevenfold rise.[122] They conclude that claims about 'an emerging "militocracy" are real but overstated'.[123] Above all, they argue that this is balanced by the increased representation of business representatives in all spheres of Russian public life, a nascent bourgeoisie that will in the long term perhaps have a far greater impact than the temporary assertion of *silovik* authority. Yeltsinite fungibility between the state and economic spheres continued, with a study by the Institute of Sociology finding that in 2001–3 some 60–70 per cent of regional assembly deputies had come from or were associated with economic activities.[124]

An indication of the importance of the *siloviki* under Putin is the significant rise in their share of funding allocations, which according to one estimate meant that total funding on domestic security agencies exceeded spending on the regular armed forces.[125] This may well have indicated fear of domestic challenges as the succession approached,[126] but it also reflected their increased role in tackling organised crime and corruption. Nevertheless, the leading 'securocrats' were well represented among the 'barons', the senior ministers and Kremlin officials, who worked closely with Putin and regularly attended the unofficial 'kitchen cabinet' held at his country home on Saturday mornings, where they

[119] On the size and role of the *siloviki* in Putin's administration, see Ol'ga Kryshtanovskaya and Stephen White, 'Putin's Militocracy', *Post-Soviet Affairs* 19, 4, October–December 2003, pp. 289–306; and for updated figures, Ol'ga Kryshtanovskaya and Stephen White, 'Inside the Putin Court: A Research Note', *Europe-Asia Studies* 57, 7, November 2005, pp. 1065–75.
[120] Andryushchenko, 'Za klanom klan?', p. 3.
[121] Kryshtanovskaya and White, 'Putin's Militocracy', p. 294.
[122] Sharon Werning Rivera and David W. Rivera, 'The Russian Elite Under Putin: Militocratic or Bourgeois?', *Post-Soviet Affairs* 22, 2, 2006, p. 136.
[123] *Ibid.*, p. 126.
[124] Andryushchenko, 'Za klanom klan?', p. 3.
[125] Julian Cooper, 'The Funding of the Power Agencies of the Soviet State', *The Journal of Power Institutions in Post-Soviet Societies* 6, 7, 2007; www.pipss.org/document562.html
[126] Blank, 'The Putin Succession', p. 243.

drank tea and discussed the fate of the nation. This group of about eight people included the heads of the force structures, as well as the prime minister and the head of the presidential administration.[127] Sechin was the most prominent of those urging Putin to amend the constitution and stay on for a third term. The *siloviki* group includes another deputy head of the presidential administration, Victor Ivanov, who worked in the KGB's domestic counter-intelligence section. Nikolai Patrushev, the head of the security service up to May 2008, is an FSB colonel general. The head of the Federal State Reserves Agency, Alexander Grigor'ev, had served with the special services in Afghanistan, and with Ivanov, was part of Putin's inner circle.

It is doubtful whether the prime minister between March 2004 and September 2007, Fradkov, can be considered a fully fledged *silovik*, although one of his sons is known to be an FSB officer and he was often considered a protégé of Sergei Ivanov, the former defence minister. Ivanov served with Putin in the KGB in St Petersburg, and in the early 1970s he studied at the KGB academy, where he learnt his excellent English, and in 1975 he spent four months at Ealing Technical College (now University of West London).[128] Between 1984 and 1990, he worked in Finland under the cover of the Soviet foreign trade office. On his return he was not part of Sobchak's team in the mayor's office and instead worked with the SVR (Sluzhba Vneshnei Razvedky, the Foreign Intelligence Service) in Moscow and he is now a retired SVR colonel general. In the late Putin years, he oversaw the military-industrial sector and various programmes for the development of high-tech industries, including nanotechnologies. It is not entirely clear whether Ivanov can be considered a member of the *silovik* faction since his loyalty was primarily to Putin personally and he thus helped Putin constrain factional conflicts. Ivanov was not trusted by the core *siloviki*, and therefore they did not rally behind his presidential ambitions. Indeed, the *siloviki* lacked their own candidate in the succession and hence advanced the 'third term' option for Putin.

The *siloviki* were well represented across the elite. The head of the Audit Chamber, Sergei Stepashin, was a former head of the FSB yet he kept his distance from the *silovik* faction. At the time of the succession, the Ministry of Internal Affairs (MVD), a crucial agency in case of unrest, was headed by Rashid Nurgaliev, an FSB army general. The

---

[127] Kryshtanovkaya and White, 'Inside the Putin Court', pp. 1067–8.
[128] Interviewed by the present author (whose home borough is Ealing) on 12 September 2007, Ivanov was enthusiastic about his time in West London and presented himself as something of an Anglophile.

MVD controls the ordinary police as well as some 180,000 internal troops. Andrei Belyaninov, a colleague of Putin's from his Dresden days in the late 1980s, headed the Federal Customs Service, while the Federal Migration Service (FMS) was headed by FSB lieutenant general Konstantin Romodanovsky. Another of Putin's colleagues from Germany is Sergei Chemezov, the director of Rosoboroneksport, the main arms export agency who went on to head one of the largest of the new state corporations. Another of Putin's colleagues from St Petersburg, although of an older generation, is FSB colonel general Victor Cherkesov, who headed the Federal Antinarcotics Committee (Gosnarkontrol', FSKN), established in 2003, and who had previously been the presidential envoy to the central federal district. Following the resignation of Igor Ivanov as head of the Security Council in July 2007, former FSB director colonel general Valentin Sobolev took over as acting head, until in May 2008 Patrushev was appointed its permanent head. FSB army general Nikolai Bordyuzha headed the Collective Security Treaty Organisation (CSTO), while SVR lieutenant general Grigory Rapota oversaw the Eurasian Economic Community (EurAsEc) until appointed presidential envoy to the southern federal district in September 2007. In general, Putin was careful to balance intra-factional sub-groupings, but he could not avert the exacerbation of factional conflict during the succession.

Vladimir Ustinov was also a key member of the *silovik* group. He was confirmed as prosecutor general on 17 May 2000 and appointed to a second term on 13 April 2005 before being summarily dismissed, as we shall see, in June 2006. In 2003, Ustinov's son Dmitry married Sechin's daughter Inga, suggesting that factional links were, at the margins, becoming clan-type relations. According to one report, this group asserted a hard line against Yukos as part of a wider plan to 'reshape the market and also strengthen state control, along with their own influence'.[129] Ustinov's ascription as a *silovik* raises a fundamental definitional question, since he is not known to have a security background. Equally, Sergei Bogdanchikov, head of the state-owned oil giant Rosneft that was instrumental in the destruction of Yukos, is ranked as one of the most influential *siloviki*, but he never served in any force structure. Thus there is a narrow meaning to the concept of *silovik*, restricted to those with a force structure background, and a broader application to encompass the group of people allied to them with non-security career structures.

---

[129] Elena Dikun, '"Delo Yukosa" v sude kreml' – Yukos neokonchennaya voina', *Moskovskie novosti*, No. 18, 21 May 2004, p. 4.

Sechin, considered the *éminence grise* behind the Yukos affair, joined the board of Rosneft on 25 June 2004 and became chairman of the board a month later on 27 July. Sechin clearly pressed for the complete liquidation of Yukos and for the continuation of the campaign against Yeltsin-era oligarchs. Born in Leningrad on 7 September 1960, Sechin was a graduate from the philological department of Leningrad State University (1977–84), specialising in Romance philology (Portuguese and French), and then served as an interpreter in Angola and Mozambique under the auspices of the GRU (Main Intelligence Directorate of the armed forces), and not with the KGB as is sometimes suggested. He then joined the directorate for foreign economic ties in the Leningrad City Soviet, and between 1991 and 1996 worked in the Committee for Foreign Economic Ties, headed by Putin, at the St Petersburg City Council. Like Putin, from 1996 he worked in the presidential and governmental apparatus in Moscow, being appointed deputy head of the presidential administration on 31 December 1999, the day that Putin became acting president. A recent book comments on Sechin as follows: 'Chief among the *siloviki* faction were two shadowy presidential deputy chiefs of staff, Victor Ivanov and Igor Sechin, both with KGB backgrounds and both long-time Putin associates who had followed him from St. Petersburg to the Kremlin. Ivanov was put in charge of personnel, and he used his power to eliminate the commission that recommended pardons for prisoners. Sechin controlled the paper flow that reached Putin and served as the president's guardian. "His main asset is his loyalty," said Valery Pavlov, who had worked with both men in St. Petersburg.'[130]

From the above it is clear that it would be fundamentally mistaken to see the *siloviki* as in any way a single coherent lobby.[131] The hostility between the FSB and the MVD, for example, has long been evident, while the regular military and its Main Intelligence Agency (GRU) were careful to keep out of politics. The civilian defence minister, Anatoly Serdyukov, pushed through a liberal reform of the military, a process that gained extreme urgency following the poor performance of the Russian armed forces as a whole in the Russo-Georgian war of 2008. Cherkesov became part of a *silovik* sub-faction locked, as we shall see, in conflict with other *siloviki*. However, although divided into various sub-factions, the *siloviki* maintained a certain group self-image as the saviours of the nation, a view that had a certain popular resonance.

---

[130] Peter Baker and Susan B. Glasser, *Kremlin Rising: Vladimir Putin's Russia and the End of Revolution*, rev. edn (New York: Scribner, 2007), p. 271.

[131] Hence the argument advanced by *The Economist* ('Putin's People', p. 11) that Russia was undergoing an 'FSBisation' was not only wrong but prompted mistaken policy-making.

A Levada Center survey in September 2007 found that 42 per cent agreed with the view that the security services were fulfilling an important role and that their powers were appropriate, but a sizeable group of 35 per cent of respondents considered that 'The Russian special services have been given too great and uncontrolled powers.'[132] We shall return to the question of the political role of the *siloviki* in the next chapter.

Neo-oligarchy: the 'family' and other beasts

The second faction is made up of the remnants of the 'family', the Yeltsin-era officials and business people oriented towards a *laissez-faire* economic policy, and a minimal role for the state. We have used the term 'family' to this point, but we concur with Simonov's view that the term is journalistic and misleading. He suggests describing it as the 'old Muscovite' *nomenklatura*-political grouping: 'old' because it represented a system with its roots in the 1990s that was eclipsed in the Putin years (although revived under Medvedev's presidency); and 'Muscovite' because it represented an alternative to the St Petersburgers (the *Pitertsy*) so prominent under Putin.[133] Elements of D'Agostino's tension between Moscow and St Petersburg policy factions have resurfaced. The key figures here are Voloshin, head of the presidential administration from 1999 until October 2003, and Kasyanov, prime minister from May 2000 until February 2004. Voloshin was credited with almost mythical political powers, and he certainly sustained a phenomenal work rate. We have already discussed his involvement with Gazprom machinations, but he was also credited earlier with having prevented Yeltsin's impeachment in 1999 and the dismissal of Primakov's government in May of that year, with establishing the Unity party in autumn 1999 and then shaping United Russia in 2002 and the associated pro-presidential majority in parliament.

The key oligarch associated with this group was Berezovsky, who fled into exile in London in 2001. Berezovsky spent much of his time plotting the downfall of Putin's government, by fair means or foul. In an interview with the radio station *Ekho Moskvy* in January 2006, Berezovsky stated: 'This regime will never permit a fair election to be held, so there is only one solution: taking power by force. It's important for people in Russia to understand that the time for empty talk has passed, and what we need now is action.'[134] Having helped fund Yushchenko's campaign

[132] 'Rossiya v tsifrakh', *Kommersant-Vlast'*, No. 40, 15 October 2007, p. 12.
[133] Simonov, *Russkaya neft'*, p. 21.
[134] Cited by Vyacheslav Kostikov, *Argumenty i fakty*, No. 49, 6 December 2006.

in Ukraine in 2004, Berezovsky now advocated an 'orange' revolution in Russia.[135] This of course exacerbated the siege mentality of Putin's entourage. Voloshin resigned four days after Khodorkovsky's arrest on 25 October 2003, indicating the weakening of the 'old Muscovite' faction with which Khodorkovsky was allied. Even those not counted among the ranks of the *siloviki* warned about the dangers of an 'oligarchic restoration', a return to the Yeltsin years when powerful business magnates stalked the corridors of the Kremlin and used political leverage for economic advantage. The partisans of the 'oligarchic underground', their opponents argued, hoped for a weak president to emerge from the succession process to allow elements of state capture to be restored.

Democratic statists

The third group comprises the democratic statists. Their leading representative is another deputy head of the presidential administration, Surkov, responsible for the management of domestic politics.[136] As we saw earlier, he is the figure most closely associated with the practice of 'managed democracy' and later advanced the notion of 'sovereign democracy'. Some of the most active 'political technologists' were associated with this idea, notably Gleb Pavlovsky and Sergei Markov of the Foundation for Effective Politics (FEP). For Markov there was no fundamental division between the liberals and the *siloviki*. As he put it, 'The *siloviki* are in charge of defending the country's sovereignty and restoring the state's institutions, while liberals deal with economic reform and the functioning of the political system, what observers have described as managed democracy. This is a clear division of responsibility.'[137] This group had a distinctive idea of how democracy should work in Russian conditions, a view that denigrated the free flow of liberal pluralism but promoted a centrist state-oriented and technocratic approach to public affairs. Recognising that in Russia democracy is faced with the need to create the conditions for its own existence, they emphasised the management of political processes and constraints on pluralism. They are classically 'democratic but not liberal'.[138] Their approach was technocratic,

---

[135] Interview with Berezovsky, 'I am Plotting a New Russian Revolution', *The Guardian*, 13 April 2007.
[136] For his views, see Surkov, *Teksty 97–07.*
[137] Press conference with Markov at *Argumenty i fakty* press centre, 16 November 2005, in *JRL*, No. 9299, 2005, Item 15.
[138] See Fareed Zakaria, 'The Rise of Illiberal Democracy', *Foreign Affairs* 76, 6, November–December 1997, pp. 22–43.

seeking to depoliticise the management of public affairs, and hence acted as the praetorian guard of the administrative regime.

The notion of 'sovereign democracy' emerged to fill the ideological vacuum and to give intellectual coherence to statism.[139] The Duma enthusiastically supported this project, in November 2005 allocating over $17 million in an amendment to the 2006 budget to support non-profit organisations involved in developing civil society. At the same time, on 8 November 2005 a bill was introduced to tighten state control of non-governmental organisations, which came into effect in April 2006 and bound NGOs hand and foot in a shroud of red tape. NGOs had a year to bring their charters in line with the new legislation and to re-register with the Ministry of Justice. All half million NGOs in Russia were required to make regular reports to the tax authorities. Convicted criminals are not allowed to establish NGOs at all, a stipulation that disqualified Khodorkovsky and his Open Russia Foundation from providing support for NGOs in the future. The bill's sponsors considered foreign-financed NGOs a 'fifth column' in the pay of foreigners who subverted the sovereignty of political space in the country. Despite the establishment of the Public Chamber and promises of greater dialogue between the authorities and society, this measure was a clear response to the perceived 'orange' threat of popular intervention in the succession process. As a protest letter signed by some leading civic rights activists put it, 'We are convinced that what civil society needs is not "stabilisation", but intensive development. Total control will not promote development.'[140]

Economic liberals and technocrats

The fourth faction is the economic liberals (alternatively dubbed the technocrats), who remained responsible for the main features of economic policy throughout Putin's presidency. In his study on the merger of the *siloviki* and the oligarchs, which gave rise to the strange hybrid beast that he calls 'the *silovarchs*', Treisman argued 'Technocrats are kept in the cabinet to provide macroeconomic stability and credibility with the West.'[141] That may have been part of the story, but they also reflected one aspect of Putin's preferences and served as a factional balance to the protectionist autarkic views of the *siloviki*. They included

[139] For a collection of documents, see Nikita Garadzha (ed.), *Suverenitet* (Moscow: Evropa, 2006).
[140] www.hro.org/ngo/about/2005/11/10–2.php, in *JRL*, No. 9298, 17 November 2005, Item 23.
[141] Daniel Treisman, 'Putin's *Silovarchs*', *Orbis* 51, 1, Winter 2007, p. 146.

Alexei Kudrin as finance minister, German Gref until September 2007 at the head of MERT and Sergei Ignat'ev, the director of the Central Bank of Russia from 2002. Kudrin and Ignat'ev, together with the economist Vitaly Naishul, had been part of the original group of St Petersburg economists headed by Chubais in the 1980s. They studied the history of economic reform and comparative experience in Yugoslavia, Poland and Hungary, together with the work of western economists, and to a remarkable extent remained a powerful influence on Russian economic policy for the best part of two decades. They were no less technocratic than the democratic statists and thus tended to lose sight of the political and social consequences of their policies.

The liberals were deeply divided by the Yukos affair, with suggestions that both Kudrin and Gref ultimately endorsed the attack (although not the manner in which it was conducted), and sought by quiet means to mitigate the worst effects. Gref in general opposed the extension of state ownership over the energy sector and other areas, describing the creeping deprivatisation as 'Neanderthal thinking'. Chubais suggested that the creation of a government holding company in the aviation industry was a good idea, as was the promotion of Gazprom as a national champion, but he criticised the diversion of billions to buy Sibneft, or to increase its stake in car maker Avtovaz. Chubais noted the essential role that Putin's support played in the liberalisation of the electricity sector.[142] The notable exception to the policy of behind-the-scenes resistance was Andrei Illarionov, Putin's never-less-than-outspoken economic adviser between 2000 and his resignation on 27 December 2005. On numerous occasions Illarionov condemned the expropriation of Yukos assets, Khodorkovsky's imprisonment and the whole drift towards greater state control over business.

In the wake of the Yukos affair, the economic liberals launched a fightback. In 2006 Gref warned that bureaucrats were engaged in a 'bacchanalia' of confiscation of private businesses.[143] They were supported by Medvedev, who clearly aligned himself with the St Petersburg liberals. He was one of the small Kremlin group of five to six individuals who in the period before Khodorkovsky's arrest and Voloshin's resignation tried to stop the Yukos affair.[144] Asked about the concept of 'sovereign democracy', Medvedev warned that

[142] *Der Spiegel*, 25 September 2007.
[143] *Vremya novosti*, 19 May 2006, quoted by Pavel K. Baev, 'Putin's Fight Against Corruption Resembles Matryoshka Doll', *EDM* 3, 99, 22 May 2006.
[144] Evgeniya Pis'mennaya, 'Medved' s chelovecheskim litsom', *Russkii Newsweek*, No. 51, 17–23 December 2007, www.runewsweek.ru/theme/print.php?tid=147&rid=2267

Playing around with terms inevitably leads to a certain simplification. I think that 'sovereign democracy' is far from ideal as a term, but then, no term is ideal. It would be a lot more correct to speak of genuine democracy or simply of democracy that goes hand in hand with all-encompassing state sovereignty. Adding words to further define the term 'democracy' creates an odd aftertaste and gives rise to the thought that perhaps what is meant is some kind of different, unconventional democracy.[145]

Medvedev thus echoed the Italian slogan of the early post-war years, when there had been vigorous debates between 'Christian' and 'socialist' democracy, in favour of 'democracy without adjectives'. It is clear that the various factions in the succession took very different views of how democratic values should be instantiated in the Russian polity. By rejecting the idea of 'democracy with adjectives', Medvedev not only rejected residual notions of a *Sonderweg* for Russia, but he also signalled that he would not align himself with any particular faction.

In July 2007 he once again insisted that 'I still don't like this term [sovereign democracy]. In my opinion as a lawyer, playing up one feature of a full-fledged democracy – namely the supremacy of state authorities within the country and their independence [from influences] outside the country – is excessive and even harmful, because it is disorienting.'[146] In his speech at the Davos World Economic Forum in January 2007, he stressed (in English) the need for the Russian economy to diversify and to reduce its dependence on energy rents. He clearly disliked labels and ideological tags, although unequivocally aligned himself with the democratic perspective: 'We are well aware that no non-democratic state has ever become truly prosperous for one simple reason: freedom is better than non-freedom.'[147] He can be taken to represent the *civiliki* (people drawn from civilian professions), and more specifically the *zakoniki* based on the legal profession and economic liberals, but he also had a technocratic dimension that precluded any sharp liberal turn on his assumption of power.

Big business

The penultimate grouping has two facets. The first are the state corporations, which we shall discuss later. The giant holdings in which the state has a majority stake are major players in the Russian political

[145] 'Interview with *Expert* magazine', 25 July 2006, www.medvedev2008.ru/english_ 2006_07_25.htm.
[146] Interview with *Vedemosti*, cited in Nabi Abdullaev, 'A Soft-Spoken, "Smart Kid" Lawyer', *Moscow Times*, 2 November 2007, p. 1.
[147] 10 December 2007, www.bbc.co.uk/news.

system. These include Gazprom, Russian Railways (RZhD), the electricity monopoly RAO UES and its successor from 1 July 2008 Inter RAO
UES, Rosoboroneksport, Rosneft, Transneft and others largely de-
scended from the Soviet era, but now lacking the integrative mechanism
of the planning system to coordinate with the state. There have been
attempts to create interest group representation, as in the establishment
of the cross-party Duma caucus called 'Russia's Energy' in February
2000 with Chernomyrdin as chair, which claimed that a fifth of deputies
were involved in the oil and gas sector.[148] The venture soon collapsed,
killed off by the Yukos affair. As Petrov notes, 'The only such [integra-
tive] "mechanism" is the president, who acts as the arbiter when corporate interests collide.'[149] We have argued that one of the structural factors
elevating the presidency, irrespective of its constitutional status, is its
role in coordinating interests and pacifying conflicts at the institutional
and informal levels. In functional terms the presidency now acts to fill
the gap left by the disappearance of the Communist Party leadership;
and this is a role that will be required even if a constitutional amendment
reduced presidential powers.

The second group is less remarked on, largely because of its lack of a
clear identity and technocratic profile, namely the sectoral industrial
'faction'. Given the predominance of raw materials in the Russian economy, this group is sometimes dubbed the *syreviki*. This group increasingly set its gaze on global markets. For example, Lukoil planned to
invest $27bn abroad by 2017. Russia's largest steel company, Evraz, in
which Roman Abramovich owned 41 per cent of stock, bought Oregon
Steel Mills for $2.3bn, while Norilsk Nickel bought the nickel assets of
another US company.[150] Russia acquired a stake in EADS, the parent
company of Airbus Industrie, but hopes that this would give them a seat
on the board were blocked. A number of companies raised significant
capital by launching IPOs in foreign money markets. Alexei
Mordashov's Severstal raised nearly €1bn for 10 per cent of his company in London in 2006. Severstal had already gone global, and had
some 90,000 employees in Europe and North America. His bid earlier
that year to take over Europe's largest steel group, Arcelor, failed, as did
his bid for the Anglo-Dutch Corus group, but the transnationalisation
strategy remained. In October 2006 Oleg Deripaska's Rusal merged with
the smaller Sual and the Swiss-based Glencore to create the giant United

---

[148] Li-Chen Sim, *The Rise and Fall of Privatization in the Russian Oil Industry* (Basingstoke: Palgrave Macmillan, 2008), p. 47.
[149] Nikolai Petrov, 'Korporativizm *vs* regionalizm', *Pro et Contra* 11, 4–5, July–October 2007, p. 75.
[150] For details, see Dmitrii Simakov, 'Pora v lidery', *Vedomosti*, 29 December 2006, p. 1.

Company Rusal, producing 16 per cent of the world's aluminium. In other words, Russian big business was going global.

Pantin notes that 'The Russian political elite consists of various groups and factions, whose interests and ideological preferences differ and often come into conflict. We are dealing not only with the well-known "economic liberals" and "siloviki", but above all the representatives and lobbying interests of the fuel and energy and military-industrial complexes … who play a large and in some ways a decisive role.'[151] The pressure from big business on state policy has been well analysed, even in conditions of the establishment of a 'power vertical'.[152] However, there was no single coherent 'business lobby', with a fundamental division between the resource-based group and a non-commodities industrial lobby, represented by Chemezov. After the Yukos affair, the oil magnates became demonstratively loyal to the Kremlin.

Russia's growing economic power has been seen as a form of 'liberal imperialism' to apply a form of 'soft power' to reassert its interests in post-Soviet Eurasia. The empirical evidence for this is thin.[153] Business groupings, however, became important players in the development of Russian foreign policy.[154] Putin's strategy since the Yukos affair was undoubtedly to build 'national champions' that could compete in international markets, but this encountered significant political resistance in the west, reinforcing Russia's concerns about the application of 'double standards'.

Regional 'barons'

The final grouping is the 'regional barons', the heads of Russia's republics and regions. The shift from election to the effective appointment of governors from 2005 deprived regional leaders of an independent political legitimacy, yet some of the more powerful remained influential not only in their regions but also in national politics. There was little chance of a repetition of the 1999 scenario, which saw a powerful coalition of regional leaders preparing to take on the Kremlin, yet a number of

---

[151] V. I. Pantin, 'Politicheskoe samoopredelenie rossii v sovremennom mire: Osnovnye factory, tendentsii, perspektivy', *Polis*, No. 5, 2007, p. 108.

[152] S. P. Peregudov, *Korporatsii, obshchestvo, gosudarstvo: Evolyutsiya otnoshenii* (Moscow: no publisher, 2003); S. P. Peregudov, N. Yu. Lapina, I. S. Semenenko, *Gruppy interesov i rossiiskoe gosudarstvo* (Moscow: no publisher, 1999).

[153] Andrei P. Tsygankov, 'If Not by Tanks, then by Banks? The Role of Soft Power in Putin's Foreign Policy', *Europe-Asia Studies* 58, 7, November 2006, pp. 1079–99.

[154] See Peter Duncan, *'Oligarchs', Business and Russian Foreign Policy: From El'tsin to Putin*, Working Paper No. 83 (London: UCL School of Slavonic and East European Studies, Centre for the Study of Economic and Social Change in Europe, October 2007).

regional leaders, above all the presidents of some of the major republics, had strong local bases of support. These include President Shaimiev of Tatarstan, President Murtaza Rakhimov in neighbouring Bashkortostan, as well as Mayor Luzhkov in Moscow, joined by Governor Valentina Matvienko in St Petersburg. By the end of her first term in power in 2006, Matvienko had been able to merge the two main competing factions in the city government.[155] In Chechnya by the end of Putin's presidency, Ramzan Kadyrov enjoyed almost undivided power in the republic. However, there was little corporate solidarity in the group, and although potentially a 'faction', in the way we have defined the term, the gutting of the Federation Council and the establishment of the toothless State Council deprived them of a collective formal platform to advance their interests, and they were careful to avoid being sucked into factional politics at the level of the administrative regime.

In conclusion, it is clear that different socio-political formations give rise to varying political outcomes. Ukraine's more strongly institutional-ised clan-type structures endows the country with an entrenched fragmentation that favours a more pluralistic political environment, resulting in greater uncertainty of political outcomes. In Russia the sphere of 'effective politics' was populated less by the Duma, political parties and regional leaders than by factions within the regime itself. Those able to wield the 'power' resource were in a particularly strong position. The left–right political spectrum was internalised within the regime, with a more liberal faction supporting macroeconomic probity and international economic integration, while a more interventionist wing favoured an active industrial policy and greater social spending. It is important to stress, however, that under Putin a 'Moscow consensus' was forged that rejected the neo-liberalism of the 1990s while remaining committed to economic modernisation and a constrained free market (the 'ordo-liberalism' that will be discussed in the next chapter), which was tempered by a greater awareness of social responsibility accompan-ied by a broad belief in Russia's status as a great power. The Moscow consensus, however, was as dualistic as the state itself and failed to create the conditions for the rule of law, secure property rights and all the other essentials of a genuinely competitive economy. When it came to power and resource issues, the factions were sharply divided, and never more so than when the succession approached.

---

[155] These were the Komsomol alliance headed by the deputy governor Viktor Lobko and the 'PSB Fraction' headed by the head of the financial-economic bloc, Mikhail Oseevsky. Daniil Tsygankov, 'Valentina Matvienko's Second Term: From Ambitious Projects to Threats of Removal', *Russian Analytical Digest*, No. 67, 9 November 2009, p. 9.

4   A genuinely political economy

Each of the main groups identified above reflect a facet of Putin's political personality and his contradictory representation of the power and modernisation challenges facing the country. Looked at another way, these factions (notably the security establishment and the liberal economists) represented real domestic constituencies to which the leadership had to respond, and the balancing strategy proved to be an effective way of managing them, even though the price was the political stalemate inherent in the passive revolution. It is quite possible that a future leader will shift from balancing to confrontation, and while this would open up a clear path in one direction or another, the disruptive effect would be high as the Caeserist strategy was implemented. Putin instead remained above faction, but all of the factions had a stake in Putin's presidency and in turn his leadership was embroiled in each of the factions. Each embodied an element of the programmatic orientations of his presidency, but in the end his presidency was less Bonapartist than hegemonic; not standing above factions but constantly acting as the faction manager to ensure that the balance within the regime was not disrupted. At certain times and over certain issues, a faction or alliance of factions would be stronger and, commensurately, their opponents eclipsed. For example, while the attack on Yukos was led by the *siloviki*, the democratic statists, concerned with the defence of the prerogatives of the state, joined in to provide ideological justification, and even certain liberals such as Kudrin, concerned about fiscal recovery, endorsed the assault. The net effect, though, was the eclipse of the liberals, and their influence never recovered under Putin's presidency to the levels of his first three years in power. When it came to the succession, however, Putin demonstrated his independence from the *siloviki*, and under Medvedev the balance of the regime tilted in favour of the liberal-technocrats.

The presidency and factionalism

Although the factional tendencies identified above existed and contributed to policy debates during Putin's presidency, his leadership was not
factionalised. By that I mean that no distinctive faction was able to
dominate his leadership, even though his leadership was shaped by the
struggle between factions. Putin certainly listened to the various views,
but in the end his policy preferences tended to predominate. While the
administrative regime was factionalised, the state was not, although this
was an ever-present danger, and the presidency could draw on the
normative resources of the unfactionalised state to retain its autonomy.
The factions interact with institutions in a relatively flexible and yet
constrained manner. As North points out, 'institutions define and limit
the set of choices of individuals'.[1] While informal relations are important, they are constrained in the Russian context by the formal rules laid
out in the constitution and subsequent normative acts. However, political institutions are unable to regulate activities with universal application to the whole population, including the elite, and there is differential
access to the policy-making process and systemic abuse of the rule of law
(especially through the procuracy). The factionalised elite constrained
the executive, but the informal nature of these shadowy accountability
mechanisms fostered systemic corruption and elements of autocratic
rule. In the first part of this chapter, we will examine the political
implications of this, and in the second the focus will be on political
economy.

Putin as faction manager

While the elite is factionalised, it is at the same time extraordinarily
homogeneous. There are no fundamental religious, ethnic or politically
represented class cleavages, the regional factor is relatively subdued
and even generational influences are mild. Indeed, the flatness of the
political landscape, quite extraordinary given the size and diversity of
the country, in part explains why factions are the main aggregative
institution. The political pluralism that is generated by social cleavages
is subsumed into intra-regime factional conflict. The factions are overwhelmingly based on professional orientation and policy preferences,
and even ideological orientations are not based on substantive value
differences. The relative ease with which Putin brought the regions to
heel reflects Soviet and imperial traditions of subordination to the strong

---

[1] North, *Institutions, Institutional Change and Economic Performance*, p. 4.

central state. As early as 1993, forty-nine regions favoured the centre reasserting itself against regional fragmentation;[2] and when it came to abolishing gubernatorial elections, regional leaders acquiesced as much for cultural as for political reasons.[3]

We have noted that already under Yeltsin the presence of 'clans' had been identified. Whatever we call these groups, their existence has been apparent since at least the mid-1990s. Yeltsin was both more susceptible to falling under their sway than Putin, but he was also more robust than the latter in dealing with them when he finally swung into action. When he became convinced of a threat to his own authority, Yeltsin did not hesitate to dismiss people whom he felt were undermining his own team or were destabilising the balance of power as a whole in the administration. The notable case of this was the sacking of his long-term confidant Korzhakov between the two rounds of the election in July 1996; the dismissal of Berezovsky as deputy head of the Security Council in 1997 is another example of the removal of an individual whom Yeltsin felt was acting too independently.[4]

The Putin administration initially drew on staff from the Yeltsin team, notably Voloshin at the head of the presidential administration and Kasyanov as prime minister. At the same time, a parallel administration was built up in the Kremlin, and gradually it dispensed with the services of Yeltsin's old guard. This was accompanied by a shift in policy priorities in the middle period of Putin's leadership. Putin's administration retained its autonomy, and his political regime did not fall prey to factional divisions. However, although Putin kept his personal autonomy, his administration was riven by factional struggles. The appointment of Fradkov as a 'technical' prime minister in March 2004 was designed in part to ensure that the factional struggles did not spill over into the work of the government.

Fradkov had no clear factional identity, although he inclined towards the *siloviki*, but from Putin's perspective his key advantage was that he was able to damp down factional conflict in the cabinet while ensuring that there would be no liberal backlash over the Yukos affair and that the government was fully subordinated to the presidency. The government remained firmly technocratic, while Fradkov himself kept a low profile

[2] Darrell Slider, Vladimir Gimpel'son and Sergei Chugrov, 'Political Tendencies in Russia's Regions: Evidence from the 1993 Parliamentary Elections', *Slavic Review* 53, 3, Fall 1994, pp. 726, 730–1.
[3] J. Paul Goode, 'The Puzzle of Putin's Gubernatorial Appointments', *Europe-Asia Studies* 59, 3, May 2007, pp. 365–99.
[4] For example, Colton, *Yeltsin*, pp. 404–6; Leon Aron, *Boris Yeltsin: A Revolutionary Life* (London: HarperCollins, 2000), pp. 640–1.

and came up with no political initiatives of his own. This in part reflected the constitutional position, which reserves political questions (above all foreign and security matters, as formulated in the 1996 law on the government) for the presidency while the government deals with the economy, budgetary issues and social programmes, but it was also a feature of his personality. His predecessor, Kasyanov, had also kept his head down on political matters, but he had a powerful political presence of his own and owed no loyalty to the Kremlin, and this in part was the reason for his dismissal on 24 February 2004.

Putin was more of a conciliator than Yeltsin and rarely resorted to the dismissal option. Putin's overriding concern was to balance the influence of the factions. For example, in November 2006 Sergei Meshcheryakov, allied with Sechin, was moved from the MVD's Economic Security Department, to head a less influential agency, the Department for Countering Organised Crime and Terrorism. This was perceived as a setback for Sechin's *siloviki*. The new head was Yevgeny Shkolov, a former intelligence officer who had served with Putin in East Germany.[5] Medvedev and Sechin were clearly rivals, although both were close to Putin. Inter-institutional rivalry constantly came to the surface, spreading disturbing ripples across the Russian political scene. Ruslan Khasbulatov had used parliament as an instrument of factional struggle (rather than wholly legitimate political contestation) in his struggle with Yeltsin in 1992–3, and this served as a powerful warning against allowing an institution to be captured by opponents of the presidency. The coincidence of factions and departments of course occurs, with economic and financial departments tending to the liberals while security agencies are the natural home of the *siloviki*. However, the ability of a faction to capture an institution and to use it as a base for its own advancement is rare.

Standard images of Putin's leadership veer between seeing him as an all-powerful strongman, dominating the political Olympus, or as balancing between the various power groups and governing on the basis of the Kremlin consensus. Neither view captures the nature of the Kremlin consensus. Putin's presidency retained its autonomy but was forced to act as a genuinely hegemonic agency, exerting the instruments at its disposal to win the consent of the ruling elite. The balance within the presidential hegemony changed over time to reflect the political conjuncture, but while the political regime over which Putin presided was factionalised, his genius was to ensure that it did not fall prey to factional

---

[5] Roman Shleinov, 'Kremlevskii kholding: Sliyaniya & poglosheniya', *Novaya Gazeta*, No. 88, 20 November 2006.

divisions. In broad terms Putin's administration maintained a consistent and coherent policy agenda. This does not mean that it was not buffeted by various factional struggles, but his administration retained an internal unity (the external autonomy defined earlier) that allowed it to consolidate an extraordinary dominance over social forces and informal interest aggregations, while at the same time remaining loyal to a state-dominated modernisation process.

Those who were at the core of his administration in most cases had nothing to do with the KGB or its successor agencies. These included Abramovich, whose wealth in the Putin years increased at least tenfold, and he remained one of Putin's closest confidants. It was Abramovich (together with Voloshin) who in the first place had recommended Putin to Yeltsin as successor, and Putin took his advice in his own succession.[6] Medvedev had no known links to the security services, and neither did the former Kremlin chief of staff Voloshin or his successor after Medvedev, Sobyanin. Even Sergei Ivanov, Putin's former KGB colleague, had a strained relationship with other security officials because of his independence of mind and ambition. Putin, moreover, was not a high-flier in the KGB and had only with great reluctance agreed to take over the directorship of the FSB in 1998–9. Despite the attack on those whom Putin considered 'criminal' oligarchs, notably Berezovsky and Gusinsky, and the politicised Khodorkovsky, Putin legitimated the property settlement of the 1990s and collaborated with most major entrepreneurs and defended the interests of big capital: not only Abramovich but also Oleg Deripaska, Mikhail Fridman, Vladimir Potanin, Victor Vekselberg, Vagit Alekperov and Alisher Usmanov, all creations of the Yeltsin era. These became so-called 'state oligarchs' in the late Putin era, ready to accommodate the interests of the regime, although this certainly did not shield them from factional attacks.

Putin's power rested on an 'internal coalition' of economic liberals, democratic statists occupying the centre ground of politics, security statists closer to the authoritarian end of the political spectrum, non-political technocrats, and regional elites. We suggest that this is an 'internal' coalition because it is not like the standard notion of a coalition as the coming together of independent political forces to create a government; but this is the 'coalescence' of factions within a regime, united in their support of the president and his patriotic-statist

---

[6] According to Stanislav Belkovsky (author's interview 3 March 2008), Putin met with Abramovich on the evening of Friday 7 December 2007, once the Duma results were out, and apparently advocated Medvedev's immediate nomination. No other source confirms this account of the meeting.

policy programme of national modernisation, but with different emphases on how best this could be achieved. The internal coalition was fragile and in the absence of a strong leader could easily disintegrate. There was some evidence that this was beginning to happen in the final period of Putin's presidency. As the succession struggle intensified, this internal coalition began to lose its stability, only to be reformed with Putin's help in a new configuration once Medvedev was inaugurated as president in May 2008.

These tendencies were often hostile to each other, and indeed the policy drift from Putin's middle period, against the background of the Yukos affair, reflected the stalemate that they had fought themselves into. Although the various strands are difficult to disentangle and tend to be pursued in the *couloirs* of power, their logic can be studied in a manner appropriate for the examination of issues of public policy. The factions represent debates and viewpoints that reflect fundamental strategies for modernisation, development and interaction with the rest of the world. This is not quite 'normal' politics, however, and Byzantine court intrigue accompanied the manipulative techniques of electoral and political management dubbed 'virtual politics' by Andrew Wilson.[7]

Two political systems operate in parallel. On the one hand, there is the system of open public politics, with all of the relevant institutions described in the constitution and pursued with pedantic regulation in formal terms. At this level parties are formed, elections fought and parliamentary politics conducted. However, at another level a second para-political world exists based on informal groups and factions operating within the framework of court politics. This Byzantine level never openly challenges the leader but seeks to influence the decisions of the supreme arbiter. This second level contains elements of 'virtual' politics, the attempt to manipulate public opinion and shape electoral outcomes through the exercise of manipulative practices. However, despite the fact that Putin strongly opposed the 'virtualisation' of politics,[8] by permitting the pseudo-politics of the second system he ensured that the formal side of political life was liable to become little more than 'show-politics', a spectacle to satisfy the formal demands of the system and the international community, but lacking the efficacy that, however limited, is one of the characteristics of modern

---

[7] Andrew Wilson, *Virtual Politics: Faking Democracy in the Post-Soviet World* (New Haven, CT: Yale University Press, 2005).

[8] A point made by Gleb Pavlovsky who, if anyone, should know, 'Predstavitel' nepredstavlennykh', p. 54.

democracies. By seeking to reduce the inevitable contradictions that accompany public politics into a matter of technocratic management, Putin inevitably exacerbated the contradictions between groups within the regime itself. Putin placed a high value on civil peace and thus opposed a return to the conflict-prone politics typical of the 1990s, but this reinforced the pseudo-politics typical of court systems. Putin failed to grasp the essence of 'the political' – agonistic public contestation over equally valid public goods and policies – and instead fostered the extended administrative regulation of public life and para-political factionalism.

The presidency was not captured by a faction or an interest group but instead was forced to operate within the framework of a 'regime' within which it tried to retain its hegemony. Putin faced numerous limitations on his power, above all through contending factions, the existence of powerful economic interests in society, the entrenched powers of some regional bosses, and the presidency's unwillingness openly to repudiate democratic procedures and continued commitment to elections as the source of the legitimacy of the Russian polity. The strong presidency in Russia solved a number of problems, above all by establishing a clear constitutional source of authority; but at the same time its use of the administrative regime created a number of new problems, notably the suffocation of civic initiative and representative politics from below and inhibiting the development of state autonomy from above (notably an independent judiciary and the separation of regime from the state). With so much power concentrated in so few hands, there was a constant problem of control and efficacy. The duality of development in Russia meant that a number of political trajectories were possible, including on the one side the consolidation of authoritarianism if the administrative regime was strengthened; or the development of autonomous demo-cratic procedures if the constitutional state could affirm its independ-ence from the regime. Hence the importance of the succession: the person who managed the regime would decide the fate of the country for the next generation.

Political role of the siloviki

Because of the salience of the issue and the misrepresentation of Putin's administration as little more than the rule of the special services, it is worth returning to the question of the political role of the *siloviki*. Putin and many of the *siloviki* he appointed to top positions were trained when Yury Andropov was head of the KGB between 1967 and 1982. He undertook a programme of modernisation in the agency and instilled it with a new sense of purpose and pride. Andropov briefly led the Soviet Union between November 1982 and February 1984, when he launched a programme of 'authoritarian modernisation', although there was far more of the former than the latter. He sought to make the Soviet Union more competitive in its struggle against the west, but without weakening any of the system's authoritarianism. On coming to power in 1985, Gorbachev quickly realised the bankruptcy of such an approach. Later he moved against the formal powers of the secret police, and by 1991 they were marginalised. As Yeltsin's popular support eroded, he came to rely on the *siloviki*, to the point that his last prime ministers all had a security background. He had begun with economic liberals, moved to economic statists and ended up with security officials.

As a result of the Yukos affair and the shock of the Beslan hostage crisis in September 2004, in which over 300 schoolchildren were killed, Putin the liberal was gradually over-shadowed by Putin the statist. Putin's étatisation programme was beset by contradictions, not the least of which was the danger that he would be captured by the bureaucratic machine that had reconstituted itself since the fall of the Soviet Union. Yet Putin did not become hostage to the system, and the presidency retained its autonomy, although embedded in the framework of fighting for hegemonic predominance over the factions within the regime. Putin certainly did not go all the way and allow the security forces free rein; this would have upset factional balance and ultimately undermined the autonomy of the presidency.

Various webs of conspiracy sought to implicate the *siloviki*, or at least a 'rogue' faction, in the slow-motion murder of Alexander Litvinenko with polonium 210, administered on 1 November 2006 and with death coming only on 23 November. Litvinenko was a former KGB officer who had fled to London in 2000 and joined the exiled oligarch Berezovsky in campaigning against Putin's regime, and together they produced a film and then a book called *Blowing up Russia*, alleging that the FSB had been behind the apartment block bombings in September 1999.[9] Coming after the murder of the journalist Anna Politkovskaya on 7 October 2006 and the mysterious illness of the economist Yegor Gaidar on a visit to Ireland on 24 November, the events appeared somehow to be linked. This certainly was the view of Chubais, the architect of the 1990s privatisation programme, who argued that the 'chain of deaths of ... Politkovskaya, Litvinenko, and Gaidar would perfectly correspond to the interests and the vision of those

---

[9] Alexander Litvinenko with Yuri Feltshtinsky, *Blowing up Russia: The Soviet Plot to Bring Back KGB Terror* (London: Gibson Square, 2007).

people who are talking about a forceful, unconstitutional change of power in Russia as a possible option'.[10] These events remain shrouded in the fog of conspiracy, but one prominent version suggests that the aim of those responsible for Litvinenko's murder was to force Putin to stay in power after 2008, by creating conditions in which it would be impossible for him to step down. This was the putative aim of the so-called 'third term' party headed by Sechin, the exemplary representative of the *siloviki*.

The alleged pre-eminent role of the *siloviki* has been challenged by a number of studies. Renz questions whether the growth in *silovik* numbers was a conscious strategy by Putin to enhance their influence and thereby to create a more authoritarian regime; and in any case she argues that there was no common 'military mindset' among them advocating relatively more authoritarian policies. In her view, they are far from dominant in the policy-making process. Only nine of forty-seven leading officials in the presidential administration in 2005 had a security background, and none of the nine was in the top echelons of power. Only two of ten presidential advisers were *siloviki*. Putin simply relied on people with whom he had worked in the past, and security officials were just one group of many. The majority of Putin's *siloviki* in any case had, like Putin, enjoyed varied careers. They certainly did not constitute a coherent clan, she insists, as the concept of 'militocracy' implies.[11]

Putin's regime was certainly oriented towards the retention and perpetuation of power, but at the same time it had a clear ideological orientation towards a state-shaped developmental agenda. The presidency sought to retain its autonomy from the factions and corporate interests. For example, early in Putin's first term Putin's old colleagues in the Lubyanka and in the Security Council developed a restrictive 'information security doctrine', but he rejected their ideas and a modified doctrine was adopted. The *siloviki*, moreover, endorsed the endeavours of the democratic statists to remould the domestic sphere, where pluralism was diminished and party life and elections were closely regulated. Pressure on NGOs, especially those concerned with the defence of human rights and public advocacy, became more intrusive, especially following the adoption of the NGO law in 2006. Even here it is important to distinguish between the military and the security establishment.

---

[10] Comments on RTR Rossiya Television, Associated Press, 29 November 2006, reported by Charles Gurin, 'Gaidar's Apparent Poisoning Fuels Conspiracy Theories', The Jamestown Foundation, *EDM* 3, 222, 1 December 2006.
[11] Bettina Renz, 'Putin's Militocracy? An Alternative Interpretation of *Siloviki* in Contemporary Russian Politics', *Europe-Asia Studies* 58, 6, 2006, pp. 903–24.

A survey of Russian military officers reported by Rivera and Rivera, for example, demonstrated their strong support for 'the basic tenets of democracy'.[12] At the same time, Putin was careful to ensure that the military was on his side. On his fifty-fifth birthday on 7 October 2007, Putin demonstratively invited a range of top military officials, and they in turn swore loyalty to him.[13]

The impact of the *siloviki* on domestic affairs is hard to demonstrate. The appointment of five *siloviki* as heads of the seven federal districts when they were established in 2000 has often been adduced as evidence that the *siloviki* had come to power, but since then the replacements to the original seven have had a diverse background. Despite much talk of a surge of generals coming to power in the regions, this has not been the case in practice. In the twenty-six gubernatorial elections held in *oblast*s and *krai*s between 26 March 2000 and January 2001, candidates from security agencies participated in only four (Kaliningrad, Kamchatka, Voronezh and Ulyanovsk) and won in only three (Vice-Admiral Valery Dorogin came a poor fourth in Kamchatka). The election of General Vladimir Shamanov, who had a tough track record in Chechnya, as governor of Ulyanovsk *oblast* seemed to be the most spectacular case of the military coming to power, but once in office his behaviour was indistinguishable from other governors and his team came from all over the country with different interests.[14] Other aspects of his identity (he had been a sociologist by training) came to the fore. Shamanov was not successful as governor and his tenure was not renewed by Putin. It would thus be an exaggeration to talk of the 'militarisation' of Russian regional politics under Putin.

Putin did, however, rely on an 'inner court' of some close advisers, but not all of them with a *silovik* background. An informal 'politburo' dominated, which included FSB director Nikolai Patrushev, Victor Ivanov, Sechin and was supported earlier by Ustinov, and which met on Saturday mornings.[15] Just beyond this *silovik* core were a number of people who were close to Putin. These include Vladimir Yakunin, who in 2005 took over as head of Russian Railways (RZhD); Victor Cherkesov, the head of FSKN; Sergei Chemezov, general director of the arms export monopoly Rosoboroneksport and later head of Russian Technologies; and Deputy Prime Minister Sergei Naryshkin, chair of the board of the

[12] Rivera and Rivera, 'The Russian Elite Under Putin', p. 128.
[13] *Nezavisimaya gazeta*, 8 October 2007.
[14] Derek S. Hutcheson, *Political Parties in the Russian Regions* (London: RoutledgeCurzon, 2003), p. 45.
[15] Kryshtanovkaya and White, 'Inside the Putin Court'.

Channel One television station and deputy chair of Rosneft who in May 2008 became head of the presidential administration under Medvedev. Other key figures beyond the *siloviki* included Yury Kovalchyuk, chairman of the board of directors of Bank Rossiya; Alexander Grigor'ev, director of Gosrezerv, the state reserve agency; Dmitry Kozak, the former presidential envoy to the southern federal district and from September 2007 the regional development minister until in October 2008 he took charge of preparations for the Winter Olympics in Sochi in 2014. These people represented an extraordinary concentration of political and economic power. While in broad terms they shared a dirigiste perspective, this did not preclude some intense factional fighting.

The issue of new power-sharing treaties with Tatarstan and Chechnya is an example of policy debate taking the form of factional conflict. Putin repudiated the system of bilateral treaties, and by July 2005 all forty-six had lapsed. However, with elections coming up and concerned about renewed separatist militancy in the region, the Kremlin needed Tatarstan's support. The renewed treaty with Tatarstan was ratified against considerable opposition by the Duma on 9 February 2007.[16] Long-drawn-out discussions with Chechnya tried to formalise its exceptional status with a bilateral treaty. Delays were provoked by Moscow's fears of granting excessive powers and privileges to the Chechenised leadership in the republic, above all in the economic and taxation spheres. The president, Ramzan Kadyrov, was particularly keen to assert the republic's control over the oil industry. The *siloviki* in the Kremlin and their allies did not trust Kadyrov. Opposition to a power-sharing treaty with the republic was led by Sechin, his close friend Mironov at the head of the Federation Council, and Victor Ilyukhin, head of the Duma's security committee. The *siloviki* lost the battle for Tatarstan, but over Chechnya they were able to have their way, and no doubt as part of the deal that brought Kadyrov to the presidency in March 2007, he abandoned the idea.

Foreign policy was a sphere relatively insulated from factional conflict. Rivera and Rivera note that 'few analysts have expressed the expectation that a Kremlin dominated by *siloviki* will behave more aggressively in the international arena or observed any actual increase in the use of force by Moscow'.[17] Indeed, foreign policy under Putin until 2007 was characterised by the search for consensus and strategic co-operation

---

[16] The debate was one of the most heated seen in the Duma for years, and even United Russia split over the issue, but in the end the motion was carried by 306 votes for, 110 against and one abstention. Andrei Smirnov, 'Tatar Treaty Suggests Dissent Inside Kremlin on Regional Policy', *EDM* 4, 33, 15 February 2007.

[17] Rivera and Rivera, 'The Russian Elite Under Putin', p. 127.

with the west, although the attempt to assert Russia's views on world issues provoked much criticism. Russia's more assertive foreign-policy stance in the late Putin years was advanced with as much vigour by the democratic statists as it was by the *siloviki*. Foreign policy was dominated by Putin personally, seeking to balance the various interests at home while advancing a policy of Russian autonomy abroad. Putin struggled to ensure that Russia was not boxed into becoming the centre of a new alternative bloc (for example, in the Shanghai Co-operation Organisation) in a putatively multipolar world. The distinction between autonomy and alternativity is crucial to understanding Russia's foreign policy in the Putin era. Russia wanted to be treated as an equal in world affairs, but it certainly did not want to become the core of a balancing anti-western pole in some sort of replay of the Cold War.[18]

The 2007–8 electoral cycle was conducted in the shadow of deteriorating relations with the west. It is not entirely clear how the factional interests map on to what undoubtedly was increased hostility to the west in the late Putin presidency. The general philosophy of the period was summed up by Pavlovsky: 'The main challenge in the contemporary world is clearly American expansion. And no one, I think, except a sovereign, resilient and modernised Russia can contain American expansion … And if America is not contained, in a friendly but firm and consistent manner, it will destroy the international system.'[19] In the light of such thinking, Putin had clearly taken the decision to assert Russia's interests, but the role of the special services in taking that decision is unknown. As we shall see, the liberals questioned the economic consequences of strained relations with the west, but there was in general a broad consensus in Moscow in favour of an independent foreign policy.

Factionalism and the new dirigisme

The 'over-mighty subjects' had been tamed and now the Kremlin went on the offensive, not only to ensure its own prerogatives in economic policy and political life, but also to forge a new model of what Karl Wittfogel called 'a genuinely political economy',[20] where the state's preferences predominated. The Yukos affair represented a major disciplinary act, not only ensuring that business leaders stayed out of politics, but also bringing the state back into the heart of business life. This was

[18] See Sakwa, *Putin*, Chapter 10.
[19] 'Chego zhdat' ot Putina?', 19 October 2007, http://www.lenta.ru/conf/pavlovsky/.
[20] Karl A. Wittfogel, *Oriental Despotism: A Comparative Study of Total Power* (New Haven, CT: Yale University Press, 1957), p. 22.

achieved not so much by renationalisation as through 'deprivatisation'. Economic policy was no longer to be a matter purely for autonomous economic agents but would have to be coordinated with the state, while the state itself became a major player in the economic arena (in particular in the energy sector) through its 'national champions', above all Gazprom and Rosneft. The equivalent of deprivatisation in the political sphere was 'de-autonomisation'. As long as the Kremlin had adequate resources, in material, political capital and authority terms, to rein in potentially fractious elites, systemic balance could be maintained, but there was an ever-present threat of defection accompanied by the stasis associated with political stalemate.

The Yukos affair and energy rents

In energy policy the dominant paradigm until the Yukos affair was the liberal one, although it was far from unchallenged, and policy in this area was driven by the struggle between rival groups for influence.[21] Russia's energy policy as a whole continues to lack detailed strategic perspectives and according to Tompson is a confused mass of tactical expediency, reflecting the struggle for economic and political power between the remnants of the old Yeltsin faction (created through the financial sector) and the new Putin elite, whose power is pre-eminently of administrative origin.[22] This broad split operated in the Yukos affair, accompanied by the structural factor identified by Tompson of 'A state characterized by weak regulatory and rule-enforcement capabilities but enjoying a hypertrophied capacity for the use of force'; facing institutional weakness, the authorities fell back on 'time-honoured methods of coercion and direct control'.[23] The standard interpretation suggests a tension between economic liberals and the *siloviki*, and there is no doubt that these were the two main factions involved. The Yukos affair was the most vivid manifestation of a faction able to pursue its policy agenda in one sphere, but in the event the Yukos affair did not signal a wholesale attack by the state on big business.

Following the exile of Berezovsky and Gusinsky, no substantial opposition remained in society. From 2003, however, Gleb Pavlovsky argues that 'the authorities encountered a new systemic opposition within itself,

---

[21] Peter Rutland, 'Oil, Politics and Foreign Policy', in David Lane (ed.), *The Political Economy of Russian Oil* (Lanham, MD: Rowman & Littlefield, 1999), pp. 163–88.
[22] William Tompson, 'A Frozen Venezuela? The Resource Curse and Russian Politics', in Michael Ellman (ed.), *Russia's Oil and Natural Gas: Bonanza or Curse?* (London and New York: Anthem Press, 2006), pp. 189–212.
[23] *Ibid.*, p. 208.

seeking to modify the president's course from within, relying on part of the state's special services under the flag of supporting and strengthening a "weak" president'.[24] The aim of the intra-systemic opposition, according to Pavlovsky, was to achieve a redistribution of property and a change of elites at the national and regional level, accompanied by the development of a state ideology that would allow the 'new oligarchy' to consolidate power. A new breed of Kremlin 'oligarchs' had already been subordinated to state and quasi-state corporations, and now the administrative regime disciplined the independent oligarchs. If these new Kremlin oligarchs won, Pavlovsky noted, Putin would become their hostage. The Yukos affair was presented as curbing predatory capitalism and thus gained a degree of popular legitimacy, but it was primarily designed to rebuff an attempt to transcend the passive revolution, and by breaking the stalemate of revolution/restoration would have challenged the privileges of the elite that exploited the ambiguities of the situation. The Yukos affair saw the destruction of the nascent bourgeoisie's ability to pursue independent policies, and instead they became a subaltern class. Big business was subordinated politically to the state through a combination of deprivatisation and de-autonomisation. The oligarchs were tamed politically, but magnates were allowed to expand their business empires and wealth, and thus continued to act as a counterweight to the *siloviki*.[25] Putin was too wily a politician to become hostage to any one group.

Putin's policy agenda got bogged down in the middle part of his presidency by the struggle over ownership questions, and in particular the belief that the 'oligarchs' represented a threat to the achievement of his goals, and thus there was the need to reassert state prerogatives in the sphere of political economy and economic policy-making.[26] This took the form of the Yukos affair, which deflected attention away from Putin's reformist agenda and exacerbated divisions within the administration. The priority appeared to be to deny oligarchs influence over the economy, politics and the media, a concern that appeared marginal to the real issues facing the country. After a long trial, Khodorkovsky was jailed and the Yukos company was

---

[24] Gleb Pavlovsky, '"Brat – 3"', *Ekspert*, No. 32, 1 September 2003, in *Ekspert: Luchshie materialy*, No. 2, 2007, pp. 63–7, at p. 63.

[25] Cf. Vladimir Shlapentokh, 'Wealth Versus Political Power: The Russian Case', *Communist and Post-Communist Studies* 37, 2, June 2004, pp. 135–60.

[26] See William Tompson, 'Putin and the "Oligarchs": A Two-sided Commitment Problem', in Alex Pravda (ed.), *Leading Russia: Putin in Perspective* (Oxford: Oxford University Press, 2005), pp. 179–202; also William Tompson, 'Putting Yukos in Perspective', *Post-Soviet Affairs* 21, 2, April–June 2005, pp. 159–82.

dismembered; the reformist agenda was blunted and factional conflict in the Kremlin exacerbated. In the new model of political economy, the regime sought to defend its claimed prerogatives against the business elite.

Except in cases where the presidency perceived an outright political threat to its position, this did not necessarily entail outright nationalisation. As Hanson notes, 'corrupt relations between big business and the state allow Russia's political elite to dispose of resource rents fairly freely without recourse to direct state ownership'.[27] Russia under Putin adopted elements of the 'ordo-liberalism' pursued in early twentieth-century Germany. One of its leading exponents, Walter Eucken, argued that the development of the economic order was too important to be left to the operation of spontaneous market forces, and thus purposive state action (*ordnungspolitik*) was required. Influenced by Carl Schmitt, ordo-liberals argued that by the end of the nineteenth century the state had been captured by private interests. Their response was not for the state to manage the economy, but to establish a framework of juridical institutions that would foster the development of the market economy while insulating the state from economic pressures and avoiding the undue politicisation of the economy.[28] In formal terms there are undoubted elements of ordo-liberalism in contemporary Russia, although given the regime's technocratic and pragmatic bias, this has emerged out of situational rather than ideological considerations. What the Russian case does demonstrate once again is that 'there is no simple correlation between the development of market forces and the emergence of the rule of law and liberalism', and thus 'The rule of law cannot be engineered; it needs to be located in a historical and political context.'[29]

Khodorkovsky was convinced that the attack on Yukos was a function of factional struggles. In an interview three months before his arrest, he argued that the struggle between Kremlin factions in anticipation of the March 2004 presidential elections lay behind the assault.[30] He was probably right, and we have identified Sechin as the main advocate of a forceful solution to the Khodorkovsky 'problem', with FSB director Patrushev tagging along. One of the main detectives working on the Yukos case, Salavat Karimov, is alleged to have reported to Sechin twice

---

[27] Philip Hanson, 'The Resistible Rise of State Control in the Russian Oil Industry', *Eurasian Geography and Economics* 50, 1, 2009, p. 14.
[28] Jayasuriya, 'The Exception Becomes the Norm', pp. 122–3.
[29] *Ibid.*, pp. 124.
[30] United Financial Group, *Morning Comment*, 7 July 2003; cited by Philip Hanson, 'The Turn to Statism in Russian Economic Policy', *The International Spectator* 42, 1, March 2007, pp. 29–42.

a week on progress on the case. However, Sechin's *silovik* credentials have been questioned,[31] and there remains disagreement over what precisely his faction sought to get out of the prosecution of Khodorkovsky. Their views overlap with those of the democratic statists, calling for greater state involvement in the economy and a more aggressive role of Russian capital abroad, where they joined forces with the industrial lobby. The *siloviki*, like the Yeltsinite oligarchs earlier, fused power and property, although now with 'business capture' taking the place of 'state capture'.[32]

The attack on Khodorkovsky was prompted less by ideological factors than by concerns about power; and property redistribution was a consequence rather than a cause.[33] Belkovsky argues that the merger of Yukos with Sibneft (in effect, the incorporation of Sibneft) 'would have entailed the beginning of the end of the Russian Federation'.[34] The Yukos affair helped catalyse a powerful but dependent distributional coalition, headed by Rosneft. It feasted on the corpse of Yukos, but did so only as long as it remained subordinate to the presidency. The independent 'oligarch' as a subject of Russian politics disappeared. Instead, dynamic coalitions between business leaders (notably the now dominant class of 'state oligarchs') and administrative officials came together to exploit opportunities. Political loyalty for both groups was the condition for their continued existence. Intensified democratisation was not in the immediate interests of any of these dependent coalitions, although in the long-term more democracy would allow them to develop as independent actors and guarantee their property rights.

The *silovik* preference for a dirigiste economic model promoted the gradual deprivatisation of the Russian oil industry. The share of state-controlled companies in oil production rose from 24 per cent in 2003 to 37 per cent in 2007.[35] The major beneficiary of Yukos's expropriation was Rosneft, which became Russia's largest oil major with a capitalisation by 2007 of $78 billion and with an annual production of 100 million tonnes. The destruction of Mikhail Gutseriev's Russneft company, the seventh largest Russian oil producer, in 2007 marked yet another milestone in the consolidation of the sector. The struggle for ownership of Russneft between Oleg Deripaska's Basic Element and

---

[31] Renz, 'Putin's Militocracy?', p. 909, fn 7.
[32] See Timothy Frye, 'Capture or Exchange? Business Lobbying in Russia', *Europe-Asia Studies* 54, 7, November 2002, pp. 1017–36.
[33] For a full discussion, see Sakwa, *The Quality of Freedom*.
[34] Stanislav Belkovskii, 'Odinochestvo Putina', in his *Imperiya Vladimira Putina* (Moscow: Algoritm, 2008), pp. 15–22, at p. 15.
[35] Hanson, 'The Resistible Rise of State Control in the Russian Oil Industry', p. 14.

Sechin's Rosneft was a proxy test of the strength of the two factions concerned, the *siloviki* and the loyal industrialists.[36] It would be a mistake to see the Yukos case as simply the exercise of monolithic state power to implement certain goals. The Russian political system is far too fluid and open-ended for that, and divided as we have seen between the aspiration to achieve genuine constitutionality and elements of the administrative regime. These tensions allowed rampant factionalism to develop, and this is well illustrated by the persecution of individuals associated with the Yukos oil company from 2003. The Yukos case in turn consolidated an environment where other cases could be launched, notably against the management of Sovkomflot, Novoship and many other companies. It did not, moreover, make decision-making any more transparent or streamlined, as the tortuous discussions to adopt the long-promised Law on Subsoil Resources demonstrates. As Fortescue notes in his study, there are plenty of cases of coherent and transparent decision-making in Putin's presidency, but this was not one of them and instead the whole process was characterised by 'bureaucratic infighting, delay, shifts and turns in policy preferences, and bitter debate'.[37] All this clearly demonstrates that there was no consensus over the state's role in the economy, and while there was an element of ideological statism at work in the Yukos affair, this was only one driver of the affair. The economic crisis from mid-2008 provided an ideal opportunity for the state to extend its control over the economy, but it did not do so.

The Yukos affair allowed Putin to centralise the collection of energy rents and ensure a stable set of priorities for their disbursement; it also allowed the administrative regime to retain control over their distribution. Not only was the state's extractive capacity enhanced, but also its insulation from social forces pressing for immediate expenditure on various social projects or the regions, or to give tax breaks to privileged groups.[38] Appel stresses that 'the ability to govern was the prerequisite

---

[36] Yuliya Latynina, 'Dvukhpartiinaya sistema Rossii: Partiya nefti protiv Partii gaza', *Novaya gazeta*, No. 69, 10 September 2007. By November 2009 it looked as if Deripaska would fail to win Russneft, accompanied by rumours that Gutseriev would return to Ingushetia in some senior capacity: Editorial, *Vedomosti*, 24 November 2009.

[37] Stephen Fortescue, 'The Russian Law on Subsurface Resources: A Policy Marathon', *Post-Soviet Affairs* 25, 2, April–June 2009, from the abstract on p. 160. See also Yuko Adachi, 'Subsoil Law Reform in Russia Under the Putin Administration', *Europe-Asia Studies* 61, 8, October 2009, pp. 1393–414, who identifies a three-way struggle between the Kremlin's changing policy priorities, bureaucratic infighting and the interests of state-controlled mineral extracting companies.

[38] Appel, 'Is It Putin or Is It Oil?', p. 315.

for the ability to tax'.[39] Control over distribution proved challenging as the succession approached, and in the event there was an 'unwise growth of spending, which duly reignited inflation in 2007–08'.[40] There were many claimants to control the rent-sharing process. As Gaddy notes:

A successor must understand Putin's concept of 'Russia, Inc.', subscribe to it, and be capable of putting it into practice. He cannot allow rent sharing to devolve into personal enrichment to the detriment of state interests. A fratricidal rivalry among the elites could threaten use of the rents for state interests.[41]

Putin was well aware that a free-for-all over the distribution of resources would allow corruption to emerge from the shadows to take over the system: venal corruption would metastise into meta-corruption and become system-forming. Putin's vaunted stability would swiftly erode, and governance deteriorate.

A new political economy?

The segmented nature of the state, reflecting its Soviet background, took the form of the development of so-called *votchiny* (derived from allodial or patrimonial estates in Muscovite Russia, as opposed to *pomest'e*, estates). These votchiny were prominent in certain sectors of the economy that, while formally controlled by the state, acted as autonomous agents. Notable examples were state-controlled bodies such as Gazprom, Rosneft, RAO UES, Alrosa (diamonds), TVEL (power engineering) and Rosoboroneksport (the arms export monopoly, later absorbed by the Russian Technologies state corporation), complemented by the state agencies Minatom, MPS (transport) and later Russian Railways. Under Putin even nominally independent companies, particularly in the energy sector, had to show loyalty, and even obeisance, to the regime to survive. Power and property were directly related in these companies, populating an unusual social landscape in which Soviet patterns of interaction were reproduced. Igor Bunin argues that this gave rise to 'internal oligarchs', each guarding its part of the 'sovereign territory of the state'.[42]

---

[39] *Ibid.*, p. 321.
[40] Hanson, *Russia to 2020*, p. 18.
[41] Statement of Clifford G. Gaddy, Senior Fellow, The Brookings Institution, Committee on House Financial Services Subcommittee on Domestic and International Monetary Policy, Trade and Technology, 17 October 2007, in *JRL*, 219/25, 2007.
[42] Igor' Bunin, 'Ot votchin k pomest'yam', *Ekspert*, No. 46, 10 December 2001, in *Ekspert: Luchshie materialy*, No. 2, 2007, p. 41.

Putin sought to undermine the power of these 'internal oligarchs', and to do this he had as it were to 'nationalise' the state. The first step was to 'deprivatise' the companies, and one of the mechanisms to achieve this was the imposition of a system of interlocking appointments between the administration and corporations. The old Yeltsinite 'unwritten contract' between powerful independent actors gave way to their transformation into informal agents of the state, what Bunin calls the *pomest'e* system. Corporate autonomy gave way to subordination to the interests of the administrative regime. In the new model of political economy, the state sought to defend its claimed prerogatives against the business elite. One of its main instruments to achieve this was by placing its representatives on the boards of leading companies, mostly with people loyal to Putin personally. The status of regime officials came to be measured as much by their boardroom position as governmental rank. Outsiders were rare, and on the whole the managers and overseers of these corporations had either known Putin earlier or came from the special services, or both. There was not much scope for independent action, unless one entered into direct confrontation, the path taken by Khodorkovsky. His fate served only to reinforce the compliance of others.

While Berezovsky boasted in 1997 that seven bankers controlled the bulk of Russia's economy, a decade later seven of Putin's barons monitored the work of a large part of the Russian economy. While the *siloviki* were prominent in this, they were by no means alone in acting as the state's eyes and ears in state companies. The resulting inter-penetration of state officials and business executives prompted much talk of the establishment of 'Kremlin, Inc.', as a type of corporation (*korporatsiya*), run by a strong chief executive (the president) but also constrained by a type of collective board (the factions). Treisman, as we have seen, described the emergence of a distinctive class of '*silovarchs*' in which security structures merged with business interests.[43] This, however, was not a system of 'state corporatism', since that would suggest a legal framework and the observance of the whole panoply of law in an institutionalised system of the incorporation of business interests. Instead, the new system is best described as 'bureaucratic capitalism', a variant of the ordo-liberalism mentioned above, where property rights were fungible, seeping between the state and private owners, in an informal assertion of regime power over the economy.

---

[43] Treisman, 'Putin's *Silovarchs*'.

The inter-penetration of the state and business to create *sui generis* 'business states' has become prevalent in the post-war era. The development in Pakistan of a 'military business' ('Milbus') has been described in a recent work by Ayesha Siddiqa. She argues that from the very inception of the Pakistani state in 1947, defence absorbed up to two-thirds of the new state's resources, something that can be explained not only by Pakistan's need to defend itself against India, but by the military's desire from the early 1950s to present itself as the moral saviour of the country. This was certainly the rhetoric of General Pervez Musharraf when he deposed the civilian regime in 1999, accusing it of corruption in its eleven years of rule since the last bout of military government under General Zia ul-Haq, and argued that the military was the last remaining viable institution in the country. The army penetrated agriculture, business, manufacturing and real estate to create a 'Milbus' empire, defined as 'military capital used for the personal benefit of the military fraternity, especially the officer cadre, which is not recorded as part of the defence budget'.[44] The military's economic empire was accompanied by the development of cronyism, the exploitation of informal networks in the award of contracts, financial bailouts by state banks to keep unprofitable enterprises working, and in general by multiple inefficiencies and the distortion of the market. The political consequences were no less dysfunctional, with a powerful incentive structure created for the military to stay in power to defend its vast economic empire. Siddiqa notes the comparison often drawn between the military's vaunted professionalism and guardianship of modernisation and Huntington's model of the 'soldier reformer'; but she argues that rather than being the 'carriers of western cultural norms', the military model in Pakistan is rather more 'feudal-authoritarian' than any Weberian model of hierarchical professionalism.

A similar argument has been applied to Russia,[45] but the application of the 'feudal' model to Russia is undoubtedly overdrawn. Others talk of the onset of an era of 'authoritarian capitalism'.[46] The new economic policy has been represented as a type of authoritarian modernisation, harking back not to the Soviet period but to the developmental states of the 1960s (notably, South Korea and Singapore). However, both models miss the mark if by 'authoritarianism' in this context we mean the

[44] Ayesha Siddiqa, *Military Inc: Inside Pakistan's Military Economy* (London: Pluto, 2007).
[45] Vladimir Shlapentokh, *Contemporary Russia as a Feudal Society* (New York: Palgrave Macmillan, 2007).
[46] Azar Gat, 'The Return of the Authoritarian Great Powers', *Foreign Affairs* 86, 4, July–August 2007, pp. 56–69.

repudiation of democratic norms. As long as the country remains committed to the development of effective and democratic governance, however tempered by the development of the dual state, it is more accurate to describe it as a type of dirigiste rather than authoritarian modernisation. Putin was keen to place Russian practices into a broader context:

If we remember the discussions during the Great Depression in the United States, then we can remember that even in the United States there were experts who believed that elements of state interference in the economy to overcome difficulties were not only possible but also desirable. President [Franklin D.] Roosevelt was precisely of that opinion. But today market tools are called for and are more efficient, though without the regulating function of the state, nothing would work, basically. This view has nothing to do with my service as a KGB officer in the Soviet Union, but it has to do with my education ... I defended my Ph.D. thesis in economics.[47]

In the period before the 2007 election, Roosevelt became something of a hero to Russia's elite, and there were frequent references to the need for state supervision of the economy.

State corporations: Kremlin Inc.

The creation of state-sponsored mega-corporations during Putin's second term reflects a combination of the consolidation of *silovik* power and Putin's own preferences. In his doctoral dissertation defended in June 1997 at the St Petersburg Mining Institute and in an article published in 1999, he argued that for Russia to make up lost economic time, it would have to create vertically integrated financial-industrial corporations 'capable of competing on equal terms with western multinational corporations'. State support would be essential to create competitive companies, and at the same time the state would defend the 'interests of society as a whole' and act as the arbiter between competing economic interests and obstruct 'monopolistic behaviour' that would otherwise predominate and which 'inhibits innovation'.[48] This was not so much an attempt to emulate the post-war authoritarian developmental states of South and East Asia, as a response to the challenge of

---

[47] 'Putin Q & A: Full Transcript', *Time*, 18 December 2007; www.time.com/time/specials/ 2007/personoftheyear/article/0,28804,1690753_1690757_1696150,00.html

[48] Harley Balzer, 'Vladimir Putin's Academic Writings and Russian Natural Resource Policy', *Problems of Post-Communism* 53, 1, January–February 2006, pp. 48–54, with Putin's article 'Mineral Natural Resources in the Strategy for Development of the Russian Economy', at pp. 49–54. See also Harley Balzer, 'The Putin Thesis and Russian Energy Policy', *Post-Soviet Affairs* 21, 3, 2005, pp. 210–25.

reviving sick industries in conditions of neo-liberal hegemony. Others were less complimentary and suggested that Putin was reverting to the modernisation strategy of the Soviet era.[49] The aircraft industry is a classic case, where the world is dominated by two huge corporations (Boeing and Airbus Industries), and without consolidation and protection the Russian industry would simply shrivel away. The official strategy for the industry envisaged the United Aviation Corporation (OAK) entering into joint ventures and strategic partnerships with the world's leading aircraft manufacturers.[50] In the context of a factionalised polity, however, the creation of giant state corporations reflected distributional coalitions within the regime.[51] Any ideological commitment to a state-sponsored development programme was blunted by the pursuit of factional advantage and awareness that autarchic developmental models would reinforce Russia's lack of competitiveness.

The late Putin regime began to create a set of developmental institutions. These included an Investment Fund and a Development Bank (Vneshekonombank), as well as the creation of a network of state corporations from which foreigners were barred. A law of 5 May 2007 banned investors from forty-two strategic industries.[52] These sectors enjoyed monopoly benefits, and it was unclear how 'hard' their budget constraints would be. Given the shortage of private investment capital (in large part, caused by the regime itself), budget funds were the only serious alternative. All of this suggested a drift back towards a neo-Soviet industrial strategy, accompanied by the recrudescence of some of the practices of the 1990s. The creation of the industrial state corporations was as much about control over cash flows as it was about development. Berezovsky had long been considered the master of this form of business activity, and it was now generalised to cover large sections of the economy. This was a neo-modernisation strategy tempered by the contradictions of Russia's fragmented state and factional conflict.

[49] Maksim Shishkin, Dmitrii Butrin, Mikhail Shevchuk, 'Prezident v kandidaty', *Kommersant-Vlast'*, 3 April 2006.
[50] I am grateful to Phil Hanson for pointing this out. OAK was created in May 2007 and brought together the leading civilian and military aircraft manufacturers including MiG, Sukhoi and Tupolev.
[51] In Belarus, Lukashenko jealously guarded his supremacy in property matters, and in particular sought to keep the *siloviki* at bay. Meeting with the republican KGB on 19 July 2007, Lukashenko claimed that KGB officials had become 'overly involved' in commercial matters and would be severely punished 'with their arms cut up to their shoulders'. Andrei Liakhovich, 'The Lukashenkas (There Could be More than One)', Belarus Public Policy Fund (Minsk: BISS, 2008), p. 3.
[52] 'Putin Signs Law on Strategic Sectors', *Moscow Times*, 6 May 2008.

Already in 2004 the law on non-commercial organisations contained a section on state corporations. The need to find an appropriate legal status for the new Deposit Insurance Agency, created to guarantee individual savings (and thus to prevent a repeat of the loss of people's savings, as had occurred in 1991–2 and again in 1998), forced the creation of this new legal form, since it was considered inappropriate for the Agency to be part of the Central Bank or a government body. The law defined a state corporation as a special form of non-commercial partnership to fulfil specified social tasks. A special federal law governs each corporation. The next to be created after the Deposit Insurance Agency was the Home Mortgage Credit Agency, then the State Air Traffic Management Agency, although the latter was really a state unitary enterprise. In the latter, property is owned by the state and all profits are returned to the state, and the director is subordinated to another state body and thus can be dismissed at any time. MERT sought to reduce the number of this type of enterprise.[53] State corporations are to fulfil the goals set out in their founding charters and each has a supervisory council, staffed in large part by presidential nominees. Assets held by state corporations are no longer owned by the state but come under the founding partnership of the corporation. Although the founders enjoy extensive privileges, they are not property rights. In a state corporation, the unique founder is the Russian Federation itself, thus allowing considerable leeway to the directors appointed by the state to manage its assets. State corporations represented the extension into economics of the para-constitutionalism that characterised politics.

This form of property was an alternative to genuine privatisation or full nationalisation. Misgivings about the creation of state corporations accompanied by factional tensions delayed the approval of Chemezov's plan in 2005, the first out of the block, to create a state corporation (Russian Technologies) on the basis of the state unitary enterprise Rosvooruzhenie. The plan to create a State Nanotechnology Corporation (Rosnanotekh), sponsored by Sergei Ivanov and the head of the Kurchatov Institute, Mikhail Kovalchuk, also encountered stiff resistance. In particular, Prime Minister Fradkov opposed the creation of state corporations, and this may well have been one of the reasons for his dismissal in September 2007. Fradkov well understood that state corporations entailed the creation of a new type of parastatal economic enterprise (the counterpart of Putin's other

[53] Dmitrii Butrin, 'Gosudarstvennye korporatsii', *Kommersant*, 24 December 2007.

experiments with para-constitutionalism and para-politics) that would, like the national projects, be removed from government control. The institutional framework whereby the state would regulate these alienated assets was not at all clear. As Pappe and Galukhina stress, 'This form differs principally from the creation of state holdings or from normal nationalisation.'[54] As economic agents they were thus 'abnormal', acting as non-profit bodies with a special law in each case setting them up. State assets granted to the corporation became its property, and it was allowed to keep the profits. Their management was also unique, with the main role taken by the Russian president.[55]

In the end seven state corporations were created, as well as a number of quasi corporations. The scale of the new development was unprecedented, with some $20 billion transferred to the six state corporations created between May and November 2007 as starting capital.

- A special law in 1999 created the Credit Restructuring Agency, which in 2003 became the Deposit Insurance Agency.
- The old Vneshekonombank, headed by Vladimir Dmitriev, was restructured to become the Development Bank – VEB, intended to finance infrastructural projects of state importance. VEB played a key part in feeding liquidity into the financial system and the stock market during the 'credit crunch' of September–October 2008, and thereafter played a central role in managing the financial sector.
- Sergei Ivanov was given the brief to revive Russia's electronics industry and to spend up to $60bn of the country's windfall oil and gas earnings over a decade to transform Russia into an advanced high-technology player in global markets. Of this, R246bn was to be spent on the development of the aerospace industry, while R130bn of the above sum was to be spent on nanotechnology (dealing with particles smaller than a billionth of a metre). He was appointed head of the Rosnanotekh state corporation, created in July 2007. In September 2008 Chubais, out of work since the liquidation of RAO UES in July 2008, was appointed head of what is now called Rosnano.
- The Housing and Utilities Reform Fund was headed by the former Federation Council member, Konstantin Tsitsin, and by its statute was to be wound up in 2012. In his speech at the eleventh congress of

---

[54] Ya. Sh. Pappe and Ya. S. Galukhina, *Rossiiskii krupnyi biznes, pervye 15 let: Ekonomicheskie khroniki 1993–2008* (Moscow: Higher School of Economics Publishing House, 2009), p. 187.
[55] Pappe and Galukhina, *Rossiiskii krupnyi biznes*, p. 188.

United Russia on 21 November 2009, however, Putin extolled its work
in improving the housing stock and suggested that it be given an extra
lease of life, to at least 2013.[56]
- The construction of the infrastructure for the 2014 Winter Olympic
  Games, to be held in Krasnaya Polyana in Sochi, was led by
  Olimpstroi, created on 10 October 2007 and headed initially by
  Semën Vainshtok. He had earlier been head of Transneft, but had lost
  his post as a result of factional manoeuvring, in this case led by a group
  in the *siloviki*. Dissatisfaction with progress led to the appointment of
  Kozak in October 2008 to take over preparations for the Olympics, a
  project in which Putin had vested considerable personal capital.
- The government planned to spend R674bn ($27.4bn) on the develop-
  ment of nuclear energy, accompanied by the creation in July 2007 of
  the Atomic Energy Industry Complex (Atomenergoprom), bringing
  together all stages from uranium mining to turbine manufacture. This
  new body was headed by the director of Rosatom, Sergei Kirienko.
- Last on the list was the creation of a corporation to take the lead in
  developing high-technology exports. Chemezov finally achieved his
  ambition in November 2007 and became the head of a new state
  corporation called 'Russian Technologies' (Rostekhnologii, Russian
  Technology Corporation, known colloquially as Rostekh), controlling
  the state arms agency Rosoboroneksport and VSMPO-Avisma, the
  world's largest titanium alloy producer and a supplier to Boeing, as
  well as other defence and manufacturing plants. As Kasianova notes,
  the company 'positioned itself for a principal role on the battlefield of
  corporate redistribution of national property'.[57] The state's takeover
  of Avtovaz, Russia's largest car manufacturer, had been achieved in
  December 2005 by appointing officials to dominate its board and
  through Rosoboroneksport's purchase of a controlling (62%) stake
  for $350 million, and later the loss-making car plant was merged
  with the Volga truck-maker Kamaz. Rostekh became a huge military-
  industrial conglomerate which by 2009 had swallowed some 400
  entities, earning it the moniker of an 'industrial Gazprom'.[58] The
  defence minister Anatoly Serdyukov was appointed head of the supervisory council of the corporation. Sergei Ivanov's absence from the
  council represented a defeat for Chemezov and was interpreted as part
  of the rollback of *silovik* influence that had begun with Serdyukov's

---

[56] http://premier.gov.ru.
[57] Alla Kasianova, 'Enter Rosoboroneksport', *PONARS Policy Memo*, No. 406, July 2006,
  p. 6.
[58] Max Delany, 'Arms Chief in Race to Grab Assets', *Moscow Times*, 19 March 2009, p. 1.

appointment as defence minister in February 2007 and Zubkov's appointment as prime minister in September of that year. Neither had a KGB background.[59]

Management of the companies was taken out of state hands, but their financial security was underwritten by the government. The lack of transparency in the operation of these non-state but not private corporations provoked criticism by liberals, and they became a controversial issue during the Medvedev succession and after. Criticism focused on Rostekh and Rosnano, which appeared to be using state funds to deprivatise whole swaths of the economy that were delivered not to the state but into the hands of what were now genuinely 'state oligarchs'. The most predatory of these corporations acted as a form of licensed 'raiding'.

Hanson, as we have seen, argues that the increased role of the state in these sectors fostered the creation of a 'dual economy', with varying rules applying to the different sectors. Market forces operated freely in the private sector, whereas in the parastatal (but not necessarily state-owned) strategic-development oriented part of the economy, more dirigiste rules would apply. In his view such intense bureaucratic interventionism would not be disastrous for the Russian economy, but it would depress economic growth rates.[60] Easter has called this a 'concessions economy', where the most valuable assets of the old command economy became state concessions and the system as a whole became an 'upstairs-downstairs economy', with strategic industries and the large state service corporations on the top floor, while the mass retail and consumer sectors are downstairs.[61] The duality runs even deeper. Frye has advanced the 'exchange' model of business–state relations, arguing that the earlier elements of 'state capture' were now reversed by a trend towards 'business capture', but neither model is satisfactory since the two spheres are deeply entwined.[62] Building on this, Libman argues that Russia now had a 'clan economy' where 'power is the source of profits and profits are the basis of power'.[63] A similar model of 'clan capitalism' in Russia is

[59] Pavel Felgenhauer, 'Chemezov to Head New Russian Arms Conglomerate', *EDM* 4, 221, 29 November 2007.
[60] Philip Hanson, 'The Russian Economic Puzzle: Going Forwards, Backwards or Sideways?', *International Affairs* 83, 5, September–October, 2007, pp. 884–7.
[61] Gerald M. Easter, 'The Russian State in the Time of Putin', *Post-Soviet Affairs* 24, 3, July–September 2008, p. 212.
[62] Frye, 'Capture or Exchange?'.
[63] Aleksandr Libman. 'Vzaimosvyaz' ekonomicheskoi i politicheskoi sistem v sovremennoi Rossii', *Svobodnaya mysl'*, No. 6, 30 June 2004, p. 101.

advanced by Leonid Kosals.[64] Political and economic power are indeed
deeply imbricated, where the earlier partial privatisation of state functions now gave way to the politicisation of the economy. In part this was
designed, as the Yukos affair demonstrated, to deprive the opposition of
economic support, as well as to ensure that business itself did not
challenge the prerogatives of the regime, but there was also an ideological component.

Contrary to the nostrums of 'Washington consensus' economists that
liberalisation was the only way ahead, and that private enterprises are
always more efficient than state-owned ones, Putin's administration
insisted that state intervention had an important role to play, although
in keeping with ordo-liberal ideas, this did not necessarily mean state
ownership. The Sredmash company, a conglomeration ranging from
defence industries to nuclear reactors, was held up as an example of a
successful state-owned company. There were special features at work
here, however, since the company had enjoyed strong investment, good
management and a competitive environment, but the case demonstrated
that the form of ownership is not always the key factor in a company's
performance. The Gazprom monopoly was a good counter-example,
able to increase output by only 0.1 per cent in the first half of 2007
when the economy as a whole was growing at 7 per cent per annum.
Nevertheless, as Vlad Ivanenko notes, despite being a state-owned monopoly that for historical reasons was not privatised, Gazprom 'proved to
be highly competitive in the global arena'.[65] Having swallowed Yukos,
Rosneft, contrary to expectations, turned into a competitive player in
domestic and foreign markets, although by late 2007 was burdened by
over $35 billion of corporate debt. Major innovation tends to come from
new or small companies, but big corporations come into their own when
it comes to applying economies of scale and entering fiercely competitive
markets. This was recognised in the plan to create about a dozen information technology industrial parks, an idea that had greatly impressed
Putin on a visit to Bangalore, India, in 2004. Russia produces some
200,000 science and technology graduates a year, and over thirty foreign
firms (including Boeing) took advantage of Russia's highly skilled but
low-paid workers. Many of course emigrated, leading to the well-known
definition of contemporary American higher education: Chinese
students taught by Russian professors.

[64] Leonid Kosals, 'Klanovyi kapitalizm v Rossii', *Neprikosnovennyi zapas*, http://www.
nz-online.ru.
[65] Vlad Ivanenko, 'Russian Global Position After 2008', *Russia in Global Affairs* 5, 4,
October–December 2007, p. 147.

Putin was well aware of these issues, and thus it would be a mistake to argue that he was a full-blooded exponent of the developmental state. Putin argued that industrial development required 'institutions of development' (the various conglomerates mentioned above), but 'I consider that the real sector of the economy should be developed above all not through institutions of development, but through creating the appropriate macroeconomic conditions.' This included keeping inflation low, creating the appropriate financial conditions and so on. Some money, he admitted, could be devoted to infrastructural investment and the institutions of development without threatening macroeconomic stability, but the priority was not so much state investment, which he admitted was not always the most efficient, but the state's lead, which would encourage private investors.[66] This was a clear indication of the ordo-liberal component of his thinking and helps explain why the liberals retained control of macroeconomic policy throughout his leadership. Soon after the Duma election, Putin committed himself once again to limiting the growth of state-owned companies and to ensuring free competition: 'We are not planning to build state capitalism', he insisted.[67] State corporations remain subordinate to the president and not the government, and thus some intriguing questions were raised by his shift to the prime minister's office. Anticipating his changed status, Putin firmly asserted that no new state corporations were needed.

This was not the language of corporatism but of someone who understood the importance of the state providing macroeconomic stability. Typical of his dualism, however, Putin failed to provide a stable and predictable institutional framework for microeconomic development. The relatively weak expansion of small and medium enterprises reflected the bureaucratic and legal problems the sector faced. More broadly, Sergei Aleksashenko, a former deputy head of the Central Bank of Russia, argued that a solid anti-reform bloc dominated at the highest levels, with systemic reform defined as 'the introduction of both political and economic competition, the establishment of independent courts, greater openness to inward foreign investment, control of corruption and the entry on to world markets of non-raw material sectors of the Russian economy'.[68] Arkady Dvorkovich, the head of the presidential administration's analysis department and later President Medvedev's

---

[66] Valdai Discussion Club meeting, Sochi, 14 September 2007, http://president.kremlin.ru/text/appears/2007/09/144011.shtml.

[67] 11 December 2007, meeting with the presidium of the Russian Chamber of Commerce and Industry, www.kremlin.ru/textappears/2007/12/154000.shtml/.

[68] Hanson, *Russia to 2020*, p. 34.

economic adviser, was well aware of these problems.[69] Earlier he had warned against creating too many state corporations: 'I view the fashion of creating state corporations as being extremely dangerous, particularly for the industries being proposed.' His comment came in response to plans to create corporations to run the fishing industry, develop medicines and build roads.[70] Particular concerns were raised by creeping state control of the oil industry, with the head of Surgutneftegaz, Vladimir Bogdanov, warning that increased state control would render the industry less competitive. His company was considered the next target for a Rosneft takeover. At the World Economic Forum meeting in Davos in January 2007, Medvedev noted:

> We aim to create big Russian corporations and will back their foreign economic activities. But the role of the state certainly should not involve telling any particular company or sector how to carry out diversification. Even if the state retains a controlling interest … we aim to create public companies with a substantial share of foreign investment in their capital.[71]

The promotion of Finance Minister Kudrin to deputy prime minister in September 2007 (see next chapter) strengthened the position of the economic liberals and their policy of economic prudence, holding down public expenditure and operating a counter-cyclical fiscal policy, channelling energy rents into the Stabilisation Fund. However, during the election campaign the attack on his deputy, Sergei Storchak (see below) revealed the high stakes and the struggle by the political elite to control economic resources. Thus while Putin remained in charge, some sort of balance between the 'patrimonial estates' and more liberal approaches was maintained, but the situation was both inherently unstable and stultifying for broad-based redevelopment of the economy, a problem with which Medvedev would grapple throughout his presidency.

---

[69] Personal notes, meeting of 12 September 2009.
[70] Anatoly Medetsky and Miriam Elder, 'Kremlin Aide Warns of State Control', *The Moscow Times*, 4 October 2007, p. 1.
[71] 10 December 2007, www.bbc.co.uk/news.

5   Managed succession

The 2007–8 elections were predictable in broad terms but accompanied by surprising shifts in tactics and unexpected *coups de main* as the cycle unfolded. As one commentator noted, 'This predictability is one of the main achievements of the Kremlin, which has spent the last two–three years consistently building its defences against any type of "orange threat". And, it has to be admitted, it has been most successful in this.'[1] It was for this reason that opposition groupings questioned the legitimacy of the elections, echoed by many in the west. However, the placid appearance of the election cycle belied the turmoil beneath the surface. The formal election process was accompanied by a second, subterranean, struggle in which Putin sought to mould the succession, while the factions sought to shape Putin's preferences and to force an outcome to their advantage. Putin's overall goal was to ensure an orderly transition not only from one leader to another but also, in his conception, from a period of stabilisation to one of modernisation. As far as the Putin elite were concerned, all this was threatened by external dangers. The 'orange revolution' in Ukraine in autumn 2004 had enormous impact on that elite, and the fear of a new Russian revolution was palpable. Opinion polls in July 2005 found that 42 per cent (up from 32 per cent a year earlier) believed that a colour revolution on the Georgian, Ukraine or Kyrgyz model was possible in Russia.[2] Fear of foreign intervention was stoked by news at that time that the US Congress had decided to allocate $85 million for 'developing democracy in Russia', to be distributed through the National Endowment for Democracy (NED).

Government reshuffles

The fundamental problem of a concentrated power system is to ensure adequate renewal to avoid rendering itself so inward-looking as to

---

[1] Vladimir Rudakov, 'Dumskaya osen'', *Profil'*, 3 September 2007, pp. 13–20, at p. 13.
[2] Data from the Public Opinion Foundation (FOM), headed by Alexander Oslon, known as 'the Kremlin's pollster', reported by Georgi Il'ichev, 'Poll Results: 42% Say That a Revolution is Possible in Russia', *Izvestiya*, 20 July 2005.

become dysfunctional. Reliance on a small coterie of trusted followers and the resulting weakness of competent personnel leads to reduced governmental capacity and poor policy performance. The chief mechanism used by the Putin administration to avoid this fate was to undertake periodic personnel reshuffles, which reflected the changing balance of forces and took on added significance as the elections approached. There were four major governmental shake-ups during his presidency. The first, on 28 March 2001, saw some of the most egregiously tainted of the Yeltsin cohort purged, notably Nikolai Aksënenko from his post at the railways ministry, and the elevation of Putin's allies, notably Sergei Ivanov, who was appointed defence minister. Coming exactly a year after his election, Putin asserted his authority over personnel, hitherto limited by the terms of a supposed transitional deal with Yeltsin. The second, on 24 February 2004, saw the nomination of Fradkov as premier to replace Kasyanov (he was confirmed by the Duma on 1 March). The third, on 14 November 2005, signalled the beginning of elite realignment in preparation for the succession in 2008. The fourth, on 12 September 2007, was part of the succession operation and saw Fradkov replaced as premier by Victor Zubkov, accompanied by a limited cabinet reshuffle. We will begin by looking at the second and third reshuffles and subsequent personnel issues, and leave the eve-of-election cabinet changes of September 2007 to later in the chapter. The way Putin undertook these periodic personnel changes was reminiscent of Yeltsin's political style – a sudden and dramatic announcement, typically coming like a bolt from the blue. At the same time, they revealed the constraints he worked under, forced to manoeuvre within the factional system.

February 2004 reshuffle

The government reshuffle of February 2004, on the eve of the presidential election of March 2004, put in place a streamlined government, with a smaller cabinet in which the number of deputy prime ministers was cut back to one, and with a clear liberal profile. The reduced cabinet was part of the administrative reform masterminded by Kozak in which government bodies were divided into three categories: ministries, agencies and oversight bodies, with what were intended to be clearly demarcated functions and greater autonomy for each (something that did not work out in practice). Fradkov had enjoyed a chequered career, but one feature undoubtedly attracted him to Putin (in addition to his unquestioning loyalty): he was a qualified economist, and thus it was assumed would be able to get a grip on government finances, a feature that was even more pronounced with Zubkov's appointment later. It was clear that Putin was becoming less tolerant of appointments made before his time, and in appointing new people he favoured loyal outsiders who would be less 'departmental' in their views. With what he hoped would be a less corporate mindset, they would enjoy a diminished capacity to extract what Putin in his 3 April 2001 address to the Federal Assembly called 'status rent';[3] material advantages gained by taking advantage of professional position.

From late 2005 the regime vigorously applied the new model of political economy that was forged by the Yukos affair. The notion of 'sovereign democracy' tried to give intellectual weight to the new statism. In terms of political administration, the period from September 2004 was marked by a reconfiguration of the federal system that saw the status of regional legislatures increase as the major parties were forced to compete for half the seats in proportional elections, accompanied by the weakening of regional executive dominance by the shift to the appointment of governors. It was also a time of national assertion, reflected in Defence Minister Sergei Ivanov's riposte to the accusation that the country was slipping back in democratic terms: 'Democracy is not just a potato that can be transplanted from one garden to another.'[4]

November 2005 reshuffle

In the 14 November 2005 reshuffle, two of Putin's closest confidants were promoted. Defence Minister Sergei Ivanov retained his ministerial portfolio but also became a deputy prime minister. The head of the presidential administration, Dmitry Medvedev, became the first deputy prime minister, while remaining Gazprom chairman. Medvedev was given the authority and resources to deliver on Putin's four 'national projects', announced on 5 September 2005, to achieve improvements in health, education, housing and agriculture. Medvedev had been elected chair of the Gazprom board on 29 June 2000 when he was a member of the presidential administration and head of Putin's presidential election campaign. Medvedev ceded the position of Gazprom board chair to Rem Vyakhirev when the latter was dismissed as CEO in May 2001, but he returned to head the board a year later. As the authors of a study of Gazprom note, Medvedev's appointment to Gazprom was never an end in itself but served to raise his political status and independence, since as head of such a large company he gained additional weight in the state hierarchy and thus could address oligarchs and ministers from a

---

[3] See www.president.kremlin.ru/events/42.html.
[4] 'That Democracy is Not a Potato', *RFE/RL Newsline*, No. 30, Part 1, 14 February 2005.

position of strength.[5] This is a devastating commentary on the relative weight of political and economic hierarchies in Russia. Vyakhirev had boasted that without Gazprom there would be no Russia; and now both Russia and Gazprom were governed from the same Kremlin tower.[6] Medvedev, however, was never deeply taken with Gazprom issues, as reflected in his rather modest office in Gazprom headquarters.[7] It was an open secret that Putin personally managed Gazprom questions, leading to the persistent rumour that after stepping down from the presidency, he would take over as the head of the company. This would have been appropriate, since Gazprom's pipelines 'distributed not just gas, but also ideology'.[8] According to Rahr, the new ideology represented a combination of 'money, resources and power'.[9]

Ivanov was long considered the front-runner in the succession stakes, and at various points he was expected to be appointed prime minister. In 1998 Putin appointed him his deputy at the FSB, and Ivanov's appointment to the defence ministry in 2001 was portrayed as an attempt to boost military reform. He was at first considered to be a defence minister with enhanced powers, rather than a deputy prime minister who also happened to be defence minister. Announcing the appointments on television, Putin stated that at a meeting a week earlier 'the participants expressed anxiety about the problems the defence ministry had encountered in achieving its plans for future development . . . these problems are connected with the lack of coordination between various ministries and departments'.[10] Ivanov gained access to resources beyond that of the military-industrial complex to enhance the potential of Russia's armed forces. At the same time, Ivanov could provide crucial support for Medvedev's advancement, if that indeed would be the Kremlin's choice; or to act as a candidate in his own right if Medvedev faltered. Ivanov established a type of election council to prepare policy positions for his putative presidency, consisting of various cultural figures and experts and which first met on 16 January 2007.[11] At the St Petersburg Economic Forum in June 2007, Ivanov projected himself as a forward-looking economic liberal with a clear agenda for Russia's economic development. He also stressed his democratic credentials, insisting that Russia would develop as a democratic state. Ivanov played a key role in the development of the new state corporations.

---

[5] Zygar' and Panyushkin, *Gazprom*, pp. 105, 251.   [6] *Ibid.*, p. 111.
[7] *Ibid.*, p. 250.   [8] *Ibid.*, p. 252.   [9] Rar, *Rossiya zhmet na gaz*, p. 6.
[10] Nick Paton Walsh, 'Putin Reshuffle Gives Clues to Choice of Heir', *The Guardian*, 15 November 2005, p. 23.
[11] Author's interview with Vitaly Shlykov, Rostov, 9 September 2008.

Medvedev took over as chair of the Council on National Projects (CNP), previously headed by Fradkov, and insisted that the aim was to avoid political intrigues and to 'make the life of the people considerably better'.[12] With an election in the offing, the government finally acceded to demands that instead of 'sterilising' the energy bounty, more should be invested in developmental goals.[13] At Medvedev's disposal was the Infrastructure Investment Fund, running at $2.44 billion in 2006 and rising to $2.56 billion in 2008.[14] The national projects sought to make a tangible difference to people's lives, and can thus be seen as part of the succession strategy, and also represented Putin's attempt to create a permanent legacy of improved welfare. The national projects were designed to achieve quick improvements in standards of living and modernised welfare services while avoiding inflation or the social protests that accompanied the monetisation of social benefits.[15] The launching of the national projects relieved the political pressure to spend some of the windfall energy rents.[16] The post was a high-profile one that would ensure extensive media coverage on issues that affected people's daily lives.

The establishment of the Council indicated once again Putin's penchant for para-constitutional solutions to problems of public administration, this time duplicating the work of the government. The creation of the State Council in 2000 undermined the Federation Council, while the creation of the Public Chamber in 2004 eclipsed the Duma's public advocacy role. Para-constitutionalism affected the cabinet no less. A similar process was at work with Sergei Ivanov's nanotechnology corporation and some of the other corporations, which handled billions of roubles outside of formal governmental structures. Functions that should properly have been the business of the cabinet were transferred to councils and corporations. In the event the CNP was brought under the aegis of the government, partly in response to widely expressed concerns about the unclear division of responsibilities. The CNP was banned from using the cabinet building to emphasise the purely

---

[12] *Kommersant*, 19 November 2005; quoted by Pavel Baev, 'Putin's Bureaucratic Response to Russia's Economic Misbalance', *EDM* 2, 217, 21 November 2005.

[13] The argument was powerfully made, for example, by Nikolai Petrakov, 'Samaya nishchaya bogateishchikh stran mira', *Svobodnaya mysl'*, No. 11, 30 November 2005, pp. 15–22.

[14] For a good analysis, see A. N. Myrynyuk, *Natsional'nye proekty v rossii: Problemy i perspektivy* (Moscow: Maroseika, 2007).

[15] This rather benign view is provided by Roi Medvedev, *Dmitrii Medvedev: Prezident Rossiiskoi Federatsii* (Moscow: Vremya, 2008), pp. 27–39.

[16] V. O. Kazantsev, *Prioritetnye natsional'nye proekty i novaya ideologiya dlya Rossii* (Moscow: Vagrius, 2007).

technical nature of the projects. As a Kremlin insider, Medvedev was familiar with factional concerns but appeared neutral in these conflicts, although he was clearly ideologically predisposed to favour liberal-technocratic solutions.[17]

The changes weakened Fradkov's position as prime minister. Until the reshuffle, moreover, the liberal economist Alexander Zhukov had been the only deputy prime minister, and now he became one of three, joined by Ivanov and Medvedev. On 20 March 2006, Ivanov's position was further strengthened by his appointment to head a powerful new commission created to oversee state military procurement, a position that was not answerable to the prime minister. At the same time, Ivanov's deputy on the defence industry commission, Vladimir Putilin, was given ministerial rank. Putilin had formerly been head of the defence and security department at MERT. In his new role Ivanov took control of a budget of $25 billion, in addition to the $17 billion he oversaw as defence minister.[18] The change further overshadowed Fradkov and appeared to give Ivanov the edge over Medvedev in the succession stakes.

Medvedev had by now established a campaign headquarters based on the Russian Information Society (RIO-Centre). Members included Nabiullina, deputy to Gref at MERT, the political commentator Vyacheslav Nikonov, and Igor Yurgens, the deputy head of the Russian Union of Industrialists and Entrepreneurs (RUIE), and they began to draft the outlines of his programme. The centre was in operation from November 2006, and it has been suggested that Medvedev had by then already been chosen to succeed Putin.[19] As part of his preparations, Medvedev sponsored the creation of the Institute for Contemporary Development (INSOR), headed by Yurgens, to provide ideas for his presidency. INSOR was the counterpart of German Gref's Strategic Studies Centre of the early Putin years but was more of an experts' assembly than the earlier prototype. As we have seen, Medvedev was sceptical about the notion of sovereign democracy, and his insistence on democracy without adjectives suggested the restoration of 'normality' associated with the constitutional state to overcome the inherent arbitrariness of the administrative regime.

The governor of the energy-producing region of Tyumen, Sergei Sobyanin, became Putin's new chief of staff. Sobyanin had been elected

---

[17] For a biography and character assessment, see Abdullaev, 'A Soft-Spoken, "Smart Kid" Lawyer', p. 1.
[18] Nabi Abdullaev, 'Defense Minister Gets Boost in Kremlin Race', *Moscow Times*, 22 March 2006.
[19] Informal discussions with Nikonov and others.

governor of Tyumen region in January 2001, and he was a member of United Russia. The personnel changes helped consolidate an echelon of leaders to fill the gap when Putin's term in office came to an end. It also suggested a new dynamism to a presidency that appeared to have lost direction in the wake of the Yukos affair, the Orange revolution in Ukraine and protests over the monetisation of social benefits in early 2005. Sobyanin's appointment drew on cadre reserves from outside the two capitals and suggested that the balance of Russia's federal relations could once again be tilted in favour of the regions. Sobyanin, like his predecessor Medvedev, was a Kremlin outsider and did not try to impose his authority on the factions and the powerful deputy heads of the presidential administration such as Sechin and Surkov.[20] The balance in the cabinet also changed, with a rather stronger 'political' bloc that had been notable for its absence earlier.[21] More broadly, the reshuffle strengthened the moderates around Putin, who had been battling certain *siloviki*, led above all by Sechin, who had long been seeking to reduce Ivanov's influence. Ivanov's enhanced profile brought him firmly into the field of contenders for the succession. Ivanov was loyal to Putin personally but was at the same time an independent figure, a quality that rendered him suspect to the *siloviki*. An Ivanov presidency, moreover, would not guarantee continuity in either personnel or policy, and it is this quality which probably lost him the crown. Medvedev appeared a strong compromise candidate who would be acceptable to democratic statists, liberal-technocrats and the *siloviki*.

The November 2005 reshuffle consolidated Putin's team within the government, but by the same token threatened to weaken the presidential administration. Already the Kremlin had begun to draw on people outside the core Putinite elite. A number of deputies to Luzhkov, the Moscow mayor, were sent out to become governors, as Putin hoped to spread Moscow's prosperity across the country, and to weaken Luzhkov. The former first deputy, Valery Shantsev, became governor of Nizhny Novgorod, Georgy Boos became governor of Kaliningrad, and Mikhail Men became governor of Ivanovo. Medvedev's move into government was compensated by drawing on talented outsiders to broaden the administration's base. The former Bashkortostan prosecutor, Alexander Konovalov, was appointed head of the Volga federal district to replace the liberal Sergei Kirienko (who became head of Rosatom), and the former mayor of Kazan, Kamil Iskhakov, became head of the Far East

---

[20] Yulia Latynina, 'What Really Happened to Medvedev', *Moscow Times*, 23 November 2005.
[21] Evgenii Strel'tsov, 'Prem'er soschital do chetyrekh', *Izvestiya*, 17 November 2005.

federal district. The dynamics within the government changed, with Fradkov now flanked by a powerful triumvirate (Medvedev, Ivanov, Zhukov), who acted as a 'collective Putin' with greater responsibility for government policy. A reconfigured power system was in the making whose final act was expected to be the appointment of a new prime minister, the traditional springboard for the presidency.

The November 2005 reshuffle created the framework for the succession and brought to the fore the leading contenders. If elections had been held in May 2006, Medvedev's vote would have equalled that of Zhirinovsky at 18 per cent, while Ivanov was 1 per cent ahead of Zyuganov at 17 per cent. Asked directly about who they would like to succeed Putin, Ivanov came in at 19 per cent, Medvedev won 16 per cent, while other candidates came in far below (Yavlinsky, for example, with only 4 per cent).[22] Putin had become increasingly trapped by the narrowness of his political base in the Kremlin and government, and by the policy contradictions engendered by the struggle between the 'liberals' and the *siloviki* in his administration, with the moderate statist line in danger of being overshadowed by the other two. By bringing in personnel from beyond his traditional recruiting grounds – pre-eminently the security apparatus and St Petersburg – Putin signalled that he was now confident of having socialised the outsider elites in the ways of his liberal statism to be able to draw on them; and that he was now moving from a power consolidation agenda to a power transfer one.

Personnel changes and personalities

If the idea of national projects was to enhance Medvedev's electoral prospects, then the tactic worked. By November 2006 Medvedev's trust rating had risen to 17 per cent, nearly double that of his rival, Ivanov, who had fallen to 9 per cent.[23] At the World Economic Forum in Davos on 27 January 2007, Medvedev outlined his policy agenda. He advanced the idea of Russia as an 'effective democracy', one based on market economics, the rule of law and governmental accountability; and thus once again distanced himself from the notion of 'sovereign democracy'. Medvedev stressed the need for the diversification of the Russian economy, reflecting concerns about excessive reliance on natural resource exports. These warnings were accompanied by boastful claims that in 2007 Russia would overtake Saudi Arabia as the world's largest oil producer and that Russia would soon overtake Britain and France to

[22] Levada Center poll, www.levada.ru/press/2006050202.html.
[23] VTsIOM poll of 11–14 November, reported by Gazeta.ru, 21 November 2006.

become the world's fifth-largest economy. He promised that foreign investors would enjoy equal treatment, to be guaranteed by a new law regulating foreign investment in strategic sectors of the Russian economy. Medvedev stressed that 'We are fully aware that no undemocratic country has ever become truly prosperous, and this for the simple reason that it is better to have freedom than not to have it.' He also rather sternly revealed his statist side in foreign-policy matters: 'We are not trying to make anyone love Russia, but we will also not allow anyone to do Russia harm. What we want is respect towards Russia's people and our country as a whole, but we will obtain this respect through responsible behaviour and through our achievements, and not through force.'[24]

On 15 February 2007, Ivanov was promoted to first deputy prime minister, responsible for overseeing Russia's military-industrial complex through the Military Industrial Commission formed in 2006 and aspects of the civilian economy, in particular the engineering sector. The defence budget sextupled, rising from R148bn ($5.8bn) in 2000 to R870bn ($34bn) in 2007, although service conditions remained poor and the increasing sums devoted to procurement (R300bn in 2007, $11.8bn) seemed to buy remarkably little: '30 new tanks, several helicopters and some missiles'.[25] Although respected, Ivanov was never popular with military officialdom. He was now elevated to the same rank as Medvedev, and his prospects of becoming the next president commensurately improved, reflected in rising poll ratings. With Medvedev well ahead, the partial reshuffle restored the balance. Ivanov was also freed of the burden of dealing with the intractable problems of military reform and released from responsibility for dealing with bullying in the army. The Andrei Sychëv case in January 2006 caused him considerable damage. Sychëv was a conscript serving at the Chelyabinsk Tank Academy who was beaten so badly and then deprived of medical assistance that his legs and genitalia had to be amputated because of gangrene. Each year over a thousand conscripts die of accidents, bullying and suicide, yet this case received wide prominence, in part because it was particularly dreadful but also apparently because Ivanov's opponents (notably Sechin, Ustinov and Patrushev) colluded to discredit him.[26] While Medvedev had gained stature in Davos, it was Ivanov who accompanied Putin to Munich and reinforced the president's tough

[24] 'Speech at the World Economic Forum', 27 January 2007, www.medvedev2008.ru/english_2007_01_27_.htm.
[25] Pavel Felgenhauer, 'Serdyukov's Fake Resignation', *EDM* 4, 178, 26 September 2007.
[26] Pavel Felgenhauer, 'Light Sentence for High-Profile Russian Hazing Case', *EDM* 3, 178, 27 September 2006.

message delivered in his speech to the security conference there on 10 February 2007, and his promotion came just five days later. Between the two of them, they were responsible for nearly half of the federal budget. Ivanov's position was further strengthened when in July 2007 he took over as head of Rosnano, the second-largest holding company after the aircraft builder OAK.

The new defence minister was Anatoly Serdyukov, who had made his fortune in the furniture business before entering public service. In 2000–1 he ran the tax inspectorate in St Petersburg in a notoriously harsh manner, bankrupting companies unable to meet their obligations, before becoming deputy tax minister and then taking over as head of the Federal Tax Service on 27 July 2004. Serdyukov (together with his deputy Sergei Shatalov) masterminded the $33 billion tax claims against Yukos that ultimately brought the company to its knees. His brief now was to sort out the financial affairs of the defence ministry, a task hardly likely to inspire devotion from the officer class. The billions of petro-dollars being invested in the armed services seemed to be going into a bottomless pit – and it was now Serdyukov's job to limit the corruption. Putin's concern over the issue had already been evident when he appointed the accountant Lyubov Kudelina as a deputy defence minister at the same time as appointing Ivanov minister in March 2001. Serdyukov's appointment meant that for the first time in independent Russia, an entirely civilian person was appointed defence minister, and it could well have reflected Putin's mistrust of career military officers (characteristic of security officials). Serdyukov's appointment and Ivanov's promotion to deputy prime minister, in Blank's view, were 'almost certainly ... tied to Putin's efforts to manage the succession up to the last moment and to balance rival clans'. Serdyukov and his father-in-law, Zubkov, were considered part of Sechin's faction.[27]

At the same time, Putin promoted cabinet Chief of Staff Naryshkin (he had occupied this post since 2004) to the post of deputy prime minister in charge of foreign trade, particularly with other former Soviet republics. Naryshkin trained together with Putin at the KGB's foreign intelligence training centre in 1978–82, and in 1988–92 he served in the Soviet embassy in Brussels, thus missing the revolutionary excitement at home as the Soviet Union collapsed. Naryshkin then ran the finances of the mayor's office in St Petersburg up to 1995, under Putin's supervision, before joining the foreign investment department of Vladimir Kogan's Promstroibank (which managed Putin's personal finances).

---

[27] Blank, 'The Putin Succession', p. 249.

Like so many of Putin's top officials, Naryshkin was part of the
interlocking network of politicians and directors: in his case he was head
of the board of directors of Russia's main TV station, Channel One, as
well as being on the boards of Rosneft and Sovkomflot, Russia's premier
international shipping company; and later in 2007 he became chair of
the new United Shipbuilding Corporation.[28] Ivanov, Serdyukov and
Naryshkin all hail from Putin's native St Petersburg, and were considered to be loyal to Putin personally. Above all, like many of Putin's
late appointments, he was an outsider and thus not aligned with any of
the factions dividing the Kremlin. Naryshkin also had the distinction of
coming from an old noble family (Peter the Great's mother was Natalya
Naryshkina) and thus represented a link with Russia's monarchical past.
The structure of the government had now changed, with two first deputy
prime ministers, and two deputy prime ministers, Naryshkin and
Zhukov. Naryshkin retained his responsibilities as cabinet chief of staff
and thus effectively enjoyed seniority over Zhukov. With this move
Naryshkin joined the exclusive club of potential successors.

On the same day, 15 February 2007, Putin dismissed the Chechen
president, Alu Alkhanov, and nominated Ramzan Kadyrov, the former
prime minister, as his replacement, whose confirmation by the Chechen
parliament was little more than a formality. There had been rumours
that Putin would take this step, since Kadyrov had turned thirty in
October 2006 and had thus become eligible for the post. Alkhanov was
appointed a federal deputy justice minister. This was yet another sign of
the weakening power of the *siloviki*, or at least one of their sub-factions,
since Kadyrov as we have seen was distrusted by the FSB.

At a press conference during the Shanghai Cooperation Organisation
(SCO) summit on 15 June 2006, Putin remarked that his nomination as
successor would be a man whose name 'is not completely unknown, but
which is simply not circulated' by the media.[29] This seemed to rule out
the two leading candidates, Ivanov and Medvedev, since they were
constantly the focus of media attention. The name of one of the less
familiar figures in Putin's administration, Vladimir Yakunin, was much
touted to fill the bill. He had been a member of the Soviet committee for
foreign trade relations and had then served with the Soviet mission in the
United Nations until, with the fall of the USSR, he moved into business

---

[28] Miriam Elder, 'Discreet With a Deceptively Shy Grin', *Moscow Times*, 26 October 2007,
p. 1. The bulk of Russia's civilian and naval shipbuilders were consolidated in this quasi-
state corporation in July 2007.

[29] SCO summit, Shanghai, 15 June 2006. These comments are not reproduced in the
official transcript of the press conference but were widely reported in the media.

and banking, before in 1997 being appointed by Putin, then head of the Main Control Department in the presidential administration, as his envoy to north-west Russia. A deputy transport minister in 2000 and then deputy railways minister, in 2005 he was appointed founding head of the reorganised Russian Railways (RZhD). This is the country's second largest enterprise after Gazprom, the world's largest railway system with 42,000 kilometres of track, 1.3 million employees and annual revenues of more than $20 billion. Hailing from St Petersburg, Yakunin is a close friend of Putin's and they have neighbouring dachas in Ivanovo (Priozersk).

In 2001 Yakunin became head of the board of trustees of the St Andrew's Foundation, established in 1992 to foster patriotic sentiments and the restoration of national values. Under Yakunin, the Foundation was involved in numerous religious-cultural events, including bringing home for reburial the émigrés Ivan Il'in, a philosopher quoted by Putin, and Anton Denikin, the tsarist and later civil war general (whose political views on issues such as Nazi Germany, incidentally, were diametrically opposed to those of Il'in). Yakunin also heads the Centre of National Military Glory. The presence of notable *siloviki* as trustees, including Sergei Ivanov, the head of the federal narcotics agency Victor Cherkesov, and Georgy Poltavchenko, gave the body a strongly Putinesque flavour, and its espousal of national-patriotic causes reflected Putin's values. Yakunin also helped broker the reconciliation in 2006 between the Moscow Patriarchate and the Russian Orthodox Church Abroad, a cause fervently supported by Putin. Yakunin was also the formal head of the World Public Forum, which since 2003 has held an annual 'Dialogue of Civilisations' convention in Rhodes. Yakunin acted as a bridge between the business world, the managerial class, the *siloviki* and the values-based group in Putin's entourage. Yakunin himself insisted that he saw 'no meaning' to the division of the Russian elite into the '*siloviki*' and 'liberal' camps.[30]

Putin's succession strategy now appeared to be to allow a contest between a number of favoured figures, with Ivanov and Medvedev at the head of the list. Whether this would be enough to prevent succession issues from paralysing the work of the administration is not clear. At the end of 2006, Putin held a conference with some key members of his team, warning them against focusing on their own problems in the transition and not on their professional duties.[31] The vagaries of the

[30] Victor Yasmann, 'Russia: Could Yakunin Be "First-Called" as Putin's Successor?', RFE/RL, *Russia Report*, 20 June 2006.
[31] Editorial, 'Podvig razvedchika', *Nezavisimaya gazeta*, 31 October 2007, p. 2.

succession process meant that there was no one to whom they could shift their loyalty, and Putin refused to become a lame duck in the interim. Putin would be leaving, but he would also be staying – and in the meantime his message was: get on with your work.

Clearing the field

The succession by definition would focus ultimately on a single individual emerging to assume the duties of the presidency, a person who would be selected by Putin. While Putin tried to ensure that the presidency retained maximum room for manoeuvre and that his choice would not be forced or his position weakened, the para-political world of factional conflict tried to influence the decision. Fearing that his control over the succession process could be challenged, either by elite factions from above or the representative system or popular movements from below, the president cleared the field.

Anti-corruption as a disciplinary method

Several cabinet ministers had become millionaires while in office, and charges of nepotism were rife, touching even Fradkov himself. In June 2007 his son Peter had been appointed to the board of directors of the state-owned Bank Razvitiya (Development Bank), while his other son, an FSB officer, was employed by the state-controlled VTB (Vneshtorgbank). Two of VTB's vice-presidents came from the *silovik* stable: Dmitry Patrushev, the son of FSB director Nikolai Patrushev, and Yury Zaostrovtsev, the former head of the FSB's economic department. Fradkov himself was on VTB's advisory council. Sergei Ivanov's son, also called Sergei, was a vice-president at Gazprombank, while his other son, Alexander, was employed by Vneshekonombank. The son of St Petersburg governor Valentina Matvienko, Sergei, was vice-president at VTB. Dmitry Patrushev, the elder son of the head of the FSB, as noted was employed by VTB and dealt with loans to oil companies, while Nikolai Patrushev's younger son, Andrei, was an adviser to Rosneft chair and deputy head of the presidential administration, Sechin.[32] The list could be extended indefinitely. With so many members of the government and administration allegedly making financial hay while the Putin sun shone, the president could not be sure that if faced by the choice between mammon and Putin, they would choose him.

---

[32] We have referred to a comprehensive list in Chapter 2, *Kommersant-vlast'*, No. 37, 24 September 2007.

Even those in the presidential administration and officialdom who espoused the 'third term' option did so less out of loyalty to Putin as out of fear that they would lose the power, privileges and property that they had amassed during his presidency. As Latynina notes, they were 'devoted not to Putin but to themselves'. Another figure would do equally well, such as Fradkov, as long as the status quo was maintained.[33] The original Putin team had developed interests of its own, which could only be guaranteed by a continuation of Putinism, preferably with Putin at the helm, but not necessarily; a replacement team as a last resort would do the job. Aware of these considerations, Putin strengthened the financial monitoring system as the succession approached. While the struggle against corruption was certainly a priority, no less important was keeping financial tabs on officialdom, to ensure that they made the right choice and did not put their own economic interests above Putin's in the succession. Over the summer of 2007, Putin on at least two occasions argued that Russia's main problem were no longer 'fools and roads' but corruption and incompetence.[34] He now sought to reduce the one while tackling the prevalence of the second.

In the 2007 Corruption Perceptions Index, Russia fell from 126th place the previous year to 143rd place out of 180.[35] The inclusion of seventeen new countries in the index pushed Russia down the league table, but there was no question that the situation was dire. The State Duma had been unable to adopt a federal anti-corruption law for some years, although it had created a Duma Commission on Corruption headed by Mikhail Grishankov. In 2007 the presidential administration decided to take the initiative and prepared the law itself, presenting the draft to the Federation Council on 8 October. By that time the General Prosecutor's Office (GPO) announced that over 700 corruption cases had been filed against officials, including some deputy governors and mayors. It is estimated that up to a quarter of money allocated for state purchases is stolen.[36]

The struggle against corruption and criminality, as is so often the case, took on a political complexion and was used as part of the covert struggle

---

[33] Yuliya Latynina, 'Novye prem'ery', *Novaya gazeta*, No. 70, 13 September 2007. She listed Sechin, Patrushev and Viktor Ivanov in this group, as well as Ustinov, who in some ways would have suited even better since he was far more resolute in the Yukos affair, according to Latynina, than the half-hearted and indecisive Putin.

[34] Quoted by Gleb Pavlovsky, *Ekspert*, No. 34, 17 September 2007.

[35] Transparency International, Corruption Perceptions Index, 26 September 2007, www.transparency.org/policy_research/surveys_indices/cpi/2007.

[36] G. P. Armstrong, *Russian Federation/CIS Weekly Sitrep*, 18 October 2007.

of one faction against another. The arrest of Vladimir Kumarin (who had changed his name to Barsukov) on 24 August 2007 provoked much comment that the case fell into this category, especially since it was linked with the attack on Cherkesov (see Chapter 6). Kumarin was the former vice-president of the St Petersburg Fuel Company (PTK) in 1998–9 and was allegedly once the head of the feared Tambov Gang (Tambovskaya gruppirovka) in St Petersburg. A book by Jürgen Roth argues that Putin was connected to the Kumarin gang through Vladimir Smirnov, the president's former associate in the city and the former head of the Petersburg branch of the German firm SPAG. The story dates back to 1994, when Putin awarded PTK the contract as sole supplier of petrol to St Petersburg, in exchange for facilitating food and other supplies.[37] Smirnov at the time was a major shareholder in the company, which was allegedly controlled by the Tambov gang, and in 1998 he took over the company, appointing Barsukov his deputy.[38] SPAG, a company for which Putin acted as adviser for seven years, was allegedly involved in a money-laundering scheme with Kumarin.[39] Since 2000 independent criminal groups had been squeezed out of strategic economic sectors, although in many cases new relations with the authorities had been established. The charge laid against Barsukov by the prosecutor general, Yury Chaika, was of banditry and organising a criminal gang, but the two charges of *reiderstvo* (raiding, see p. 207) were only the tip of the iceberg of his supposed criminality.[40] The trial was delayed until after the March 2008 election, but the case exposed Putin to a smear campaign and revealed the vulnerability of his position.

Neutralising the regions

In 1999 the regions had been the source of one of the most powerful threats to the incumbent regime. As we have seen (Chapter 1), the alliance of All Russia and Fatherland with Primakov threatened to bring outsider forces to power. As the 2007–8 electoral cycle approached, it was clear that the ruling regime had no intention of allowing a repetition of this sort of insurgent elite threat. A major step in neutralising the regions as a source of autonomous upward political mobility was the

---

[37] Rosemary Mellor, 'Through a Glass Darkly: Investigating the St. Petersburg Administration', *International Journal of Urban and Regional Studies* 21, 3, September 1997, p. 488.

[38] Jürgen Roth, *Die Gangster aus dem Osten* (Hamburg: Europa Verlag, 2003).

[39] *Der Spiegel*, June 2003.

[40] Igor' Timofeev, 'Banditskii Peterburg v otgoloskakh istorii', *Argumenty i fakty*, No. 37, 11 September 2008, p. 13.

shift in 2004 to the appointment of governors. With the new system in which presidential nominations have to be confirmed by regional legislatures firmly in place from 2005, independent regional political entrepreneurs were much weakened. The most effective way now for them to make a political career was to join the dominant party, UR, just as in the Soviet period bureaucrats had entered the Communist Party to advance up the career ladder. Some leaders remained powerful actors, notably the '*krepkie khozyaistvenniki*' (strong business managers) like Luzhkov in Moscow, Shaimiev in Tatarstan, and Rakhimov in Bashkortostan, but unlike 1999, they could no longer dream of intervening in the succession operation as autonomous agents.

The simultaneous removal of four senators in May 2006 revealed the continued assertiveness of Sechin's *silovik* faction. The police and the GPO coordinated their actions in the Nenets autonomous district, Khakassia and St Petersburg to force the removal of the representatives to the Federation Council from these regions. At the same time, the Nenets governor, Alexei Barinov, the last to be popularly elected (on 23 January 2005, with the second round on 6 February, running against the Kremlin's favoured candidate), was taken into custody, without much in the way of evidence. He had apparently threatened the interests of Rosneft. The governor of the Republic of Khakassia, Alexei Lebed, was also the subject of legal action to force him out. It was now clear that appointed governors were little more than ordinary bureaucrats, no longer accountable to the wishes of the electorate but dependent on the hierarchy of power.[41] The weakening of the electoral legitimacy of regional executives threatened to undermine the very basis of the federal separation of powers. At the federal and regional levels, neo-patrimonial features were gaining prominence.

In the run-up to the succession, regional executives and city mayors were changed in forty-nine regions, with many finding themselves under arrest or investigation. A notable victim was Konstantin Titov, who after sixteen years as governor of Samara was dismissed on 27 August 2007, and two days later the head of the Avtovaz car plant (located in the region), Vladimir Artyakov, was confirmed as the new governor. Titov had never been accepted as part of Putin's team, and indeed had run against him in the March 2000 elections, and had later sponsored the Social Democratic Party of Russia (SDPR) rather than United Russia. Although he later joined the ranks of the latter, it was clear that his heart was not in it; and the region as a whole, moreover, had always been

---

[41] Nikolai Petrov, 'Undercutting the Senators', *Moscow Times*, 30 May 2006.

proud of its independence. By contrast, Artyakov was part of Chemezov's team at Rosoboroneksport before going to manage the car plant. His appointment represented a significant strengthening of central power. It was also part of the succession calculations, since the regime needed to guarantee the loyalty of the region's leadership while ensuring that they would not be able to undertake any political initiatives on their own. A network of regional leaders loyal not only to the regime but also to Putin personally was created.[42]

In Sakhalin, Putin appointed a Gazprom loyalist as governor. The long-time head of Novgorod region, Mikhail Prusak, was also dismissed in August 2007 after having been accused by the presidential envoy of having ignored corruption. For good measure, he was voted off UR's general council on 1 October. Soviet appointment patterns became ever stronger, with leaders sent to regions with which they had no or very little association (the so-called *varyagi*). A former factory director in Kazan was sent to govern Amur region, while the deputy governor of Tomsk region became president of Buryatia. Regional leaders now joined the UR bandwagon en masse, with sixty-four heading the party lists in their regions (more on this later).

Stability in the transition period was one issue, as was securing the loyalty of governors in the election season, but a larger point was being made. By launching a wave of gubernatorial changes, with the replacement of some executives who had been in power since the early Yeltsin years, Putin was signalling that it was time for a change of regional elites. The aim was to rejuvenate regional politics but at the same time to stress the dependence of those who remained. The stipulation that half the membership of local assemblies had to be elected from party lists further undermined local power systems based on the governor. Putin's imminent departure from the presidency denoted that it was also time for governors to go, while those who remained were to deliver the vote for Putin's successor.

Continuity, not succession: the September 2007 reshuffle

As the election season moved into full swing from the summer of 2007, the administration made it clear that it was engaged less in a succession operation than in 'operation continuity'. The idea was to ensure that Putinism would remain even after Putin left office. That this would be the leitmotif of the campaign was already pointed out as early as

---

[42] Ol'ga Popova, 'Konets samarskoi vol'nitsy', *Ekspert*, No. 32, 3 September 2007, p. 76.

May 2005: 'We should understand that the rotation of power in 2008 will be called not operation "successor" but operation "continuity" . . . there will be a civilised transfer of power and policy continuity along a certain corridor will arise automatically, and players, who want to deprive us of our future, will simply not stand a chance.'[43] It was clear even then that the successor would have to be entirely reliable and controllable, and that the whole process would not be allowed to take on an autonomous character. The regime's aim was to ensure that the hard-won stability would not be squandered in an electioneering bounty, and that fundamental policy priorities would remain in place once Putin left office. A whole raft of initiatives ensured that the administration was thinking beyond the immediate 2007–8 electoral cycle.

The state budget adopted in 2007 covered not the usual twelve months but the three years up to 2010. The national projects overseen by Medvedev operated on a timescale that lasted several years. The ambitious plans outlined by Ivanov at the St Petersburg Economic Forum in June 2007 stretched well into the future, and the talk was of propelling Russia into the ranks of the world's top five economies by 2020. The presidential demographic strategy of October 2007 entailed plans to encourage births, reduce mortality and encourage immigration until 2025, once again tying the hands of Putin's successor. On a more directly political level, United Russia's programme entitled 'Putin's plan' (see Chapter 1) spoke of the long-term transformation of Russia into a competitive and socially just society. All of this was now threatened as 'Competition within the ruling group could become a serious struggle for power and provoke instability.' Putin now seriously began to think of finding a way to remain the arbiter even after the end of his term. 'This would allow him to strengthen the foundations of his foreign and economic policy in a way that continuity would be maintained after his departure.'[44]

The replacement of the prime minister in connection with the elections had long been anticipated, but the manner was typically Putinite and unexpected. Fradkov resigned on 12 September 2007, and less than two hours later Putin nominated a new prime minister. His choice was Victor Zubkov, head of the Federal Financial Intelligence Agency, whose appointment was easily ratified by the Duma two days later.[45] Fradkov's resignation had clearly been coordinated with Putin, and thus the whole

---

[43] Andrei Gromov and Tat'yana Gurova, 'Kapital'nyi remont konservatizma', *Ekspert*, No. 17, 9 May 2005, in *Ekspert: Luchshie materialy*, No. 2, 2007, pp. 106–113, at pp. 106, 8.

[44] Rar, *Rossiya zhmet na gaz*, p. 218.

[45] With 381 votes in favour, 47 against and 8 abstentions.

process was 'depoliticised', becoming a purely administrative matter.[46] As Putin argued, the change was to a large degree of a purely 'technical character', so as to allow the central and regional governments to work without interruption 'like a Swiss watch', not only up to the presidential elections in March but also to May 2008, when the new president would be inaugurated. As for why he changed the government at that time, Putin noted: 'Unfortunately, members of the government, like the rest of us are people. I noticed that they were easing off work and beginning to think about their own fate after the elections.'[47]

The choice of Zubkov as prime minister was unexpected, since his name had figured on few lists of potential candidates.[48] Putin argued that Zubkov was 'a true professional, an effective administrator with a pleasant personality, and with a lot of professional experience', and noting the vast amount of financial information at his disposal, Putin stressed: 'Not once, I would like to emphasise, did Victor Zubkov abuse this trust ... I believe that in this quite critical pre-election period for Russia, we need precisely this sort of person: a superb professional, a decent person, cool-headed and, I would add, wise.'[49] Zubkov's nomination foreclosed the appointment of the two leading candidates to this post, to be then used as the springboard for the presidency – the route taken by Putin in 1999. If Ivanov was disappointed, he hid his feelings well, and appeared before the Valdai Discussion Club hours after the announcement and expounded his ideas in a relaxed and robust manner, and even commented favourably on Zubkov's appointment.[50] In his first statements on 13 September as premier-designate, Zubkov stated that 'if I achieve something as prime minister' then he would think of standing for the presidency,[51] a sentiment that sounded suspiciously rehearsed and one that he would never have expressed without Putin's agreement. The comment was endorsed by Putin at the Valdai Discussion Club meeting in Sochi on 14 September, although Putin stressed that Zubkov had not said that he would stand, but that if he worked successfully then he may do so, which was a 'balanced, sensible answer' in Putin's view. He stressed that there were now at least five serious candidates for the presidency.[52]

---

[46] The argument is made by Alexei Zudin, *Moskovskie novosti*, No. 36, 14 September 2007.
[47] Valdai Discussion Club meeting, Sochi, 14 September 2007, http://president.kremlin. ru/text/appears/2007/09/144011.shtml.
[48] Vladimir Pribylovsky's Panorama was one exception.
[49] http://president.kremlin.ru/text/appears/2007/09/144011.shtml.
[50] Personal notes.
[51] Clifford J. Levy, 'Putin's Pick Hints at Run for Russian Presidency', *International Herald Tribune*, 14 September 2007, p. 3.
[52] http://president.kremlin.ru/text/appears/2007/09/144011.shtml.

Zubkov's age was certainly one factor in the calculations. Born in 1941 in the Urals, he turned sixty-six on 15 September 2007. Also pertinent was the fact that he was not a member of any of the existing factions (although he was close to Victor Ivanov, responsible for presidential appointments) and had never served in the intelligence services. An economist by training, he graduated in 1965 from Leningrad's Institute of Agriculture. He worked as director of a collective farm in the village of Razdol'e in the Leningrad Region, making it one of the best in the country, and from 1991 headed the Executive Committee of the Soviet of People's Deputies in the Priozersk district of Leningrad Region, where Putin, Patrushev and Chemezov built their dachas. In 1992–3 he worked for ten months as Putin's deputy in the external affairs committee of the St Petersburg mayor's office, before taking over the St Petersburg tax inspectorate in 1993.[53] He impressed Putin with his administrative capacities and lack of political ambitions. As Putin noted, he 'practically had no dealings with ideological work'. This did not preclude running for governor of Leningrad region in 1998, when Boris Gryzlov was his campaign manager, winning a modest 8.6 per cent of the vote. A classic Soviet mid-level functionary, Zubkov at the same time was one of the few who did not succumb to the pervasive corruption.[54]

In 2001 he was appointed the inaugural head of the newly established Financial Intelligence Agency (FMS, now Rosfinmonitoring), helping to take Russia off the Financial Action Task Force (FATF) 'at-risk' register. Russia had been placed on the blacklist in June 2000 because of its links with offshore black holes and was taken off in October 2002, and in 2003 Russia joined FATF as a fully fledged member.[55] He was also involved in Putin's early assault against the oligarchs. As head of the FMS he had more information about the movement of legal and illegal funds than anyone else in the country, and as Putin noted, 'the concentration of so much confidential information in one body could have had a negative effect on business, but this did not happen'.[56] Zubkov was a soviet-style leader who retained some of the best features of the old system's morality, but by the same token he was not a public politician.

---

[53] 'Biografiya Viktora Zubkova', *Novaya gazeta*, 13 September 2007.

[54] A useful biographical note is 'An Ideal Soviet Man has Putin's Trust', *Moscow Times*, 14 December 2007, p. 1.

[55] Ol'ga Proskurnina and Vasilii Kuginov, 'Chelovek bez chastnoi zhizni', *Vedemosti*, 13 September 2007, p. A06.

[56] http://president.kremlin.ru/text/appears/2007/09/144011.shtml.

In his nomination speech to the Duma on 14 September, Zubkov focused on Putin's priorities for economic growth and social welfare, but he also dwelled on the problem of corruption. He argued that new legislation was required that clearly defined the problem and suggested that a special body, similar to the FMS, should be established to lead the fight, an idea that Medvedev later took up. Coming at a time when Russia had plunged down the Corruption Perceptions Index, Zubkov's concern with the issue was appropriate. He also pledged firm controls over the federal funds allocated to the defence sector and to the various mega-corporations in the aircraft and ship-building sectors. Soon afterwards Yury Chikhanchin, Zubkov's former deputy in the FMS, was appointed to head the government secretariat.

Intense speculation surrounded Zubkov's appointment. Although it was in keeping with Putin's style to launch unexpected initiatives, he never did so simply for the fun of it. Zubkov had a number of characteristics sought by Putin: he had strong financial expertise, as well as successful experience as a manager, and in addition he was part of the St Petersburg group on which Putin relied, without being aligned with any faction. With corruption allegations swirling around Putin's administration, and with the flood of petro-dollars showing no signs of abatement, someone who could keep a tight rein on public and not-so-public finances was crucial in the run-up to the election. By appointing Zubkov, Putin was signalling to the elite not to dip their hands into the public till. He would also dampen the faction fights and ensure that Putin remained firmly in control until the end of his term. Zubkov was also a token of the commitment to continuity in the transition. In the short-term his appointment removed the question of prime ministerial change: the issue was now closed and Zubkov would serve as prime minister up to the presidential elections. He would ensure the implementation of Putin's policy priorities in a typically Putinite technocratic manner. The new premier, moreover, was not allowed to appoint 'his' team in the government 'for fear of upsetting the existing balance of clan interests'.[57]

Firm action at the beginning of the electoral season dampened the increasingly frenzied speculation about governmental changes, changes that had begun to threaten the system's stability. By appointing Zubkov, Putin drew the sting from the prime ministerial question without creating a competitor. Putin reshaped the political situation and removed the successor question from the immediate agenda while maintaining his

---

[57] This had been predicted by Igor' Fedyukin, 'God pered rozhdestvom', *Kommersant-Vlast'*, 22 January 2007, p. 16, in his analysis of scenarios for the succession.

own room for manoeuvre. Zubkov's appointment also postponed the moment when Putin's presidency would enter the 'lame duck' phase. From a longer-term perspective, his appointment did not foreclose the chances of the other candidates, notably Medvedev and Ivanov, who remained senior deputy prime ministers, roles that were only a little less powerful as a launching pad than the prime ministerial seat itself. Neither did it queer the pitch for any of the other potential presidential candidates, including a potential 'third option' that had been hinted at by various presidential aides and Putin himself in the summer of 2007.

Above all, Zubkov's appointment helped establish the framework for policy and personnel continuity after Putin left office. This was evident in the minimal cabinet changes that followed Zubkov's appointment. The announcement on 24 September of the new cabinet saw only three ministers dropped: trade and economic development minister German Gref, health and social development minister Mikhail Zurabov, and regional development minister Vladimir Yakovlev. With elections coming up, Putin sacrificed the three most unpopular ministers: Gref because of his liberal pro-western views (he had also made clear his desire to enter private business); Zurabov for his mishandling of the monetisation of social benefits; and Yakovlev for problems in the housing sector. Gref was the most consistent and eloquent advocate of World Trade Organisation (WTO) membership and his departure dealt a blow to this long-term aspiration, which would help consolidate property rights in Russia. Gref was replaced as minister of trade and development by his deputy Nabiullina, who had been part of the team developing Medvedev's economic strategy even before his election and thus ensured that Gref's broad approach at MERT would be maintained. In 1999 Nabiullina had worked at Gref's Centre for Strategic Research, and at the same time was vice-president of the Strategic Research Centre, which drew up a medium-term strategy for Russia's socio-economic development to 2010, which the Russian government followed. She was concerned with making Russian business more transparent while reducing the tax and administrative burden.[58] She was also reputed to be rather more sympathetic to the national projects than Gref.[59] Tatyana Golikova, formerly a deputy finance minister and the wife of the industry and energy minister, Victor Khristenko, took over the health and social development portfolio. Renowned for her mathematical prowess, she was a strong supporter of Kudrin's macroeconomic policies, but her

---

[58] *Rossiiskaya gazeta*, 28 September 2007.
[59] Dmitry Babich, 'A Government Reshuffle', *Russia Profile* 4, 9, November 2007, pp. 7–8, at p. 8.

new portfolio found her on the other side of the barricades, calling for increased social spending.

Kozak, Putin's veteran St Petersburg confidant, was brought back into central government as the regional development minister with enhanced powers and extra resources from the Investment Fund. The Fund had been created in 2005 and in 2007 was allocated $4.4bn, and Kozak was now to select and oversee all its projects. Since September 2005 he had been presidential envoy to the troubled southern federal district, fire-fighting in numerous conflict situations and endemic social crisis. Before that he had advanced municipal reform, including the radical law No. 131 that changed the whole system of Russian local government, as well as the rather unsuccessful administrative reform, which had seen endless disputes between ministries and agencies. The attempt to restrict the number of deputy prime ministers to one had also not worked, with Fradkov having four deputies at the time of his resignation, while Zubkov began with five.

Other ministers kept their posts, notably Ivanov and Medvedev as first deputy prime ministers, as well as the foreign minister, Sergei Lavrov. Finance minister Kudrin was promoted to deputy prime minister, thus strengthening his ability to defend the government's macroeconomic policies and sending a clear signal to markets that the succession would not be allowed to undermine Putin's monetary policy.[60] Deputy prime ministers Naryshkin and Zhukov kept their jobs. Serdyukov was Zubkov's son-in-law, and on 18 September he resigned as defence minister because of possible conflicts of interest, a decision applauded as signalling that Russia would not be taking the nepotistic path characteristic of Central Asia.[61] However, in announcing the new cabinet on 24 September, Putin refused to accept the resignation. Putin's decision is understandable: technically, the defence minister, like other security and foreign-policy ministers, is directly subordinate to the president and not the prime minister. Appointed little more than half a year earlier, Serdyukov had only begun the struggle against corruption, waste and mismanagement in the defence ministry. He was now given the clear signal to continue the fight against 'parquet generals' and to restore financial and economic order in the armed forces, now reinforced by the appointment of another financial expert as premier. Serdyukov's reappointment strengthened the position of the 'financial manager' proto-faction (the *finansisty*).

---

[60] Neil Buckley, 'Reformers Gain Ground in Russian Reshuffle', *The Financial Times*, 25 September 2007.
[61] *Moscow Times*, 19 September 2007.

The government therefore did not undergo any major changes either in membership or in structure, and thus the vaunted Putinite 'stability of cadres' was continued. If anything, the liberal tone to the government was reinforced. The appointment of two women in a cabinet of twenty slightly reduced the overwhelming masculine tone. The tried and tested team was largely kept in place, and thus in a sense a 'collective Putin' was created, a system that would inevitably relieve the pressure on the one individual and limit the options of the successor, at least for the first period. A 'collective Putin' obviated the need for 'another Putin' and thus allowed the actual Putin to influence policy after the succession, both to ensure continuity and to minimise the risk of destabilisation. At the same time, the pre-emptive change of prime minister ensured that the government would not become the election headquarters for a presidential candidate and would continue to function normally. In Russian terms, this meant the government retaining its overwhelming technocratic character and not becoming politicised, as had so often been the case in the 1990s.[62] The election campaign office would remain firmly in the Kremlin and no second centre would be allowed. The business of government would not be distracted by the election campaign.

In terms of our factional model, it is important to note that Zubkov does not have a background in the intelligence services. His appointment reinforced Putin's strategy of creating a parallel team, not beholden to the *silovik* lobby. In party terms, the sacking of the unpopular ministers strengthened the position of the leftist Just Russia, which was locked in a struggle with the Communist Party over issues of 'social justice'. Although Putin was adept at balancing one faction against another, he was no less skilled in ensuring that a second centre of governance and authority did not emerge, especially in the dangerous succession period. Above all, Putin built an intricate intra-regime system of checks and balances that made it difficult for any one faction to predominate, while at the same time ensuring that his successor would have to continue his policy line.

---

[62] Notably when Anatoly Chubais and Boris Nemtsov transformed the cabinet into an election campaign office, until they were dismissed by Prime Minister Viktor Chernomyrdin, who had his own presidential ambitions.

6   War of the Putin succession

Once Putin made clear that he would be standing down in 2008, the struggle for the presidency began. The intensification of factional wars reflected personal rivalries and the positioning of the various groups in anticipation of a change in the administration. The battle for the succession, it should be stressed, took place on two levels: the formal level of elections and public politics; and the subterranean level of group conflict within the administrative regime. Our model of Kremlin politics is of a non-public sphere of competing groups seeking to influence policy to advance their own interests within the framework of the rules of the game established by Putin to ensure his own autonomy and ultimate ability to trump the various projects of his subordinates. At the same time, the formal open election process rumbled on in parallel. There were two separate campaigns in the 2007–8 elections: one hidden from view but occasionally breaking into view; and the open formal process. The two interacted with each other, but ultimately it was the shadow system that was decisive.

Neutralising threats

While the liberals had a number of possible candidates, including Dmitry Medvedev and even Sergei Ivanov, the *siloviki* had no credible candidate of their own whom they could advance, and it is for this reason that they sought to persuade Putin, by fair means or foul, to stay on. Already in early 2007, Gleb Pavlovsky was arguing that the *siloviki* could resort to a strategy of 'managed instability' to ensure that Putin was forced to stay on for a third term.[1] In the event, the succession crisis exposed the divisions within the *siloviki* as much as it did between them and other factions.

---

[1] Robert Coalson, 'Russia: Why the Kremlin Likes the CIA', RFE/RL, *Russia Report*, 1 October 2007.

The factions line up

The struggle between Sechin and Victor Zolotov, the shadowy head of the presidential security service, dates back to the 1990s, when Zolotov was part of Mayor Sobchak's guard and Sechin was an assistant to Putin, who was then vice-mayor. Zolotov trained with the KGB's ninth main directorate, responsible for protecting the Soviet leadership. When Putin was appointed head of the FSB in 1998, he took with him a whole cohort of associates from St Petersburg, and on his appointment as prime minister in August 1999 Zolotov became head of his guard, and Sechin took charge of the premier's secretariat. At this point their business strategies diverged. While Zolotov remained on friendly terms with remnants of the 'family' faction, notably Roman Abramovich and Oleg Deripaska, Sechin developed links with Rosneft, whose board chair he became in 2004. Zolotov's ally Cherkesov, who had headed the FSB in St Petersburg between 1993 and 1998, became first deputy to Putin when he headed the FSB, but he failed to take over as director when Putin moved on to the premiership in August 1999. Instead, the Sechin ally Nikolai Patrushev took over, while Cherkesov was shunted sideways shortly afterwards as envoy to the north-west federal district, although he remained an active figure and later returned to national politics as head of the Federal Anti-Narcotics Agency (FSKN).

The feuding between the Sechin and Zolotov subgroups was evident in the Yukos case. In 2003–4 it was Sechin who drove the case forwards, allied with the GPO headed by the forceful Vladimir Ustinov. In due course, as noted, the alliance became a family one, when Sechin's daughter married Ustinov's son. Zolotov took a very different view of how to resolve the Yukos question, fearing that Khodorkovsky's arrest would not only damage Russia's reputation in the west, but would also harm Putin personally. Sechin ignored these concerns, and while the west did not react to the Yukos affair with any immediate démarches, such as expulsion from the G8, the case did indeed cause long-term damage to Russia's credibility as a democratic rule-of-law state and contributed to the onset of elements of a new cold war in the final years of Putin's presidency. At the same time, the Yukos affair undermined the sphere of public politics and consolidated the importance of factional relations as the drivers of policy, although no single faction was able to seize the policy initiative across the spectrum.

As the Yukos affair developed, Zolotov reinforced his position by bringing in his former St Petersburg security colleague Roman Tsepov, with whom he had worked when providing security for the mayor's office. Since then Tsepov had become head of the security company

Baltik-Eskort, which was now formally contracted to provide security for the St Petersburg mayor's office. Tsepov in turn placed his own team into important posts, including Andrei Novikov as a deputy MVD minister (2005–6). According to the Ukrainian political analyst (and Belkovsky's wife), Olesya Yakhno, Zolotov asked Tsepov to start negotiations with Yukos representatives to see whether there was an alternative to Sechin's approach to resolving the case. Tsepov put out feelers, but in September 2004 he was poisoned and died soon after.[2] As so often in the mysterious deaths of Russian politicians, officials and journalists, investigations dragged on for years and the case remains unresolved. Reports in the St Petersburg media suggest that he was poisoned while visiting the St Petersburg FSB, where he had a cup of tea (there are clear echoes here with Litvinenko's visit to the Millennium Hotel on 1 November 2006). Zolotov heeded the warning and ended contacts with Yukos.

Looking for a way to re-enter national politics, Cherkesov convinced Putin in 2003 to create FSKN, drawing on the operational resources of the dissolved Tax Police as well as the MVD's anti-drug units. Some two-thirds of the 50,000-strong tax police were transferred to the new agency. The FSKN had the right to tap telephones to fight the drug business, but it was common knowledge that the agency was engaged less in fighting narcotics smuggling than in wiretapping and gathering material about the FSB, the MVD, the GPO and Sechin personally. Wiretapping operations were overseen by Lieutenant-General Alexander Bulbov, effectively Cherkesov's deputy. Materials collected by Cherkesov and Zolotov were used to persuade Putin to dismiss Ustinov from the post of prosecutor general in June 2006 (in which among other things the Tri Kita (Three Whales) case figured, see below). Ustinov was shifted over to the post of minister of justice, accompanied by a shake-up in the FSB. The new prosecutor general, Yury Chaika, was considered an associate of Abramovich and Deripaska, who allied with Zolotov's team in the common struggle against Sechin.

Sechin's sub-faction included Alexander Bortnikov, the FSB deputy director (who would go on to head the agency in May 2008), Ustinov and Alexander Bastrykin, a former law-school classmate of Putin's and the first head of the Investigative Committee established in September 2007 (see below). Sechin sponsored Bortnikov in 2004 to head the

---

[2] 'Pundits Explore History, Outcome, Near Future of Chekist Wars in Russia', FORUM/ Moscow/Russia, www.forum.msk.ru, 19 November 2007. Feature by Natalya Royeva, with quotations from CNN correspondent Nick Peyton Walsh, political expert Lilia Shevtsova, *The New Times*, and Ukrainian political expert Olesya Yakhno: 'Putin Is a Hostage to His Own Retinue, Which Will Do Anything Just to Make Certain that He Remains in Power', in *JRL*, No. 242, 2007, Item 25.

FSB's economic security department to replace Yury Zaostrovtsev, who was implicated in the Tri Kita furniture store scandal.[3] Putin's aide Victor Ivanov was at the centre of an allied group comprising Patrushev, Gryzlov and Nurgaliev. Ranged against them were Prosecutor General Chaika, who by all accounts enjoyed good relations with Medvedev, and Finance Minister Kudrin. The group was also supported by Putin's long-standing friend Yury Kovalchuk, the head of Bank Rossiya, as well as Timchenko, one of the key partners in the oil trader Gunvor, the head of the presidential administration Sobyanin, the former chief of staff Voloshin, and former Sibneft owner Abramovich.[4]

Coup d'état foreclosed

As the succession approached, the factions tried to impose their views on the process. Cherkesov's deputy, Bulbov, had apparently tapped a phone conversation between Sechin and Ustinov, in which the idea had been mooted for Ustinov to become Putin's successor as president (this may well have been the reason for Bulbov's arrest in October 2007, see below). Putin, however, was not a black belt judo master for nothing, and he was quite capable of the surprise counter-attack to ensure that he retained the initiative.

The unexpected dismissal of Ustinov as prosecutor general on 1 June 2006, approved by a surprised Federation Council on the following day, can be interpreted as Putin's continuing resistance to the consolidation of factions into clans. Ustinov's appointment in July 1999 had originally been sponsored by the Yeltsinite 'family', and he had certainly not been the first choice as prosecutor general in 2000, but for unknown reasons Putin was unable to achieve the appointment of his preferred choice, his St Petersburg colleague Kozak. Ustinov pursued a number of high-profile and politically motivated cases, including the alleged fraud and tax evasion charges against Gusinsky in 2000 and Khodorkovsky in 2003, with a single-minded zeal. He did not show the same enthusiasm for investigating corruption until his final days in office. The procurator's office remained a powerful force in Russian politics, operating in much the same way it did in the Soviet era, although it, too, reflected the duality of the state. As a recent study puts it, 'In cases of street crime and crimes not touching the elite's economic and political interests, the Procuracy functions appropriately ... But in cases treading on

[3] Andrei Lavrov, Maksim Tovkailo and Evgenii Belyakov, *Gazeta*, 13 May 2008.
[4] Francesca Mereu, 'Sechin's Clan the Loser in a Week of Surprises', *Moscow Times*, 17 December 2007, p. 1.

government interests and those of high-level officials ... the Procuracy reflects the interests of the Presidential Administration and the elites within it.'[5]

Following what he considered the successful prosecution of the Yukos affair, it is reported that Ustinov took to chairing meetings of the GPO's collegium with an increasingly presidential air, boasting that, unlike Putin, he would not have stopped at half-measures.[6] A profile of Ustinov noted that 'in recent years he made a name for himself and his office as a staunch fighter of the oligarchs who are "inconvenient" to the Kremlin', and his handling of the Yukos case was another 'hour of triumph' for him.[7] Ustinov allegedly shielded officials accused of smuggling furniture and other goods for the Moscow furniture retailers Tri Kita and Grand, and thus avoided paying millions in import duties. Soon after Ustinov's removal from the GPO, prosecutors arrested Sergei Zuev, the head of Tri Kita and Grand, as well as four others, for alleged involvement in the smuggling operation.[8] More than this, as the succession approached it appeared that the Sechin–Ustinov alliance was gaining adherents, including possibly the prime minister, Fradkov, and even Moscow mayor, Luzhkov.[9] The consolidation of this group would have deprived Putin of freedom of manoeuvre in the succession, and this is something that he would not allow. It was also suggested that Putin was tired of dealing with the family relations between Sechin and Ustinov.[10] It was Sechin who had forced through Ustinov's appointment for a second term. Sechin's attempt to turn his brother-in-law Ustinov into a major political player was defeated by a counter-alliance which included Cherkesov, Chaika and Zolotov.

Ustinov's removal now, quite apart from other issues (including the battle against corruption), was a delayed indication of Putin's consolidation of power. In an interview with Radio Liberty, the never less than provocative Stanislav Belkovsky provided an interesting angle on Ustinov's dismissal, arguing that 'Vladimir Ustinov got too involved in the political and bureaucratic battle against Dmitry Medvedev, serving Igor Sechin's interests in this case. The Prosecutor General's office was

---

[5] Ethan S. Burger and Mary Holland, 'Law as Politics: The Russian Procuracy and Its Investigative Committee', *Columbia Journal of East European Law* 2, 2, 2008, p. 162.

[6] Yuliya Latynina, 'Novye prem′ery', *Novaya gazeta*, 13 September 2007.

[7] *Moscow News*, 21 January 2005; on his role see also 'Kremlinology Makes a Comeback in Putin's Russia', *The Financial Times*, 4 March 2005.

[8] *Moscow Times*, 19 June 2006.

[9] Pavel K. Baev, 'Ustinov's Firing Reveals Clan Maneuvering Inside Kremlin', *EDM* 3, 108, 5 June 2006, pp. 1–2.

[10] Aleksei Levchenko and Dmitry Vinogradov, 'Putin Abandoned Ustinov's Family', Gazeta.ru, 7 June 2006; in *JRL*, No. 132, 2006, Item 18.

seeking incriminatory evidence against Medvedev and preparing to launch a number of criminal prosecutions. Such actions did not fit in with Vladimir Putin's view of team ethics and the rules of the game within a clan.' Belkovsky concluded that the dismissal revealed *nomenklatura*-style divisions within the ruling elite, which 'could soon have some unpredictable consequences'.[11] Ustinov's dismissal demonstrated that Sechin's position in the Kremlin administration had weakened.

Putin now placed his relations with the *siloviki* on a new footing. The selection of the new prosecutor took place without Sechin's participation, but the change also affected Putin's relations with other security bodies, including the MVD and even the FSB. Kozak appeared to be one of the strongest candidates for the post, having gained experience of politics in the southern federal district since late 2004. Kozak, moreover, had no connections with the *siloviki* and was clearly committed to the reform of the GPO. In the event a professional was appointed, the incumbent minister of justice, Yury Chaika. Chaika had worked as deputy prosecutor general in 1995–9 and had then served as acting prosecutor general in 1999 following Yury Skuratov's suspension in February of that year. He was famously at odds with Ustinov, who had taken over the job full-time in July 1999 despite Chaika's hopes to have been appointed. Instead, Chaika was appointed justice minister by Putin on 17 August 1999.

Chaika was a supporter of moderate judicial reform, and under his leadership the justice ministry carried out a reform of the penitentiary system that was praised by the Council of Europe. It was Chaika, as the overseer of the work of the Federal Penitentiary Service (FSIN), who in October 2005 was ultimately responsible for sending Khodorkovsky to faraway Chita, even though the Russian Criminal Code requires people to serve their sentences as close as possible to their home region. Despite the appointment of this respected figure, it was clear that the prosecutor's office would remain a highly political office, even though formally the body does not have political functions. Chaika soon began a purge of the GPO, including the dismissal of the deputy prosecutor Vladimir Kolesnikov, who had been deeply involved in the Yukos case.[12] The GPO's deputy head, Yury Biryukov, a key member of the informal 'politburo' behind the Yukos affair, also resigned, only to become a senator in the Federation Council.[13] Ustinov's key lieutenants who had

---

[11] Oleg Dement'ev, *Rossiiskie vesti*, No. 22, June 15, 2006.
[12] Alek Akhundov and Yurii Senatorov, 'Chistka Mundirov', *Kommersant*, 28 June 2006, pp. 1, 3.
[13] *Novaya gazeta*, 8–11 February 2007.

supervised the Yukos affair were removed, although the reshuffle in the
GPO was accompanied by 'soft landings' for all concerned. This was
possibly in recognition of their services in the Yukos affair, accompanied
by concern that their alienation would expose the regime to the danger
that the hidden story would be told.

Although it appears that Putin's administration was by and large in
agreement over the Yukos affair (and those who disagreed, like Voloshin,
resigned, while others, like Kasyanov, kept silent), the procurator's office
was now identified as a threat to the regime itself. The new Criminal
Procedure Code (UPK) of July 2001, masterminded by Kozak, transferred some power from prosecutors to judges, weakening their rights to
issue arrest and search warrants, and attempted to boost judicial responsibility by rendering judges more accountable. The overall effect, however, was far less than intended. In November 2003 Kozak and
Medvedev drew up further plans to change the GPO's status accompanied by a sharp reduction in its powers, above all removing its investigative
authority and creating a special investigations committee.[14] The initiative was blocked at the time by a combination of Ustinov and Sechin. As
Baker and Glasser put it, 'Every step along the way, though, Kozak ran
into virulent opposition from the man who had beat him out of the job of
prosecutor general, Ustinov.'[15] However, when in spring 2006 the procuracy under Ustinov once again began to demonstrate its power and
autonomy, with cases launched against customs officials, regional
authorities and some members of the Federation Council itself, the
administration was alarmed. With the GPO's help, it would not be
difficult to seize power in the country. For this reason Ustinov was
dismissed from this key post, although he remained in the administration
and, to maintain factional balance, was appointed minister of justice,
Chaika's old post.[16] This astonishing personnel merry-go-round belies
the seriousness of the affair. Given Putin's reliance on security structures, it was not surprising that they should become the focus of
bureaucratic-factional power struggles, but the intensity of the conflicts
within the law-enforcement and secret services was extraordinary and
ultimately posed a threat to the presidency itself.

---

[14] Unattributed interview with Alexander Bastrykin, *Izvestiya*, 5 October 2007.
[15] Baker and Glasser, *Kremlin Rising*, p. 240.
[16] In that post he once again gathered his old team from the GPO, including Nikolai
Savchenko and Sergei Vasil'ev; Sergei Varshavchik, 'Proverrye lyudi', *Nezavisimaya
gazeta*, 1 September 2006, p. 3.

The Investigative Committee (Sledstvennyi komitet, SK)

The idea of creating a special investigative committee was now revived. In June 2007 Alexander Bastrykin, the head of the St Petersburg University law school group and reputed to be an associate of Sechin's, was appointed head of the newly created Investigative Committee (Sledstvennyi komitet, SK) *in* the General Prosecutor's Office (but note, not *under*), and he formally took office on 7 September. The head of the SK is appointed not by the prosecutor general but by the Federation Council, following nomination by the president. The SK took over many of the GPO's powers and 18,000 of its investigators, as well as responsibility for some 60,000 criminal cases. The prosecutor general lost the power to initiate investigations (including into the affairs of Duma deputies or top officials), seize property or start criminal cases. The head of the SK can launch an investigation into the affairs of the prosecutor general, but the latter cannot return the compliment (this requires the approval of three Supreme Court judges at the president's request). To demonstrate the SK's autonomy, it was given a number of prestigious office buildings, and its own teaching and research institutes. The SK also enjoys the right of legislative initiative, working through the president and government. The new body took over all politically sensitive investigations, including those into politicians and officials.

The establishment of the SK suggested an enhanced role for the security agencies, with the FSB officer Yury Nyrkov appointed deputy director in October 2007. This was part of a larger pattern. In 2006 Oleg Safonov was appointed as an MVD deputy minister and Alexei Anichkin became head of the interior ministry's own investigative committee, and in August 2007 Nurgaliev established special regional police teams with the power to reopen old corruption investigations. Bastrykin and Sechin became allies, since both were ranged against the GPO and Zolotov. Sechin's position was reinforced by the support of Cherkesov's long-time opponent from his St Petersburg FSB days, Bortnikov, now the head of the economic security service of the FSB (the SEB). Sechin also weakened the FSNK by restricting its wiretapping rights and thus appeared to be regaining ground lost after the defeat of summer 2006, when Ustinov was removed as prosecutor general.

The emergence of a group of financial and other experts who owed personal loyalty to Putin had the effect of balancing the influence of the *siloviki* as a group, however torn by intra-factional conflict. Already the appointment of the head of the Federal Tax Service, Serdyukov, as minister of defence had signalled Putin's intention to impose state control over financial flows, as did the appointment of Zubkov, who had headed the Financial Intelligence Agency, as premier in September 2007. Serdyukov's replacement as head of the Federal Tax Service was Mikhail Mokresov, who was an old friend of Zubkov's from his days in St Petersburg's city hall. Baev argues that these appointments represented the 'carefully orchestrated ... rise of a new political clan [the *finansisty*] in the shadows of the seemingly all-powerful siloviki'.[17] As well as tackling corruption in the armed forces, Serdyukov's mission was to ensure that the military stayed out of the succession struggles, both in their open and covert manifestations, and this he achieved.[18] No 'military' candidate was even hinted at, and thus the long-term strategy to depoliticise the military had succeeded and the Russian tradition of demilitarised politics was maintained.

The replacement of Ustinov as prosecutor general by Chaika represented a major blow to Sechin's position. The creation of the SK, which in turn reduced Chaika's powers, was Sechin's response. Neither Chaika nor Bastrykin had the authority once enjoyed by the unified GPO headed by an all-powerful prosecutor general. As Khodorkovsky's lawyer, Yury Schmidt, puts it, 'Out of one powerful figure two weak ones were created, and both are dependent on the Kremlin administration and personally on the president, since he nominates both.'[19] The attempt to launch an investigation into the work of Bastrykin's committee in December 2007 (see below) by Chaika and his reformist colleagues, just a few months after its establishment and before it could make significant changes, marked yet another bout in the struggle.

As long as Putin was in power, he was able to control the beast of factional conflict, but the events of spring 2006 obviously alarmed him. One of the main tasks in ensuring stability in the succession, therefore, was to reduce the power of the procuracy, but not too much. The creation of the SK effectively deprived the GPO of its ability to conduct investigations and to initiate criminal proceedings. There was much talk of creating an entirely independent investigations committee, possibly bringing together not only the GPO's work in this area but also that of the MVD and the FSB. This would have the effect of achieving a powerful separation of powers in the force structures, since none on its own would be able to pursue the whole cycle of gathering evidence, initiating proceedings and pursuing court actions, and the power of

---

[17] Pavel K. Baev, 'Zubkov: The Tax Man Cometh', *EDM* 4, 173, 18 September 2007.
[18] Stephen Blank, 'Serdyukov's Authority Grows at Ministry of Defense', *EDM* 5, 10, 18 January 2008.
[19] Yurii Schmidt, 'Chto dal'she', 25 October 2007, www.khodorkovsky.ru/cassation/comments/7430.html.

each would be limited. This would make another Yukos affair more difficult, but not impossible. Only when politics was taken out of the administrative 'power' sphere and returned to social actors such as parties and other centres of accountability could one speak of 'normal political life'.[20]

Factionalism goes public

Matters came to a head over the Tri Kita furniture case, a scandal that had rumbled on since August 2000 when customs inspectors confiscated a consignment of furniture and other consumer goods from China, in the end accusing those involved of evading customs duties, of money-laundering, arms smuggling and even assassinations. The case involved both active and retired officials at the highest levels. It was alleged that Tri Kita was patronised by the FSB, notably Yevgeny Zaostrovtsev, a former superior of the current FSB director Nikolai Patrushev and the father of then FSB deputy director Yury Zaostrovtsev. The affair 'entwined the interests of clans, agencies, honest and shadowy business' and was one in which the president had become personally involved.[21] The case may well have provoked the poisoning of Duma deputy Yury Shchekochikhin, who after a sudden swiftly acting illness died on 3 July 2003 after he had published an article on the affair in *Novaya gazeta* in June. Following research with the GPO, FSB, the MVD and the State Custom's Committee, Shchekochikhin had come to the view that the case encompassed far more than contraband but involved the laundering of millions of dollars through the Bank of New York (BONY), and possibly arms sales as well. In June 2003 he met with FBI officials in Moscow and he planned to travel to the United States for further investigation.[22] In their notorious report of 4 June 2003 'The State and the Oligarchs', which warned of a 'creeping oligarch coup', Belkovsky and his colleagues in the Council for National Strategy warned that the elite was ignoring the law when it suited them, as in the Tri Kita case when even the president's order for the case to be investigated properly was ignored. They noted that 'the president in this new system no longer has the function or right to act as arbiter, and thus

[20] Cf. Editorial, 'Perekrestnaya neutralizatsiya silovikov', *Ekspert*, No. 32, 3 September 2007, p. 19.

[21] Natal'ya Kozlova, '"Tri Kita" doplyli do suda', *Rossiiskaya gazeta*, 29 January 2008, p. 6.

[22] Jonas Bernstein, 'Deaths of Corruption Fighters Overshadows New Anticorruption Campaign', *EDM* 5, 101, 28 May 2008.

one can assume is a weaker institution than even during Boris Yeltsin's rule'.[23] A trial dealing with the main issue in the Three Whales scandal, the importation of furniture from China, finally reached a court in Naro-Fominsk in January 2008.

The Bulbov case and Cherkesov's hook

With the investigation going nowhere, in 2006 Putin insisted that the Tri Kita case should be pursued more vigorously. The new investigation by Bulbov led in spring 2006 to widespread dismissals in the GPO and the FSB, including the arrest of five senior officers including Colonel Yury Gaidukov, an FSB official who worked in the defence ministry. The FSKN once again demonstrated that it had less to do with controlling drugs than acting as a body to keep an eye on other special services. In response, on 2 October 2007 Bulbov, who worked closely with Cherkesov, was arrested by agents of the FSB and the newly established Investigative Committee and accused of corruption and monitoring the calls of fifty-three business people and journalists.[24] He was charged with illegal wiretapping, illicit business activities and receiving bribes.

This was more than normal inter-institutional rivalry; it revealed the intense struggle between factions behind the scenes. Cherkesov was lined up against FSB director Patrushev, while away from this particular conflict no love was lost between Sergei Ivanov, on the one side, and Sechin and Ustinov on the other. The arrest of some top officials in the Audit Chamber, headed by the former FSB director Stepashin, suggested yet another dimension to the factional struggles. Stepashin had been investigating the disappearance of some $4bn in IMF loans in 1998, and apparently he had gathered a considerable body of evidence against government officials. Cherkesov's key ally was the head of the presidential security service, Zolotov. The arrest of Barsukov (see Chapter 5), considered an ally of Cherkesov and Zolotov, in August 2007 was also part of the intrigue. Cherkesov apparently had business ties with Semen Vainshtok, the head of the Transneft oil and pipeline company, who was

---

[23] The full version of 'Gosudarstvo i oligarkhiya' is available (accessed 7 November 2007) at www.strategeia.ru/news_453.html. A slightly shortened version was republished as 'Gosudarstvo i oligarkhiya', *Zavtra*, 27 June 2003, p. 3.

[24] Vladimir Perekrest, 'General zaderzhali u trapa samoleta', *Izvestiya*, 4 October 2007, p. 1; Roger McDermott, 'Russian General Implicated in Narcotics Sting', *EDM* 4, 186, 9 October 2007. Three of Bulbov's colleagues were also arrested. The key accusation was that Bulbov paid a certain Mikhail Yanykin $50,000 a month to listen in to conversations of major business people, politicians and journalists.

replaced, perhaps not coincidentally, in October 2007 by Nikolai Tokarev, who had served with Putin in East Germany in the 1980s.

On 9 October Cherkesov brought the tensions into the open in a lengthy article titled 'We Must Not Permit Warriors to Become Merchants' in *Kommersant*, which warned against 'internecine feuds' in the security services, noting that 'Any corporation, including the Chekist one, should respect norms in order to be healthy ... If these norms disappear and there is arbitrariness, then the corporation collapses.' He singled out the Investigative Committee for attack, although the FSB was clearly his target. He also talked in terms of the elite being a 'caste', suggesting interlocked networks of family and other ties, and noted that 'You cannot be a trader and a warrior at the same time', highlighting the commercial aspects of the case.[25] He suggested that Bulbov had been arrested to prevent investigation into corruption and smuggling in the special services. Cherkesov had long espoused the ideology of 'Chekism', the view that the security services had a special role and had saved the Russian state in the 1990s. The security service was a 'hook' that had been grabbed by post-Soviet society as it was 'tumbling into an abyss'. Now the unity of the special services had dissolved and they were torn by rivalries: 'A "war of all against all" will result in a complete disintegration of the network ... We must avoid scandals and an all-out war.' The degeneration of the warrior caste into merchants was a rather romantic way of describing the interpenetration of politics and business in Putin's Russia.

Sechin once again appeared to be at the heart of struggle, with his opponents (notably Cherkesov) trying to curb his influence as the putative head of the *siloviki*. The fact that the struggle under the carpet had now moved into the open indicated the intense nature of this intra-factional power struggle. It also suggested that Cherkesov was losing ground, and by going public was ready to exercise the nuclear option of *glasnost'* ('openness'). The audience probably was not the public at large but Putin personally, to whom he appears to have lost access. Patrushev's FSB also suddenly became more public, listing in October how many foreign spies it had stopped in 2007 and exposing the alleged plot to assassinate Putin on his visit to Tehran that month.

This was not the first time that Cherkesov had argued that the Chekists had a special role in Russia. In an earlier article in 2004, however, he had been both more circumspect and triumphalist, attacking those who sought to undermine the security services and

---

[25] Viktor Cherkesov, 'Nel'zya dopustit', chtoby voiny prevratilis' v torgovtsev'', *Kommersant*, 9 October 2007, p. 1.

their staff, and he described former KGB/FSB personnel as 'the bulwark estate'.[26] He proudly stated: 'I remain faithful to the main thing, to my sense of work as a Chekist, to the understanding of my Chekist destiny. It is well-known that I did not reject this faith during the peak of the democratic attacks in the early 1990s, and I will not reject it now.' The burden of saving Russian statehood, he insisted, had fallen to the lot of the Chekists.[27] Cherkesov perhaps revealed more than he intended, since in appealing to the corporate duties of a special group he not only admitted the existence of a type of state within the state, but also its limited coherence. Contrary to those who argue that a unified group of *siloviki* exists, guided by an ideology of Chekism, Cherkesov revealed a permanent war over influence and resources. As so often in Putin's Russia, the struggle between state agencies entailed a struggle to control the flow of resources. The Chekist view, as far as we can ascertain, was that Putin had to remain in power to guarantee that the chaos of the 1990s would not return and that there would be no property redistribution at the elite level.

As Putin's second term came to a close, the struggle to shape the succession threatened the stability of the whole administration. The machine that Putin had created appeared now to threaten his ability to shape the transition. As Vladimir Kryuchkov, the head of the KGB at the time of the August 1991 attempted coup, and some other KGB officials warned in an open letter at this time, all sides in the conflict must 'take steps towards each other! Otherwise, as our experience shows, a terrible misfortune may occur, and we must not allow this.' They argued that Cherkesov's letter had been the first step in overcoming the conflict, and they called for more moves in that direction. As they noted, 'We know from experience that conflict between respected and worthy people can be used for dark ends', and they stressed that 'all sides are united in their faith in Putin as a national leader, as the factor of stability in the country'.[28] Putin also fought back and warned Cherkesov that airing dirty linen in public was 'incorrect': 'It is wrong to bring these kinds of problems to the media. When someone behaves that way and . . . claims

[26] Viktor Cherkesov, 'Nevedomstvennye razmyshleniya o professii: Moda na KGB?', *Komsomol'skaya pravda*, 29 December 2004, p. 6.
[27] Viktor Cherkesov, 'Vmesto poslesloviya: Chekistov byvshikh ne byvaet', *Komsomol'skaya pravda*, 29 December 2004, p. 7.
[28] 'Ne dovesti do bedy!', signed by Vladimir Kryuchkov, Nikolai Leonov, a Duma deputy and former head of a KGB department, Vagif Guseinov, director of the Institute of Strategic Evaluations and Analysis and former head of the Azerbaijan KGB, and Vyacheslav Generalov and Yevgeny Kalgin, also former heads of KGB departments, *Zavtra*, 31 October 2007, p. 1.

that there is a war between security agencies, he should, first of all, be spotless.'[29] Putin now appointed Cherkesov to head a new agency, the State Anti-Narcotics Committee (GAK). Cherkesov's powers were expanded, making him head of an organisation comparable to the National Anti-Terrorism Committee (NAK) created in 2006, headed by FSB director Patrushev.[30] Kryuchkov and his colleagues in the special services had played a catastrophic role in 1990–1 in feeding Gorbachev fearsome stories about internal and foreign subversion, encouraging Gorbachev's turn to the conservatives in winter 1990 and thus losing the confidence of the democrats. It would be ironic if the very same process now led to Putin's isolation.

Cherkesov had been angling to be appointed head of the Security Council, a post vacant since the resignation of the former foreign minister Igor Ivanov in July 2007, or even to head the FSB. In not doing so, Putin signalled that he would be even-handed in the factional and inter-agency conflicts, and would not allow one complete victory over any other. The Security Council session planned for 8 October, where the new secretary was to have been announced, was repeatedly postponed. Putin kept the post vacant rather than making a choice, which would have limited his ability to balance one group against the other and entailed the danger of him becoming hostage to them. The unity that had characterised the regime during the Yukos affair had now given way to open conflict, and as his presidency came to an end there was a danger that he would lose the power to mediate.

More broadly, if in 1997 the country was wracked by a 'banker's war', when the major oligarchs fell out over the spoils of the Svyazinvest communication company privatisation and used the media to fight their respective corners, it was a measure of how much things had changed that the struggle now was between factions of the *siloviki*. The earlier war had pitted Berezovsky and Gusinsky against Potanin and the so-called 'young reformers' (Chubais, Nemtsov and Alfred Kokh), but within a year the whole system of oligarchic power had collapsed in the partial default of August 1998. The oligarch factional struggle over Svyazinvest proved suicidal for all concerned, forcing Chubais and his team of 'young reformers' to leave their posts and severely weakening the oligarchs themselves. Fear of a re-enactment of toxic internecine strife prompted Putin to warn against conducting such faction fights in public.

[29] Andrei Kolesnikov, 'Prezident ne sognul svoyu "liniyu"', *Kommersant*, 19 October 2007, p. 1.
[30] Natal'ya Melikova and Marina Obrazkova, 'Vtoroi, antinarkoticheskii: Putin skazal svoe slovo v voine spetssluzhb', *Nezavisimaya gazeta*, 22 October 2007, pp. 1, 3.

With the disposal of the energy rents at stake, as well as policy continuity and the property settlement, the factions sought to consolidate their positions in the transition. Putin feared that the whole system could be consumed by fraternal warfare between rival elite factions. The warring camps, however, would remain in conflict until the succession was resolved.

The siloviki *over-reach: the Storchak affair*

Factional conflict during the succession crisis intensified with the arrest of the deputy finance minister, Sergei Storchak, on the eve of the election. He was arrested on 15 November and charged with embezzling $43.4 million from the state budget. According to Rahr, the arrest was the outcome of 'A mass attack against the reformist wing at the top of the government' by Sechin.[31] Storchak had been in charge of negotiations to pay off Soviet-era debts, and he was one of the leading experts in the field. The embezzlement charges focused on the settlement of one of these debts to the commercial firm Sodexim. The case focused on an Algerian debt that Sodexim had purchased from the Russian government in 1996 for $26 million, to be repaid to Sodexim in the forms of various goods and services. When the Algerians stopped supplying these, Sodexim sought compensation from the Russian government. The director of Sodexim, Victor Zakharov, was also arrested, along with the president of the Moscow-based Inter-Regional Investment Bank. The Investigative Committee took the lead in pursuing the case, and indeed threatened its parent body, the GPO, with legal action after the latter blocked a second case (focused on debt negotiations with Kuwait in January 2005) against Storchak.[32]

Kudrin, who at the time of the arrest was about to leave for South Africa with Storchak, strongly backed his deputy: 'I don't understand the measure taken regarding this man, who for many years worked and every day fought for every kopeck, asserting Russia's interests in every debt negotiation.'[33] The lesson may well have been precisely this – to teach Kudrin just how weak he was in the real hierarchy of power. Kudrin's poor relations with security officials in Putin's entourage were well known, but Storchak's arrest was also a blow against Zubkov,

---

[31] Rar, *Rossiya zhmet na gaz*, p. 352.
[32] Max Delany, 'Siloviki Clash in the Storchak Affair', *Moscow Times*, 7 December 2007, p. 1. A sum equivalent to $1 million was allegedly found in Storchak's apartment.
[33] Quoted by Anna Arutunyan, 'Deputy Finance Minister Held in Corruption Probe', *Moscow News*, 23 November 2007, p. 2.

discrediting one of his officials. The arrest may also have been a blow directed against Chemezov, since the officials arrested with Storchak, Vadim Volkov and Victor Zakharov, were linked with the Inter-Regional Investment Bank on whose board of directors Chemezov's deputy, Alexei Alëshin, sat. Soon after Igor Kruglyakov, another director of the same bank, was arrested. For Yasin, the former economics minister, Storchak's arrest, accompanied as we shall see by virulent attacks against the SPS, were clear 'actions of Sechin's *siloviki* against the liberals'.[34]

The balance of factional power appeared to be shifting against the liberals in the government. Coming when the electoral campaign was reaching its peak, the arrest was clearly designed as a public relations act cloaked in the struggle against corruption.[35] It revealed the methods of the parallel universe of faction-fighting, where voting and popular support were irrelevant. As in the Yukos affair, the key tools were 'the ability to launch criminal cases, arrests and trials'.[36] Indeed, it appeared that elite relations had reached such a dead end that no methods other than forceful ones were available. Already in 2001 a criminal case had been launched against Aksënenko, someone who had stood against Putin in 1999–2000, for having allegedly exceeded his authority resulting in large financial losses for the state; the case only ended with his death in autumn 2003. Other cases had been started against officials in the State Customs Committee and other agencies. The method was already familiar from the Yeltsin years when, for example, in 1998 the first deputy minister of finances, Vladimir Petrov, was arrested and accused of financial malfeasance; he was later rehabilitated (no doubt because of factional intervention) and became a member of the Federation Council.[37]

The public nature of the struggle over the Storchak affair, however, revealed the intensity of the struggle accompanying the SK's attempt to carve out an independent sphere of action for itself. The Storchak case revealed that the division of labour between the two bodies remained unclear. The GPO was clearly dissatisfied with the loss of its

---

[34] Irina Timofeeva, 'Golosovanie orkestrom', *Novaya gazeta*, No. 93, 6 December 2003. He also noted that 'powerful forces opposing the *siloviki*' lay behind Shvartsman's interview (see below).

[35] The 2003 parliamentary campaign had also been accompanied by an ersatz anti-corruption campaign, called 'werewolves in epaulettes'. Few gave credence to the assertion by senior Public Chamber member Anatoly Kucherena that Storchak's arrest gave 'real proof that the country's leadership has stepped up the fight against corruption in government agencies'; see Miriam Elder, 'Deputy Finance Minister Arrested', *Moscow Times*, 19 November 2007, p. 1.

[36] Editorial, 'Izbirateli i sledovateli', *Ekspert*, No. 44, 26 November 2007, p. 21.

[37] Maksim Agarkov and Andrei Gromov, 'Arest', *Ekspert*, No. 44, 26 November 2007, pp. 23–8, at p. 28.

investigative functions and sought to do more than simply monitor the judicial process. The Storchak case saw Bastrykin run headlong into the opposition of Chaika and the prosecutor's office: Bastrykin was considered an ally of Sechin and the Kremlin *siloviki*; while Chaika was affiliated with the rival Cherkesov faction. The Investigative Committee went public with its condemnation of the GPO,[38] yet another sign of the fragmentation of Putinite elite structures at the close of his presidency. Bastrykin demanded greater independence, while Chaika called for the SK to be fully subordinated to the GPO, and they criticised each other in public.[39]

A further blow to Sechin and his faction was the review announced on 14 December 2007 by the GPO into whether the SK had conducted its work according to the law.[40] Coming just a few months after its establishment, the political motives behind the move were clear. The investigation would look at the keeping of personnel files, the solving of serious crimes such as murder, and the informing of embassies and relatives when foreign citizens were detained.[41] If violations needed to be found, they undoubtedly would be. The review signalled the continued fight back by Cherkesov and Zolotov, and possibly also the liberal faction, alarmed by the Bulbov and Storchak arrests.

The Storchak case had broad ramifications, including control of Russia's $150 billion Stabilisation Fund and setting spending priorities. By weakening Kudrin, the guardian of macroeconomic probity, there would be easier access to these funds.[42] His arrest, at the climax of the election campaign, revealed perhaps an even more disturbing tendency: the conduct of politics in the second sphere took the form of spectacular arrests and démarches. As an editorial in *Ekspert* magazine put it, there could be different views on the most appropriate way to dispose of stabilisation funds, but 'a situation where the chief argument in fighting Kudrin is the arrest of his deputy minister cannot be considered normal'. The article went on to argue that force had become basically the only way to resolve arguments within the elite, and the costs of the breakdown of normal procedures was becoming increasingly disruptive. An assault on one group ricocheted into attacks on others.[43] In this context, Putin's

[38] Dmitrii Dogov, *Izvestiya* (online version), 5 December 2007.
[39] Alexei Nikol'skii, 'Chaika Bastrykinu ne ukaz', *Vedomosti*, 1 February 2008, p. A02.
[40] Ekaterina Zapodinskaya, 'Sledstvennyi komitet proveryaet na vyzhivaemost'', *Kommersant*, 15 December 2007, pp. 1, 3.
[41] Mereu, 'Sechin's Clan the Loser in a Week of Surprises', p. 1.
[42] Nika Viktorova, 'Skandal: Minfin protiv MVD?', *Argumenty i fakty*, No. 48, 28 November 2007, p. 2.
[43] *Ekspert*, No. 44, 26 November 2007.

attempts to ensure a strong majority for United Russia can be seen as a way of escaping the logic of internecine power struggles and to root the formal institutions not only in the legitimacy of law but also of popular politics. In the 2007–8 electoral cycle, he sought to break out of the isolation of a popular president accompanied by weak instruments of popular representation (parties and parliament). The covert system came into open confrontation with the system of public politics, and fearing rampant intra-elite conflict within the administrative regime, Putin drew on the institutional resources of the normative state. The instrumental way in which the formal political order was mobilised, however, negated its transformational potential. The Putinite system could not reintegrate the two dimensions and thus transcend itself.

Putin under attack

Belkovsky, at the time the head of the National Strategy Council whose report 'The State and the Oligarchs' in 2003 had provided the intellectual rationale to launch the campaign against Khodorkovsky and Yukos, later stated that he was deeply dissatisfied with the way that the case had developed.[44] He had favoured a revision of the privatisations of the 1990s but instead, he argued, all that had happened was a redistribution of property carried out by the same controversial methods.[45] The Putin elite had used their turn in power to enrich themselves rather than establishing a more just political system. Valery Khomyakov, who had taken over as the head of the National Strategy Council, argued that while the distancing of big business from the corridors of power under Putin was to be welcomed, economic interests would nevertheless try to influence the succession. He insisted that the race would not be a pleasant stroll but an 'intense struggle both within elite groups and between them'. The main players would be regional elites, political parties, including UR, 'which has recently demonstrated independence', and above all big business. He singled out the Alfa Group, headed by the former minister Petr Aven, as the most likely to attempt to influence the succession. He noted the group's deep integration into the power system, the international community and the media, and with apparent ambitions to place one of its own into the top echelon of power, the premiership or as speaker of the

[44] Belkovsky by now had left the National Strategy Council and headed the National Strategy Institute.
[45] BBC Monitoring, NTV Moscow, 0720 GMT 26 December 2004, in *JRL*, No. 8517, 2004, Item 10.

State Duma.[46] In the event, no company or individual was willing to step into Khodorkovsky's shoes in the 2007–8 campaign, and there was no new Yukos affair or even a hint of a regional *fronde*. Instead, factional conflict took intensely personalised forms.

As the focus of the new system of power and property, Putin himself came under increasing scrutiny. Åslund notes that in February 2004 Rybkin had named three people as Putin's financial intermediaries, notably Gennady Timchenko, possibly a former KGB officer and a member of Putin's dacha collective in Priozersky district of Leningrad region.[47] Timchenko is alleged to have acted as the intermediary between Putin and Sobchak after the latter had been smuggled into exile by Putin in November 1997. Timchenko and Putin supported Zubkov's gubernatorial bid in Leningrad region in 1998, although they lost to the outsider Valery Serdyukov, an incident that provided further grounds for Putin to be wary of the unconstrained electoral process.

Timchenko was a co-founder of the Gunvor oil trading company, with apparently a net worth of $20 billion on the eve of the Yukos affair, which acted as the trading company for four Russian oil companies.[48] On the back of Rosneft's acquisition of the main Yukos assets, the Geneva-based Gunvor group became the world's third largest oil trader, after Glencore (making $116.5 billion in 2006) and Vitol ($113.9 billion), posting profits of $8 billion on a turnover of $43 billion in 2007. Gunvor handled a third of Russia's seaborne oil exports on behalf of Surgutneftegaz, Gazprom-Neft, TNK-BP and Rosneft.[49] Earlier Yukos had traded through its own Swiss subsidiary, Petroval, but with the company's bankruptcy, its main assets had been transferred to Rosneft, and its foreign trading activities to Gunvor. There had long been speculation about Gunvor's main shareholders. Torbjohn Tornqvist, Gunvor's Swedish managing director, in October 2007 revealed that he and

---

[46] Roundtable held on 6 June 2006, 'Sud'ba Khodorkovskogo koe-kogo nichemu ne nauchila', *Izvestiya.ru*, 6 June 2006, www.izvestia.ru/press/article3093549/index.html.

[47] Rybkin argued that Timchenko had taken over from Roman Abramovich as the Kremlin's banker in the 2003–4 electoral cycle. Timchenko controlled not only the Swiss-based Gunvor, but also other oil traders: Russia's Transoil, Estonia's Tarcona, and Finland's International Petroleum Products (IPP) and dozens of other companies and offshore firms, with his transactions protected not only by Estonian bureaucrats but also by Russia's *siloviki* (he had allegedly worked in the KGB's First Directorate, but there is uncertainty over this). There is no doubt that his links with Putin go back to at least the early 1990s, including joint stakes in the 'Rossiya' bank.

[48] Åslund, 'Unmasking President Putin's Grandiose Myth', p. 9.

[49] Elena Vrantseva, Igor' Prokop'ev and Andrei Demenkov, 'Komu kto povezet', *Russkii Newsweek*, 15 January 2007. For more details see Catherine Belton and Neil Buckley, 'On the Offensive: How Gunvor Rose to the Top of Russian Oil Trading', *The Financial Times*, 14 May 2008.

Timchenko had founded the company in 1997 but denied that its rise had anything to do with Putin.[50] In a letter to the *Financial Times* on 22 May 2008, Timchenko reiterated the point: 'Media suggestions about the extent of any ties between me and Mr. Putin are overblown.' He conceded that he and Putin had together opened a judo club, but he stressed that 'My career of more than 20 years in the oil industry has not been built on favors or political connections. When it comes to price – ask our rivals and study our record in open tenders.' Commentators clearly were influenced by the development of a whole series of corrupt trading relationships that had developed after the nationalisation of Aramco between 1976 and 1980 in Saudi Arabia where, for example, the Petromonde oil trading company had allegedly been used to skim profits for the benefit of members of the Saudi royal family.

More details were provided by Belkovsky, the ideologist of the early Yukos campaign. He had hoped to use the Yukos affair to establish himself as the Kremlin's favoured PR campaigner, but having failed in this endeavour, he turned into a harsh critic of Kremlin politics. In an astonishingly direct attack on 12 November 2007, Belkovsky claimed that Putin had amassed enormous personal wealth. He alleged that Putin controlled 37 per cent of the shares in Surgutneftegaz (worth $20bn), 4.5 per cent of Gazprom's shares ($13bn) and 'at least 50%' of Timchenko's Gunvor company, 'which last year had a turnover of $40 billion and profits of $8 billion' (possibly worth $10 billion).[51] This would give Putin personal assets worth over $41bn, which if true would make him one of history's greatest kleptocrats, casting president Mobuto of Zaire or Marcos of the Philippines in the shade. Allegations of this type have been made against Putin since the time of his work in the mayor's office in St Petersburg in the early 1990s, and none of them have been confirmed.[52]

---

[50] Luke Harding, 'Putin, the Kremlin Power Struggle and the $40bn Fortune', *The Guardian*, 21 December 2007, pp. 1–2.
[51] '"Man sollte die active Rolle Putins nicht überschätzen": Der russische Politologe Belkowski sieht wirtschaftliche Kräfte am Werk im Kreml und prophezeit den Niedergang Russlands', *Die Welt*, 12 November 2007.
[52] On 10 January 1992, Marina Sal'e was appointed by the St Petersburg legislature to head a working group of deputies to investigate Putin's work as head of the Foreign Relations Committee of the St Petersburg mayor's office. The charges against him focus on malpractices associated with various food for oil barter arrangements. She argued that Putin engaged in a criminal conspiracy with various associates to defraud the city, and as a result very little food was brought in, forcing the city in October 1991 to introduce ration cards. She sums up: 'In 1991–1992 Putin firmly entered the criminal world and there established his "great state". Today he has been called upon to lead it.' Marina Sal'e, 'V. Putin – "president" korrumpirovannoi oligarkhii!', obshchestvenii fond 'Glasnost'', 18 March 2000, www.glasnostonline.org/fond/sviazi.htm.

Following the repetition of Belkovsky's claims in the *Guardian*, by which time Putin's alleged stake in Gunvor had risen to 'at least 75%' with his total assets 'at least $40 billion', but he also may have held assets in other companies so the total could be 'much more',[53] Tornqvist denied that Putin was in any way a 'beneficiary of its activities' and refuted allegations that the company had benefited from a close relationship with the Kremlin. The majority shares in the company were held by himself, Timchenko, and 'with a minority of the shares held by a third investor' (the identity of this 'third man' aroused considerable speculation). He insisted that the profits of Gunvor ran into the 'hundreds of millions, not billions' and conceded that Timchenko 'did indeed know President Putin in the days before the latter became famous'. This at least was new information, since Timchenko was notoriously reclusive. He went on to note: 'However, suggestions that they share a KGB heritage or have been in business together are wide of the mark.'[54] The informational war about Putin's alleged wealth had clearly been unleashed as part of the struggle between Kremlin factions.

Just before the New Year, in an interview with a Kazakh website (Pozitsiya.kz), Belkovsky repeated his charges against Putin, now insisting that Medvedev was chosen as the favoured candidate to succeed Putin so that he could complete the task of 'legalising' the funds that the Russian elite had accumulated in western accounts. In this interview Belkovsky noted, as he had done in the *Guardian* earlier, that Putin had not tried to sue him. He also argued, as he had done several times before, that Putin would give up power entirely, and that he would not serve as Medvedev's prime minister. It is worth quoting at length from the interview since it provides a useful corrective to the usual portrayal of Putin as a power-hungry leader intent on staying in office at all costs:

Putin never sought after the presidential post; he was persuaded, and he has always had difficulty making decisions in complicated situations. He has put off all painful and hard decisions until later. And he has showed himself to be a leader who does not want to remain in power for a long time. He is frightfully tired of that power. Therefore, I have always believed and [continue to] believe that he will not remain in power in any form, although he will have a certain ceremonial post that guarantees him not so much power as security after leaving office. What post? Thus far, I don't know.[55]

---

[53] Harding, 'Putin, the Kremlin Power Struggle and the $40bn Fortune'.

[54] Torbjohn Tornqvist, 'Putin Owns no Part in Gunvor', *The Guardian*, 22 December 2007, p. 31.

[55] Stanislav Belkovsky, 'Menya ob'yavyat vragom svobody', interview with Aigul' Omarova, 28 December 2007, http://http://posit.kz/?lan=ru&id=100& pub=4904;

The source of Belkovsky's information about Putin probably originated with Sechin, and we know from the Yukos affair that the two had worked together. On 30 November 2007, the long-suppressed report by Marina Sal'e and Yury Gladkov on Putin's actions as head of the foreign affairs committee of the St Petersburg mayor's office, commissioned by the St Petersburg Soviet of People's Deputies on 10 January 1992, came back into the public domain. Resurfacing two days before the Duma election, probably with the help of Sechin operatives, the publication of the document indicated that the taboo on personal criticism of Putin by the regime's factions had definitively been lifted. The Sal'e report suggested that Putin had embezzled some $92 million dollars in a failed barter scheme to import food in exchange for oil and other natural resources. The report recommended Putin's dismissal and for the materials to be passed over to the city prosecutor's office, but this was ignored by Sobchak.[56] The issue of corruption was caught up in the struggle between the mayor's office and the pretensions of the city soviet to supreme power in the city, a microcosm of the struggle between Yeltsin and the Congress of People's Deputies, which ended in the bloodshed of October 1993.

It seems clear that the Sechin faction, having lost the battle for the succession, now turned their *kompromat* guns against Putin himself. What they hoped to gain is not clear, but the episode reveals both the intensity of the factional struggles in the late Putin presidency, as well as the pressure he was facing in his final period in the Kremlin, and helps explain his extraordinary edginess in this period.

Counter-attack

A further indication of the covert struggle accompanying the formal parliamentary election was the appearance of an interview with Oleg Shvartsman in Kommersant on 30 November 2007, this time an attack directed against Sechin.[57] Shvartsman, the head of Finansgroup,

---

reported in Jonas Bernstein, 'Belkovsky predicts Medvedev Will Tighten the Screws', *EDM* 5, 1, 7 January 2008.
[56] 'Doklad Mariny Sal'e i Yuriya Gladkova o deyatel'nosti V. V. Putina na postu glavy komiteta po vneshnim svyazyam merii Sankt-Peterburga', copyright 'Okalman', 28 November 2007, available at www.compromat.ru/main/putin/saliedokl.htm.
[57] Åslund suggests that the venue of the attack on Sechin, the *Kommersant* newspaper, was probably not accidental. It is owned by Alisher Usmanov, who is connected to Gazprom, the company chaired by Medvedev. Anders Åslund, 'Purge or Coup?', *Moscow Times*, 9 January 2008, p. 7. Rahr agrees that the Shvartsman incident was part of a counter-attack against Sechin, Rar, *Rossiya zhmet na gaz*, p. 353.

claimed that his $3.2bn fund management company handled the finan-
cial affairs of 'certain political figures', using a variety of instruments
including offshore companies, and had close links with people in the
presidential administration, the FSB and the SVR. He claimed that his
company had the backing of the state to conduct corporate raids on
private companies to force them back into state ownership, what he
called the 'velvet reprivatisation' of assets initially privatised in the
1990s. The methods used, according to Shvartsman, were what he
termed 'voluntary-coercive instruments', applied with the assistance of
the MVD's departments fighting organised and economic crime.[58]
Although soon after Shvartsman sought to distance himself from his
comments, the damage was done.[59] The key point of the article, and
probably its entire purpose, was to attack Sechin, the *éminence grise* of the
siloviki and allegedly behind the whole exercise.[60] Valentin Varennikov,
one of the masterminds behind the anti-Gorbachev coup of August 1991
and the only one who had refused an amnesty, had been named by
Shvartsman as his intermediary to Sechin, but Varennikov condemned
Shvartsman as a 'rascal of the highest order'.[61] The troubles for Shvartsman were far from over, with five regions later cancelling venture capital
tenders won by his company, and Rosoboroneksport, the company
named as the beneficiary of his dealings, filing a lawsuit against both
Kommersant and Shvartsman for damaging its reputation.[62]

The whole episode was interpreted as an attempt to discredit Sechin,
possibly by his rivals Cherkesov and Zolotov. Even if this was the case,
the fundamental question remains: how true were the allegations?
Chubais stated: 'Intentionally or not, Mr Shvartsman told the truth.
Truth about unavoidable diseases of such social and political systems as
"sovereign democracy".'[63] Chubais was characteristically blunt about
the dangers attendant on making the Kremlin the sole source of power.
No less pertinent a question was the timing of the article, removing yet

---

[58] Interview with Oleg Shvartsman by Maksim Kvasha, 'Partiyu dlya nas olitsetvoryaet
silovoi blok, kotoryi vozglavlyaet Igor′ Ivanovich Sechin', *Kommersant*, 30 November
2007.
[59] Following publication two of the companies mentioned in Shvartsman's article, a
Russian venture capital company and the Israeli finance group Tamir Fishman, which
had been engaged in enormous financial transactions, withdrew from all dealings with
the company. Shvartsman then argued that *Kommersant* had edited his comments in a
misleading manner, something that the paper denied. George Bovt, 'Using Pull of FSB
Patrons to Make Deals', *Moscow Times*, 13 December 2007, p. 8.
[60] *Kommersant*, 30 November 2007. Later Shvartsman claimed that the newspaper had
misinterpreted his comments, and in response *Kommersant* planned to sue Shvartsman.
[61] *Moscow Times*, 5 December 2007.
[62] 'Shvartsman Fund Deals Canceled', *Moscow Times*, 20 February 2008, p. 6.
[63] Reuters, 4 December 2007, in *EDM* 4, 227, 7 December 2007.

again a corner of the rug covering elite faction fights. The article also placed the spotlight on the widespread practice of *reiderstvo* by business rivals, which is a fundamental problem in contemporary Russia. The term 'raiding' is derived from practices on Wall Street common in the 1980s, but has now entered the Russian lexicon. A report on the subject defines raiding as:

> The illegal . . . seizure of property . . . The winning of control in the widest sense by one company of another using both illegal and legal methods; the seizure of shares by provoking business conflicts; . . . a way of redistributing property, which in essence is banditry, but which formally conforms to some sort of judicial procedure.[64]

Criminal proceedings are used to force a business competitor to relinquish their stake to the raider, usually at a considerable discount or for no value at all. State agencies and officials are often complicit in such corporate raids, and the integrity of the courts is undermined.

Sechin had picked fights with almost everyone, and ultimately with his own boss, Putin, as well as his closest associate, Bogdanchikov at the head of Rosneft. The company had grown fat at the expense of Yukos, but had accumulated enormous debts. As the faction fights intensified with the approach of the parliamentary election, three Rosneft vice-presidents were forced to resign and a number of others faced dismissal, in a purge apparently inspired by Sechin to remove Bogdanchikov's supporters, and even the latter's position appeared under threat. Rosneft had long been in competition with Gazprom, having narrowly escaped being swallowed by the gas giant in 2005. Faced with a January 2008 deadline to restructure the debt, it appears that Sechin was throwing his Rosneft colleagues to the wolves, blaming them for Rosneft's financial difficulties. With the emergence of the Gazprom team as winners in the presidential race, with Medvedev advancing together with Surkov, a supporter of Gazprom's interests, the political terms of trade turned against Sechin.

The arrest of the Ukrainian Semën Mogilevich in late January 2008 was variously interpreted. The organised crime boss had for years been on the wanted list in the United States and Russia for fraud and racketeering, although he had apparently long been living openly in the prestigious Rublëvka district. He had married a Russian citizen in 1999 and taken on Russian citizenship, and thus could not be extradited to

[64] *Reiderstvo kak sotsial'no-ekonomicheskii i politicheskii fenomenon sovremennoi Rossii: Otchet o kachestvennom sotsiologicheskom issledovanii* (Moscow: Tsentr politicheskikh tekhnologii, May 2008), p. 13.

America.[65] He was also suspected of being involved with the Swiss-registered gas trading intermediary RosUkrEnergo, handling since 2005 Russia's gas exports (sourced mainly from Turkmenistan) to Ukraine. Mogilevich's arrest, together with that of Vladimir Nekrasov, the majority owner of Arbat Prestige, a chain of cosmetic shops, on the eve of the presidential election, was seen as yet another sign of inter-factional conflict (as well as another example of *reiderstvo*), although it was not clear whether the blow was directed by the *siloviki* against Medvedev (head of the Gazprom board of directors), or vice versa. Most likely the arrest was sanctioned by Putin to protect Medvedev by resolving problems that could harm his presidency. The arrest was not carried out by the FSB or Bastrykin's SK but by officers from the MVD's economic security department, formerly headed by Yevgeny Shkolov, Putin's trusted former associate from his Dresden days in the KGB, and where he remained influential. Thus like the arrest of Barsukov in August 2007, the idea was to put people who could threaten the new regime behind bars before they could damage the reputation of the new president.[66]

From under the carpet

Elections act as a catalyst for factional conflict. Throughout the convoluted struggles described above, Putin acted in a strategic manner. He had castigated as 'inappropriate' Cherkesov's public airing of factional struggles, yet he appointed him to head the new State Anti-Narcotics Committee. He did not allow any one subgroup to become predominant, and maintained the balance between the main players. This neutral position allowed the president to act as arbiter and judge, while avoiding the need to align decisively with one faction or another. It also meant that Putin could keep his options for the succession open until the last moment.

The factions had their own preferences. The Zolotov–Cherkesov group initially supported Medvedev, and then Sergei Ivanov. Sechin's group opposed these candidates, while Zubkov appeared to be an acceptable compromise candidate for all groups, while not the top preference of any. The main criterion appeared to be the perpetuation of Putinist balancing, to prevent the triumph of any one line. This aspect

---

[65] 'Militsionery naryli amerikantsam Mogilevicha', *Izvestiya*, 28 January 2008, p. 3.
[66] This argument is advanced, among others, by Vladmir Milov, the former deputy energy minister and now head of the Institute of Energy Policy, in Jonas Bernstein, 'Semyon Mogilevich's Arrest: A Blow to Medvedev, or Favor?', *EDM* 5, 16, 28 January 2008.

of the continuity strategy, however, was thrown into disarray by Putin aligning himself with United Russia in the Duma election (see Chapter 7), at a stroke transforming the parliamentary election into a 'referendum' on Putin and removing the 'primary' element. Factional conflict, moreover, stymied necessary appointments, as with the postponement of a decision over the new head of the Security Council.

The rivalry between the various factions influences personnel appointments and will do so long into the future. It also reflects struggles between various financial-political groups, and factionalism has become part of Russia's political economy. Indeed, as we have argued, the parallel world of administrative feuds and conflicts threatens to substitute for the world of public politics. However, Russian politics remains dual track, and while public platforms were indeed damaged by the displacement of political competition into the *apparat* sphere, the institutions of the public sphere (elections, parliament, parties, a civil society and independent mass media) remain vitally important. There are thus two categories of actors in the Russian political process: representatives of shadowy financial-political groups; and the institutions of public politics. The two intersect in the office of the president, who remains outside and above both and struggles to retain his role as arbiter, not only between factions but also between the two spheres of politics.

His ability to do so weakened as the succession crisis intensified. The prevalence of personalised balancing politics imbued both spheres with growing elements of chaos, possibly irrationality, and certainly suffocated the spirit of open debate and the institutionalisation of mechanisms for political arbitration and resolution. The principle of legitimisation of a political order is hardly stable when it depends on the preferences of one individual. This was a very fragile foundation on which to build a political order. The existence of the secret succession struggle undermined the sphere of public politics and the importance of open elections. No less significant, open conflict between warring factions suggested that the Putin era was coming to an end even as he tried to manage the succession. The balance between factions that Putin had been able to maintain was coming apart, and the discipline and coherence that had dominated the public image of his regime was now eroding.

7 Duma selection

All Russian parliamentary elections, apart from the first in December 1993, were overshadowed by the even greater prize of the presidency. The presidential succession and the parliamentary election campaign are organically interlinked. Traditionally, Duma elections acted as a type of primary for the later presidential poll, acting as a filter for potential presidential candidates. The relatively poor performance of his Fatherland-All Russia (OVR) electoral bloc in December 1999 forced Primakov to withdraw from the succeeding presidential campaign. In the 2003–4 electoral cycle, however, Putin's overwhelming predominance meant that no serious alternatives to his candidacy emerged, and the primary element declined. By 2007 the Duma election of 2 December did not serve in any real sense as a 'primary' (since the identities of the possible presidential candidates were unknown), but it was turned by Putin into a 'referendum' on his rule to give him authority to shape politics after his term in office expired. Although factionalised internally, the regime placed a high premium on the concept of 'loyalty' from officialdom and the public, with defectors quickly being tarred with the 'dissident' brush while supporters were demonstratively to display their conformity. The neo-Soviet mentality was still reflected in electoral practices.[1]

The normative framework

Although the presidential administration managed the electoral process, there remained a number of unresolved issues. It was unclear how many parties would be represented in the Duma and which would be filtered out. One of Putin's priorities on coming to power was a restructuring of the party system, intended to reduce the number of parties and to ensure

---

[1] A feature already noted in Russia's first post-communist election in 1993. See Michael Urban, 'December 1993 as a Replication of Late-Soviet Electoral Practices', *Post-Soviet Affairs* 10, 2, 1994, pp. 127–58.

Table 7.1 *Parties with the right to participate in the elections*

Name of party (listed in order of decreasing membership)	Leader
1 United Russia (UR)	Boris Gryzlov
2 Just Russia (JR)	Sergei Mironov
3 Communist Party of the Russian Federation (CPRF)	Gennady Zyuganov
4 Agrarian Party of Russia (APR)	Vladimir Plotnikov
5 Liberal Democratic Party of Russia (LDPR)	Vladimir Zhirinovsky
6 Democratic Party of Russia (DPR)	Andrei Bogdanov
7 Patriots of Russia	Gennady Semigin
8 Union of Right Forces (SPS)	Nikita Belykh
9 Yabloko	Grigory Yavlinsky
10 Civic Force	Alexander Ryavkin
11 Party of Social Justice	Alexei Podberëzkin
Other parties involved	
Party of Russian Rebirth★	Gennady Seleznev
Socialist United Party of Russia★★	Vasily Shestakov
Party of Unity and Concord (PRES)★★★	Sazha Umalatova
People's Union ★★★	Sergei Baburin
Russian Green Party ★★★	Anatoly Panfilov

Notes:
★On 26 January 2007 a party congress decided to rename the party Patriotic Forces: For the Homeland!, but the change was not approved by the Federal Registration Service. In the event, Rebirth of Russia ran with Gennady Semigin's Patriots of Russia.
★★The party reformed as a non-governmental organisation.
★★★Parties denied registration to fight the election because of problems with their applications.
Source: www.cikrf.ru/elect_duma/politpart/party_tabl.jsp, from Federal Registration Service, www.rosregistr.ru; *Moscow Times*, 29 October 2007, p. 3.

that those remaining actively participated in national and regional elections. In September 2007 the Federal Registration Service published a list with only fifteen parties eligible to fight the election, down from thirty-five in 2003 (see Table 7.1). Notable victims of the cull included Ryzhkov's Republican Party of Russia, a number of left parties and the disparate 'Other Russia' grouping.

Changes to the rules

We have discussed the main electoral provisions in Chapter 2. Although electoral rules had evolved between 1994 and 2004, their basic principles had remained the same, but between 2005 and 2007 the whole system changed fundamentally. While the right to vote had been little modified, it was now much harder to be elected. Substantial barriers were imposed on entering the political field, with the Duma barrier raised to 7 per cent, cross-party blocs forbidden, and the stipulation imposed that a member of one party could not ballot on the list of another. Electoral observation was restricted to registered parties, thus banning direct non-party activity, and the number of signatures needed to be nominated had risen to 200,000 while the proportion of allowable invalid signatures had been reduced, the electoral deposit doubled and the 'against all' category abolished. The ban on electoral blocs enhanced the position of established parties.

A minimum of 60 per cent of the vote had to be represented in parliament, and no fewer than two parties. Votes cast for parties making it across the threshold are redistributed proportionally according to the Hare formula, which tends to reflect voter preferences most accurately. Parties eligible to fight the election nominated a maximum of three individuals on their national list and formed between 80 and 135 regional lists, with a maximum number of 600 people in total. With the abolition of single-mandate constituency seats, independent MPs were excluded. The Duma would lose some of its outstanding figures, including well-known personalities such as Ryzhkov, Rogozin and Glaz'ev. The new system of full PR accompanied by filters on independent parties meant that there was no niche for them in these elections. Others to go included Victor Pokhmelkin, who led a crusade against corruption in law-enforcement agencies and for the rights of motorists, and Anatoly Yermolin, a former KGB officer who had become a powerful critic of Putin's consolidation of power. Ryzhkov was particularly critical of the 'pre-selection' before the election: 'This is the first time in post-Soviet history when only the Kremlin decides who can participate and who can't.'[2]

The Central Electoral Commission (CEC) was established to manage the 1993 election, and afterwards it became a permanent 'ministry of elections' to regulate the whole process. The CEC consists of fifteen members: five chosen by the president, five by the State Duma and five by the Federation Council. Following his appointment in March 1999, Alexander Veshnyakov presided over major changes to the electoral system, until the endless tinkering became too much even for him. He opposed the abolition of the 'against all' category and the minimum turnout requirement, and favoured the abolition of what he considered were superfluous obstacles in elections. With the number of parties reduced to a dozen and the minimum membership requirement raised

---

[2] Clifford J. Levy, 'With Tight Grip on Ballot, Putin is Forcing Foes Out', *New York Times*, 14 October 2007.

from 10,000 to 50,000, he saw no need for parties to lodge bonds or collect signatures before elections.[3] Veshnyakov's attempts to impose penalties on candidates in the top troika of the federal list and leaders of regional parties who cede their seats after having been elected to the Duma were defeated. In a crucial move in anticipation of the succession elections, he was dismissed as head of the CEC in March 2007.

His replacement was Vladimir Churov, a former member of the LDPR and a physicist by training with no legal background. His main recommendation for the post was that he hailed from St Petersburg and was Putin's former classmate. He made no secret of his view that 'Putin is always right.' He was also astonishingly frank about the whole process. In an interview with NTV on 31 August 2007, he argued that Russia had formed a 'corporate state', and on that basis: 'We have a state corporation and we are electing the top management of our state corporation.'[4] At the same time, he declared that these would be the fairest elections held in Russia so far. Meeting with the Valdai Club on 14 September, he stressed the care with which electoral commissions at all levels were being formed, the number of domestic and foreign electoral observers, and that the ballot papers would be kept until the next electoral cycle (rather than being destroyed rather speedily, as in the past). Measures had been introduced to prevent the falsification of the results when transmitted from polling stations to the CEC in Moscow.[5]

Regional elections had been held on set dates twice a year since 2005. The one on 11 March 2007, as noted, acted as the dress rehearsal for the parliamentary elections, with fourteen regions involved comprising one-third of the electorate. United Russia had won an average of 44 per cent of the PR vote, the Communists won 16 per cent but came second in only half the regions, Just Russia gained 15 per cent and won seats in thirteen regions, while the LDPR won seats in eleven regions with 9 per cent of the vote. The SPS ran in nine regions, but it had been disbarred in Dagestan, Vologda and Pskov (after initial disqualification it ran in Samara) and its strong performance in crossing the 7 per cent threshold in five regions and narrowly missing in another two suggested that it had positioned itself to be the main liberal party.[6] On 2 December elections were also held for the regional legislatures in nine regions. On that day Chechnya held a referendum on changing its constitution to bring the

---

[3] *Izvestiya*, 21 February 2007.
[4] Victor Yasmann, 'Russia: From Silovik Power to a Corporate State', RFE/RL, *Russia Report*, 25 September 2007.
[5] Personal notes, 12 September 2007.
[6] J. Paul Goode, 'The Regional Dimension of Russia's 2007–2008 Elections', *Russian Analytical Digest*, No. 19, 17 April 2007, pp. 15–17, at p. 16.

republic's legislation into line with federal norms. The presidential term would be increased from four to five years, but the head of the republic would no longer be elected but instead be nominated by the federal president and confirmed by the Chechen parliament.

The changes described above, notably the shift to a full PR system and the abolition of gubernatorial elections, led to expectations that the scope for the 'virtual politics' associated with Russia's highly developed market for political technologies would gradually decline. In the event, the market changed its forms but remained as important as ever. As a perceptive study put it, the market for *piarshchiki* (PR managers) 'has achieved a degree of stability, unthinkable in recent years. Professionals, who for many years have suffered from competition from amateurs, who earned easy money in the sphere of "black" technologies, can now breathe more easily; there are far fewer casuals in the market.'[7] Special-ists in electoral campaigning branched out into other activities, including journalism, business public relations and social organisations. The anarchy of the electoral consulting market gave way to the dominance of fewer and more professional agencies, although the scope for black technologies in the political process did not commensurately decrease.[8] Only more competitive and transparent elections would strip political consultancy of its manipulative connotations. The notion of 'virtual politics' from our dual state perspective, however, deals only with the epiphenomena of a profoundly hybrid political order.

Election monitors

The December 2003 Duma election had been attended by 1,168 foreign observers, the highest number ever, from forty-nine states and thirty-six international and national organisations, while the March 2004 presi-dential elections had been attended by 771 observers from fifty states. Now Churov affirmed that foreign observers would once again be invited, although he hoped that they would be 'higher quality and more experienced'.[9] He also called for more Russian observers. In the event, over 1.5 million observers from the eleven parties involved monitored the election, and they also enjoyed the right to send a representative to district election commissions. Putin's main fear, as it had been in 2003–4, was that a negative report by foreign observers would undermine the legitimacy of the elections. At the same time, in keeping with his broader

[7] A. Sanaev, *Vybory v Rossii: Kak eto delaetsya* (Moscow: Os'-89, 2007), p. 237.
[8] *Ibid.*, p. 238.
[9] Vladimir Rudakov, 'Vremya "Ch"', *Profil'*, 3 September 2007, pp. 20–4, p. 24.

philosophy of 'normalising' Russia's relations with the world, he resented Russia being treated as a second-rate country which had to be 'inspected' and 'observed' by foreign agencies. Russia had long complained that the Organization for Security and Co-operation in Europe (OSCE) had departed from its original mission to act as a pan-European security agency and had become little more than the self-appointed monitor of elections and judge on the state of democracy in the post-communist area. The organisation concentrated on human rights, and in Russia's view neglected its role in military-political co-operation and security. The OSCE's Office for Democratic Institutions and Human Rights (ODIHR), based in Warsaw, had issued particularly fierce criticism of the 2003 Duma election,[10] perhaps in compensation for its rather indulgent approach to the bitterly fought December 1999 election and its whitewash of the 1996 presidential election. On 18 September 2007, Russia tabled proposals to the OSCE to limit monitoring missions to fifty people, with no more than 5 per cent from any one country; to prohibit missions from commenting on the elections before the results were officially announced; ensuring that the content of assessments were subject to approval by the OSCE Permanent Council (where Russia enjoys veto power); monitoring elections across the OSCE membership and not just post-Soviet countries; and appointing more senior staff and monitors from Russia and the CIS to ODIHR monitoring missions. ODIHR practice was to issue a needs assessment report before the election, followed by a preliminary statement shortly after the election, followed by a full report within six weeks.[11] Russia was particularly irked by the fact that extensive election monitoring was held only in countries 'east of Vienna', while electoral violations elsewhere were dealt with at the national level.[12]

At the EU-Russia summit on 26 October 2007 in Mafra (Portugal), Putin went further and suggested that Russia would establish a human rights monitoring agency in Brussels, to deal with the alleged lack of adequate rights for the Russian-speaking populations in Estonia and Latvia, among other issues. It was clear that the Putin administration was thoroughly fed up with being constantly lectured by people whom it believed had more than a mote in their own eye. It was for this reason that the invitation for foreign monitors to observe the 2007 election was

---

[10] See www.osce.org/news/show_news.php?id=3757.
[11] See www.osce.org/odihr-elections.
[12] Vladimir Shkolnikov, 'Russia and the OSCE Human Dimension: A Critical Assessment', in *Russia, the OSCE and European Security, EU-Russia Centre Review*, No. 12, 2009, pp. 21–9, provides a good overview of the issues.

delayed, although the Russian press stressed that countries like Bulgaria and Turkey had invited observers only a month before their respective elections, while France issued invitations only seventeen days in advance, and the UK still had no provision for external election monitoring at all. In Russia's case the invitation letter was faxed on 31 October, a little more than a month before the election. The number of monitors invited was sharply reduced to about 400 in total, as were the terms. The OSCE/ODIHR alone in 2003 had sent 400 short-term and 56 long-term observers (who stayed for about six weeks), but now it could send no more than 70. Despite the OSCE's outraged reaction, Churov insisted Russia's actions were in line with international practice.[13] There would be an equal number of observers from the CIS Executive Committee, and smaller delegations from the CIS Inter-Parliamentary Assembly, the Parliamentary Assembly of the Council of Europe (PACE), the Shanghai Cooperation Organisation (SCO), the Nordic Council and some dozen other national electoral commissions with which the Russian CEC had worked. There would also be over a million domestic observers. Although the electoral law now banned NGOs from sending observers directly, there was nothing to prevent them being delegated by registered parties.

In the event, on 16 November the ODIHR decided not to send its delegation, on the grounds that it had faced difficulties in receiving visas for its observers.[14] The majority of OSCE mission observers did not require visas since they were diplomats, while others were already in the CIS and thus were also not in need of further travel documentation. On the eve, the director of the ODIHR, the Austrian diplomat Christian Strohal, visited America, 'which was seen even by western diplomats as provocative',[15] although the OSCE denied any American involvement in the decison. It is hard to avoid the conclusion that the ODIHR was looking for an excuse to provoke a scandal, although the Russian side provided no shortage of grounds for it to take offence. The lack of trust on both sides was complete, and that by far was the most disturbing message to emerge from the sorry business. The quota of election observers designated for the OSCE was redistributed to PACE, the OSCE Parliamentary Assembly and the CIS Inter-Parliamentary Assembly. Speaking to a group of UR activists on 26 November in St Petersburg, Putin reacted harshly to the OSCE's decision: 'These

[13] *Gazeta*, 1 November 2007, p. 3.
[14] Nikolaus von Twickel, 'OSCE Body Cancels Vote Monitors', *Moscow Times*, 19 November 2007, p. 1.
[15] Shkolnikov, 'Russia and the OSCE Human Dimension', p. 27.

actions cannot disrupt the elections in Russia. Their aim is to delegitimise the vote, but they will not achieve this goal.'[16] The incident added to Russia's disenchantment with the OSCE and reinforced its aspirations to recast the security architecture of post-Cold War Europe through some sort of 'Helsinki 2' process, a theme advanced by Medvedev later, in a speech in Berlin on 5 June 2008, where he proposed a comprehensive and inclusive European security treaty.

The parties line up

As the election approached two issues remained unknown – the number of parties that would make it across the threshold and the size of the pro-presidential majority. A number of other questions remained to be settled, including whether Just Russia would make it into second place. Parties had to submit their candidate lists by 5 October to be eligible. Of the fourteen registered political parties, eleven entered the race for the lower house. Three parties – UR, the CPRF and the LDPR – were registered automatically without signature lists or election deposits as they were already in parliament. Four parties – JR, SPS, Yabloko and the Patriots of Russia – provided an electoral deposit of 60 million roubles. The deposit is returned to parties winning at least 4 per cent of the vote. Another four parties – the Democratic Party, the Agrarian Party, Civic Force and the Party of Social Justice – collected 200,000-long signature lists in their support. The CEC denied registration to three parties (Table 7.1). The Party of Unity and Concord (PRES), one of the oldest in Russia and the only one led by a woman, was excluded because the number of faulty signatures allegedly exceeded the permissible 5 per cent by 0.16 per cent (some 100 signatures). The Green Party had the largest percentage of invalid signature lists, 17.27 per cent, while 8.56 per cent of the signature lists of Baburin's People's Union were declared invalid. The three parties had the right to appeal to the Supreme Court. Gennady Seleznev's Rebirth of Russia pulled out and ran with Gennady Semigin's Patriots of Russia.

United Russia (UR, Edinaya Rossiya)

Earlier parties of power, despite the administrative resources that were tilted in their favour, failed to sustain themselves for much more than a single electoral cycle. United Russia enjoyed incommensurably greater

---

[16] Nabi Abdullaev, 'Putin Says U.S. Pressured OSCE', *Moscow Times*, 27 November 2007, p. 1.

administrative support than earlier versions, yet even as a 'catch-all' party it still needed to attract the vote.[17] All polls agreed that UR would gain the plurality of seats in the Fifth Duma and possibly even an outright majority. In 2003 UR had received 37.6 per cent of the vote on a 55.7 per cent turnout, giving it 223 seats, which rose to over 300 with the addition of single-mandate seats. The abolition of constituency seats now threatened to reduce the party's constitutional majority. The party was by far the largest, overshadowing all the others with its 1.6 million members.[18] The party entered the election with the simple slogan: 'Putin's Plan: A Worthy Future for a Great Country', the title of its election manifesto adopted at its eighth congress on 1–2 October 2007. The document argued that 'Russia is confidently pursuing a course that will turn it into one of the world's centres of political and economic influence, cultural and moral attraction, and guarantees a new quality of life for all of its citizens.' The stress was on Russia as a 'unique civilisation', an echo of the concept of 'sovereign democracy', although the term was not used in the document.[19] As mentioned, an accompanying book, *Putin's Plan*, brought together Putin's eight annual addresses to the Federal Assembly, some of his major speeches, and a speech by UR's leader, Gryzlov, to party activists, reviewing the achievements of the party under Putin, and its plans for the future.[20] United Russia was established for a number of functional reasons, but under the guidance of Surkov it began to develop an ideological identity. In his annual address to the Federal Assembly on 26 April 2007, Putin stressed the need to make Russia a more competitive economy, through investment in high-tech industries, innovative companies and by improving infrastructure and encouraging small and medium businesses.[21] One aspect of 'Putin's plan', as we have seen, was the creation of mega-corporations, designed to act as the drivers in their sectors.

---

[17] A point made by Laverty, 'Limited Choices', p. 374.

[18] *Izvestiya*, 28 November 2007.

[19] 'Plan putina: Dostoinoe budushchee velikoi strany', adopted 1 October 2007, www.edinros.ru/news.html?id=124255.

[20] The programmatic speech by Boris Gryzlov was called 'O realizatsii Plana Putina partiei "Edinaya Rossiya"', which lay at the basis of the party's election programme; and Putin's materials comprised his 'Russia at the Turn of the Millennium' manifesto of 30 December 1999, his post-Beslan speech of 13 September 2004 and his Munich speech of 10 February 2007: *Plan Prezidenta Putina: Rukovodstvo dlya budushchikh prezidentov rossii* (Moscow: Evropa, 2007). The selection of materials reflects a hard line both at home and abroad, combined with a reformist bent, the paradoxical combination at the heart of the notion of sovereign democracy.

[21] http://president.kremlin.ru/text/appears/2007/04/125401.shtml.

United Russia was one of the last to select its party lists. At the opening session of the eighth congress on 1 October, Putin warned that 'power and money should be kept separate', and thus business people should be kept off the ballot, and stressed how important it was for the party to have a decisive win in the election.[22] There were rumours that the party would place one of the leading presidential contenders at the top. This would give additional exposure to the candidate, while endowing their bid with the supplementary legitimacy of a public contest. In a surprise move on 1 October, Putin's plan became clearer: he accepted the nomination to head the party's national list into the election, and his was the only name on the list. It was not clear how far this had been planned, since even Surkov had not been informed.[23] This was a classic case of stage-managed spontaneity, with the Soviet-style woodenness of the congress now offset by Putin's extraordinary démarche. Factional conflict was certainly one reason for Putin placing himself at the head of the UR campaign, although this incommensurately enhanced the party's status and prepared the way for the possible emergence of a second centre of political power in the country: 'Putin's seeming inability to single out a chosen candidate without roiling the competing Kremlin clans could have been a factor in his decision to position himself for a new role within United Russia.'[24]

Putin noted that 'I not only supported the creation of the party in 2001, I was among its initiators', and he called UR 'a uniting force' that 'provided political stability and implemented all our programmes'.[25] In his final speech, after having accepted the nomination, Putin also hinted that he was thinking of taking over as prime minister in the next parliament: 'To head the government is an entirely realistic proposal, but it's too early to think about this.' Two conditions would have to be met: UR would have to win a substantial majority in the December elections; and the president would have to be someone who was a 'worthy, capable and effective figure with whom I could work'. He made it clear, however, that he would not be joining the party: 'Like the overwhelming majority of my countrymen, I am not a member of any party, and I do not wish to change this.'[26] Delegates voted unanimously to amend UR's charter to

[22] 'Vstupitel'noe slovo na VIII s″ezde partii "Edinaya Rossiya"', V. V. Putin, *Izbrannye rechi i vystupleniya* (Moscow: Knizhnyi mir, 2008), pp. 447–54.
[23] Neil Buckley and Catherine Belton, 'An Apparatchik President?', *The Financial Times*, 12 December 2007, p. 1.
[24] Paul Abelsky and Dmitry Babich, 'Russia's Parties Name Their Top Candidates', *Russia Profile* 4, 9, November 2007, pp. 8–9, at p. 9.
[25] www.kremlin.ru/text/appears/2007/10/146479.shtml.
[26] www.kremlin.ru/text/appears/2007/10/146477.shtml.

allow a non-party member to run on its ticket. Once elected, Putin would have to choose between taking up the seat and resigning the presidency, something still allowed by the rules despite Veshnyakov's attempt to ban the practice.[27] One option mooted at the time was that as head of the parliamentary majority, Putin could take over as Duma speaker.

By a single *coup de théâtre* Putin transformed the election campaign. His unequivocal endorsement of UR had the effect of immeasurably raising its status. As president, he was not technically allowed to campaign when performing his duties, although it was difficult to see how this could be avoided. Russian presidents are faced by what Henry Hale calls the 'dilemma of partisanship': elected as non-party individuals, the incentive to identify with a party is only strong when they are faced by threats that cannot be effectively countered by presidential institutions. Yeltsin in 1996 had responded to the dilemma by creating the Gazprom-sponsored Our Home is Russia, but still hedged his bets and failed fully to endorse the party. With the onslaught from regional and other leaders in 1999, the Kremlin with greater commitment established a presidential party that would insure against such a threat emerging in the future.[28] However, it is unclear what perceived threat in autumn 2007 prompted Putin to take such a radical step and to identify so closely with the party. After all, by then UR already enjoyed an overwhelming predominance, the opposition was weak and fragmented, and regional and business leaders cowed. In part, Putin's dramatic move was a way of outflanking factional conflict and reinforcing his position as arbiter.

In the regional lists, Gryzlov headed the St Petersburg nominations, pushing the city's governor, Valentina Matvienko, into second place. The popular Sergei Shoigu (the long-serving head of the emergency situations ministry), who had been expected to enter the top three on the national list, was sent to bump up UR's prospects in Stavropol *krai*, the only region where JR had beaten UR into second place in the March 2007 regional elections. Luzhkov took the top spot in Moscow, followed by Deputy Prime Minister Zhukov, one of the four UR cabinet members. A total of sixty-three of the party's eighty-three regional lists were headed by regional leaders, and in two they were second (St Petersburg and Khakassia), compared to the twenty-nine governors

---

[27] Nabi Abdullaev et al., 'Putin Will Run on United Russia Ticket', *Moscow Times*, 2 October 2007, p. 1.
[28] Henry E. Hale, 'The Upcoming 2007 Duma Elections and Russia's Party System', *Russian Analytical Digest*, No. 31, 2007, pp. 2–4.

that headed UR lists in 2003. The governors acted as 'locomotives' (*paravozy*), pulling out the vote.[29] Regional leaders with a security service background were kept off the lists, since they were not considered attractive to voters.[30] The party's list also included 20 mayors of regional capitals, 5 Federation Council members, 192 current Duma members, some 80 members of regional parliaments, and about 20 federal officials and almost 40 regional officials.

In keeping with Putin's injunction, the lists were purged of some businessmen with dubious reputations. Already at the UR congress, Bogdanchikov, the head of Rosneft, had been quietly dropped from the list of candidates, and later Suleiman Kerimov (who had defected from the LDPR), the owner of the holding company Polimetall and Mosstroiekonbank, with assets of $12.8bn, was dropped, as well as Vladimir Krupchak, the head of the Arkhangel Pulp and Paper Combine. Even so, at least 72 of UR's 600 candidates (12 per cent) had direct links to large or medium-size businesses. Eighteen of them came from the oil business, 14 had links to metals and mining companies, while 6 worked in the financial sector.[31]

Just Russia (JR, Spravedlivaya Rossiya)

The inclusion of Putin on the UR list was bad news for all the other parties and in particular for JR, which in any case would have struggled to garner the requisite 7 per cent.[32] Founded out of the merger of a number of smaller parties (including the nationalist Rodina group) in autumn 2006 (see Chapter 1), Just Russia was very much a project party designed by the regime to occupy the centre-left niche. It was established with Putin's blessing when he met key leaders of the new group in August 2006, but he clearly became disenchanted by the populist, nationalist and socialist turn it took under Mironov. At the Valdai Discussion Club meeting in Sochi on 14 September 2007, Putin noted

[29] Vladimir Gel'man, 'Political Trends in Russian Regions on the Eve of the State Duma Elections', *Russian Analytical Digest*, No. 31, 2007, pp. 6–7.
[30] This group comprises Viktor Maslov in Smolensk, Vladimir Kulakov in Voronezh (since 2000), Murat Zyazikov in Ingushetia (from 2002) and Valery Potapenko in Nenets okrug; see Andrei Balov and Yurii Chernega, 'Vtoraya zhertva "Edinoi Rossii"', *Kommersant*, 15 December 2007, p. 2. Other governors kept off the UR lists include Nikolai Kiselev in Arkhangelsk, Georgi Shpak in Ryazan, Oleg Chirkunov in Perm, Pavel Ipatov in Saratov, Nikolai Maksyuta in Volgograd, Alexander Chernogorov in Stavropol, who was replaced by Sergei Shoigu. Nikolai Petrov, 'The Faces of United Russia', *Moscow Times*, 23 October 2007, p. 11.
[31] Details are in Francesca Mereu, '72 United Russia Hopefuls Linked to Business', *Moscow Times*, 2 November 2007, p. 1.
[32] For the impact on JR, see March, 'Managing Opposition in a Hybrid Regime', pp. 522–4.

that he had hoped that JR would occupy the social democratic niche. The aim clearly had been to establish a two-party system, but JR's radical turn (intended to win the protest and communist vote and to distinguish it from UR) rather undermined this plan. Instead Putin more closely identified himself with UR. The Kremlin appeared to have washed its hands of JR, but at the last moment it gave the green light for the party to enter parliament.

The party's national list consisted of Mironov, Svetlana Goryacheva, a former member of the CPRF and well known for her stringent views, and Sergei Shargunov, a 27-year old popular fiction writer at the head of the party's youth organisation. The heterogeneous nature of the party, however, was starkly revealed by the presence of the August 1991 putschist Varennikov at the top of the Saratov regional list, although he later removed himself, ostensibly at the request of the Communists, with whom he had long been affiliated. Just Russia talked of a 'new socialism of the twenty-first century'. Mironov announced his 'October theses' on socialism 'version 3.0' on the eve of his party's first anniversary.

Communist Party of the Russian Federation (CPRF)

The CPRF was always confident of being able to enter the Fifth Duma, as it had done all the previous ones. Putin's decision to head the UR party suggested that Russia would end up with a two-party system, with only the CPRF challenging UR's predominance – as the farthing to UR's penny. Despite a number of damaging splits and the lack of programmatic renewal, the party under the veteran leadership of Zyuganov (he became the party's head when it was re-established in 1993) stabilised with a support base of around 15 per cent, although as we shall see Putin's popularity diverted some to UR in these elections. The party chose Zyuganov, the former kolkhoz chairman Nikolai Kharitonov, and the left-inclined Nobel prizewinning physicist Zhores Alfërov to head its national list. The election manifesto adopted at its twelfth congress on 22 September 2007 showed just how little the CPRF had changed ideologically, vowing to renationalise 'strategic' industries, promising to restore elements of Soviet power and to reunite Russia with some of its former Soviet allies like Belarus, Ukraine and Kazakhstan. It argued that 'capitalism is killing Russia', that 55 out of 74 million economically active people earned less than R5,000 (about €125) a month, and despite the constitution declaring that power belongs to the people, in fact Russia was run by 'the bourgeoisie, the bureaucracy and bandits'.[33]

---

[33] 'Za vlast' trudovogo naroda!', www.kprf.ru/party_live/51880.html?print.

This populist appeal to the disenchanted was enough for the party to keep its traditional leftist electorate and appealed to those alienated by Putin's centrist managerialism. It was not enough, however, to render the party a viable opposition with a coherent programme and answers to the fundamental problems facing the country. Indeed, in comparison it made United Russia look like the acme of a modern, forward-looking and progressive party.

Liberal Democratic Party of Russia (LDPR)

Two other parties hovered around the threshold. The LDPR, headed by Zhirinovsky, presented itself as an oppositional force, although it consistently voted for the government. Suffering some damaging splits in the run-up to the election, including the defection of a former deputy chair, Alexei Mitrofanov, to Just Russia in August, the LDPR appeared to be the target of a Kremlin attack. Nevertheless, Zhirinovsky's vote-winning capacity was not to be underestimated, demonstrated once again by placing Andrei Lugovoi (wanted by London for his alleged involvement in Litvinenko's death) in second place on the LDPR's national list, after Zhirinovsky. The third slot at the party's nineteenth congress on 17 September was allocated to Igor Lebedev, Zhirinovsky's son and head of the LDPR group in the Duma. The party entered the election with its usual programme of the innovative and the absurd. Zhirinovsky urged a constitutional change to extend the presidential term to five years, and that the head of state should be elected by parliament. Some of the former 'against all' vote in the end went to the LDPR as it mopped up what was left of the 'protest' vote.

Union of Right Forces (SPS, Soyuz Pravykh Sil)

The two main classically liberal parties, the Union of Right Forces (SPS) and Yabloko, failed to cross what was then the 5 per cent threshold to enter the Duma in 2003, and since then, despite repeated attempts, have not united. There has not yet been a case in post-communist Russia's short experience of parliamentarianism for a party that failed to enter the Duma in one election returning from limbo. The SPS, under the dynamic and intelligent leadership of Nikita Belykh, recast itself as less a party of the successful bourgeoisie than one with strong social liberal credentials. However, as the election approached, the party adopted a more populist agenda, apparently disappointed that the Kremlin had reneged on a deal to allow it to enter the Duma. Both Yabloko and the SPS had been careful not to alienate the Kremlin and distanced themselves from the anti-systemic Other Russia movement. There had been indications that the regime wanted to see a strong liberal presence in the Duma, if only to counter accusations that a dominant party system was being created,[34] but in the event other priorities came to the fore, provoking SPS's radicalisation.

There was considerable controversy over the selection of the SPS national troika. At one point it appeared that Sychëv, the draftee who had suffered dreadful torments at the Chelyabinsk Tank Academy, would be chosen. However, the use of the poor man's suffering for political purposes was condemned by many party members, including Maria Gaidar (the daughter of the economist Yegor Gaidar) in an open letter, and in the event, on 21 September a more conventional choice was made. There were also persistent rumours that Ryzhkov would be placed on the SPS list,[35] although Belykh denied that he had ever been considered.[36] In the number 2 slot after Belykh was the veteran Boris Nemtsov, and in third place Marietta Chudakova, a literary critic and philologist renowned for her studies of writers critical of the Soviet system, notably Andrei Platonov and Mikhail Bulgakov. Chubais was absent from the conference, following some open criticism from Putin (see below). Maria Gaidar was placed at the top of the Moscow list, while Leonid Gozman, a board member of UES and Chubais's loyal associate, headed the St Petersburg list. The SPS party lists included 316 candidates, and the party's campaign platform was called 'freedom and humanism'.

The SPS had traditionally been relatively well disposed to Putin's administration, especially in his first term when he had pursued a policy of liberal economic reform. Indeed, this was one of the issues that prevented unification with Yabloko, as well as the role of some SPS leaders (notably Chubais) in the 'black privatisation' of the 1990s. Following SPS's strong showing in the March 2007 elections, when it had adopted some 'leftist' policies, it appeared that the party was on course to enter the Duma. The SPS leadership also believed that the Kremlin had given its tacit assent to the SPS having a clear run. The first signal that this would not be the case was Putin's comment to the Valdai Discussion Club meeting in Sochi on 14 September 2007. He noted that Chubais, at the head of the electricity giant RAO UES generating 70 per cent of Russia's electricity and employing 470,000, could influence

[34] Vladimir Rudakov, 'Dumskaya osen'', *Profil'*, 3 September 2007, pp. 13–20, at p. 19.
[35] *Novaya gazeta*, 10 September 2007.
[36] Francescu Mereu, 'Belykh, Nemtsov but no Chubais', *Moscow Times*, 24 September 2007.

electoral outcomes: 'As you know this company, with its huge resources ... is able to provide not only moral and administrative, but also financial backing. I hope they do it according to the law.'[37] He noted that this was a form of state support, but it was not entirely clear why he should pick up on this, since no shortage of companies and official agencies were supporting UR without Putin reading the riot act about the need to remain within the law. In the event, Chubais withdrew his company's funding and kept a low profile, and this was one of the reasons for the party's poor performance.[38] The SPS still tried to avoid displeasing the Kremlin and decided not to place Ryzhkov on its national list. As the parliamentary campaign got under way in autumn 2007, it became clear that the Kremlin was taking a far from benign view of the party, inflicting withering criticism from its media outlets. Feeling cheated, in a sharp reversal the SPS joined the 'irreconcilable' opposition, notably Other Russia, and took an active part in 'dissenters' marches', hoping to garner the protest vote.[39]

Yabloko

Although the Kremlin on the whole was neutral towards Yabloko, from the beginning its chances of re-entering parliament were slight. The survival of Yabloko as a party was a notable achievement since its defeat in December 2003. As we saw in Chapter 1, following what Ryzhkov called the 'liberal débâcle' in 2003, Khodorkovsky had written of a 'crisis of Russian liberalism'. Nevertheless, Yabloko survived, and by 2007 it had a network of seventy-seven organisations and fought numerous regional elections, although its finances were parlous. The party was undoubtedly a defender of western-style democracy, but it was often perceived to be rather authoritarian in its internal governance under Yavlinsky's leadership.

Yabloko chose a distinctive line-up. The party's leader, Yavlinsky, took the number 1 slot, but the choice of the veteran human rights campaigner Sergei Kovalëv (whose virulent criticism of Putin we discussed earlier) at number 2 was a clever move. A scientist and a Soviet-era dissident, at seventy-seven Kovalëv was one of the most respected public figures in Russia. A co-founder of the Russia's Choice party in 1992, between 1994 and 1996 he was the outspoken head of the presidential

[37] http://president.kremlin.ru/test/appears/2007/09/144011.shtml.
[38] *Kommersant*, 15 December 2007, p. 1.
[39] Francescu Mereu, 'Kremlin Accused of Duping SPS', *Moscow Times*, 28 November 2007, p. 1.

human rights commission and a severe critic of Yeltsin's war in Chechnya. By aligning itself with a human rights agenda, Yabloko drew attention to an issue of concern to many Russians; by the same token, however, it made few friends in the Kremlin.

Other parties

By 5 October all fourteen political parties running in the parliamentary elections had filed their registration documents with the CEC. Only UR submitted fewer than the three allowed on its national list – as we have seen, their single candidate was Putin. In addition to the major parties listed above, the smaller parties also sought to attract figures with some popular resonance. The liberal Civic Force party, based on the Free Russia (Svobodnaya Rossiya) party created in 2004 but renamed at an extraordinary congress in March 2004, sought to draw the vote away from other liberal parties. It was headed by the presidential representative to the Supreme Court, the well-known lawyer and publicist Mikhail Barshchevsky, and officially had some 60,000 members. The party placed Barshchevsky at the top of its list, together with Maria Arbatova, a liberal feminist who often appeared on TV. There was much talk in Kremlin circles about backing this party as the genuine centre-left party, to counter JR's excessive leftward tilt. Other parties fighting the election included Patriots of Russia, established in October 2004 by Gennady Semigin as a result of a split in the CPRF, as well as the Greens, the Democratic Party of Russia, the Party of Peace and Unity and the Agrarian Party.

A number of peripheral parties were unable to enter the ballot. A candidate list submitted by Other Russia, co-led by Kasparov, was refused registration because it was not registered as a political party. Legislation adopted since the 2003 election stipulates that only registered political parties can fight elections, and thus Other Russia submitted the list for purely propagandist purposes. Kasparov's United Civic Front (OGF) remained an uncomfortable presence as part of the anti-systemic opposition. Kasparov argued that 'The state apparatus has been subverted to serve a corporate apparatus that operates above the law and behind the scenes. The Putin regime has steadily channelled funds into state-controlled corporations that serve the ruling clique. It is a super-oligarchy that has largely superseded the state.'[40] As for Kasyanov, having left the Other Russia bloc in summer 2007 when it

---

[40] Garry Kasparov, 'The Board Members of Russia, Inc.,' *Wall Street Journal*, 20 September 2007, p. A13.

refused to back his presidential ambitions, in September he established a new liberal opposition party 'People for Democracy and Justice', claiming that it had 30,000 members. Kasyanov stated that the party would boycott the Duma elections but would fight the presidential elections. The Great Russia grouping was denied official registration and, like Sergei Baburin's People's Alliance and Gennady Semigin's Patriots of Russia, supported United Russia because of its 'patriotic' defence of sovereignty and the country's independence.

To the starting gate

Following condemnation of corruption in his 1 October speech to the UR congress, Putin went on to argue that 'power and money should stay separated'. Although stressing that he meant 'nothing personal', he argued that representatives of big business had no place on party lists.[41] The Fourth Duma had twenty deputies who were among the top 500 wealthiest business people, mostly in the UR faction. At the congress Putin signalled that 'oligarchs' should not be chosen: 'The presence of big business on candidate lists and in the federal parliament is counter-productive.' He had in mind in particular those placed in the top 50 of Forbes's Russian list (with assets over $1.3bn), and in the event the proscription was only partially applied. Contrary to expectations, Alexander Lebedev, whose fortune approached $3.6bn, did not make it onto the JR slate, while the LDPR chose no oligarchs for their pass-through lists. The Communists, however, stuck with two: Sergei Muravlenko, a former top manager of Yukos, and Victor Vidmanov, the party's treasurer, although neither made it into the Forbes top 50. United Russia, as we have seen, made some moves to comply with Putin's injunction, but in the end a number of top 50 people entered its pass-through lists, including Victor Rashnikov, the director of the Magnitogorsk Metallurgical Combine, coming in at number 11 on the Forbes list with a fortune of $9.1bn.

Many of the business people were existing deputies seeking re-election. The law states that deputies are prohibited from holding a second job other than teaching and research. Although the letter of the law was observed, some transferred their business interests to family members or to trusts held by associates. A deputy mandate provides the holder with immunity from prosecution, something that was particularly attractive for the six people connected with Yukos elected in 2003,

[41] www.kremlin.ru/text/appears/2007/10/146479.shtml.

three of whom entered the ballot in 2007. A seat in parliament is also a good venue to advance one's business interests, hence the willingness of many to pay the alleged 'entry fee' (the donation ranged between $2 and $4 million according to some estimates) to be placed on the UR lists. While radicals of all stripes would be missing from the Fifth Duma, it would be flooded not only with business people but also singers and actors.

A total of 4,684 candidates were registered, just over ten per available seat. Only three parties – UR, CPRF and the LDPR – did not need 200,000 signatures or a deposit of 60 million roubles to enter the race since they had demonstrated their political standing by entering the Duma in 2003. This phase of the election ended on 28 October. Up to that date parties were able to expel candidates, as could the CEC. United Russia nominated the maximum 600 candidates, more than any other party. The second largest contingent was the Democratic Party, with 578 candidates, while Just Russia had 556 and the Communists 515. Fifty-two of UR's candidates, including Putin, were not members of UR (eight had nominated themselves). This was the first time that self-nomination was allowed to the lists of parties to which they did not belong, an innovation designed to compensate in part for the abolition of single-mandate seats. A total of sixty-eight people used this right as independent candidates, and nineteen were included on party lists as self-nominated candidates. A close look at the UR list demonstrates just how heterogeneous its deputy group would be, and in the event its parliamentary majority consisted of a number of disparate minority blocks. On 30 October lots were drawn to distribute gratis and paid time on television and the radio, and then a second time, on 31 October, to allocate the party's number on the ballot paper.[42] The race was on.

The context of the election

At the UR congress on 1 October 2007, Putin signalled his intention to stay at the centre of power. At a stroke he changed the balance of forces, as well as the strategic importance of the elections. The parliamentary vote became less a question of which parties would enter than the size of the UR majority. Similarly, the name of the individual who would take

---

[42] The ballot paper listed parties in the following order: Agrarian Party, Civil Force, the Democratic Party of Russia, the Communist Party, the Union of Right Forces (SPS), the Party of Social Justice, the Liberal Democratic Party of Russia, Just Russia, Patriots of Russia, United Russia, and Yabloko.

over the presidency was matched by concern over what powers could be transferred to the prime minister and the role that Putin would play in that office. It was now clear that Putin was not coming to the end of his leadership; only its form would change. The danger of him turning into a lame duck had receded, and he remained the force around which the whole political constellation revolved. Nevertheless, Putin delayed naming his preferred successor until after the parliamentary election. Polls consistently showed that some 30 per cent of the electorate would vote for whomever Putin suggested; he would now garner this vote for himself, even if by proxy. There would be no political vacuum as his authority ebbed away, and indeed his position strengthened.

The Putin deflation

By unequivocally signalling his intention to stay on in some high political capacity, Putin deftly took the heat out of the faction fights. He would remain in authority, if not in power, and thus the opportunity for anyone else to emerge into the limelight was blocked. The whole political class could breathe a sigh of collective relief: there would be no changing of the guard, and thus no redistribution of power and property. The threat of dual power remained, but this depended on the role that Putin would assume after May 2008. His spectacular announcement that he would head the UR national list was designed to enhance its performance, but it risked Putin's popularity being damaged by association with a party that represented officialdom and alienating those opposed to United Russia. Putin had always been risk averse, although not afraid of the occasional bold move, but the question now was whether this was a classic master-stroke or whether he was suffering from hubris and beginning to believe in his own invulnerability. The loss of independent feedback channels threatened to leave him dangerously exposed, and it is at this point typically that a politician becomes most vulnerable. Putin, however, appeared once again to be able to defy the laws of political gravity and to recreate himself in a new role.

Putin's announcement that he would head the UR list changed all previous calculations. Nikonov noted that the greatest sensation of the campaign began at its very beginning and represented 'a crushing blow to the opposition' as the 'presidential locomotive' gathered steam. In his view, placing Putin at the top of its list was practically the only way that UR could retain its majority, given the shift to a wholly PR system. He stressed the medium-term consequences, notably a strong presidential majority in parliament that would provide a foundation of stability for the next presidency and act as 'a bulwark against populism', while at the same time advancing the institutionalisation of the party system. By uniting the majority party and the authorities, something that is taken as the norm in other countries, the move in his view represented a step forwards for democracy.[43]

The decision reflected Putin's long-term belief that Russian politics needed to be structured more along party lines. The role of party substitutes had been undermined and the formal role of parties had been enhanced, but the competitiveness of the party system as a whole had sharply declined. As Gorbachev noted at the time, with his own social democratic party being wound up: 'Laws have been passed which restrict the possibilities of free democratic choice and political competition. This significantly narrows the space for public politics.'[44] Putin's decision threw a spanner in the party works, dealing a blow to the pseudo-party system that his leadership had created. The Kremlin's aim from the first had been to ensure a strong pro-regime majority in the Fifth Duma, but now the tactics changed. If at first UR, JR and Civic Force had been designated to achieve this, the Kremlin now decided to put all of its eggs into the UR basket. This of course put JR in a difficult situation, since it would not do to attack a party with which Putin not only identified but effectively led. This rendered JR redundant, while UR's overwhelming predominance opened up new dangers.

Putin's decision to head UR's federal list has been called possibly 'the worst bungle in his biography as a statesman'. Up to that time the so-called 'provisional electoral authoritarianism' could have been accepted as a crude but perhaps necessary way to modernise the country. However, with the prospect of the creation of an effectively one-party parliament, all excuses for deviations from acceptable democratic principles, 'such as political pluralism, division of power, checks and balances, an independent mass media and a strong civil society', were exhausted, and Russian political development diverged not only from western political systems, 'but also from countries such as Poland, Bulgaria and Ukraine'.[45] The early parliamentary elections in Ukraine of September 2007, provoked by a governmental crisis and followed by a long period of paralysis while a new coalition was formed, was precisely something that the Russian political class tried to avoid. Presidential power had been weakened as a result of the constitutional amendments adopted in

---

[43] Vyacheslav Nikonov, 'Putin i "Edinaya Rossiya"', *Izvestiya*, 31 October 2007, p. 6.
[44] Luke Harding and Tom Parfitt, 'Putin wants to Go On and On, and the Voters Agree', *The Guardian*, 6 October 2007, p. 28.
[45] Andreas Umland, 'A Modern-Day Don Quixote', *Moscow Times*, 19 October 2007, p. 8.

December 2004, and Ukraine was considered by much of the Russian elite as a warning to be avoided rather than an example to be emulated. Putin's mindset was that of a technocratic moderniser, based largely on the principle that what works best is best; whereas in Ukraine following the Orange revolution, genuine democratic politics had been restored, although undermined by Byzantine power-brokering between economic, regional and political interests.

The technocratic vision was reflected in Putin's defence of his decision. In his 'direct line' question and answer session on 18 October 2007, Putin returned to his customary condemnation of the 1990s: 'With an ineffective parliament, an ineffective Duma, it was impossible to adopt the slightest decent decision. Populist resolutions were adopted that led the country's economy and social sphere into a dead end.' Now with elections due, 'There will be a new person in the Kremlin.' Hence, in his view, 'In these conditions it is essential to maintain the strategic course of development of our state, to maintain continuity in the implementation of those decisions taken recently.' After listing the national projects and other programmes, he warned: 'just imagine if people came who do not respect these decisions'. 'For this reason', he went on, 'it is very important that we should have a capable parliament after the 2007 elections. The key element in the effectiveness of parliament in recent years was United Russia. It is for this reason that I decided to head its list.'[46] Thus Putin considered a strong parliamentary majority for his party as the anchor to weather the storms as his successor cast out on his own. From a technocratic perspective the logic was impeccable, but this was the logic of a new monistic political system.

Putin's partisanship in favour of UR took much of the spice out of the election. United Russia would undoubtedly win by a landslide, squeezing out all the other parties. Polls gave different estimates of the Putin bounce, but all agreed that Putin's engagement with UR pushed its rating well above the 50 per cent mark, with some polls showing support close to 70 per cent.[47] It was now clear that Just Russia did not figure centrally in the Kremlin's calculations. It had been designed for a different situation, above all to steal left-wing votes from the CPRF, but this UR could now do itself. The Kremlin had been disappointed by JR's

[46] 18 October 2007, www.kremlin.ru/text/appears/2007/10/148629.shtml.
[47] For example, a VTsIOM poll released on 11 October 2007 saw UR's rating rise to 54%, up 6% from late September. The same poll, conducted 6–7 October, found that the number supporting a third term for Putin rose from 60% to 66%. A Levada Center poll in late October found that UR support was up to 68%, JR's falling from 7% to 4%, the LDPR's from 11% to 6%, while only the Communists held at around 17%. 'Putin Boosts Popularity of UR to 68%', *Moscow Times*, 25 October 2007, p. 3.

populism, and its failure to direct its fire in the approved direction. Just Russia had attacked the 'evil boyars' in UR, but now the 'good tsar' had aligned himself with them, and the party was adrift without a compass. The idea of running two approved candidates against each other (Medvedev and Ivanov) had been abandoned, and now the idea of running two approved regime parties of roughly equal weight in the parliamentary ballot was also dropped.

At the same time, much of the 'democratic' vote would also be scooped up by UR. As Valery Fëdorov, head of VTsIOM, argued, democratic values were 'associated primarily with a higher quality of life and the understanding that civil society cannot exist without this', and from this perspective UR most accurately reflected this view of democracy.[48] This 'social' definition of democracy was one espoused by Putin, placing less emphasis on such classically 'liberal' issues as media freedom. The patriotic vote was also swept into the UR bag by its advocacy of 'sovereign democracy', stressing its robust foreign policy in defence of Russia's perceived interests while at the same time asserting its democratic credentials.

If UR took up to 60 per cent of the vote, there was not much left for the other parties. Following his 'direct line' question and answer session, Putin stressed that, in his view, 'the presence of oppositional forces both from the left and the right liberal flanks would be extremely useful',[49] but his actions had the opposite effect. Like the attempt by Yeltsin in 1995 to create a two-party system from above, with Chernomyrdin's right-centre bloc Our Home is Russia matched by Ivan Rybkin's left centre grouping, as soon as the political conjuncture changed, both were abandoned: the Rybkin bloc almost immediately, and NDR once Chernomyrdin was dismissed from the premiership in March 1998, although NDR limped on into the December 1999 parliamentary election. The consolidation of UR prompted the defection of regional leaders from JR, although some left because they had not been placed on JR's regional lists for the December election. Just Russia had quite explicitly placed national leaders on regional lists 'to avoid being too closely tied to regional interests', as a spokesperson put it.[50] Putin's affiliation with UR effectively destroyed an alternative for regional leaders.

---

[48] A VTsIOM poll found that up to 70 per cent of the democratic electorate, which represented about 13 per cent of the voters, were ready to cast their votes for UR. *Izvestiya*, 2 October 2007.

[49] www.kremlin.ru/text/appears/2007/10/148675.shtml.

[50] Alexander Osipovich and Nabi Abdullaev, 'A Just Russia Facing Defection in the Regions', *Moscow Times*, 15 October 2007, p. 1.

The CPRF would retain much of its electorate since its voters are disciplined and turn out to vote, whatever the occasion. Demographic trends were working against it in the long term, however, with its ageing electorate not adequately balanced by the recruitment of younger members. Just Russia, fighting on similar issues, would find it hard going to win support without the Kremlin's backing. The LDPR remained very much on the cusp, with Zhirinovsky's bravura showmanship helping to bolster its vote. The LDPR was one of the primary benefi-ciaries of the shift to a fully proportional system, since it had never won more than a handful of single-mandate seats. With 12 per cent of the vote in 2003 it won thirty-six seats, whereas even if it barely scraped over the 7 per cent threshold in 2007 it would win some forty-eight seats. As for the 'democratic' opposition (i.e. Yabloko and SPS), it was clear that they were marginal to Putin's calculations. The announcement that he would head the UR list represented effectively the death knell of their chances of returning to parliament.

It did not appear to be in the Kremlin's interests to see the whole party system reduced to a single overwhelmingly predominant party. Although the rules insisted that a minimum of two had to enter the Duma, a penny farthing system would be no more balanced than the original four-party vehicle. Most other parties had positioned themselves in opposition to UR and not to Putin personally; now this stance was untenable. With the rug pulled out from under JR, and to a degree the LDPR, they were disoriented. More broadly, as we have seen these open calculations were accompanied by the hidden power struggle between Kremlin factions, which surfaced at various points during the campaign. The question of power would be resolved in a brutal struggle between groups in the back alleys of the power system as much as in open political contest.

Putin's role

Putin's status after the end of the electoral cycle was at the heart of electoral discussions. Many noted that his direct association with UR weakened rather than strengthened his position. Yeltsin had always stressed that he was president of all Russians, hence he had not identified with any one party. Now Putin had stepped down from the presidential Olympus and entered the tawdry business of party politics, and thus some of the sanctity of the presidential office was lost. The Duma poll was now transformed from an election into a referendum on Putin – both on his actual performance as incumbent president and on his future role, including possibly as prime minister. The referendum factor eclipsed the electoral element. Fought as a referendum, there would be a stampede of voters from the other parties to Putin. At the same time, the more ideological parties (the CPRF, SPS and Yabloko) could take advantage of the new circumstances to challenge the erosion of electoral responsibility. There was also another problem. It was certain that Putin would be elected to the Duma, but it was equally clear that he would not resign the presidency to take up his parliamentary seat. Thus his participation in the parliamentary election only reinforced the charade element of the poll, with top political executives leading lists as 'locomotives' across the country and contesting seats that they had no intention of filling. The practice had been criticised by the OSCE in its report on the 2003 election, but proposals to ban it were defeated by UR.

By assuming leadership of the UR campaign, Putin in part was responding to elite aspirations for him to stay in power, since it undermined the risks of a disruptive transition to a new leader. The two main fears for Putin were the return of the 1990s and an outbreak of 'colour revolution'. Putin, moreover, was the source of the legitimacy of the system and had become the object of factional intrigue to keep him in office. Taking on the UR slot could well have been a way of keeping them satisfied. As Boris Kagarlitsky notes, 'The truth of the matter is that, despite Putin's immense power and prestige, he has become a hostage to the very bureaucratic elite that he himself created. Bureaucracy has won and the politician has lost.'[51] Putin was also responding to the phenomenal high popular ratings, which also wished him to remain leader in one form or another. Gleb Pavlovsky argued that on 2 December 'the confidence vote' would transform the notion 'leader of the nation' from 'a metaphor into a constitutionally-entrenched fact'. He also argued that it was fanciful to think that Russia would become a parliamentary republic, since that would require a stable elite instead of 'one as in Ukraine, with every coalition leading to the fragmentation of the political system as a whole'.[52]

Putin played an active part in the campaign, appearing as both the president and a candidate. Indeed, the confusion between his role as president and as UR's top candidate prompted SPS in mid-November to lodge an appeal with the Supreme Court, which on 20 November swiftly rejected the claim that Putin was using his official position to boost UR in the campaign, without a full examination of the arguments.[53] Each

---

[51] The point is made by Boris Kagarlitsky, 'A Hostage of the Elite', *Moscow Times*, 11 October 2007, p. 8.

[52] 'Chego zhdat' ot Putina?', 19 October 2007, www.lenta.ru/conf/pavlovsky/.

[53] David Nowak, 'Court Refuses SPS Case Against Putin', *Moscow Times*, 21 November 2007, p. 3. On 11 September 2008, the cassation instance of the Supreme Court finally rejected the SPS case that the parliamentary elections were invalid. Viktoriya

level in the campaign had its own fears and concerns as the tensions of 'double adaptation' played themselves out: the appeal to the formal letter of electoral legislation and universal norms of free elections came into conflict with the specific demands of the regime. With the ballot becoming less an election than a referendum, a simple win in favour of 'Putin's plan' would not be enough: the margin of victory became crucial.[54]

Meeting with construction workers in Krasnoyarsk on 13 November 2007, Putin defended his participation on the grounds that only a strong UR victory would ensure that his political programme continued after his second term. He was, nevertheless, scathing about the inadequacies of the party. Putin noted that it 'lacked a stable ideology or principles for which the great majority of party members are prepared to fight', but since it was close to power at the federal and regional levels all sorts of 'freeloaders' tried to 'worm their way into such structures, and they are partially successful'. He added, 'Nevertheless we have nothing better.'[55] The contrast between support for Putin and for the party reflected the broader problem: trust in Putin at this time did not spill over into growing trust in other political institutions.

In his speech of 21 November to a 5,000-strong rally of supporters, the climax of the 'For Putin' campaign (see below) at the Luzhniki stadium in Moscow, Putin observed that 'In the next few months a complete renewal of Russia's highest state power will take place', but he left the details vague. The speech stressed that the parliamentary elections were not only important in their own right but preceded the election of a new head of state a few months later. The main task, he once again insisted, 'was to maintain policy continuity for the stable and steady development of the country' by reducing 'political risks'. He reiterated his dislike of political campaigning and remarked that United Russia 'is not at present the ideal political instrument', but he had 'absolutely consciously' decided to head the UR list because in that way he could help create 'an authoritative and effective legislative body'. He warned that he could not allow the Duma to become 'a gathering of populists, paralysed by corruption and demagogy, repeating the situation that the country had once endured'. The country needed 'not a populist but a responsible parliament', and the best way of achieving this

Kruchinina, 'SPS ne uspokaivaetsya', *Nezavisimaya gazeta*, 12–13 September 2008, p. 3.

[54] Andrei Lipskii, 'Chego oni boyatsya', *Novaya gazeta*, 22 November 2007, pp. 1–2.

[55] www.kremlin.ru/text/appears/2007/11/151504.shtml.

was to give UR a majority, even though the party itself needed to be 'renewed and reformed'.

He noted that nothing in politics was predetermined, and social stability, economic growth and the like 'was not yet, unfortunately, working in an automatic, unconditional regime' but was the result of 'intense political struggle', both at home and abroad. He accused western governments of supporting 'destructive forces' in Russia that 'scavenge like jackals for money at foreign embassies', but he would not allow a return to the situation of the late 1980s when basic services were destroyed or the 1990s when top officials acted 'against the interests of society and the state'. Warming to the theme, he lashed out against all those who 'at the end of the last century led Russia into mass poverty, to endemic corruption, to that against which we are still struggling':

And, dear friends, we should have no illusions! These people have not left the political scene. You will find their names among the candidates and sponsors of certain parties. They wish to take revenge, to return to power and influence, and gradually restore the oligarchic regime, based on corruption and lies. They are still lying today. They will do nothing for anyone, despite their promises.[56]

Even accepting that Putin was speaking at an election rally, the virulence of the tone and the harsh condemnation of opponents was something new in Putin's public rhetoric. His anti-orange paranoia was getting the better of him. It was clear that he had little respect for the opposition, which may have been justified, but more dangerous was the implication that opposition as a whole was dangerous for Russia, and little more than an emanation of foreign powers. That way lay full-scale imposition of an authoritarian system.

Issues

The sterility of debate in this electoral cycle was marked. The 1999 parliamentary election focused on the restoration of order in Chechnya, while in 2003 the struggle against the oligarchs predominated. The situation in 2007 was radically different, with a confident and popular leader and several years of solid economic growth and improvements in social welfare to the government's credit. Socio-economic issues were at the top of the list in 2007, although with a less anti-oligarch edge than in 2003. In the wake of the campaign against Yukos and Khodorkovsky's arrest, the 2003 election took place in the

---

[56] 'Vstuplenie V. V. Putina na forume storonnikov', *Argumenty i fakty*, No. 48, 28 November 2007, p. 3.

shadow of the 'redistribution of natural rent'. Voters were faced with a clear choice between supporting the assault against the oligarchs or voting against the authorities. In the event, in giving such strong support to the pro-presidential party, the assault against Yukos was endowed with a degree of popular legitimacy. No such issue predominated in 2007.[57] Economic development and the question of 'social justice' figured prominently. The question now was how to spend the bounty derived from economic growth wisely; allowing the country to develop economically while devoting an appropriate share to popular welfare.

With a sharp rise in the price of staple foods and services before the election, and fear of living standards under threat, all parties made appeals to defend the interests of the common people, although none was able to define specific measures that would rectify the situation. The SPS, traditionally the party of the successful middle class, entered the unfamiliar territory of paternalistic social welfare. The centrepiece of UR's campaign was criticism of the 1990s, just as Putin repeatedly returned to this theme. As noted, United Russia's manifesto, 'The Putin Plan: A Worthy Future for Our Country', focused on Putin's various statements and committed itself to continuing Putin's course. The strategic aim was 'to build Russia into a great power' as befitted Russia as a 'unique civilisation'; to support strategic sectors of the Russian economy, to cut inflation to 5 per cent by 2011, to achieve membership of the World Trade Organization and to foster the development of small and medium business; to raise living standards, wages and pensions, and boost birth-rates; to strengthen the country's defences, and to ensure that Russia could play its part in a multipolar world, and to prevent nuclear proliferation; and to strengthen the state, cut bureaucracy and develop civil society and openness.

Surkov's warnings about the danger of 'colour technologies' being applied to Russia were echoed in a programme aired on the state-owned Rossiya channel on 30 September 2007 called 'Barkhat.ru' ('Velvet.ru') by Arkady Mamontov. He argued that the CIA was working to overthrow the Kremlin elite through an orange-style popular movement. He listed the usual catechism – Serbia, Georgia, Ukraine, Kyrgyzstan – and the next stop for the 'revolution express', he warned, was Russia. He ascribed opposition groupings such as Kasparov's Other Russia to a CIA plot and asserted that the Russian opposition was supported by western bodies such as Freedom House. Such reportage said less about western

---

[57] Konstantin Sonin, 'Election Still Waiting for the Big Question', *Moscow Times*, 11 September 2007.

intentions than it did about the fears that gripped the Russian elite as the succession approached.

Detailed issues of foreign policy did not figure prominently in party programmes. United Russia devoted just two paragraphs to the issue, combining a commitment to the resolution of world problems such as the defence of human rights and freedom and preventing WMD (weapons of mass destruction) proliferation, accompanied by the vigorous defence of Russia's sovereignty. The CPRF lacked a special section on foreign policy, but warned of capitalism's inevitable collapse and called for a new 'Union of Soviet Peoples' to replace the CIS. Just Russia warned of the threat of international terrorism and called for more justice in international affairs. The SPS's programme contained perhaps the most considered analysis of Russia's role in the world, including the call for the country to integrate into NATO's political organisation. Zhirinovsky exploited the deep resentment against Britain's suggestion that Russia should change its constitution (the extradition of Russian citizens is something explicitly forbidden by Article 61.1) to allow Lugovoi to be tried in London by placing him on its list. Lugovoi was charged with committing an act of nuclear terrorism, and thus his presence in the new Duma would do little to enhance the legitimacy of Russia's parliament. In mid-December 2007, Russia formally withdrew from the Conventional Forces in Europe (CFE) treaty at the end of a six-month moratorium, an event that was accompanied by a sullen resignation in the west rather than the anticipated harsh criticism of Russia.

The general issue of Russia's place in the world figured prominently, and there appeared to be public support for Russia's more assertive foreign policy. West-bashing emerged as a popular theme, with Putin taking the lead in anti-western rhetoric, although he personally, like Medvedev, was sceptical about the term 'sovereign democracy'. As the campaign progressed, Putin's speeches adopted an ever more shrill anti-western edge. His thinking was clearly reflected in the speech he gave to heads of the diplomatic service in the Kremlin on 28 November: 'We have done everything to safeguard Russia from internal disturbances and to put it firmly on the track in evolutionary development . . . And I am forced to repeat myself – we will not allow this process to be changed from outside.' He noted that for Russia 'The CIS is not a "chessboard" [a reference to Zbigniew Brzezinski's book of that title, *The Grand Chessboard*] on which geopolitical games are played', but an area where peaceful development is an imperative for all those living in the region.[58]

---

[58] www.kremlin.ru/text/appears/2007/11/152426.shtml.

At the same time, he once again reasserted the democratic credentials of the election: 'Our political course is clear and invariable', he said. 'We follow the path of democratic development. We know the value of true democracy and want to conduct elections that are honest, as transparent as possible and open. We are sure this is the way these elections will be.'[59]

Managed elections

Although there were justified concerns about the competitiveness of the poll, in particular with the elimination of the whole category of single-mandate seats, Russian elections always have an element of the unexpected. Putin himself was clear that he wished to see 'all points of view represented in the next parliament. It would make it livelier, and conditions would be created for the adoption of more balanced decisions.'[60] United Russia was not aiming to eliminate all competition but to win a substantial parliamentary majority to enable it to pass or block any legislation. Even Khodorkovsky, from his jail in Chita where he waited for his second trial, posted a letter in which he conceded that a crushing victory for UR was a foregone conclusion. He opposed a boycott (proposed by Kasyanov and others) and called on people to make their voice heard:

The bureaucracy, and today this is precisely our main opponent, exploits social apathy. For this is a confirmation of its monopolistic right to rule the country according to its own discretion. That is to say that the readiness of the citizen to give his vote, his fate to a distant bureaucrat (*chinovnik*) testifies in their eyes to the utter uselessness of taking the people's opinion into consideration. That is, the person who votes 'with their feet', still to a large degree is one who votes for UR, and encourages the bureaucratic class towards despotism and contempt for the 'herd'. Therefore it is imperative that you vote not for those who evoke contempt; it's better to vote for any of the small parties. This will be your own clear and personal gesture: I am a citizen, I have the right to vote and I will; I am not a slave and I am not a beast.[61]

The campaign

Campaigning officially began only twenty-eight days before the election (4 November), with free access to the media for contending parties. In

[59] Oleg Shchedrov, 'Putin Says "Forced" to Repeat Warnings', *Moscow Times*, 29 November 2007, p. 3.
[60] Valdai Discussion Club meeting, Sochi, 14 September 2007, http://president.kremlin.ru/text/appears/2007/09/144011.shtml.
[61] 'The Khodorkovsky Letter', posted by Robert Amsterdam on 9 November 2007, modified translation, www.robertamsterdam.com/2007/11/the_khodorkovsky_letter.htm#more.

the past a party had to spend at least half of the allotted airtime debating, but changes to the electoral law removed this stipulation. United Russia devoted all of its allotted time to promoting its platform and refused to enter into debate with any of its rivals. During the campaign there was much discussion of the various ideological wings in the party, with some talk of refashioning them as 'platforms': liberal, social and conservative-patriotic. United Russia's refusal to debate allowed its competitors to direct their fire at UR without any direct response, but they were heavily constrained in their ability to do so by new laws. Candidates were no longer allowed to exhort voters to cast their ballots against another candidate or party, or suggest 'potentially negative consequences' of voting for them.[62] These were quite extraordinary restrictions on freedom of discussion, although motivated in part by the desire to stop *ad hominem* attacks.

The split in the liberal vote between SPS and Yabloko was again fatal for both. A VTsIOM poll in late October gave them a combined total of 7.5 per cent, taking them over the threshold if the vote was concentrated in a single party; but split between the two, neither would enter. During the campaign SPS emerged as the most vigorous in attacking the regime, while Yabloko was rather more reserved. The SPS campaigned on the basis of harsh criticism of Putin personally as well as on a broader populist platform. Having been allegedly betrayed by the Kremlin reneging on its promise to allow SPS a clear run back into the Duma, the SPS decided to play the opposition card.[63] The SPS was subject to a remorseless negative propaganda and harassment campaign, with searches, slurs in the media, the seizure of promotional literature and the exclusion of candidates from regional voting lists. Although polls suggested that SPS stood little chance of passing the representation threshold on its own, its unequivocal stance against Putin provoked the use of 'administrative resources' against the party.[64]

The party was even willing to campaign with Other Russia, and SPS leaders Belykh and Nemtsov joined in the protest demonstrations on the eve of the vote. Belykh was arrested at a so-called 'dissenters' march' in St Petersburg on 25 November, while his deputy Gozman had his arm broken in the fracas attending his arrest. Opinion polls suggested, however, that SPS voters were second only to UR in their satisfaction with

---

[62] Karen Dawisha, 'A Restricted Election', *Russia Profile* 4, 10, pp. 7–9, at p. 9.
[63] Francesca Mereu and Natalya Krainova, 'SPS Finds New Place Closer to Kremlin', *Moscow Times*, 3 October 2008.
[64] Konstantin Sonin, 'Truly Strange Duma Elections', *Moscow Times*, 20 November 2007, p. 10.

Putin's leadership.[65] In an open letter to his supporters, Belykh declared that the Kremlin had declared war against the SPS, that 'Putin's plan' would lead to the 'restoration of Soviet-style statehood' and that the Duma election had unleashed 'a real bacchanalia of black technologies and the administrative resource'.[66] By adopting such brash campaigning, SPS alienated its natural constituency, the growing middle class, threatened by a weakening of the precarious stability achieved by Putin's leadership. The real target of the SPS campaign, however, was more profound than a simple denunciation of Putin's regime: its aim was 'To reveal the crisis of the ruling regime that has been maturing in the unique conditions of "petro-prosperity".'[67] The essence of the crisis was the increasingly overt struggle between warring factions accompanied by the centralisation of power designed to ensure administrative control over public politics.

The heavy-handed policing of the various dissenters' marches and other demonstrations during the campaign was evidence of the twitchiness of the authorities. The SPS took the brunt of the harassment, with prosecutors confiscating 15 million campaign newsletters, calendars and fliers. Following a political rally in Moscow on 24 November, Kasparov was arrested for resisting arrest and taking part in an unsanctioned march (permission had been given for a rally, but not a march), and spent five days in the Petrovka 38 jail. On the eve of his arrest, he had taken to calling Putin a 'dictator', but on his arrest he addressed the cameras in English, a fact which incensed Putin, arguing in his *Time* 'man of the year' interview that Russian politicians should at least try to address their own people in their own language.[68] This is a point that Khodorkovsky had made earlier in his 'Crisis of Russian Liberalism' article. Limonov, leader of the banned National Bolshevik Party, and Maria Gaidar, at the head of the SPS list in Moscow, were also briefly detained and then released. Shenderovich ended up in a police van after a demonstration was dispersed that had allegedly deviated from the agreed route. It was clear that the authorities had decided not to allow street demonstrations to gain a momentum of their own, the pattern of earlier colour revolutions. Public space was colonised by pro-regime movements such as Nashi, Molodaya Gvardiya (UR's youth association)

[65] Cited by Vyacheslav Nikonov, *Rossiiskaya gazeta*, 3 December 2007.
[66] 'Nikita Belykh obratilsya s pis'mom k storonnikam', 2 December 2008, http://sps.ru/?id=206905£cur_id=224452.
[67] *Ezhednevny zhurnal*, 30 November 2007; cited by Pavel K. Baev, 'Russia Has Voted as Ordered, Now What?', *EDM* 4, 223, 3 December 2007.
[68] *Time*, 18 December 2007; www.time.com/time/specials/2007/personoftheyear/article/0,28804,1690753_1690757_1696150,00.html.

and other pro-Putin movements. Within three years, membership of Nashi, the successor to Vasily Yakemenko's Walking Together (Idushie Vmeste) organisation, had grown to over 120,000, but instead of the vague aims of the earlier organisation oriented on Putin personally, the new body was strongly focused on combating the 'orange peril'.[69] Talk of a 'fifth column' and foreign support for groups was taken seriously by the government, if by no one else.

The 'keep Putin' movement

We have seen in Chapter 2 that Putin had repeatedly vowed to leave office, if not power, in 2008. However, even before the presidential campaign Putin's assumption of the number 1 slot on the UR list thrust him into the limelight. Meeting with the UR leaders at his Zavidovo residence on 17 November, Putin made clear that while he had consented to lead the list, he did not want the public to identify him too closely with the party. The UR leader, Gryzlov, then immediately emphasised that Putin was the 'national leader', something that was even more important than winning an election.[70]

It was at this time that the 'For Putin' ('Za Putina') movement reached its climax with a forum of Putin supporters in Moscow on 21 November. Since its inception in October, the movement had been rolling across the country, with various rallies, marches and demonstrations expressing 'confidence in Putin' held in about thirty regions between 23 October and 15 November.[71] On the latter date, a nationwide forum of initiative groups was held in Tver, which appealed to Putin not to leave politics and which formally established the 'Za Putina' movement headed by the lawyer Pavel Astakhov, the doctor Renat Akchurin and dairymaid Natalya Agapova. Astakhov informed the Tver meeting that he had already collected 30 million signatures for a petition to keep Putin, an astonishing fifth of the Russian population if the figures can be believed. This was buttressed by various resolutions of regional and municipal legislative assemblies, as in Yamal-Nenetsk and Sverdlovsk, calling on Putin to 'preserve his role as the national leader and continue his active participation in the life of the country'.[72]

---

[69] Regina Heller, 'Russia's "Nashi" Youth Movement: The Rise and Fall of a Putin-Era Political Technology Project', *Russian Analytical Digest*, No. 50, 18 November 2008, pp. 2–4.

[70] Sergei Mikhailov and Anastasia Novikova, 'Potomy chto nel'zya', *Gazeta*, 19 November 2007, p. 7.

[71] Jonas Bernstein, 'Putin, Post-March 2008: De Facto "National leader", or Back in the Kremlin', *EDM* 4, 210, 12 November 2007.

[72] Nikolai Petrov, 'For Putin, Anti-Democracy', *Moscow Times*, 20 November 2007, p. 11.

The 'third term' movement was designed to remind people of the high stakes in the election.

Putin repeatedly confirmed that he would not leave politics, although quite what he would do remained unclear. United Russia's ethnic policy coordinator, Abdul-Khakim Sultygov, in a message posted on the UR website on 13 November but then quickly removed, suggested that a 'civic council for the Russian nation' be convened in the spring following the presidential election at which Putin could be elected 'national leader'. The article, entitled 'The Phenomenon of National Leader in Russia', argued that the national leader is the highest personification of representative power in Russia, and while after May 2008 a new president and government would enter office, the national leader in the shape of Putin would oversee affairs.[73] The idea was wholly in the spirit of Gryzlov's article of 17 October in *Rossiiskaya gazeta* arguing that 'Putin will remain leader of Russia'. The constitution, of course, contains no mention of such an office, although Putin's para-constitutional modifications (including the establishment of the seven federal districts, the creation of the State Council and the Public Chamber) were legion. There was no way that the post of 'national leader' could be created without some serious rethinking of the constitutional division of powers. The idea was reminiscent of a 'guardianship council' of the Turkish sort, where to defend the secular constitution, the military stood above the constitution, or Lee Kuan Yew's position as 'minister mentor' in Singapore.

More broadly, Putin's willingness to go along with the 'for Putin' wave probably damaged more than helped his cause. The fact that the ratings of UR did not rise much beyond what they were when he joined their campaign suggested a certain voter resistance to being steam-rollered in a direction sought by the regime. Any advantage was outweighed by resentment to being treated as part of a herd. The For Putin movement was designed to offset the impression that Putin represented the interests of only one party, even though he was the sole name on UR's national list, but the method only reinforced the view that he represented a manipulative regime.

Outcomes

The development of parallel political spheres was characteristic of Putin's presidency, and this was spectacularly displayed in this election.

---

[73] Dmitrii Kamyshev, 'I. o. tsarya', *Kommersant-Vlast'*, No. 44, 12 November 2007, pp. 15–18 has extensive extracts and commentary.

The country was not just choosing a new parliament; the vote became a type of surrogate poll on Putin's leadership. The interplay of party politics and genuine competition between programmes was occluded by the meta-vote on the continuation of Putinite stability and achievements. As so often in Russia's brief history of electoral politics, the vote was as much a referendum on the regime as a choice between parties. The establishment of normal quotidian politics was once again postponed, despite Putin's repeated plea for 'normality' to be restored in Russia.

The vote

A total of 107 million people were registered to vote, down by 600,000 since the 2003 Duma elections. The figure includes 1.7 million abroad, for which 350 polling stations were opened outside the Russian Federation in 140 countries. In Russia, the eighty-five constituent territories were divided into 153 districts for regional groups. Moscow city was divided into ten, Moscow *oblast'* into eight, while St Petersburg city and the Sverdlovsk, Rostov and Krasnodar regions each had five. The 'cost' of a seat differed for every political party, reflecting the ratio between the number of votes cast and the number of seats to which it is entitled. Voting took place in 95,000 polling stations, subordinated to 2,747 territorial electoral commissions. With eleven parties on the ballot paper, the voter had significant choice across the political spectrum.

The abolition of the minimum turnout requirement meant that there was no technical reason now artificially to inflate the figures. The former head of the CEC, Veshnyakov, had feared that the abolition of minimum turnout requirements would result in the 'delegitimisation' of elections, but with a turnout of 35.8 per cent in the October 2006 regional election and 40.1 per cent in March 2007, the fall was not as great as he had feared. The regime in December 2007, however, for political reasons was intent on a high turnout. With the vote turning into a referendum on Putin's leadership and future role, the higher the turnout, the Kremlin reasoned, the greater the legitimacy. However, the pressure to achieve the result had the paradoxical effect of undermining the legitimacy of the outcome. A poll by the Levada Center found that 17 per cent of respondents had experienced pressure during the campaign, compared to only 9 per cent in 2003.[74] There is plentiful evidence indicating that

[74] Dmitrii Kamyshev, 'The Year of Doubling the President', *Kommersant-Vlast'*, No. 50, 24 December 2007.

local authorities and state agencies were encouraged to ensure a high turnout.

Liliya Shibanova of the Golos monitoring organisation, which mobilised 2,500 volunteers to visit over 20,000 polling stations in thirty-eight regions, noted: 'We have seen an unprecedented attempt to manipulate the vote. There has been mass forced voting and a raft of other violations.'[75] The Golos organisation, established in 2000 to protect voter rights and to develop civil society and which receives EU Commission and American funding, also found itself at the sharp end of administrative pressure during the campaign.[76] Golos launched a long-term election monitoring programme in July 2007 and received information from its *Civic Voice (Grazhdanskii golos)* newspaper network in forty regions. The use of absentee certificates rose markedly in comparison with 2003 to ensure that people voted. According to Ryzhkov, the number of absentee ballots in his Siberian constituency rose from 1,500 in 2003 to 20,000 in 2007. There were also complaints that election officials toured housing estates with ballot boxes to ensure a high turnout for UR.[77] There were persistent allegations that state employees and students were instructed to vote for UR, and numerous reports of ballot box stuffing.

In the event, the turnout of 64.4 per cent exceeded the 55.8 per cent reached in 2003. As usual, turnout was particularly high in agrarian regions, where it was relatively easy to organise the vote. Some rural districts in the south of Tyumen region registered a 100 per cent turnout. By contrast, the UR vote in Moscow (54.15 per cent) was lower than in the country as a whole, and it was even lower in St Petersburg (50.33 per cent). In some of the North Caucasian republics, as we shall see, the order was over-fulfilled. There was a remarkable uniformity in the result across the country, both between regions and within them. Parties that failed to gain representation in the Duma did not win in any region except the Agrarians in the Ust-Orda Buryat autonomous *okrug*, in its last outing as an independent region before merging with Irkutsk *oblast'*. As Petrov notes, a number of regions had effectively become one-party systems, while a handful (where the CPRF did well) emerged as two-party systems.[78]

---

[75] Tom Parfitt and Luke Harding, 'Intimidation and Dirty Tricks Help Putin to Massive Landslide', *The Guardian*, 3 December 2007, p. 1.

[76] Natalya Krainova, 'Russian Election Observers Sidelined', *Moscow Times*, 29 November 2007, p. 1.

[77] Parfitt and Harding, 'Intimidation and Dirty Tricks Help Putin to Massive Landslide', p. 2.

[78] Nikolai Petrov, 'The Consequences of the State Duma Election for Russia's Electoral System', *Russian Analytical Digest*, No. 32, 2007, pp. 5–8, at p. 8.

Table 7.2 *State Duma election of 2 December 2007*

Name of party	Percentage vote	Votes (mln)	Seats
1 United Russia (UR)	64.30	44.71	315
2 Communist Party of the Russian Federation (CPRF)	11.57	8.05	57
3 Liberal Democratic Party of Russia (LDPR)	8.14	5.66	40
4 Just Russia (JR)	7.74	5.38	38
Subtotal	**91.75**	**63.8**	**450**
Seven per cent representation threshold			
5 Agrarian Party of Russia (APR)	2.30	1.60	–
6 Yabloko	1.59	1.11	–
7 Civic Force	1.05	0.73	–
8 Union of Right Forces (SPS)	0.96	0.67	–
9 Patriots of Russia	0.89	0.62	–
10 Party of Social Justice	0.22	0.15	–
11 Democratic Party of Russia	0.13	0.13	–
Subtotal	**7.14**	**5.01**	–
TOTAL	**100** (rounded)	**68.81**	**450**
Number of registered voters		109,145,517	
Number of valid votes		68,777,136	
Number of spoilt ballots		759,929	
Turnout		69,537,065 (64.1%)	

Source: Central Electoral Commission: www.cikrf.ru; http://www.vybory.izbirkom.ru.

Four parties crossed the 7 per cent threshold, between them garnering 91.7 per cent of the votes cast (Table 7.2). The gulf between the winning party and the other three groups had never been so wide. United Russia received nearly two-thirds of the vote (64.3 per cent), putting all its competitors in the shade. Putin received the endorsement that he sought to stay on in some sort of leadership position. He was quick to take the credit for the achievement, telling aviation workers in Khimki that 'I headed this party's ticket, and [the result] was definitely a demonstration of [the voters'] trust.' He argued that the win came 'not only in appreciation of what has been done but, most of all, as a result of voters' expectations that United Russia will continue to solve social problems'. Gryzlov reiterated Putin's argument, noting that 'Vladimir Putin has won the first round', suggesting that the election was indeed a primary for the presidential contest. In a press conference on election night, he argued that 'This is support for our national leader. A referendum has been held';[79] and later he stressed 'The victory belongs to Putin.'[80] However, the gap between the vote Putin received in the 2004 presidential election (71 per cent, 49.53 million votes) and his popularity ratings (approaching 80 per cent), and the vote won now by UR (44.71 million) with so much effort revealed that personal support could not so easily be transferred. The difference of just over 6 million votes revealed a certain deficit of trust in the party. Out of the total electorate, only 41 per cent voted for UR (44.71 million), indicating that the ruling regime did not enjoy overwhelming support.

The victory of UR had a number of dimensions. First, as a referendum, the result not only confirmed confidence in Putin but was also a judgment on the 1990s, and endorsed his largely negative view of that decade. Second, the electoral base of UR's victory signalled a clear shift from Putin as 'the president of hope', as it had been earlier, towards a largely positive assessment of his period as leader, with a pragmatic endorsement of the 'Putin plan' for the future. The Putin majority was less fragile than it had been earlier, notably at the time of unrest over the monetisation of social benefits, but now appealed across the ideological divide to encompass liberals, conservatives and patriots. While polls suggest that liberalism in Russia is supported by between 10–15 per cent of the population, much of this vote was cast for Putin's party in this election and not for the professed liberal parties, SPS and Yabloko.[81] In other words, the result was a defeat for the liberals but not of liberalism as such, which to a degree had been incorporated into the UR machine.

The CPRF had been expected to enter, and its vote of 11.6 per cent was what most opinion surveys had predicted. In fact, across the board the outcome of the election was firmly in line with poll predictions and with exit polls,[82] suggesting that the dirty tricks at the ballot box did not substantively affect the result. The 'red belt' still survived, although much weakened. In Altai, Krasnodar, Bryansk, Orël, Omsk and Novosibirsk, the Communist vote at 17 per cent was well above its national average, while 19 per cent were cast for them in Samara and 22 per cent in Voronezh.

In third place with 8.14 per cent came the LDPR, with Zhirinovsky having once again pulled off the trick of entering parliament with a vote almost identical with that achieved in 2003. With him came Lugovoi,

---

[79] Anna Smolchenko, 'Party Ponders Life After Landslide', *Moscow Times*, 3 December 2007, p. 1.
[80] Nabi Abdullaev, 'Putin Praises Voters, Himself', *Moscow Times*, 4 December 2007, p. 1.
[81] Dmitrii Orlov, *Izvestiya*, 10 December 2007.
[82] 'Pozdravlenie kollegam', 7 December 2007, www.levada.ru/press/2007120705.html.

who was looking for a post in the new Duma's security or defence committee. Membership of the Duma gave him immunity from prosecution, although the British authorities stubbornly vowed to continue the case. The LDPR did well in its traditional area of support in the Far East, winning 13 per cent in Primorsk and Khabarovsk, and 11 per cent in Chita and Magadan regions. As always, the LDPR picked up some of the protest vote, in this case those who were dissatisfied with UR and the authorities but who did not wish to rock the boat. In voting for the LDPR, people could demonstrate their opposition to policies while endorsing the system.

The entry of Just Russia with 7.74 per cent was perhaps the greatest surprise, with polls having suggested that it would with difficulty cross the representation threshold. We have noted the 'Putin deflation', the blow to the party struck when Putin took up the top slot with UR. The party in subsequent weeks suffered a number of high-profile defections, accompanied by administrative pressure against its candidates. The most blatant attack against the party took place in Stavropol, where the JR mayor and leading candidate, Dmitry Kuzmin, was disbarred from standing because of a series of apparently fabricated charges, including corruption and the keeping of Nazi insignia.[83] The JR vote was highest in Astrakhan (20 per cent), and an impressive 16 per cent in St Petersburg, followed by 13 per cent in Stavropol, despite the various scandals. The support of the former Party of Pensioners in the Just Russia alliance and the Party of Life undoubtedly helped, given the country's demographics. Although formally positioned as a centre-left alternative to UR, the party under Mironov was in fact a socialist alternative to the CPRF. Just Russia was always balanced on the threshold, and credible leaks from the Kremlin suggest that in the last weeks of the campaign the administration relented and helped it get over the barrier. The new party's breakthrough was less impressive than Rodina's had been in 2003, when it had won 9.02 per cent with forty-five seats, but it was more durable.

Just over 8 per cent of the ballot went to the seven parties that failed to cross the representation threshold, the lowest proportion of 'wasted' votes in Russia's electoral history. Support for these seven fell far short of the 7 per cent threshold, and none even managed to reach the 3 per cent of the vote necessary for the return of their 60 million roubles, or $2.4 million, election deposit. The general rule that no party has been able to return to parliament once it failed to make the threshold was

---

[83] Alexander Osipovich, 'Early Voters Support a Just Russia', *Moscow Times*, 3 December 2007, p. 3.

confirmed. On this occasion it was even worse, with both Yabloko and SPS not only excluded but humiliated, winning just 1.9 and 0.96 per cent of the vote, respectively. Even in its St Petersburg heartland, Yabloko won only 5.1 per cent of the vote.

The Kremlin sponsored a number of 'spoiler' parties, designed to siphon votes away from more established parties. The fake parties in the 2007 election were apparently financed through a special fund operating in Vneshekonombank supervised by Surkov and Sobyanin.[84] In normal circumstances a percentage point could have meant the difference between crossing the representation threshold or not. The Civic Force and the Democratic Party had been designed as spoilers for the SPS, while the Party of Social Justice mimicked the rhetoric of JR. Civic Force was explicitly a liberal party and in most respects shared the SPS view on economic and social policy. The significant vote garnered by these peculiar parties, unknown a few months before the election, came as a shock to the traditional liberal parties, coming within an ace of overtaking them. The long-established SPS, in particular, was humiliated by the result in which a virtual creation received nearly as many votes as the real party.

The SPS had moved deeper into opposition to the Kremlin as the campaign progressed, and now it denounced not only the results but the whole political system that had taken shape since 1991. Chubais, who had been one of the founders of the party and remained one of its key sponsors (although not financially this time round), condemned the lack of media access for the opposition parties and the predominance of UR: 'This party has become a monopoly using a Soviet mentality, the Soviet soul and a Soviet atmosphere.' He went on to note that 'I know how a monopoly works', being the head of the electricity monopoly: 'In 1991, we had two tasks to accomplish: one was to reform the economy, and the other was to reform the political system. The first task we have accomplished, the second one we have not.' Belykh conceded defeat in what he described as rigged elections but argued that in the long run justice would prevail: 'The important thing is that we won a moral victory in the country. There are people ready to come out against the cynicism of those in power. That means all is not lost.' Another key SPS leader, Nemtsov, argued that 'This is the most dishonest election that Russia has seen.'[85]

---

[84] Andrew Wilson, *Meeting Medvedev: The Politics of the Putin Succession*, European Council on Foreign Relations, *Policy Brief*, No. 5, February 2008, p. 3.
[85] Anatoly Medetsky, Catrina Stewart and Nikolaus von Twickel, 'Disappointment and Defiance in Party Camps', *Moscow Times*, 3 December 2007, p. 1.

The election gave a crushing victory to Putin and UR, but the manner in which it was achieved undermined the legitimacy of the whole process. Even though the CPRF managed to enter the new parliament, immediately after the elections Zyuganov issued a statement: 'The nation has never seen such dirty and unlawful elections: whole new areas of total election fraud appeared in Russia.' The North Caucasus and Volga regions were listed as the source of most complaints from the party's election observers. The CPRF argued that up to 10 per cent of its vote had been stolen, although the result was only a little below the 12.6 per cent won in 2003, but this was the worst result for the CPRF since 1993. Yavlinsky argued that the whole election was 'a special kind of violence against the nation. Victory is when you have fair competition ... I am very sorry for my country, very sorry.' [86]

There were indeed some freakish results. The Kremlin managers were well aware of the correlation between a high turnout and votes for UR.[87] Administrative pressure resulted in a turnout of between 80 and 90 per cent in Chechnya, Ingushetia, Kabardino-Balkaria, Mordovia, Karachaevo-Cherkessia, Dagestan, Bashkortostan and Tatarstan, exceeding by far the national average of 64 per cent, with a commensurately high vote for United Russia. In Chechnya, official figures showed that 99.21 per cent went to the polls (576,729 out of 580,918 registered voters) and UR received 99.36 per cent of the vote. The media had shown nothing but exhortations by Kadyrov to turn out and vote for UR, whose regional list he headed, and this was achieved in a classically Soviet 'voluntary-compulsory' manner. At the same time, the referendum saw 96.15 per cent vote, of which 96.88 per cent supported extensive amendments to the republic's constitution that allowed the local parliament to make constitutional changes, extended the presidential term from four to five years, reduced the size of the parliament to a single 41-deputy chamber from the old 61-deputy bicameral assembly, and made Russian and Chechen the two state languages.[88] Few were ready to incur the wrath of the region's strong-willed leader, and thus the once rebellious republic registered the highest 'loyalty' vote for UR in the country.

It was run closely by a number of other North Caucasus republics. Turnout in Ingushetia was 98.35 per cent, with 98.72 allegedly voting

[86] Nabi Abdullaev, 'Putin Praises Voters, Himself', *Moscow Times*, 4 December 2007, p. 1.
[87] The correlation according to Nikolai Petrov was 0.9, 'The Consequences of the State Duma Elections for Russia's Electoral System', *Russian Analytical Digest*, No. 32, 2007, pp. 5–8, at p. 8.
[88] www.kavkaz-uzel.ru/newstext/news/id/1203008.html.

for UR; turnout in Kabardino-Balkaria was 97 per cent, and 94 per cent in Karachaevo-Cherkessia, with a similar percentage voting for UR. In Dagestan, turnout was about 92 per cent, with 89 per cent supporting UR. Only North Ossetia, the scene of the Beslan massacre in September 2004, was the odd one out, with turnout of just 60.3 per cent, with 71.6 per cent voting for UR while 10.88 per cent voted for the Communists. Observers in Ingushetia later claimed that no more than 8 per cent of the population had voted.[89] The North Caucasus has a long-established reputation for overwhelming official victories to have little relationship with reality. Such results resolve none of the pressing social and political problems in the region, although they do send important signals to Moscow. Sergei Markedonov, head of the Inter-Ethnic Relations Department of the Institute for Political and Military Analysis, notes, 'It is not even a matter of mass falsification (even though the election headquarters of other parties are already presenting proof of this) … Or even of administrative resources, which, of course, are practically limitless there. From our point of view, the main problem is the significant gap between the formal and the real in the Caucasus region.'[90] And, we may note, this gap is not confined to the North Caucasus alone.

A below average turnout was registered in Moscow, St Petersburg, Volgograd, Nizhny Novgorod and some other Russian cities, which some have taken as being a more accurate reflection of voter preferences when administrative resources are subtracted.[91] Turnout in St Petersburg was only 50 per cent, significantly lower than it had been in 2004. In regions where the vote was particularly low, some of those responsible, as in Udmurtia, lost their jobs.[92] Officials and public sector workers were pressured to ensure a high turnout, and at least fourteen municipal heads or their deputies were sacked and others reprimanded if they failed to do so. Retribution at the gubernatorial level also was not long in coming. The governor of Smolensk *oblast'*, where the turnout had been particularly low (54 per cent, the fourth lowest after the Nenets *okrug*, Petersburg and Yaroslavl), Victor Maslov, 'resigned' soon after the election. He had been one of the first 'Chekists' to become a governor in 2002 and now fell victim to the system that he had helped create. The governor of Yaroslavl *oblast'*, Anatoly Lisitsyn, was also

[89] Jonas Bernstein, 'More than 80,000 Ingush Deny that They Voted in State Duma Elections', *EDM* 5, 5, 11 January 2008.
[90] *Chechnya Weekly* 8, 47, 6 December 2007.
[91] Hans-Henning Schröder, 'Sufficient Legitimation for "Shadow President"?', *Russian Analytical Digest*, No. 32, 2007, p. 3.
[92] *Kommersant*, 5 December 2007.

forced out of office and took up his Duma seat. As we have seen, none of the four main Chekist-governors headed the UR list in their regions. We have seen that the outcome coincided remarkably with the prognoses of opinion polls, although turnout was 10 per cent higher than the Levada Center had predicted. The original Levada figures are probably correct, since in the North Caucasian republics bar one the figures were drastically inflated. As Petrov notes, 'If the predictions are correct, then either the pollsters learned how to take the use of administrative resources into account or the administrative system works according to the predictions, which thereby play a normative role.' He notes the expert view that the UR vote was possibly inflated by 12–15 per cent, the Communist vote reduced by 2–5 per cent, the JR vote significantly increased to take it over the threshold, that Civic Force was given some extra votes, while the Yabloko and SPS votes were reduced by 2–3 per cent, although he stresses there is no reason to believe that even in the best of circumstances they would have crossed the 7 per cent barrier.[93]

Neither free nor fair?

The use of 'selection' techniques before the election has been criticised as much as the election itself. The rigid normative framework filtered out numerous potential participants. The regime was quite open about its intention of preventing extremists and nationalists entering the race, but its 'selectivity' went far further than this. The attack against Chubais effectively deprived the opposition of access to legitimate campaign funds, just as the attack against Khodorkovsky in 2003 had done.[94] During the campaign the dominance of UR on the airwaves was marked, with Putin and UR commanding around 60 per cent of all prime-time political news coverage between 1 October and 22 November 2007.[95] A total of 350 foreign observers monitored the election. Observers from the CIS on 3 December reported that the Duma elections had been 'democratic, free and transparent', but the OSCE and the Council of Europe were less positive and declared that the poll 'was not fair and failed to meet many OSCE and Council of Europe commitments and standards for democratic elections'.[96] The CPRF announced that its

[93] Petrov, 'The Consequences of the State Duma Elections', p. 8.
[94] Editorial, *Vedomosti*, 20 November 2007.
[95] Report of Centre for Journalism in Extreme Situations, in Nabi Abdullaev, 'United Russia Rules the Airwaves', *Moscow Times*, 30 November 2007, p. 1.
[96] RIA Novosti, 3 December 2007.

300,000 observers had found some 10,000 violations, and that it would appeal to the Supreme Court to rule on the validity of the vote. On 4 December Golos issued a statement which accused the Duma elections of having been riddled with violations that deprived them of legitimacy. 'The lack of political competition, the pressure on the voting process, the mass casting of absentee ballots and the unprecedented use of administrative resources' all cast serious doubt on whether the elections met international standards.[97] Surprisingly, the actual counting of the vote and the transmission of collated figures to Moscow was not singled out for criticism, although it is precisely here that the greatest abuses had previously taken place. A later study of the results found anomalies in the returns, with a disproportionate tally of figures ending in round numbers (ending in zero or five), which gave a higher turnout and UR vote than a normal distribution would have predicted.[98]

The conduct of the election was the subject of intense international criticism. At a joint press conference on the day after the election, the president of the OSCE's Parliamentary Assembly, Göran Lennmarker, noted that 'These elections failed to meet many of the commitments and standards that we have.' He was supported by Luc van den Brande, the head of the PACE delegation, who argued, 'If Russia is a managed democracy, then these were managed elections.'[99] The joint declaration issued by the two missions, which had sent a total of 147 observers, listed four main concerns. The first was UR's links to the Kremlin. Van den Brande noted that, 'May I say that for us, it is an unprecedented situation that a sitting president is running in an election.' He obviously had in mind an incumbent president running in a *parliamentary* election, since American and French presidents usually run for a second *presidential* term. The other concerns were: 'media bias in favour of the president; restrictive election laws that make it difficult for small parties to develop and to register new ones; and the reported harassment of opposition parties'.[100] A notable case of the media reporting a campaign speech as news was that sixteen minutes of Putin's emotional 25-minute 21 November speech was broadcast in news programmes on state channels that day.

---

[97] www.golos.org/a1055.html; David Nowak, 'Golos Sees Serious Violations', *Moscow Times*, 5 December 2007, p. 3.
[98] Nabi Abdullaev, 'Voting Figures Look a Bit Too Round', *Moscow Times*, 29 February 2008, p. 1.
[99] Luke Harding, 'Russian Election Unfair and Biased Towards Putin, Observers Say', *The Guardian*, 4 December 2007, p. 2.
[100] David Nowak, 'Observers Criticize "Managed Elections"', *Moscow Times*, 4 December 2007, p. 1.

The OSCE based its observations on a detailed analysis of electoral laws and the campaign that had begun well before the delegation arrived in Russia. In a more detailed defence of its view that the elections had been 'not fair', it highlighted the following issues (following the points made by the joint report, above):

- the merging of the state and a political party;
- media bias in favour of Putin and United Russia;
- complicated procedures and prohibitively high fees for registering political parties, which made it particularly difficult for smaller parties to run;
- the harassment of opposition parties and movements.

The widespread use of state resources in favour of one party over the others was described as

> an abuse of power and a clear violation of the Copenhagen commitments, which, in paragraph 5.4, say that there should be 'a clear separation between the state and political parties; in particular, political parties will not be merged with the state'. The extensive use of administrative resources and the active role of the head of state, President Vladimir Putin, on behalf of United Russia, even though he was not officially a party member, violated the OSCE and PACE commitments and standards and turned the parliamentary elections into a referendum on the president.

The OSCE also criticised changes in electoral legislation that prohibited 'negative campaigning' except in debates, but since UR refused to participate in the debates any criticism of the party could technically be classified as 'negative campaigning'.[101]

Golos divided the complaints it had received into the following categories: 23 per cent involved officials and police impeding election monitors; 22 per cent involved accusation of illegal campaigning; 15 per cent dealt with the manipulation of voter lists; 11 per cent reported pressure on voters; 9 per cent reported the violation of voter privacy; and 4 per cent claimed outright bribery.[102] An election campaign should be the opportunity for a genuine discussion about the issues facing the country, but the restrictive rules prevented an open debate of these issues. The election turned into a referendum on the president and a test of loyalty not only of the population but also of the regime's

---

[101] www.oscepa.org/, 3 December 2007; with the gloss supplied by Klas Bergman, 'Why the Vote Was Not Fair', *Moscow Times*, 6 December 2007, p. 10. Bergman was the director of communications and spokesperson of the OSCE Parliamentary Assembly.
[102] 4 December 2007 press release: www.golos.org/a1055.html.

appointees; and at the same time, it demonstrated the way that the regime maintained itself in power. Voting turned into a para-election as the counterpart of the para-political processes that accompanied public life as a whole.

The flaws in the electoral process prompted comparisons with Yeltsin's re-election campaign in 1996, which had also been intensely managed and had tried to rally the nation against a common enemy to maximise support. In 1996 the threat of the return of communism was played for all it was worth, while in 2007 the alleged danger posed by the return of oligarch power was highlighted. The high turnout and strong vote for UR indicated intense administrative pressure. The official turn-out figure of 64.1 per cent probably exaggerated the real figure, although it was undoubtedly increased by the febrile atmosphere cultivated during the campaign, encouraged by Putin's speeches warning of a return to the past and foreign intervention. A detailed study by Buzin and Lyubarev sought to quantify the impact of administrative resources. If the elections had been free and fair, they calculated that UR would have received 30.88 million votes and won 278 seats, 56 per cent of the Duma total; but the use of administrative pressure boosted UR's tally by 13.83 million additional votes, and thus gave them an extra 37 seats and a constitutional majority.[103]

The Kremlin vigorously denounced the accusations. The usual claims of western 'double standards' were advanced, including the argument – not entirely without foundation – that western observers had made up their minds about the election long before they were held. It also noted that there were only sixteen observers at the 2004 US presidential election, twelve at the parliamentary election in Poland in 2007, and that Austria failed to invite any European observers at all, but the OSCE failed to 'see anything reprehensible about it'.[104] During the campaign Putin frequently warned against foreign intervention, and it appears that the Kremlin believed that international condemnation of the election would be the signal for some sort of colour revolution – the scenario in popular uprisings against alleged stolen elections elsewhere. This was more than mere rhetoric, and the Kremlin really did believe that some

---

[103] Aleksandr Melenberg, 'V Dume 37 lishnikh deputatov', *Novaya gazeta*, No. 23, 6 March 2009, p. 8. The book, outlining three different models for the calculations, by Andrei Buzin and Arkady Lyubarev is called *Prestuplenie bez nakazaniya: Administrativnye tekhnologii federal'nykh vyborov 2007–2009 godov* (Moscow: Nikkolo-M, 2009).
[104] The argument was advanced by Lyubov Sliska, a deputy speaker in the Fourth Duma, Itar-Tass, 5 December 2007.

sort of physical confrontation was on the cards.[105] Berezovsky's crowing about funding the opposition did not help, especially since he had earlier made typically exaggerated claims about having bankrolled the Orange revolution. It was for this reason that the Kremlin engaged in pre-emptive repression, including the forcible dispersion of demonstrations on the eve of the election, although the Kremlin only after the Duma election agreed to increase the wages of the armed forces to ensure their loyalty.

There is no doubt that 'administrative resources' were used, and that media coverage was heavily biased in favour of the incumbent and his party. However, in broad terms the result did reflect the way that Russians felt, and thus there was no gulf between popular aspirations (or at least of a large and coherent group) and outcome, the gap that elsewhere had provoked popular unrest of the colour variety. In every Russian election, the authorities have overtly, although to varying degrees, supported the pedestal party of the day: Russia's Choice in 1993 (15 per cent), Our Home is Russia in 1995 (10 per cent), but up to 1999 this had generally been ineffective.[106] Administrative measures on their own could not guarantee desired outcomes, although no doubt the regime had become more adept at their application and was in a stronger position to shape the whole process. This should not occlude the fact that Putin enjoyed a high degree of popular support and approval, and some of this rubbed off on to his acolytes. There was no shortage of information available in Russia, with the internet becoming the primary source of news for at least 10 per cent of the population. Visions of an embattled and unpopular regime manipulating the electoral process in its entirety to cling on to power are mistaken. The Kremlin would have won an open contest, but as we have seen it was pursuing a number of aims, only one of which was simply to win the election. This it could easily have done without intervening, but the Kremlin was also seeking plebiscitary approval for its party and policies, and this required more active intervention.

A number of court cases challenged the outcome. In particular, the SPS took its case to the Constitutional Court, arguing that in the Vologda regional elections the whole list had been removed when one of its groups had withdrawn, a provision copied from national electoral legislation. The SPS claimed that the threshold to enter elections was

---

[105] Pavel Felgenhauer, 'Kremlin Landslide will Promote Confrontation', *EDM* 4, 225, 5 December 2007.
[106] A point made by Patrick Armstrong, *Russian Federation/CIS Weekly Sitrep*, 6 December 2007.

thus rendered excessively high.[107] The SPS case went all the way through the Russian court system and up to the ECtHR. Kasyanov also appealed to Strasbourg, challenging the CEC's refusal to register his political party. On a number of occasions in early 2008, Gorbachev returned to the theme, noting in particular in a meeting in London that the Duma and presidential elections demonstrated that the Russian electoral system 'needed serious modification'. He was part of a team that prepared a highly critical report for the Independent Institute for Elections, which included the body's head, Alexander Ivanchenko. The executive authorities, contrary to basic principles of a level playing field, intervened to support the party of power (the 'administrative resource'), and there was unequal access to the media, giving rise to some 'anomalous results', as in the North Caucasus. The report's authors considered that in broad terms Russian electoral legislation was in conformity with the constitution and international standards, but lacked serious elements of both freedom and fairness. How the necessary corrections could be made was left vague, although they saw no reason why an evolutionary modification could not take place. Unlike some of the opposition, notably the Communists who talked of a 'socio-political crisis' or Yabloko, which insisted that a democratic system could not be built in Russia by parliamentary means, they did not consider that a change of regime was necessary, or that Russia found itself in a 'revolutionary situation'.[108]

Many of these points were confirmed by the Liberal Mission Foundation's report on the subject, chaired by Yasin, which argued that Russia's first elections (notably in 1993) had been the most democratic, and the competitiveness of elections had declined thereafter. The electoral system had adapted to the needs of the regime as part of the 'dual adaptation' discussed in Chapter 1. They noted that even small changes in electoral legislation could have significant deleterious effects. The report compared the regional elections of 8 October 2006 with those held on 11 March 2007, with the latter less competitive and democratic. The number of parties and candidates fell between the two events, with three times more groups being prevented from participating: in the October elections almost 90 per cent of the proposed lists were accepted, whereas in March only 91 out of 130 were accepted, with over a third

[107] Igor' Romanov, 'Konstitutsionnyi sud mozhet podderzhivat' liberalov', *Nezavisimaya gazeta*, 1 February 2008, p. 4; Yurii Chernega, 'Konstitutsionnyi sud rassmotrit partspiski', *Kommersant*, 1 February 2008, p. 3.
[108] Viktor Khamraev, 'Izbiratel'nyi protsess ne tuda poshel', *Kommersant*, 20 January 2008, p. 4.

rejected. The fundamental flaw in the experts' opinion was the law on the parties, which made it hard for groups to form and place themselves before the electorate.[109] An interesting aspect of the whole process is that most Russians considered the election fair, a view that has to be seen in the context of appreciation for what was perceived to be satisfactory government performance.[110] There is of course no single measure of what constitutes 'unfairness', although the usual indicator is the ability of the government to be defeated. However, perceptions and attitudes play a large role, and those who held a positive view of post-communist Russia and its political system were more likely to consider the elections fair, and thus disagreed with the view of international observers.[111] A major comparative study, however, categorised the 2007 Duma ballot as one of the most fraudulent of Russia's elections.[112] The conclusion is clear: Russian elections have been the subject of endless and concerted fiddling, but it would be an exaggeration to say that they have been fixed; however, by 2007 the cumulative administrative interventions meant that electoral politics were close to the tipping point. Unless there was a qualitative improvement in the quality of elections, the crisis of Russian democracy would give way to its demise.

The Fifth Duma

The strong vote in favour of UR was nevertheless a resounding vote in support of Putin and his policies. As Putin stated in a cabinet meeting on the day after the elections, the vote was a demonstration of confidence in his rule, and he stressed that Russians would 'never allow their country to follow the destructive path taken by some post-Soviet countries', a reference to the 'colour' revolutions elsewhere. Despite enjoying Putin's undivided support and basking in the mantle of his popularity, UR had only with great effort (and with the help of administrative resources) managed to win 64 per cent of the vote. There was thus a gap between this figure and the popularity ratings of Putin, which at this time were consistently around 80 per cent. This suggests that UR was not as strong

---

[109] Report by Alexander Kynev, in *Nauchnyi seminar Yevgeniya Yasina, Stepen' demokratichnosti rossiiskikh vyborov: Kriterii otsenki* (Moscow: Fond 'Liberal'naya missiya', 7 July 2007).
[110] Richard Rose and William Mishler, 'How Do Electors Respond to an "Unfair" Election? The Experience of Russians', *Post-Soviet Affairs* 25, 2, April–June 2009, pp. 118–36.
[111] Rose and Mishler, 'How Do Electors Respond to an "Unfair" Election?', p. 128.
[112] Myagkov, Ordeshook and Shakin, *The Forensics of Election Fraud*, p. 31.

as it appeared and that this prompted Putin to campaign for the party. He was nevertheless open in his criticism of UR, suggesting that it was not really a party but an association of careerists interlaced with criminals. However, in terms of the 'referendum' strategy on his policies, he received the popular endorsement that he sought and shaped an instrument to ensure policy continuity.

The new Duma maintained many features from the previous one. Once again, four parties were represented, with Rodina's place now taken by Just Russia. The overwhelmingly masculine tone of the body remained, even though the number of women increased from forty-four to sixty-three (from 9.8 to 14 per cent), with the gender imbalance exacerbated by the fact that 53 per cent of the Russian population are women. The number of women increased in large part because of the refusal of a large proportion of people higher up the lists to take their seats (see below).[113] With the abolition of single-mandate seats and independent deputies, however, the composition of the parliamentary groups changed radically. United Russia had achieved its constitutional majority in the Fourth Duma by scraping together independent deputies and defectors from other parties. Now deputies were selected by the party leadership, which improved discipline and factional coherence in Duma politics. It also rendered deputies more malleable.

A total of sixty-five governors ran on UR's eighty-three regional lists, taking the top spot in all but Khakassia, Stavropol and St Petersburg and acting, as we have seen, as 'locomotives' for the party. In twenty-seven cases governors were allowed to appear on the same poster as Putin in regions where they were especially popular and UR successful.[114] Thus the vote was not only a national referendum on Putin's rule but also a series of referendums on regional leaders. Like Putin himself, none were willing to give up their executive posts to take up their Duma seats. In 2003 only four of UR's fifteen-person federal list actually took up their seats, although all fifteen on the federal lists of the three other parties crossing what was then the 5 per cent threshold entered parliament (CPRF, LDPR and Rodina).[115] An amendment to the election law in 2007 allowed a candidate who declined to fill their seat to take up the option later, with the party's approval (the so-called 'postponed mandate'), opening the way for significant rotation of the Duma's membership. Whereas in 2003, thirty-seven heavyweights on UR lists declined to

---

[113] Carl Holmberg, *Managing Elections in Russia: Mechanisms and Problems* (Stockholm, FOI: Swedish Defence Research Agency, February 2008), p. 68.
[114] Holmberg, *Managing Elections in Russia*, p. 28.
[115] Clark, 'Russia at the Polls', p. 28, fn 11.

take up their seats,[116] in 2007 over a hundred candidates who ran on the federal and regional lists of winning parties did not take up their mandates. An extraordinary total of 31 per cent of UR MPs declined to take up their seats, and 25 per cent of all MPs withdrew.[117] They included not only Putin himself, but also three federal ministers, all governors except Anatoly Lisitsyn of Yaroslavl (whose choice was rather less than free), many mayors and speakers of regional legislatures. As Petrov observes, 'This is shameful. It is a hypocritical shell where Kremlin political strategists dragged political heavyweights onto the ballots to serve nothing more than a decorative function. Then, after the elections, they were replaced by others who are unknown or even unpopular with the voters.'[118] The parliamentary election provided an opportunity for the regime to remove inconvenient politicians from the regions (for example, the mayor of Norilsk, the speaker of the Ryazan regional legislature and many more) and sent them into 'honourable retirement' to the Duma, a process that had been long-established in filling the ranks of the Federation Council but did nothing to enhance the status of either body.

The Duma was turned into an arena to cement the factional deals made in the Kremlin and became the instrument through which the Kremlin could deliver on its policy obligations. United Russia received the mandate to implement the 'Putin plan'. The challenge now was for the party to begin to act like a real party, with an inner life of its own and ready to engage in open and fair competition with its opponents, without relying on the advantages of administrative resources. The party, however, had won its super-majority precisely with the assistance of its semi-governmental position. This undermined the legitimacy of the Duma as a whole. As Konstantin Sonin put it:

The crucial reason for this lack of legitimacy is that the laws that governed these elections did not meet even the minimum democratic standards. Furthermore, compliance with these laws was extremely selective. On top of this, the majority of international observers were excluded from monitoring the elections. Although the positions of foreign governments have little influence on the dynamics of Russian politics, this decision undermined the legitimacy of the elections.[119]

---

[116] Ol'ga Kryshtanovkaya, *Anatomiya rossiiskoi elity* (Moscow: Zakharov, 2005), p. 251.
[117] Holmberg, *Managing Elections in Russia*, p. 7.
[118] Nikolai Petrov, 'Great Shell Game in Duma', *Moscow Times*, 18 December 2007, p. 11.
[119] Konstantin Sonin, 'Kremlin Wins a Duma with No Legitimacy', *Moscow Times*, 4 December 2007, p. 10.

Putin took a very different view. In a meeting with the cabinet on 3 December, he insisted that:

Our parliament has gained greater legitimacy. The previous parliament reflected the votes of 70 per cent of voters, while the new parliament represents 90 per cent of the voters, as just 10 per cent of votes went to parties which failed to make it into parliament, considerably fewer than in previous elections. This is one of the highest results in Europe in terms of broad-based support for the parties represented in the parliament. This also entails great responsibilities, especially for the party that has obtained the majority, the constitutional majority, in the Duma, namely, United Russia. People will be expecting serious results and active work from United Russia and from the other parties in the State Duma.

He called on the Duma to meet earlier than the thirty-day time period set by law. He also suggested that the new parliament consider the question of changing the spacing between the parliamentary and presidential elections, since in his view 'People are no doubt tired of campaign tactics and political agitation.'[120]

United Russia retained its constitutional majority (see Table 7.2). With 315 seats (up from the 302 it had in the previous Duma), it could push through constitutional amendments and changes to federal constitutional laws, create new federal subjects, impose states of emergency, decide on nominations to the Constitutional Court and other issues; while a simple majority (226 votes) allowed it to take the lead on budgetary and tax issues. Although enjoying a constitutional majority in the previous parliament, UR had not amended the constitution even though it could have done so since it also had a majority in the Federation Council and regional assemblies. The inviolability of the formal letter of the constitution had become a shibboleth for Putin, although he had freely engaged in para-constitutional innovation.

In a strange paradox, the Communists now emerged as the bastion of pluralism and the last redoubt of opposition. As Zyuganov put it immediately after the election, 'The chamber provides an opportunity to outline our point of view ... We are the last remaining guarantee of the freedom of speech, democracy and human rights in our country.'[121] With 57 seats, the party had five more deputies than the fifty-two in December 2003 at the beginning of the Fourth Duma (forty from the PR list and twelve from single-mandate districts), but it remained a beleaguered minority. Zhirinovsky's LDPR saw its total of seats rise from the 36 it had won in 2003 to 40, while JR entered for the first time

---

[120] www.kremlin.ru/text/appears/2007/12/152978.shtml.
[121] Anatoly Medetsky, Catrina Stewart and Nikolaus von Twickel, 'Disappointment and Defiance in Party Camps', *Moscow Times*, 3 December 2007, p. 1.

with 38 seats. The presence of JR made possible one of the presidential scenarios: for each of the Kremlin's pedestal parties to nominate a favoured successor, and then to let them battle it out for the presidency. On 7 December Gryzlov was nominated by UR's council to lead the party's faction in the Fifth Duma and to hold the speaker's post, positions that he had held in the outgoing assembly, a decision confirmed by the UR congress on 17 December.[122] On 24 December the Fifth Duma convened for the first time, heeding Putin's recommendation that it should meet without delay. The number of committees was increased from twenty-nine to thirty-two, with six of the chairs coming from parties other than UR.[123] Seventeen heads kept their positions, but not always the ones that were most appropriate.[124] The old 'packet agreements' operating in the first three Dumas, whereby appointments were part of a broader deal reflecting the strength of each group, no longer operated. Personal status replaced the party principle in allocating committee chairs.[125] In this as in so many other spheres of public life, a type of 'status rent' was levied, whereby appointment became dependent on loyalty rather than political representation or technical professionalism.

Gryzlov was confirmed as speaker, and he entered along with nine other deputies into the Duma presidium, seven from UR and one each from the CPRF and LDPR. Oleg Morozov from UR once again became first deputy speaker, while Lyubov Sliska lost that title to become just one of the deputy speakers. The CPRF delegated their deputy leader Ivan Mel'nikov to become a deputy speaker, while the LDPR nominated Zhirinovsky himself, and JR nominated the former head of the Rodina faction, Alexander Babakov. Two UR deputy speakers in effect ranked alongside Gryzlov, with Yury Volkov considered the representative of the Sechin faction in the Duma's leadership, while Valery Yazev was the Gazprom representative and thus acted on behalf of Medvedev.[126] The factional divisions within the Putin elite now reached into the very heart of parliamentary politics.

---

[122] RIA Novosti, 11 December 2007.
[123] The number of Duma committees and deputy speakers has grown with every new convocation: there were 23 committees and 5 deputy speakers in the First Duma; 28 and 6, respectively, in the Second; 28 and 9 in the Third; and 29 and 10 in the Fourth.
[124] For example, Andrei Kokoshin was reduced to deputy head of the CIS committee, whose new chair was Alexei Ostrovsky of the LDPR.
[125] Dmitrii Kamyshev, 'Dumokraticheskii protsess', *Kommersant-Vlast'*, 28 January 2008, pp. 15–20, at p. 15.
[126] Ivan Rodin, 'Gryzlov podelilsya Dumoi s zamestitelyami', *Nezavisimaya gazeta*, 29 January 2008, p. 3.

8 Presidential succession

The Duma election provided Putin with what he wanted – a vote in support of the system he had created and a referendum endorsing his views on policy continuity. The plebiscitary element in the parliamentary elections clearly undermined the typical purpose of an election, which is to choose between independent alternatives, and thus the legitimacy of the post-election order was both confirmed while at the same time impaired by the manner in which it had been achieved. Despite the endorsement that he received in the parliamentary vote, and public expressions of the view that 'Putin saved us from catastrophe so let's keep him in power',[1] Putin remained committed to his pledge not to run for more than two consecutive terms. In choosing his successor, as with the Duma election, two processes ran in parallel. In the words of Konovalov, 'The specific feature of the Russian election campaign is that the real election struggle is being waged among various power groups rather than among officially registered candidates for the post of president.'[2]

Rules and stratagems

The reshuffle of September 2007 signalled that Putin would seek to retain a guiding role in the transition until the very last moment. The lack of an independent political base of any of the leading candidates meant that he remained arbiter to the very end. All viable candidates presented themselves as emanations of the Putin plan to ensure elite and policy continuity. At the same time, the careful management of the succession undermined what is usually taken to be the point of elections – uncertainty of outcome. The vexed issue of Putin's succession turned out not to be such a problem after all. If the Yeltsin succession focused

[1] The title of a 'no comment' feature in *Izvestiya*, 5 October 2007, p. 2.
[2] Aleksandr Konovalov, head of the Institute of Strategic Assessments, 'Monopoliya na demokratiyu', *Nezavisimaya gazeta*, 19 February 2008, p. 15.

on the personality of the individual who would take over from him, the Putin succession was both more complex and more simple. It was more complex because the whole system had evolved, and no single individual could incorporate the interests of the various factions and bureaucratic layers. It was simpler because structures had been put in place to ensure continuity as the baton was passed to the successor. The country was no longer in crisis as it had been in 1999, when the very existence of the state was threatened by domestic insurgency in the Caucasus and its capacities had been undermined by ambitious business and regional interests. All this had changed, while in the world at large Russia had returned as an independent force.

The rules

The federal law on presidential elections ran to 169 closely printed pages. The law was adopted by the State Duma on 24 December 2002 and came into force on publication in *Rossiiskaya gazeta* on 16 January 2003.[3] An amendment to the law banned a party nominating someone belonging to a different party. As with the parliamentary election, there was no longer a minimum turnout requirement, and the 'against all' category had been abolished. The funding limit had been raised from R250 million in 2003 to R400 million.

The constitution stipulates that a Russian citizen of twenty-five years or older is eligible for nomination, provided that he or she has lived in the country for at least ten years. Those with dual citizenship or with a resident permit abroad, or incapable for one reason or another, or serving a custodial sentence, cannot stand. The presidential campaign began officially on 28 November, when the Federation Council resolution giving notice of the 2 March 2008 presidential election was printed in *Rossiiskaya gazeta*. A list of all parties eligible to nominate their candidates was published by the CEC by 1 December. The deadline for self-nominated candidates, sponsored by an initiative group of at least 500 supporters, was 18 December, whereas parties had until 23 December 2007 to announce their candidates. All registration documents had to be submitted to the CEC by 16 January, and the registration of candidates was to be completed by 27 January 2008. Parties and initiative groups had to collect at least 2 million signatures in support of their candidates, and the number of signature errors was not to exceed 5 per cent. Parties in the Duma were exempt from

---

[3] Reprinted as *O vyborakh Prezidenta Rossiiskoi Federatsii* (Moscow, Os'-89, 2003).

collecting signatures. No deposit was required from candidates. The formal campaign lasted from 2 to 29 February, and the latest a candidate could withdraw was 25 February.

Para-political possibilities

Putin had never made any secret of his impatience with public politics, and in particular with what he considered the inherent demagogy associated with electioneering in the modern age. In his view, it was best to sort these things out behind the scenes, in the cool light of rational consideration of what was best for Russia, and only then should the choice be put to the people. This technocratic approach clearly met with popular approval. Polls consistently showed around 70 per cent *approval* rating, with a *support* level that rarely fell far below 50 per cent. This carried over into strong support for a continuation of Putin's presidency, even though he was barred from standing for an immediate third term. The proportion of Russians supporting a third term grew from 27 per cent in mid-2006 to 42 per cent a year later, with over half of UR's supporters in favour, and even a quarter of CPRF's supporters wanting Putin's policies to continue.[4] Another poll in September 2007 revealed the contrast with other potential candidates, with Ivanov scoring only 3 per cent and Medvedev 2 per cent if an election had been held at that time, while Zyuganov reached the dizzying heights of 4 per cent – at a time when 63 per cent would have voted for Putin. He became the object of a wave of 'loyalty' declarations, ranging from obsequious soliloquies from President Ramzan Kadyrov of Chechnya to United Russia's 'How can we live without you, Vladimir Vladimirovich?'[5]

Lacking a candidate of their own, it appears that Sechin and his branch of the *siloviki* moved behind a Zubkov candidacy, while Surkov and the 'democratic statists' were lining up behind Ivanov.[6] Ivanov was the bugbear of the 'third term' party and was not the favourite of any of the Kremlin factions. He was not obliged to them for anything, and neither did he promise them anything. He also apparently felt that the *siloviki* had set him up over the Sychëv affair, having failed to inform him of the gravity of the event, and had then allowed details of his son's car accident in which a pedestrian had been killed to be splashed all over the

---

[4] VTsIOM, *Press-vypusk*, No. 764, 10 September 2007, http://wciom.ru/novosti/press-vypuski/press-vypusk/single/8758.html.
[5] A. A. Mukhin, *Tainyi pravitel'* (Moscow: Tsentr politicheskoi informatsii, 2007), p. 91.
[6] Mikhail Rostovsky, *Moskovskii komsomolets*, 7 December 2007; in *JRL*, No. 252, 2007, Item 11.

media (see below). There had been much speculation that he would be chosen to head the UR national list, but as we have seen, Putin was chosen on 1 October. By early November, 26 per cent of Russians said that they would vote for Medvedev, compared with 25 per cent for Ivanov.[7] The two had become the clear front-runners.

This was a period when endless permutations for the succession were being played out in the media. The secrecy with which Zubkov's appointment had been prepared was explained by the need to pre-empt opposition from even within his entourage, notably Surkov and presidential chief of staff Sobyanin. Zubkov's declaration that he would consider running for president provoked speculation that with such a loyal figure as prime minister and potential president, Putin could activate several options: a pre-term resignation that would allow him to stand again; or Putin's appointment as prime minister, to place him in poll position for a putative presidential bid at a time of his own choosing. Zubkov was the only potential president who could be absolutely trusted to play his allotted role in any of these scenarios. The option of some sort of collective leadership, or a strong prime minister (Putin) and a loyal president (Zubkov) was considered.[8] All this was accompanied, as we have seen, by the secret 'war of the Putin succession'.

This encouraged speculation on various ingenious ways of circumventing Article 81.3, which clearly states that 'one person cannot occupy the position of the president of the Russian Federation for more than two successive terms'. Alexander Shokhin, head of the RUIE, for example, argued that a loophole in the regulations could be exploited to allow Putin to run as president. All he would have to do is resign as president, since this was incompatible with his Duma mandate; and then the dominant party in the Duma, UR, could nominate its candidate for the presidency – Putin.[9] In 1999 Shokhin had been one of the few to have predicted Yeltsin's resignation on 31 December 1999,[10] but in 2007 he was not able to repeat the trick. The plan was rejected by Churov, who cited Article 6.3 of the presidential election law, which states unequivocally that 'A citizen of the Russian Federation who has been occupying the office of the president of the Russian Federation and has stopped fulfilling the duties of the president of the Russian Federation before his term's expiration due to resignation, inability to perform

---

[7] Abdullaev, 'A Soft-Spoken, "Smart Kid" Lawyer', p. 1.
[8] The various contestants are nicely described by Mukhin, *Tainyi pravitel'*, pp. 97–123.
[9] Alexander Shokhin interviewed by Natal'ya Kalashnikova, 'Vykhod est'', *Itogi*, 12 November 2007, pp. 30–4.
[10] *Segodnya*, 19 December 1999.

his duties for health reasons or impeachment cannot be nominated as a candidate at elections held due to his pre-term termination of presidential powers.'[11] Quite apart from the legality of the question, there is also the question of legitimacy; and as we have seen, Putin was not willing to join some of his CIS colleagues to stay on indefinitely. One of the framers of the 1993 constitution, Oleg Rumyantsev, warned that any attempt to bypass the constitutional ban on more than two successive terms would represent 'a blow to the constitutional order and the legitimacy of the Constitution itself'.[12]

Among the myriad theories of Putin's strategy towards the change of leader, the simplest were probably the most accurate. At the Sochi meeting with the Valdai Discussion Club, when asked about the possibility of a 'technical' president taking over to allow him to rule from behind the scenes, Putin insisted that he 'was not interested in the president of Russia being weak . . . I want our president not only to be self-sufficient, but they have to be a person who can effectively fulfil the obligations and duties they take up on behalf of the people.' He went on to stress that he would not be leaving the country, and that his presence should be taken into account by his successor, and thus 'we will come to some sort of agreement about how to function'. But Putin stressed that he would do all in his power 'to ensure their independence and effectiveness. After all, I worked for all these years for Russia to be strong. Russia cannot be strong with a weak president. I do not intend to destroy what has been achieved in recent years.' Responding to another question, he revealed that he had taken the 'firm decision' long ago, 'from the very beginning', that 'a person in power should not change the conditions of that power while in office'. Putin thus decisively rejected changing the constitution to allow him to remain in office, something that a number of presidents had done in other post-Soviet republics. It was too early to talk of what could happen in 2012 or 2016, he insisted, but in the meantime he was not going anywhere, and certainly would not go abroad, although 'I have not yet decided what I will do.' Whatever he did, he recognised that he would retain a certain 'moral influence', reminiscent of Deng Xiaoping's role following his formal retirement from office. Putin acknowledged that he was concerned that too much in Russia depended on one person, hence his attempt 'to broaden the field'. While he supported United Russia, he was not sure that he was

---

[11] Interfax, 26 November 2007.
[12] Nabi Abdullaev, 'Authors Warn About Constitutional Games', *Moscow Times*, 22 November 2007, p. 3.

interested in taking over as its head.[13] The notion of some sort of puppet president, as Putin acknowledged, would be humiliating for both the puppet and the puppeteer, as well as destructive for Russia.

Although he was not an official contestant, Putin made clear that he would retain a significant political post after stepping down from the presidency. He thus became a type of 'shadow' candidate. While Yeltsin in the 1999 project had been concerned with finding a successor who would be able to guarantee his personal security, this was less salient in 2007–8 since Putin's prestige remained so high. However, Putin was highly risk-averse, and he would not leave the process of finding an appropriate successor to chance. Unlike in 1999, there was little possibility of a substantial challenge to the Kremlin by regional leaders, oligarchs or Duma politicians, and neither would there be a credible outsider candidate. As for an insider, Putin had neutralised any faction's ability to advance a candidate of its own; or even to bounce him into an involuntary third term – the plan of the 'third term' party.[14] Putin delayed naming his chosen successor to the last minute to avoid placing the candidate in the spotlight too early. Well aware of the factional struggles, he sought to shield the formal succession process from the informal struggle of elites. Only when he had gained a renewed mandate in the Duma elections did Putin reveal his hand; and his preference would be decisive. The role of public politics and open democratic choice was marginalised. Polls, however, suggested that for at least half the Russian population, the Mexican or Japanese (or indeed British) path of institutionalised intra-governmental succession was certainly not the worst option.

The candidates

Putin's towering presence dominated the succession, even though he was not himself a candidate. His popularity rating at the end of 2007, after nearly eight years in power, had risen to an astonishing 85 per cent, with most indicators of trust and approval on a rising gradient.[15] On that basis, Putin asserted that he retained the right to ensure that a candidate was chosen who would continue his work. On the eve of the September 2007 cabinet reshuffle, moreover, Putin commented that like a good hockey player he would 'play down to the last second'.[16] It was clear that

[13] http://president.kremlin.ru/text/appears/2007/09/144011.shtml. The comment about not being prepared to take over as party leader is from my personal notes.
[14] Yuliya Latynina, 'Novye prem'ery', *Novaya gazeta*, No. 70, 13 September 2007.
[15] Levada Center polls, www.levada.ru/prezident.html.
[16] *Rossiiskaya gazeta*, 17 September 2007.

Putin did not want the nominated candidate to start building an independent power base too soon, something that would erode his authority. It was equally clear that Russia's next president effectively boiled down to Putin's choice.

The Medvedev candidacy

Rather than waiting for UR's reconvened congress to choose its nominee, on 10 December Putin made known his favoured candidate – Medvedev. At a meeting in the Kremlin with the leaders of United Russia (Gryzlov) and three other parties that had just fought the election – Just Russia (Mironov), the Agrarian Party (Vladimir Plotnikov) and Civic Force (Mikhail Barshchevsky) – UR announced that it would nominate Medvedev. Rather than advancing its own candidate, as it was entitled to do, JR supported Medvedev's candidacy. This was then warmly endorsed by Putin and the others present. Commenting on the choice, Putin said: 'I have known him [Medvedev] for more than 17 years, I have worked with him very closely all these years, and I fully and completely support this candidacy.'[17] It was clear that this rather stage-managed performance denoted Putin's choice. He also stressed that 'we have the opportunity to establish stable government after the 2008 election, and not just stable government but government that will continue the policies that have delivered positive results over these last years'. At a cabinet meeting later that day, Putin announced the result of the earlier meeting but insisted that the government had to continue to work 'like a good watch, rhythmically, letting all state mechanisms work effectively, and not allowing any perturbations associated with political events in the country'.[18] Later Medvedev argued that his candidacy had been UR's idea and not Putin's: 'Naturally, I discussed this with the president. I am a person whom the president has led, who has worked with the president for 17 years ... But the initiative came from the party.'[19]

Medvedev's candidacy may have been less of a surprise than either he or Putin suggested. According to reliable sources, the stake had been placed on Medvedev as far back as 2005, and in November 2006, as we have seen, a type of pre-election staff was established. The idea

[17] 'Vstuplenie na zavershayushchem zasedanii VIII s"ezda partii "Edinaya Rossiya"', Putin, *Izbrannye rechi i vystupleniya*, p. 471.
[18] www.kremlin.ru/text/appears/2007/12/153801.shtml.
[19] David Nowak, 'Sobyanin to Manage Medvedev Campaign', *Moscow Times*, 21 December 2007.

that 'freedom is better than unfreedom' had already been voiced by Medvedev at Davos in January 2007, as well as his emphasis on the rule of law. Medvedev was not alone in creating such a group since Ivanov headed an analogous body, and even Yakunin had apparently established a centre to define a programme for his leadership.

Medvedev's only clear affiliation was to Putin personally, to whom, it is reported, he looked up to as some sort of father figure (Medvedev was born on 14 September 1965, thirteen years after Putin, 7 October 1952). It was therefore not surprising that Medvedev's first act as candidate on 11 December, meeting with the four parties that had nominated him, was to propose Putin as his prime minister. He announced this live on television that day: 'As I confirm my readiness to run for Russian president, I request that he [Putin] gives his consent in principle to head the Russian government after the new president is elected.'[20] The two conditions that Putin had stipulated on accepting the UR nomination on 1 October had been fulfilled: for United Russia to gain a convincing victory, and for the next president to be a 'worthy' person with whom he could work. Putin's nomination as prime minister of course had a campaigning purpose, seeking to exploit Putin's popularity. Medvedev at the same time signalled that his leadership would maintain the existing elite structure: 'It is important to keep the effectiveness of the team created by the incumbent president.' He stressed that the social development of the country would be his priority.[21]

At the reconvened UR congress on 17 December, Medvedev's candidacy was endorsed by 478 votes to one. Putin announced that 'If Russian citizens express their confidence in Dmitry Medvedev and elect him president of the country, then I will be ready to head the government', and he once again affirmed that he would not change the balance of power between the president and prime minister.[22] Rather than Putin throwing his enormous prestige behind the UR candidate chosen at its congress, it was UR that fell into line and supported Putin's candidate. Medvedev would nevertheless fight as an independent and would not in the narrow sense be a 'party man'. Crucially, however, the support of the party meant that he was shielded from factional opposition to his nomination. Putin's strategy in so warmly endorsing UR now became clear. With the party enjoying its overwhelming win in the Duma election, it made any alternative bid from within the administrative regime

---

[20] RIA Novosti, 11 December 2007.
[21] Nabi Abdullaev, 'Medvedev Offers Putin a New Job', *Moscow Times*, 12 December 2007, p. 1.
[22] www.kremlin.ru/text/appears/2007/12/154552.shtml.

impossible, while of course carrying all before it in the country at large. The strategy of fielding two or more regime-sponsored candidates had clearly been abandoned.

Medvedev was a compromise candidate acceptable to the 'democratic statists' and the *siloviki*, as well as to liberals and industrialists. He was also the choice of the remnants of the 'the family' (the Muscovites), and of Abramovich personally.[23] At the same time he lacked a power base of his own. He was acceptable to the maximum number of the competing Kremlin factions, and the least threatening to most. However, he was not a consensus candidate, since he had clear views of his own. Like Putin, Medvedev was not a member of UR or any other party. He was one of the St Petersburg lawyers who occupied important posts at the federal level after Putin came to power. His close allies included Igor Shuvalov, presidential economic adviser, Arkady Dvorkovich, head of the presidential expert council, and in the cabinet, Finance Minister Kudrin, Regional Development Minister Kozak, Economic Development and Trade Minister Nabiullina, Agriculture Minister Alexei Gordeev, and Education and Science Minister Andrei Fursenko. Others considered close to Medvedev included Sergei Stepashin, head of the Audit Chamber, Alexander Voloshin, the former head of the presidential administration, Alexander Konovalov, presidential envoy to the Volga federal district, and above all Anton Ivanov, a former university classmate, co-author and close friend who had been appointed head of the Supreme Arbitration Court in January 2005.

Medvedev's policy approach can be described as 'controlled liberalism', accepting that the state had a role to play in resolving questions beyond the capacity of the market and to establish strategic priorities, but allowing society to solve its own problems elsewhere. Like Putin, he viewed Yeltsin's court politics in the 1990s, as the economy and society headed for the rocks, with distaste.[24] Medvedev's candidacy was widely interpreted as a 'triumph for the liberals', and 'a defeat for the *siloviki*'.[25] Åslund reinforces this view, noting that KGB people had come to the fore because of their friendship with Putin, 'But by appointing Medvedev as his heir apparent, Putin has carried out a coup against his KGB friends, betraying them all.' He argued that the primary beneficiaries were 'the surviving family oligarchs led by Roman Abramovich,

[23] As presciently argued by Stanislav Belkovsky on Ekho Moskvy on 13 May 2006, in *JRL*, No. 112, 2006, Item 5. By the same token, according to Belkovsky he was unacceptable to Sechin and the *siloviki*, and Belkovsky predicted an 'all-out war' before Medvedev could be brought to the presidency.
[24] Dmitry Babich, 'A Controlled Liberal?', *Russia Profile*, 11 December 2007.
[25] The title of Natal'ya Melikova's article, *Nezavisimaya gazeta*, 11 December 2007.

who have been losing out politically since the Yukos confiscation in 2003'.[26] In other words, with Medvedev's candidacy Putin had launched a type of counter-coup against his erstwhile colleagues and restored balance within the administrative regime.

Sechin, as we have seen, wanted Putin to stay on for a third term and opposed the naming of a successor; or at worst, favoured Zubkov assuming an interim presidency to allow Putin to return in pre-term elections. While Zubkov owed his primary loyalty to Putin, he was reputed to be close to the Sechin group of *siloviki*. Throughout the Duma campaign there had been rumours that Putin was angry with Sechin for having exceeded his authority, provoking the clash with Cherkesov and the subsequent public airing of factional conflicts, for attempting to force Vladimir Solovëv, a commentator on NTV, off the air, and for driving the campaign against foreign oil companies.[27] The leakage of information about Putin's alleged wealth to Belkovsky, and the resurrection of the Sal'e report, probably came from the Sechin faction. On the very day that the Sal'e report resurfaced, the Shvartsman interview on 30 November portrayed Sechin as the head of a *silovik* faction intent on 'reprivatisation' and filtering money abroad into secret accounts. Another sign of Sechin's weakening position was the investigation launched into the work of Bastrykin's Investigative Committee, just three months after its establishment. In early December a reshuffle of the leadership of the Rosneft oil company, of which Sechin was head of the board of directors, appeared to indicate Sechin's attempt to strengthen his hold on the company in anticipation of him having to leave the Kremlin and moving fully into business. Sechin was notoriously secretive, having only appeared twice in public during his eight years in office. On the first occasion, on 30 June, he addressed a meeting of Rosneft shareholders, and on the second, on 12 December, he spoke to the widows of security personnel, in the company of the FSB director Patrushev.[28] His appearance on that occasion was intended to show that he remained a political player.[29]

A rather darker interpretation is also possible. We noted in Chapter 6 the allegations made against Putin by Marina Sal'e and colleagues. A recent article suggested that it was precisely Medvedev who transferred funds on Putin's behalf for various construction projects,

---

[26] Anders Åslund, 'Purge or Coup?', *Moscow Times*, 9 January 2008, p. 7.
[27] Mikhail Fishman and Artem Vernibud talk of 'Sechin in mourning', 'Ruchnaya peredacha', *Russkii Newsweek*, No. 51, 17–23 December 2007.
[28] *Kommersant*, 13 December 2007.
[29] *Vedomosti*, 13 December 2007.

including several million dollars for the restoration of an Orthodox church in Greece, with the 'Rossiya' bank, headed by the notorious Koval′chuk brothers, acting as intermediary.[30] In other words, Medvedev was one of the few individuals with detailed information about Putin's years in the St Petersburg mayor's office, around which so many allegations and insinuations swirl; while Putin had detailed information on Medvedev's dealings, notably with Ilim Pulp, linking them into a common community of fate. In the interview we referred to earlier, Belkovsky took up this theme. Asked why Medvedev was chosen to be Putin's successor, he responded:

One of the most important problems for the Putin government has not yet been solved – namely, the legalisation of the Russian politico-economic elite, its capital, in the west. Precisely for that reason Putin was forced to stake on a candidate with the image of a liberal, who will have a certain carte-blanche from and credit of trust with the west. And a person with the image of a *silovik* or a Soviet leader – that is, Sergei Ivanov or Viktor Zubkov – would not have such a credit of trust, which would complicate fulfilling this task, perhaps the only unresolved task of Putin's rule.

Belkovsky voiced considerable scepticism about whether Medvedev would turn out to be a liberal or advance significantly the cause of democracy in Russia. He noted that those who know him characterised Medvedev as 'tough and strong-willed', and not the 'soft, good-natured' person that he was sometimes portrayed to be. Medvedev, like Putin, had no solutions to Russia's problems and would thus be forced to take repressive actions, even if disguised by liberal rhetoric.[31]

The choice of Medvedev was a way of shaping Putin's legacy. It also signalled to the world outside that Russia was looking for co-operation and would remain committed to the path of democratisation and international integration. Putin had clearly decided that he could not depend on any one of the factions, and instead looked for an independent figure. As noted, Medvedev remained aloof from all factions and factional conflicts, although his image was that of an economic liberal and a democratic moderniser. He had questioned Surkov's notion of 'sovereign democracy', insisting that democracy was a concept that needed no qualifying adjectives. Although free from the taint of factional affiliation, and with no military or security service background, Medvedev was if anything a technocratic moderniser, and in that sense he could be ascribed not to a faction but to a class – the rampant Russian

[30] 'Polkovnik KGB Putin pustil po miru Piter', *New Times*, 13 June 2007, author not indicated; in www.compromat.ru/main/putin/trest20ptentsy.htm.
[31] Belkovsky, 'Menya ob″yavyat vragom svobody'.

bureaucracy. The *siloviki*, who appeared so powerful on the eve of the electoral cycle, had been stymied by Putin's convincing win in the parliamentary elections and Putin's advancement of Medvedev. As Shokhin put it, Medvedev's nomination put an end to talk of 'velvet privatisation'.[32] It also helped dampen talk of a new 'cold war'. The nomination was part of the attempt to restore the balance in Putin's inner circle that had been disrupted by the succession problem. Nevertheless, Putin would have to remain the arbiter in the faction fights for some time to come.

The Medvedev succession differed from all others in Russian and Soviet history, where newcomers 'campaign' as the antithesis of their predecessor. Each new leader has created a distinctive regime whose central feature in most cases is its difference from what had gone before. Putin never attacked Yeltsin personally, but his whole political programme was built on a negative assessment of the 'disastrous' 1990s. Medvedev lacked an independent power base in the Kremlin and, unlike Putin when he came to power in 1999–2000, stressed not dissimilarity with what had gone before but continuity. Having long been a member of the Security Council, Medvedev was familiar with defence and security issues. Above all, Medvedev's nomination confirmed what Putin had long asserted: that he would be looking for legitimate institutional methods to resolve the succession and continuity problems.

On 21 January 2008, Medvedev was officially registered as a candidate, and his campaign officially began. Medvedev needed just 50 per cent of the vote on 2 March to avoid a second round, but the Kremlin election managers clearly wished him to receive a resounding endorsement (which would at the same time be an endorsement of Putin's strategy); but Medvedev's ballot should not put Putin in the shade or exceed his vote in March 2004 (71 per cent). Medvedev remained in post during the campaign and his ratings soon reached Putinesque proportions. Indeed, one poll saw his support exceed the vote Putin received in 2004 at 75 per cent, although in terms of trust Putin was still ahead at 62 per cent while Medvedev followed at 36 per cent.[33] Putin's declaration that he would take up the offer of the premiership helped swell support for Medvedev as a type of surrogate vote for Putin. Medvedev's popularity was endowed by his closeness to Putin and his nomination as the official candidate. At least three-quarters of

---

[32] Interfax, 10 December 2007; in *JRL*, No. 253, 2007, Item 27.
[33] VTsIOM poll of 30 January 2008, 'Preemnik prevzoidet prezidenta', *Kommersant*, 1 February 2008, p. 3.

Medvedev's vote was Putin's electorate.[34] Surveys confirmed this, revealing that if Putin had also been running in the election Medvedev's support would have fallen to 9 per cent.[35]

Much of Medvedev's support came from his closeness to Putin, thus his main challenge was to present himself as an independent personality with an agenda of his own.[36] It was anticipated that Medvedev would push through reforms that had stalled in Putin's second term, notably administrative and social reforms. The monetisation of welfare benefits in early 2005 had been badly mishandled threatening a 'grey revolution' of pensioners and others who feared losing out, but with a strong popular mandate and Putin as prime minister, the declared programme of the modernisation of Russia could continue.

Other contenders

By mid-December 2007, over two dozen potential candidates had announced their intention to run. They included Victor Gerashchenko, the head of the Central Bank from 1998 to 2002 and from 2004 head of Yukos, Nemtsov from the SPS, and Oleg Shenin, the head of the CPSU's apparatus and Politburo member in the final days of the Soviet Union and an active participant in the August 1991 coup. In the end, on 22 December the CEC only approved six candidates, one of whom (Nemtsov) subsequently withdrew. In 2000 there had been eleven candidates, a number that had fallen to six by 2003. The other main possible official candidate, Sergei Ivanov, threw his weight behind Medvedev: 'I had known about the decision that was announced yesterday [10 December] in advance. I supported it then, and I support it now.'[37] The Kremlin had abandoned the idea of running two official candidates. Quite why Ivanov, the front-runner for so long, was not chosen is not clear. Foreign-policy issues may have played a part, with Ivanov taking a rather more hawkish view, and possible disappointment on Putin's side that he had been unable to get the Glonass satellite positioning system in place.[38] There was also the mishandling of the death, on 20 May 2005, of the 68-year-old Svetlana Beridze as she

[34] 'Preemnik prevzoidet prezidenta', *Kommersant*, 1 February 2008, p. 3.
[35] Georgy Bovt, 'The 100 Percent Guarantee', *Russia Profile*, 7 February 2008.
[36] A Levada Center poll in late December 2007 found that 43 per cent of voters said that Medvedev's strength came from Putin's trust in him; *Moscow Times*, 16 January 2008, p. 3.
[37] Itar-Tass, 11 December 2007.
[38] Pavel Felgenhauer, 'Did Glonass Failure Sink Ivanov's Chance at the Presidency?', *EDM* 5, 23, 6 February 2008.

crossed the street, struck down by one of Ivanov's son's speeding car. No criminal charges were brought against him, and there appeared attempts to intimidate the dead woman's family.[39]

In announcing his withdrawal on 26 December, Nemtsov called on other candidates to do likewise or risk legitimising what he called a 'farcical' election. His withdrawal was in part prompted by the failure of the opposition to field a joint candidate: 'I had always hoped there would be a single candidate from a united democratic opposition, and this has not happened.' There were also doubts whether he would have been able to collect the requisite signatures in time.[40] Nemtsov's withdrawal left Kasyanov the only liberal in the election. On 12 February Nemtsov announced the suspension of his membership in SPS, possibly to spare the party any reprisals as he launched a blistering critique of Putin's Russia.[41] The report, brought out with Vladimir Milov, who had been a former deputy energy minister, in 2002, and head of the Institute of Energy Policy, was called *Putin: The Results*, and it painted a devastating picture of failures in pension and military reform, huge debts by state companies, and unprecedented corruption.[42]

The four parties that entered the Fifth Duma had the automatic right to nominate a candidate. On 17 December the Communist Party nominated its leader, Zyuganov, to run, and this marked a change in tactics from 2004, when they had chosen a substitute, Nikolai Kharitonov, to make a symbolic run against the Putin steam-roller. Zyuganov condemned low pensions and growing social inequality: 'The Communist Party insists on nationalisation of natural resources and strategic sectors of industry.'[43] Limonov, one of the leaders of Other Russia, commented that if the CPRF had chosen Mel'nikov, the chair of the party's central committee, then Other Russia would have backed him;[44] an endorsement that is unlikely to have improved the chances of the Communists. The LDPR's twentieth congress on 13 December nominated their leader Zhirinovsky, and thus, like the CPRF, Zhirinovsky did not repeat the strategy of March 2004 when the former heavyweight boxer Oleg

[39] Julia Latynina, 'Open Season: Life in Putin's Russia', *Washington Post*, 22 June 2008.
[40] Nabi Abdullaev, 'Nemtsov Ditches Bid for Kremlin', *Moscow Times*, 27 December 2007, p. 1.
[41] Natalya Krainova and David Nowak, 'Nemtsov Walks Away from His Party', *Moscow Times*, 13 February 2008, p. 3.
[42] Boris Nemtsov and Vladimir Milov, *Nezavisimy ekspertnyi doklad: Putin – Itogi* (Moscow: Novaya gazeta, 2008).
[43] Dmitry Solovyov, 'Zyuganov Promises to Fight Medvedev', *Moscow Times*, 17 December 2007, p. 17.
[44] Francesca Mereu, 'Kasyanov Chosen Kremlin Hopeful', *Moscow Times*, 10 December 2007, p. 3.

Malyshkin had stood in for him. Zhirinovsky's 2008 campaign was fought under the ambiguous slogans 'I'll Clean the Whole Country', and 'You Will Answer for Everything', suggesting that he had bureaucrats in mind, as well as the pointedly unambiguous promise to abolish ethnic republics and the Federation Council.[45] Just Russia did not nominate a candidate of its own but, as we have seen, was part of the consortium that nominated Medvedev.

The three other candidates had to collect at least 2 million signatures by 16 January. On 8 December the Russian People's Democratic Union (Rossiiskii narodno-demokraticheskii soyuz, RNDS) nominated its leader, former premier Kasyanov, as its candidate. Various obstacles had been placed in the way of the Union gathering (as it had in November when delegates found that their conference hall in Tver was closed because of an alleged bomb threat), but in the end nearly 700 delegates found a venue willing to open its doors to them. Kasyanov declared: 'We are approaching a decisive moment: either we follow the mainstream path of building a civilised state, or we continue to fall into the abyss where the current authorities are taking us – the dead end of totalitarianism.'[46] Having submitted over 2 million signatures, Kasyanov's team was accused of forging thousands of signatures in the Mari El republic and Yaroslavl region. A candidate could not be registered if more than 5 per cent of the signatures were found to be invalid. Of the 2,067,000 signatures Kasyanov submitted, some 80,000 were declared invalid (13.36 per cent), taking his total below the required 2 million, and thus he was denied registration. Even in the best of circumstances, it would have been difficult to gather 2 million genuine signatures in not much more than a fortnight. The signature-collection agencies had undoubtedly been careless, although whether this rendered his nomination invalid remains controversial. The vote in the CEC was unanimous, although

---

[45] *Vladimir Zhirinovskii: Kandidat v prezidenty rossiiskoi federatsii* (Moscow: LDPR, 2008) contains the article 'Za vse otvetite!' (pp. 4–5), as well as a summary of the main programmatic issues advanced by the party, 'Osnovnye pozitsii LDPR' (pp. 9–23), which included an attack on the oligarchs and a call for the renationalisation of their energy assets (point 3, p. 9); the liquidation of all stabilisation-type funds, which in Zhirinovsky's view were propping up western economies when they should be spent immediately in Russia (point 4, pp. 9–10); a policy of 'state egoism', putting Russia at the centre of everything (point 8, p. 10); they noted that the LDPR was the only party that voted against the disintegration of the USSR and the dissolution of the CPSU, and called for a return to Soviet equality (point 9, pp. 10–11); the programme attacked corruption and the proliferation of civil servants (points 15 and 13, pp. 11–12); it also called for the division of Russia into fifty regions (*krais*) based on population alone (no fewer than 3 million), the abolition of all national-territorial divisions and a return to pre-revolutionary administrative-territorial units (point 48, p. 19).

[46] Mereu, 'Kasyanov Chosen Kremlin Hopeful', p. 3; modified translation.

the margin of ineligible signatures was quite small. The CEC had been upset by Kasyanov's failure to send a representative not so much to answer queries over alleged fake signatures as to explain why the lists had been filed incorrectly.[47] His popularity at the time, according to VTsIOM, was less than 1 per cent. On 5 February Kasyanov lost his appeal to the Supreme Court, and on 9 February the RNDS presidium resigned itself to his disqualification.

Kasyanov received another blow at this time when his party, the People for Democracy and Justice (Narod za Demokratiyu i Spravedlivost'), was refused registration by the FRS and thus had to disband.[48] The reason given was the large number of 'dead souls' listed as party members. Kasyanov earlier had left the All-Russian Civic Congress, bringing together some 1,000 leading civil society activists, and at this time the two other main leaders, Ludmila Alekseeva and Georgy Satarov, also left, arguing that it was impossible to work with Kasparov.[49] Meanwhile Nemtsov announced the creation of a democratic bloc comprising the SPS, Yabloko, Kasyanov's RNDS, Kasparov's United Civic Front and Ryzhkov's liquidated Republican Party. Limonov's National Bolsheviks were not invited to the party, and in response he noted that the new body had 'A lot of generals and no lieutenants'.[50] A conference called 'A New Agenda for the Democratic Movement' on 22 March in St Petersburg brought together the disparate strands of the non-systemic opposition. The new umbrella movement fared no better than any of its predecessors. 'Committee 2008', established during the 2003–4 electoral cycle to ensure free elections next time round, expired in 2005 and thus did not reach its eponymous year. The Other Russia organisation, intended to act as a broad democratic bloc, had long been little more than a paper organisation and had failed to back Kasyanov's presidential bid. Undoubtedly exogenous factors were crucial, but endogenous failings were also important. Russia continued to lack an effective and above all united oppositional grouping. Kasyanov's failure to be registered cannot unequivocally be interpreted as a token of Russia's authoritarian turn.

[47] Nataliya Antipova, 'Zachem kandidaty "risuyut" podpisi', *Izvestiya*, 28 January 2008, p. 2; 'Pri polnom neprotivlenii storon', *Ekspert*, No. 4, 28 January–3 February 2008, p. 10. The clear implication is that the Kasyanov campaign was not really interested in taking part in the election but sought to exploit the public relations advantage of being blocked. The Kasyanov camp, however, was adamant that it genuinely tried to participate in the election.
[48] Mariya-Luiza Tirmaste, 'Partiyu Mikhaila Kas'yanova ob"yavili vne zakona', *Kommersant*, 29 January 2008, p. 3.
[49] Interfax, 17 January 2008.
[50] Sergei Arkhipov, 'Opyat' pererugalis'', *Izvestiya*, 20 Janaury 2008, p. 2.

The other candidate approved by the CEC to collect the signatures was Andrei Bogdanov, the head of the Democratic Party of Russia (DPR), which had come last in the Duma elections with 0.13 per cent of the vote although it was one of the oldest parties in the country. In 2005 Kasyanov tried to use the party as his platform to stand in the forthcoming election, and had then tried to take over some of the party's regional branches, prompting the DPR to sever all ties with him at its congress in December 2005. Bogdanov had worked as a political strategist for much of the 1990s and thus was experienced in drawing up voter lists. In June 2007 Bogdanov was elected Grand Master of the Grand Lodge of Russia, founded by the French Grande Loge Nationale of the freemasons in June 1995. No major irregularities were found with Bogdanov's signatures, and he was, as anticipated, registered to stand in the 2 March ballot. His participation was clearly designed to ensure at least one other candidate to make Medvedev's win legal in case all the others withdrew. He was also considered a 'spoiler' candidate, to draw votes away from other putative candidates. At thirty-eight, he was the country's youngest ever presidential contender. He insisted he was not a liberal but a conservative.[51]

All the other potential contestants were not approved to run by the CEC. Vladimir Bukovsky announced his candidature in May 2007, and in October he returned to Russia for the first time since 1992. He had spent twelve years in Soviet camps and psychiatric hospitals, and had been deported in 1976 for his dissident activity in an exchange with the Chilean communist Luis Corvalan. He devoted his first visit in 1992 to urge Yeltsin to establish a Nuremburg-style trial of the former Soviet security services to prevent the restoration of the Soviet regime. His efforts failed, and in his view after 1993 Yeltsin had become a captive of the *siloviki*. He called his eight-page electoral manifesto 'Russia on the Chekist Hook', a clear reference (discussed in Chapter 6) to Cherkesov's 2004 article, repeated in 2007, which argued that the special services in the 1990s had provided a 'hook' to stop Russia's headlong fall into the abyss.[52] Bukovsky's manifesto argued that if decommunisation had been completed in the early 1990s, the *chekists* would not have been able to return to power. Later he warned that, if elected, he would order an investigation into the crimes committed by the Soviet and Russian security service, and more broadly 'all the crimes of the Soviet regime and its heirs'. He would also drop the country's traditional antagonism

---

[51] Nabi Abdullaev, 'Not Your Standard Presidential Candidate', *Moscow Times*, 8 February 2008, p. 1.
[52] Vladimir Bukovskii, 'Rossiya na chekistskom kryuke', www.bukovsky.org.

to the west.[53] Before he could get on the ballot paper, however, he had numerous hurdles to cross, notably the stipulation that candidates are not allowed to have dual citizenship, and that they should have lived in Russia for ten years before the election.[54] The CEC rejected his application on three counts: not having lived in Russia for ten years; holding a British residency permit; and failing to prove his occupation as a writer. Bukovsky condemned the decision as politically motivated: 'The Chekist regime failed to accept our challenge, having retreated cowardly behind the barbed wire of legal scholastic' (sic).[55] Bukovsky had probably never intended a serious run for the presidency (there are rumours that he was put up to it by Kasparov); and his programme was more of an ethical declaration than a serious political platform, 'a rallying cry for justice and decentralization rather than a detailed policy programme'.[56]

The institutional framework of the election was undoubtedly skewed in favour of the Kremlin, thinning out the field and placing almost insuperable obstacles in the way of independent candidates. Already from 2003 the regime had ensured that perhaps the most formidable potential candidate, Khodorkovsky, was out of the race by launching a selective but effective attack on Yukos and associated figures. In October 2007 Khodorkovsky became eligible for parole, having served half his sentence, but this was blocked on technicalities, and instead a new criminal case was prepared against him. Thus at the time of the election in March 2008, Khodorkovsky was sitting in a pre-trial detention centre in Chita and played no part in the 2007–8 electoral cycle other than the occasional comment.

This electoral cycle once again exposed the weakness of organised opposition in Russia. We have noted the failure of the main liberal parties, Yabloko and SPS, to unite before the Duma election. On 14 December Yabloko decided that it would not support Yavlinsky to run for the presidency and instead backed Bukovsky's candidature, even though it clearly infringed international eligibility norms. The decision can only be rated an act of folly. Following Bukovsky's disqualification, Yabloko called on its members to boycott the election. In Table 1.3 we saw the secular decline in the vote for liberal parties falling from 27 per cent

[53] Natalya Krainova, 'Bukovsky Vows Probe of FSB, KGB', *Moscow Times*, 18 October 2007, p. 3.

[54] Kevin O'Flynn, 'Beyond Opposition, Beyond a Chance', *Moscow Times*, 21 September 2007, p. 1.

[55] Nabi Abdullaev, '6 Candidates Will Run for President', *Moscow Times*, 24 December 2007, p. 3.

[56] Philip Boobbyer, 'Vladimir Bukovskii and Soviet Communism', *The Slavonic and East European Review* 87, 3, July 2009, p. 484.

in 1993 to under 4 per cent in 2007. Lev Gudkov, the head of the Levada Center polling agency, noted that 'Liberal voters are fed up of the leaders of these parties' and went on to observe that 'These parties have lost the ability to communicate with the electorate.'[57] The spread of relative affluence and the political stability of the Putin years had clearly won over the middle class and much of the liberal vote to government parties. The decision to postpone Yabloko's fifteenth congress from February to the summer was justified by the heavy debts (some 140 million roubles) that the party had incurred as a result of the parliamentary elections, but it also gave Yavlinsky time to rally support behind his fading leadership.[58] In the event, Yavlinsky was replaced by his long-time deputy, Sergei Mitrokhin.

Ryzhkov had been a deputy since 1993 but lost his seat in December 2007. He insisted that Russia had become a typical authoritarian state, with 'heavy policy control, censorship in the main media channels and the systemic hounding and persecution of nongovernmental organizations, human rights groups and opposition parties ... Not a trace of these elements of pluralism has remained under Putin's presidency.' He argued that Russia 'has created a Soviet-oligarchic model: a synthesis of Soviet monopoly on political power combined with the nepotism and corruption from the 1990s' and warned that the period of 'stability' was coming to an end.[59] More practically, the short period between the parliamentary and presidential elections was undoubtedly a problem, giving little time for candidates to prepare and above all to collect the necessary 2 million signatures. In the wake of the Duma elections, Putin had called for a longer gap between the two bouts. One practical way to do this would be to extend the presidential term, something that Medvedev later enacted.

The campaign

In France the presidential campaign precedes parliamentary elections, and thus the newly elected leader can appeal to the country to give them a workable majority in the National Assembly to support the mandate and programme of the newly elected president. In Russia a wholly different dynamic is at work, with parliamentary elections preceding

---

[57] David Nowak, 'Changes Loom for Yabloko and SPS', *Moscow Times*, 17 December 2007, p. 1.

[58] Igor' Romanov, 'Yavlinskii tyanet vremya', *Nezavisimaya gazeta*, 30 January 2008, p. 3.

[59] Vladimir Ryzhkov, 'A Bad Blend of Brezhnev and Abramovich', *Moscow Times*, 17 December 2007, p. 10.

the presidential ones. Parliamentary elections are accompanied by far greater uncertainty, especially when the two terms of an incumbent president are coming to an end. In 2007 the Duma contest became part of the succession campaign and specific parliamentary issues were obscured.

The race begins

Medvedev's campaign got off to a flying start. Already by the end of December, a Levada Center poll found that if the election was held at that time, 79 per cent would vote for him; Zyuganov and Zhirinovsky were running neck and neck at 9 per cent; while Kasyanov enjoyed the support of 2 per cent; and all the rest (including Nemtsov, Bukovsky and Bogdanov) were at 1 per cent.[60] On 20 December Medvedev appointed the presidential chief of staff, Sergei Sobyanin, to head his campaign. As recounted in Chapter 5, Sobyanin had taken over the post from Medvedev in November 2005, after the latter became a deputy prime minister. Surkov had been touted as a possible campaign manager and in the event assumed much of the responsibility for devising Medvedev's strategy on the back of his success in winning UR such a large majority in the Duma election. The next step was to enlist governors, and since the majority were affiliated with UR, they became his natural allies.[61]

On 25 December Medvedev pledged that the government would increase spending on the national projects to R300 billion ($12 billion) in 2008, up from R260 billion in 2007. He noted that 'Investment into human capital has proved to be most effective. The national projects paid back not only in terms of development of these industries but the economy and society as a whole.' He stated that the projects would be integrated into a larger programme of social development up to the year 2020, and would be ended in 2009, three years after being launched, although education, agriculture and health would remain government priorities.[62]

Medvedev refused to take part in the televised debates, and thus he perpetuated the tradition of both his predecessors, as well as UR, which also refused to take part in television debates in 2003 and 2007. He cited

---

[60] Poll of 1,600 people conducted 21–24 December, 27 December 2007, www.levada.ru/press/2007122701.html.

[61] For details, see Nikolaus von Twickel, 'Governors to Get Votes for Medvedev', *Moscow Times*, 10 January 2008, p. 3; see also Nikolai Petrov, 'Medvedev's Regional Policy', *Moscow Times*, 22 January 2008, p. 11.

[62] *Moscow Times*, 27 December 2007, p. 5.

his heavy workload as first deputy prime minister.[63] The campaign was kept deliberately low-key: 'His [Medvedev's] campaign handlers have made a pragmatic choice to ensure that his popularity does not eclipse that of President Vladimir Putin and to prevent voters from feeling manipulated.'[64] To compensate, he presented his views on a website dedicated to the campaign, although there was not much personal information available and instead the stress was on his social policies.[65] Unlike the parliamentary campaign, the final two months before the presidential election were remarkably quiet, with the various *silovik* factions keeping their heads down. Sechin's group had always been able to exploit tactical opportunities, but they had no strategic vision for Russia and were no match for Medvedev's allies, notably Alisher Usmanov, the owner of *Kommersant* the paper that had carried Cherkesov's anti-Sechin article and the interview with Oleg Shvartsman. Preparations were also made for an orderly handover of responsibility in Gazprom. Nominations to the Gazprom board in late January included Zubkov, who had loyally acted as cover for Medvedev's advancement since his appointment to the premiership in September 2007. With Medvedev's elevation to the presidency, Zubkov replaced him as head of Gazprom's board. Gazprom at the time provided 13 per cent of budgetary revenue, with a capitalisation of about $330 billion.

At the same time, the volume control on anti-western rhetoric coming from the Russian authorities was sharply turned down, with only Yury Baluevsky, the chief of the general staff, reminding the world that Russia would take the appropriate 'counter-measures' if the United States went ahead and deployed its ballistic missile defence (BMD) system in Poland and the Czech Republic. Medvedev's candidacy was part of Russia's reaction to the changing international situation. Following Putin's Munich speech on 10 February 2007, the scenario of a new cold war would have favoured Ivanov's candidacy. However, the US response to Munich was to ease its strident tone, and the personal relationship between Bush and Putin remained strong. Medvedev's advancement was a clear signal that Moscow, like Washington, Paris and Berlin, was not ready to engage in a new cold war; although it would defend its perceived interests as appropriate.

[63] Arina Borodina, Irina Nagornykh, Alla Barakhova and Yurii Chernega, 'Dmitrii Medvedev budet agitirovat' v rabochem poryadke', *Kommersant*, 29 January 2008, p. 3.
[64] Nabi Abdullaev, 'Medvedev Aiming for Low-Key Campaign', *Moscow Times*, 1 February 2008, p. 1.
[65] www.medvedev2008.ru.

This was confirmed by speeches by Kudrin and Chubais during the campaign. At the Davos World Economic Forum in late January 2008, Chubais warned of the difficulties facing the Russian economy, above all capital flight and a negative trade balance.[66] Addressing an investment forum on 30 January, Kudrin called on Russia to pursue its international goals through international engagement, above all through joining the WTO: 'Our dependency on global economic ties, on our exports, is felt so strongly, that in the nearest future we need to adjust our foreign-policy goals to guarantee stable investment.' Chubais, with his typical bluntness, at the same event insisted that with a shrinking current account surplus, a hawkish foreign policy was simply unsustainable: 'We really have to think about how much our foreign policy costs our economy.' He also condemned the Russian decision to close the British Council offices in St Petersburg and Ekaterinburg, actions taken in retaliation for the expulsion of four Russian diplomats in July 2007 in response to Russia's refusal to extradite Lugovoi.[67] A hardline foreign policy could damage Russian economic interests, as well as being finan-cially unsustainable.

Programmes and plans

In his address to the second Civic Forum (the first had been held in November 2001, but this time it was sponsored by the Public Chamber) on 22 January 2008, which in effect represented his first major campaign speech, Medvedev outlined his views on key issues facing the country. He was positive about Russia's prospects, but when it came to develop-ing democracy he stressed the need to combine 'our national traditions with a functional selection of democratic values. We have been working on this for at least 150 years, and Russian society is now closer than ever to resolving this problem.' The national idea for Russia had to be based on 'freedom and justice', accompanied by the 'civic dignity of the individual' and 'the individual's prosperity and social responsibility'. He stressed that 'The most important requirement for our country's development is the continuation of calm and stable development. What we need quite simply is a decade of stable development – something that our country never had in the twentieth century', and like Putin he noted the 'great trials of the 1990s, and many mistakes were made – but our country wasn't destroyed'. He then stressed the development of social

---

[66] Mikhail Sergeev, 'Apokalipsis ot Chubaisa', *Nezavisimaya gazeta*, 28 January 2008, p. 6.
[67] Mikhail Sergeev, 'Liberal'no-pravitel'stvennyi opportunizm', *Nezavisimaya gazeta*, 31 January 2008, pp. 1, 6.

policy to allow individual development. In relations between state and society, he talked of 'a social contract between the authorities and society – a contract in which they have duties to each other, rendering the authorities fully accountable to the people'.

Reflecting his earlier opposition to the attack on Yukos, he stressed that 'We shall pursue a firm policy of free development for private enterprise, protecting property rights, and reinforcing the common principles of a market economy', accompanied by the need to turn the struggle against corruption into a national campaign. This was hampered by the fact that 'Russia is still suffering from legal nihilism. No European country can boast this degree of contempt for the law. This phenomenon is rooted in our country's distant past. The state cannot be a law-based state, or a just state, unless the authorities and citizens know and respect its laws, and citizens have sufficient awareness of the law to monitor the actions of state officials effectively.' In foreign policy the strategic goal of 'reinforcing Russia's international status, so that it holds a proper position worthy of our country and its people', would be continued. It would engage in 'dialogue and cooperation with the international community', but 'Russia's actions will be based on its own interests, combined with an understanding of the degree to which Russia is responsible for rational development of a democratic world order and solutions to global problems, economic and otherwise.'[68] The tone of the speech represented a significant de-escalation of the harsh rhetoric of Putin's last year, although in substance it did not differ from much of what Putin had been saying for years. It was clear that the main policy lines would continue as before, but they would now be pursued in a milder manner.

At the Civic Forum, Medvedev called for the struggle against corruption to become a 'national programme', noting that 'legal nihilism' took the form of 'corruption in the power bodies'. He returned to this idea in his 29 January speech to the Association of Russian Lawyers, of which he was chair of the board of trustees, when he called on his fellow lawyers to take a higher profile in society and to combat 'legal nihilism'.[69] He clearly had two evils in mind: corruption in the traditional venal sense, characterised by the abuse of public office for private gain; and meta-corruption, where the judicial process is undermined by political interference, the 'telephone law' that we have discussed earlier, and

---

[68] www.medvedev2008.ru/english_2008_01_22.htm; *Nezavisimaya gazeta*, 23 January 2008.

[69] 'Vystuplenie na vneocherednom s″ezde Assotsiatsii Yuristov Rossii', 29 January 2008, www.medvedev2008.ru/live_press_01_29_law.htm.

which had been most prominently in evidence during the Yukos case, which itself had given rise to the term 'Basmanny justice'. He made no mention of the need to change the constitution, the only practical way in which the gap between parliamentary and presidential elections could be lengthened, and instead announced the creation of a new public holiday, the 'day of the jurist'.[70]

In his Civic Forum and other speeches, Medvedev advanced a liberal-conservative programme for the modernisation of the country, arguing that Russia needed 'decades of stable development' since, as he put it in a Putinite turn of phrase, the country had 'exhausted its share of revolutions and social upheavals back in the twentieth century'. Medvedev's sentiments echoed those of Russia's conservative prime minister between 1906 and 1911, Petr Stolypin, who famously said: 'Give the state twenty years of peace both at home and abroad and you will then not recognise Russia.'[71] He clearly was not advocating another programme of 'modernisation from above', since he was at pains to emphasise the need for the controlled development of civic initiative and civil society. He was sanguine about the achievements: 'Our civil society was born in the pains and upheavals of the last 20 years, but now it is an indisputable fact that it has become an important factor in political life.' In a speech in Voronezh on 24 January, he insisted, as Putin had done before him, that civil society could advance either through the path of confrontation with the state or 'the path of cooperation', based on a type of social contract, the path that he insisted was the most constructive.[72] He was thus not in favour of 'modernisation from below' either, and instead clearly favoured what can be called a programme of 'modernisation from the middle': based on a developing middle class, secure property rights, the independence of the courts, and a free but responsible public sphere (Medvedev personally was an aficionado of the internet, logging into news sites daily).

On 30 January 2008, addressing the RUIE in Krasnodar, Medvedev called for Russian business not to be afraid to stake out international positions, and to be confident of the state's support. Already in 2007 Russian direct investment abroad had doubled over the record-making 2006 to $45 billion, just a little below FDI into Russia of $47.1 billion. The biggest deal had been Norilsk Nickel's 100 per cent purchase of

---

[70] Natal'ya Melikova, 'Ni slova o pravke Konstitutsii', *Nezavisimaya gazeta*, 20 January 2008, pp. 1, 3.
[71] Petr Stolypin, interview in *Volga* newspaper, 1 September 1909; in E. V[erpakhovskaya], *Gosudarstvennaya deyatel'nost' P. A. Stolypina*, Vol. I (St Petersburg, 1909), p. 8.
[72] Interfax, 24 January 2008.

Canada's LionOre in 2007 for $6.4 billion, followed by Evraz's purchase of Oregon Steel Mills in 2006 for $2.3 billion, and Oleg Deripaska's Basic Element's purchase of the Austrian construction company Strabag for $1.6 billion. Russian capital was not always welcomed abroad, with estimates suggesting that some $50 billion had been blocked by that time, including obstacles to Gazprom's expansion into downstream distribution systems in Europe.[73]

In a keynote speech to the fifth Krasnoyarsk Economic Forum on 15 February, Medvedev outlined not only his economic programme but also his broad view of the challenges facing Russia. He focused on an unwieldy bureaucracy, corruption and lack of respect for the law. In a decisive tone, he insisted that 'Freedom is better than lack of freedom – this principle should be at the core of our politics. I mean freedom in all of its manifestations – personal freedom, economic freedom and, finally, freedom of expression.' He repeated earlier promises to ensure personal freedoms and an independent and free press. He repeatedly returned to the theme of 'the need to ensure the independence of the legal system from the executive and legislative branches of power' and once again condemned the country's 'legal nihilism' and the need to 'humanise' the country's judicial system. He promised to reduce red tape and the number of bureaucrats, and stated that he was against the practice of placing state officials on the boards of major corporations. The state would continue to play a role, however, but state appointees 'should be replaced by truly independent directors, which the state would hire to implement its plans'. Thus the trauma of the factional conflicts of the 1990s was finally transcended, although how he would deal with those of the 2000s remained unclear. He insisted that 'Respect for private property has to be one of the foundations of the government's policies' and called for an end to corporate raids. He also proposed an overhaul of the tax system to reduce the burden in some areas, including cuts in VAT and export duties on energy exports to allow oil firms to invest in new facilities. Medvedev's plans for economic modernisation focused on the four 'I's: institutions, infrastructure, innovation and investment. In foreign policy he also sounded a rather more emollient tone than Putin had latterly, emphasising co-operation rather than competition: 'If before we could ... build walls to insulate ourselves, in today's globalised world, when states share, in effect, a common set of values, such co-operation should continue.'[74]

[73] Svetlana Ivanova, 'Pora pokupat'', *Vedomosti*, 31 January 2008, p. 1.
[74] 'Vystuplenie na V Krasnoyarskom ekonomicheskom forume "Rossiya 2008–2020: Upravlenie rostom"', www.medvedev2008.ru/live_press_15_02.htm.

He demonstrated a rather more personal tone in a paid-for interview with *Itogi* magazine published on 18 February. He revealed that his family had been ordinary Soviet people, sharing a 40-metre apartment in the St Petersburg suburb of Kupchino. His father taught at a polytechnic institute, and Medvedev had supplemented his meagre student stipend by working as street cleaner and on building sites. His ancestors included a blacksmith and a hat-maker. His maternal grandfather was called Venyamin Shaposhnikov, which could be a Russian or a Jewish name, a fact which much exercised certain Russian nationalists.[75] Medvedev was baptised into the Russian Orthodox Church at the age of twenty-three, a decision he insisted that he had made himself, although at the time the Soviet authorities repressed all religions. The purchase of his first flat, a three-room apartment in a Moscow suburb, was a major event: 'I remember feeling unbelievable happiness. It was not comparable to anything else.' His father died in 2004 and his mother moved near to him in Moscow. He admitted that 'When I moved to Moscow in 1999, I could not imagine that eight years later I would be running for the post of president.' If elected, he insisted that he would be in charge: 'Our country was and remains a presidential republic. It cannot be any other way. There cannot be two, or three or five power centres. The president is in charge of Russia, and under the constitution there can only be one president.' He insisted that he would work well with Putin as prime minister: 'This union will only work in an atmosphere of complete trust and partner-like relations.'[76] The 55-year old Putin would take up his post as a subordinate to his 42-year-old protégé Medvedev after having been the supreme power in Russia for eight years. As we shall see below, in his final press conference on 14 February Putin viewed the prime ministerial office as Russia's top executive post, which is not quite the view of the constitution (which envisages at best a dual executive system); and Putin noted that he would not be hanging Medvedev's portrait in his office.

Medvedev's campaign sought to combine themes of continuity and stability with ideas of change and renewal. These contradictory aspirations were embedded in Putin's handover of power: a three-year budget due to run until 2010, and with the outlines of 'Putin's plan' set in numerous policy documents. From his Civic Congress and other speeches, it was clear that Medvedev was particularly concerned with

[75] Alexander Osipovich, 'Nationalists Obsess Over Medvedev's Roots', *Moscow Times*, 20 February 2008, p. 1.
[76] *Itogi*, No. 8 (610), 21 February 2008; www.itogi.ru/Paper2008.nsf/Article/Itogi_2008_02_17_01_1958.html.

the quality of economic growth, reducing dependence on foreign technology and boosting Russian exports, the development of human capital and establishing a stronger legal framework to overcome 'legal nihilism'. The national projects were a way of improving the quality of life, and he stressed the state's social responsibility towards its citizens. On foreign policy Medvedev emphasised that Russia was one of the few countries in the world able to act independently, although the theme of Russia as a sovereign actor was one that Putin had made his own in his second term. Medvedev advanced the same idea, but in rather more temperate tones. Medvedev favoured evolutionary development. Although a liberal in economic terms, he was rather more of a conservative in the political sphere.[77]

Although he was not running in any election, Putin appeared to be campaigning for the right to take up the premiership. In a keynote address to an extended session of the State Council on 8 February, he outlined his vision of the fundamental tasks facing the government. The address acted as both a farewell speech and a manifesto. Putin announced ambitious plans, including making Russia the 'best place to live' and a country where human capital would be developed and the quality of life substantially improved. He admitted that he had not been able to wean the country off 'inert' dependence on natural resources and argued that a 'strategy of innovative development' was essential to diversify the economy and to allow a fourfold increase in the economy's competitiveness by 2020. He returned to the theme that had so exercised him in his final two years as president, namely the appalling demographic indices, and pledged a comprehensive overhaul of Russia's healthcare system. He committed himself to reducing inequalities between regions by creating regional innovation centres and by developing a modern transport infrastructure.

Turning from the ambitious domestic agenda, his analysis of the international situation was gloomy: 'It is clear that a new arms race has been unleashed in the world', but he warned against Russia responding in kind and thus allowing itself to be drawn into a costly confrontation. The policy of containment, with NATO moving ever closer to Russia's border, was driven by an attempt to gain access to Russia's natural resources. As Putin noted, 'We closed down our bases in Cuba and Vietnam, and what did we get? New American bases in Romania, Bulgaria, and a new third missile defence system in Poland.' Russia was forced to respond, and he called for a new security strategy to

[77] Vyacheslav Nikonov, 'Dmitrii Medvedev – konservator', *Izvestiya*, 6 February 2008.

address emerging threats. Putin asserted that democracy was the cornerstone of Russian society, but he stressed once again his 'wager on the strong', and that only a few large parties would be allowed to compete to govern the country. He also warned against foreign interference while condemning political parties that took money from foreign governments as 'immoral' and 'demeaning for the Russian people'.[78]

In his 14 February press conference, Putin effusively praised Medvedev as an 'honest, decent and good man', insisting that he could 'feel confident and unashamed about handing over the main reins of power in this country to such a person', a colleague of fifteen years who was 'progressively oriented and modest'. He predicted that 'I'm sure he will be a good president and an efficient leader. Besides, there is personal chemistry [between us]. Simply speaking, I trust him.' However, he interpreted the constitution to mean that the president and the prime minister shared equal executive powers, giving the premier 'many opportunities' including responsibility 'for devising the budget and presenting it to parliament', 'forming the foundations of monetary and credit policy', and 'resolving social, healthcare, education and environmental issues', as well as 'creating the conditions for our country's defence and security' and 'carrying out our economic and trade policies abroad'. He did not challenge the president's role as 'the head of state, guarantor of the constitution', as well as the person who 'establishes the main domestic and foreign policy guidelines', but he asserted that 'the highest executive power in the country is in the hands of the government'.

On issues of policy, Putin gave a clear indication that he would not be afraid to advance his own views. He argued that state corporations were necessary 'when there is a need for major long-term investment that private business is not yet ready to undertake', but, echoing Medvedev's concerns, a time would come when this was no longer necessary and then 'we will gradually list these companies on the stock market and make them part of the market economy'. He noted that Medvedev would have the last word in decision-making but insisted his role as prime minister was not a subservient one: 'I would of course never act as a substitute head of state. But of course I reserve the right to express my views.' He stressed that he had never been tempted to stay on for a third term and that he was not 'addicted' to power. He also scoffed at rumours of his great wealth. On the painful issue of election observers, he insisted that 'We will not allow anyone to dictate any terms to us, but we will honour every commitment', and accused the ODIHR of

---

[78] www.kremlin.ru/text/appears/2008/02/159528.shtml.

inventing discriminatory rules vis-à-vis Russia: 'Let them teach their wives to make fish soup', was his pithy conclusion. He branded western attempts to build pipelines bypassing Russia as 'incorrect, stupid and unprofessional'. Ultimately, he insisted, Russia was 'not interested' in a return to the Cold War: 'Our main tasks are internal development, the resolution of social and economic problems.'[79] Putin's authoritative tone was that of a world leader of eight years, whereas Medvedev's tone was of a novice in international politics.

Zyuganov's campaign was low-key. Unveiling his election programme, he insisted that the presidential election could not be fair since the country was run by 'thieves': 'Because privatization itself was unfair, because everything has been stolen and because thieves can't call fair elections', and he revealed that he had considered pulling out of the contest but decided to stay on because 'I don't want to give the country away to a group of nouveaux riches.'[80]

Election monitors

As in the parliamentary election earlier, the CEC came into conflict with the OSCE. On 28 January 2008, the CEC announced that 400 international observers would be invited to monitor the election, reduced two days later to 350. Of these, 70 would be accredited to the OSCE/ODIHR mission, and an equal number to the CIS Executive Committee's observation mission – a parity principle that was introduced now for the first time. The joint mission of the OSCE's Parliamentary Assembly and PACE would get 30 places, the same as the 30 each for the CIS Parliamentary Assembly and the SCO. Thus the balance in numerical terms shifted to regional observers and away from international missions. At the same time, the proposed arrival date of 28 February excluded any scope for long-term observation, which usually lasted six weeks. Strohal requested the accreditation of more observers, the removal of restrictions on their activity, and the immediate issuance of visas to allow some long-term observation. The official response by CEC member Igor Borisov was robust: 'Russia has been and is a sovereign state and has the right to define the form and manner of monitoring on its territory without affecting its outcome, as long as international law does not establish otherwise.'[81] Churov and the CEC were explicit in

[79] www.kremlin.ru/eng/text/speeches/2008/02/14/1011_type82915_160266.shtml.
[80] 'Zyuganov Says Vote Won't be Fair', *Moscow Times*, 5 February 2008.
[81] Aleksandr Samarina, Natal'ya Kostenko and Andrei Terekhov, 'Argument Curova', *Nezavisimaya gazeta*, 1 February 2008, p. 1.

their view that they considered some western observers biased, while Lavrov in Minsk on 29 January once again criticised the OSCE for failing to take into account the positive experience of elections and electoral systems in the CIS and repeated his call for a common evaluative methodology.[82] On 7 February the ODIHR announced that it would not be sending observers, and the OSCE's parliamentary assembly also cancelled plans to send a monitoring mission. PACE, however, decided to send a mission headed by Andreas Gross.

According to Pavlovsky, the cancelled missions were part of a US plan to undermine the legitimacy of the election: 'This plan is aimed at undercutting the new president at the very beginning of his work.' Fyodor Lukyanov, the editor of *Russia in Global Affairs*, took a rather more subtle approach, arguing that the conflict over the monitoring missions reflected Russia's changing self-perception as a country no longer ready to submit itself to a regime of inspection: 'Election monitoring was initially meant as something to certify the legitimacy of elections in countries in transition ... Russian rulers believe that we are not in transition anymore, that we have arrived where we want to be.'[83]

The outcome

While the name of the victor had long been known, the margin of victory, the turnout, and the rank order of the other candidates and the strength of their vote were all issues that would be decided on 2 March. The succession was run like a special operation, but that did not mean that the conductor would have it all his own way. In the event, the vote delivered the required result in the manner that the Kremlin desired. In making his choice, the outgoing president had taken into account domestic and international challenges, and now the electorate endorsed his choice. While the offering was somewhat circumscribed, the winning candidate gained an unambiguous mandate from the Russian people.

The result

Medvedev won 70.28 per cent of the popular vote, representing over 52 million people (see Table 8.1). By any standard this was an impressive

---

[82] Vladimir Socor, 'Russia Reinforces Restrictions on OSCE/ODIHR Ahead of Presidential Election', *EDM* 5, 19, 31 January 2008.

[83] Nabi Abdullaev, 'European Observers Will Skip Election', *Moscow Times*, 8 February 2008, p. 1.

Table 8.1 *Presidential election of 2 March 2008*

Candidate	Vote		Percentage
Medvedev, Dmitry	52,530,712		70.28
Zyuganov, Gennady	13,243,550		17.72
Zhirinovsky, Vladimir	6,988,510		9.35
Bogdanov, Andrei	968,344		1.30
Electorate		107,222,016	
Number of valid ballots		73,731,116	
Turnout		69.81%	

Source: Central Electoral Commission: www.vybory.izbirkom.ru/region/region/izbirkom.

endorsement and meant that there was no need for a second round. The outcome fell just short of Putin's win in March 2004, when he had been re-elected with 71.3 per cent, so the necessary hierarchy had been maintained; but with 52.5 million votes cast for Medvedev, he exceeded Putin's 49.6 million in 2004. The turnout also exceeded that of the preceding Duma election: at 69.81 per cent, this was exactly the same turnout as in the bitterly contested first round of Yeltsin's bid for re-election for a second term on 16 June 1996. Surveys revealed that most of Putin's electorate had shifted to Medvedev, but he had scored particularly strongly among young people. Without an attractive alternative, voters plumped for the safe choice.

The strongest vote for Medvedev came in Dagestan, where he won 91.92 per cent, coming in just ahead of Ingushetia, where 91.66 per cent voted for him. His weakest performance was in Smolensk where only 59.26 per cent came in on his side. He won 71.59 per cent in Moscow and 72.27 per cent in his native St Petersburg. The Communists also had reasons to feel pleased. Zyuganov's personal vote exceeded that won by the party in the Duma election, and the CPRF remained firmly positioned as the main opposition grouping. Over 13 million people (17.72 per cent of turnout) voted for a party whose programme was highly retrograde yet represented an alternative to the stifling conformity of the Putin system. The strongest vote for the Communists was in Bryansk region, where they won 27.08 per cent, and the weakest performance was in Ingushetia at 1.47 per cent. With 5 million more votes than the party had won on 2 December, Zyuganov was justified in arguing that the CPRF had 'significantly strengthened its position'.[84]

---

[84] Aleksandr Latyshev, 'Dvoe v galere', *Izvestiya*, 4 March 2008, p. 2.

Zhirinovsky was rather less satisfied, having fallen into third place with only some 7 million votes. He demonstrated that his core electorate remained loyal, but he had been squeezed by the powerful rallying effect behind the official candidate. Nearly a million people voted for Bogdanov, which was quite an achievement. The so-called protest vote went mainly to Zhirinovsky and Bogdanov.

Regional elections

In addition to voting for a new president, legislative elections were also held in eleven regions on 2 March. In Rostov the LDPR list for the regional assembly was headed by Andrei Lugovoi, who had already proved himself a vote winner in the Duma elections and ran against the UR list headed by the regional governor, Vladimir Chub. Elections were also held in Kalmykia, Ingushetia, Yaroslavl, Ivanovo, Ulyanovsk, Sverdlovsk, Bashkortostan, Altai region, Sakha and Amur (see Table 8.2). In the majority of regions, the elections were fought by the four parties that had made it through to the Duma in December 2007 (Rostov, Ul'yanovsk, Altai *krai*, Ingushetia and Bashkortostan). The other parties lacked the finances or were squeezed out because of 'administrative resources', with, for example, the Agrarian Party of Russia and Civic Force refused registration in Altai *krai*, allegedly because of too many incorrect signatures.[85] Just Russia's support for Medvedev did not prevent it being excluded from the ballot in the Yaroslavl regional Duma and the Yakutia legislative assembly.[86] Yabloko was not able to run in a single region, while SPS fought only in Ivanovo.

In some regions a split proportional and majoritarian system operated, allowing some independent deputies to enter the regional legislative assemblies. Without Putin at its head, UR performed rather worse than in the Duma elections, yet its victory was overwhelming. Its best performance was in the national republics, with 88.14 per cent in Bashkortostan, 74.1 per cent in Ingushetia, 54.58 per cent in Kalmykia and 52.62 per cent in Yakutia, but even these impressive figures fell short of those in December, with their weakest performance in Yaroslavl (49.7 per cent compared to 53.2 per cent in December), even without JR competing for the vote. The JR vote weakened everywhere, barely crossing the threshold in Ul'yanovsk with 7.77 per cent and failing to do so in Amur (5.62 per cent), as well as in Rostov, Sverdlovsk, Kalmykia and Bashkortostan. The absence of any significant JR input into Medvedev's presidential

---

[85] 'Malye partii ne nakhodyat sebe mest na vyborakh', *Kommersant*, 1 February 2008, p. 3.
[86] *Novaya gazeta*, No. 15, 3 March 2008, p. 10.

Table 8.2 *Regional elections of 2 March 2008*

Region	Thr'd	UR	CPRF	JR	LDPR	APR	SPS	PR	NS	CF	Greens	PPU
Bashkortostan	7	88.14	7.03	3.46	1.66							
Ingushetia	7	74.09	7.34	7.39	11.06							
Kalmykia	7	54.58	22.49	4.99	3.64						4	
Yakutia	7	52.62	15.79	14.56	6.51	7.61						
Altai *krai*	7	53.46	19.61	7.7	16.46	8.14						
Amur *oblast'*	7	62.36	17.51	5.62	11.06							1.15
Ivanovo *oblast'*	5	60.30	15.34	10.27	8.61		3.03					
Rostov *oblast'*	7	71.68	15.88	5.13	5.81							
Sverdlovsk *oblast'*	7	58.43	12.2	6.26	16.07					4.04		
Ul'yanovsk *oblast'*	7	66.37	15.94	7.77	7.39							
Yaroslavl *oblast'*	5	49.7	14.59	7.77	12.56	4.83		5.94	0.34	1.01	2.98	

Key: UR – United Russia; CPRF – Communist Party of the Russian Federation; JR – Just Russia; LDPR – Liberal Democratic Party of Russia; APR – Agrarian Party of Russia; SPS – Union of Right Forces; PR – Patriots of Russia; NS – Popular Union (Narodnyi soyuz); GS – Civic Force; PPU – Party of Peace and Unity (Partiya mira i edinstva).

Source: 'Partiya regional'noi vlasti', *Kommersant*, 4 March 2008, p. 4.

campaign damaged the party's performance in the regions. The CPRF's performance improved across the board. In Amur region the CPRF vote rose from 10.16 per cent to 17.51 per cent, in Yakutia from 9.48 per cent to 15.79 per cent, and in Kalmykia from 11.72 per cent to 22.49 per cent.[87] In short, the 7 per cent barrier allowed only the 'big four' Duma parties to enter regional assemblies, confirmed by the exception of Patriots of Russia in Yaroslavl, where the barrier was only 5 per cent.[88]

Free but not fair – again

In broad terms the figures reflected popular preferences. Medvedev had made a number of important policy speeches during the campaign, and his plans in regards to his predecessor were in the public domain and represented a popular commitment to policy continuity laced with an element of innovation to achieve his declared goals. However, his status as Putin's nominated successor undoubtedly detracted from the sweetness of victory, and it is for this reason that the authorities tried to compensate by ensuring an exceptionally strong vote for him (as long as it did not eclipse Putin's achievement four years earlier), based on a high turnout. In addition, as we saw in the Duma election, regional and local authorities were pressured to ensure that the result in their region did not fall short of the desired outcome, a system of pressure that worked its way down to the level of enterprises and offices.[89] In Vladivostok, for example, each district was effectively given a target to meet, and elsewhere a whole range of incentives were devised to entice voters to the polling station. In some, products were sold at a discount, and in many, amateur concerts were staged.[90] In part, this was a response to the calls for a boycott issued by Yabloko, SPS and Other Russia.[91] It also reflected the system's need to test the loyalty of the pro-Kremlin elite, but in doing so it undermined the legitimacy of an election that it would have won in any case.[92]

---

[87] Elena Ivanova and Anton Utekhin, 'Bez prezidenta ne vykhodit', *Vedomosti*, 4 March 2008, p. 2.

[88] Nikolai Petrov, 'Of Mayors and Interlopers', *Moscow Times*, 18 March 2008, p. 11.

[89] Churov admitted that there had been 'blatant' incidents of students and employees being pressured to vote; 'Elections Chief Acknowledges Violations', *Moscow Times*, 5 March 2008, p. 3.

[90] Afanasii Sborov, '"Ya i Galochka budem zhdat' vas"', *Kommersant-Vlast'*, No. 8, 3 March 2008, pp. 17–21.

[91] Boris Vishnevskii, 'Ot"yavlennyi elektorat', *Novaya gazeta*, No. 14, 28 February 2008, p. 7.

[92] Daniel Treisman, 'What Keeps the Kremlin Up All Night', *Moscow Times*, 18 February 2008, p. 10.

The main criticism of the election lies not in the procedures on the day itself, which at most altered the result by 5 per cent and did not change the outcome, but in restricting access to the ballot of independent candidates. We have seen that Kasyanov was not allowed to register his candidacy; but in any case pollsters suggested that he would have received no more than 2–3 per cent of the vote. No serious country, let alone one with nuclear weapons, would have accepted Bukovsky's candidature since he held a foreign residency. Neither Yabloko nor SPS were in a position to advance a candidate, and the 'democratic' opposition could not agree on someone who could carry the liberal flag. The barrier of 2 million signatures for non-Duma parties is undoubtedly set very high, but in itself is a technical question that is not insuperable.

Another major criticism is unfair access to the mass media, and Medvedev's refusal to participate in the televised debates. This is another technical issue, and each candidate has the right to decide the issue themselves. Clearly an incumbent or leading candidate is hesitant to endow their opponents with the patina of seriousness by engaging them in debate. The quality of discussion, as US elections show, is usually very low, so not much is added in terms of policy detail. Medvedev did gain incommensurable media coverage during the election as he went about his business, and this undoubtedly gave him an advantage. Medvedev had 17.3 times more airtime on NTV, for example, than the three other candidates combined, while his advantage on Channel One was 4.2.[93] However, even outside the debates, many of which were staged at inconvenient times (Moscow time; in Vladivostok ten time zones away some were shown prime time), both Zyuganov and Zhirinovsky gained considerable coverage – too much, in fact, for many. The Slovenian presidency of the EU had some positive words to say about the calm manner in which the election had been conducted but regretted that the OSCE/ODIHR had not been able to conduct a meaningful election observation mission or that the situation did not allow for genuinely competitive elections. The absence of equal media access for the opposition was an issue of particular concern.[94]

Kasparov, the remaining head of the Other Russia movement, conceded that the opposition was fragmented, but as far as he was concerned the fundamental point was that the authorities were

[93] Nabi Abdullaev, 'Medvedev Slammed for Airtime Monopoly', *Moscow Times*, 28 February 2008, p. 1.
[94] 'Declaration by the Presidency on Behalf of the European Union on the Presidential Elections in Russian Federation on 2 March 2008', www.eu2008.si/en/News_and_Documents.

illegitimate. For this reason he urged his supporters to boycott the
election and join the 'dissenters' marches' organised by Other Russia
on 3 March. The one in Moscow was not sanctioned since the organisers
had been unable to reach agreement with the Moscow mayor's office on
the venue, and after seven minutes dozens of arrests were made from
among the few hundred who gathered in Turgenev Square. The
St Petersburg march was licensed and about five hundred people, of
whom two hundred were journalists, marched peacefully to condemn
what they insisted had been an electoral farce.[95] Kasparov argued that
Medvedev's election, even if accompanied by a 'thaw', would make no
difference: 'The regime will remain the same – illegitimate. The regime
will possibly simply change its tasks. If Putin's aim was to strengthen the
redistribution of property and the total destruction of democratic institutions, Medvedev will have to resolve the problem of legitimating all of
this abroad.'[96] Kasparov convened the National Assembly on 23 March
in yet another doomed attempt to unite the opposition.

The preliminary report by Gross, the head of the 22-member PACE
election-monitoring mission, summed up its findings as follows: 'The
results of the presidential election held on March 2 are a reflection of the
will of a people whose democratic potential was, unfortunately, not
tapped.'[97] The election had the character of a plebiscite on Putin's
presidency, Gross noted, and the people voted for stability. The inadequacies, however, meant that the 'fairness' of the election was in
question, as well as the degree to which they could be considered free.
The criticisms focused on the registration of candidates, unequal access
to the media and increased transparency in campaign financing, and less
on falsification on the day of the election itself.[98] The Golos election-
monitoring group argued the election was unfair and fell below western
democratic standards, but conceded that whatever the manipulations
Medvedev would have won anyway.[99]

Ryzhkov argued that the election was 'carried out in a classic authoritarian tradition': 'The widespread, popular myth is that President

[95] Andrei Borsobin, 'Oppozitsiya proshlas' po zhizni marshem', Izvestiya, 4 March 2008,
p. 2; Andrei Kozenko, Ekaterina Savina and Mikhail Shevchuk, '"Nesoglasnye" proshli
v nogu s militsiei', Kommersant, 4 March 2008, p. 5.
[96] Mariya-Luiza Tirmaste interview with Garri Kasparov, '"My voyuem s sistemoi,
kotoraya formiruet nelegitimnuyu vlast'"', Kommersant-Vlast', No. 8, 3 March 2008,
pp. 34–5, at p. 35.
[97] Andreas Gross, 'A Missed Opportunity', Moscow Times, 4 March 2008, p.10.
[98] Mariya-Luiza Tirmaste, 'PASE prisnala Dmitriya Medvedeva', Kommersant, 4 March
2008, p. 2.
[99] Nabi Abdullaev and Francesca Mereu, '"Not Free, Not Fair, But Accurate All the
Same"', Moscow Times, 4 March 2008, pp. 1–2.

Vladimir Putin has abided by the Constitution by stepping down from office and holding an election. Just the opposite is true: Sunday's vote was the latest, and most significant, chapter in a whole series of actions taken by the Kremlin to eliminate free and fair elections in the country.'[100] Vladimir Frolov takes a very different view, arguing that even though the result may have been predetermined, that did not render the election undemocratic or Medvedev's victory illegitimate. He insists that 'the lack of competition is caused mostly by a lack of credible alternatives to Putin's course rather than by the Kremlin's manipulations'. The CPRF had stuck with the three times loser Zyuganov, Kasyanov would have received no more than 2 per cent even if he had been registered, and ultimately the main problem had been 'not procedural but substantive. Medvedev's rivals simply did not have any political platforms that could be viewed as plausible alternatives to Putin's course.'[101] Although lacking competitiveness, the election effectively legitimised the transfer of power. This was in keeping with all the presidential elections in post-communist Russia; never once have they achieved a change of leadership and instead have provided popular endorsement for the existing authorities.

While economic factors were an important element in Putin's and Medvedev's electoral success, this did not necessarily mean that individual voters benefited from the long period of growth. Instead, as Colton and Hale demonstrate, 'economy-related factors do have a major impact, they work through multiple channels and in tandem with other factors',[102] which in this case means association with a range of policy preferences, including the shift to the market and pro-western international integration. Membership of United Russia was an important factor in determining voter preferences, with the party channelling mass support for the two leaders. The study found no link between specific social constituencies and the Putin vote, although the youth and female vote for him was higher than average. Colton and Hale recognise the existence of fraud and administrative pressure on voters, but they argue that this is 'not the exclusive or even the main story of Russian presidential elections',[103] noting instead that 'Putin has quite consistently garnered ballots through his agreement with voters on some of the biggest issues of the day and through leadership qualities and the sense

[100] Vladimir Ryzhkov, 'A Dull and Boring Show', *Moscow Times*, 3 March 2008, p. 10
[101] Vladimir Frolov, 'An Election Can Be Boring and Democratic', *Moscow Times*, 3 March 2008, p. 11.
[102] Timothy J. Colton and Henry E. Hale, 'The Putin Vote: Presidential Electorates in a Hybrid Regime', *Slavic Review* 68, 3, Fall 2009, p. 474.
[103] *Ibid.*, p. 474.

of competence he has managed to project.'[104] Putin and Medvedev, in their view, actually resonated with the electorate in a vote in which there was at least some genuine opposition and competition, and thus Russia was a hybrid regime rather than a fully-fledged authoritarian one. The 2007–8 electoral cycle confirmed the rough balance between the two pillars of the dual state, and it would now be up to Medvedev to deliver on his promise of strengthening the constitutional wing.

[104] *Ibid.*, p. 502.

9   Medvedev's challenge

Putin was a hard act to follow. In comparison with Yeltsin, Putin enjoyed almost every possible advantage – youth, dynamism and vision – and any successor would labour in his enormous shadow. The double elections for parliament and the presidency gave Russia's leadership a renewed mandate while embedding continuity across the divide. The Medvedev succession remained true to the letter of the constitution: the constitution was not changed, and Putin did not succumb to calls to stay on for a third term. However, Putin remained, but in a new capacity. On 7 May 2008, Medvedev was sworn in as president, and the following day the Duma confirmed Putin as prime minister by an overwhelming majority (392 to 56, with the Communists voting against and two abstentions), and thus the succession operation was complete. The constitution establishes a dual executive (although technically the president stands above the executive), and now this was reinforced by political realities. Even with Putin as prime minister, Russia would not be transformed into a parliamentary republic, but a new centre of power was created outside the Kremlin: a popular prime minister at the head of the dominant party backed by a parliamentary majority. Russia remained a presidential republic, but the role of the government was enhanced since it was now led by an authoritative figure with enormous political capital of his own. Medvedev's election represented the partial triumph of the *civiliki* and reflected the failure of the security apparatus to consolidate its position. It also represented an opportunity to move beyond the Putin era, but unlike so often in Russia's past when a new leader repudiates the legacy of his predecessor, the succession operation was designed to ensure that this would be done with Putin and not against him. Medvedev's presidency, above all, represented an opportunity to transcend the dual state by enhancing the effective powers of the constitutional state against the aggrandised powers of the administrative regime.

Tandemocracy

The hidden succession process had been unnerving for Putin. As factional conflict in late 2007 intensified, the 'third term' party hoped that Putin would align with them and crush opposing factions. Since the unstable equilibrium was in danger of being destroyed, the only way for continuity to be maintained was for the regime to realign itself along the line of a single factional axis. The alternative, of course, was to crush all factions and to rule by appealing to the normative resources of the constitutional state. This high-risk strategy would have meant Putin's repudiation of everything that had constituted the inner spring of his leadership, and this he was not ready to do. The choice in the event was to select a single party to win an overwhelming victory in the parliamentary elections and to nominate a single candidate for the presidency, and at the same time to remain a powerful political arbiter. Thus the Putin system remained intact, and while this endowed the new presidency with a powerful political resource, it also perpetuated the dual state and thereby constrained the new leader. Medvedev had a 'Putin problem', which did not necessarily have to take crisis forms but which constrained his political options and limited his ability to grow into the presidency. While continuity had been achieved, the political stalemate threatened to turn into stagnation.

Soviet wine in a Russian bottle?

The relationship between the president and prime minister in Russia is one of permanent vulnerability for the latter. Russia is one of the few semi-presidential systems where the constitution allows the government to be dismissed at the president's whim (Article 117.2, see also Article 83.c).[1] Putin was once again a subordinate whose status was clearly below that of the president. There is a conventional division of responsibilities between the two posts, with the president enjoying priority in foreign and security affairs, while the prime minister deals with current matters relating to economic and social matters. However, having dealt with foreign policy for so long, Putin's views in this area remained influential. There were numerous issues over which potential conflicts could emerge, including over the strategic development of big business, the appointment of key officials, as well as any attempts to impose major

---

[1] There was much speculation in 2008 that the constitutional law on the government would be changed so that the prime minister could only be dismissed by a four-fifths majority of the Duma and a two-thirds majority of the Federation Council, but no such amendment was adopted.

elite restructuring. The composition of the new cabinet was also a matter of compromise. While the appointment of the foreign, defence and security ministers is unequivocally a presidential prerogative, other ministers are usually appointed in consultation with the prime minister.

To balance this, without Putin's support Medvedev would be a much weaker president. The tandem of a strong leader and a strong prime minister is not unique in Russian history and was in evidence earlier when Putin served as Yeltsin's premier from August 1999.[2] Putin now took office as Russia's thirty-first prime minister, and according to Nikonov (Molotov's grandson) there was nothing in Russia's historical experience that would suggest that the tandem would not work.[3] The constitutional boot, however, remained firmly on Medvedev's foot, and he made it clear that he intended to exercise his powers. The view that Medvedev would be little more than 'Putin's poodle' proved exaggerated.

Following the presidential succession, many spoke of the return of the atmosphere of the late Brezhnev years – of relatively low-level repression accompanied by a dull sense of fear and caution. The two-stage United Russia congress in October and December 2007 reminded many of the bad old Soviet days of stiffly formalised political occasions, with the token milk maid and representatives of the workers and peasants voting as instructed. In addition to a constitutional majority in the Duma (385 out of 450 seats), UR by 2009 also enjoyed a similar predominance in the Federation Council, with 111 out of 166 senators members of the party. By late 2009, seventy-eight of the country's eighty-three governors were members of United Russia, a figure that rose to seventy-nine when Matvienko officially joined the party and its Supreme Council at UR's eleventh congress on 21 November. Although the opposition tried to find new ways to work in reaction to the consolidation of the regime, its self-image became that of a marginalised dissident movement. The Putinite power system had been created to reduce the administrative regime's dependence on the institutions of popular representation, but as Afanasiev notes, by the same token it 'drove themselves and society into an institutional trap, because the bureaucratic mechanisms of

---

[2] Other notable pairings were Sergei Witte (Russia's first premier in 1905–6) and then Petr Stolypin (1906–11) with the wilful Nicholas II; Lenin at the head of Sovnarkom (1917–24) in which he effectively served as prime minister; Vyacheslav Molotov (1930–41) and Stalin; Alexei Kosygin (1964–80) and Brezhnev; and Primakov and Yeltsin in 1998–9 (not a successful relationship). See I. M. Avramenko, *Prem'er-ministry (predsedateli pravitel'stva) Rossii (1905–2005): Biograficheskii spravochnik* (Rostov-on-Don: Feniks, 2005).
[3] Vyacheslav Nikonov, *Izvestiya*, 14 May 2008; and personal discussion.

systemic stability, when tested, may prove to be mechanisms of systemic inadequacy that only worsen the crisis'.[4]

With the threat of popular anti-regime mobilisation of the colour type having passed, the regime visibly relaxed. The youth group Nashi declared that after the presidential election it planned to transform itself into a political party. Having reared this home-grown 'Taliban' movement to occupy the streets, the Kremlin announced the movement's demobilisation, although its annual summer camp at Lake Seliger continued.[5] The authorities wished to clear the streets of all public activity, although Nashi survived in a new form and was called on by the administrative regime when necessary. The election had been conducted as a Soviet-style 'special operation'; and now having achieved its goals, life could return to the old routine.[6]

A flood of commentary argued that Putin's decision to head the UR list and to assume the premiership represented a conclusive turn to authoritarianism, with Putin trying to hang on to power for life. Typical of this was *The Economist*: 'Nowhere in these manoeuvrings is there a trace of democracy as understood and practised in the west: it is far more reminiscent of the old Soviet Union.'[7] Putin's intentions, however, were misunderstood. If he had really wanted to stay on as president he could easily have amended the constitution. Of course, the fact that the decision whether to abide by the spirit of the constitution was a personal one illustrates the vulnerability of the constitutional order. Putin, moreover, was quite clear at the Valdai Discussion Club meeting on 14 September 2007 that he had no intention of weakening the status of the presidency.

At the Sochi meeting with the Valdai Club, Putin insisted that he was not interested in seeing a weak president:

I have no intention of undoing with my own hands everything that has been achieved over these last years ... There is a well-established expression that has passed down the ages from one generation to another: victory does not go to the one with power but to the one who has truth. What does this mean? It refers to the fact that in our society the strength of moral influence on society is always greater than the influence associated with the official rank or position of that person. This incidentally is in large measure one reason for the success of the dissident movement in Russia. These people were honest towards their country and its citizens, and the citizens felt it. It's absolutely clear: my actions will have

---

[4] Afanasiev, 'Is There a Demand for Modernization in Russia?', p. 32.
[5] Maya Atwal, 'Evaluating *Nashi's* Sustainability: Autonomy, Agency and Activism', *Europe-Asia Studies*, 61, 5, 2009, pp. 743–58.
[6] Aleksandr Konovalov, 'Kogda sipyashchii prosnetsya', *Nezavisimaya gazeta*, 22 January 2008, p. 13.
[7] Editorial, 'Russian Democracy, Soviet Style', *The Economist*, 6–12 October 2007.

an influence. But I say again that I am not planning to destabilise or weaken the authorities. My goal is to ensure that power in Russia remains stable. And I have every reason to believe that it will.[8]

Praise for the dissident movement from a former KGB officer reminds us of Putin's political background as a *semidesyatnik*, a man of the 1970s when the Soviet Union drifted into stagnation.[9] As for the form in which his influence would be exercised, this was to remain secret until after the parliamentary elections. Following his 'direct line' on 18 October 2007, we have seen that Putin stressed that 'I am against limiting the president's powers', noting that there was no need to redistribute powers between the two branches of the executive while insisting that there was no 'dual power' in the system.[10] The Ukrainian experience of permanent political crisis since 2006, when the constitutional amendments came into force that reduced presidential powers while enhancing those of the prime minister, was very much on Russian minds. President Yushchenko came into conflict with his prime ministers, Yuliya Timoshenko, Viktor Yanukovich, and then again Timoshenko. This sort of 'dual power' system, even though it provided a powerful impulse for pluralism in Ukrainian politics, was one that Putin sought to avoid.

Then why did Putin stay on? While many former presidents retire to write their memoirs and comment on public affairs, Putin had no intention of leaving public life. The question was not so much Putin after Putinism, but Putinism after Putin: his system would remain even though he was no longer president. Ultimately, the answer lies in our factional model: Putin may have been 'unable to quit' since, as an editorial in *Nezavisimaya gazeta* put it, no one else was 'capable of effectively controlling the elites', and a 'struggle between influential clans could get out of control' leading to 'degradation'.[11] This became a common view among commentators, who noted that Putin was left with little choice but to continue in some sort of high office to limit the infighting among the elites and to 'remain the guarantor of the checks and balances of the system'.[12] Before the outbreak of open factional conflict in late 2007, Putin may well have planned to leave, but in the end his decision to head the government was a forced move.[13] Putin

---

[8] http://president.kremlin.ru/text/appears/2007/09/144011.shtml.
[9] Sakwa, *Putin*, Chapter 1.
[10] www.kremlin.ru/text/appears/2007/10/148675.shtml.
[11] 'Putin ostaetsya', *Nezavisimaya gazeta*, 28 December 2007, p. 1.
[12] Dmitrii Kamyshev, *Kommersant*, 18 December 2007.
[13] *Gazeta*, 5 May 2008, quoted by Jonas Bernstein, 'Newspaper Reports all Key Powers Will Shift to the White House', *EDM* 5, 85, 5 May 2008.

acted as a shield against the security faction and in general the factionalism that waxed so strongly during his presidency.

The 2007 Duma election fulfilled its goals, which was not only to elect a new parliament but also to legitimise what would soon be former President Putin in a new role. As premier, Putin would not be in charge of foreign affairs and diplomacy, a presidential prerogative, and would thus be denied an official voice in a sphere that he had made his own. Putin would have to immerse himself in routine socio-economic matters, a rather less exciting task than managing foreign policy, while at the same time sharing not only his authority but also his political capital. As premier, Putin enjoyed a strong parliamentary majority at his back, and thus in political terms he could not be easily dismissed. Equally, in constitutional terms Putin did not need to redistribute authority – the premier's office simply took back powers that had been arrogated by the presidency. This is a point made by Medvedev in his interview with the *Financial Times* on 25 March 2008. The president-elect stressed that the country's constitution 'predetermines the answer to the question on who takes decisions on what issues'. While the strategic direction of national and foreign policy was set by the president, Medvedev stressed that the government headed by the prime minister 'has its own extensive areas of competence'.[14] Like Putin, he insisted that there would be no redistribution of powers between the president and the prime minister.

At the ninth (extraordinary) congress of United Russia on 15 April 2008, Putin agreed to head the party as its chairman, but he refused to become a party member. Putin noted that he was 'ready to take added responsibility' and promised to do everything to strengthen the party. However, he declared that the party needed to be reformed: 'United Russia must become more open for discussion, it has to be completely debureaucratised, purged of people who are pursuing their personal aims.'[15] On the same occasion, Medvedev was also invited to join the party by Gryzlov, but he turned down the offer as 'untimely'. Putin endorsed Medvedev's decision, agreeing that it was not 'advisable' for the president to become a party member; but for a prime minister to lead a party was 'a practice that is natural and traditional for democratic states'.[16] Putin's decision meant that he was in a position to control the party, but the party was not in a position to exercise influence over

---

[14] Lionel Barber, Neil Buckley and Catherine Belton, 'Laying Down the Law: Medvedev Vows War on Russia's "Legal Nihilism"', *The Financial Times*, 25 March 2008.

[15] Rustem Falyakhov, 'Dvazhdy predsedatel'', *RBK Daily*, 16 April 2008, p. 2.

[16] Personal notes; Anna Smolchenko, 'Putin to Lead, but Not to Join Party', *Moscow Times*, 16 April 2008, pp. 1–2.

him. In other words, the decision was an instrumental one and was unlikely to do anything to advance the party as a functioning democratic organisation. Despite Gryzlov's attempts to raise UR's standing, the party did not become an autonomous subject of the political process. United Russia remained an instrument *of* power but not a party *in* power. Putin had solved a tactical problem at the expense of taking advantage of the strategic opportunities created by the new presidency to reinvigorate political life.

Putin created a system that guaranteed the preservation of his power under the Medevedev presidency. He now had two major formal instruments at his disposal: the premiership and the dominant party, as well as enjoying a Putinite majority in the Federation Council. Those who wished Putin to take up a third successive term were getting their way, but not in the form they had anticipated. As the analyst Dmitry Oreshkin noted, 'Putin was relieved of the presidential post on condition that he did not give up the levers of power.'[17] This was not a party government, but an administration that used the party as an instrument of power. Its subordination to the prime minister was now formalised. United Russia was the dominant party, but it was not allowed to become the core of a dominant power system and it could not independently dispense patronage and formulate policy.[18] The administrative regime, with Putin and Medvedev at its new dual heart, retained its autonomy.

Medvedev was far from being a 'technical president' subordinate to Putin. Instead, Putin was probably genuine in his desire to strengthen the party base of the regime and exploited his popularity to the full, like any politician worth his or her salt. However, by endowing UR with an overwhelming majority, he withdrew the oxygen on which a genuine pluralistic multi-party system could thrive. Indeed, his continuing presence, while indeed ensuring a smooth succession and stability, created new problems, notably the absence of elite renewal and government rotation. Above all, Putin's continued power inhibited the new president from growing into an autonomous and authoritative figure.

The Medvedev succession represented elite recombination accompanied by policy continuity. Medvedev did not belong to the KGB network, and he was the first Russian leader since Lenin whose parents had a higher humanities education. He represented a new post-Soviet generation. For Sergei Markedonov, however, this represented the onset of a period of 'velvet stagnation'. Putinite centralisation in his view had solved none of the problems of the north Caucasus while encouraging a

---

[17] Falyakhov, 'Dvazhdy predsedatel'', p. 2.
[18] Cf. Carothers, 'The End of the Transition Paradigm', p. 11.

new period of confrontation with the west, somewhat akin to the last period of Brezhnev's rule in the early 1980s.[19] Shevtsova argues that a more aggressive foreign policy was a way of maintaining the status quo by consolidating the country around its leadership.[20] The succession operation had solved the problem of perpetuating the power of the regime, but it had not opened up the system to genuine contestation and political pluralism. However, with Medvedev as the new incumbent, the evolutionary resolution of the problems facing Russia remained possible, and thus this electoral cycle did not represent the conclusive consolidation of an authoritarian regime. The succession operation consolidated the status quo, but in a new format.

Diarchy, dual power or tandem

With the new dual leadership, Russia entered uncharted territory. While Putin enjoyed overwhelming *political* support, the bulk of *constitutional* power lay with Medvedev, a mismatch that inevitably generated tensions. Putin was the man with the authority, while Medvedev was the person in power. A duumvirate does not necessarily entail diarchy, and this was nothing like the dual power between February and October 1917 where two separate systems of power and legitimacy competed. Neither was it necessarily *dvoetsarstvie* (the rule of two tsars). However, the balance of power between the president and prime minister had clearly changed. First, Putin enjoyed unprecedented popularity and prestige. This no doubt was a wasting asset, since as the manager of the economy he was responsible for economic and social problems. He was vulnerable as domestic energy and other utility prices rose, and indeed, as world energy prices fell and the economy suffered the shocks of the world financial crisis from autumn 2008. The RTS stock market index suffered a fivefold fall from its peak of 2,500 in May 2008 to 555 in late October. Second, the bureaucracy owed its loyalty to Putin. Already in the interregnum between December 2007 and May 2008, presidential staff drifted from the Kremlin to the White House, the seat of the government. Third, the constitutional majority in parliament, with around 70 per cent of the seats, owed loyalty not to Medvedev but to Putin and acted as a constraint on presidential power.

[19] Sergei Markedonov, 'Stsenarii "barkhatnogo zastoya"', Caucasus.Times.com, www.caucasustimes.com/article.asp?id=13578.
[20] Liliya Shevtsova, 'Konets epokhy: Antitezis Gorbachevy', *Vedomosti*, 17 September 2008.

United Russia also enjoyed extensive support in regional assemblies, which translated into an overwhelming majority in the Federation Council. The Federal Assembly provided Putin with a powerful independent political base. It was unlikely that this majority would adopt constitutional amendments, let alone ones counter to Medvedev's wishes, but in the eventuality of such a clash the presidential veto could be over-ridden by a three-quarters vote in the Federation Council and two-thirds of the Duma. It would be a misnomer, however, to describe the new system as 'cohabitation' on anything like the French model, since Russia does not have a government based formally on the parliamentary majority, and thus a situation when the president and prime minister are of opposing parties does not arise. The closest Russia came to this was during Primakov's premiership between September 1998 and May 1999. Instead, Russia now entered a period of 'tandemocracy', in which the anticipated shift from stabilisation to modernisation would be guaranteed by Putin, in partnership with the new president.[21] In effect, the establishment of the tandem restored the factional balance that had been disrupted as a result of the Yukos affair, with a more stable liberal-statist configuration to the power system. There were two centres of authority, but not two opposed centres of power. This was therefore not a 'co-presidency' but an arrangement unique in Russian history. Whether it could muster the dynamism necessary to implement the modernisation agenda was another matter, and a duumvirate is obviously a recipe for stagnation.

Elgie argues that 'the highly presidentialised form of semipresidentialism in Russia has played a part in the country's sharp decline in the area of democratic governance'.[22] The presidency now had to share authority with the prime minister, an arrangement that logically created space for greater pluralism. In institutional terms, Russian semi-presidentialism reflects the traditional Soviet division of labour between strategic management functions, above all policy formation and personnel appointments, which was the responsibility of the Politburo and the Central Committee, and managerial functions, focusing above all on socio-economic issues, handled by the Council of Ministers. The 2007–8 operation, however, blurred this division, and strategic and managerial functions were no longer so clearly delineated. This would

---

[21] The term 'tandemocracy' was first used by Dmitrii Kamyshev, 'Chetyre voprosa pro dvukh prezidentov', *Kommersant-Vlast'*, No. 10, 17 March 2008, pp. 30, 32, under the rubric 'Tandemokratiya'.

[22] Robert Elgie, 'A Fresh Look at Semipresidentialism: Variations on a Theme', *Journal of Democracy* 16, 3, July 2005, p. 104. For a broader view, see Robert Elgie (ed.), *Semi-Presidentialism in Europe* (Oxford: Oxford University Press, 1999).

not necessarily lead to conflict, since the new 'team' had long worked together, and thus dual power could be avoided. Medvedev insisted that he had long been part of Putin's St Petersburg group 'and do not separate myself from them'.[23] The two had worked together since the early 1990s and shared not only a legal education in common but also views that coincided on most substantive issues. Thus endless discussions about who would be the dominant partner and take the final decisions rather missed the point: the constitutional position was clear, while political practice would be a matter of experimentation, there was little reason to believe that the relationship in normal circumstances would not work well. Even when tested by the Georgian war in August 2008, the formal division of labour was applied. It was Medvedev who conducted the negotiations with President Nicolas Sarkozy of France, representing the EU; while Putin focused on practical matters, dealing with the refugee crisis and then the reconstruction of South Ossetia.

In Ukraine and elsewhere, Elgie notes that upon assuming office prime ministers 'have immediately achieved the status of a potential presidential candidate'.[24] In his first premiership in 1999, this was certainly the case with Putin, but as president he was careful to stymie any such independent ambitions by his prime ministers; however, on retaking the office in 2008, the latent potential of the office once again resurfaced. Putin was clearly going to be an activist but self-limiting prime minister. As he told *Time* magazine, 'I intend to handle current economic and social affairs like roads, housing, education. As for key matters of defense and international nature, they will remain the prerogative of the president of course.' He also noted that there would be no redistribution of responsibilities from the presidential administration: 'Russia is a nation, like the United States, with a balanced but strong presidential power, and I am adamantly against stifling and restricting the authority of the president.'[25] Article 83 of the constitution allows the president to chair cabinet meetings, while Article 86 grants them control over foreign policy. Nevertheless, the constitution allows considerable scope for the prime minister, and thus Putin would only be activating the powers that were already vested in the premier's office. This was already the case in his first premiership, between December 1999 and May 2000, when he took the initiative in a number of policy areas, notably in launching the second Chechen war. The 1996 federal law on the

---

[23] Svanidze, *Medvedev*, p. 215.
[24] Elgie, 'A Fresh Look at Semipresidentialism', p. 109.
[25] 'Putin Q & A: Full Transcript', *Time*, 18 December 2007;www.time.com/time/specials/ 2007/personoftheyear/article/0,28804,1690753_1690757_1696150,00.html

government did not need to be changed to allow such activity. Article 32 does not preclude the prime minister taking control of the FSB, the MVD, the GPO, the justice ministry and so on. The prime minister also has the authority to create and chair advisory bodies, like the Defence Council that existed briefly in 1996 as a counter-weight to the Security Council. There was a danger, however, of power migrating to whatever post Putin held; but an even greater danger (certainly in his own mind) was that if he held no post, the power system would dissolve.

Putin insisted that the premiership had perfectly adequate powers and there would be no need to create new ones; while Medvedev declared that he was deeply opposed to the creation of a parliamentary republic and favoured a strong presidency.[26] He stressed that 'Never in Russian history has the former head of state, whatever he was called, taken a subordinate position', and thus Putin's decision to take on the premiership was unique.[27] There was no indication that either would cede authority to the other, and both repeatedly committed themselves to a political partnership based on experience of working together and trust. It was clear that the era of a 'technical' prime minister, accompanied by a super-strong presidency, was over for as long as Putin occupied the premiership. The constitution endows the prime minister with considerable powers at the head of part of the dual executive, and under Putin the potential of the post was exploited to the full. The shift also entailed a change in political style, since the work of the government is much more transparent than that of the presidential administration. There is at least a law on the government, whereas none regulates the work of the presidential administration.[28] Although some of the para-constitutional practices migrated to the White House, they operated in a very different environment. Putin lost direct contact with the force ministries, while Medvedev's relationship with them was very different from that of his predecessor. Not only did he not come from that environment, his legal background prompted his calls to overcome 'legal nihilism'.

The system remained personalistic, but now based on two leaders. The combination of two powerful leaders, as French experience repeatedly demonstrated, is never easy. Medvedev's lack of affiliation with any of the factions gave him room for political manoeuvre, but the lack of a power base of his own meant that he lacked the political weight and strategic resources to replace Putin as the ultimate referee. Medvedev was not able to adjudicate between the various factional conflicts, and

---

[26] Svanidze, *Medvedev*, p. 217.   [27] *Ibid.*, p. 223.
[28] Nikolai Silaev, 'Modernizatsiya moshchi', *Ekspert*, No. 9, 3–9 March 2008, pp. 21–6, at p. 26.

thus it was left to Putin to exercise this function. Putin was thus not just the PM, but he also became the FM – the faction manager, covering for Medvedev and ensuring that none of the factions became predominant or threatened the tandem's policy agenda. Without Putin to defend him, for example, it is unlikely that Kudrin would survive in post. In his book of interviews, Medvedev admitted that some people might wish to challenge his presidency, a rare public acknowledgement of the factional struggle that attended his rise.[29] Putin is alleged to have declared that he stayed on 'because I know what my friends the siloviki are planning for the country if I leave completely'.[30] In the wake of the elections, the *siloviki* were preoccupied with their internecine conflicts and unable to mount a sustained challenge to the course charted by the tandem leadership, yet they remained a powerful force.

Tandemocracy represented an attempt to move away from the dual system, where formal institutions were accompanied by covert power struggles, towards a more fully-fledged and operational *political* system where public politics would predominate. By placing himself at the head of United Russia and occupying the fully legitimate post of prime minister rather than taking up some sort of *éminence grise* role, Putin contributed to the consolidation of the institutions of Russian governance. The contradictions of the dual state, however, would not be overcome so easily since it was more than an emanation of personal will but reflected profound social realities. Medvedev is not cut out for the role of supreme political arbiter, a function that Putin performed brilliantly, so it is quite possible to envisage a trend towards greater political pluralism – but only if Putin withdrew from active politics. This could take a pathological form, primarily through rampant factional conflict (an eventuality that Putin so feared, accompanied possibly by Carothers's 'feckless pluralism'); or a more benign form through greater autonomy for political parties and a livelier parliament. Growing sections of the elite were no longer satisfied with the stultifying hegemony of the Putinite system.

[29] Svanidze, *Medvedev*, pp. 320–1. Medvedev's comments are extremely guarded and couched in terms of avoiding conflict between the presidential and prime ministerial bureaucracies. Elsewhere in the book, he stressed that he did not feel that 'some sort of corporation' (he had in mind 'people with epaulettes') 'existed as some sort of alien body or had put everything under its control'. He compared them with discussion over whether the 'Dnepropetrovsk' or 'Sverdlovsk' group had been better than the *Pitertsy*, stressing that the existence of such groups was highly conditional; *ibid.*, p. 227. However, the gloss by the editors suggests a different conclusion, noting that 'the bureaucracy in Russia is traditionally the ruling class. Struggle within it, when it goes beyond certain limits, provokes widespread instability'; *ibid.*, p. 228.

[30] Quoted from Alexander Sungurov, a human rights activist, by Graham Stack, 'Promises Made to Be Broken', *Russia Profile* 5, 3, April 2008, pp. 8–10, at p. 9.

One study of elite views revealed that 61 per cent considered that the concentration of power was reducing the regime's effectiveness and ability to implement a developmental agenda.[31]

The new model of governance was predicated on co-operation, but a competitive dynamic was inherent in the situation. At a certain point a new model would be appropriate, and it would be a test for both to ensure that this took place consensually. Although tension mounted as Medvedev's presidency advanced, the ideological gulf between the two leaders should not be exaggerated. Putin after all could have chosen from any number of more conservative statists if not outright *siloviki* if his aim had been to preserve his system intact, and with it the power of the bureaucracy and his allies. Instead he chose the professor of law Medvedev, with whose views he was entirely familiar, to advance a moderate programme of modernisation.

Personnel changes and factional reshuffling

Putin was the master at picking and reshuffling personnel and ensuring that loyalty became the fundamental virtue in the elite pecking order. As long as the pie was growing, each faction could enrich itself in its own way and competition was restrained, but if there was a shift to zero-sum competition in conditions of economic downturn, then the outcome would be destabilising. The mercantilisation of the *siloviki*, as we have seen, had already been a matter of concern for Cherkesov; and the viciousness of the feuds between and within factions became apparent as the succession dragged on. The FSB director Patrushev had come into open conflict with the 'drug tsar' Cherkesov; and the tension between Prosecutor General Chaika and his nominal subordinate Bastrykin at the head of the Investigative Committee took open forms. The creation of a new 'financial' faction headed by Prime Minister Zubkov and Defence Minister Serdyukov outflanked the traditional factions, and opened the political field sufficiently to allow Medvedev's candidacy. In all of this Putin struggled to maintain the autonomy of the presidency, and as faction manager he would do the same on the tandem's behalf.

The acid test of the new system, according to Hedlund, 'will lie in the Kremlin's ability to maintain a balance among rival factions, a task that will not be made easier by the cohabitation of Putin and Medvedev'.[32] Even before Putin had left office, the tide had turned against the *siloviki*.

---

[31] Editorial, *Vedomosti*, 22 September 2008.
[32] Stefan Hedlund, 'Rents, Rights, and Service: Boyar Economics and the Putin Transition', *Problems of Post-Communism* 54, 4, July–August, 2008, p. 37.

The system of attaching security officials from the MVD, FSB and the defence ministry to the presidential administration and the government, which had been in full flood between 2001 and 2005, was ended by a presidential decree of 16 January 2008.[33] The upper reaches of Russian government were being 'desecuritised' in preparation for the transition to a Medvedev presidency. The fundamental question was how far Medvedev would go against the *siloviki*. Soon after Medvedev's inauguration on 7 May 2008, Åslund noted that

> The scourge of the Putin administration was the Sechin group, which spearheaded the confiscation of Yukos and reinforced repression. It seemed invincible, but now its four top members have been demoted: Sechin, Victor Ivanov, Patrushev, and Justice Minister Vladimir Ustinov. Apparently, their only support was Putin's presidency. The worry was that the competing St. Petersburg KGB clan headed by Cherkesov would come to the fore, but Cherkesov has also lost standing. Medvedev has delivered a remarkable double blow.[34]

There are two ways for a new leader to consolidate their position. The first is to advance allies to key positions in the heartland of the para-constitutional system, in the presidential administration, the security agencies and the government. The problem here was Medvedev did not have an extensive team of his own, and what he did have in part over-lapped with Putin's. The only constituency that came to him naturally were the remnants of the Yeltsin family, the 'old Muscovite' elite. The notable figure here was Voloshin, the former presidential chief of staff. The alternative, for normative and strictly political reasons, was to restrict the scope of the para-political order and to fill constitutional institutions, including the party system and parliament, with real political content and weight. In other words, Medvedev could adopt a strategy based on building his own team, or the path of institutional reform. In the event, Medvedev adopted mild versions of both but tended towards the latter. He was certainly not ready to enter into full-blooded conflict with the Putinite establishment.

Putin's team was divided into two. Putin brought with him to the White House some of his staff from the Kremlin. When first appointed prime minister, on 17 August 1999, Putin had appointed Sechin to head his secretariat before taking him into the Kremlin to become a deputy head of the presidential administration, and now Sechin once again followed his patron back to the White House to become a deputy

---

[33] Vladimir Ukhov, 'Up the Stairs Leading Down', *The New Times*, No. 6, February 2008.
[34] Anders Åslund, 'Unlike Putin, Medvedev Took Charge Quickly', *Moscow Times*, 21 May 2008.

premier. Putin is not known for his love of bureaucratic detail, and thus the role and number of deputy prime ministers increased. This undoubtedly was a response to workload pressures, but it may also have been a continuation of Putin's unwillingness to commit himself where sensitive factional issues are involved. As Fortescue notes, Putin was constrained 'by the need of dominant leaders in faction-ridden political systems to be careful in the degree of support that they give to any single faction'.[35] Fortescue argues that Putin as prime minister found himself 'in the same no-man's land as the Putin presidency', struggling to 'deal with important but less than first-order priority issues', and thus in terms of policy-making Russia once again 'floundered' as it had in the Brezhnev era.[36]

Putin raised the number of deputy prime ministers to seven, and they assumed the bulk of the administrative burden. There were two first deputy prime ministers: former presidential aide Igor Shuvalov, who in Putin's absence stood in for him, joined by Zubkov, the former prime minister. The five normal deputy prime ministers were Putin loyalists: Sergei Ivanov, who was effectively demoted, Sechin and Sobyanin, while Zhukov and Kudrin gave the new team a liberal flavour. Deputy prime ministers traditionally provide strategic direction while ministers are more technical figures implementing policy; and now the deputy prime ministers gained some greater powers. On 18 May 2008, a fifteen-member 'presidium' was created consisting of the seven deputy prime ministers plus eight ministers, including the foreign, interior, defence, health and social development, economic development, agriculture and regional development ministers. The presidium meets weekly and comprises a quorum with the power to adopt decisions on behalf of the whole cabinet, which meets monthly. Some of the administrative reforms of March 2004 were reversed, with the relative independence of agencies (executive organs) and services (supervisory bodies) abolished as they were once again subordinated to ministries.

Sobyanin shifted to become the government's chief of staff. The personnel changes broke up the Sechin 'faction', although its position in the Security Council was strengthened and now included Patrushev, who headed the body; Bortnikov, the new head of the FSB; Nurgaliev heading the MVD; and Fradkov, now at the head of the SVR, the centre of foreign intelligence information. The Security Council, however, provides only strategic advice and is not a policy-making body, and its head has typically been a parking lot for politicians on their way up or down. Sechin lost his informal power over administration staff and

---

[35] Fortescue, 'The Russian Law on Subsurface Resources', p. 173.
[36] Ibid., p. 179.

ramified connections to other agencies. He was now just one of a group of deputy premiers, responsible for civilian shipbuilding and energy policy (excluding Gazprom), nuclear power and most private oil companies. He was now a publicly accountable official with an onerous portfolio of responsibilities, and thus moved from the shadow world into the sphere of public politics. Without Sechin in the Kremlin, Bortnikov lacked direct access to power. Equally, Victor Ivanov lost his control over personnel policy, and his arrival at the FSKN meant that Bulbov's intelligence operation in the agency would conclusively be dismantled. His former victim, Ustinov, was appointed presidential envoy to the southern federal district, and the existing envoy, Grigory Rapota, went to the Volga federal district, replacing Konovalov, who became justice minister.

There was also movement the other way. Deputy prime minister and cabinet chief of staff, Sergei Naryshkin, Putin's classmate from the KGB intelligence school who since 2005 had been chair of Channel One (formerly ORT), became Medvedev's new presidential chief of staff. Naryshkin had always been more of an economic administrator than a security official, yet his appointment now made him Putin's eyes and ears in the presidential team. Naryshkin's appointment helped coordinate the work of the presidential administration and the government, but there is also a darker interpretation – it may also have been a way of constraining Medvedev.[37] Medvedev had undoubtedly been chosen because he was one of the few plausible candidates who would not seek to create an independent power base or to overshadow the former president, but Putin would not be Putin unless he imposed personal and institutional constraints on his successor.

By contrast, Medvedev sought to strengthen formal institutions, and thus his own autonomy. He lamented that 'Politics in Russia has always been excessively personalised', adding that 'The sooner we can depersonalise power, the more civilised we will become.'[38] However, in the first instance he was forced to deal with personnel matters. Naryshkin was supported in his new role by two senior deputies: Alexei Gromov (formerly the presidential press secretary, now replaced by Dmitry Peskov) and Surkov, two close associates of Putin's. The president's press secretary, Natalya Timakova, and his liberal economics adviser, Arkady Dvorkovich, became part of his core team. Medvedev's former university classmate and latterly a senior official in Gazprom, Konstantin

---

[37] Medvedev himself dismissed such concerns and insisted that Naryshkin's appointment would facilitate relations between the presidential and prime ministerial staffs; Svanidze, *Medvedev*, pp. 320–1.
[38] Svanidze, *Medvedev*, p. 234.

Chuichenko, was Medvedev's new personal assistant and head of the Control Directorate. Sechin's old post was taken by Alexander Beglov, also a St Petersburger and former head of the Control Directorate. Overall, while there was much movement, it is remarkable how little personnel turnover there was in the presidential administration. Many of its existing members had been appointed by Medvedev when he had earlier worked in the Kremlin, first as deputy chief of staff from December 1999 to October 2003 and then as head to November 2005, thus he already had part of his own team in place.

Medvedev steered well clear of upsetting the factional balance. He sought good relations with all wings of the regime, including confirming Bastrykin in his post as head of the Investigative Committee while allowing the GPO to hire 2,000 new staff.[39] That in part was an attempt to restore factional balance following Victor Ivanov's appointment to head the FSKN – Ivanov belonged to an opposed *silovik* sub-faction to Cherkesov. Ivanov now lost control over personnel appointments, the core of *silovik* power under Putin. Cherkesov himself on 12 May was appointed head of Rosoboronpostavki (the arms delivery agency). Medvedev's victory did not represent the end of the *silovik* faction, but it did see their influence in the presidential administration weakened and their influence overall diminished.[40] For the first time in twenty years, the influence of the *siloviki* in Russian governance weakened.[41] By contrast, Medvedev's presidency confirmed the rise of the '*civiliki*', reflecting his status as a civil law scholar.[42] This was reflected in his close relationship with Chaika, who became the main executor of Medvedev's struggle against corruption and legal nihilism. The tension between the various factions remained, but as long as each retained a stake in the system, the tandem would remain stable.

The change of presidency was accompanied by a slow renewal of regional leaders, although heavyweights like Luzhkov in Moscow, Shaimiev in Tatarstan and Rakhimov in Bashkortostan remained in post.[43] In a speech on 23 July 2008, Medvedev expressed dissatisfaction

---

[39] Nikolai Petrov, 'Medvedev prishel, Putin ostalsya', *Nezavisimaya gazeta*, 1 July 2008, p. 9. The SK, however, was denied its request to hire new staff.
[40] See Åslund, 'Unlike Putin, Medvedev Took Charge Quickly'.
[41] The peak of their influence, according to Olga Kryshtanovskaya, was in 2007 when they comprised two out of every three members of the president's administration, and thereafter their influence ebbed. Charles Clover, 'Shift to the Shadows', *The Financial Times*, 17 December 2009, p. 13.
[42] For details, see Graham Stack, 'Dmitry Medvedev's Civiliki', *Russia Profile* 5, 2, March 2008, pp. 8–10.
[43] Andrei Riskin, 'Gubernatorskaya perezagruzka', *NG Regiony*, No. 001 (184), 28 January 2008, p. 13.

with the work of regional governors and declared that Russia was suffering from a 'famine of personnel'. He called for the creation of a 'presidential reserve' of candidates for top regional posts and suggested the rotation of bureaucrats to fight corruption and improve effectiveness.[44] In August he created a presidential commission on recruitment, and in his address to the nation in November he called on 'the most talented, creative-thinking and professional people' to be recruited to state service. A competitive database of some 1,000 people was selected, drawn from across the political spectrum. Putin's system of relying on personal networks now gave way to an attempt to professionalise recruitment into government service. This was accompanied by a shift away from reliance on members of the Soviet-era *nomenklatura*. They made up 38 per cent of officials in Putin's administration but comprised only 16 per cent of Medvedev's government.[45] The new administration moved cautiously, but gradually turnover in regional leaderships gained momentum. The 'resignation' of the president of Ingushetia, Murat Zyazikov, on 30 October 2008, removed one of Russia's least successful regional leaders, and the new governor, Yunus-Bek Yevkurov, was strongly critical of the region's law-enforcement agencies. The overall ambition appeared to be to implant a new generation of 'Medvedevite' governors with a profile similar to his. As one report put it, Medvedev planned a mass rotation of regional heads to implant businessmen under fifty-five years of age who could break up clan loyalties.[46] Notable early examples of the Medvedevite generation of governors were Nikita Belykh, appointed to Kirov (Vyatka) region, and Boris Ebzeev, the former Constitutional Court judge, appointed to Karachai-Cherkessia.

From crisis to reform?

Medvedev came to power promising reform in three key areas: politics and the party system; corruption in the form of 'legal nihilism'; and the modernisation of the economy. In keeping with his legalistic style, progress in all three areas was slow.

[44] 'Vstupitel'noe slovo na soveshchanii po voprosam formirovaniya rezerva upravlencheskikh kadrov', 23 July 2008, Gorki, Moscow *oblast'*, www.kremlin.ru/text/appears/2008/07/204467.shtml.

[45] Data from Olga Kryshtanovskaya, director of the Centre for Elite Studies of the Russian Academy of Sciences. Anna Malpas, 'Medvedev Looks to Fill Senior Posts', *Moscow Times*, 22 January 2009.

[46] *Vedomosti*, 24 July 2008.

Parties and politics

For much of Putin's second term, there had been considerable debate over whether the administrative regime was planning to institutionalise itself in the form of a predominant party system. It was unclear whether the model would be Mexico, Japan or even Italy of the *partitocrazia* period. Some even talked of the Chinese model of 'authoritarian capitalism' as one that would be appropriate for a Russia in which power and property were formally interlinked in some form of state capitalism. Any of these models would signify the authoritarian transcendence of the dual state.

From 2003 Putin institutionalised his political prestige in the form of United Russia as a powerful aggregative party, and in turn the election gave Putin a stable majority in the legislature. In 2007–8 this agenda was broadened and UR was used as an instrument to facilitate executive succession. Thereafter UR assumed some of the functions of a governing party while modestly extending its role in patronage distribution, ideological propagation and as a source of popular legitimacy for the new course. The 2007–8 electoral cycle consolidated UR's role as a privileged part of the governing system. However, there remained considerable ambivalence about the extent to which UR would become the dominant party. It was not an autonomous agent, and the representative subsystem remained subordinate. The administrative regime remained firmly in control of UR and inhibited its development into a genuine dominant party, while the ability of the dominant party to exercise control over the administrative regime remained limited. Russia did not follow the path taken, for example, by the PRI in Mexico, where the president was effectively chosen by the party before subjecting himself to the popular vote, or Japan, where the LDP traditionally chose the prime minister. In Russia the executive certainly did not require the independent approval of the party, and factionalism, unlike in Mexico and Japan, was not internalised in the party.

The 2007–8 elections proved fateful for the whole party system (the scale of the shift is reflected in Tables 1.1 and 1.3). Under Putin the regime had reformed the party system with great zeal, but although the rhetoric under Medvedev changed, little was done to reduce the manual management of political processes. The regime did not give up its attempts to engineer the party system. In particular, the Kremlin considered the CPRF (with 160,000 members) under Zyuganov an anachronism, and in early summer 2008 the idea of replacing him by his first deputy, Ivan Mel′nikov, was floated, but the war in Georgia put all such plans on hold. Surkov, although reluctant to accept JR as one of the Russias – United and Just – now sponsored the party as a centre-left alternative to the Communists, and indeed as a party that could in time occupy the CPRF's niche.[47] Even without Surkov's intervention, the CPRF was in long-term decline, just as the Communist Party of France (PCF) had been a generation earlier under the leadership of the neo-Stalinist Georges Marchais. Support for the CPRF peaked in December 2000 (29 per cent) and reached a nadir in January 2007 (10 per cent).[48]

In his first state of the nation speech to the Federal Assembly on 5 November 2008, Medvedev called for the mandatory rotation of party functionaries.[49] There was speculation that such a change to the law on political parties would see both Zyuganov and Zhirinovsky forced to give up the leadership of their respective parties, which they had held for over fifteen years. While the rotation of party officials was no doubt a healthy phenomenon, this is not a matter usually subject to state regulation, and the idea represented yet more intrusive state interference in the internal affairs of civic associations. At that time various mergers and absorptions reduced the number of registered political parties from fourteen to just seven. Some of the smaller parties disappeared, with Alexei Podberezkin's Party of Social Justice joining Just Russia, and the larger Agrarian Party joining United Russia. Sergei Baburin's People's Union and Sazha Umalatova's PRES failed to meet registration requirements and in due course dissolved. In his speech Medvedev also suggested that parties winning 5 per cent of the vote could be given a seat or two in parliament, while in a meeting with party leaders on 10 November the idea was mooted of reducing the representation threshold, possibly as low as 3 per cent.[50]

It is easy to blame the liberal parties for having failed to respond adequately to the changing political circumstances, the view of those who consider endogenous factors as decisive. In 2003 Yabloko and SPS had narrowly missed passing the 5 per cent threshold, and it was obvious that only a concerted effort could propel them over the 7 per cent barrier. They went into the election still at loggerheads and paid the corresponding penalty. Once Putin identified himself with UR on 1 October, the rules of political trade changed dramatically, and even if they had united, it is not clear that this would have propelled them across the threshold. It would certainly have meant both losing their political

---

[47] Vladimir Zaleski, 'Partii pod snos', *The New Times*, No. 36, 8 September 2008, p. 29.

[48] Data from the Levada Center, www.levada.ru/tabl06.html.

[49] 'Poslanie Federal'nomu Sobraniyu Rossiiskoi Federatsii', 5 November 2008, www. kremlin.ru/text/appears/2008/11/208749.shtml.

[50] Maryam Magomedova, *Novye izvestiya*, No. 205, 11 November 2008.

identity. Putin's critique of the 'chaotic 1990s' could not but reflect badly on the liberal architects of the economic policies of that period. The long-term decline of the liberal vote must also be taken into account.

More immediately, organisational issues came to the fore. The second electoral defeat in a row provided the parties with an opportunity to reflect on their failings. By June 2008 Yabloko had 58,548 members, SPS 58,538, while Civic Force had 68,300 and the Democratic Party of Russia 79,000.[51] The shortcomings of Yabloko and SPS were in part responsible for their poor electoral performance, but clearly regime-sponsored attacks on the programmatic opposition, poor access to the media and the huge disparities in access to resources played a large part.[52] Yabloko had been losing ground in every election since the first in 1993, when it won 7.8 per cent of the vote, falling to 1.6 in 2007. Already in July 2003, a movement had emerged called 'Yabloko without Yavlinsky' (SPS was accused of having played a hand in this), and now immediately after the 2007 election Yavlinsky's grip was challenged by the head of Yabloko's youth movement, Ilya Yashin. He called for major changes to the party's organisation and tactics, and condemned the party's participation in the Duma election, granting it an air of spurious legitimacy. Yashin had been active in organising opposition rallies in Moscow and other cities, and now called for Yavlinsky's parliamentary politics to give way to 'the kind of leader that can bring people onto the streets to fight against the system'.[53]

At Yabloko's congress on 21 June 2008, the Moscow City Duma deputy, Mitrokhin, took over from Yavlinsky, who had led the party since its inception in 1993. The latter, however, retained his influence in the party at the head of a new Political Committee. Indeed, Yavlinsky was likened to a miniature Putin: arranging for a hand-picked successor while he retained influence through a parallel body.[54] Like Yavlinsky, Mitrokhin represented the moderate wing of the party ready to co-operate with the authorities, and thus his election represented a defeat for the radicals.[55] Mitrokhin had taken a tough stance against unity with

---

[51] Ul'yana Makhkamova, 'Pitertsy zamakhnulis′ na kreslo Yavlinskogo', *Nezavisimaya gazeta*, 20 June 2008, p. 4.

[52] David White, 'Victims of a Managed Democracy? Explaining the Electoral Decline of the Yabloko Party', *Demokratizatsiya* 15, 2, 2007, pp. 209–29.

[53] David Nowak, 'Yashin Says He's Ready to Replace Yavlinsky', *Moscow Times*, 6 December 2007, p. 3.

[54] Zaleski, 'Partii pod snos', p. 29.

[55] These included the head of the St Petersburg branch, Maxim Reznik, its leader in Karelia, Vasily Popov, and its youth leader, Ilya Yashin, who as we have seen favoured street demonstrations and affiliation with Other Russia protests. Mitrokhin was

other liberals, notably SPS, and thus his election did not augur well for opposition unity; but by the same token, he considered Other Russia's co-operation with the 'red-browns' to be 'political suicide'. In his view, only a clear commitment to European-style democracy could overcome what he identified as 'the crisis of Russian democracy'.[56] With the economic downturn from mid-2008, however, business became even more dependent on the Kremlin and was therefore less inclined to fund opposition parties. Nevertheless, the party stuck to its view that a policy of 'small deeds' based on 'a democratic alternative to the Putin-Medvedev course' was viable, based on the defence of free entrepreneurship, independent courts and a free media. On this basis, in Mitrokhin's words, 'a mass civil non-violent opposition to legal and social arbitrariness' could be organised.[57]

The SPS had campaigned on a leftist platform of social welfare, increased pensions and benefits, but the liberal parties failed to connect with the concerns of the Russian people. The political philosopher Boris Kapustin argues that various 'pseudo-explanations' (which mostly lie in exogenous factors), such as the repressive nature of the regime or the 'innate hostility of the Russian "cultural tradition" toward liberalism', could not explain the 'calamity' of organised liberalism's disappearance from the Russian political scene. This only obscured liberalism's own failings, which he identified as its inability to free itself from 'the burden of the Boris Yeltsin legacy – its unabashed neoliberalism – and confront the type of economic order expressed by the present regime's "authoritarian capitalism"'. The liberal opposition was good at articulating the faults of the regime but was unable to present 'an attractive and politically mobilizing ideology'. The death of Yeltsinite democracy passed unlamented, while Putin offered tangible benefits: 'political life is no longer insultingly grotesque, even though it has become boring . . . Order is by no means an ultimate political good, but it is an indispensable prerequisite of all political progress and is appreciated as such.'[58] On 17 December 2007, Belykh threatened to resign as party leader, a post he had held since 2005, arguing that his major 'strategic mistake' was that

supported by 75 of the 125 delegates, 24 voted for Reznik and 20 for Popov. Natalya Krainova, 'Yavlinsky Resigns as Yabloko Leader', *Moscow Times*, 23 June 2008.

[56] Sergei Mitrokhin, 'Izobretatel'nost' d'yavola', *Nezavisimaya gazeta*, 20 June 2008, p. 11.

[57] Report on the meeting of Yabloko's Political Committee, 26–27 September 2009, Viktor Khamraev, '"Yabloko" vozlozhila bol'shie nadezhdy na malye dela: Partiya prigotovilas' k nenasil'stvennoi bor'be s rezhimom', *Kommersant*, 28 September 2009, p. 3.

[58] Boris Kapustin, 'After Putin: How Russia's Liberalism Might Be Revived', *Europe's World*, No. 10, Autumn 2008, pp. 100–7.

the SPS had adopted its tough stance against the Kremlin 'too late'.[59] With less than 3 per cent of the vote, the 2005 election law stipulated that the party had to repay the free television airtime during the campaign, leaving it with debts of R159 million ($8 million) which had to be reimbursed within a year. Seven parties found themselves in this position, with Yabloko's debts even higher at R170 million.[60] Belykh finally resigned on 26 September 2008 amid tensions within the party between those seeking reconciliation with the Kremlin and those, like Belykh, who wished to continue independent opposition. The SPS was not forgiven its attacks on the Kremlin during the election, and when the party condemned Russia's incursion into Georgia during the five-day war of August 2008, it was relegated even further to the category of a 'fifth column'.[61] The godfather of the party, Chubais, was open about his desire to transform the party into a liberal pro-Kremlin organisation. At the same time, and probably not coincidentally, Chubais in late September was appointed head of Rosnano, having completed the transformation of the electricity industry. Gozman took over as interim leader on a platform of co-operation with the regime.

On 3 October plans were announced for the party to merge with the two small liberal groupings, Bogdanov's Democratic Party and Barshchevsky's Civil Force. All three parties would dissolve and create a new organisation. The aim of the new configuration was to attract 'an intelligentsia loyal to the Kremlin',[62] while at the same time filling the political vacuum in the liberal part of the political spectrum. On 15 November, against the advice of Nemtsov, SPS voted by 97–11 to disband, and the next day, with the two other bodies, joined the new party called Right Cause (Pravoe Delo), headed by Gozman, the journalist Georgi Bovt, and Boris Titov, the head of the business group Delovaya Rossiya.[63] Once again, as in 1999 when SPS had been created, the Kremlin sponsored the creation of a 'project' party, whose chances of entering the Duma in 2011 were high if support was maintained. Right Cause may well have been a Kremlin project, but it probably had sufficient policy independence to retain some programmatic character.

---

[59] David Nowak, 'SPS Leader Resigns over Duma Elections', *Moscow Times*, 18 December 2007, p. 3.

[60] Natalya Krainova, 'Duma Losers Scramble to Pay Debts', *Moscow Times*, 19 March 2008, p. 3.

[61] Zaleski, 'Partii pod snos', p. 28

[62] Jonas Bernstein, 'Chubais Reportedly Behind Kremlin Bid to Tame SPS', *EDM* 5, 186, 29 September 2008.

[63] Francesca Mereu, 'Liberals Form Party with State Support', *Moscow Times*, 17 November 2008.

Plans continued to unite the non-systemic opposition in a new movement called Solidarity, one of whose founders at a special congress in Khimki on 13 December 2008 was Nemtsov, together with Vladimir Milov, the former deputy energy minister.[64] Solidarity sought to exploit the 'opportunity of crisis' to gain ground.[65] When oil prices fell by two-thirds in 1985–6 (from $30 to $10 a barrel), the Soviet regime had been brought to its knees, and the opposition now envisaged a similar scenario. According to the political analyst Dmitry Oreshkin, the 'irreconcilable' stance adopted by Solidarity meant that it 'can come to power only when the vertical power structure, built by Putin, collapses', an eventuality that in his view was neither desirable nor likely.[66] This was a classic example of the 'Leninist liberalism' to which we have referred earlier. Belykh, however, now left the ranks of the opposition and accepted the post of governor of Kirov *oblast'*. Belykh had earlier served as deputy governor of Perm region in 2004–5 and thus had managerial experience. Facing criticism from his erstwhile colleagues, Belykh argued that 'I think that it is right and useful that there are people who think like us in the structures of power', and he praised liberals like Finance Minister Kudrin, Central Bank chief, Sergei Ignat'ev, and Federal Anti-Monopoly Service head, Igor Artem'ev (formerly of Yabloko).[67] The appointment demonstrated that the Medvedev administration would continue Putin's practice of co-opting liberals willing to work with the regime.

Gorbachev now teamed up with the billionaire Alexander Lebedev to launch what was provisionally called the Independent Democratic Party.[68] The two were already partners in supporting the independent newspaper, *Novaya gazeta*. The 'irreconcilable' opposition headed by Kasparov continued to condemn the regime, especially as the global financial meltdown worsened and began to affect the 'real' economy, accompanied by rising prices and unemployment. The 'other side' of the succession was the barely veiled contempt for Putin and the regime by the irreconcilable opposition, who increasingly adopted a dissident mentality and called for the overthrow of the system in its entirety.

---

[64] www.rusolidarnost.ru.
[65] Vladimir Milov, 'Can Russia's Opposition Rise to the Opportunity of Crisis?', RFE/RL, *Russia Report*, 30 December 2008.
[66] 13 December 2008 broadcast on Ekho Moskvy, in BBC Monitoring; reproduced in *JRL*, No. 226, 2008, Item 26.
[67] Nabi Abdullaev, 'From Kremlin Critic to Governor', *Moscow Times*, 10 December 2008.
[68] Conor Sweeney, 'Gorbachev to Form Independent Party with Russian Billionaire', *The Guardian*, 1 October 2008, p. 24.

Their arguments were reinforced by continued abuses of the electoral process. In the mayoral elections in Sochi on 26 April 2009, Nemtsov tested the strength of the liberal vote, and against innumerable instances of administrative pressure he won a respectable 13.5 per cent of the vote, against 77 per cent for the official UR candidate.[69] The local elections of 11 October 2009, held in seventy-five of Russia's eighty-three regions and entailing 6,696 different votes, were marked by the consolidation of UR's dominance and egregious cases of fraud. New convocations of deputies were elected to the Moscow City Duma, the Duma of Tula region and the State Assembly of the Republic of Mari-El. In Moscow, UR won a landslide victory, winning thirty-two of the thirty-five party-list seats with 66 per cent of the vote, while the CPRF was the only opposition party to cross the 7 per cent qualification barrier (with 13 per cent) and gained three seats, with the LDPR coming third with 6 per cent, Just Russia with 5 per cent and Yabloko, which had an active presence in the old City Duma, now failing to enter with just under 5 per cent of the vote. United Russia also won all seventeen of the single-mandate districts, with independent candidates facing major challenges to register. Turnout was only 35.02 per cent, up slightly from the 34.75 per cent four years earlier. In Tula, UR, JR and the CPRF entered the new regional parliament, while in Mari-El the LDPR entered instead of JR. In the municipal elections held in ten regional capital cities, UR won the day everywhere, winning between 50 and 75 per cent of the vote and 189 out of 235 mandates. In Derbent in Dagestan, one-third of the thirty-six polling stations did not open, intimidated by local security officials, while in the first mayoral elections in Grozny, the incumbent, Muslim Khuchiev, was re-elected with over 87 per cent of the vote on a turnout of 91.5 per cent. The main charge of fraud focused on the vote count rather than the use of the primitive method of forging ballot papers, with observers in the capital and elsewhere noting a wide variance between their calculations and the declared results.[70] Above all, as a Levada poll revealed, only a third of Muscovites believed that the Duma had any serious decision-making powers.[71]

---

[69] For details and analysis, see Robert W. Orttung, 'Can Russia's Opposition Liberals Come to Power?, *Russian Analytical Digest*, No. 60, 19 May 2009, pp. 2–5.

[70] Out of Moscow falsification was more prevalent but even here, as Mitrokhin himself witnessed (even his vote for himself failed to register in the count), it was certainly widespread, accompanied by 'the misuse of absentee ballots, the improper use of administrative resources and pressure on people to vote for United Russia'. Nikolaus von Twickel, 'Yabloko Leader's Vote Not Counted', *Moscow Times*, 19 October 2009.

[71] 'Moskvichi o vyborakh v Moskovskuyu gorodskuyu Dumu', 2 October 2009, www.levada.ru/press/2009100200.html.

In terms of both process and substance, the crisis of Russian democracy was palpable. Another Levada poll at that time found that only 4 per cent considered that democracy was firmly in place in Russia and 33 per cent considered that it partially existed, while 33 per cent thought that it had not yet taken root and 20 per cent thought that in recent times it had been decreasing.[72] Although the signals coming out of Medvedev's Kremlin was not to obstruct opposition parties, the fate of regional leaders depended on how UR fared at the ballot box. In 2008 Stavropol governor Alexander Chernogorov was dismissed after Just Russia beat United Russia in regional legislature elections, while in 2009 Murmansk governor Yury Yevdokimov lost his job after UR's candidate failed to become mayor of the city of Murmansk, and the head of the Nenets autonomous *okrug*, Valery Potapenko, was sacked after UR scored less than 49 per cent in regional elections. Not surprisingly, Luzhkov was gleeful when he surveyed his almost clean sweep in the city Duma election.[73] The two branches of the dual state now vividly came into contradiction, and the weak signals in favour of clean elections were trumped by the practices of the administrative regime, leading to popular alienation.

As Mitrokhin put it in the wake of the elections, 'Society has finally learned to live with the idea that absolutely nothing depends on it. It leaves the authority's hands untied. The recent election was rigged in the most outrageously arrogant manner.'[74] In response the CPRF, LDPR and JR opposition parliamentary deputies staged an unprecedented two-day walk-out in protest on 14–15 October 2009, and even Zhirinovsky became a passionate defender of democracy.[75] Just Russia in particular had reason to feel aggrieved, abandoned by its Kremlin sponsors who dropped the idea of creating a two-party system and instead plumped for a predominant one-party system (although with the limitations we have noted earlier). The egregiously farcical nature of this round of regional elections, which suggested that in all of 10-million-strong Moscow with a strong liberal voting record, support for only three independents, and Communists at that, could be found. This was clearly nonsense. The political juggernaut created by the administrative system rendered elections little more than a legitimating mechanism of the regime – but this now backfired and instead delegitimated the whole system.

[72] 'Predstavleniya rossiyan o demokratii', www.levada.ru/press/2009101501.html.
[73] Nabi Abdullaev, 'United Russia Win Raises a Dilemma', *Moscow Times*, 13 October 2009.
[74] Anatolii Stepovoi, '"We Are Wounded, Not Dead"', *Izvestiya*, 13 October 2009.
[75] Pavel Felgenhauer, 'Massive Vote-Rigging Exposed in Russia', *EDM* 6, 189, 15 October 2009.

Gorbachev was unequivocal in his condemnation, noting that if even parties with a long history of supporting the regime were protesting, then 'trust in the political institution of elections has been conclusively lost'. He went on to note that 'Elections have palpably turned into a mockery of the people and demonstrated a deep disrespect for their voices.' 'The party of power gained the result it wanted by discrediting political institutions and the very party itself.' There would in his view now be a return to non-parliamentary forms of struggle, since 'It is pointless to expect anything from this Duma', with a heightened role for the press.[76] Official para-constitutionalism would now be challenged by unofficial para-politics. The situation in the country was not pre-revolutionary, but the crisis of the existing political system was evident. The 1 March 2009 regional elections had been followed by the usual charges of fraud and administrative manipulation, with Mironov particularly bitter on behalf of JR. In response, Medvedev met with Churov and urged moderation in the use of administrative resources, and in August talked of 'ensuring greater competition' in the next regional elections.[77] In August 2009 the Kremlin had declared that 'new democratic times are beginning' in Russia and threatened to break UR's near monopoly.[78] In the event, even the last two remaining independent television channels, REN TV and St Petersburg Fifth Channel, risked being taken under state control. The gulf between Medvedev's promises of greater political pluralism and the reality of an increasingly controlled political system was widening. Various liberal statements had not been backed up by sustained political or personnel renewal. The question now was whether Medvedev had the desire or ability to renew Russia's political and economic system.

Legal nihilism in the open

The constitutional state is the source of normative and political renewal. The tension between the instrumental use of law and the normative principles inherent in the rule of law characterise the Russian polity, where the managerial impulses of the administrative regime were far from consolidated in a fully authoritarian system. The selective and politically inspired use of law in the Putin era was confirmed by Medvedev's recognition of 'legal nihilism'. On 20 May 2008, Medvedev

[76] Dmitrii Muratov, 'Mikhail Gorbachev: Na glazakh u vsekh vybory prevratili v nasmeshku nad lyud'mi', *Novaya gazeta*, No. 116, 19 October 2009.
[77] Afanasii Sborov, 'Otbiratel'noe pravo, *Kommersant-Vlast'*, No. 36, 14 September 2009, pp. 11–14.
[78] Conor Sweeney, 'Polls Show Russians Back Crisis Plan: Putin's Party', Reuters, 12 October 2009; in *JRL*, No. 187, 2009, Item 9.

called for an independent court system when he addressed a meeting with senior judges and legal officials in the Kremlin: '[Unjust] decisions, as we all know, do happen and come as a result of different kinds of pressure, like telephone calls and – it cannot be denied – offers of money.'[79] Both types of perversion of justice were in evidence at that time. In late 2006 Anton Ivanov, head of the Supreme Arbitration Court, shocked a meeting of judges when he declared that the Federal Tax Service (FSN) was pressuring judges. The FSN in that year managed to get a few judges dismissed who had been dealing with the tax affairs against TNK-BP.[80] The Just Russia State Duma deputy, Gennady Gudkov, argued that the corruption of the judicial system had provoked the sharp rise in the number of convictions, with cases 'often a symptom of raiding and competitive struggles, achieved with the help of the corrupt law enforcement apparatus'.[81] Gudkov was convinced that 'Clans, the so-called *siloviki* and liberals, will retain their position and continue their internecine warfare hidden from the public.'[82]

With the new leadership in place, the judiciary could at last now fight against its political subordination. Indeed, in his *Financial Times* interview on 25 March 2008, Medvedev stressed that 'The security services were not created in order to fight against each other but to follow their constitutional obligation to defend the social order.' In late April Bastrykin dismissed Dmitry Dovgy, the head of the SK's investigative administration who was leading the case against Bulbov, as well as against Storchak and three of his subordinates in the finance ministry, together with the case against Barsukov (Kumarin). Dovgy was accused of failing to fulfil his duties according to the law and for revealing confidential information, but informal reports suggest that his real offence was to reveal the pressure that his superiors had put on him to fabricate evidence against Storchak. For Ryabov, the case against Storchak was a form of pressure on Kudrin, the gatekeeper of stabilisation funds.[83] In October 2008, after a year of investigation, Storchak was released on bail and 'the TV channels showed his greeting by friends and

[79] www.kremlin.ru/text/appears/2008/05/201007.shtml.
[80] Olga Pleshanova, 'Sud vysshego dostoinstva', *Kommersant*, 13 May 2008.
[81] 'Kommentarii: Rabotu nado nachinat' nemedlenno', Newsru.com, 20 May 2008.
[82] Pavel Burmistrov, Dmitrii Velikovskii, Viktor Dyatlikovich, Vitalii Leibin, Mikhail Romanov, Ruslan Khestanov, Vladimir Shpak, 'Kapital prezidenta', *Russkii reporter*, No. 7 (37), 28 February–6 March 2008, pp. 20–6, at p. 22.
[83] Interview with Andrei Ryabov, *Novaya gazeta*, No. 26, 14 April 2008, p. 10. In the end Dovgy was charged with taking €750,000 in bribes and for exceeding his authority. 'Dmitriya Dovgiya ostavili v tyur'me', *Vremya novostei*, 10 February 2009, p. 3.

family as if a hero had returned from enemy captivity'.[84] Bulbov faced a very different fate, and on 31 October 2008 he was charged with thirty-five criminal acts, notably illegal phone-tapping and taking bribes worth $3.2 million.[85]

These cases had been bound up with succession struggles and had little to do with the genuine struggle against corruption. Medvedev returned to the theme on numerous occasions and tried to find ways to deliver, including the creation of an Anti-Corruption Council. Addressing the body's inaugural meeting on 30 September 2008, he likened corruption to a grave illness: 'I will repeat one simple, but very painful thing. Corruption in our country has become rampant. It has become commonplace and it characterises the life of Russian society.'[86] He outlined his 'National Plan Against Corruption', consisting of a new anti-corruption law and amendments to twenty-five existing laws that had earlier been submitted to parliament. The veteran corruption fighter at the head of the INDEM think tank, Satarov, was sceptical, noting that the plans failed to address corruption where it was most prevalent, among elected officials and law-enforcement bodies. The plan, he argued, 'is just another internal method to fight this society-wide contagion', and the measures would be useless in the absence of a free media, independent courts, transparent government and competitive politics.[87] In the event the new anti-corruption legislation was signed into law by Medvedev on 25 January 2009, although only after attempts by the Duma to postpone its implementation. Russia now at last had serious, if flawed, legislation against corruption, which in the context was quite an achievement, although preliminary results were meagre.[88] At the same time, the equivalent of a freedom of information act required officials to disclose, upon request, information controlled by the

[84] Pavel K. Baev, 'Qaddafi and Zyazikov: Reality Checks for Russia's Petro-Politics', *EDM* 5, 210, 3 November 2008. The fact that this was shown on the main channels is also significant and indicates the quiet resistance of the normative state against the arbitrariness of the prerogative state.
[85] Ekaterina Butorina, 'Tridtsat′ pyat′ prestuplenii generala', *Vremya novostei*, No. 204, 1 November 2008.
[86] Interfax, 30 September 2008. In April 2009 Storchak was finally charged with fraud 'in what was widely seen as a politically motivated vendetta'. Charles Clover, 'Dismissal Puts Spotlight on Kremlin Rivalry', *The Financial Times*, 22 December 2009.
[87] Georgy Satarov, 'Throw Anti-Graft Plan in the Trash Heap', *Moscow Times*, 15 October 2008.
[88] Transparency International's Corruption Perception Index published on 17 November 2009 saw Russia move up from 2.1 in 2008 to 2.2 in 2009, a marginal improvement which acknowledged the new legislation and attempts to fight corruption; however, Russia remained firmly in 146th place on a par with Zimbabwe and Sierra Leone.

government, such as budget expenditures, court rulings and government permits.[89] This was a considered step in the battle against 'legal nihilism'.

In an important signal that the new administration was serious about fighting corruption, on 12 May 2008 Anton Ivanov filed a request to have Lyudmila Maikova, the chair of the Federal Arbitration Court in the Moscow District, suspended from her duties for 'damaging the authority of the judicial branch and the reputation of the judiciary'. Ivanov charged that Maikova, who had presided over a number of legal disputes involving the city administration, received help from City Hall in 2004 to swap her own apartment for two others and to buy another from a developer at less than market price.[90] On the political front, on 27 May 2008 in its first major judgment in its new home in St Petersburg, the Constitutional Court dismissed the lawsuit against Manana Aslamazyan, the head of a media-related NGO that had earlier been funded by Open Russia, who was accused of smuggling foreign currency.[91]

The Boev affair in the early months of Medvedev's presidency demonstrated the way that law had been instrumentalised in the Putin years. Legal action was taken against the media commentator Vladimir Solovëv, a reporter for the Serebryannyi Dozhd' radio station, who had declared that 'There are no independent courts in Russia – there are courts dependent on Boev.'[92] As if to prove his point, the case against him was brought by Valery Boev, an adviser on personnel appointments in the former Putin administration, in particular dealing with the appointment of judges. Boev dropped the claim after three other judges declared that they were ready to testify against him.[93]

Soon after, Yelena Valyavina, since October 2005 first deputy chair of the Supreme Arbitration Court, testified that Boev had threatened to damage her career if she refused to reverse a ruling handed down on 22 November 2005 against the Federal Property Fund involving shares in Togliattiazot (Toaz), the country's biggest producer of ammonia. With a view to coercing her into acceding to his request, Boev warned her: 'Elena Yurievna, you still have to be re-appointed.'[94] In her evidence to

[89] Anna Malpas, 'Bill Gives People Right to Know', *Moscow Times*, 21 January 2009.
[90] Bruce Bean, 'Give Putin a Break', *Moscow Times*, 6 June 2008.
[91] 'Gadis Gadzhiev – Konstantinu Katanyanu', *The New Times*, No. 24, 16 June 2008, pp. 26–8.
[92] Olga Pleshanova, '"Sud vysshego dostoinstva"', *Kommersant*, 13 May 2008.
[93] *Ibid.*; Yevgeny Kiselëv, 'Cracks in Putin's Vertical Power Fortress', *Moscow Times*, 5 June 2008.
[94] Ekaterina Butorina, 'Independence War: Arbitration Courts Acknowledge Pressure from Executive Authorities', *Vremya novostei*, 21 May 2008.

Moscow's Dorogomilovsky District Court on 12 May 2008, she noted that she ran into Boev on a number of occasions when she took up her post, since as the deputy presiding judge she was responsible for co-operation with the Supreme Qualifications Board. In her judgment on the contentious case of Toaz shares sold in 1996 (a case which other judges tried to avoid), she ruled in favour of suspending provisional measures associated with the ban on holding general meetings. When Valyavina requested the case file, a call came from Boev, and then he came for a meeting. She was astonished at the way that the conversation turned out, anticipating a discussion of personnel issues. Instead, Boev 'spoke at length about state interests, adding that I was probably failing to understand them correctly'. She reminded him that she was the judge in the case and 'that he had no right to give me instructions'. He was asking her to annul her determination in this case. She told him that she was ready to work as an ordinary judge if she was not reappointed for another six-year term as a presiding judge. Boev continued to try to exert pressure on the court by visiting senior members.[95] It is unlikely that Boev was acting on his own initiative, which suggests that his actions were prompted by his superiors in the presidential administration.

Valyavina's declaration was considered 'unprecedented'. As one lawyer noted, 'For the first time at such a high level we heard how the presidential administration through its officials tries to influence high judicial proceedings.'[96] With the new leadership in place, the scale of political interference in judicial matters could at last be brought to light, and this was indeed a 'litmus test' for the rule of law.[97] A former judge of the Samara Region Arbitration Court, Nadczhda Kostuchenko, was dismissed from her post by the qualification board of judges in March 2006 after being accused of making 'illegal' judgments in the Toaz case. She had adjudicated that steps taken to confiscate a 6.1 per cent tranche of Toaz shares were illegal, as the stock no longer belonged to the defendant. There were persistent press reports that prior to the hearing she had been pressured by the chair of the court not to return a judgment in favour of Toaz.[98] Kostuchenko appealed against her dismissal to the ECtHR.

Medvedev's declarations against 'legal nihilism' encouraged more open discussion about political and allied business pressure against the courts, and at least brought the issue into the open. At the seventh

---

[95] Transcript of the Dorogomilovsky District Court session of 12 May 2008, mimeo.
[96] Pleshanova, 'Sud vysshego dostoinstva'.
[97] Editorial, 'A Litmus Test for the Rule of Law', *Moscow Times*, 7 June 2008, p. 10.
[98] Interfax, 24 June 2008.

all-Russian congress of judges in December 2008, Medvedev promised a whole range of reforms to humanise the judicial system, and by September of the following year a range of practical measures had been drafted to ensure that people were not kept in pre-trial detention without due cause.[99] As we saw in Chapter 1, a rise in cases handled by the civil courts suggested greater trust in judicial procedures. However, in high-profile cases achievements were minimal. The death in pre-trial detention of the lawyer Sergei Magnitsky, who had been caught up in the attack on William Browder's Hermitage Capital investment fund, on 16 November 2009, demonstrated just how little had changed. He had been denied adequate medical care, and the whole case against Hermitage Capital reflected the worst aspects of 'raiding' in which the courts were used to pursue group interests. Medvedev responded by sacking the head of the MVD's tax crimes department and demanded a full investigation. The case demonstrated that the dual system remained firmly entrenched in the judicial system, as it was in the state as a whole.

Modernisation from the middle

Medvedev's defence of the rule of law and freedom in his Krasnoyarsk and other speeches indicated that the trauma of the 1990s, when democracy had become a dirty word, was finally over. An editorial in *Ekspert* noted that 'Russia's choice in favour of democratisation, taken in the late 1980s and early 1990s, has been rehabilitated and reconfirmed.'[100] Russia under Medvedev entered a new stage of development. With the restorative agenda having been secured by Putin, the way was opened for a new wave of modernisation, including democratisation. As the editorial notes, while Putin was often criticised in the west for his 'authoritarianism', these criticisms fail to take into account a fundamental issue that an earlier generation of political scientists had well understood: 'There is no such thing as simply a "democracy" in the world; but there are "democratic states". It is impossible to build democracy without an effective state. Democracy without a state is like Iraq, where there is no state but elections are conducted.' [101] The stabilisation agenda under Putin had focused on state strengthening, whereas under Medvedev the modernisation agenda was more socially oriented. As Yurgens argued,

---

[99] Ivan Rodin and Aleksandra Samarina, 'Ugolovnyi kodeks podvergnut liberalizatsii', *Nezavismaya gazeta*, 30 September 2009, p. 3.
[100] 'Luchshe, chem nesvoboda', *Ekspert*, No. 8, 25 February 2008, p. 19.
[101] *Ibid.*

any programme of complex modernisation could not be achieved by state action alone. This was not only because the state machine itself was ineffective, but because it also required initiative and innovation by individual citizens and society as a whole.[102] Indeed, Yurgens and his INSOR associates went so far as to argue that the Medvedev modernisers had to create an alternative 'power vertical' to operate in parallel to the entrenched Putin elites.[103]

Putin's power base lay in the administrative system, but this was precisely where the greatest problems in terms of corruption and bureaucratism lay – hence in trying to deal with the latter pathologies, Medvedev would find himself implicitly attacking Putin. State strengthening under Putin had taken on authoritarian aspects, assuming the form of regime strengthening at the expense of democracy, but this was only part of the story. As far as Putin was concerned, the exercise of state power was the essential prerequisite for modernisation. This tension reflected the bivalency of the dual state: conforming to the constitutional order, but managing the political arena through para-constitutional and para-political processes shaped and manipulated by the administrative regime. The potential for further democratic development, however, was facilitated by the very act of state strengthening, even if the restoration of the state took a perverse form and was distorted by the incubus of the administrative regime. Now the modernisation agenda shifted the focus to the development of human capital, the rule of law, the struggle against corruption, and above all fighting the excesses of bureaucratic regulation and state intervention. Shuvalov, at an investment conference in Moscow, called for higher standards of corporate governance at both state-owned and private companies,[104] and at the St Petersburg Economic Forum soon after (see below), he called for 'limits on the state's damaging interference in the economy', which could not but be an implicit criticism of Putin's administration. With the focus now on the four 'I's – institutions, investment, innovation and infrastructure – Medvedev's reforms began to transcend the limits of 'Putin's plan'.

The motor of modernisation under Yeltsin, as it had been under Alexander II, was the liberal bureaucracy. In Putin's second phase this force had taken a *silovik* inflection, but there was no other agency on

---

[102] Igor' Yurgens, *Ocherednye zadachi Rossiiskoi vlasti* (Moscow: Rosspen, 2009), pp. 43–4.
[103] The report was called 'The Modernisation of Russia as the Construction of a New State', reported by Elina Bilevskaya and Aleksandra Samarina, 'Modernizatsiya kak predlog', *Nezavisimaya gazeta*, 30 October 2009, p. 1.
[104] Paul Goncharoff, 'Bringing Trust into Russia's Business Culture', *Moscow Times*, 7 June 2008, p. 11.

which Medvedev could rely.[105] The authoritarian elements of the Putinite reconstitution could be overcome only by the implementation of the Krasnoyarsk agenda, including the development of genuinely free courts, the completion of administrative reform to transform officialdom from a Soviet-style bureaucracy into a real civil service, accompanied by genuine decentralisation of powers to regional federal authorities and the transfer of certain functions to non-state agencies. In the event, despite much talk of a reform agenda, the shift from restoration to modernisation was impeded by the systemic stalemate.

The dilemmas of Russia's developmental path were aired at the twelfth St Petersburg Economic Forum on 6–8 June 2008, just weeks before the economic storm hit Russia. Medvedev noted 'how illusory it is to suppose that a single country, even if it is the most powerful, can assume the role of global government' and stressed the gap between the formal role played by the United States in the world economic system and its actual capabilities. He observed that major financial companies 'underestimated risk and the aggressive fiscal policies in the world's largest economy', and criticised the existing system of institutions of international governance while calling for a reform of the global financial structure. Russia would play its full part in this, he insisted, and he proposed an international conference to discuss a new architecture of international financial governance.[106] In his speech, Shuvalov provided a robust defence of property rights, arguing that their protection was the state's central task and that the government would be judged on how effectively it fulfilled this role. He stressed that the government should 'limit the injurious meddling of the state in the economy'. He announced that the number of partially state-owned strategic enterprises (in which foreign investment was prohibited) would be reduced, although some new state corporations could be created in sectors where market mechanisms were unable to function effectively. Their operation, he stressed, would have to be absolutely transparent, a feature not noted hitherto. He repeated the promise to replace federal officials on the boards of state-owned 'national champions' with independent directors. He boasted that Russia could become the world's sixth largest economy by the end of 2008.[107] Since commodities make up 85 per cent of Russian exports, even if in purely numerical terms Russia rises up the league table, its lack

---

[105] Maksim Rubchenko and Nikolai Silaev, 'Zayavka kandidata', *Ekspert*, No. 8, 25 February 2008, pp. 21–5, at p. 22.
[106] 'Vystuplenie na XII Peterburgskom mezhdunarodnom ekonomicheskom forume', 7 June 2008, www.kremlin.ru/text/appears/2008/06/ 202221.shtml.
[107] Igor Tomberg, 'XII St. Petersburg Economic Forum', *Essays & Analyses* 15, Moscow, June 2008, p. 11; Alexander Osipovich, 'Investors Back Call for Eased State Role',

of diversification makes it very much a one-dimensional international economic player.

Medvedev's pitch for Russia to become a new international economic and political centre identified undoubted failings in the existing order, but the financial crisis from autumn 2008 mercilessly revealed not only global inadequacies but also Russia's. Having since 1999 enjoyed nine consecutive years of economic growth averaging an annual 7 per cent, with healthy budget surpluses accompanied by a sharp rise in real incomes together with the accumulation of some $590 billion in hard currency reserves, Russia's leaders were lulled into a sense of complacency, reflected in their view that the country would be insulated from the crisis besetting western Europe and America. In the event, Russia's economy proved extremely vulnerable. The price of oil fell precipitously from the peak of $147.27 a barrel on 11 July to $47.36 on 2 December 2008.[108] With oil and gas rents comprising one-fifth of Russia's GDP and 50 per cent of federal budget revenues, the government's budget projections were in disarray. Facing a $150 billion shortfall in its spending plans, the state budget in 2009 had a 3–4 per cent deficit. Stock values fell by some 70 per cent in 2008, accompanied by a 25–30 per cent fall in the value of the rouble. By November 2008 the Central Bank had spent $57.5 billion propping up the rouble as the government vacillated between defending the currency and allowing its devaluation, while over $200 billion was committed to boost liquidity. The idea of the rouble becoming a reserve currency was exposed for the bombast that it was. The rouble had only achieved full convertibility in July 2006, and the Russian economy comprised no more than 2.5 per cent of global GDP. Moreover, quite apart from corruption and poor competitiveness, it lacked the macroeconomic stability, financial depth (Russia's banking system was notoriously undeveloped, with a minuscule bond market) and secure property rights, the rule of law and a robust regulatory framework that are essential for any bid for global economic leadership to be taken seriously.[109] The exogenous shock of the crisis in a sense proved salutary in exposing the endogenous weakness of Russia's financial structures and economic system as a whole.

Moscow Times, 10 June 2008, pp. 1, 2; Editorial, 'Put the Brakes on Russian Technologies, *Moscow Times*, 10 June 2008, p. 10.

[108] Javier Blass and Chis Flood, 'Oil Prices Hit 3.5-Year Lows on Concerns over OPEC Output Levels', *The Financial Times*, 3 December 2008, p. 15. In early 2009 prices bumped along at around $40 a barrel, before starting to rise again from mid-year.

[109] Anders Åslund, 'The Ruble as a Reserve Currency? No!', *Moscow Times*, 23 September 2009.

Russia had long suffered from a serious lack of investment credits, prompting companies to enter international financial markets. Russia's reserves were basically intermediated through G7 banks back to Russia's real economy. Even Russian sovereign savings derived from the taxation of windfall energy revenues (which had greatly increased as a result of the Yukos affair) were invested abroad and then intermediated back into the domestic corporate sector through western financial institutions. The external indebtedness of Russia's major corporations had reached some $275 billion by May 2007, with refinancing costs in 2008 alone estimated at $111 billion.[110] By June 2008 Russia's total external debt was $527 billion, while its reserves by November were down to $475 billion.[111] Rosneft and Gazprom alone had wracked up corporate debts of $90 billion, much of which was short-term, while the rest comprised debts accumulated by private 'oligarchic' businesses. Loss of confidence led to sharp falls in market capitalisation, provoking 'margin calls' for debts to be repaid since the collateral had lost value. The government provided $50 billion for the refinancing of foreign debts, but this was little more than a short-term palliative. Liquidity was also pumped into the system to prop up the banking sector, but access to the credit lines was opaque and prompted Standard & Poor's to reduce Russia's sovereign credit rating from 'stable' to 'negative' in late October 2008. Inflation in 2008 reached 13.3 per cent, instead of the anticipated 8.5 per cent. The response in Russia, as elsewhere, was more government intervention.

The financial crisis had profound effects on the 'real economy', with cuts in wages, stagnant real gains in living standards and rising unemployment, raising the prospect of a growth in industrial militancy. In response, on 25 December 2008 the government approved a list of 295 companies of strategic importance that could apply for financial assistance from a specially designated fund of some $200 billion, designed to reduce the social and economic consequences of the crisis. The state-owned VEB (whose board is chaired by Putin) purchased shares to support the stock market and a range of measures were introduced to support the banking sector, with over a dozen saved from collapse, although only five were nationalised. VEB managed the $50 million fund to help enterprises refinance their debts to foreign creditors. Enormous sums were expended to allow a gradual devaluation of the

---

[110] Dmitrii Dokuchaev and Dmitrii Krylov, 'Indeks RTS', *The New Times*, 8 September 2008, p. 33.

[111] 'The Long Arm of the State', in 'Enigma Variations', Special Report on Russia, *The Economist*, 29 November 2008, p. 7.

rouble, which had fallen more than 50 per cent against the dollar by early 2009 compared to its value in July 2008. These and other measures allowed a stabilisation of the economic system while preventing a collapse of the 1998 type. The crisis, moreover, while certainly exacerbating factional conflict, did not in the end fundamentally shift the balance between the two pillars of the dual state.[112] In that sense, the opportunity offered by the crisis was wasted.[113]

There were also coercive measures. The administration's heavy-handed response to protests, including the brutal suppression of protest actions (against a rise in imported vehicle tariffs) in Vladivostok on 21 December 2008, revealed its fears that the economic crisis could be exploited by an outsider group to mobilise public discontent to launch an orange-style assault on the system. Planned cuts to MVD internal troops were abruptly halted on 16 December, although cuts in the regular army continued. The middle class had acquiesced in the government's heavy-handed paternalism when times were good, but they could now turn against the regime. The possibility of increased labour activism prompted Yevgeny Gontmakher, a member of the board and a leading researcher at INSOR and the deputy director of the Institute of International Economy and International Relations (IMEMO), to refer to the events in Novocherkassk on 1–2 June 1962, when workers' protests were crushed by the army with the loss of twenty-three lives and dozens imprisoned. For many Russia's difficulties amounted to something more than just a crisis, but something 'immeasurably worse'.[114]

The events in Pikalevo, one of Russia's 460 company towns, or 'monotowns', where a single enterprise provides not only most of the jobs but also social services, made evident the social impact of the crisis. Pikalevo's population grew desperate six months after the shutdown of the town's cement plant, and finally on 2–4 June 2009 the residents

---

[112] The political analyst Dmitry Oreshkin argued that 'Putin used to act as arbiter standing above the two main clans – the siloviki and the rational economists. ... Now he has been dragged down into the fight and he's under fire from both sides.' Quoted by Tom Parfitt, 'Putin and Medvedev Factions Locked in Kremlin Financial Power Struggle', *The Guardian*, 3 March 2009, p. 15. In the event this analysis proved to be premature.

[113] As the economist Paul Romer is famous for arguing, 'A crisis is a terrible thing to waste.'

[114] Yuri Zarakhovich, 'Mismanagement of Russian Economy Could Lead to Social Unrest', *EDM* 5, 228, 1 December 2008. The article by Gontmakher was called 'Novocherkassk 2009', published in *Vedomosti* on 6 November 2008. The Federal Mass Media Inspection service later warned Gontmakher that the publication 'could be considered an attempt to incite extremist activities', although an official from Putin's White House telephoned the author on the day the article was published thanking him for raising an important issue. Yevgeny Gontmakher, 'When Writing About the Crisis is Extremism', *Moscow Times*, 17 December 2008.

blocked the main road and thus gained the attention of the federal authorities. In what was obviously a public relations stunt, Putin flew in by helicopter and forced the plant's owner, Oleg Deripaska (the head of what had become a heavily indebted Basic Element), to sign a pledge to reopen the plant.[115] The episode raised some fundamental issues about the nature of Russian capitalism. No one was threatening Deripaska's property, yet it was not clear what he and his fellow oligarchs had done with the billions loaned from state-controlled banks to help cover their debts. Between 2005 and 2008 he had paid himself dividends of $8.2 billion.

A controversial report in August 2009 called *Post-Pikalevo Russia: The New Political and Social Reality* argued that in autumn 2008, at the peak of the crisis, Russia's magnates doubled the amount of cash flow diverted offshore while at the same time demanding assistance from the government.[116] They threatened that otherwise their employees would suffer, threatening social stability and even the existence of the administration. The authors recommended resolute measures, including a review of how the oligarchic enterprises had been able to extort assistance in late 2008, the nationalisation of companies unable to meet their debt obligations to the state accompanied by the restructuring into government bonds of their foreign liabilities. The aim was to turn post-Pikalevo Russia into a post-oligarch country. The oligarchs of the 2000s were very different from those of the 1990s: no longer imposing their will on the state but acting on behalf of the state. Private oligarchs (Roman Abramovich, Oleg Deripaska, Victor Vekselberg, Alisher Usmanov and many more) had now been joined by powerful quasi-state oligarchs acting on behalf of the state (Sergei Bogdanchikov, Alexei Miller, Sergei Chemezov). The whole 'oligarch' class behaved like temporary bosses, holding their main assets abroad. The majority of Basic Element's enterprises were registered in Jersey, while the company's main affiliate was registered in the British Virgin Islands. The report provides data on the extensive 'offshorisation' of the Russian economy, with the flight to register abroad in part a response to the dangers of 'raiders' at home. The credit history of these companies is no less astonishing. Between January 2002 and June 2009, their foreign debts rose by 12.3 times, from $23.9 to $294.4 billion. At the same time, they neglected the

---

[115] Leon Aron, *Russia's "Monotowns" Time Bomb* (Washington, DC: American Enterprise Institute, 2009), p. 2.

[116] Nikita Krichevskii, *Postpikalevskaya Rosiiya: Novaya politico-ekonomicheskaya real'nost'*, with Vladislav Inozemtsev (Moscow: no publisher, 2009); www.krichevsky.ru/images/book/doklad.pdf.

needs of their workers, and at the first test at Pikalevo the state had capitulated.[117] Thus, in the Putin years, Russian capitalism had developed a dualism of its own: an offshore leg and a national capitalist one; but both formed part of a corporate order characterised by a mutual dependency between the state and business. The ensuing conservative mentality, in which elites sought to defend their entrenched interests, hardly provided a dynamic foundation for developmental projects.

The modernisation idea, however, remained central to Medvedev's presidency and generated precisely the reflection that is inherent in our definition of 'crisis'. Medvedev repeatedly argued that the Russian economy had no future unless its structure was changed, above all by reducing its dependence on the raw materials sector.[118] Iosif Diskin, for example, subjected Russian economic development to a devastating critique, and at the same time located his discussion firmly in the context of international trends. The economic crisis from 2008, in his view, had exposed the weakness of Russian institutional development in the Putin era, although it marked an improvement on the 'oligarch-organised chaos' that it replaced.[119] The notion of 'globalisation' and its neoliberal postulates was now overshadowed, in his view, by the need to forge a strategy for the 'national-democratic' modernisation of Russia, which included consideration of the ethical bases of modern capitalism and political coherence as much as any more narrowly economic agenda.[120] Diskin's work falls into the mainstream of what had become the 'Moscow consensus' of economic thinking: the need for a competitive economy integrated into world markets and processes, but reflecting the long tradition from Emile Durkheim onwards of 'embedding' the economy into an ethical socio-political system responsive to national peculiarities. This was a reprise of the 'embedded capitalism' tradition that in Russia, as in Germany earlier, assumed an 'ordo-liberal' inflection, a trend that assumed new life as a result of the manifest crisis of Anglo-American neo-liberal capitalism from 2008.

The 2000s had represented a period of stability after the crisis of the late 1990s, and as a sociological analysis by the Institute of Sociology demonstrated, the population's concerns turned to more humdrum issues, but the economic crisis from 2008 marked a turning point in which old forms of state organisation and economic management

---

[117] The report is summarised by Nikita Krichevskii and Vladislav Inozemtsev, 'Besperspektivnye proekty', *Vedomosti*, 17 and 20 August 2009.
[118] For example, 'Present Structure of the Russian Economy Has No Future', Itar-Tass, 10 August 2009.
[119] Iosif Diskin, *Krizis ... i vsë zhe modernizatsiya!* (Moscow: Evropa, 2009), p. 162.
[120] *Ibid.*, pp. 169–86 and *passim*.

exhausted their potential and the demand for radical change once again began to rise.[121] According to Diskin, a 'new Russia' had emerged out of the ashes of the Soviet system with new concerns and enhanced expectations for the future.[122] This was part of the truth, especially in the major cities, but the Institute of Sociology study found that the majority still lived within the framework of traditional precepts.[123] Even in conditions of crisis, protest behaviour was considered a last resort when all other legal mechanisms had failed.[124] A new generation had emerged who expected little from the authorities and relied on themselves;[125] and at the same time their interest in social and political life was low, as was the demand for legal forms of political participation.[126] A national consensus had been established around the key principles of 'Putin's plan' (a strengthened state, establishing order, restoration of the basic principles of social justice, and an increased role for Russia in world affairs), and Medvedev was expected to operate within this framework.[127] The 'Putin course' endowed the country with a certain reserve of stability, with a degree of social optimism, but the crisis from 2008 provoked calls not for radical change but for ameliorative improvements to the existing system. This was the Medvedev agenda.

It was clear that the economic good fortune that had accompanied Putin's presidency now gave way to what would be a prolonged crisis that threatened the stability that had been trumpeted for so long as the main achievement of the 2000s. As an editorial in *Ekspert* put it, however, 'Crises are an essential part of living systems' that, however painful, should be used to improve effectiveness since 'they reveal how the economy really works'.[128] As I have argued in this book, these strictures apply not just to the economy. The crisis now meant that Russia's ambitious economic modernisation plans accompanied by assertive foreign-policy rhetoric would have to be scaled back. Exaggerated ambitions and expectations were the first casualties of the global financial crisis, and in that sense proved salutary.[129] The crisis could also have a positive effect in international affairs, since as Lukyanov, the editor of

[121] M. K. Gorshkov, R. Krumm and V. V. Petukhov (eds.), *Rossiya na novom perelome: Strakhi i trevogi*, Friedrich Ebert Foundation and RAN Institute of Sociology (Moscow: Al'fa-M, 2009).
[122] I. E. Diskin, *Revolyutsiya protiv svobody: Sbornik* (Moscow: Evropa, 2007), p. 224.
[123] Gorshkov *et al.* (eds.), *Rossiya na novom perelome*, p. 12.
[124] *Ibid.*, p. 27.   [125] *Ibid.*, p. 28.   [126] *Ibid.*, p. 29.   [127] *Ibid.*, p. 69.
[128] 'S krizisom vas!', *Ekspert*, No. 1, 29 December 2008, p. 38.
[129] For an examination of the relationship between great power ambitions and energy prices, see William Zimmerman, 'Russian National Interests, Use of Blood and Treasure, and Energy Price Assessments: 2008–2009', *Post-Soviet Affairs* 25, 3, 2009, pp. 185–208.

Russia in Global Affairs, argued, 'All of the institutions that are called upon to deal with this have their roots back in the era of the Cold War. That is, they were created for an entirely different reality.'[130] In domestic politics the balance between liberal-technocrats and the *siloviki* was threatened, with the latter encouraged to enhance the role of state corporations by consolidating the energy sector in government hands while strengthening the barriers to foreign competition.

Integrating the two states

Putin's eight years as president had been accompanied by the consolidation of a dual system. To the formal constitutional order, a number of para-constitutional accretions were added. We described the dual state in Chapter 1. All sorts of informal processes, ranging from an opaque system of regional transfers, the use of *kompromat* and the development of 'Basmanny' justice (as in the Yukos affair), ensured the loyalty of the bureaucracy, the subordination of business leaders and elite groups and the quiescence of the population. The election of a new president offered the opportunity for systemic renewal, but with Putin installed as premier, Medvedev's room for manoeuvre was severely circumscribed. As Andrei Piontkovsky acidly observes, it is as if Khrushchev delivered his 'secret speech' to the Twentieth Party Congress in 1956 with Stalin sitting in the front row.[131] An administrative regime-based model of economic modernisation came into conflict with a broader programme for the renewal of Russian democracy. A covert duel now began between the two leaders. Winning the election was the easy part; the new president would have to test his strength within the framework of the balance of power within the dual state and the tandem.

Following Medvedev's election there was much talk of a new 'thaw' (*ottepel'*), concerned primarily with domestic politics of the sort that had followed Stalin's death in 1953. The analogy is far-fetched, since the political situation in Russia after Putin's two terms was very unlike the one that followed three decades of Stalin's dictatorship. Yet the notion of a thaw does reflect the aspirations of a new modernising coalition, the end of the manual control over political processes, greater pluralism in the media and politics, and the release of a new generation of what could be called 'political prisoners': Khodorkovsky and his associates,

---

[130] Fedor Lukyanov, 'Financial Crisis May Benefit Russia', Gazeta.ru, 23 October 2008; in *JRL*, No. 195, 2008, Item 11.
[131] Evgeniya Albats, Il'ya Barabanov and Lyubov Tsukanova, 'Piontkovskii protiv Pavlovskii', *New Times*, 28 September 2009; http://newtimes.ru.

Igor Sutyagin, jailed for allegedly passing secret material to the United States and China, and many others. Milov noted that 'Medvedev undoubtedly has the option of liberalising the political and economic sphere as one way of quickly making his mark. He can gain political authority if he starts really to free the country. But for him and those who stand behind him, open competition entails serious risks.'[132] The notion of 'liberal' in the Russian context is a relative term. For Medvedev it certainly did not mean giving up the drive to assert Russia's status in the world or to manage a developmental project that would transform Russia into a modern state. Under Medvedev sovereignty would be defended, although the notion of sovereign democracy was dropped. There would be greater emphasis on property rights, the rule of law, seeking consensus in international politics (but not at the expense of Russia's perceived interests), and greater pluralism in the public sphere. There would be continuity in foreign policy, while legal processes would not be bypassed to allow the release of Khodorkovsky or anyone else.[133] To have done so, from Medvedev's perspective, would have been to perpetuate, although in reverse, the legal nihilism that he condemned during the election campaign.

Medvedev came to power as Putin's nominated successor, and this clearly placed him in a position of dependency vis-à-vis his patron and by the same token reduced his sense of obligation to the electorate. However, Putin had also come to power as the nominee of the Yeltsinites, but soon established his independence. The situation, of course, had changed, and the elements of the dual state had become more clearly delineated. Medvedev was the outcome of both a public contest and a shadow war, and thus he was beholden to both the constitutional state and the administrative regime. In the Putin years, power had fused ever more with the bureaucratic class and its associated factionalism, thus the challenge facing Medvedev to establish his own political identity was greater than that faced by Putin eight years earlier, leaving aside Putin's continuing popularity and active engagement in politics. No less significant was the fact that both Putin and Medvedev reflected an underlying 'Putin consensus'. Thus as a study by the European Council on Foreign Relations (ECFR) stressed, '[F]raming the competition of ideas solely as an opposition between supporters of democracy and the forces of authoritarianism masks a far more complex reality.'[134] The Putin

---

[132] *Novaya gazeta*, No. 15, 3 March 2008, p. 10.
[133] 'Press-konferentsiya po okonchanii rossiisko-germanskikh peregovorov', Berlin, 5 June 2008, www.kremlin.ru/text/appears/2008/06/ 202120.shtml#.
[134] 'Introduction' by the editors, in Mark Leonard, Ivan Krastev and Andrew Wilson (eds.), *What Does Russia Think?* (London: ECFR, 2009), p. 2.

consensus, supported by some 70 per cent of the population, had been forged through the experience of Soviet collapse, the difficult 1990s and the recovery of the 2000s.[135] Medvedev's support was in a sense on loan from Putin, but once in office his standing in popularity polls quickly rose to exceed 70 per cent, a trend reinforced by what was seen as his effective handling of the Georgian war and its aftermath. Medvedev already had the embryo of his own team, with seventeen full-time staffers working for him by mid-2007, and this was now extended and formalised. Talk of Putin being the puppet-master was ill-placed, and the idea of a simple control model was fundamentally misconceived. Although Putin's nominal superior, in fact Medvedev allowed Putin to act as his guide, and thus the relationship was balanced as a trade-off between formal powers and informal respect. The relationship reproduced in new forms Putin's relationship in the 1990s with his boss, Sobchak, whom Putin described as 'a friend and mentor to me'.[136] The transfer of power to a trusted successor preserved the status quo, but it did so in new ways. Not only was Medvedev's political personality different from Putin's, but the operation of a power tandem was unprecedented in Russian politics.

In his Federal Assembly address of 5 November 2008, Medvedev outlined a programme for Russia's development accompanied by a critique of the state-bureaucratic system. The speech wove a careful balance between liberal and *silovik* positions, reflecting the continued systemic stalemate.[137] The bulk of the speech was devoted to a cautious modernisation of Russian political space, with twelve specific proposals to modify the political system, but commentary focused on his proposal to extend the presidential term to six years and parliament's to five years, to apply after the current terms ended.[138] Golosov, for example, argued that the proposal was about 'the minimisation of risk … As empty as elections are in contemporary Russia, they are still risky for

[135] Vyacheslav Glazychev, 'The "Putin Consensus" Explained', in Leonard *et al.* (eds), *What Does Russia Think?*, pp. 9–13.
[136] Samuel Charap, 'The Petersburg Experience: Putin's Political Career and Russian Foreign Policy', *Problems of Post-Communism* 51, 1, January–February 2004, p. 59.
[137] Dmitry Kamyshev and Sergei Minaev argue that Medvedev had no choice but to maintain the balance between these two factions, a fact which determined the structure of the speech. 'Zheleznaya ottepel'', *Kommersant-Vlast'*, No. 44, 10 November 2008, pp. 14–16.
[138] It appears that in 2007 Surkov had drafted a plan to extend the presidential term to six years, including the election of a successor who would push through all the necessary constitutional amendments, paving the way for Putin to return to the Kremlin for a new six-year term. However, Putin decided that 'changing the constitution in the interests of the incumbent president would not be "ethical"', Dmitry Babich, 'One Step Forward, Two Steps Back', *Russia Profile* 5, 10, p. 7.

power-holders.'[139] The inherent risks in holding elections, however well managed, could be reduced by holding them less frequently. This may well have been a factor, but it was also a way of ensuring a gap between parliamentary and presidential elections, the issue raised by Putin in the cabinet meeting of 3 December on the morrow of the 2007 Duma elections. The changes required amendments, and thus the taboo on changing the constitution was finally broken fifteen years after its adoption.[140]

In his speech, Medvedev promised to reduce the number of signatures that parties have to collect to run in regional legislatures, but the proposal had a sting in its tail since money deposits would no longer be allowed as a substitute for signatures. Medvedev also talked of ensuring access to the media for Duma factions and of changing the way that the Federation Council is formed, to be selected from people elected to regional assemblies and local government bodies. Medvedev quoted Petr Stolypin's famous formulation: 'First the citizen, then citizenship'; although he noted, 'But in our country we usually have the opposite.' In other words, the development of a civic sphere would allow the development of an engaged public based on free and responsible citizens. This was an implicit admission that civil society was stymied and the exercise of civic rights constrained. It was not, however, a repudiation of Putin's great power statist liberalism, and thus the continuity with others in that tradition, notably Witte and Stolypin, was reaffirmed. Most of Medvedev's concrete proposals were in due course adopted, including the requirement for the government to provide an annual report to parliament (although without a compulsory vote of confidence), that the nomination of regional governors be linked to electoral success, that procedures to dismiss mayors be simplified, that financial deposits be abolished[141] and that the number of signatures required for a political party to participate in elections be reduced. A number of other measures were also introduced to make it easier for parties to run for office. From 1 July 2009, the new system required the majority party in a regional parliament to propose three candidates for the post of governor,

---

[139] Grigory V. Golosov, reported in Luke Harding, 'Critics Alarmed as Medvedev Reveals Plan to Extend Russian Presidential Term to Six Years', *The Guardian*, 6 November 2008, p. 26.
[140] The requisite legislation was rushed through the Federal Assembly within three weeks in November, ratified by the eighty-three regional legislatures within a month and signed into law by Medvedev on 30 December 2008.
[141] On 23 January 2009, the Duma voted to abolish monetary bond requirements for federal, regional and local elections. As Vladimir Ryzhkov pointed out, it was hard for electoral commissions to refuse registration if the monetary bond had been paid, whereas it was much easier to claim that over 5 per cent of signatures were invalid. 'Medvedev the Sham Liberal', *Moscow Times*, 3 February 2009.

and the president then has thirty days to approve one of the candidates or to ask for three more nominations, and the nominee then has to be approved by the regional legislature. Medvedev also pushed through legislation that one or two representatives of parties that received between 5 and 7 per cent of the vote would be allowed into parliament. This at best was a half measure, and the restoration of the old 5 per cent threshold would allow parties winning 5–7 per cent of the vote to form a group of some twenty-three to twenty-five deputies, with some real impact in parliament.

The dualism in Medvedev's political personality, combining both hawk and liberal, was in evidence in his foreign-policy statements. Medvedev's declaration on deploying nuclear missiles in Kaliningrad to 'neutralise' the installation of a BMD system on the very day that Barack Obama was declared the forty-fourth president of the United States was a clear indication that Russia had little faith in an imminent improvement in Russo-American relations. Indeed, Medvedev lambasted the United States for its 'arrogant course' and 'unilateralism', insisting that Russia had to respond to the security challenge posed by the United States and NATO expansion to Russia's borders: 'These are forced measures ... We have told our partners more than once that we want positive cooperation ... but unfortunately, they do not want to listen.'[142] Overall the speech disappointed those who had, rather unrealistically, anticipated a Khrushchev-style 'secret speech' condemning his predecessor, or even overt manifestations of a thaw; but at the same time, while continuity was reaffirmed, there were powerful indications of a desire for change.

In a series of increasingly bold steps, Medvedev began to project a political personality of his own. In early 2009 he established a Commission for Modernisation, another para-constitutional innovation created to coordinate actions to push through his modernisation plans. On 29 January 2009, he met with the editor of *Novaya gazeta*, Dmitry Muratov, and its part-proprietor, Gorbachev, in a public act of sympathy following the murder of the human rights lawyer Stanislav Markelov and the paper's freelance correspondent Anastasia Baburova on 19 January. In that month he instructed his staff to rework a controversial bill that broadened the definition of treason and espionage, which had attracted fierce criticism, to ensure that it did not violate human rights.[143] On

---

[142] 'Poslanie Federal'nomu Sobraniyu Rossiiskoi Federatsii', 5 November 2008, www. kremlin.ru/text/appears/2008/11/208749.shtml.

[143] Brian Whitmore, 'Medvedev Scuttles Putin's Espionage Law', *Russia Report*, 28 January 2009.

15 April 2009, he granted an exclusive interview with *Novaya gazeta*, which he recognised as a paper that did not 'lick up' to anyone.[144] The interview did not move beyond generalities, although Medvedev rejected the idea that 'democracy' needed to be rehabilitated in Russia, but the choice of forum signalled a commitment to political diversity. Asked about the second Khodorkovsky trial, the president insisted that he had no right to comment on the case or to predict its outcome, given the independence of Russia's judicial system. He also defended the principle of the president remaining 'non-party' in the medium term since Russia's 'political system is not yet developed'. His fundamental point was that any idea of a new 'social contract' in which people gave up democracy in exchange for prosperity was unacceptable, and he promised Russia both.

Medvedev was becoming more than a figurehead, a fact recognised by a poll in May 2009 in which 41 per cent believed that power was shared equally between the two.[145] On 14 April he visited INSOR, established as a think tank to prepare for his presidency but now focused on engaging 'the world's leading academics, corporate and government leaders in open and candid dialogue on practical ways of creating a modern Russian society'.[146] INSOR was reformed in March 2008 when Medvedev took over at the head of its board of trustees, but Yurgens remained its executive head, who as deputy director of RUIE brought the business lobby behind Medvedev's leadership. One of INSOR's first reports, entitled 'Democracy: Developing the Russian Model', criticised Russia's political system, notably the lamentable condition of Russia's political parties, a weak and servile parliament, limits on party competition, excessive hierarchical centralisation and an electoral system that delivered neither free nor fair elections. Russia had focused more on modernisation than democratisation, which froze institution-building and restricted pluralism, but the 'hands-on' style of political management, in the report's view, had exhausted its potential. While a strongly presidential system should be retained, the country needed a 'top-down liberalisation of Russian politics'.[147] Yurgens was unequivocal in his view that 'Medvedev is conducting an intense struggle with hostile Kremlin clans to fulfil his programmatic promises to establish the supremacy of

---

[144] Dmitrii Muratov, 'Deklaratsiya Medvedeva: God 2009', *Novaya gazeta*, 15 April 2009, pp. 2–4.
[145] BBC Russian Service poll, 22 April 2009, http://surveys.globescan.com/ bbc_russia09/.
[146] www.riocenter.ru/en/_programs.
[147] The report, published as *Demokratiya: Razvitie rossiiskoi modeli* (Moscow: Ekon-Inform, 2008), was commissioned from the Centre of Political Technologies headed by Igor Bunin and Boris Makarenko.

law, to fight against corruption and to extend freedoms.' Medvedev could only win if he was able to forge a coalition, otherwise he would go the way of so many earlier Russian reformers.[148] Yurgens did not specify where Medvedev would find his allies or how the modernising coalition could be forged in conditions of factional and systemic stalemate.

Tutelary politics remained, but Medvedev was beginning to carve out a defined programme of controlled democratisation. Medvedev's latent liberalism now reportedly took the form of a 'silent war' with the Putinite administrative regime.[149] This was reflected in Medvedev's programmatic article 'Forward, Russia!', published on a liberal website (Gazeta. ru) in September 2009.[150] Although the form was original, the style resembled Putin's lengthy question and answer sessions with domestic and foreign media. Both allowed the leader to communicate in a relatively free format while at the same time retaining control of the agenda and were thus another type of para-political behaviour. The article reflected the Kremlin's growing perception that continued political drift was no longer an option, but it also suggested uncertainty over what was to be done. The article was presented as a discussion document for the president's annual state of the nation address to the Federal Assembly, but the harshly critical tone went beyond what would be acceptable on such a formal occasion.[151] He characterised Russian social life as a semi-Soviet social system, 'one that unfortunately combines all the shortcomings of the Soviet system and all the difficulties of contemporary life'.[152] Underlying the article was the view that the rent-extraction model of the Russian political economy was unsustainable in the long run. The fundamental question was whether Russia, with its 'primitive economy' and 'chronic corruption', has a future. Medvedev attacked not Putin but the system that Putin represented, a balancing act that blunted his message.

The article listed a devastating series of Russian problems, although it was weaker in suggesting ways in which the situation could be remedied. First, Medvedev argued that the country was economically

[148] Yurgens, *Ocherednye zadachi Rossiiskoi vlasti*, p. 7.
[149] Aleksandr Ryklin, 'Medvedev Requires Opposition Tolerance', *Ezhednevny zhurnal*, 22 July 2008; in *JRL*, No. 136, 2008, Item 17.
[150] Dmitrii Medvedev, 'Rossiya, vpered!', www.gazeta.ru/ comments/2009/09/ 10_a_3258568.shtml.
[151] Something that Medvedev himself admitted in his meeting with the Valdai Club, when he argued that 'The actual Address is of course a much more conservative document.' 'Beginning of Meeting with Valdai International Club Participants', 15 September 2009, http://eng.kremlin.ru/ speeches/2009/09/15/1647_type82914type84779_221 667.shtml.
[152] *Ibid.*

backward and distorted by dependence on extractive industries. Who would act as the modernising force, however, was not clear: the state or private enterprise? Second, corruption had long been one of Medvedev's bugbears, and here he once again condemned the phenomenon. It would require a wholly impartial and independent judiciary to achieve a breakthrough, yet as the endless cases of judges working closely with business 'raiders' demonstrated, little progress had been made in the Medvedev years. Third, Medvedev condemned the 'paternalist mindset' prevalent in Russian society. A similar charge could be made against most advanced democracies, where a widespread political passivity has set in; but in Russia, a society that underwent at least two revolutions in the twentieth century, the charge was misleading. However, there was a noticeable rise in social paternalism, reflected in the most desirable careers for young people shifting from business to administration, indicating a return to a 'quasi-Soviet social contract'.[153]

Medvedev sought to break away from such neo-Soviet attitudes, viewing innovation, democracy and freedom as the responsibility of the individual; but he recognised that entrenched interests stymied popular initiative. With businesses under attack from bureaucrats, it was safer to join the latter. More broadly, it was all very well blaming the elite for having driven Russia up a dead end, but that same elite retained its full powers and it would take an act of political courage from above or a revolution from below to remove its grasp on power. It was precisely a revolutionary approach that Medvedev rejected in his article, but that only placed a greater weight of expectation on changes from above. The absence of a social subject of modernisation was a weakness noted by Khodorkovsky in his commentary on the article, insisting that 'it takes a whole stratum, a real modernising class, to achieve genuine modernisation', and he outlined a 'Generation M' that could achieve this.[154] The fundamental weakness of Medvedev's reform programme was its failure to devise a process of modernisation from the middle, mobilising not a centrist political coalition (that was Putin's constituency) but social forces that could provide substance to the ground between the two pillars of the dual state, and thus establish a dynamic to transcend the division.

[153] Andrei Kortunov, 'The New Russia', Kennan Institute, event summary, 5 February 2009; in *JRL*, No. 71, 2008, Item 10.
[154] Mikhail Khodorkovskii, 'Modernizatsiya: Pokolenie M', *Vedomosti*, 21 October 2009, p. 4. Medvedev's press secretary, Natalya Timakova, revealed that Medvedev read the article as he prepared his annual address.

Tensions with the White House were evident at the Yaroslavl conference on 'The Contemporary State and Global Security' on 14 September 2009. With Russia's leading politicians in attendance, but without Putin himself, some 700 delegates gathered to devise an alternative programme for Russia's development and international security. INSOR was one of the sponsors of the event, together with the Institute for Social Planning and Yaroslavl State University. The idea, as Yurgens put it, was to examine the models of democracy in the world and the principles of co-operation between democratic countries.[155] The meeting was addressed by Medvedev, Prime Minister François Fillon of France, Prime Minister Jose Luis Rodriguez Zapatero of Spain and scholars such as Immanuel Wallerstein, the journalist Fareed Zakaria and the futurologists Alvin Toffler and John Neisbitt. The Yaroslavl conference was planned to become an annual event and would represent one of the few distinctly Medvedevite initiatives.

Surkov maintained a resolute silence, preserving his careful balance between Medvedev and Putin. At the Strategy 2020 forum celebrating Medvedev's first year in power, Surkov argued that 'I'm confident that our political system is working', a view that did not preclude some modernisation, but he insisted that the main challenge was simply to make the existing system more efficient.[156] He repeated this view in a later interview discussing the meaning of 'modernisation' and 'innovation', but he insisted that 'it is important not to confuse a liberal, democratic society with chaos and disorder'; 'Weak democratic institutions cannot guarantee economic recovery.'[157] Addressing the Public Chamber on 20 October 2009, he insisted on a 'non-violent evolutionary' path for Russia.[158] For Gontmakher, Surkov's dismissal was the essential precondition for genuine political reform, but this was not the official position of INSOR.

The latent struggle between Putin and Medvedev focused on the next succession. The issue came to the fore in the 2009 Valdai Discussion Club interviews. Asked by Nikolai Zlobin on 11 September whether he would compete with Medvedev in the 2012 presidential election (now for a six-year term), Putin rhetorically asked: 'And did we compete in 2008? And in 2012 we won't either. We will sit down and reach

[155] Elina Trukhanova and Tat'yana Panina, interview with Igor Yurgens, *Rossiiskaya gazeta*, 14 September 2009, p. 4.
[156] Vladislav Surkov, 'The Political System Is Working', *Russian Journal*, No. 17 (31), 1 July 2009, p. 9.
[157] Aleksandr Chudoev, 'Obnovlyaites', gospoda!', *Itogi*, No. 44, 26 October 2009.
[158] 'Evolyutsiya bez revolyutsiya', on the UR website, 20 October 2009, http://er.ru/news/text.shtml?10/3948,110566.

agreement, because we are people of the same blood and with the same political views.' Closer to the time, Putin averred, he and Medvedev would 'decide among ourselves' on what should be done, depending on the 'particular circumstances' and the situation of United Russia: but, Putin insisted, 'We definitely will not fall out with each other.'[159] When the same question was posed to Medvedev on 15 September, he also gave an equivocal and rather clumsy answer: 'With regard to biological characteristics, I will try to find out in the near future and declare officially which blood group he is and which I am'; but he stressed that he 'dreams of nothing and excludes nothing'.[160] His tone and bearing suggested that his candidature was by no means excluded.

In his comments Putin failed to mention that the decision ultimately should be that of the people, and thus smacked of hubris. The succession debate now involved two people, and to that extent the dynamics of succession in 2012 would differ from earlier ones. Both leaders were well aware that any premature announcement of their intentions (if known at that point) would destabilise elite balance and could even threaten the stability of the system in its entirety: the bureaucracy and its economic partners would immediately shift to the future power source and unbalance the dual leadership, rendering one a lame duck and the other the crown prince. Uncertainty was one of the essential rules of the power system created by Putin. Both leaders from 2009, nevertheless, entered what appeared to be a covert succession struggle, characterised by an almost permanent campaigning mode of governance. The prospect of Putin returning to power in 2012 for two six-year terms, which would take him to 2024 when he would be almost seventy-two, provoked fears of a new era of stagnation. Yurgens warned that 'The analogy with Brezhnev is not altogether stupid.' In Yurgens's view, Putin's first eight years had been 'very good' for Russia and his choice of Medvedev as successor demonstrated that he did not want to become another Brezhnev-type figure. The best way to avoid this happening, Yurgens argued, was for an 'open, transparent competition between Putin and Medvedev' in 2012, as leaders of two distinct factions in Russian government.[161]

Medvedev continued his programme of modest incremental reform in his second address to the Federal Assembly on 12 November 2009. He insisted that 'The strengthening of democracy does not mean the

---

[159] Personal notes; P′er Sidibe, 'Kod 2012', *Rossiiskaya gazeta*, 14 September 2009, p. 3.
[160] Personal notes.
[161] Michael Stott, 'Putin Risks Becoming "New Brezhnev": Medvedev Aide', Reuters, 16 September 2009; in *JRL*, No. 172, 2009, Item 25.

weakening of law and order.' He sternly warned that 'Any attempt to rock the situation under democratic slogans, to destabilise the state and split society will be stopped.' In international affairs the tone was less confrontational than the previous year, and instead he called for an 'exclusively pragmatic' foreign policy since Russia needed to attract foreign capital, technology and ideas. 'There is no point us puffing up our cheeks', he insisted, although he promised a range of modern equipment for the armed forces. The focus of his speech was on economic modernisation: 'We have still not overcome the primitive structure of the economy', he noted. Once again he condemned the idea of state corporations, arguing that 'this legal form of enterprise has no future in the modern world'. The state's role in the economy, 'which has never fallen below 40 per cent', would be reduced, but the details were to be worked out, as in a range of other measures, by the government headed by Putin. There was to be more state support for socially oriented NGOs, and some limited changes to electoral rules, designed according to Medvedev to increase political competition. He focused on 'strengthening democratic organisations at the regional level', including equalising the number of deputies in regional legislatures, allowing all parties in them to form factions, ensuring that all parties receiving more than 5 per cent of the vote were represented, and parties not represented in the State Duma but with a faction in the regional legislature were to be exempted from having to collect nomination signatures for elections in that region; and in the long term the collection of signatures in national elections was also to be abolished since parties already needed to prove that they had significant membership and national coverage.[162]

Both Medvedev and Putin evinced concerns about the status of United Russia at its eleventh congress in November 2009. Putin praised UR for having been instrumental in 'gathering the state' in the early 2000s, and 'in putting an end to anarchy and restoring a common legal space in the country', but he had stern words for 'those who have come to see the party as an elite and prestigious club membership which paves the way to furthering one's ambitions, one's career and solving other problems'.[163] Putin's imprecations were reminiscent of a long line of speeches by CPSU general secretaries. In his speech Medvedev, with the recent scandalous regional elections in mind, warned against 'administrative excesses' committed by the party: 'Elections are intended to be an

[162] 'Poslanie Federal'nomu Sobraniyu Rossiiskoi Federatsii', 12 November 2009, www.kremlin.ru/transcripts/5979.
[163] 'V. V. Putin vystupil na XI s"ezde Vserossiiskoi politicheskoi partii "Edinaya Rossiya"', 21 November 2009, http://premier.gov.ru.

expression of the popular will, a contest of ideas and programmes, but as a result they sometimes turn into exercises in which democratic procedures are confused with administrative ones', and he once again stressed the need 'to revamp the entire system of social relations'.[164] The congress approved a new 'programme document' for the next ten years, superseding the 'Putin plan' and the 'Strategy-2020' document. The idea was to depersonalise the programme, which was now explicitly based on an ideology of modernisation and a 'Russian socially-oriented conservatism'.

Russian democracy may well be suffering from crisis, but a certain recuperative capacity within the framework of the existing constitutional order remains. As long as the actions of the administrative regime were considered reprehensible, the gap with a functioning constitutional state could be bridged. Medvedev's presidency, however, was unable to mobilise the normative resources that were potentially available to him to achieve political and legal renewal, and instead he equivocated, generating disappointment and eventually anger.

---

[164] 'XI s″ezd partii "Edinaya Rossiya"', 21 November 2009, www.kremlin.ru/transcripts/6066.

10   Conclusion: transcending the dual state

The succession operation was brought to a successful conclusion. The parliamentary elections ensured the predominance of United Russia, accompanied by a limited choice of other parties. In the presidential contest, scenarios that had envisaged a third term for Putin or an orange revolution gave way instead to one in which a single nominated successor won an overwhelming mandate, while Putin retained considerable power as prime minister. Putin gained a third term by default, without infringing the letter of the constitution. Presidential succession both opened up the possibility of democratic renewal while limiting the political options. In his keynote speech to the World Policy Conference in Evian, France, on 8 October 2008, Medvedev noted that 'Any crisis offers at the same time a chance to resolve systemic contradictions.'[1] Opportunities, however, are not always taken. The formal constitutional election had been accompanied by a para-political struggle between elite factions. Putin had achieved his fundamental goal – leadership, and elite and policy continuity.

No sooner was the tandem in place than it was challenged by economic and foreign policy crises. The stability of the system was now tested, but the fundamental challenge was to reduce the arbitrariness of the administrative regime while enhancing the hegemony of the normative state. Genuine constitutionalism, accompanied by free elections and an independent judiciary, would constrain the shadow state and allow the autonomous operation of political institutions and social forces. Institutional rules would gain a life of their own and undermine the 'manual' operation by the regime. That was the promise of Medvedev's election, but the reality was of a president with limited room for manoeuvre. The fundamental challenge facing his leadership was to find a way of overcoming system stalemate. His reforms would make heavy weather since the ruling bureaucratic-political class saw no need for systemic reform,

---

[1] www.kremlin.ru/eng/text/speeches/2008/10/08/2159.

and the pressure for within-system change lacked a developed political constituency. His modifications to the political system and judicial practices as well as modernisation of the economy were incremental and hesitant. A conservative ideology prevailed that stymied attempts to achieve structural change.

In the press conference following his 18 October 2007 'direct line' session, Putin was asked by a journalist about the implementation of the 'Putin plan' and when the country would be able to shift from the 'manual' mode of management to an automatic one. Putin recalled the way that Roosevelt during the depression had governed in an interventionist manner, much criticised at the time, but which had allegedly set the country back to prosperity. Thus, Putin insisted, 'We are not doing anything unusual.'

We are just coming out of a profound systemic crisis, and have to do much in the so-called manual mode. When will the time come when much or most will function automatically? Only after the completion of these plans. Only after we have created the necessary legal conditions, created legal mechanisms, when all the elements of a market economy are fully working . . . This needs time. This requires thought-out plans for the diversification and strengthening of the economy. The growth of a middle class in the country, undoubtedly, will stabilise both the political system and social life. All this needs time. When the legal, economic and social foundations develop and become stable, then we will no longer require manual management.

Asked how long that would be, Putin suggested that the country would be ruled in the manual mode for some fifteen to twenty years.[2] Putin referred to Roosevelt in his 2006 annual address to the Federal Assembly, noting that 'The toes of some people are being stepped on, and are going to be stepped on' – the line came from one of Roosevelt's fireside talks in 1934. Russian television (RTR) showed a ninety-minute documentary showering praise on Roosevelt on 14 October, and the late Putin years were marked by the development of a Roosevelt cult. The historical example was an obvious analogue for contemporary developments in Russia, including the need for business to stick to business and not politics and for an interventionist state – a 'neo-Keynesian' theme taken up by western leaders in response to the global crisis from 2008.

Putin's comments reflected the temporal displacement of sovereignty from the people to the regime. While predicated on a benign tutelary role, the postponement of the open pluralism of a genuinely competitive system fostered corruption and shadow politics. Factional conflicts undermined formal mechanisms based on institutions to reconcile

---

[2] www.kremlin.ru/text/appears/2007/10/148675.shtml.

differing interests and sucked life from public contestation. The institutions of public politics created in the Yeltsin era, above all the Duma and the Federation Council, had been systematically undermined: internally, they had lost dynamism as Putinite managerialism stifled their vitality and autonomy; and externally, they were forced to share their role with para-constitutional bodies such as the State Council and the Public Chamber. Real power lay not with one or the other but with unelected officials in the presidential administration. The institutions designed for competitive politics were rendered empty shells. There was not much political debate in the Duma, the Federation Council had become a depositary for superannuated politicians and the forum for business lobbies, while the mass electronic media avoided controversial political questions. Putin's management style rested on a series of informal agreements with key individuals in the elite. In turn, these elites constrained his room for manoeuvre. Public and open political competition for real power was secondary in this system.

The succession crisis weakened discipline within the elite, as evidenced by the open outbreak of factional struggle demonstrated in the Bulbov affair, when Cherkesov's right-hand man had been arrested, as well as in the Storchak and other cases, and which took institutional form in the struggle between the GPO and its own agency, the Investigative Committee. Policy differences also took on a more open form, with Kudrin and Chubais warning of the economic costs of a new cold war, while Kudrin, who spoke after Putin at the State Council on 8 February 2008, advocated tax reductions as soon as possible. This disarray certainly reflected the passions attending the succession, but as Silaev notes, it also signalled something deeper: 'The system of informal power mechanisms in Russian politics have gained such a critical mass that the centre where decisions are taken is in danger of shifting from the elected president to the appointed higher bureaucracy. All the more so since the president changes and the bureaucracy remains.'[3]

Medvedev had limited scope to restructure the political elite but he could influence the systemic balance. It is, however, misleading to designate Putin the defender of the administrative regime and Medvedev the champion of the normative state. Although elements of such a division exist, neither leader was ready unequivocally to align with either system. Putin and his networks, moreover, were a presidential resource that Medvedev was forced to use to consolidate his own power, lacking extensive social support and a political base of his own. Pavlovsky argued

---

[3] Silaev, 'Modernizatsiya moshchi', p. 22.

that this was 'a demonstration of Russian political strength, not weakness';[4] but it was also a recipe for policy paralysis and continued political stalemate.

The December 2007 election weakened all political institutions in Russia, including the presidency, since Putin's emergence as 'national leader' began to transcend the constraints of the particular office that he held. Putin expended considerable political capital in pushing through the succession operation and he achieved his main goal: an orderly succession of power without disrupting the established pattern of factional interests. His successor was in no position to challenge the powerful factions, even though he represented none of them. Instead of the constraints on public politics taking the form of street demonstrations, as in Ukraine in 2004, it intensified the factional conflict within the political machine itself. The gulf between the two systems remained as wide as ever. The regime had reduced much of politics to bureaucratic intrigues, while the opposition 'refused to see in the plans and actions of the authorities anything other than the pursuit of self-interested gain of specific officials and were simply not ready to discuss substantive issues with the authorities'.[5] When such a gulf between elite and representative politics emerged in Ukraine in 2004, the result was a 'revolutionary coup'. Leaders throughout the CIS feared the emergence of a third force, sick of the gulf between formal politics and real power relations. This could take the form of strikes, demonstrations and all the way up to a mass movement and popular mobilisation. This was the nightmare that haunted Putin throughout the 2007–8 electoral cycle.

Although the regime had perpetuated itself, it had done so in a largely technocratic way. The Putinite order drew on the institutions and practices of the constitutional state to formalise itself to win genuine legitimacy at home and abroad, but its parasitic relationship drew the life blood from the latter. Any attempt to politicise the Putin system would entail, as Pavlovsky argued, 'establishing its political outlines and naming his own new place within it'.[6] Instead, while the formal rules had been obeyed, the spirit of open public politics and the electoral competitiveness had been undermined. However, by relinquishing the presidency in the prescribed manner, Putin remained a figure of unrivalled national authority and enhanced his international reputation. Michael McFaul, who had been critical of Russia's 'democratic backsliding', noted: 'By committing to stepping down as president by naming a successor, Putin

[4] Gleb Pavlovsky, 'Afterword', in Leonard et al. (eds.), What Does Russia Think?, p. 74.
[5] Editorial, 'Uvidet' perspektivu', Ekspert, No. 9, 3–9 March 2008, p. 19.
[6] Gleb Pavlovsky, Ekspert, No. 34, 17 September 2007.

has taken a small but important step toward democratization. Since December 1993, political forces of all ideological persuasions have acquiesced to the political rules of the game spelled out in the Constitution. Putin's decision to adhere to these rules will make it more costly for future leaders to transgress them.'[7] The succession was conducted with constant reference to the constitution, and the decision ultimately was made within its framework. Nussberger comments that the 'Russian model' demonstrated that if political elites stick to constitutional rules, personal changes and a break in the succession could be avoided.[8] Term limits are an important constraint on the decline of an authoritarian regime into outright despotism. As Maltz notes, 'if Vladimir Putin is still governing Russia in twenty years, that country will likely be more authoritarian than if power is simply transferred within the ruling coterie'.[9] The extension to the length of presidential (and parliamentary) terms, moreover, was in conformity with democratic norms in stipulating that the amendment would only apply to the incumbent's successor.[10]

The tension between public politics and the closed shadow world of para-politics, populated by factions, intrigues and informal relations, came to characterise the Putin era. The political system, as in the Yeltsin years, remained liminal, in the sense that the concept of transition barely begins to describe the characteristics of the social order. The legal system, for example, retained the potential to transcend para-politics and to conform to the normal exigencies of constitutional politics. As Richard Lourie puts it:

> If the case of Mikhail Khodorkovsky proved anything, it was that the judiciary will, if need be, serve the interests of the Kremlin regardless of the truth and the law. But Russian society today is authoritarian, not totalitarian. Not everything is or can be subjugated, and there is evidence that some people who have adopted the law as a profession actually believe in its precepts. Judges here and there have been displaying signs of independence. A Sakharov of the courts has to be one of the Kremlin's nightmares.[11]

The Putin system combined two opposed processes, which were not so easily distinguished because of their interrelated characteristics. There was a weak but not negligible pressure from the electorate, with

---

[7] Michael McFaul, 'Small Democratic Step', *Moscow Times*, 13 December 2007, p. 8.
[8] Nussberger, 'Ogranicheniya prezidentskoi vlasti v postkommunisticheskikh stranakh', p. 60.
[9] Gideon Maltz, 'The Case for Presidential Term Limits', *Journal of Democracy* 18, 1, January 2007, p. 131.
[10] Cf. *Ibid.*, p. 141.
[11] Richard Lourie, 'Putting the Whip in Their Own Hands', *Moscow Times*, 12 November 2007, p. 10.

preferences to a degree shaped by civic organisations, including political parties, while the business class continued to exert pressure on the bureaucratic ruling elite. In a contradictory manner, this continued social pressure on the regime was proto-democratic and forced it to remember that at some point it could be forced to cede power. However, for that to take place a genuine opposition would have to emerge. The old democratic movement, the one born in the last years of *perestroika* based on the radical intelligentsia but which failed to consolidate its power in the 1990s and which under Putin became ever more marginal, would have to give way to a new democratic movement, rooted in the new realities of a resurgent Russia in a complex world and reflecting the new social realities of a capitalist democracy and a strengthened state. The old Soviet intelligentsia traditions would be of little use now, and instead a sober attempt to find real social constituencies would be essential. In practice, the pace of the decline of the old democratic movement (the former SPS and Yabloko) and systemic opposition (notably the CPRF and LDPR) far exceeded the creation of new ones, accentuating the palpable features of democratic decline.

The two-term presidential limit had not been breached, but the former incumbent retained power. The succession problem had been resolved within the regime itself while formally ensuring that the transfer of power was achieved within the framework of the constitution. The institutional design of the 1993 constitutional settlement had never sought to give a pre-eminent role to the cabinet, and even then its powers were further limited in 1994 when Yeltsin subordinated the power and security ministers directly to the president, eroding the authority of the prime minister. However, Putin was a master of para-constitutional solutions, and he now revitalised the premier's office.

The continuity operation had been successful, and danger of instability accompanying the succession had been avoided. While it is easy to denigrate, from a narrow instrumental perspective, this was no mean achievement. There had been a real danger that faction-fighting would spill over into public confrontation and could have taken very damaging forms. As it was, we shall probably never know the details of the various machinations of the behind-the-scenes struggle as the succession approached. Those who favoured a third term for Putin tried to force him into staying, and the various murders (notably of Politkovskaya and Litvinenko) may have been part of these factional machinations. However, the chance to apply a clear competitive succession mechanism was missed, and once again court intrigues took the place of public politics. At the same time, the overwhelming majority of the Russian people wanted Putin to stay and supported his nominated successor, and the views of this 'democratic' majority in the event prevailed. The settlement of the succession within the regime was not accompanied by elite splits or by popular revulsion; thus two of the main conditions for colour revolutions, as experienced earlier in Serbia, Georgia, Ukraine and Kyrgyzstan, were simply not present in Russia. However, even though Putin's support remained extraordinarily high, a desire for change was also apparent. His emergence in 1999–2000 reflected a desire for change, and so too in 2007 when 'once again the moment has come when mass psychology demands something new'.[12]

In a paradoxical way, Putin presented himself as an instrument of both continuity and change, and to a degree he acted as the embodiment of an anti-elite strategy. The regime internalised political processes and tendencies of the society at large. As the succession approached Putin conducted a number of government reshuffles, and he also created a number of bodies largely independent of existing structures, notably Bastrykin's Investigative Committee. He advanced a financial inspectorate that had nothing to do with the old factional scene, and promoted outsiders like Serdyukov and Churov to important posts. This was done with a minimum of consultation with the old elites. According to one commentator, 'These appointments are anti-elite per se; they reflect, above all, Putin's deep disappointment in the country's current political elite in general and its ruling clique in particular.'[13] The appointment of Zubkov and the others reflected a trend to reach beyond the existing elite groups, and instinctively Putin drew on his St Petersburg contacts. Putin's strategy in the final period of his second term was thus both anti-factional and anti-establishment; he had clearly become frustrated at the venality of much of the existing system. This was reflected in his 1 October 2007 UR congress speech, when he spoke of the danger of 'squandering' road-building funds, asserted that money should not be 'wasted' in the housing programme, and then tackled the issue head on, noting that corruption had 'become a major social and political problem'. Despite 'replacing staff and pursuing thousands of legal cases', he admitted that 'we have not been able radically to change the situation', and a 'systematic programme of action', including financial, organisation and personnel measures, was needed, something he hoped that UR would develop.[14]

---

[12] Elena Shestopal', interviewed in Viktor Khamraev, 'Chto takoe suverennaya demokratiya, ponyatno tol'ko Surkovu', *Kommersant-Vlast'*, No. 39, 8 October 2007, pp. 32–4, at p. 33.

[13] Georgy Bovt, 'The Anti-Elite: New Government Leaders Come from Outside the System', 3 October 2007, www.russiaprofile.org.

[14] www.kremlin.ru/text/appears/2007/10/146479.shtml.

Putin's stake on United Russia had the potential in the long-run to bring factional struggles from under the carpet and into the open, by formalising them in the form of intra-party conflict. As the *Ekspert* editorial cited before argued, it could signal the attempt to create 'fully-fledged and effective political instruments instead of criminal cases and arrests',[15] a route to escape the logic of factional struggles. The main challenge facing Russia was not the threat of a return to the anarchy of the 1990s but the struggle between two systems: the subterranean politics of factional conflict and a system based on public politics.

Even before the 2007–8 electoral cycle, there had been signs of political stagnation, and this now accelerated. Stability inevitably has a tendency to lead to stasis, where problems are ignored and swept under the carpet. Although Putin was no Brezhnev, his emphasis on social and political stability took the form of a profound fear of popular mobilisation accompanied by an institutional conservatism that avoided changing formal arrangements to avoid unleashing broader demands for constitutional change. Since coming to political prominence, anti-revolutionism was one of the recurring themes of Putin's discourse. It sounded once again in his UR speech on 1 October:

In the last century, our homeland went through a series of upheavals. We cannot afford to repeat old mistakes, and we cannot lose the historic chance for peace and stable development. And therefore United Russia, a party that accepts its political responsibility for the course it has adopted, can have only one objective: victory in the forthcoming elections, a victory won in a fair fight. But we don't need victory for its own sake. We need it to guarantee the stable development of the country, in order to make all the plans a reality and justify the expectations of millions of Russian citizens. Their hopes for a better lot cannot be disappointed. The time has come to prove that Russia is indeed a great country. A country that is proud of its citizens and respected by its neighbours, a country where human dignity and rights are respected. This is precisely why we have worked together, enjoyed success together and sometimes faced adversity. I am sure that United Russia is ready and, supported by society, will fight for its programme of transformation, a programme designed for the prosperity of Russia and its people.[16]

The anti-revolutionary theme was taken up by Medvedev, accompanied by a renewed modernisation strategy. This generation of post-communist leaders across the former Soviet Union has an aversion to mass politics, except when it propels them to power in the form of colour revolutions. Medvedev's reforms were thus unable to transform

---

[15] Editorial, 'Izbirateli i sledovateli', *Ekspert*, No. 44, 26 November 2007, p. 21.
[16] www.kremlin.ru/text/appears/2007/10/146479.shtml.

managed democracy into a competitive democracy, accompanied by the development of a flexible civil society responsive to new challenges. Medvedev remained committed to a top-down model of democratisation, considered a function of the modernisation process itself based on elites learning how to compete democratically between themselves. The fear of a popular revolution weighed heavily on the minds of the Medvedevites, as it did on the Putinites.[17]

Under Putin Russia underwent the classic consolidation phase of a period of revolutionary transformation. The effervescence of popular mobilisation died away, and Putin quite explicitly sought to suppress any manifestation of revolutionary behaviour. In the most profound sense Putin had a horror of revolutions, having seen at first hand two systems perish (the GDR and the Soviet Union), and thus his distaste of the orange revolution was genuine. He was an anti-revolutionary, opposed to the revolutionary approach to political change, but not a counter-revolutionary, and he did not seek to restore anything approximating the Soviet system. Putin's anti-revolutionism took the form of a strong technocratic bias, but the lack of a vibrant political process and public politics threatened the stability of the system by allowing the administrative regime, with its associated factionalism, to expand its prerogatives, and thus weakened the ability of the normative state to reproduce itself. Putin tried to finesse the danger by advocating modernisation without mobilisation, combined with the management of associative life to ensure that the latter remained controlled and systemic. Putin succeeded in controlling the succession process, but the underlying problem of the passive revolution was not resolved.

It was clear from early October 2007 that the fate of Just Russia was no longer a major concern for Putin, and even less so the ability of SPS or Yabloko to enter parliament. Instead, the key line of fracture now was how Putin, as an insider who posed as the embodiment of opposition to a corrupt and suffocating bureaucracy, could muster sufficient resources to influence events once he handed over the presidency in May 2008. In the shadow of UR, the country would at best be endowed with a one-and-a-half party system. Putin had an ambivalent relationship with the administrative regime, and although ready to exploit it as a political resource he understood the long-term limits of a political order based on arbitrariness and closed politics. He recognised that a powerful party

---

[17] These issues were the subject of an INSOR report of early 2010, *Rossiya XXI veka: Obraz zhelaemogo zavtra* (Moscow: Econ-Inform, 2010); with critical pre-publication commentary by Elina Bilevskaya and Aleksandra Samarina, 'Suverennuyu demokratiyu zamenyat sostyazatel'noi', *Nezavisimaya gazeta*, 30 September 2009, p. 4.

system offered an escape route, but his own partial understanding of a genuine competitive public politics trapped him within the logic of the administrative regime. His successor offered a way for the Putinite system to escape from its own contradictions and for Putin himself to avoid a destiny not of his own making.

Medvedev's election represented a gradual change of generations in the elite. Although trained in the communist era, most of his professional career was spent in post-Soviet conditions. As we have seen, however, the new generation was less enamoured of the west and readier to defend Russia. In that context Medvedev was 'Putin plus', with a wider spectrum of political responses. On the one side, he had a stronger liberal side, and this could well provide space for the renewal of political institutions, the independence of the judiciary, greater media freedom and the general reassertion of the authority of the normative state. On the other side, however, Medvedev reflected the more assertive consciousness of younger Russians and thus was readier even than Putin to stand up to what was perceived to be the west's overbearing behaviour and hypocritical application of double standards. The personalisation of power continued against the background of the maintenance of imposed consensus, and thus there would be no sharp reduction in the influence of the administrative regime.

The succession operation had avoided unconstrained intra-elite conflict, although at the margins there were some dangerous outbreaks of open factional warfare. Public competition was also limited and managed by the regime, and apart from some small demonstrations, the whole process was kept an elite affair. Competition was controlled and the public played a limited role, and all mass actors played their allotted role. In the long run, however, a factionalised elite was unlikely to be able to exercise control over the executive, which in turn fosters corruption and elements of autocratic rule. The paradox in Russia is that the elite is highly factionalised but at the same time extraordinarily homogeneous. In this context political changes can have major institutional consequences. The emergence of a politically powerful prime minister accompanied by an institutionally strong president offered the prospect of a more transparent and balanced political system operating according to known rules of the game. 'Russia could achieve something unique: on its own and in an evolutionary manner grow into a strong democratic European state.'[18]

[18] Editorial, 'Uvidet' perspektivu'.

Our dual state model envisages precisely this possibility; but it also stresses the obstacles to an evolutionary transcendence of the authoritarian, arbitrary and informal elements of the administrative regime. The programme to strengthen a functioning legal state is rather different from earlier liberalisation projects. Thus models of Russian politics that cast Medvedev in the role of a Khrushchev or Gorbachev miss the crucial dynamics of what he was trying to achieve. The aim was not to achieve a liberalisation of the system but to attempt to reforge a new type of social contract that would guarantee civil and property rights. This entailed the strengthening of a certain type of state power that had been undeveloped, the infrastructural power of due process and transparency, while reining in the hypertrophy of its administrative features. Medvedev's brand of legalistic conservativism precluded any populist appeal to the people or even a programme for the revival of democracy and civil associations from below that could have been used to exert pressure on the administrative system. His attempt to improve the quality of governance did not necessarily, at least in the first instance, entail a radical enhancement of political pluralism. That at least was Medvedev's gambit, and it was one that he essentially was forced to make, given the constraints imposed on him by tandemised leadership.

A legitimacy crisis emerges when one or both of the following circumstances hold: the principles on which a political leader or leadership group are questioned or rejected by the mass of the population over whom government is exercised; and/or an alternative approach to the principles on which the political order operates is generated from below and gains a certain degree of acceptance as the basis on which a preferable social order can be built. The 2007–8 elections demonstrated that neither of these conditions held, although they did reveal the possibility of such a crisis. There was no fundamental challenge to 'the belief in the rightfulness of [the] state',[19] the awareness of the potential for such a challenge and the grounds on which the elements of an alternative way of managing the existing social order could be grounded revealed the tension between the Putinite manual mode of managing social relations and the prospect of greater automaticity grounded in the independence of the rule of law and political actors.

The most dangerous moment for any relatively closed political system is the moment of succession. Successful regimes devise a method that does not threaten to destroy the system, while less successful authoritarian systems endure the transitional process as a series of crises. In the

---

[19] Vilho Harle, *Ideas of Social Order in the Ancient World* (Westport, CT: Greenwood Press, 1998), p. 88.

Russian case in 2007–8, the regime emerged intact from the succession process and demonstrated its ability to survive, but the election cycle exposed a whole range of problems. First, the extreme dependence on the will and preferences of a single individual revealed a dangerous narrowing of the decision-making process. Second, the inability to transform factional politics into open and structured political contestation over different policy choices generated tensions within the regime that at times threatened to tear it apart. Third, the formal institutions of political democracy – the parties, parliament and electoral process – were overshadowed by secret factional struggles and thus took on a pseudo quality that undermined the relevance of formal public politics. Two succession processes operated in parallel: one confined to the Kremlin and associated power centres; and the other in which the public were allowed to participate, although their preferences were advisory rather than binding.

The interaction between the two levels was important, and thus the public process should not be discounted. The open political process lost some of its 'virtual' character, whereby in the past political technologists used all sorts of tricks and clever tropes to ensure the victory of their candidates.[20] In this election the dark arts of virtual politics were marginalised, and instead the clunking mechanism of the regime-engineered election process rumbled into life and predominated in the open part of the election. The preferences of voters here did play a role, although not quite in the way that would be typical of a single-plane open election. The 'referendum' factor mediated electoral choices, and thus the vote in the Duma election was less about a choice between political parties and different ideologies, than about the fate of the incumbent president and his policies. In this electoral cycle, therefore, the 'primary' element in the parliamentary ballot almost entirely disappeared, and the 'referendum' factor was highlighted.

Although successful in achieving its short-term goals – managing the succession without systemic crisis and ensuring personnel and policy continuity – the whole process damaged the credibility of the regime. The factional side of Russian politics was exposed and did little to bolster trust in the efficacy of public institutions. In that sense, although accompanied by none of the rhetoric and effervescence that accompanied the orange revolution in Ukraine, these elections signalled a qualitative transformation of the regime in Russia. By revealing its hidden workings, it may not have become more transparent but it did become

---

[20] Wilson, *Virtual Politics*.

more exposed. By that token, an involuted colour revolution was set in motion whose long-term effects could transform the system. Although the Putinite order proved resilient, the succession crisis demonstrated the lack of unity among elites and the inadequate integration of public and regime politics. Once the gulf was revealed, it would be only a matter of time before there would be attempts to transcend it. This was the fundamental challenge facing Medvedev's presidency.

The elections allowed the regime to perpetuate itself, but they did not resolve fundamental questions about Russia's future. The elections appeared only to postpone solutions to the crisis, which would once again become manifest in the next electoral cycle in 2011–12. There was a paradox at the heart of Medvedev's leadership, as there was in Putin's. Both came to power as a result of a nomination process rather than the outcome of an unpredictable contest at the ballot box; yet both were able to win democratic legitimacy through an electoral process and to win over public opinion to support their leaderships. The only way out of this and other impasses was to create a genuine public politics based on an active citizenry. The administrative regime would have to relax its tutelary hold and trust that democracy *could* create the conditions for its own existence without threatening internal order or foreign-policy interests. By pursuing liberal economic policies and effective macroeconomic management that ensured sustained economic growth, Putin's administration was creating the social basis for a more inclusive type of politics in the future. The gulf between regime and society has not been transcended in Russian history, despite numerous revolutions and coups, but there remains the possibility of an evolutionary transcendence of the traditional gap between Russia's rulers and ruled. The 2007–8 electoral cycle did not bring the country any closer to transforming the Russian polity by bridging the rift between the normative state and the administrative regime, but by starkly revealing the problem, it played a part in finding a solution.

Bibliography

Adachi, Yuko, 'Subsoil Law Reform in Russia Under the Putin Administration', *Europe-Asia Studies* **61**, 8, October 2009, pp. 1393–414.

Afanas'ev, M. N., *Klientizm i rossiiskaya gosudarstvennost'*, 2nd edn (Moscow: MONF, 2000).

Nevynosimaya slabost' gosudarstva (Moscow: Rosspen, 2006).

Afanasiev, Mikhail, 'Is There a Demand for Modernization in Russia?', *Russia in Global Affairs* **7**, 3, July–September 2009, pp. 22–33.

Ahrend, Rudiger, 'Russia's Post-Crisis Growth: Its Sources and Prospects for Continuation', *Europe-Asia Studies* **58**, 1, January 2006, pp. 1–24.

Albats, Yevgenia, *KGB: State Within a State* (London: I. B. Tauris, 1995).

Altaiskii Forum, *Rossiya 1993–2008: Itogi transformatsii*, ed. Reinhart Krumm and Vladimir Ryzhkov (Moscow: Moskovskaya shkola politicheskikh isseldovanii, 2009).

Amsterdam, Robert R., *The Dual State Takes Hold in Russia*, mimeo, Royal Institute for International Affairs, 7 February 2008.

Anokhina, N. V. and E. Yu. Meleshkina, 'Proportsional'naya izbiratel'naya sistema i opasnosti prezidentsializma: Rossiiskii sluchai', *Polis*, No. 5, 2007, pp. 8–24.

Appel, Hilary, 'Is it Putin or Is It Oil? Explaining Russia's Fiscal Recovery', *Post-Soviet Affairs* **24**, 4, October–December 2008, pp. 301–23.

Aron, Leon, *Boris Yeltsin: A Revolutionary Life* (London: HarperCollins, 2000).

'After the Leviathan', *Journal of Democracy* **18**, 2, April 2007, pp. 120–1.

The Vagaries of the Presidential Succession, Russian Outlook (Washington, DC: American Enterprise Institute, 2007).

'Was Liberty Really Bad for Russia? (Part I)', *Demokratizatsiya* **16**, 1, 2008, pp. 27–36; 'Part II', Demokratizatsiya **16**, 2, 2008, pp. 131–42.

Atwal, Maya, 'Evaluating *Nashi*'s Sustainability: Autonomy, Agency and Activism', *Europe-Asia Studies* **61**, 5, 2009, pp. 743–58.

Avramenko, I. M., *Prem'er-ministry (predsedateli pravitel'stva) Rossii (1905–2005): Biograficheskii spravochnik* (Rostov-on-Don: Feniks, 2005).

Baev, Pavel K., 'The Evolution of Putin's Regime: Inner Circles and Outer Walls', *Problems of Post-Communism* **51**, 6, November–December 2004, pp. 3–13.

Baker, Peter and Susan Glasser, *Kremlin Rising: Vladimir Putin's Russia and the End of Revolution* (New York and London: Scribner, 2005; revised edn 2007).

Balmaceda, Margarita M., *Energy Dependency, Politics and Corruption in the Former Soviet Union: Russia's Power, Oligarchs' Profits and Ukraine's Missing Energy Policy, 1995–2006* (London and New York: Routledge, 2008).

Balyer, Harvey, 'Managed Pluralism: Vladimir Putin's Emerging Regime', *Post-Soviet Affairs* **19**, 3, 2003, pp. 189–227.

'The Putin Thesis and Russian Energy Policy', *Post-Soviet Affairs* **21**, 3, 2005, pp. 210–25.

'Vladimir Putin's Academic Writings and Russian Natural Resource Policy', *Problems of Post-Communism* **53**, 1, January–February 2006, pp. 48–54, with Putin's article 'Mineral Natural Resources in the Strategy for Development of the Russian Economy', at pp. 49–54.

Basmannoe pravosudie: Uroki samooborony: Posobie dlya advokatov (Moscow: Publichnaya reputatsiya, 2003); www.ip-centre.ru/books/Basmannoe.pdf.

Baudoin, Marie-Elisabeth, 'Is the Constitutional Court the Last Bastion in Russia Against the Threat of Authoritarianism?', *Europe-Asia Studies* **58**, 5, July 2006, pp. 679–99.

Belkovskii, Stanislav, *Imperiya Vladimira Putina* (Moscow: Algoritm, 2008).

Beumers, Birgit, Stephen Hutchings and Natalia Rulyova (eds.), *The Post-Soviet Russian Media: Conflicting Signals* (London: Routledge/BASEES, 2009).

Bialer, Seweryn, *Stalin's Successors, Leadership, Stability, and Change in the Soviet Union* (Cambridge: Cambridge University Press, 1980).

Biryukov, Nikolai and Viktor M. Sergeev, *Russia's Road to Democracy: Parliament, Communism and Traditional Culture* (Aldershot: Edward Elgar, 1993) *Russian Politics in Transition: Institutional Conflict in a Nascent Democracy* (Cheltenham: Ashgate Publishing, 1997).

Bjorkman, Tom, *Russia's Road to Deeper Democracy* (Washington, DC: Brookings Institution Press, 2003).

Blank, Stephen, 'The Putin Succession and Its Implications for Russian Politics', *Post-Soviet Affairs* **24**, 3, July–September 2008, pp. 231–62.

Blauvelt, Timothy, 'Abkhazia: Patronage and Power in the Stalin Era', *Nationalities Papers* **35**, 2, May 2007, pp. 203–32.

Bobkov, F. D., *KGB i Vlast'*, 2nd enlarged and updated edn (Moscow: EKSMO, Algoritm, 2003).

Boobbyer, Philip, 'Vladimir Bukovskii and Soviet Communism', *The Slavonic and East European Review* **87**, 3, July 2009, pp. 452–87.

Bremmer, Ian and Samuel Charap, 'The Siloviki in Putin's Russia: Who They Are and What They Want', *The Washington Quarterly* **30**, 1, Winter 2006–7, pp. 83–92.

Brooker, David C., 'Kravchuk and Yeltsin at Re-Election', *Demokratizatsiya* **16**, 3, 2008, pp. 294–304.

Bryant, Christopher and Edmund Mokrzycki (eds.), *The New Great Transformation?* (London: Routledge, 1994).

Brym, Robert J. and V. Gimpelson, 'The Size, Composition and Dynamics of the Russian State Bureaucracy in the 1990s', *Slavic Review* **63**, 1, Spring 2004, pp. 90–113.

Buck, Andrew D., 'Elite Networks and Worldviews During the Yel′tsin Years', *Europe-Asia Studies* **59**, 4, June 2007, pp. 643–61.

Bunce, Valerie, 'Should Transitologists be Grounded?', *Slavic Review* **54**, 1, Spring 1995, pp. 111–27.

Subversive Institutions: The Design and the Destruction of Socialism and the State (Cambridge: Cambridge University Press, 1999).

Bunich, Andrei, *Osen′ oligarkhov: Istoriya prikhvatizatsii i budushchee Rossii* (Moscow: Yauza-Eksmo, 2006).

Burger, Ethan S. and Mary Holland, 'Law as Politics: The Russian Procuracy and Its Investigative Committee', *Columbia Journal of East European Law* **2**, 2, 2008, pp. 142–93.

Burlatsky, Fyodor, *The Modern State and Politics* (Moscow: Progress Publishers, 1978).

Burnell, Peter (ed.), *Democratization Through the Looking Glass* (New Brunswick, NJ: Transaction Publishers, 2006).

Burrett, Tina, *Covering the President: Presidential Power and Television in Putin's Russia* (London: Routledge/BASEES, 2010).

Buzin, Andrei and Arkady Lyubarev, *Prestuplenie bez nakazaniya: Administrativnye tekhnologii federal′nykh vyborov 2007–2009 godov* (Moscow: Nikkolo-M, 2009).

Carnaghan, Ellen, *Out of Order: Russian Political Values in an Imperfect World* (University Park: Pennsylvania State University Press, 2007).

Carothers, Thomas, 'The End of the Transition Paradigm', *Journal of Democracy* **13**, 1, January 2002, pp. 5–21.

Chaisty, Paul, *Legislative Politics and Economic Power in Russia* (Basingstoke: Palgrave, 2006).

Chaisty, Paul and Petra Schleiter, 'Productive but Not Valued: The Russia State Duma, 1994–2001', *Europe-Asia Studies* **54**, 5, 2002, pp. 701–24.

Charap, Samuel, 'The Petersburg Experience: Putin's Political Career and Russian Foreign Policy', *Problems of Post-Communism* **51**, 1, January–February 2004, pp. 55–62.

'Inside Out: Domestic Political Change and Foreign Policy in Vladimir Putin's First Term', *Demokratizatsiya* **15**, 3, 2007, pp. 335–52.

'No Obituaries Yet for Capitalism in Russia', *History Today*, October 2009, pp. 333–8.

Chebankova, Elena, 'The Evolution of Russia's Civil Society Under Vladimir Putin: A Cause for Concern or Grounds for Optimism?', *Perspectives on European Politics and Society* **10**, 3, September 2009, pp. 394–416.

Chirikova, A. E., 'Ispolnitel′naya vlast′ v regionakh: pravila igry formal′nye i neformal′nye', *Obshchestvennye nauki i sovremennost′*, No. 3, 2004, pp. 71–80.

Chubais, Igor′, *Rossiya v poiskakh sebya: Kak my preodoleem ideinyi krizis* (Moscow: Izd-vo NOK 'Muzei bumagi', 1998).

Clark, William A., 'Russia at the Polls: Potemkin Democracy', *Problems of Post-Communism* **51**, 2, March/April 2004, pp. 22–9.

Collier, David and Steven Levitsky, 'Democracy with Adjectives: Conceptual Innovation in Comparative Research', *World Politics* **49**, 1997, pp. 430–51.

Collins, Katherine, 'Clans, Pacts, and Politics in Central Asia', *Journal of Democracy* **13**, 3, July 2002, pp. 137–52.

'The Logic of Clan Politics: Evidence from the Central Asian Trajectories', *World Politics* **56**, 2, January 2004, pp. 224–61.

Clan Politics and Regime Transition in Central Asia (New York: Cambridge University Press, 2006).

Colton, Timothy J., 'Putin and the Attenuation of Russian Democracy', in Alex Pravda (ed.), *Leading Russia: Putin in Perspective* (Oxford: Oxford University Press, 2005), pp. 103–18.

Yeltsin: A Life (New York: Basic Books, 2008).

Colton, Timothy J. and Henry E. Hale, 'The Putin Vote: Presidential Electorates in a Hybrid Regime', *Slavic Review* **68**, 3, Fall 2009, pp. 473–503.

Colton, Timothy J. and Michael McFaul, *Are Russians Undemocratic?* Working Paper No. 20 (Washington, DC: Carnegie Endowment for International Peace, Russian Domestics Politics Project, Russian and Eurasian Program, June 2001); republished in *Post-Soviet Affairs* **18**, 2, 2002, pp. 91–121.

Popular Choice and Managed Democracy: The Russian Elections of 1999 and 2000 (Washington DC: Brookings Institution Press, 2003).

Colton, Timothy J. and Cindy Skatch, 'The Russian Predicament', *Journal of Democracy* **16**, 3, July 2005, pp. 113–26.

Cooper, Julian, 'The Funding of the Power Agencies of the Soviet State', *The Journal of Power Institutions in Post-Soviet Societies* **6**, 7, 2007; www.pipss.org/document562.html

Corruption Process in Russia: Level, Structure, Trends. Diagnostics of Corruption in Russia, Indem Foundation, 20 July 2005, www.indem.ru/en/Publicat/2005diag_engV.htm.

Cox, Robert W., 'Civil Society at the Turn of the Millennium: Prospects for an Alternative World Order', *Review of International Studies* **25**, 1999, pp. 3–28.

Crick, Bernard, *In Defence of Politics* (Harmondsworth: Penguin Books, 1964).

D'Agostino, Anthony, *Soviet Succession Struggles: Kremlinology and the Russian Question from Lenin to Gorbachev* (Boston: Unwin Hyman, 1988).

Dahl, Robert, *Polyarchy: Participation and Opposition* (New Haven, CT: Yale University Press, 1971).

Daugavet, A. B., 'Neformal'nye praktiki rossiiskoi elity (Aprobatsiya kognitivnogo podkhoda)', *Polis*, No. 4, 2003, pp. 26–38.

Diamond, Larry, *Developing Democracy: Towards Consolidation* (Baltimore and London: The Johns Hopkins University Press, 1999).

'Thinking About Hybrid Regimes', *Journal of Democracy* **13**, 2, 2002, pp. 21–35.

Diskin, Iosif E., *Revolyutsiya protiv svobody: Sbornik* (Moscow: Evropa, 2007).

Krizis . . . i vse zhe modernizatsiya! (Moscow: Evropa, 2009).

Duncan, Peter, *'Oligarchs', Business and Russian Foreign Policy: From El'tsin to Putin*, Economics Working Paper No. 83 (London: UCL School of Slavonic and East European Studies, Centre for the Study of Economic and Social Change in Europe, October 2007).

Dunlop, John B., *The Rise of Russia and the Fall of the Soviet Empire* (Princeton, NJ: Princeton University Press, 1993).

Easter, Gerald M., 'Personal Networks and Postrevolutionary State Building: Soviet Russia Reexamined', *World Politics* **48**, July 1996, pp. 551–78.

Reconstructing the State: Personal Networks and Elite Identity in Soviet Russia (Cambridge: Cambridge University Press, 2000).

'The Russian State in the Time of Putin', *Post-Soviet Affairs* **24**, 3, July–September 2008, pp. 199–230.

Elgie, Robert, 'A Fresh Look at Semipresidentialism: Variations on a Theme', *Journal of Democracy* **16**, 3, July 2005, pp. 98–112.

(ed.), *Semi-Presidentialism in Europe* (Oxford: Oxford University Press, 1999).

Evans, Alfred B., Jr, 'The First Steps of Russia's Public Chamber: Representation or Coordination?', *Demokratizatsiya* **16**, 4, Fall 2008, pp. 345–62.

Evans, Alfred B., Jr., Laura A. Henry and Lisa McIntosh Sundstrom (eds.), *Russian Civil Society: A Critical Assessment* (Armonk, NY: M. E. Sharpe, 2005).

Evans, P., D. Rueschemeyer and T. Skocpol, *Bringing the State Back In* (Cambridge: Cambridge University Press, 1985).

Ezhegodnye poslaniya prezidenta RF federal'nomu sobraniyu 1994–2005 (Novosibirsk: Sibirskoe universitetskoe izdatel'stvo, 2006).

Fainsod, Merle, *How Russia is Ruled* (Oxford: Oxford University Press, 1963).

Federal'nyi zakon: O Vyborakh deputatov gosudarstvennoi dumy federal'nogo sobraniya rossiiskoi federatsii (Moscow: Os'-89, 2005).

Fish, M. Steven, *Democracy Derailed in Russia: The Failure of Open Politics* (New York: Cambridge University Press, 2005).

'Stronger Legislatures, Stronger Democracies', *Journal of Democracy* **17**, 1, January 2006, pp. 5–20.

Fortescue, Stephen, 'The Russian Law on Subsurface Resources: A Policy Marathon', *Post-Soviet Affairs* **25**, 2, April–June 2009, pp. 160–84.

Fraenkel, Ernst, *The Dual State: A Contribution to the Theory of Dictatorship*, trans. from the German by E. A. Shils, in collaboration with Edith Lowenstein and Klaus Knorr (New York: Oxford University Press, 1941; repr. The Lawbook Exchange, Ltd, 2006).

Frye, Timothy, 'Capture or Exchange? Business Lobbying in Russia', *Europe-Asia Studies* **54**, 7, November 2002, pp. 1017–36.

'Vladimir Putin and the Succession Dilemma', *Problems of Post-Communism* **54**, 6, November–December 2007, pp. 59–60.

Furman, Dmitrii, 'A Silent Cold War', *Russia in Global Affairs* **4**, 2, April–June 2006; http://eng.globalaffairs.ru/ numbers/15/1020.html.

'Imitation Democracies: The Post-Soviet Penumbra', *New Left Review*, No. **54**, November–December 2008, pp. 29–47.

Politicheskaya sistema Rossii v ryadu drugikh postsovetskikh system, Report No. 233 (Moscow: Institute of Europe, 2009).

Gaman-Golutvina, Oksana, 'Regional'nye elity Rossii: Personal'nyi sostav i tendentsii evolyutsii (I)', *Polis*, No. 2, 2004, pp. 6–19.

Garadzha, Nikita (ed.), *Suverenitet* (Moscow: Evropa, 2006).

Gat, Azar, 'The Return of the Authoritarian Great Powers', *Foreign Affairs* **86**, 4, July–August 2007, pp. 56–69.

Gel′man, V. Ya., 'Institutsional′noe stroitel′stvo i neformal′nye instituty v sovremennoi rossiiskoi politike', *Polis*, No. 4, 2003, pp. 6–25.

'The Unrule of Law in the Making: The Politics of Informal Institution Building in Russia', *Europe-Asia Studies* **56**, 7, 2004, pp. 1021–40.

'Political Opposition in Russia: A Dying Species?', *Post-Soviet Affairs* **21**, 3, July–September 2005, pp. 226–46.

'From "Feckless Pluralism" to "Dominant Power Politics"? The Transformation of Russia's Party System', *Democratization* **13**, 4, August 2006, pp. 545–61.

'Out of the Frying Pan, into the Fire? Post-Soviet Regime Changes in Comparative Perspective', *International Political Science Review* **29**, 2, 2008, pp. 157–80.

Gel′man, V. Ya. (ed.), *Tretii elektoral′nyi tsikl v Rossii, 2003–2004 gody: Kollektivnaya monografiya* (St Petersburg: European University, 2007).

Gel′man, V. Ya., G. V. Golosov, E. Yu. Meleshkina (eds.), *Vtoroi elektoral′nyi tsikl v Rossii: 1999–2000gg* (Moscow: Ves′ mir, 2002).

Getty, J. Arch and Oleg V. Naumov, *Yezhov: The Rise of Stalin's 'Iron Fist'* (New Haven, CT: Yale University Press, 2008).

Gill, Graeme, *The Origins of the Stalinist Political System* (Cambridge: Cambridge University Press, 1990).

Glaz′ev, Sergei, *Vybor budushchego* (Moscow: Algoritm, 2005).

Gleason, Gregory, 'Fealty and Loyalty: Informal Authority Structures in Soviet Asia', *Soviet Studies* **43**, 4, 1991, pp. 613–28.

Glebova, I. I., 'Politicheskaya kultura sovremennoi Rossii: Obliki novoi russkoi vlasti i sotsial′nye raskoly', *Polis*, No. 1, 2006, pp. 33–44.

Goode, J. Paul, 'The Puzzle of Putin's Gubernatorial Appointments', *Europe-Asia Studies* **59**, 3, May 2007, pp. 365–99.

Gorlizki, Y. and O. Khlevniuk, *Cold Peace: Stalin and the Soviet Ruling Circles 1945–53* (Oxford: Oxford University Press, 2004).

Gorshkov, M. K., R. Krumm and V. V. Petukhov (eds.), *Rossiya na novom perelome: Strakhi i trevogi*, Friedrich Ebert Foundation and RAN Institute of Sociology (Moscow: Al′fa-M, 2009).

Gramsci, Antonio, *Selections from the Prison Notebooks of Antonio Gramsci*, ed. and trans. Quintin Hoare and Geoffrey Nowell Smith (London: Lawrence & Wishart, 1971).

Grigor′ev, Maksim, *Fake-struktury: Prizraki rossiiskoi politiki* (Moscow: Evropa, 2007).

Gromov, Andrei and Tat′yana Gurova, 'Kapital′nyi remont konservatizma', *Ekspert*, No. 17, 9 May 2005, in *Ekspert: Luchshie materialy*, No. 2, 2007, pp. 106–13.

Gryzmala-Busse, Anna, *Rebuilding Leviathan: Party Competition and State Exploitation in Post-Communist Democracies* (Cambridge: Cambridge University Press, 2008).

Hahn, Jeffrey W. and Igor Logvinenko, 'Generational Differences in Russian Attitudes Towards Democracy and the Economy', *Europe-Asia Studies* **60**, 8, October 2008, pp. 1345–69.

Hale, Henry E., *Why Not Parties in Russia? Democracy, Federalism and the State* (Cambridge: Cambridge University Press, 2006).

'Democracy or Autocracy on the March? The Colored Revolutions as Normal Dynamics of Patronal Presidentialism', *Communist and Post-Communist Studies* **39**, 2006, pp. 305–29.

Handelman, Stephen, *Comrade Criminal: The Theft of the Second Russian Revolution* (London: Michael Joseph, 1994).

Hanson, Philip, 'The Turn to Statism in Russian Economic Policy', *The International Spectator* **42**, 1, March 2007, pp. 29–42.

'The Russian Economic Puzzle: Going Forwards, Backwards or Sideways?' *International Affairs* **83**, 5, September–October 2007, pp. 869–89.

'The Resistible Rise of State Control in the Russian Oil Industry', *Eurasian Geography and Economics* **50**, 1, 2009, pp. 14–27.

Russia to 2020, Occasional Paper (Rome: Finmeccanica Occasional Paper, RIIA, November 2009).

Harasymiw, Bohdan, *Political Elite Recruitment in the Soviet Union* (London: Macmillan, 1984).

Harle, Vilho, *Ideas of Social Order in the Ancient World* (Westport, CT: Greenwood Press, 1998).

Haughton, Tim (ed.), *Constraints and Opportunities of Leadership in Post-Communist Europe* (Aldershot: Ashgate, 2005).

Hedlund, Stefan, 'Vladimir the Great, Grand Prince of Muscovy: Resurrecting the Russian Service State', *Europe-Asia Studies* **58**, 5, July 2006, pp. 775–801.

'Rents, Rights, and Service: Boyar Economics and the Putin Transition', *Problems of Post-Communism* **55**, 4, July–August 2008, pp. 29–41.

Heller, Regina, 'Russia's "Nashi" Youth Movement: The Rise and Fall of a Putin-Era Political Technology Project', *Russian Analytical Digest*, No. 50, 18 November 2008, pp. 2–4.

Helmke, Gretchen and Steven Levitsky, 'Informal Institutions and Comparative Politics: A Research Agenda', *Perspectives on Politics* **2**, 4, 2004, pp. 725–40.

Henderson, Sarah L., *Building Democracy in Contemporary Russia: Western Support for Grassroots Organizations* (Ithaca and London: Cornell University Press, 2003).

Hendley, Kathryn, '"Telephone Law" and the "Rule of Law": The Russian Case', *Hague Journal on the Rule of Law*, No. 1, 2009, pp. 241–62.

'Rule of Law, Russian-Style', *Current History*, October 2009, pp. 339–40.

Hill, Fiona and Clifford Gaddy, *The Siberian Curse: How Communist Planners Left Russia Out in the Cold* (Washington: Brookings Institution Press, 2003).

Holmberg, Carl, *Managing Elections in Russia: Mechanisms and Problems* (Stockholm: FOI, Swedish Defence Research Agency, 2008).

Hough, J. F., *The Soviet Prefects: The Local Party Organs in Industrial Decision-Making* (Cambridge, MA: Harvard University Press, 1969).

Howard, Marc Morje, *The Weakness of Civil Society in Post-Communist Europe* (Cambridge: Cambridge Uiversity Press, 2002).

Huntington, Samuel, *Political Order in Changing Societies* (New Haven, CT: Yale University Press, 1968).

The Third Wave: Democratization in the Late Twentieth Century (Norman: University of Oklahoma Press, 1991).

Huskey, Eugene, 'The State-Legal Administration and the Politics of Redundancy', *Post-Soviet Affairs* **11**, 2, 1995, pp. 115–43.

Presidential Power in Russia (Armonk, NY: M. E. Sharpe, 1999).

Hutcheson, Derek S., *Political Parties in the Russian Regions* (London: RoutledgeCurzon, 2003).

Hyde, Sarah, *The Transformation of the Japanese Left: From Old Socialists to New Democrats* (London: Nissan Institute/Routledge Japanese Studies, 2009).

Isaacs, Rico, 'Between Informal and Formal Politics: Neopatrimonialism and Party Development in Kazakhstan', Ph.D., Department of IR, Politics and Sociology, Oxford Brookes University, 2009.

Ivanenko, Vlad, 'Russian Global Position After 2008', *Russia in Global Affairs* **5**, 4, October–December 2007, pp. 143–56.

Ivanov, Vitalii, *Partiya Putina: Istoriya 'Edinoi Rossii'* (Moscow: Olma Media Grupp, 2008).

Jayasuriya, Kanishka, 'The Exception Becomes the Norm: Law and Regimes of Exception in East Asia', *Asian-Pacific Law & Policy Journal* **2**, 1, Winter 2001, pp. 108–24.

Kapustin, Boris, 'After Putin: How Russia's Liberalism Might be Revived', *Europe's World*, No. 10, Autumn 2008, pp. 100–7.

Karl, Terry Lynn, 'The Hybrid Regimes of Central America', *Journal of Democracy* **6**, 3, 1995, pp. 72–87.

The Paradox of Plenty: Oil Booms and Petrostates (Berkeley: University of California Press, 1997).

Kasparov, Garry, 'Battling KGB, Inc.', *Journal of Democracy* **18**, 2, April 2007, pp. 114–19.

Katz, Richard S. and Peter Mair, 'Changing Models of Party Organization and Party Democracy: The Emergence of the Cartel Party', *Party Politics* **1**, 1, 1995, pp. 5–28.

Kazantsev, V. O., *Prioritetnye natsional'nye proekty i novaya ideologiya dlya Rossii* (Moscow: Vagrius, 2007).

Khanin, V., 'Political Clans and Political Conflicts in Contemporary Kyrgyzstan', in Yaacov Ro'i (ed.), *Democracy and Pluralism in Muslim Eurasia* (London: Frank Cass, 2004), pp. 215–32.

Khlevniuk, Oleg V., *Master of the House: Stalin and His Inner Circle* (New Haven, CT: Yale University Press, 2009).

Khodorkovskikh chtenii, Konferentsii 'Rossiiskie al'ternativy', 10 July 2007, www.polit.ru/dossie/2007/10/05/conf.html.

Kilavuz, Idil Tunçer, 'The Role of Networks in Tajikistan's Civil War: Network Activation and Violence Specialists', *Nationalities Papers* **37**, 5, September 2009, pp. 693–717.

Klebnikov, Paul, *Godfather of the Kremlin: Boris Berezovsky and the Looting of Russia* (New York: Harcourt, 2000); the Russian version is Pavel Khlebnikov, *Krestnyi otets Kremlya Boris Berezovskii, ili Istoriya razgrableniya Rossii* (Moscow: DetektivPress, 2001).

Klyamkin, Igor' and Liliya Shevtsova, *Vnesistemnyi rezhim Borisa II: Nekotorye osobennosti politicheskogo razvitiya postsovetskoi Rossii* (Moscow: Carnegie Centre, 1999).

Knight, Alan and Wil Panster (eds.), *Caciquismo in Twentieth-Century Mexico* (London: Institute for the Study of the Americas, 2006).

Knight, Amy, *Spies Without Cloaks: The KGB's Successors* (Princeton, NJ: Princeton University Press, 1996).

Knoops, Geert-Jan Alexander and Robert R. Amsterdam, 'The Duality of State Cooperation Within International and National Criminal Cases', *Fordham International Law Journal* 30, 2007, pp. 260–95.

Korzhakov, Aleksandr, *Boris Yeltsin: Ot rassveta do zakata* (Moscow: Interbuk, 1997).

Boris El'tsin: Ot rassveta do zakata – Posleslovie (Moscow: DetektivPress, 2004).

Kovalëv, Sergei, 'Why Putin Wins', trans. Jamey Gambrel, *New York Review of Books*, 22 November 2007, pp. 64–6.

Kozhevnikova, G. V., O. A. Sibireva and A. M. Verkhovskii, *Xenophobia, Freedom of Conscience and Anti-extremism in Russia in 2007: A Collection of Annual Reports by the SOVA Center for Information and Analysis* (Moscow: Informatsionno-analiticheskii tsentr 'Sova', 2008).

Krasnov, Mikhail, 'Konstitutsiya v nashei zhizni', *Pro et Contra* 11, 4–5, July–October 2007, pp. 30–42.

Krasnov, M. A. and I. G. Shablinskii, *Rossiiskaya sistema vlasti: Treugol'nik s odnom uglom* (Moscow: Institut prava i publichnoi politiki, 2008).

Krichevskii, Nikita, *Postpikalevskaya Rosiiya: Novaya politico-ekonomicheskaya real'nost'*, with Vladislav Inozemtsev (Moscow: no publisher, 2009); www.krichevsky.ru/images/book/doklad.pdf.

Kryshtanovskaya, Ol'ga, *Anatomiya rossiiskoi elity* (Moscow: Zakharov, 2005).

Kryshtanovskaya, Ol'ga and Stephen White, 'Putin's Militocracy', *Post-Soviet Affairs* 19, 4, October–December 2003, pp. 289–306.

'The Rise of the Russian Business Elite', *Communist and Post-Communist Studies* 38, 3, September 2005, pp. 293–307.

'Inside the Putin Court: A Research Note', *Europe-Asia Studies* 57, 7, November 2005, pp. 1065–75.

Kurginyan, Sergei, *Kacheli: Konflikt elit – ili razval Rossii?* (Moscow: Eksperimental'nyi tvorcheskii tsentr, 2008).

Kynev, Alexander, *Vybory parlamentov rossiiskikh regionov 2003–2009: Pervyi tsikl vnedreniya proportsional'noi izbiratel'noi sistemy* (Moscow: Panorama, 2009).

Lane, David, 'The Orange Revolution: 'People's Revolution' or Revolutionary Coup', *The British Journal of Politics & International Relations* 10, 4, November 2008, pp. 525–49.

Laruelle, Marlène, *Inside and Around the Kremlin's Black Box: The New Nationalist Think Tanks in Russia*, Institute for Security and Development Policy, Stockholm Paper, October 2009, pp. 25–31; www.isdp.eu.

Laverty, Nicklaus, 'Limited Choices: Russian Opposition Parties and the 2007 Duma Election', *Demokratizatsiya* **16**, 4, Fall 2008, pp. 363–81.

Ledeneva, Alena V., *Russia's Economy of Favours: Blat, Networking and Informal Exchange* (Cambridge: Cambridge University Press, 1998).

How Russia Really Works: The Informal Practices that Shaped Post-Soviet Politics and Business (Ithaca, NY, and London: Cornell University Press, 2006).

'Telephone Justice in Russia', *Post-Soviet Affairs* **24**, 4, October–December 2008, pp. 324–50.

'From Russia with *Blat*: Can Informal Networks Help Modernize Russia?', *Social Research* **76**, 1, Spring 2009, pp. 257–88.

Leonard, Mark, Ivan Krastev and Andrew Wilson (eds.), *What Does Russia Think?* (London: European Council on Foreign Relations, 2009).

Leshchenko, Natalia, 'The National Ideology and the Basis of the Lukashenka Regime in Belarus', *Europe-Asia Studies* **60**, 8, October 2008, pp. 1419–33.

Libman, Aleksandr, 'Vzaimosvyaz' ekonomicheskoi i politicheskoi sistem v sovremennoi Rossii', *Svobodnaya mysl'*, No. **6**, 30 June 2004, pp. 97–111.

Limonov, Eduard, *Takoi president nam ne nuzhen!* (Moscow: no publisher indicated, 2005).

Limonov protiv Putina (Moscow: Novyi Bastion, 2006).

Litvinenko, Alexander with Yuri Feltshtinsky, *Blowing up Russia: The Soviet Plot to Bring Back KGB Terror* (London: Gibson Square, 2007).

Livshin, Aleksandr and Igor' Orlov, *Vlast' i obshchestvo: Dialog v pis'makh* (Moscow: Rosspen, 2002).

Lukin, Alexander, *The Political Culture of the Russian 'Democrats'* (Oxford: Oxford University Press, 2000).

'Putin's Regime: Restoration or Revolution?', *Problems of Post-Communism* **48**, 4, July–August 2001, pp. 38–48.

Lust-Okar, Ellen, 'Competitive Clientalism', in Anthony J. Langlois and Karol Edward Soltan (eds.), *Global Democracy and Its Difficulties* (London and New York: Routledge, 2008), pp. 130–45.

Makarenko, Boris, '"Nanopartiinaya" sistema', *Pro et Contra* **11**, 4–5, July–October 2007, pp. 43–57.

Makarkin, A., *Politiko-ekonomicheskie klany sovremennoi Rossii* (Moscow: Tsentr politicheskikh tekhnologii, 2003).

Makarychev, Andrey S., 'Politics, the State, and De-Politicization: Putin's Project Reassessed', *Problems of Post-Communism* **55**, 5, September–October 2008, pp. 62–71.

Maltz, Gideon, 'The Case for Presidential Term Limits', *Journal of Democracy* **18**, 1, January 2007, pp. 128–42.

March, Andrew F., 'From Leninism to Karimovism: Hegemony, Ideology, and Authoritarian Legitimation', *Post-Soviet Affairs* **19**, 4, 2003, pp. 307–36.

March, Luke, 'The Contemporary Russian Left after Communism: Into the Dustbin of History?', *The Journal of Communist Studies and Transition Politics* **22**, 4, December 2006, pp. 431–56.

'Managing Opposition in a Hybrid Regime: Just Russia and Parastatal Opposition', *Slavic Review* **68**, 3, Fall 2009, pp. 504–27.

Marshall, Dorothy, *Eighteenth Century England* (London: Longman, 1962).

Matsuzato, Kimitaka, 'A Populist Island in an Ocean of Clan Politics: The Lukashenko Regime as an Exception Among CIS Countries', *Europe-Asia Studies* **56**, 2, March 2004, pp. 235–61.

'Semipresidentialism in Ukraine: Institutionalist Centrism in Rampant Clan Politics', *Demokratizatsiya* **13**, 1, Winter 2005, pp. 45–58.

Mazo, Boris, *Preemnik Putina, ili kogo my budem vybirat' v 2008 godu* (Moscow: Algoritm, 2005).

McAllister, Ian and Stephen White, '"It's the Economy, Comrade!" Parties and Voters in the 2007 Russian *Duma* Election', *Europe-Asia Studies* **60**, 6, August 2008, pp. 931–58.

McFaul, Michael, *Russia's Unfinished Revolution: Political Change from Gorbachev to Putin* (Ithaca and London: Cornell University Press, 2001).

Medushevskii, Andrei, 'Bonapartistskaya model' vlasti dlya Rossii?', *Konstitutsionnoe pravo: Vostochnoevropeiskoe obozrenie*, No. 4 (33)/No. 1 (34), 2001, pp. 161–7.

Medvedev, Roi, *Vladimir Putin: Tret'ego sroka ne budet?* (Moscow: Vremya, 2007).

Dmitrii Medvedev: Prezident Rossiiskoi Federatsii (Moscow: Vremya, 2008).

Meeting Medvedev: The Politics of the Putin Succession, European Council on Foreign Relations, Policy Brief, No. 5, February 2008; www.ecfr.eu.

Mellor, Rosemary, 'Through a Glass Darkly: Investigating the St Petersburg Administration', *International Journal of Urban and Regional Studies* **21**, 3, September 1997, pp. 481–503.

Mickiewicz, Ellen, *Television, Power, and the Public in Russia* (Cambridge: Cambridge University Press, 2008).

Mikhailovskii, E. (ed.), *Rossiya Putina: Ruiny i rostki oppozitsii* (Moscow: Panorama, 2005).

Mukhin, A. A., *Tainyi pravitel'* (Moscow: Tsentr politicheskoi informatsii, 2007).

Munck, Gerardo L. and Jay Verkuilen, 'Conceptualizing and Measuring Democracy: Evaluating Alternative Indices', *Comparative Political Studies* **35**, 1, February 2002, pp. 5–34.

Murphy, Jonathan, 'Illusory Transition? Elite Reconstitution in Kazakhstan, 1989–2002', *Europe-Asia Studies* **58**, 4, June 2006, pp. 523–54.

Myagkov, Mikhail, Peter C. Ordeshook and Dimitry Shakin, 'Fraud or Fairytales: Russia's and Ukraine's Electoral Experience', *Post-Soviet Affairs* **21**, 2, 2005, pp. 91–131.

The Forensics of Election Fraud: Russia and Ukraine (Cambridge: Cambridge University Press, 2009).

Myrynyuk, A.N., *Natsional'nye proekty v rossii: Problemy i perspektivy* (Moscow: Maroseika, 2007).

Nemtsov, Boris and Vladimir Milov, *Nezavisimy ekspertnyi doklad: Putin – Itogi* (Moscow: Novaya gazeta, 2008).

North, Douglass, *Institutions, Institutional Change and Economic Performance* (Cambridge: Cambridge University Press, 1990).

Nussberger, Angelika, 'Ogranicheniya prezidentskoi vlasti v postkommunisticheskikh stranakh', *Sravnitel'noe konstitutsionnoe obozrenie*, No. 5 (66), 2008, pp. 53–68.

OECD, *Russia: Building Rules for the Market*, OECD Reviews of Regulatory Reform (Paris: OECD Publishing. 2005).

'Improving the Quality of Public Administration', in *Russian Federation, OECD Economic Surveys* (Paris: OECD Publishing, 2006), pp. 115–46.

O'Dwyer, Conor, *Runaway State-Building: Patronage Politics and Democratic Development* (Baltimore, MD: The Johns Hopkins University Press, 2006).

Ogushi, Atsushi, 'Toward a Government-Party Regime? United Russia in Perspective', paper delivered to the Annual Convention of the AAASS, New Orleans, 15 November 2007.

Ordzhonikidze, Maria, 'Russians' Perceptions of Western Values', *Russian Social Sciences Review* **49**, 6, November–December 2008, pp. 4–29.

Orenstein, Mitchell A., Stephen Bloom and Nicole Lindstrom (eds.), *Transnational Actors in Central and East European Transitions* (Pittsburgh: University of Pittsburgh Press, 2008).

Orttung, Robert W., 'Russia', in *Nations in Transit 2008* (Washington, DC: Freedom House, 2008), pp. 495–518.

'Can Russia's Opposition Liberals Come to Power?, *Russian Analytical Digest*, No. 60, 19 May 2009, pp. 2–5.

Ottaway, Marina and Thomas Carothers (eds.), *Funding Virtue: Civil Society Aid and Democracy Promotion* (Washington, DC: Carnegie Endowment for International Peace, 2000).

Oversloot, Hans, 'Reordering the State (Without Changing the Constitution): Russia Under Putin's Rule, 2000–2008', *Review of Central and East European Law* **32**, 2007, pp. 41–64.

O vyborakh Prezidenta Rossiiskoi Federatsii (Moscow: Os'-89, 2003).

Pappe, Ya. Sh. and Ya. S. Galukhina, *Rossiiskii krupnyi biznes, pervye 15 let: Ekonomicheskie khroniki 1993–2008* (Moscow: Higher School of Economics Publishing House, 2009).

Pastukhov, V. B., 'Temnyi vek: Postkommunizm kak "chernaya dyra" russkoi istorii', *Polis*, No. 3, 2007, pp. 24–38.

Pearce, Edward, *The Great Man: Sir Robert Walpole – Scoundrel, Genius and Britain's First Prime Minister* (London: Jonathan Cape, 2007).

Peregudov, S. P., *Korporatsii, obshchestvo, gosudarstvo: Evolyutsiya otnoshenii* (Moscow: no publisher, 2003).

Peregudov, S. P., N. Yu. Lapina and I. S. Semenenko, *Gruppy interesov i rossiiskoe gosudarstvo* (Moscow: no publisher, 1999).

Petrakov, Nikolai, 'Samaya nishchaya bogateishchikh stran mira', *Svobodnaya mysl'*, No. 11, 30 November 2005, pp. 15–22.

Petrov, Nikolai, 'Korporativizm *vs* regionalizm', *Pro et Contra* **11**, 4–5, July–October 2007, pp. 75–89.

Pivovarov, Yurii S., *Russkaya politika v ee istoricheskom i kul'turnom otnosheniyakh* (Moscow: Rosspen, 2006).

'Russkaya vlast' i publichnaya politika: Zametki istorika o prichinakh neudachi demokraticheskogo tranzita', *Polis*, No. 1, 2006, pp. 12–32.

'Mezhdu kazachestvom i knutom: K stoletiyu russkoi konstitutsii i russkogo parlamenta', *Polis*, No. 2, 2006, pp. 5–26.

Pivovarov, Yurii S. and A. I. Fursov, 'Russkaya sistema i reformy', *Pro et Contra*, **4**, 4, Autumn 1999, pp. 176–97.

Plan prezidenta Putina: Rukovodstvo dlya budushchikh prezidentov rossii (Moscow: Evropa, 2007).

Plattner, Marc F., 'A Skeptical Perspective', in Larry Diamond and Leonardo Morlino (eds.), *Assessing the Quality of Democracy* (Baltimore, MD: The Johns Hopkins University Press, 2005), pp. 77–81.

Pogorelsky, Alexander, 'Russian Bureaucracy Needs to be Brought Back to Reality', interviewed by Liubov Ulianova, *Russian Journal*, No. 23 (37), 30 September 2009, pp. 6–7.

Proekt Rossiya: Vybor puti, vtoraya kniga (Moscow: Eksmo, 2007).

Putin, V. V., *Izbrannye rechi i vystupleniya* (Moscow: Knizhnyi mir, 2008).

Putnam, Robert D. and Kristin A. Goss, 'Introduction', in Robert D. Putnam (ed.), *Democracies in Flux: The Evolution of Social Capital in Contemporary Society* (Oxford: Oxford University Press, 2002), pp. 3–19.

Ra'anan, Uri (ed.), *Flawed Succession: Russia's Power Transfer Crises* (Lanham, MD: Lexington Books, 2006).

Raeff, Marc, *Understanding Imperial Russia* (New York: Columbia University Press, 1984).

Rar, Aleksandr, *Rossiya zhmet na gaz: Vozvrashchenie mirovoi derzhavy* (Moscow: Olma, 2008); trans. from Alexander Rahr, *Russland gibt Gas (Die Rückkehr einer Weltmacht)* (Munich: Carl Hanser Verlag, 2008).

Remchukov, Konstantin (ed.), *Lektsiya Vladislav Surkova 'Russkaya politicheskaya kul'tura: Vzglyad iz utopii': Materialy obsuzhdeniya v 'Nezavismoi gazete'* (Moscow: Nezavisimaya gazeta, 2007).

Remington, Thomas F., *The Russian Parliament: Institutional Evolution in a Transitional Regime* (New Haven, CT: Yale University Press, 2001).

'The Russian Federal Assembly, 1994–2004', *The Journal of Legislative Studies* **13**, 1 March 2007, pp. 121–41.

Richter, James, 'Putin and the Public Chamber', *Post-Soviet Affairs* **25**, 1, January–March 2009, pp. 39–65.

Rigby, T. H., 'The Origins of the Nomenklatura System', in T. H. Rigby, *Political Elites in the USSR* (Aldershot: Edward Elgar, 1990).

Rigby, T. H. and Bohdan Harasymiw (eds.), *Leadership Selection and Patron-Client Relations in the USSR and Yugoslavia* (London: Allen & Unwin, 1983).

Riggs, F., 'The Survival of Presidentialism in America: Para-Constitutional Practices', *International Political Science Review* **9**, 4, 1988, pp. 247–78.

Riggs, Fred W., 'Bureaucrats and Political Development: A Paradoxical View', in Joseph LaPalombara (ed.), *Bureaucracy and Political Development* (Princeton, NJ: Princeton University Press, 1993).

Riggs, Jonathan W. and Peter J. Schraeder, 'Russia's Political Party System as an Impediment to Democratization', *Demokratizatsiya* **12**, 2, Spring 2004, pp. 265–93.

'Russia's Political Party System as a (Continued) Impediment to Democratization: The 2003 Duma and 2004 Presidential Elections in Perspective', *Demokratizatsiya* **13**, 1, Winter 2005, pp. 141–51.

Rimsky, V. L., 'Bureaucracy, Clientelism and Corruption in Russia', *Russian Polity: The Russian Political Science Yearbook (2007–2008)* (Moscow: Politeia, 2009), pp. 99–117.

Rivera, Sharon Werning and David W. Rivera, 'The Russian Elite Under Putin: Militocratic or Bourgeois?', *Post-Soviet Affairs* 22, 2, 2006, pp. 125–44.

Renz, Bettina, 'Putin's Militocracy? An Alternative Interpretation of *Siloviki* in Contemporary Russian Politics', *Europe-Asia Studies* 58, 6, 2006, pp. 903–24.

Robertson, Graeme B., 'Managing Society: Protest, Civil Society, and Regime in Putin's Russia', *Slavic Review* 68, 3, Fall 2009, pp. 528–47.

Roeder, Philip G., *Red Sunset: The Failure of Soviet Politics* (Princeton, NJ: Princeton University Press, 1993).

Romanov, Petr, *Preemniki ot Ivana III do Dmitriya Medvedeva* (St Petersburg: Amfora, 2008).

Rose, Richard, 'The Impact of President Putin on Popular Support for Russia's Regime', *Post-Soviet Affairs* 23, 2, April–June 2007, pp. 87–117.

Rose, Richard and William Mishler, 'How Do Electors Respond to an "Unfair" Election? The Experience of Russians', *Post-Soviet Affairs* 25, 2, April–June 2009, pp. 118–36.

Rose, Richard and Neil Munro, *Elections Without Order: Russia's Challenge to Vladimir Putin* (Cambridge: Cambridge University Press, 2002).

Rose, Richard, William Mishler and Neil Munro, *Russia Transformed: Developing Popular Support for a New Regime* (Cambridge: Cambridge University Press, 2006).

Rose, Richard, Neil Munro and William Mishler, 'Resigned Acceptance of an Incomplete Democracy: Russia's Political Equilibrium', *Post-Soviet Affairs* 20, 3, 2004, pp. 195–218.

Ross, Michael L., 'Does Oil Hinder Democracy?', *World Politics* 53, 3, April 2001, pp. 325–61.

Roth, Jürgen, *Die Gangster aus dem Osten* (Hamburg: Europa Verlag, 2003).

Russia's Wrong Direction: What the United States Can and Should Do, Independent Task Force Report No. 57, chaired by John Edwards and Jack Kemp, with Stephen Sestanovich as Project Director (New York: Council on Foreign Relations, 2006).

Rustow, Dankwart A., 'Transitions to Democracy: Toward a Dynamic Model', *Comparative Politics* 2, 3, 1970, pp. 337–63.

Rutland, Peter, 'Oil, Politics and Foreign Policy', in David Lane (ed.), *The Political Economy of Russian Oil* (Lanham, MD: Rowman & Littlefield, 1999), pp. 163–88.

Ryabov, Andrei, 'Vybory v Moskve i politicheskaya perspektiva', *Svobodnaya mysl'*, No. 1, January 2006, pp. 44–52.

Ryzhkov, Vladimir, 'The Liberal Debacle', *Journal of Democracy* 15, 3, July 2004, pp. 52–8.

'Lenivye i truslivye', *Pro et Contra* 11, 4–5, July–October 2007, pp. 58–74.

Sakwa, Richard, 'The Russian Elections of December 1993', *Europe-Asia Studies* 47, 2, March 1995, pp. 195–227.

'The Regime System in Russia', *Contemporary Politics* 3, 1, 1997, pp. 7–25.

'The 2003–2004 Russian Elections and Prospects for Democracy', *Europe-Asia Studies* 57, 3, May 2005, pp. 369–98.

Putin: Russia's Choice, 2nd edn (London and New York: Routledge, 2008).

Russian Politics and Society, 4th edn (London and New York: Routledge, 2008).

'Two Camps? The Struggle to Understand Contemporary Russia', *Comparative Politics* **40**, 4, July 2008, pp. 481–99.

The Quality of Freedom: Khodorkovsky, Putin and the Yukos Affair (Oxford: Oxford University Press, 2009).

Salmi, Anna-Maria, *Social Networks and Everyday Practices in Russia* (Helsinki: Kimora Publications, 2006).

Sanaev, A., *Vybory v Rossii: Kak eto delaetsya* (Moscow: Os'-89, 2007).

Schatz, Edward, *Modern Clan Politics: The Power of 'Blood' in Kazakhstan and Beyond*, Jackson School Publications in International Studies (Seattle: University of Washington Press, 2004).

'Reconceptualizing Clans: Kinship Networks and Statehood in Kazakhstan', *Nationalities Papers* **33**, 2, 2005, pp. 231–54.

Schmitt, Carl, *Political Theology: Four Chapters on the Concept of Sovereignty* (Chicago and London: University of Chicago Press, 1985).

Schneider, Eberhard, 'Putin's Successor', *The EU-Russia Review*, No. 3, *After Putin ... What Next?* (Brussels: The EU-Russia Centre, March 2007), pp. 5–14.

Schraeder, Peter J., *Exporting Democracy: Rhetoric vs. Reality* (Boulder, CO: Lynne Rienner, 2002).

Segbers, Klaus (ed.), *Explaining Post-Soviet Patchworks*, 3 vols. (Aldershot: Ashgate, 2001).

Semonov, V. E., 'The Value Orientations of Today's Young People', *Russian Social Sciences Review* **49**, 6, September–October 2008, pp. 38–52.

Sestanovich, Stephen, 'Putin's Invented Opposition', *Journal of Democracy* **18**, 2, April 2007, pp. 122–4.

Sharlet, Robert, 'Stalinism and Soviet Legal Culture', in Robert C. Tucker (ed.), *Stalinism: Essays in Historical Interpretation* (New York: W. W. Norton, 1977), pp. 155–79.

Sheinis, V. L., 'Dvizhenie po spirali: Prevrashcheniya rossiiskogo parlamenta', *Obshchestvennye nauki i sovremennost'*, No. 5, 2004, pp. 43–52.

Shepilov, Dmitri, *The Kremlin's Scholar: A Memoir of Soviet Politics Under Stalin and Khrushchev*, ed. Stephen V. Bittner (New Haven, CT: Yale University Press, 2007).

Shevtsova, Liliya, *Rezhim Borisa El'tsina* (Moscow: Rosspen, 1999).

Yeltsin's Russia: Myths and Reality (Washington, DC: Carnegie Endowment for International Peace, 1999).

'Russia's Hybrid Regime', *Journal of Democracy* **12**, 4, October 2001, pp. 65–70.

Russia – Lost in Transition: The Yeltsin and Putin Legacies (Washington, DC: Carnegie Endowment for International Peace, 2007).

Shkolnikov, Vladimir, 'Russia and the OSCE Human Dimension: A Critical Assessment', *The EU-Russia Review*, No. 12, *Russia, the OSCE and European Security* (Brussels: The EU-Russia Centre, 2009), pp. 21–9.

Shlapentokh, Vladimir, 'Wealth Versus Political Power: The Russian Case', *Communist and Post-Communist Studies* **37**, 2, June 2004, pp. 135–60.

Contemporary Russia as a Feudal Society (New York: Palgrave Macmillan, 2007).

'Big Money as an Obstacle to Democracy in Russia', *Journal of Communist Studies and Transition Politics* **24**, 4, December 2008, pp. 512–30.

Shleifer, Andrei, *A Normal Country: Russia After Communism* (Cambridge, MA: Harvard University Press, 2005).

Shleifer, Andrei and Daniel Treisman, 'A Normal Country', *Foreign Affairs* **83**, 2, March–April 2004, pp. 20–39.

Shugart, Matthew Soberg and John M. Carey, *Presidents and Assemblies: Constitutional Design and Electoral Dynamics* (Cambridge: Cambridge University Press, 1992).

Siddiqa, Ayesha, *Military Inc: Inside Pakistan's Military Economy* (London: Pluto, 2007).

Sim, Li-Chen, *The Rise and Fall of Privatization in the Russian Oil Industry* (Basingstoke: Palgrave Macmillan, 2008).

Simonov, Konstantin, *Russkaya neft': Poslednii peredel* (Moscow: Eksmo Algoritm, 2005).

Slider, Darrell, 'Putin's "Southern Strategy": Dmitriy Kozak and the Dilemmas of Recentralization', *Post-Soviet Affairs* **24**, 2, April–June 2008, pp. 177–97.

Slider, Darrell, Vladimir Gimpel'son and Sergei Chugrov, 'Political Tendencies in Russia's Regions: Evidence from the 1993 Parliamentary Elections', *Slavic Review* **53**, 3, Fall 1994, pp. 711–32.

Smith, Gordon B., *Reforming the Russian Legal System* (Cambridge: Cambridge University Press, 1996).

Smyth, Regina, Anna Lowry and Brandon Wilkening, 'Engineering Victory: Institutional Reform, Informal Institutions, and the Formation of a Hegemonic Party Regime in the Russian Federation', *Post-Soviet Affairs* **23**, 2, April–June 2007, pp. 118–37.

Startsev, Yaroslav, '"Informal" Institutions and Practices: Objects to Explore and Methods to Use for Comparative Research', *Perspectives on European Politics and Society* **6**, 2, 2005, pp. 331–51.

Stern, Jonathan P., *The Future of Russian Gas and Gazprom* (Oxford: Oxford University Press for the Oxford Institute for Energy Studies, 2005).

Stockwin, J. A. A., *Governing Japan: Divided Politics in a Resurgent Economy*, 4th edn (Oxford: Blackwell Publishing, 2008).

Stoner-Weiss, Kathryn, *Resisting the State: Reform and Retrenchment in Post-Soviet Russia* (Cambridge: Cambridge University Press, 2006).

Strigin, Evgenii, *Vladimir Putin: Vnedrenie v kreml'* (Moscow: Algoritm, 2006). *Boris Berezovskii i londonskii shtab* (Moscow: Algoritm, 2006).

Suleiman, Ezra N., 'Presidential and Political Stability in France', in Juan J. Linz and Arturo Valenzuela (eds.), *The Failure of Presidential Democracy: Comparative Perspectives* (Baltimore, MD: The Johns Hopkins University Press, 1994), pp. 137–62.

Surkov, Vladislav, *Teksty 97–07* (Moscow: Evropa, 2008).

Svanidze, Nikolai and Marina Svanidze, *Medvedev* (St Petersburg: Amfora, 2008).

Telen, Ludmila, 'The Kingmakers: Oligarchs Jockey for Position Behind Their Candidates of Choice', *Transitions*, June 1998, pp. 32–4.

Tilly, Charles, *Democracy* (Cambridge: Cambridge University Press, 2007).

Titkov, Alexei, *'Party Number Four' – Rodina: Whence and Why?* (Moscow: Panorama, 2006).

Tomberg, Igor, 'XII St. Petersburg Economic Forum', *Essays & Analyses* **15** (Moscow), June 2008, pp. 5–16.

Tompson, William, 'Putin and the "Oligarchs": A Two-Sided Commitment Problem', in Alex Pravda (ed.), *Leading Russia: Putin in Perspective* (Oxford: Oxford University Press, 2005), pp. 179–202.

'Putting Yukos in Perspective', *Post-Soviet Affairs* **21**, 2, April–June 2005, pp. 159–82.

'The Political Implications of Russia's Resource-Based Economy', *Post-Soviet Affairs* **21**, 4, October–December 2005, pp. 335–59.

'A Frozen Venezuela? The Resource Curse and Russian Politics', in Michael Ellman (ed.), *Russia's Oil and Natural Gas: Bonanza or Curse?* (London and New York: AnthemPress, 2006), pp. 189–212.

Treisman, Daniel, 'Putin's *Silovarchs*', *Orbis* **51**, 1, Winter 2007, pp. 141–53.

Tret'yakov, Vitalii, *Nuzhen li nam Putin posle 2008 goda? Sbornik statei* (Moscow: Rossiiskaya gazeta, 2005).

Trochev, Alexei, *Judging Russia: The Role of the Constitutional Court in Russian Politics 1990–2006* (Cambridge: Cambridge University Press, 2008).

'All Appeals Lead to Strasbourg?: Unpacking the Impact of the European Court of Human Rights on Russia', *Demokratizatsiya* **17**, 2, Spring 2009, pp. 179–92.

Tsygankov, Daniil, 'Valentina Matvienko's Second Term: From Ambitious Projects to Threats of Removal', *Russian Analytical Digest*, No. 67, 9 November 2009, pp. 9–12.

Uhlin, Anders, *Post-Soviet Civil Society: Democratization in Russia and the Baltic States* (London: Routledge, 2006).

Urban, Michael, 'December 1993 as a Replication of Late-Soviet Electoral Practices', *Post-Soviet Affairs* **10**, 2, 1994, pp. 127–58.

Varese, Federico, *The Russian Mafia: Private Protection in a New Market Economy* (Oxford: Oxford University Press, 2001).

Verkhovskii, Aleksandr (ed.), *Demokratiya vertikali* (Moscow: Inform.-analiticheskii tsentr 'Sova' and Issled. tsentr 'Demos', 2006).

Vishnevskii, A. G., 'Modernizatsiya i kontrmodernizatsiya: Ch'ya voz'met?', *Obshchestvennye nauki i sovremennost'*, No. 1, 2004, pp. 17–25.

Vladimir Zhirinovskii: Kandidat v prezidenty rossiiskoi federatsii (Moscow: LDPR, 2008).

Volkov, Vadim, *Violent Entrepreneurs: The Use of Force in the Making of Russian Capitalism* (Ithaca, NY: Cornell University Press, 2002).

Walker, Christopher and Jeannette Goehring, 'Nations in Transit 2008: Petro-Authoritarianism and Eurasia's New Divides', in *Nations in Transit 2008* (Washington, DC: Freedom House, 2008), pp. 25–35.

Walker, Martin, 'After Yeltsin: Russia Faces Free-Fall', *Transitions*, June 1998, pp. 20–2.

Way, Lucan A., 'Authoritarian State Building and the Sources of Regime Competitiveness in the Fourth Wave: The Cases of Belarus, Moldova, Russia, and Ukraine', *World Politics* **57**, January 2005, pp. 231–61.

Wedel, Janine R., *Collision and Collusion: The Strange Case of Western Aid to Eastern Europe 1989–1998* (Basingstoke and London: Macmillan, 1998).
'Flex Organizing and the Clan-State', in William Alex Pridemore (ed.), *Ruling Russia: Law, Crime, and Justice in a Changing Society* (Lanham, MD: Rowman & Littlefield, 2005), pp. 101–16.

Wegren, Stephen K. and Andrew Konitzer, 'Discussion Article: Prospects for Managed Democracy in Russia', *Europe-Asia Studies* 59, 6, September 2007, pp. 1025–47.

White, David, *The Russian Democratic Party Yabloko* (Aldershot: Ashgate, 2006).
'Victims of a Managed Democracy? Explaining the Electoral Decline of the Yabloko Party', *Demokratizatsiya* 15, 2, 2007, pp. 209–29.

White, Stephen, Matthew Wyman and Sarah Oates, 'Parties and Voters in the 1995 Russian Duma Election', *Europe-Asia Studies* 49, 5, 1997, pp. 767–98.

Whitefield, Stephen, 'Putin's Popularity and Its Implications for Democracy in Russia', in Alex Pravda (ed.), *Leading Russia: Putin in Perspective* (Oxford: Oxford University Press, 2005), pp. 139–60.
'Russian Citizens and Russian Democracy: Perceptions of State Governance and Democratic Practice, 1993–2007', *Post-Soviet Affairs* 25, 2, April–June 2009, pp. 93–117.

Willerton, John P., *Patronage and Politics in the USSR* (Cambridge: Cambridge University Press, 1992).

Wilson, Andrew, *Virtual Politics: Faking Democracy in the Post-Soviet World* (New Haven, CT: Yale University Press, 2005).

Wilson, Kenneth, 'Party-System Development Under Putin', *Post-Soviet Affairs* 22, 4, October–December 2006, pp. 314–48.

Wittfogel, Karl A., *Oriental Despotism: A Comparative Study of Total Power* (New Haven, CT: Yale University Press, 1957).

Wolin, Sheldon S., *Democracy Incorporated: Managed Democracy and the Specter of Inverted Totalitarianism* (Princeton, NJ: Princeton University Press, 2008).

Yasin, Yevgeny, *Prizhivetsya li demokratiya v Rossii?* (Moscow: Novoe izdatel'stvo, 2005).

Yeltsin, Boris, *Midnight Diaries* (London: Weidenfeld & Nicolson, 2000).

Yurgens, Igor Y., *Russia's Future Under Medvedev*, English edn, ed. Professor Lord Skidelsky (Warwick: Centre for Global Studies, 2008).
Ocherednye zadachi rossiiskoi vlasti (Moscow: Rosspen, 2009).

Zakaria, Fareed, 'The Rise of Illiberal Democracy', *Foreign Affairs* 76, 6, November–December 1997, pp. 22–43.
The Future of Freedom (New York: W. W. Norton, 2003).

Zassoursky, Ivan, *Media and Power in Post-Soviet Russia* (Armonk, NY: M. E. Sharpe, 2004).

Zaznaev, O. I., *Poluprezidentskaya sistema: Teoreticheskie i prikladnye aspekty* (Kazan: Kazanskii gosudarstvennyi universitet, 2006).
'Indeksnyi analiz polyprezidentskikh gosudarstv Evropy i postsovetskogo prostranstva', *Polis*, No. 2, 2007, pp. 146–65.

Zimmerman, William, 'Russian National Interests, Use of Blood and Treasure, and Energy Price Assessments: 2008–2009', *Post-Soviet Affairs* **25**, 3, 2009, pp. 185–208.

Zygar′, Mikhail and Valeri Panyushkin, *Gazprom: Novoe russkoe oruzhie* (Moscow: Zakharov, 2008).

Index

Abakumov, V. S., 88
Abkhazia, 88
Abramovich, Roman, 94, 101, 128, 135, 185–7, 271, 338
administrative regime, 1, 6, 8, 10, 13, 19, 21, 28–9, 30, 33, 35, 38, 41–2, 45, 47, 51–2, 85, 89, 93–4, 101–2, 105, 107–8, 114, 116, 125, 130, 132, 137, 144, 147, 149, 165, 184, 201, 270, 272, 301, 303–4, 307, 319, 326–7, 333, 341–2, 347, 352–3, 355, 361–3, 365
Afanasiev, Mikhail, 78, 303
Afghanistan, 120
Agapova, Natalya, 242
Agrarian Party, 4, 211, 217, 226, 246, 269, 294, 320
Akaev, Askar, 21
Akchurin, Renat, 242
Aksenenko, Nikolai, 161, 199
Alekperov, Vagit, 135
Aleksashenko, Sergei, 158
Alekseeva, Ludmila, 278
Aleshin, Alexei, 199
Alfa Group, 201
Alferov, Zhores, 222
Aliev, Heidar, 114
Alkhanov, Alu, 170
Alrosa (diamonds), 148
Altai region, 294
Amsterdam, Robert, 40, 41
Amur region, 176, 294–5
Andijan, 67
Andropov, Yuri, 7, 137
Angola, 122
Anichkin, Alexei, 191
Anti-Corruption Council, 329
Appel, Hilary, 147
Aramco, 203
Arbatova, Maria, 226
Arbitration Court of Samara Region, 331
Arcelor (steel group), 128

archaisation of Russian politics, 101
Argentina, 57
Arkhangel'skaya, Natal'ya, 101
Aron, Leon, 56, 82
Artem'ev, Igor, 324
Artyakov, Vladimir, 175
Aslamazyan, Manana, 330
Åslund, Anders, 72–3, 202, 271, 314
Association of Russian Lawyers, 285
Astakhov, Pavel, 242
Atatürk, Kemal, 27
Atomic Industry Complex (Atomenergoprom), 155
Audit Chamber, 120, 194, 271
authoritarian capitalism, 150, 319, 322
authoritarianism, 31, 37, 73, 76–7, 137–8, 150, 230, 304, 332, 342
autonomy
  external, 109, 135
  internal, 109, 116
Aven, Petr, 94, 201
Avisma (VSMPO), 155
Avtovaz, 126, 155, 175
Azerbaijan, 114

Babakov, Alexander, 19, 262
Baburin, Sergei, 211, 217, 227, 320
Baburova, Anastasia, 345
Baev, Pavel K., 100, 192
Baker, Peter, 190
ballistic missile defence (BMD), 283, 345
Balmaceda, Margarita, 110
Baltik-Eskort (security company), 186
Baluevsky, Yuri, 283
Bank of New York (BONY), 193
Bank Rossiya, 141, 187
Barinov, Alexei, 175
Barshchevsky, Mikhail, 226, 269, 323
Barsukov, Vladimir, see also Kumarin, 174, 194, 208, 328
Bashkortostan, 130, 166, 175, 250, 294–5, 317